Development of Distributed Systems from Design to Application and Maintenance

Nik Bessis
University of Derby, UK & University of Bedfordshire, UK

Information Science
REFERENCE

Managing Director:	Lindsay Johnston
Editorial Director:	Joel Gamon
Book Production Manager:	Jennifer Romanchak
Publishing Systems Analyst:	Adrienne Freeland
Assistant Acquisitions Editor:	Kayla Wolfe
Typesetter:	Alyson Zerbe
Cover Design:	Nick Newcomer

Published in the United States of America by
Information Science Reference (an imprint of IGI Global)
701 E. Chocolate Avenue
Hershey PA 17033
Tel: 717-533-8845
Fax: 717-533-8661
E-mail: cust@igi-global.com
Web site: http://www.igi-global.com

Library of Congress Cataloging-in-Publication Data

Development of distributed systems from design to application and maintenance / Nik Bessis, editor.
     p. cm.
  Includes bibliographical references and index.
  Summary: "This book is a collection of research on the strategies used in the design and development of distributed systems applications"--Provided by publisher.
   ISBN 978-1-4666-2647-8 (hbk.) -- ISBN 978-1-4666-2678-2 (ebook) -- ISBN 978-1-4666-2709-3 (print & perpetual access) 1. Electronic data processing--Distributed processing. 2. Distributed operating systems (Computers) I. Bessis, Nik, 1967-
  QA76.9.D5D424 2013
  004'.36--dc23
                                2012029178

British Cataloguing in Publication Data
A Cataloguing in Publication record for this book is available from the British Library.

The views expressed in this book are those of the authors, but not necessarily of the publisher.

Associate Editors

List of Reviewers

Habib M. Ammari, *Hofstra University, USA*
Vassiliki Andronikou, *National Technical University of Athens, Greece*
Eleana Asimakopoulou, *formerly Loughborough University, UK*
Tatiana Atanasova, *Bulgarian Academy of Sciences, Bulgaria*
Mehmet Aydin, *University of Bedfordshire, UK*
Marina Burakova-Lorgnier, *University of Montesquieu-Bordeaux IV, France*
Jessica Chen-Burger, *University of Edinburgh, UK*
Marc Conrad, *University of Bedfordshire, UK*
Rogério Costa, *University of Coimbra, Portugal*
Alfredo Cuzzocrea, *University of Calabria, Italy*
Violeta Damjanovic, *University of Belgrade, Austria*
Alicia Diaz, *La Plata University, Argentina*
James Dooley, *City University, UK*
Marco Fargetta, *Consorzio COMETA - Catania University, Italy*
Tim French, *University of Bedfordshire, UK*
Pedro Furtado, *University of Coimbra, Portugal*
Michael Gardner, *University of Essex, UK*
Jeni Giambona, *Reading University, UK*
Sergei Gorlatch, *University of Münster, Germany*
Ye Huang, *University of Fribourg, Switzerland*
Ejub Kajan, *State University of Novi Pazar, Serbia*
Samee University Khan, *North Dakota State University, USA*
Valery Kuriakin, *Intel, Russia*
Krzysztof Kurowski, *Poznan Supercomputing and Networking Center, Poland*
Dimosthenis Kyriazis, *National Technical University of Athens, Greece*
Rania Labaki, *University of Montesquieu Bordeaux IV, France*
Maozhen Li, *Brunel University, UK*
Wen-Yang Lin, *National University of Kaohsiung, Taiwan*
Athanasios Loukopoulos, *TEI of Lamia, Greece*
Lu Liu, *University of Derby, UK*
Zaigham Mahmood, *University of Derby, UK*
Areti Manataki, *University of Edinburgh, UK*
Roco Martnez Torres, *University of Seville, Spain*
Sati McKenzie, *University of Greenwich, UK*
Milan Milanovic, *University of Belgrade, Serbia*
Anton Minko, *OKTAL, France*
Navonil Mustafee, *Swansea University, UK*
Jovita Nenortaitë, *Kaunas University of Technology, Lithuania*
Peter Norrington, *University of Bedfordshire, UK*
Mariusz Nowostawski, *University of Otago, New Zealand*
Elpiniki Papageorgiou, *TEI of Lamia, Greece*

Table of Contents

Section 1
Advanced Techniques and Methods for Distributed Systems

Chapter 1

Stelios Sotiriadis, University of Derby, UK
Nik Bessis, University of Derby, UK & University of Bedfordshire, UK
Ye Huang, University of Fribourg, Switzerland
Paul Sant, University of Bedfordshire, UK
Carsten Maple, University of Bedfordshire, UK

Chapter 2

Andreea Visan, University Politehnica of Bucharest, Romania
Mihai Istin, University Politehnica of Bucharest, Romania
Florin Pop, University Politehnica of Bucharest, Romania
Valentin Cristea, University Politehnica of Bucharest, Romania

Chapter 3

Zahid Raza, Jawaharlal Nehru University, India
Deo Prakash Vidyarthi, Jawaharlal Nehru University, India

Section 2
State-of-the-Art Distributed Systems Applications

Section 3
High-End Design Concepts for Future Distributed Systems

Detailed Table of Contents

Section 1
Advanced Techniques and Methods for Distributed Systems

Chapter 1
    Stelios Sotiriadis, University of Derby, UK
    Nik Bessis, University of Derby, UK & University of Bedfordshire, UK
    Ye Huang, University of Fribourg, Switzerland
    Paul Sant, University of Bedfordshire, UK
    Carsten Maple, University of Bedfordshire, UK

This paper focuses on defining the minimum requirements to support the inter-cooperation between various scales, dynamically evolved Virtual Organizations (VOs). This proposed method is able to assign a weighted value to each pair-wise path that each member (node) can select in order to locate neighbouring nodes according to their preferences. The method also takes into account the communication overhead between each node interaction. The weight of each path is to be measured by the analysis of prerequisites in order to achieve a mutually agreed interaction between nodes. Requirements are defined as the least parameters or conditions that a node needs to achieve in order to determine its accessibility factor. The motivation behind this work is the vision of the Critical Friends Community model, which is a suitable topology for interoperable grid environments. The topology suggests that capturing inter-cooperated nodes interactions that can be publicly available could lead to knowledge of neighbouring VO members which, in turn, could be used for facilitating a more effective resource discovery and selection decision.

Chapter 2

The state prediction of resources in large scale distributed systems represents an important aspect for resources allocations, systems evaluation, and autonomic control. The paper presents advanced techniques for resources state prediction in Large Scale Distributed Systems, which include techniques based on bio-inspired algorithms like neural network improved with genetic algorithms. The approach adopted in this paper consists of a new fitness function, having prediction error minimization as the main scope. The proposed prediction techniques are based on monitoring data, aggregated in a history database. The experimental scenarios consider the ALICE experiment, active at the CERN institute. Compared with classical predicted algorithms based on average or random methods, the authors obtain an improved prediction error of 73%. This improvement is important for functionalities and performance of resource management systems in large scale distributed systems in the case of remote control ore advance reservation and allocation.

Chapter 3

Computational Grid attributed with distributed load sharing has evolved as a platform to large scale problem solving. Grid is a collection of heterogeneous resources, offering services of varying natures, in which jobs are submitted to any of the participating nodes. Scheduling these jobs in such a complex and dynamic environment has many challenges. Reliability analysis of the grid gains paramount importance because grid involves a large number of resources which may fail anytime, making it unreliable. These failures result in wastage of both computational power and money on the scarce grid resources. It is normally desired that the job should be scheduled in an environment that ensures maximum reliability to the job execution. This work presents a reliability based scheduling model for the jobs on the computational grid. The model considers the failure rate of both the software and hardware grid constituents like application demanding execution, nodes executing the job, and the network links supporting data exchange between the nodes. Job allocation using the proposed scheme becomes trusted as it schedules the job based on a priori reliability computation.

Chapter 4

In this paper, the authors investigate how the sensor network performs when the event moves with special movement path. Simulation results are compared with four scenarios: when the event is stationary, moving randomly, moving with simple 4 path, and boids path. The simulation results show that for the case when the event is moving randomly, the performance is the worst in the four scenarios. The characteristic of goodput decreases with the increase of number of sensor nodes. In the case of the boids model, the goodput is unstable when the T_r is lower than 10 pps. The consumed energy characteristic increases with the increase of T_r Simulation results show that the consumed energy of random movement is the worst among the four scenarios. The consumed energy of boids model is the lowest in four cases. This shows that the event movement with boids model can decrease the consumed energy in large scale WSNs.

Chapter 5

Zhihua Lai, University of Bedfordshire, UK

Nik Bessis, University of Derby, UK & University of Bedfordshire, UK

Guillaume De La Roche, University of Bedfordshire, UK

Pierre Kuonen, University of Applied Science of Western Switzerland, Switzerland

Jie Zhang, University of Bedfordshire, UK

Gordon Clapworthy, University of Bedfordshire, UK

Propagation modeling has attracted much interest because it plays an important role in wireless network planning and optimization. Deterministic approaches such as ray tracing and ray launching have been investigated, however, due to the running time constraint, these approaches are still not widely used. In previous work, an intelligent ray launching algorithm, namely IRLA, has been proposed. The IRLA has proven to be a fast and accurate algorithm and adapts to wireless network planning well. This article focuses on the development of a parallel ray launching algorithm based on the IRLA. Simulations are implemented, and evaluated performance shows that the parallelization greatly shortens the running time. The COST231 Munich scenario is adopted to verify algorithm behavior in real world environments, and observed results show a 5 times increased speedup upon a 16-processor cluster. In addition, the parallelization algorithm can be easily extended to larger scenarios with sufficient physical resources.

Chapter 6

Parveen Kumar, Meerut Institute of Engineering & Technology, India

Rachit Garg, Singhania University, India

Minimum-process coordinated checkpointing is a suitable approach to introduce fault tolerance in mobile distributed systems transparently. In order to balance the checkpointing overhead and the loss of computation on recovery, the authors propose a hybrid checkpointing algorithm, wherein an all-process coordinated checkpoint is taken after the execution of minimum-process coordinated checkpointing algorithm for a fixed number of times. In coordinated checkpointing, if a single process fails to take its checkpoint; all the checkpointing effort goes waste, because, each process has to abort its tentative checkpoint. In order to take the tentative checkpoint, an MH (Mobile Host) needs to transfer large checkpoint data to its local MSS over wireless channels. In this regard, the authors propose that in the first phase, all concerned MHs will take soft checkpoint only. Soft checkpoint is similar to mutable checkpoint. In this case, if some process fails to take checkpoint in the first phase, then MHs need to abort their soft checkpoints only. The effort of taking a soft checkpoint is negligibly small as compared to the tentative one. In the minimum-process coordinated checkpointing algorithm, an effort has been made to minimize the number of useless checkpoints and blocking of processes using probabilistic approach.

Section 2
State-of-the-Art Distributed Systems Applications

Chapter 7

Tri Minh Tran, University of Vermont, USA

Byung Suk Lee, University of Vermont, USA

This paper presents an adaptive framework for processing a window-based multi-way join query over distributed data streams. The framework integrates distributed plan modification and distributed plan migration within the same scope by using a building block called the node operator set (NOS). An NOS is housed in each node that participates in the join execution, and specifies the set of atomic operations to be performed locally at the host node to execute its share of the global execution plan. The plan modification and migration techniques presented are for the case of updating the NOSs centralized at a single node and the case of updating them distributed at each node. The plan modification is triggered by the change of stream statistics and adjusts the join execution order and placement greedily to satisfy a cost invariant. The plan migration uses the distributed track strategy to accelerate the migration of window extents to new nodes. The migration of all window extents is synchronized. Experiments confirm the effectiveness of the developed adaptive framework on reducing the join execution cost and indicate a small additional adaptation-overhead for distributing the NOS update.

Chapter 8

Andrei Lavinia, University Politehnica of Bucharest, Romania

Ciprian Dobre, University Politehnica of Bucharest, Romania

Florin Pop, University Politehnica of Bucharest, Romania

Valentin Cristea, University Politehnica of Bucharest, Romania

Failure detection is a fundamental building block for ensuring fault tolerance in large scale distributed systems. It is also a difficult problem. Resources under heavy loads can be mistaken as being failed. The failure of a network link can be detected by the lack of a response, but this also occurs when a computational resource fails. Although progress has been made, no existing approach provides a system that covers all essential aspects related to a distributed environment. This paper presents a failure detection system based on adaptive, decentralized failure detectors. The system is developed as an independent substrate, working asynchronously and independent of the application flow. It uses a hierarchical protocol, creating a clustering mechanism that ensures a dynamic configuration and traffic optimization. It also uses a gossip strategy for failure detection at local levels to minimize detection time and remove wrong suspicions. Results show that the system scales with the number of monitored resources, while still considering the QoS requirements of both applications and resources.

Thomas Moser, Vienna University of Technology, Austria
Stefan Biffl, Vienna University of Technology, Austria
Wikan Danar Sunindyo, Vienna University of Technology, Austria
Dietmar Winkler, Vienna University of Technology, Austria

The engineering of a complex production automation system involves experts from several backgrounds, such as mechanical, electrical, and software engineering. The production automation expert knowledge is embedded in their tools and data models, which are, unfortunately, insufficiently integrated across the expert disciplines, due to semantically heterogeneous data structures and terminologies. Traditional integration approaches to data integration using a common repository are limited as they require an agreement on a common data schema by all project stakeholders. This paper introduces the Engineering Knowledge Base (EKB), a semantic-web-based framework, which supports the efficient integration of information originating from different expert domains without a complete common data schema. The authors evaluate the proposed approach with data from real-world use cases from the production automation domain on data exchange between tools and model checking across tools. Major results are that the EKB framework supports stronger semantic mapping mechanisms than a common repository and is more efficient if data definitions evolve frequently.

Maximilian Schirmer, Bauhaus-University Weimar, Germany
Tom Gross, University of Bamberg, Germany

Cooperative ubiquitous environments support user interaction and cooperative work by adapting to the prevalent situation of the present users. They are typically complex and have many environment components—interconnected devices and software modules—that realise new interaction techniques and facilitate collaboration. Despite this complexity, users need to be able to easily adapt their environments to the respective needs of the workgroups. In this paper, the authors present the CollaborationBus Aqua editor, a sophisticated, yet lightweight editor for configuring ubiquitous environments in groups. The CollaborationBus Aqua editor simplifies the configuration and offers advanced concepts for sharing and browsing configurations among users.

Stijn Dekeyser, University of Southern Queensland, Australia
Jan Hidders, Delft University of Technology, The Netherlands

Collaboration on documents has been supported for several decades through a variety of systems and tools; recently a renewed interest is apparent through the appearance of new collaborative editors and applications. Some distributed groupware systems are plug-ins for standalone word processors while others have a purely web-based existence. Most exemplars of the new breed of systems are based on Operational Transformations, although some are using traditional version management tools and still others utilize document-level locking techniques. All existing techniques have their drawbacks, creating opportunities for new methods. The authors present a novel collaborative technique for documents which is based on transactions, schedulers, conflicts, and locks. It is not meant to replace existing techniques; rather, it can be used in specific situations where a strict form of concurrency control is required. While the approach of presentation in this article is highly formal with an emphasis on proving desirable properties such as guaranteed correctness, the work is part of a project which aims to fully implement the technique.

Liliana Ardissono, Università di Torino, Italy
Gianni Bosio, Università di Torino, Italy
Anna Goy, Università di Torino, Italy
Giovanna Petrone, Università di Torino, Italy
Marino Segnan, Università di Torino, Italy
Fabrizio Torretta, Università di Torino, Italy

This paper describes a framework supporting the development of open collaboration environments which integrate heterogeneous business services. The framework facilitates the user cooperation in the execution of shared activities by offering a workspace awareness support which abstracts from the business services employed to operate. The management of the workspaces of the user's collaborations is based on the functions offered by the Collaborative Task Manager (CTM), which offers a lightweight and flexible model for handling more or less complex collaborations. The CTM is integrated with business services in a loosely coupled way which supports the management of parallel workspaces for accessing the user's collaboration contexts, their objects and the related awareness information.

José G. Hernández Ramírez, Universidad Metropolitana, Venezuela
María J. García García, Minimax Consultores C. A., Venezuela
Gilberto J. Hernández García, Minimax Consultores C. A., Venezuela

An easy to apply multi-criteria technique is the Matrixes Of Weighing (MOW), but many of the professionals that use it, in their respective fields, do it in intuitive fashion. In this regard, applications are rarely reported in specialized literature, which explains how few references exist about them. One of the application areas for MOW is the handling of catastrophes, in particular the pre-catastrophe and post-catastrophe phases where a series of problems are usually handled which solution leads to a choice, which could be done by using multi-criteria techniques.The objective of this investigation is to present the MOW with multiplicative factors, and showing their application in the pre-catastrophe phase, when choosing possible shelters and in the post-catastrophe phase, by aiding to hierarchies which infrastructures to be recovered after a catastrophe.

Section 3
High-End Design Concepts for Future Distributed Systems

Chapter 14

Sarsij Tripathi, Motilal Nehru National Institute of Technology, India
Rama Shankar Yadav, Motilal Nehru National Institute of Technology, India
Ranvijay, Motilal Nehru National Institute of Technology, India
Rajib L. Jana, Motilal Nehru National Institute of Technology, India

The world has become a global village. Today applications are developed which require sharing of resources dispersed geographically to fulfill the need of the users. In most cases applications turn out to be time bound thus leading to Real Time Distributed System (RTDS). Online Banking, Online Multimedia Applications, Real Time Databases, and Missile tracking systems are some examples of these types of applications. These applications face many challenges in the present scenario particularly in resource management, load balancing, security, and deadlock. The heterogeneous nature of the system exacerbates the challenges. This paper provides a widespread survey of research work reported in RTDS. This review has covered the work done in the field of resource management, load balancing, deadlock, and security. The challenges involved in tackling these issues is presented and future directions are discussed.

Chapter 15

Li Zhu, Università degli Studi di Milano, Italy
Barbara Rita Barricelli, Università degli Studi di Milano, Italy
Claudia Iacob, Università degli Studi di Milano, Italy

As collaboration in creating software systems becomes more complex and frequent among multidisciplinary teams, finding new strategies to support this collaboration becomes crucial. The challenge is to bridge the communication gaps among stakeholders with diverse cultural and professional backgrounds. Moreover, future uses and issues cannot be completely anticipated at design time, and it is necessary to develop open-ended software environments that can be evolved and tailored in opportunistic ways to tackle co-evolution of users and systems. A conceptual meta-design model, the Hive-Mind Space (HMS) model, has been proposed to support multidisciplinary design teams' collaboration and foster their situated innovation. The model provides localized habitable environments for diverse stakeholders and tools for them to tailor the system, allowing the co-evolution of systems and practices. The authors explore the possibility of utilizing boundary objects within the HMS model to facilitate the communication amongst stakeholders as well as their participation in the creative distributed design process. Two concrete case studies, a factory automation and the Valchiavenna Portal, demonstrate the implementation of the HMS model and provide a possible solution to overcome the complex, evolving and emerging nature of the collaborative design.

Heiko Thimm, Pforzheim University, Germany
Karsten Boye Rasmussen, University of Southern Denmark, Denmark

Well-informed network participants are a necessity for successful collaboration in business networks. The widespread knowledge of the many aspects of the network is an effective vehicle to promote trust within the network, successfully resolve conflicts, and build a prospering collaboration climate. Despite their natural interest in being well informed about all the different aspects of the network, limited resources, e.g. time restrictions of the participants, often prevents reaching an appropriate level of shared information. It is possible to overcome this problem through the use of an active information provisioning service that allows users to adapt the provisioning of information to their specific needs. This paper presents an extensible information modeling framework and also additional complementary concepts that are designed to enable such an active provisioning service. Furthermore, a high-level architecture for a system that offers the targeted information provisioning service is described.

Isamu Tsuneizumi, Seikei University, Japan
Ailixier Aikebaier, Seikei University, Japan
Makoto Ikeda, Seikei University, Japan
Tomoya Enokido, Risho University, Japan
Makoto Takizawa, Seikei University, Japan

To realize the cooperation of a group of multiple peer processes (peers), messages sent by peers must be causally delivered to every peer. In a scalable group, it is necessary to reduce the communication overhead to causally deliver messages. In this paper, the authors take advantage of the linear time (LT) and physical time (PT) protocols, as the message length is $O(n)$ for the number n of peers. However, some pairs are unnecessarily ordered, that is, even if a pair of messages is ordered in the protocols, the messages may not be causally ordered. The greater the number of messages that are unnecessarily ordered, the larger the overhead is implied since the messages must be kept in a receipt queue if a message is lost or delayed. This paper discusses a hybrid time group communication (HT) protocol that reduces the number of messages unnecessarily ordered. The HT protocol is evaluated in terms of the number of unnecessarily ordered messages compared with the PT and LT protocols. It is demonstrated that the number of unnecessarily ordered messages can be reduced in the HT protocol compared with the LT and PT protocols.

This paper presents some aspects of the 'communication' processes within a Systemic Disaster Management System (SDMS) model. Information and communication technology (ICT) plays a key part in managing natural disasters. However, it has been contended that ICT should not be used in 'isolation' but it should be seen as 'part' of the 'whole' system for managing disaster risk. Further research is needed in order to illustrate the full application of the ICT within the context of the developed model.

Much work is underway within the broad next generation technologies community on issues associated with the development of services to support interdisciplinary domains. Disaster reduction and emergency management are domains in which utilization of advanced information and communication technologies (ICT) are critical for sustainable development and livelihoods. In this article, the authors aim to use an exemplar occupational disaster scenario in which advanced ICT utilization could present emergency managers with some collective computational intelligence in order to prioritize their decision making. To achieve this, they adapt concepts and practices from various next generation technologies including ad-hoc mobile networks, Web 2.0, wireless sensors, crowd sourcing and situated computing. On the implementation side, the authors developed a data mashup map, which highlights the criticality of victims at a location of interest. With this in mind, the article describes the service architecture in the form of data and process flows, its implementation and some simulation results.

Preface

While distributed systems have been the subject for many years they continue to be a very vibrant area for intense research.

This is mainly due to the fact that they are very often heterogeneous and geographically distributed. Notably enough, technologies are and in fact, meant to be used by several communities of users, which are also geographically distributed. Hence, the ability to make technologies interoperable remains a crucial factor for the development of several types of our society systems. Clearly, one of the challenges for such facilitation is the identification of methods and techniques that are required in order to design, implement and maintain these geographically distributed systems in a sustainable manner.

Even though the advantages of several distributed computing paradigms such as of Web and Web 2.0, grid and cloud computing, it is only recently that their applicability into the real world of the information society has been realized. While scientists have almost exclusively used these for their own research and development purposes, there has been a clear shift to application domains that are closer to everyday life. Hence, these paradigms have an increased focus on the integration of distributed systems, resources and technologies, which are available within and across various collaborative communities or organizations. As such, the size and complexity of integrating and applying cutting-edge distributed technologies are enormous and thus, there is a particular need to acknowledge progress made with a specific reference to their design, implementation and maintenance.

The goal of the Development of Distributed Systems from Design to Application and Maintenance book is to provide such a focus for the presentation and dissemination of new research results within the aforementioned area.

THE PURPOSE OF THE BOOK

The book aims to demonstrate a network of excellence in distributed computing and by doing so to provide progress made with relevance to their design, application and maintenance. Its mission is to introduce and thus, to highlight a feasible and applicable arrangement within business and other research and development sector's e-infrastructures.

It also deepens its focus by highlighting strengths, weaknesses, opportunities, and threats when these are deployed within a real-world organizational setting. Contributions in this book pay particular attention to presenting topics that are diverse in scale and complexity, as well as written by and for a technical minded audience.

More importantly, the goal of the book is to prompt and foster further development for best practices in identifying opportunities and thus, it provides an excellent source for future applicable directions and technology innovative adoptions in the society.

WHO SHOULD READ THIS BOOK?

The content of the book offers state-of-the-art information and references for research work undertaken in the challenging area of distributed computing by focusing on the design, application and maintenance of such systems. The areas covered include large-scale networking and distributed systems, distributed collaborative computing, cloud computing, ubiquitous environments, wireless and real-time systems and finally, work on applying distributed computing for the specific setting of disaster management. With this in mind, the book offers an excellent source for the technical audience and the computer science minded scholar. Thus, the book should be of particular interest for:

Researchers and doctoral students who are fully engaging in the area of distributed computing, distributed data technologies, and integration technologies. The book should be also a very useful reference for all researchers and doctoral students working in the broader fields of high performance computing, grid and cloud computing, applicable computational technologies, distributed computing, object and service oriented architectures, web services, collaborative technologies, agent intelligence and data mining.

Academics and mainly postgraduate students engaging in research informed teaching and/ or learning in the aforementioned emerging technologies fields. The view here is that the book can serve as a good reference offering a solid understanding of the integration and distributed computing subject area.

Professionals including computing specialists, practitioners, managers and consultants who may be interested in identifying ways and thus, applying a number of well defined and/or applicable cutting edge techniques and processes within the aforementioned domain areas.

BOOK ORGANIZATION AND OVERVIEW

Nineteen self-contained chapters, each authored by experts in the area, are included in this book. The book is organized into three sections according to the thematic topic of each chapter. Having said that, it is possible that a chapter in one section may also address issues covered in other sections.

Section 1: Advanced Techniques and Methods for Distributed Systems

This section includes six chapters. It introduces both principles and progress made in advanced techniques and methods for distributed systems. While these stand as a state-of-the-art reference, most chapters present experimental scenarios and approaches on how these methods and techniques can be applied in the real-world. As such, they underpin future development and implementation of relevant services.

In Chapter 1 – *Defining Minimum Requirements of Inter-Collaborated Nodes by Measuring the Weight of Node Interactions* – authors focus on defining the minimum requirements to support the inter-cooperation between various scales, dynamically evolved Virtual Organizations (VOs). Their proposed method is able to assign a weighted value to each pair-wise path that each member (node) can select in order to locate neighbouring nodes according to their preferences. The weight of each path is be measured by the analysis of prerequisites in order to achieve a mutually agreed interaction between nodes. The information gathered from an interaction is then stored in a snapshot, a profile that is made available during the discovery stage. The topology suggests that capturing inter-cooperated nodes interactions that can be publicly available could lead to knowledge of neighbouring VO members which in turn, could be used for facilitating a more effective resource discovery and selection decision. Work here is applicable to grids, clouds, and inter-clouds (federated clouds).

In Chapter 2 – *Bio-Inspired Techniques for Resources State Prediction in Large Scale Distributed Systems* – authors advance available techniques for resources state prediction in large scale distributed systems by using bio-inspired algorithms (i.e. neural network improved by genetic algorithms). The new approach herein consists in a new fitness function, having as a main scope the prediction error minimization. The proposed prediction techniques are based on monitoring data, aggregated in a history database. The experimental scenarios consider the ALICE experiment, active at CERN Institute. Compared to the classical predicted algorithms based on average or random methods, authors obtained an improvement considering prediction error of 73%.

In Chapter 3 – *Reliability Based Scheduling Model (RSM) for Computational Grids* – authors present a reliability based scheduling model for the jobs on the computational grid. The model considers the failure rate of both the software and hardware grid constituents like application demanding execution, nodes executing the job and the network links supporting data exchange between the nodes. Job allocation using the proposed scheme thus becomes a trusted one as it schedules the job based on a priori reliability computation.

In Chapter 4 – *Performance of Wireless Sensor Networks for Different Mobile Event Path Scenarios* – authors investigate how the sensor network performs in the case when the event moves with special movement path. Authors compare the simulation results for four specific scenarios: when the event is stationary, moving randomly, moving with simple 4 path and boids path. The simulation results have shown that for the case when event is moving randomly the performance is the worst in the four scenarios. Simulation results also show that the consumed energy of random movement is the worst among four scenarios. The consumed energy of boids model is the lowest in four cases. This shows that the event movement with boids model can decrease the consumed energy in the large scale WSNs.

In Chapter 5 – *The Development of a Parallel Ray Launching Algorithm for Wireless Network Planning* – authors focus on the development of a parallel ray launching algorithm based on an intelligent ray launching algorithm (IRLA). Simulations are implemented, and evaluated performance has shown that the parallelization has greatly shortened the running time. Moreover, the COST231 Munich scenario has been adopted to verify algorithm behavior in real world environment, and observed results have shown a 5 times increased speedup upon a 16-processor cluster. In addition, the parallelization algorithm can be easily extended to larger scenarios with sufficient physical resources.

In Chapter 6 – *Soft-Checkpointing Based Hybrid Synchronous Checkpointing Protocol for Mobile Distributed Systems* – authors propose a hybrid checkpointing algorithm, wherein an all-process coordinated checkpoint is taken after the execution of minimum-process coordinated checkpointing algorithm for a fixed number of times. In coordinated checkpointing, if a single process fails to take its checkpoint, all the checkpointing effort goes waste, because each process has to abort its tentative checkpoint. In order to take the tentative checkpoint, an MH (Mobile Host) needs to transfer large checkpoint data to its local MSS over wireless channels. Hence, the loss of checkpointing effort may be exceedingly high. Therefore, authors propose that in the first phase, all concerned MHs will take soft checkpoint only. Soft checkpoint is similar to mutable checkpoint, which is stored on the memory of MH only. In this case, if some process fails to take checkpoint in the first phase, then MHs need to abort their soft checkpoints only. The effort of taking a soft checkpoint is negligibly small as compared to the tentative one. In the minimum-process coordinated checkpointing algorithm, an effort has been made to minimize the number of useless checkpoints and blocking of processes using probabilistic approach.

Section 2: State-of-the-Art Distributed Systems Applications

This section includes seven chapters. The content of this section is particularly valuable to those whose interest resides within the application area of distributed systems advances.

In Chapter 7 – *Distributed Adaptive Windowed Stream Join Processing* – authors present an adaptive framework for processing a window-based multi-way join query over distributed data streams. The framework integrates distributed plan modification and distributed plan migration within the same scope by using a building block called the node operator set (NOS). An NOS is housed in each node that participates in the join execution, and specifies the set of atomic operations to be performed locally at the host node to execute its share of the global execution plan. Experiments confirm the effectiveness of the developed adaptive framework on reducing the join execution cost and indicate a small additional adaptation-overhead for distributing the NOS update.

In Chapter 8 – *A Failure Detection System for Large Scale Distributed Systems* – authors present a failure detection system based on adaptive, decentralized failure detectors. The system is developed as an independent substrate, working asynchronously and independent of the application flow. It uses a hierarchical protocol, creating a clustering mechanism that ensures a dynamic configuration and traffic optimization. It also uses a gossip strategy for failure detection at local level in order to minimize detection time and remove wrong suspicions. Authors present results showing that the system scales with the number of monitored resources, while still considering the QoS requirements of both applications and resources.

In Chapter 9 – *Integrating Production Automation Expert Knowledge across Engineering Domains* – authors introduce the Engineering Knowledge Base (EKB), a Semantic-Web-based framework, which supports the efficient integration of information originating from different expert domains without a complete common data schema. Authors evaluate the proposed approach with data from real-world use cases from the production automation domain on data exchange between tools and model checking across tools. Major results are that the EKB framework supports stronger semantic mapping mechanisms than a common repository and is more efficient if data definitions evolve frequently.

In Chapter 10 – *Lightweight Editing of Distributed Ubiquitous Environments: The CollaborationBus Aqua Editor* – authors present the CollaborationBus Aqua editor, a sophisticated, yet lightweight editor for configuring ubiquitous environments in groups. The CollaborationBus Aqua editor simplifies the configuration and offers advanced concepts for sharing and browsing configurations among users.

In Chapter 11 – *Guaranteeing Correctness for Collaboration on Documents Using an Optimal Locking Protocol* – authors present a novel collaborative technique for documents which is based on transactions, schedulers, conflicts, and locks. It is not meant to replace existing techniques; rather, it can be used in specific situations where a strict form of concurrency control is required. While their approach is highly formal - with an emphasis on proving desirable properties such as guaranteed correctness - the work is part of a project which aims to fully implement the technique.

In Chapter 12 – *Collaboration Support for Activity Management in a Personal Cloud Environment* – authors describe a framework supporting the development of open collaboration environments which integrate heterogeneous business services. The framework facilitates the user cooperation in the execution of shared activities by offering a workspace awareness support which abstracts from the business services employed to operate. The management of the workspaces of the user's collaborations is based on the functions offered by the Collaborative Task Manager (CTM), which offers a lightweight and flexible model for handling more or less complex collaborations. The CTM is integrated with business services in a loosely coupled way which supports the management of parallel workspaces for accessing the user's collaboration contexts, their objects, and the related awareness information.

In Chapter 13 – *Matrixes of Weighing and Catastrophes* – authors propose the use of a multi-criteria technique, namely the Matrixes Of Weighing (MOW) for the handling of catastrophes, in particular the pre-catastrophe and post-catastrophe phases, where a series of problems are usually handled which solution leads to a choice, which could be done by using multi-criteria techniques. The objective of this investigation is to present the MOW with multiplicative factors, and showing their application in the pre-catastrophe phase, when choosing possible shelters and in the post-catastrophe phase, by aiding to hierarchies which infrastructures to be recovered after a catastrophe.

Section 3: High-End Design Concepts for Future Distributed Systems

This section includes six chapters. This section goes beyond and builds upon current theory and practice, providing cutting edge and visionary real-world directions on how distributed computing technologies are and could be used in the near future to the benefit of various settings.

In Chapter 14 – *Resource Management in Real Time Distributed System with Security Constraints: A Review* – authors provide a widespread survey of research work reported in RTDS. This review covers the work done in the field of resource management, load balancing, deadlock and security. Authors also present the challenges involved in tackling these issues and prompt future directions in these areas.

In Chapter 15 – *A Meta-Design Model for Creative Distributed Collaborative Design* – authors acknowledge that collaboration in creating software systems becomes more complex and frequent among multidisciplinary teams. The challenge is to bridge the communication gaps among stakeholders with diverse cultural and professional backgrounds. Authors also argue that future uses and issues cannot be completely anticipated at design time and developers must provide open-ended software environments that can be evolved and tailored in opportunistic ways to tackle co-evolution of users and systems. With this in mind, authors propose a conceptual meta-design model, the Hive-Mind Space (HMS) model to support multidisciplinary design teams' collaboration and to foster their situated innovation. The model provides localized habitable environments for diverse stakeholders and tools for them to tailor the system, allowing the co-evolution of systems and practices. Two concrete case studies demonstrate the implementation of the HMS model and provide a possible solution to overcome the complex, evolving, and emerging nature of the collaborative design.

In Chapter 16 – *Adaptable Information Provisioning in Collaborative Networks: An Object Modeling Framework and System Approach* – authors argue that the widespread of knowledge across a network can be used as an effective vehicle to promote trust within the network, successfully resolve conflicts, and build a prospering collaboration climate. With this in mind, authors present an extensible information modeling framework and also further complementary concepts that are designed to enable such an active provisioning service. Furthermore, a high-level architecture for a system that offers the targeted information provisioning service is described.

In Chapter 17 – *Design and Implementation of Hybrid Time (HT) Group Communication Protocol for Homogeneous Broadcast Groups* – authors were concerned with the number of messages sent within a group of multiple peer network. Herein, authors take advantage of the linear time (LT) and physical time (PT) protocols since the message length is $O(n)$ for the number n of peers. Authors discuss a hybrid time group communication (HT) protocol to reduce the number of messages unnecessarily ordered by taking advantage of the linear time and physical time. They evaluate the HT protocol in terms of the number of unnecessarily ordered messages compared with the PT and LT protocols. Authors show the number of unnecessarily ordered messages can be reduced in the HT protocol compared with the LT and PT protocols.

In Chapter 18 – *Information Communication Technology and a Systemic Disaster Management System Model* – authors present some aspects of the communication processes within a Systemic Disaster Management System (SDMS) model. Authors are focused on that ICT should not be used in isolation but it should be seen as part of the whole system for managing disaster risk. Further research is needed in order to illustrate the full application of the ICT within the context of the developed model.

In Chapter 19 – *A Next Generation Technology Victim Location and Low Level Assessment Framework for Occupational Disasters caused by Natural Hazards* – authors discuss the use of an exemplar occupational disaster scenario in which advanced ICT utilization could present emergency managers with some collective computational intelligence in order to prioritize their decision making. To achieve this, authors adapt concepts and practices from various next generation technologies including ad-hoc mobile networks, Web 2.0, wireless sensors, crowd sourcing, and situated computing. On the implementation side, they developed a data mashup map, which highlights the criticality of victims at a location of interest. Authors also present the service architecture in the form of data and process flows, its implementation, and some simulation results.

Nik Bessis
University of Derby, UK & University of Bedfordshire, UK

Acknowledgment

It is my great pleasure to comment on the hard work and support of many people who have been involved in the development of this book. It is always a major undertaking but most importantly, a great encouragement and somehow a reward and an honor when seeing the enthusiasm and eagerness of people willing to advance their discipline by taking the commitment to share their experiences, ideas and visions towards the evolvement of collaboration like the achievement of this book. Without their support the book could not have been satisfactorily completed.

First and foremost, I wish to thank all the authors who, as distinguished scientists, despite busy schedules, devoted so much of their time preparing and writing their works, and responding to numerous comments and suggestions made from the reviewers, and myself. I trust this collection of chapters will offer a solid overview of current thinking on these areas and it is expected that the book will be a valuable source of stimulation and inspiration to all those who have or will have an interest in these fields.

I wish to gratefully acknowledge that I was fortunate to work closely with an outstanding team at IGI Global. Specifically and with no particular order, I wish to thank Erika Gallagher, Heather Probst, Joel Gamon, Jamie Wilson and Jan Travers who were everything someone should expect from a publisher: professional, efficient, and a delight to work with. Thanks are also extended to all those at IGI Global who have taken care with managing the design and the timely production of this book. The editor wishes to apologize to anyone whom they have forgotten.

Finally, I am deeply indebted to my family for their love, patience, and support throughout this rewarding experience.

Nik Bessis
University of Derby, UK & University of Bedfordshire, UK

Section 1
Advanced Techniques and Methods for Distributed Systems

Chapter 1
Defining Minimum Requirements of Inter-Collaborated Nodes by Measuring the Weight of Node Interactions

Stelios Sotiriadis
University of Derby, UK

Ye Huang
University of Fribourg, Switzerland

Nik Bessis
*University of Derby, UK &
University of Bedfordshire, UK*

Paul Sant
University of Bedfordshire, UK

Carsten Maple
University of Bedfordshire, UK

ABSTRACT

This paper focuses on defining the minimum requirements to support the inter-cooperation between various scales, dynamically evolved Virtual Organizations (VOs). This proposed method is able to assign a weighted value to each pair-wise path that each member (node) can select in order to locate neighbouring nodes according to their preferences. The method also takes into account the communication overhead between each node interaction. The weight of each path is to be measured by the analysis of prerequisites in order to achieve a mutually agreed interaction between nodes. Requirements are defined as the least parameters or conditions that a node needs to achieve in order to determine its accessibility factor. The motivation behind this work is the vision of the Critical Friends Community model, which is a suitable topology for interoperable grid environments. The topology suggests that capturing inter-cooperated nodes interactions that can be publicly available could lead to knowledge of neighbouring VO members which, in turn, could be used for facilitating a more effective resource discovery and selection decision.

DOI: 10.4018/978-1-4666-2647-8.ch001

INTRODUCTION

The vision of this work is to pose a new approach to extend current VO node inter-cooperation practices as originally introduced and explained by Bessis in Huang et al. (2009). Our research leverages grid technology as a framework which emphasizes an open environment of self-motivated and acting members. For achieving this endeavour, we employ graph theory as the method to represent the interconnection of nodes and aiming at defining weighted paths that nodes can choose for future job assignments as we illustrated in Sotiriadis et al. (2010). Within a typical grid VO it is common that the number of the nodes and their communication is previously acknowledged and are connected in random topologies composing cliques of members. A widely accepted vision, initially stated by Foster et al. (2001), is that grid is about resource sharing and problem solving in multi-institutional VOs. These multi-tenancy environments of nodes may have interconnections with other VOs participants by composing an extended and scalable environment. Bessis in Huang et al. (2009) call these neighbouring of nodes as Critical Friends Community (CFC) and each specific member as a Self-led Critical Friend (SCF) which plays the role of mediator in the communication by reflecting inter-connections to any trusted node. On a similar vein, Huang et al. (2010) addressed a notable case namely how a SCF topology should be the means to realize interoperability and clarifies that a grid community can communicate within their VOs, thus they can form and manage their own perceptions about neighbouring nodes based on previous interactions, such as communication and delegation records. In other words, by using SCF, the discovery of nodes is based on a nodes internal knowledge independent of its VO domain. In this paper, we aim to utilize the fact that each VO is a specific neighbourhood of nodes composing a clique of vertices. By defining each path weight we aim to identify several paths between pairs of nodes. Eventually, the measured weight of path

edges will be supportive to the resource discovery method. The model appreciates that by assigning a value to each path we may then calculate the best job assignment selection based on the minimum requirements that a node should achieve. The effect of these is extracted from a node's necessities in order to achieve a job delegation, including the following:

- Policy management control, as the mean communication authorization.
- Knowledge coupling for delegating a specific job.
- Physical resources data stored within an announcement profile.
- Execution time constraints as history data from previous jobs delegations.

In a rational way, node communication is achieved firstly by attaining policies, followed by pairing knowledge background, and finally by physical resource and time information coupling. Data gathered from minimum requirements analysis is stored in a public profile of each node called a metadata snapshot profile. Finally, nodes will be able to decide the weight of each edge and make use of the weight at a later stage of resource selection.

There have been various attempts for realizing communication within such uncertain distributed environments. In general grids are categorised in centralized management VOs and open environments of self-motivated and acted members. This distinction is a key to understand the novel challenges posed by the inter-cooperated self-led members. Centralized management grids have received considerable attention in academia in recent years. Ma et al. (2008) suggest that efforts within the Grid community that address centralized or hierarchical models such MDS in Globus and MatchMaker in Condor have high efficiency and reduce the response time. In contrast, Czajkowski et al. (2001) propose that when the system extends to a large scale the performance will be affected by a single point of failure. Recently a new scheme has received the attention of the academic community; the fully decentralized model which turn clusters of collaborating enterprises into an efficient community of cluster member. In this model, every VO participant needs to embrace any partner in order to provide a more autonomous solution. A representation model of such network can be achieved utilizing graph theory. Any large network without apparent design principles can be described as random graphs that are the simplest and straightforward realization of complex networks. Marcus (2008) discuss that graphs consists of points (in our case the nodes), which are indicated by line segments (in our case the inter-connections) joining certain pairs of vertices (p. 1).

In order to develop such an open grid environment it is crucial to identify a grid VOs minimum requirements (Foster et al., 2004; De Roure et al., 2005) primarily including policy management control, resource discovery and representation mechanisms. Another fundamental aspect that needs to be considered is presented by Winton (2005), who suggests that nodes may be members of any number of VOs, may have any number of roles within a given VO, and their VO membership must remain confidential as well as being able to select and deselect VOs and roles (p. 57). It should be also possible to list resources and actions to which a VO member or role has access to carry out specific actions. This can be achieved by storing resources in a public profile namely by Huang et al. (2009) as the metadata snapshot profile of nodes that is accessible to everyone either member of the VO or external co-operators. The profile is then made available through advertising information directly to the inter-connected SCF nodes without having to be controlled by a central administrator or a fixed infrastructure.

It is vital to determine if a VO member has access to a certain resources, in other words the authorisation to carry out specific actions. On the other hand a VO must be able to specify a membership policy and user authorisation method. It is particularly important to realize that, a resource owner must be able to allow or forbid authorisation by VO and VO role membership. Our vision herein is based on the grid main concept, i.e. sharing resources among several VOs. Specific research questions are focused on the importance of assigning a value to a path, the method of considering the weight and the novelty of the study scheme. But most importantly, this work aims to deliver an inter-collaboration plan, by utilizing SCF as a novel notion of a resource discovery method. Clearly, the proposed architecture allows us to treat a grid community as an inter-collaborating group of users in which everyone can access and delegate jobs with respect to minimum requirements articulated by VO cliques.

In order to achieve a highly scalable cooperative community, Liu et al. (2007) propose a small world networking strategy based on randomly rewiring of all path edges via exchanging their end nodes' neighbourhood in an initially regular graph. This small world community strategy realises two expected features: highly clustered groups of nodes and shorter diameter between nodes. However, the strategy is applicable on small grid networks using graph theory as a means of network illustration. On the other hand, a very early study by Harris (2008) considers a dynamical network system that proves a balanced load distribution and efficient resource discovery. In order to design such a dynamical system, they analysed the degree distribution of nodes in a stochastic network system with a fixed number of nodes and fixed average number of path edges using a graph theoretic model. In the following sections we start off with describing the resource discovery method and the strategy of the resource selection. Then we analyse the minimum requirements by translating them to a sequence of steps for achieving interactions as well as their algorithmic structure. Finally, to demonstrate this, we present two scenarios of the inter-cooperation method; the first one presents typical grid VO nodes interactions and the second utilize the SCFs paradigm among two different VOs.

THE STRATEGY

It is fundamental for grid computing that resources of newly added nodes can be utilized by nodes already existing within the same VO. We call internal nodes of a specific VO as a *clique* which typically have the same policy preference and knowledge background. Moreover, once gaps between multi-institutional VOs are bridged by CFC members belonging to multi-VOs, collaboration of job sharing can be achieved between nodes from either the same or different VOs. In this context, the formality of communication issues is playing a vital role in the perspective of high-quality cooperation. By defining clique paths, we aim to exploit the impact on VO topology led by newly added SCF nodes. The newly regenerated VO will be a new topology of an ad-hoc nature, which will result in a new open pool of resources available to several VOs.

Within a cooperative community and from the service perspective of nodes there are mainly two kinds of communication as discussed by Liu et al. (2007); point to multipoint broadcasting and searching within the community. The point to multipoint broadcasting can be achieved by a node through an advertised information profile that it is willing to share to the community members. In this way capabilities of a node are published internally to a VO domain and each member could be aware of possible roles and actions of any VO participant. On the other hand, any community member can discover directly the information or services by searching within a neighbourhood. In a previous work we have presented a detailed discussion of a mobility agent based model including broadcasting and searching in Sotiriadis et al. (2010). Originally, Foster et al. (2004) states that the agents are widely used in the area of distributed systems; as they mutually

support efforts for exhibit intelligent behaviour involving reasoning, perception and communication on heterogeneous and robust environments as described by Russel and Norvig (2003). In both solutions VO members could establish some ad hoc, short-term relationships with one another so they can be provider, requestor, or both. Its aim is to indirect communication, independently to each own status either idle or equipped. Primary challenging goal in building an ad hoc grid is supplying each grid member with specific directions for continuously maintained information that is related to each community participant, therefore act as an intermediate. Such information will be stored on each VO member public profile and be able for advertising at the resource discovery progress. Formerly, in this work the advertising method is selected for node cooperation and each member could be able to broadcast its public profile data to the entire community by searching within the community. Howbeit, the ad hoc configuration can be achieved by presenting a self-configuring model for providing computing resources on demand utilizing each member public profile. In this way community members could be able to define their own locally administrative rules for communication and delegation within an inter-cooperative grid. A specific and detailed discussion concerning the searching resource discovery method is presented in the following sections. Before that, the next step is to translate the minimum requirements to a sequence of rational steps for achieving the inter-collaboration.

TRANSLATION OF REQUIREMENTS

In this section we trace the inter-cooperation minimum requirements, so emphasis has been on presenting fundamentals from the perspective of an open and interoperable grid environment. So, to achieve inter-cooperation by means of finding out the minimum requirements, we defined them as a sequence of reasonable steps in a specific order. Understanding the reasons behind the development of these logical key components of each step gives us an appreciation for what tasks a member can perform and how it does them. To ensure orderly access to a member we define the following sequence of steps as the data including within a public metadata snapshot profile:

1. **Policy Management Control (PMC):** The internal authorization and membership procedure happened within a VO and can be extended to an open grid environment of mutually willing members.
2. **Knowledge Base Pairing (KBP):** The knowledge background of internal members' capabilities including roles and actions as well as specific jobs that nodes can carry out.
3. **Physical Resource Announcement (PRA):** The place of the snapshot profile which contains the advertised information of hardware and software capabilities. More specifically, computational power as well as software potentials is stored here.
4. **Time Constraints Management (TCM):** The mean of realizing execution and communication times from previous jobs delegations as a record of history data.

The PMC is defined as the permissions that need to be addressed and obtained from nodes. Typically, clique nodes may have already decided and accepted a common PMC. Secondly, the KBP is critical for decisions to a node's task capabilities. The results are realized from the PRA, whose task is to classify hardware resources before the job delegation. A node with the best characteristics will be the candidate for the work assignment. Finally, the TCM will be used to determine the expected time of job completion and communication duration based on previous interactions. These requirements consist of a set of generated reports stored in a public profile of each node, namely as a metadata snapshot profile. Data stored in the profile will be announced

to each node after a request and kept up-to-date after a completed interaction. By combing data from the snapshot profile the weight of the node edges will be measured and a value will be assigned to each path. In the following sections we trace the aforementioned methodology, so as we move through the various stages, we see how the components are combined for achieving inter-collaboration of members.

A. Policy Management Control (PMC)

It is important for each VO to contain a PMC, which is shared by all nodes of a clique. The assumption is that most of the existing clique nodes have a unique account which is shared at the first time of VO construction. There are two vantage points from which to view an interaction among members, the Host and the Operators. We define as *Host* node a node which requests a job submission and *Operators* the nodes which are available for job assignment.

Each time a job delegation appears the clique nodes are identified by their account. Newly added nodes to the clique are assigned by contracting agreements after the first initialisation. If the new node belongs to the clique, then it is assigned by an internal agreement. In any other case it is a SCF and a new agreement is created. Specific policy measures include logon procedure, clique contract, SCF contract, and reference contract, which are stored within a node's public profile. The logon procedure allows clique nodes to be identified by utilizing accounts assigned to the administrator. The clique contracts are agreements signed from the internal VO nodes and their functionality is to arrange interactions for newly added nodes to the clique. The SCF contracts are agreements signed by the SCFs and clique nodes. These agreements are an indication for inter-collaboration of both parties at the time of initialization. Finally, the reference contracts are suggestions to a SCF contract which is settled by the clique VO in case a SCF needs to communicate with a node which is not aware of its existence. Figure 1 demonstrates the process sequence starting from the login and terminating when permission is granted. During the procedure the Operator is capable of performing specific tasks such as contract validation and account creation for clique nodes. Virtually, the procedure validates contract agreements of SCF and the reference contracts as the mean to realize the interoperation of nodes. The contracts functionality is to guarantee that nodes are either clique or SCF nodes. The plan is that a Host delegates a job to an Operator. Firstly, the Operator checks the Host account and decide if it is registered in the profile considering accepting the connection. If the permission is granted then the Host is successfully logged on and moves to the next step. If the logon is unsuccessful the Host responds by sending the Operator a clique contract or an SCF contract. If the agreement does not exist in both contracts then the Host may be a critical friend of a clique node and it is suggested to respond with a reference contract. It is now clear that both nodes are now able to sign an agreement protocol while the permission is successfully granted.

Figure 1. Use case of a node PMC interaction

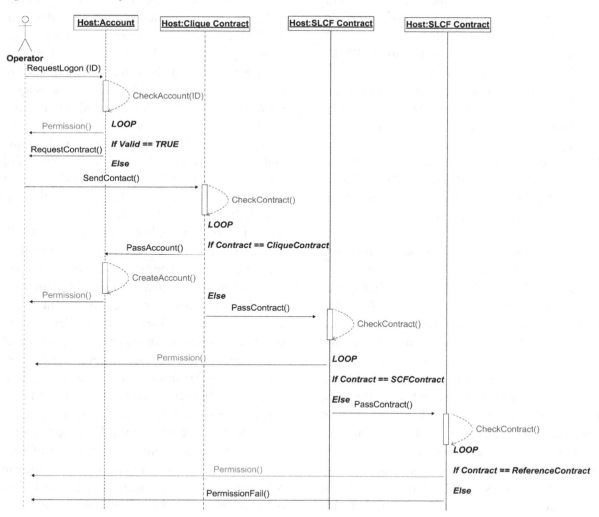

B. Knowledge-Based Pairing (KBP)

The public snapshot profile of a node should be able to provide information concerning its knowledge and capabilities. The pairing procedure is important as the node should be able to decide which node matches the needed job delegation. KBP includes current knowledge data, statistics information and suggestions for future familiar knowledge native interfaces which may be available.

The plan is that the Operator request specific actions that could be carried out from the Host node. If the knowledge does not exist then the Operator returns an error message to the Host and the job fails; otherwise, the Operator retrieves a ranking for the specific knowledge awarded by previous jobs interactions. The native knowledge interface aims to decide which job could be assigned from existing native libraries concerning particular job delegation. In this stage we define knowledge as the capability of performing specific jobs. Ranking and native knowledge interface will

be studied in future work. Figure 2 illustrates the sequence of the Host requesting the knowledge background and the Operator retrieving the rankings and native knowledge information.

C. Physical Resource Announcement

The physical resources of an Operator include information about hardware and software capabilities. These records are essential and are required to be announced to the public profile of each node. In general much information can be captured by a public profile such as CPU, Memory Space, Disk Space, Operating System, Processor Architecture, Operating System Architecture, Processor Product, Resource Cache, Number of Processors etc and heuristic information concerning network devices and capabilities. The allocation of resources happened either when the processes –such as jobs- are created or while it is executed as described by Silberschatz (2000). Due to the huge number of physical resources the PRA advertise resources

Figure 2. Use case of a node KBP interaction

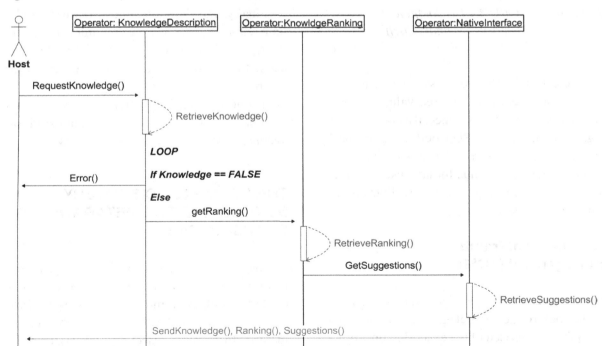

stored at each node public profile by including the following:

- CPU Power as the maximum available CPU for job delegation.
- Memory Space as the maximum allocated memory.
- Disk Space as the maximum allocated hard disk space.

A public operation is utilized by the PRA which generates a list with meets the requirements discussed above. The list is then passed to the Host which determines job assignments. The necessary prerequisites of this process are that the PCM and KBP already exist. When the Host requests an interaction, the Operator will be able to send a list of available physical resources. The data will be obtained from each node's internal procedure. If a job already exists, then it is obvious that node resources will be limited. Finally, the Host informs the Operator if it is capable of executing the job. The following mathematical Equation 1 calculates the physical resource ranking:

$$Ranking = 1 / (CPU * CPUCoefficient$$
$$+ Memory * MemoryCoefficient$$
$$+ HD * HDCoefficient) \qquad (1)$$

The coefficient value is assigned by the Operator as a measure of required values for each physical resource. For instance, if a node requests high CPU power the CPU Coefficient will be 1, in other case will be from 0,1 to 0,9. Finally, the minimization of the value for later use in a graph theoretic model is achieved by the division of 1 with the formula.

D. Time Constraints Management (TCM)

Time management is an important issue to be settled before the job delegation. The due time of a job is comprised of the execution time of the Operator and the communication time through the selected path. If a node requests a job submission via an Operator then time is affecting its decision of selecting paths. The expected execution time and the link duration will also affect the communication weight as it is the most important feature after the PRA pairing.

In order to define the expected execution time we need to identify the Optimistic Completion Time (OCT) for a job. The OCT value is defined as the best completion time achieved for a specific job and is stored in the public profile of the snapshot. The pessimistic completion time (PCT) is the worst time which the same job completes the post. The most likely completion (MLCT) time is the averaged value of jobs. When a Host requests the expected execution time, the Operator calculates the value according to the information stored in the public profile based on previous interactions. The expected execution time (EET) between events is calculated based upon the Marasovic and Marasovic (2006) as the following Equation 2:

$$ET = (MPT + 4MLCT + OCT) / 6 \qquad (2)$$

Finally, the duration link is defined as the time required achieving the communication, and is calculated by summing up the linked duration needed from one node to another. A method for determining the duration is by calculating the ping time of each interaction. We assume that each node's total distance in a certain path is an average of 1000 pings multiplied by two.

THE RESOURCE DISCOVERY METHOD AND THE METADATA SNAPSHOT PROFILE

We need to have a general knowledge of the resource discovery and selection in order to conclude to an efficient model for large scale Grid VOs. El Samad et al. (2008) discuss the current methods for resource discovery and classify them into two main categories. One is by the leader and worker –also known as master/slave approach as detailed presented by Padmanabham et al. (2005) and Ramos et al. (2006). The second one is the peer to peer approach –P2P– as it is also discussed by Cai et al. (2003) and Adeep et al. (2005).The first leader/worker approach, every leader keeps up to date information for a specific number of resources, however when the system extends to a large scale, the leaders phases the problem of scalability. On the other hand, the P2P approach suggests that a distributed hash table (DHT) is utilized be each resource, so members maintain dynamically updated data. Similar to the hash table we present the metadata snapshot profile, a storage place for rapid access from everyone.

In our case the resource discovery method starts with a node requesting information from the metadata snapshot profile of any connected member. The profile contains several data but initially we are seeking for the addresses of well known and trusted nodes.

In Figure 3 we assume that n_1 can access n_2 as well as any other member of VO1. However n_2 contains a new address of the related (and interconnected) member b_1, so n_2 assigns a reference contract to the SCF contract and updates the profile of n_1. At this stage n_1 is capable of establishing a connection with b_1. However n_1 then requests information from b_1 as they are both trusted members so they follow the same procedure and the new updated profile of n_1 contains the addresses of all members of VO_2. The procedure continues and all members from both VOs have access to any resource available to the mutually interconnected VOs. The snapshot profile is formed according to the minimum requirements gathered after the first initialization of a VO. We assume that each VO clique is managed by a VO administrator component which is able to assign clique contracts and knowledge background to each node. Then, physical resources are extracted internally and announced to the snapshot profile. Execution time data are collected from completed jobs within a node. Figure 4 demonstrates the snapshot profile attributes and operations, as well as the pairing procedure. The Host node sends its public profile data to the Operator and the procedure starts. Finally, the Operator returns a new record to the Host. If the pairing is successful, then the job delegation process starts, in any other case the pairing fails. Updated profiles of Host and Operator are stored in the metadata snapshot profile of each node.

Figure 3. The resource discovery method

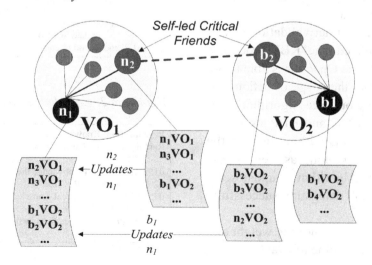

Figure 4. Snapshot profile interaction

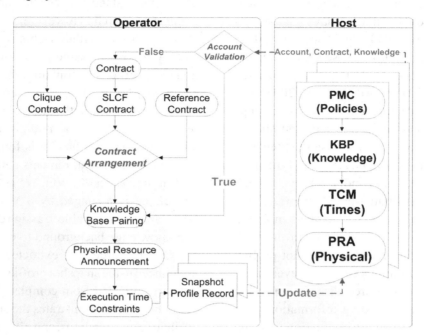

The weight of a specific job is measured by combining data collected from the profile. These data are determined by contract agreements, pairing of knowledge, physical and time constraints respectively for Host and Operators. The following initializes the above algorithm:

1st Phase: Algorithm 1 initializes the PMC routine which determines the policy of connection and validates contract.

2nd Phase: Once the contract validation is successfully completed, the KBP procedure defines whether the Operator is able to accept the job from the scope of actions capable of carrying out. See Algorithm 2.

3rd Phase: Once the PMC and KBP are paired successfully the algorithm defines the physical resource ranking as well as data about duration. Algorithm 3 updates the profile when a job delegation successfully completes.

4th Phase: Algirthm 4 calculates the weight of a path by multiplying time and ranking.

Algorithm 1. Policy control management

Precondition: Account acc, Contract con, Permission PCM, con ∈ {CliqueContract, SCFContract, ReferenceContract}

```
01: if account exists in Snapshot Profile then
02:     utilize PCM = True
03: else if contract = CliqueContract then
04:     utilize PCM = True
05:     create Account acc for new node
06:     else if contract = SCFContract then
07:         PCM = True
08:         else if contract = ReferenceContract then
09:         PCM = True
10:             update SCFContract with Reference Contract
11: end if, end if, end if, end if
```

Algorithm 2. Knowledge base pairing

Precondition: Knowledge Description kd, Knowledge Ranking kr, Knowledge Pairing KBP, PCM = True

```
01: if kd = Current Knowledge then
02:     utilize KBP = True
03:     kr = Extract Current Knowledge Ranking
04: else KBP = False
05:     create Account acc for new node
06: end if
```

Algorithm 3. Physical resource announcement and execution time management

> **Precondition**: Physical Resource Description Ranking, expected time et, most pessimistic time MPT, most optimistic time OCT, most likely completion time MLCT, Duration pingTimes, Time T, Constant a, b, c, PCM = True, KBP = True
>
> 01: Ranking = = a * CPU + b* Memory + c* HD
> 02: Ranking = = 1/ Ranking
> 03: ET = (MPT + 4MLCT + OCT) / 6
> 04: dur = sum of durations
> 05: T = ET + 2 * ping
> 06: Update ET when job completes
> 07: if ET < OCT then
> 08:   OCT = ET and store in the profile flag1= true
> 09: end if
> 10: if ET > MPT then
> 11:   PCT = ET and store in the profile flag2 = true
> 12: end if
> 13: if (flag1 = false and flag2=false) then
> 14:   MLCT = (MLCT+ET)/2
> 15: end if

Algorithm 4. Weight calculation

> **Precondition**: Edge Weight w, Physical Resource Description Ranking, completion time t, PCM = True, KBP = True, Ranking<>0
>
> 01: w = T * Ranking

The algorithms demonstrate the procedure with the appropriate sequence. First of all, the PMC and KBP algorithms utilize a procedure in which we aim to define a pairing of policies and knowledge background. Once this has been established, the TCM algorithm defines a way to measure execution and communication duration within a node. Finally, we assign a weight to a path according to the minimum requirements.

SCENARIOS

The following scenarios illustrate the minimum requirements pairing procedure in order to calculate the weight of each path. The first scenario illustrates a VO internal interaction; and the second one explains the interaction process between two VOs by utilizing SCFs as mediators of inter-collaborated nodes.

Scenario 1

The first scenario demonstrates grid node interaction amongst 3 clique nodes (O_1, O_2, and O_3), one new added node to the clique (O_4) and two SCF nodes (O_5, O_6). It is assumed that the aforementioned nodes have already initialized and specifications of values concerning PMC, KBP, PRA and TCM have been assigned by a manager component.

Figure 5 demonstrates the interconnected nodes to the Host. The plan is that the Host node requests information for job assignment of nodes O_1 to O_6. The nodes respond with data contained in each public profile and the pairing procedure starts. Table 1 contains Contracts and Knowledge of the snapshot profile of Host and Operators.

The Host requires a job submission for knowledge; a job with high processor, memory and low hard disk space requirements. Table 2 contains the data setup in conformity with Host requirements.

According to the aforesaid algorithms the pairing procedure will occur in four phases respectively for each node.

1st Phase: PCM authentication happens directly for nodes O_1, O_2 and O_3 where the PCM validates their accounts. Node O_4 is checked for its contract and after the successful pairing a new account is attributed. Finally, Nodes O_5, O_6 are critical friends and are recognised by their SCF Contracts. So permissions are arranged for all nodes.

2nd Phase: It is assumed that nodes within a clique will be able to share the same knowledge background. In this scenario knowledge pairing for job A is decided by the assumption that each node is capable of performing the particular job.

Figure 5. Scenario 1: clique nodes interaction

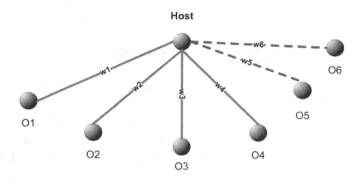

3rd Phase: The PRA is defined by an internal calculation of each node. Each ranking is calculated by the Equation 1: Consequently, Table 3 contains the calculated ranking value of each node.

The execution time for job A is stored in each node TCM profile. It is calculated by Equation 2.

Finally, we need to calculate the ping time of each interaction in order to calculate the path distance. The assumption is that the value is the average of 1000 pings performing by the Host to each Operator.

4th Phase: The following Equation 3 calculates the final weight:

$W = T*Ranking$, so
$$W = (ET+ Ping * 2) * Ranking \qquad (3)$$

Finally, the values shown in Table 4 could be assigned to each path edge as the measured weight of each interaction.

Table 1. Contracts and knowledge

Node	Contracts	Knowledge
Host	CliqueContract, SCFContract	A,B,C
O_1	Clique Contract	A,B
O_2	Clique Contract	A,B,C
O_3	Clique Contract	A
O_4	Clique Contract	A,C
O_5	SCF Contract	A,B
O_6	SCF Contract	A,B,C,D

Table 2. Coefficient values

Required Knowledge	Processor Coefficient	Memory Coefficient	Hard Disk Coefficient
A	1	1	0,01

Table 3. Rankings

Node Name	CPU	Memory	HD	Ranking
O_1	3	2	300	0,125
O_2	2.5	4	250	0,111
O_3	2	3	280	0,128
O_4	3	1	350	0,133
O_5	2.8	2	500	0,102
O_6	3.2	4	400	0,089

Table 4. Weight calculations

Node	O_1	O_2	O_3	O_4	O_5	O_6
ET	2,29	2,57	2,23	2,14	2,8	3,2
Ping	2	3	3,3	2,4	2,8	3,1
W	0,78	0,95	1,13	0,92	0,85	0,83

Scenario 2

The plan is that the Host node requests information for job assignment for nodes O1 to O6, while O5, O6 propose connection with nodes O10, O11, O12 as they form internal clique nodes of clique 2.

Table 5 contains Contracts and knowledge of Host and Operators.

Figure 6 illustrates the interaction between two cliques when a Host of Clique 1 requests access to profile information from clique nodes and SCF of Clique 2.

The emphasis has been on providing the communication link among the Host and the SCFs O_5 and O_6. Inter-connected nodes are proposed for inter-collaboration with the Host according to reference contracts signed by SCF parties from both cliques. The Host requires a job submission similar to Scenario 1. The next phases should be carried out in order to calculate path weights.

1st Phase: PCM authentication occurs automatically for nodes O_1 to O_9 where the PCM validate their accounts. Nodes O_5, O_6 are SCF and are recognised by their SCF Con-

Table 5. Contracts and knowledge

Node	Contracts	Knowledge
Host	Clique Contract, SCF Contracts	A,B,C
O_1	Clique Contract	A,B
O_2	Clique Contract	A,B,C
O_3	Clique Contract	A
O_4	Clique Contract	A,C
O_5	SCF ContractO_5	A,B
O_6	SCF ContractO_6	A,B,C,D
O_7	Clique Contract	A,B,C,D
O_8	Clique Contract	A,B,C,D
O_9	Clique Contract	A,B,C,D
O_{10}	ReferenceContract to O_6	A,B,C,D
O_{11}	ReferenceContract to O_6	A,B,C,D
O_{12}	ReferenceContract to O_5	A,B,C,D

tracts and O_{10} to O_{12} are recognised by their reference contracts.

2nd Phase: It is assumed that knowledge pairing for job A is successfully paired from all nodes.

3rd Phase: The PRA is defined by an internal calculation of each node. Table 6 contains

Figure 6. Scenario 2: two cliques' interaction

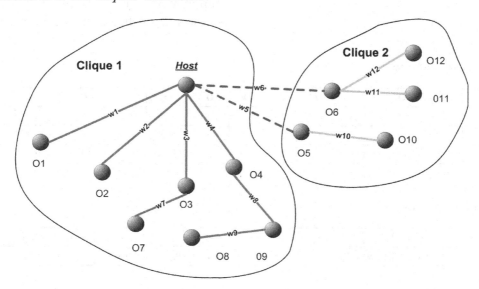

Table 6. Rankings

Node	CPU	Memory	HD	Ranking
O_1	3	2	300	0,125
O_2	2.5	4	250	0,111
O_3	2	3	280	0,128
O_4	3	1	350	0,133
O_5	2.8	2	500	0,102
O_6	3.2	4	400	0,089
O_7	3.36	3	467	0,092
O_8	3.58	3	492	0,088
O_9	3.8	3	517	0,084
O_{10}	4.02	3	542	0,080
O_{11}	4.24	3	567	0,077
O_{12}	4.46	3	592	0,074

calculated physical resource ranking of each node. For this reason the Equation 1 is utilized.

The execution time for job A is stored in each node TCM profile. Finally it is calculated by Equation 4. The following data are calculated according to the above formula and shown in Table 7.

4th Phase: So weight is calculated by the Equation 3 and Table 8 shown calculated values.

In this case study we have calculated the weights of paths for each pair-wise group of members. Moreover we assume that each member is in idle condition and each time of the weight calculation, data are stored within the public profile for future job delegations.

CONCLUSION AND FUTURE WORK

In this exploratory paper we have addressed a notable opportunity to see grid VOs as a huge graph encompassing nodes and vertices. The work here utilizes the notion of the critical friends' community model as a way to achieve the inter-cooperation of distributed Grid nodes. Our proposed method is illustrated by making use of two scenarios each one aimed at demonstrating a SCF interaction. We empirically assign a value by assuming that knowledge is standard. The philosophy of the proposed mechanism corresponds with ad hoc grid characteristics. In this direction the planned authorization mechanism and knowledge pairing does not apply to specific grid architecture as also they are independent of any centralized control. The future evolution of our work (Sotiriadis et al., 2010) addresses the minimum requirements of inter-collaborated nodes into a genetic algorithm infrastructure. Once

Table 7. Time calculations

Node	O_1	O_2	O_3	O_4	O_5	O_6	O_7	O_8	O_9	O_{10}	O_{11}	O_{12}
ET	2,29	2,57	2,23	2,14	2,8	3,2	3,11	3,26	3,41	3,56	3,71	3,87
PING	2	3	3,3	2,4	2,8	3,1	3	3,2	3,25	3,4	3,5	3,45
T	6,29	8,57	8,83	6,94	8,4	9,4	9,11	9,66	9,91	10,36	10,71	10,77

Table 8. Weight calculations

w_1	w_2	w_3	w_4	w_5	w_6	w_7	w_8	w_9	w_{10}	w_{11}	w_{12}
0,786	0,951	1,132	0,923	0,856	0,836	0,864	0,850	0,832	0,828	0,824	0,782

the weighted paths have been determined, the desired best selected paths are provisioned by the specific model. In our earlier studies we have suggested an agent based methodology for resource discovery within such uncertain environments. These investigate the possibilities for integrating mobility agents in the area of the Grids. The key component is the migration mechanism of the metadata snapshot profile into the unknown VO nodes. By performing migration of the snapshot data we recognised that the vision of Grid was closely related to that of the intelligent agents. As such, we have proposed an interoperable mobility agent model that performs migration to any interacting VO member by travelling within each domain. The originality of our approach is the mobility mechanism based on traveling and migration which stores useful information during the route to each visited individual. The method is considered under the Foundation for Intelligent Physical Agents (FIPA) standard which provides an on demand resource provisioning model for autonomous mobile agents. Finally the decentralization of the proposed model is achieved by providing each member with a public profile of personal information which is available upon request from any interconnected member during the resource discovery process. In the aforementioned works we frame important questions for engaging resource discovery within inter-cooperated grid VOs. The solutions we propose aims at integrating an inter-collaborated environment of self-directed and autonomous VO members.

REFERENCES

Bessis, N. (2009). *Grid technology for maximizing collaborative decision management and support: Advancing effective virtual organizations.* Hersey, PA: IGI Global. doi:10.4018/978-1-60566-364-7

Cai, M., Frank, M., Chen, J., & Szekely, P. (2003). MAAN: A multi-attribute addressable network for grid information services. In *Proceedings of the Fourth International Workshop on Grid Computing* (pp.184-191). Washington, DC: IEEE Computer Society.

Cheema, A. S., Muhammad, M., & Gupta, I. (2005). Peer-to-peer discovery of computational resources for grid applications. In *Proceedings of the 6th International Workshop on Grid Computing* (pp. 179-185). Washington, DC: IEEE Computer Society.

Czajkowski, G. K., Fitzgerald, S., Foster, I., & Kesselman, C. (2001). Grid information services for distributed resource sharing. In *Proceedings of the 10th IEEE Symposium on High Performance Distributed Computing* (pp. 181-194). Washington, DC: IEEE Computer Society.

Data Grid. (2002). *EU DataGrid WP6: VOMS vs. EDG security requirements.* Retrieved from http://marianne.in2p3.fr/

De Roure, D., Jennings, N. R., & Shadbolt, N. R. (2005). The semantic grid: Past, present and future. *Proceedings of the IEEE, 93*(3), 669–681. doi:10.1109/JPROC.2004.842781

El Samad, M., Hameurlain, A., & Morvan, F. (2008). Resource discovery and selection for large scale query optimization in grid environment. In Sobh, T. (Ed.), *Advances in computer and information sciences and engineering* (pp. 279–283). Berlin, Germany: Springer-Verlag. doi:10.1007/978-1-4020-8741-7_51

Foster, I., Jennings, N. R., & Kesselman, C. (2004, July 19-23). Brain meets brawn: Why grid and agents need each other. In *Proceedings of the Third International Joint Conference on Autonomous Agents and Multiagent Systems,* New York, NY (pp. 8-15). Washington, DC: IEEE Computer Society.

Foster, I., Kesselman, C., & Tuecke, S. (2001). The anatomy of the grid: Enabling scalable virtual organizations. *International Journal of High Performance Computing Applications, 15*(3), 200. doi:10.1177/109434200101500302

Foundation for Intelligent Physical Agents (FIPA). (n. d.). *Welcome to FIPA*. Retrieved from http://www.fipa.org

Harris, J., Hirst, L. J., & Mossinghoff, M. (2008). *Combinatorics and graph theory*. New York, NY: Springer.

Huang, Y., Bessis, N., Brocco, A., Sotiriadis, S., Courant, M., Kuonen, P., et al. (2009). Towards an integrated vision across inter-cooperative grid virtual organizations. In Y.-H. Lee, T.-H. Kim, W.-C. Fang, & D. Slezak (Eds.), *Proceedings of the 1st International Conference on Future Generation Information Technology and the 2nd International Conference on Grid and Distributed Computing*, Jeju Island, Korea (LNCS 5899, pp.120-128).

Huang, Y., Bessis, N., Kuonen, P., Brocco, A., Courant, M., & Hirsbrunner, B. (2009). Using metadata snapshots for extending ant-based resource discovery functionality in inter-cooperative grid communities. In *Proceedings of the International Conference on Evolving Internet*, Cannes, France.

Huang, Y., Brocco, A., Bessis, N., Kuonen, P., & Hirsbrunner, B. (2010). Community-aware scheduling protocol for grids. In *Proceedings of the 24th IEEE International Conference on Advanced Information Networking and Applications* (pp. 334-341). Washington, DC: IEEE Computer Society.

Liu, S., Yu, J., Liu, Y., Wei, J., Gao, P., Li, W., et al. (2007). Make highly clustered grid a small world with shorter diameter. In *Proceedings of the Sixth International Conference on Grid and Cooperative Computing*, Xinjiang, China (pp. 109-116). Washington, DC: IEEE Computer Society.

Ma, Y., Gong, B., & Zou, L. (2008). Resource discovery algorithm based on small-world cluster in hierarchical grid computing environment. In *Proceedings of the 7th International Conference on Grid and Cooperative Computing*, Lanzhou, China (pp. 110-116). Washington, DC: IEEE Computer Society.

Marasovic, J., & Marasovic, T. (2006, September). CPM/PERT project planning methods as e-learning optional support. In *Proceedings of the International Conference on Software in Telecommunications and Computer Networks*, Dubrovnik, Croatia (pp. 352-356). Washington, DC: IEEE Computer Society.

Marcus, D. (2008). *Graph theory: A problem oriented approach*. Washington, DC: Mathematical Association of America.

Padmanabham, A., Wang, S., Ghosh, S., & Briggs, R. (2005). A self-organised grouping (SOG) method for efficient grid resource discovery. In *Proceedings of the International Workshop on Grid Computing* (p. 6). Washington, DC: IEEE Computer Society.

Ramos, T. G., & de Melo, A. C. M. A. (2006). An extensible resource discovery mechanism for efficient grid resource discovery. In *Proceedings of the Sixth IEEE International Symposium on Cluster Computing and the Grid* (pp 115-122). Washington, DC: IEEE Computer Society.

Russel, S., & Norvig, P. (2003). *Artificial intelligence: A modern approach*. Upper Saddle River, NJ: Pearson Education.

Silberschatz, A., Galvin, P., & Gagne, G. (2000). *Applied operating system concepts*. New York, NY: John Wiley & Sons.

Sotiriadis, S., Bessis, N., Huang, Y., Sant, P., & Maple, C. (2010, February). Defining minimum requirements of inter-collaborated nodes by measuring the heaviness of node interactions. In *Proceedings of the International Conference on Complex, Intelligent and Software Intensive Systems*, Krakow, Poland.

Sotiriadis, S., Bessis, N., Huang, Y., Sant, P., & Maple, C. (2010). Towards decentralized grid agent models for continuous resource discovery of interoperable grid virtual organizations. In *Proceedings of the 3rd International Conference on the Applications of Digital Information and Web Technologies: Distributed Information and Applied Collaborative Technologies,* Istanbul, Turkey (pp. 530-535). Washington, DC: IEEE Computer Society.

Sotiriadis, S., Bessis, N., Sant, P., & Maple, C. (2010). A mobile agent migration strategy for grid interoperable virtual organisations. In *Proceedings of the 1st International Conference on Collaborative Technologies*, Freiburg, Germany.

Sotiriadis, S., Bessis, N., Sant, P., & Maple, C. (2010). Encoding minimum requirements of ad-hoc inter-connected grids to a genetic algorithm infrastructure. In *Proceedings of the 1st International Conference on Collaborative Technologies*, Freiburg, Germany.

Winton, L. J. (2005). A simple virtual organisation model and practical implementation. In *Proceedings of the Australasian Workshop on Grid Computing and e-Research* (Vol. 44, pp. 57-65).

This work was previously published in the International Journal of Distributed Systems and Technologies (IJDST), Volume 2, Issue 3, edited by Nik Bessis, pp. 19-36, copyright 2011 by IGI Publishing (an imprint of IGI Global).

Chapter 2
Bio-Inspired Techniques for Resources State Prediction in Large Scale Distributed Systems

Andreea Visan
University Politehnica of Bucharest, Romania

Mihai Istin
University Politehnica of Bucharest, Romania

Florin Pop
University Politehnica of Bucharest, Romania

Valentin Cristea
University Politehnica of Bucharest, Romania

ABSTRACT

The state prediction of resources in large scale distributed systems represents an important aspect for resources allocations, systems evaluation, and autonomic control. The paper presents advanced techniques for resources state prediction in Large Scale Distributed Systems, which include techniques based on bio-inspired algorithms like neural network improved with genetic algorithms. The approach adopted in this paper consists of a new fitness function, having prediction error minimization as the main scope. The proposed prediction techniques are based on monitoring data, aggregated in a history database. The experimental scenarios consider the ALICE experiment, active at the CERN institute. Compared with classical predicted algorithms based on average or random methods, the authors obtain an improved prediction error of 73%. This improvement is important for functionalities and performance of resource management systems in large scale distributed systems in the case of remote control ore advance reservation and allocation.

DOI: 10.4018/978-1-4666-2647-8.ch002

INTRODUCTION

The size of distributed systems followed an ascending trend during the last decade leading to today's Large Scale Distributed Systems (LSDSs). As a result, resource management has richened more and more importance, being considered a main component used to improve the system performance.

Monitoring can improve the performance of resource management systems (Shoorehdeli et al., 2009) in various ways, and for this reason most of the current resource management systems use monitoring instruments. A monitoring module should satisfy several important functional requirements, namely, to provide accurate information for all relevant parameters, to support various data delivery models, to offer an extensible data representation, to have access to real-time and history data, and to be easily ported. We have also to mention the scalability, a minimal monitoring overhead and the ability to process and distribute, in real-time, large amounts of gathered data.

Resource management also relies on prediction mechanisms (Loc et al., 2006), used to estimate what the resources utilization will be in the near future, or how many resources are likely to fail. The prediction mechanisms use monitoring data that have been collected from the system and usually stored in repositories. Based on a set of previous values for a certain parameter, the next value is forecasted and sent to the resource manager. Classical prediction algorithms are based on mean, median and standard deviation theory, but approaches inspired from natural models can also be successfully used. Our research uses a framework for distributed system monitoring, real time prediction and also a real-time error analyzer for different prediction approaches.

The paper is organized in the following way: First we briefly introduce the components of the monitoring and state prediction tool used in our research. Next, we give a definition of the prediction problem. Next, different performance criteria are expressed. In the following section, different prediction algorithms are described: from simpler one such as those based on simple mean or advanced, bio-inspired. Next, a performance comparison between all algorithms is made for different system parameters describing one system's state. The experimental tests were made in both one-step ahead and multi-step ahead prediction.

THE MONITORING AND STATE PREDICTION TOOL

This section briefly describes the monitoring and state prediction tool used in our research. Its main design goals were the scalability, the flexibility and the ease-of-use. In the meantime, we assured that the main requirements of a monitoring module are satisfied. Figure 1 presents the architecture of the monitoring and state prediction tool taken into account. Its main components are represented by the monitoring module, the repository server, the prediction server, the database and the web server. These components will be briefly introduced in the current section.

A. The Monitoring Module

The purpose of the monitoring module is to provide accurate information about the current states of different system parameters. We have considered only dynamic system that presents various aspects from the monitored systems that usually vary in time. These parameters refer to the percent of the time spent by the CPU in user, system, nice and idle mode, CPU usage percent, average system load over the last 1,5 or 15 minutes, amount of free memory and swap memory, number of total, blocked and running processes, waiting time for IO operations, number of interrupt requests and software interrupt requests, etc (Yang et al., 2003).

There are also general (static) system parameters, collected only once. They measure characteristics that do not vary in time, such as the

Figure 1. Architecture of the monitoring and state prediction tool

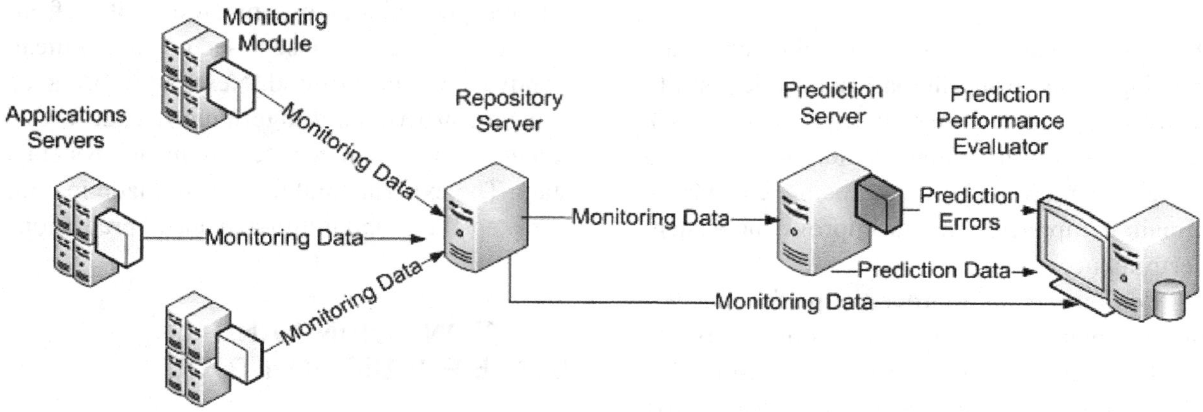

machine's hostname, model name, CPU frequency, number of CPUs and total cache size.

At the base of the monitoring service is a multithreaded system that independently executes various data collection tasks in parallel. Each thread is responsible to dynamically load and execute the modules that collect different sets of information. Threads initially created are reused when a task assigned to a thread is completed, in order to reduce the load on systems running MonALISA (Legrand, Voicu, Cirstoiu, Grigoras, Betev, & Costan, 2009). Due to the independent threads that compose the system, a failure in one monitoring task will not affect the execution of other tasks. The tasks that need to be periodically executed are kept in a priority queue, thus, monitoring a large number of heterogeneous nodes with different response times can be done without difficulty.

B. The Repository Server

The repository module gathers monitoring information from different systems, forwarding them to a prediction server and also to a repository, storing the history of each monitored station, information that can be further analyzed.

C. The Prediction Module

The prediction module receives different monitoring data and predicts the future values of the parameters, for both one-step and multi-step ahead prediction. The predictions can be made using different algorithms that will be presented in a future section. The prediction module also provides a performance evaluator useful to compare the results of different algorithms on the same time series in order to choose the fittest algorithm for each parameter.

D. The Web Server

The web server provides a flexible and intuitive interface that offers a real time perspective of both gathered and predicted parameters. It gives the possibility to inspect the behavior of the monitored hosts, offering real time information of different parameters that characterize the system's state, utilization and availability.

More, the web server provides an evaluation framework for the different prediction solution, comparing their performance. The comparison is done according to the previously described criterion.

DEFINITION OF THE PREDICTION PROBLEM

We consider for the prediction problem $P(V_{t+1})$. that denotes the predicted value for the $t+1^{th}$ measurement and is computed using the following formula:

$$P(V_{t+1}) = f(V_t, V_{t-1}, V_{t-2}, ...)$$

where f can be a linear function such as mean, median, standard deviation or a more complex one, bio-inspired for instance, implying computations based on neural networks or genetic algorithms. Different prediction solutions will be discussed later in the paper.

The problem is to determine the function such as the error, measuring the distance between the real value and the predicted value to tend to zero.

ERROR EVALUATION

Prediction can be made using different approaches and algorithms, and thus, it is important to have a measure of prediction performance, to be able to choose the fittest algorithm. We can use several performance criteria such as those listed here.

The Normalized Mean Squared Error (NMSE) is defined as:

$$NMSE(p, r) = \frac{\sum_{i=0}^{n} (p_i - r_i)^2}{n \cdot \sum_{i=0}^{n} (\frac{r_i}{n})^2}$$

The cross product is defined as follows:

$$< p, r >= \sum_{i=0}^{n} |p_i - r_i| \cdot |mean - r_i|, mean = \frac{1}{n} \cdot \sum_{i=0}^{n} r_i$$

Absolute Percentage Error (APE) is computed using the following formula:

$$APE(p, r) = \sum_{i=0}^{n} \frac{|p_i - r_i|}{r_i}$$

where:

- r_i is the real value at the ith measurement of V.
- p_i is the predicted value for r_i.
- n represents the number of measurements taken into account.

The NMSE represents in fact a sum of the absolute errors for all test examples, offering a simple moving average of the error values. The cross product is defined similarly to a weighted moving average where the biggest weights are offered to the errors obtained for the modulation values - graphical points where the time series' tendency is changing.

APE offers a simple moving average of the percentage errors of the predicted series. Our purpose is to develop an algorithm offering prediction errors very close to zero. The predictions are based on historical information gathered by MonALISA (Jarvis, Spooner, Lim Choi Keung, Cao, Saini, & Nudd, 2006) monitoring system.

The results and errors for different system parameters and prediction algorithms are presented further in this paper.

PREDICTION ALGORITHMS

This section briefly introduces the main characteristics of different prediction algorithms proposed in literature and makes a brief critical analysis. All algorithms' performances will be further analyzed. Different methods are based on linear models (Dinda & O'Hallaron, 2009), homeostatic and tendency based (Yang et al., 2003) or bio-inspired (Pop, Costan, Dobre, & Cristea, 2009; Visan, Istin, Pop, & Cristea, 2010).

Moving Averages

Dinda and O'Hallaron (2009) evaluated multiple linear models autoregressive moving average, autoregressive integrated moving average, and autoregressive fractionally integrated moving average models. A moving average is used to analyze a set of data points by creating a series of averages of different subsets of the full data set. Mathematically, a moving average is a type of convolution and it is similar to the low-pass filter used in signal processing. Several methods of computing the next value have been developed.

Simple Moving Average (SMA) is the unweighted mean of the previous n data points of the time series V:

$$SMA = \frac{1}{n} \sum_{i=l-n}^{l} V_i$$

Weighted Moving Average (WMA) is the average that has multiplying factors to give different weight to different data points. The weights are decreasing arithmetically as the values are older in time:

$$EMA = \frac{2}{n \cdot (n+1)} \sum_{i=1-n}^{l} (l-i) \cdot V_{l-n+i}$$

Exponential Moving Average (EMA) applies weighting factors which decrease exponentially, giving much more importance to recent data values.

The random prediction is based on the standard prediction theory. In statistics, the standard deviation is a simple measure of the dispersion of a data set and is defined as the square root of the variance. The variance is the average of the squared differences between data points and the mean. Standard deviation measures the spread of data about the mean. The random prediction algorithm computes one step ahead value as a random real number contained in the interval (m-s; m+s) where m is the mean of the set of values and s is the standard deviation.

Bio-Inspired Approaches

Natural models inspired researchers in different study areas. Neural networks (Miikkulainen & Stanley, 2009; Peck & Dhawan, 1995), for instance, have been used in economics and financial prediction because of their ability to learn from historical data. Another reason for this choice is that a neural network is also capable of a multi-step ahead prediction model.

Neural networks are complex modeling techniques, able to shape nonlinear functions, used in situations when there exists a dependency between the known input and the unknown output, but the nature of that relation cannot be expressed exactly. In the case of CPU prediction, for instance, the future value will always depend on the current and the past behavior, but is impossible to define the exact relation between those two. These properties make the use of neural network ideal for prediction purposes.

An artificial neural network receives a number of input neurons, from original data or from the output of other neurons. The connections between the neurons have weights associated, representing the connection's strength. To produce the output, the weighted sum is passed through an activation function. Each neuron is able to accept inputs and to produce output. The neurons accept their input from other neurons or from the user program. In a similar way, the output is sent to other neurons or to the user program.

The received information is computed by the neuron primitive function – usually just by adding the different signals – and the result is then evaluated. A neuron activates, or fires, when produces output. When the sum of its inputs satisfies the neuron's activation function, the neuron will activate.

A common type of network has a feed forward structure, where neurons are only connected forward. Each layer is connected only to the next layer. For instance, the input layer is connected to the hidden layer. This hidden layer must be connected to other hidden layer or to the output layer. The external environment passes a pattern to the neural network through the input layer. In other words, the number of neurons that compose the input layer will be chosen consequently. The output layer of the neural network is the one that presents a pattern to the external environment. The input and output patterns are similar, therefore the output of the neural network can be directly traced back to the input layer.

In order to train the neural network, the back propagation algorithm is used. Being a form of supervised training, the network receives, along with sample inputs, the anticipated outputs. The anticipated outputs will be compared against the outputs produced by the network. For each training pattern, the error between the actual output of the neural network and the output that was expected is computed. The weights of the layers are then adjusted backwards from the output layer all the way back to the input layer.

Pop, Costan, Dobre, and Cristea (2009) proposes for prediction the structure of the back-propagation neural network established based on a trial and error approach (Figure 2 presents the network's architecture used for one-step ahead prediction). The number of input neurons has been chosen as a consequence of the simple moving average prediction. It can be observed that five values are sufficient for evaluating the performance of one parameter for a short period of time. The number of neurons in the output layer is determined by the number of steps that will be predicted. The number of hidden layers as well as the number of neurons in each of the hidden layers

Figure 2. Feed-forward neural network

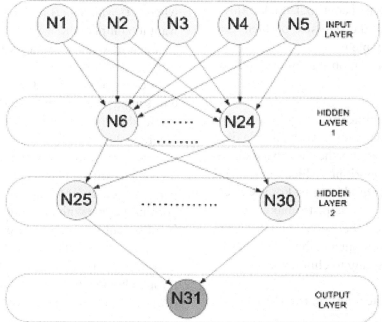

was established by conducting tests. Two hidden layers can approximate any non-linear function that would describe the relationship between past and current values and future behavior.

CasCor GA

This section describes a more complex bio-inspired prediction algorithm (Visan, Istin, Pop, & Cristea, 2010) based on the Cascade Correlation neural network architecture that uses a genetic algorithm in order to initialize the weights for all candidate units (Cirstoiu, Grigoras, Betev, Costan, & Legrand, 2007).

The Cascade Correlation learning algorithm (Fahlman & Lebiere, 1990) was developed in an attempt to overcome certain problems and limitations of the popular back-propagation learning algorithm. The most important of these limitations is represented by the slow pace at which back-propagation learns from examples. It is known that, even on simple benchmark problems, a back-propagation network may require many thousands of epochs to learn the desired behavior from examples, where an epoch is defined as one pass through the entire set of training examples. Two major problems that contribute to that slowness were identified: the step-size problem and the moving target problem.

The Cascade-Correlation algorithm combines two key ideas:

1. The cascade architecture, in which hidden units are added to the network one at a time and do not change after they have been added.
2. The learning algorithm, which creates and installs the new hidden units. For each new hidden unit, we attempt to maximize the "magnitude" of the correlation between the new unit's output and the residual error signal we are trying to eliminate.

The cascade architecture is illustrated in Figure 3 where:

- $window$ is the number of previous values used in prediction.
- $V(t - window), ..., V(t)$ are the previous measured values.
- $P(V(t + 1))$ is the predicted future value.
- Filled bullets represent connections that are trained repeatedly.

It begins with some inputs and one or more output units, but with no hidden units (Figure 3a). The number of inputs and outputs is dictated by the problem. Every input is connected to every output unit by a connection with an adjustable weight. In the experiments we have run, we use *window* input units and one output unit. We add hidden units to the network one by one (Figure 3b) where unfilled bullets represent connections that are frozen.

The weights' initialization uses the weighted moving average: every input unit was the weight computed as following:

$$weight(V(t - window + i), P(T(t + 1))) = \frac{i}{window \cdot (window + 1)}$$

where $V(t\text{-}window+i)$ is the input for which we want to compute the weight.

Each new hidden unit receives a connection from each of the network's original inputs and also from every pre-existing hidden unit. The hidden unit's input weights are frozen at the time the unit is added to the net; only the output connections are trained repeatedly.

Each new unit therefore adds a new one-unit "layer" to the network, unless the network's performance do not improves. The learning algorithm begins with no hidden units. The direct input-output connections are trained as well as possible over the entire training set, as shown in Algorithm 1. With no need to back-propagate through hidden units, we can use the "delta" rule or any of the other well-known learning algorithms

Figure 3. Cascade correlation architecture: a) initial state, b) second step, c) after adding 2 hidden units

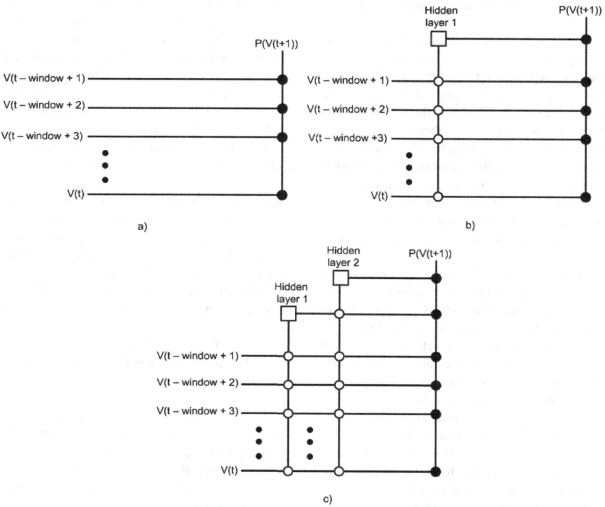

Algorithm 1. Main steps of weights training

1: **for** each training example **do**
2:     Compute Y-the network output
3:     Compute D-the real output
4:     $E = D - Y$ (the error)
5:     **for** each input unit $V(i)$ and the output unit P **do**
6:         Recompute the weight as following:
7:             $weight_{t+1}(V(i), P) = weight_t(V(i), P) + weight_t(V(i), P) * E * Value(V(i)) * a_t$
8:     **end for**
9: **end for**

for single-layer networks. In our simulations, we use the "delta" rule to train the output weights as following:

At some point, this training will approach an asymptote. When no significant error reduction has occurred, we run the neural network one last time over the entire training set to measure the error. If we are satisfied with the network's performance, we stop; if not, there must be some residual error that we want to reduce further. We attempt to achieve this by adding a new hidden unit to the network. The new unit is added to the net, its input weights are frozen, and all the output weights are once again trained using "delta" rule. This cycle repeats until the error is acceptably small.

To create a new hidden unit, we begin with a candidate unit that receives trainable input connections from all of the network's external inputs and from all pre-existing hidden units. The output of this candidate unit is not yet connected to the active network. In order to compute the candidate unit's input weights we use the genetic algorithm described in the following section.

In fact, we simulate a pool of candidate units, each with a different set of initial weights. All receive the same input signals and see the same error for each training pattern. Because they do not interact with one another or affect the active network during training, all of these candidate units can be trained in parallel. Whenever we decide that no further progress is being made, we install the candidate whose correlation score is the best.

The use of this pool of candidates is beneficial in two ways: it greatly reduces the chance that a useless unit will be permanently installed because an individual candidate got stuck during training, and it can speed up the training because many parts of weight-space can be explored simultaneously. The process of adding new hidden units stops when the error is acceptably small or the programmer defined patience is reached.

In order to find out fittest weights for candidate units' inputs we use a genetic algorithm. The purpose is to maximize the correlation between the inputs of the training examples and the errors obtained for the current configuration of the Cascade Correlation network in order to minimize the errors for the future configuration that is composed by the current configuration and the hidden layer we are trying to add. In the following section, the chromosome's encoding, the two genetic operators and the fitness function are described.

In a genetic algorithm, a chromosome represents a possible solution to the problem. In the case of computing the weights for a new candidate unit, each chromosome represents the weights corresponding with every input unit and every previous hidden layer. The initial population is built by generating the weights according to the exponential moving average algorithm.

We used the representation presented in Figure 4, where each gene represents a weight:

- *Weight* 1 is assigned to the first input unit.
- *Weight n* is assigned to the last added hidden unit.

In order to obtain high performances it is essential to find the proper genetic operators. It is important to have a balance between exploitation (obtained using the crossover operator) and exploration (obtained using the mutation operator).

Single point crossover was used, with a randomly generated crossover point. The offspring is obtained by joining the head segment of the first parent with the tail segment of the second parent. Also, the parents used in crossover are randomly generated in a way explained below.

All chromosomes resulted after the reproduction processes have a certain probability of being

Figure 4. Chromosome's representation

Weight 1	Weight 2	…….	Weight n

affected by mutation. The search space expands to the vicinity of the population by randomly altering genes. As a result, the population tends to converge to a global optimum rather than to a local optimum. We randomly choose the position of the gene to be "mutated" and we randomly generate *dW* the value used in mutation.

The selection process chooses the individuals of the current population that will reproduce. The proposed algorithm uses the roulette wheel selection method, which proved to offer good solutions in other learning problems. Also, in order to obtain a faster convergence we use the CHC selection method described in the following lines:

- If the population size is N, we generate N children by using roulette wheel selection.
- We combine the N parents with N children.
- Sort these $2 \cdot N$ individuals according to their fitness value.
- Choose the best N individuals to propagate to the next generation.

When using traditional roulette wheel selection, the best individual has the highest probability of survival but does not necessarily survive. Using CHC selection, we guarantee that the best individuals will always survive in the next generation and the population converges quickly compared to roulette wheel selection and the performance is also better. The chance (*prob(i)*) of n individual to reproduce is directly proportional to its fitness value *fitness(i)* and is computed using the following formula:

$$prob(i) = \frac{fitness(i)}{F_t}$$

where F_t represents the total fitness of the population

$$P: \ F_p = \sum_{i=0}^{|p|} fitness(i)$$

The fitness function is the essential element in a genetic algorithm because it gives the appreciation of the quality of a potential solution according to the problem's specification. The goal is to obtain fittest input weights for the next candidate unit in order to minimize the errors previously obtained for the training examples. Every population receives a list of training examples and a list containing the corresponding errors obtained for the current network configuration. The population's purpose is to produce an individual that maximize the correlation between the inputs and the errors.

According to the chromosome's encoding and genetic operators previously presented, the fitness of the ith chromosome and the training set E is computed as following:

$$fitness(i) = \left(\sum_{j=0}^{|E|} (value(i,j) - error(j))^2 \right)^{-1}$$

where *error(j)* is the error obtained for the jth training example using the current neural network's configuration, and

- $value(i,j) = \sum_{k=0}^{|I|} weight_k \cdot input_k(j)$.
- I is the chromosome's number of genes (equal with the number of inputs).
- $weight_k$ is the value corresponding to the kth chromosome's gene.
- $input_k(j)$ is the kth input corresponding to the jth training example.

Decomposition Based Prediction

All prediction algorithms previously discussed take into account the last consecutive *window* values in order to predict the next future value of the time series that describes the resource's behavior. This approach is represented in Figure 5, where the goal is to predict the next future value, *V(t+1)*, taking into account the marked values. *P(V (t+1))*, the prediction in the classical approach, is made according to the following formula:

$$P(V(t+1)) =$$
$$f_{pred}(V(t-(window-1)),...,V(t-1),V(t))$$

where f_{pred} is the used prediction algorithm and may be an algorithm based on mean, median, standard deviation or a complex one, inspired from artificial intelligence methods.

We proposed (Visan, Istin, Pop, & Cristea, 2010) a different prediction approach that takes into account not only the last *window* values as the classical solution previously described, but also considers older values with different sampling rates. This model is inspired from the decomposition of a complex wave into simpler waves with fixed frequencies.

Thus, we divide the time series that describes the current state of one resource, into multiple time series using different sampling steps. This represents in fact the decomposition stage presented in Figure 6. The number and values of sampling step should be carefully chosen. For each of the obtained series, we predict the value of *V(t+1)* using one of the classical algorithms. Then, in the composition stage of the algorithm, all these prediction results are combined into a single value using methods inspired from artificial intelligence, namely neural networks.

Figure 8 presents the time series decomposition considered by the prediction algorithm, where:

- f_{pred_1}, f_{pred_2},..., f_{pred_n} are the prediction algorithms applied on the first, second,... n^{th} sampling series, and can be either of the prediction algorithms. f_{pred_i} with $i \in 1..n$ computes P_i, the predicted future value.

- $P_1, P_2,..., P_n$ are the predicted values of *V(t+1)* of the first, second,... n^{th} step.

Different sampling steps (denoted by s in Figure 7) can be taken into account. Customizing the new prediction approach (represented in Figure 8) and considering only one sampling step, equal to 1, we obtain the classical prediction approach, previously presented.

For each sampling step (the current sampling step being denoted by i), the partial prediction is computed using the following formula:

$$P_i(t+1) =$$
$$f_{pred_i}(V(t-i(window-1)),...,V(t-i),V(t))$$

As previously mentioned, those partial results ($P_i(t+1)$ with $i \in 1..step$) are further combined for the final computing of the predicted value for the moment *t*+1 according to the following formula:

$$P(V(t+1)) = f_{pred}(P_1(t+1),...,P_{step}(t+1))$$

In our experimental tests, we use three different sampling steps (one, two, and three) in the decomposition stage (Figure 8), solution moti-

Figure 5. Classical prediction approach

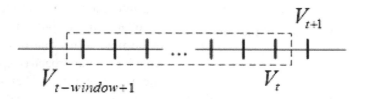

Figure 6. Wave decomposition inspired approach

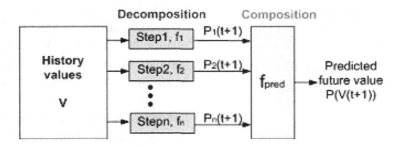

vated further in the paper. In order to predict each branch (P_1, P_2, P_3) we use a prediction algorithm based on average and in order to compose all those results (instead of f_{pred} in Figure 6) we use a learning algorithm based on NNs: a perceptron or a complex architecture inspired for the Cascade Correlation NN architecture (Fahlman & Lebiere, 1990; Girgin & Preux, 2008).

The first learning algorithm uses a perceptron which is the simplest kind of feed-forward NN: a linear classifier. We considered the architecture presented in Figure 9, containing three real inputs (corresponding to each partial prediction result $– P_1, P_2, P_3$) and one real output and trained using the delta rule. The threshold is considered zero

Figure 7. Decomposition based prediction

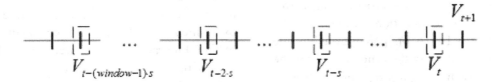

Figure 8. Time series decomposition

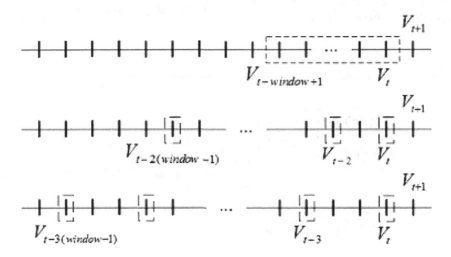

and accordingly, the output is computed using the following formula:

$$P(V(t+1)) =$$
$$Weight_{out} \cdot \sum_{i=0}^{n} (P_i(t+1) \cdot Weight_i)$$

where

$$Weight_{out} \cdot \sum_{i=0}^{n} Weight_i = 1$$

and n represents the branching number (here equal to 3).

The second learning algorithm uses a complex architecture inspired for the Cascade Correlation NN architecture (Fahlman & Lebiere, 1990; Girgin & Preux, 2008) (Figure 3), dynamically adapted to the properties of the function to be learned by adding multiple hidden layers until the correlation between the input weights of those hidden layer and the previously obtained errors. Another important advantage of the Cascade Correlation NN is that is requires no back-propagation of error signals through the connections of the network.

The solution based on perceptron has the advantage of simplicity; the time needed for the structure to learn the weight corresponding to each sampling step value is low, having a negligible overhead. Due to the fact that it has only one layer, the architecture is very sensitive to fast input variations. Thus, this solution is the best choice

for the prediction of parameters presenting very fast tendency modifications.

In contrast, the solution based on Cascade Correlation Neural Network architecture presents a complex structure, which is dynamically created according to the evolution of the inspected parameter. The response to unexpected behavior will be less accurate than the perceptron case because the convergence of this solution is slower, as it needs to modify not only the weights on a single layer, but the weights corresponding to multiple layers. Thus, it perfectly suits for the prediction of parameters having fast variations but no rapid tendency modifications.

We have also to mention that the overhead implied by our approach is comparable to the overhead of any other time series prediction algorithm. Basically, at each prediction step, we will compute the next value for each sampling step we take into account. The number of different time series to consider is a tradeoff between the overhead and the precision of the resulting estimation. As the number of different sampling steps increases, both the overhead and the accuracy also increase. The experimental results have proved that the number of sampling rates equal to three is best choice.

The time complexity for each sampling series is *O(window), window* having the same meaning as before. The time complexity for the entire algorithm using the Cascade Correlation approach in the composition stage is

Figure 9. The perceptron's architecture used in the composition stage

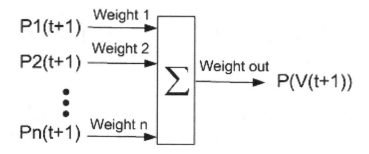

$$O(window \cdot n) + O(h \cdot n + h^2)$$

where n is the number of sampling steps considered and h is the number of hidden layers dynamically added to the network. The first term $\left(O(window \cdot n)\right)$ denotes the complexity of the decomposition stage while the second $\left(O(h \cdot n + h^2)\right)$ shows the overhead of the composition stage.

The experiments have shown that the number of necessary hidden layers is always lower than the number of network inputs, in our case equal to n. Thus, we can suppose that

$$O(window \cdot n) + O(h \cdot n + h^2) =$$
$$O(window \cdot n) + O(n^2 + n^2) =$$
$$O(window \cdot n + n^2)$$

In the second case, using a perceptron, the resulting time complexity is

$$O(window \cdot n) + O(n) = O(window \cdot n)$$

Considering that $n=3$, the overhead implied by our approach, is comparable to the overhead of other similar algorithms.

EXPERIMENTAL TESTS AND ANALYSIS

This section presents the experimental results obtained using all prediction approach previously discussed. Performance comparison between them is made for different types of representative parameters describing one station's state, information very important and useful in a distributed environment. All experimental tests are made for both one-step ahead and multi-step ahead prediction. The performance criteria used in order to evaluate the results were previously described.

We have chosen to monitor systems involved in the ALICE (Cirstoiu, Grigoras, Betev, Costan, & Legrand, 2007) project, one of the largest experiments in the world devoted to research in the physics of matter at an infinitely small scale.

A prediction based scheduler can improve considerable the time necessary to schedule tasks with dependencies. Using predictions, we can presume that the idle time of tasks can be reduced significantly, resulting a completely resource utilization and load balance. In order to tune a scheduler with a state prediction component, we have to choose the minimum, but the sufficient set of system parameters that is able to provide a correct image over the system state and also a relevant entry for the scheduling component but without a considerable overhead.

In our experimental testing, we considered the parameters set composed by the CPU usage, the free memory, the swap memory and the load averages. In the following paragraphs we make a comparison between the results of all prediction algorithms proposed in the current literature.

One-Step Ahead Prediction

This section discusses the experimental results obtained by different prediction algorithms in the situation of one-step ahead prediction for the earlier described parameters. The presented graphics highlight the errors obtained by the following prediction approaches: SMA (simple moving average), EMA (exponential moving average), WMA (weighted moving average), Random (random prediction), CascorGA (the prediction algorithm proposed in (Visan, Istin, Pop, & Cristea, 2010) based on the Cascade Correlation NN and genetic algorithms), FA (the decomposition based prediction approach based on composition using a perceptron), FC (the decomposition based prediction approach based on composition using the Cascade Correlation NN architecture).

Table 1 presents the absolute percentage errors obtained using those prediction algorithms for different system parameters where the minimum error for each parameter is bolded. As the table emphasized, in each situation the minimum error is obtained using the new prediction approach using the Cascade Correlation NN architecture. Figures 10 and 11 show the percentage of error for cpu usage and cpu idle respectively.

Because of the fact that the *idle* parameter's behaviors don't vary very fast, the errors obtained are very small (less than 0.12% for all algorithms). There aren't large differences between the results obtained using the decomposition based prediction approach using a perceptron (marked with FA in the graphic) and the results obtained by the decomposition based algorithm using a Cascade Correlation NN architecture (marked with FC in the graphic). The difference between those two is 1.8%. The improvement offered by this new approach compared to the algorithm proposed in (Visan, Istin, Pop, & Cristea, 2010) is more than 51% and more than 90% compared to the classical prediction algorithms (Dinda & O'Hallaron, 1999).

The fast variations of the *load5* parameter's behavior cause larger errors than the first presented experiment (7% or less). The decomposition prediction approach using the Cascade Correlation NN architecture proved to offer better results than the one using a perceptron, obtaining an error reduced with 30%. Here, this approach offers a great improvement compared to the classical prediction algorithms: more than 38%.

The *cpu usage* parameter has fast variations and tendency modifications. The decomposition prediction approach using one perceptron proved

Table 1. Average percentage errors (%) for one-step ahead prediction

Parameter	SMA	EMA	WMA	Random	CascorGA	FA	FC
cpu idle	0.103	0.116	0.099	0.098	0.019	0.010	0.009
cpu usage	6.672	7.284	6.898	8.472	6.433	6.994	5.645
load5	0.721	0.832	0.561	0.911	0.481	0.456	0.266
free mem	12.107	12.766	9.886	14.266	12.458	8.749	7.400

Figure 10. Percentage errors for cpu usage and free memory

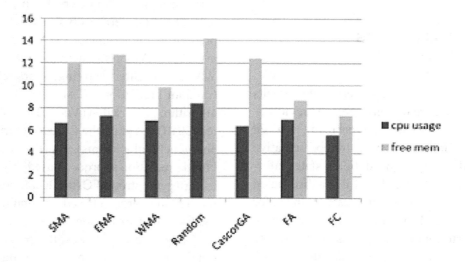

Figure 11. Percentage errors for cpu idle and load5

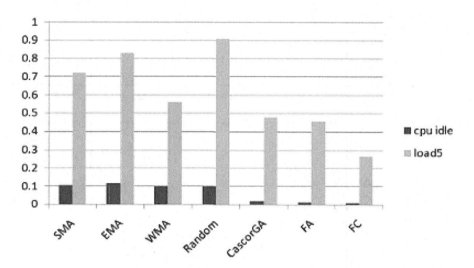

to offer better results, obtaining an error reduced with 12.8%.

A very interesting situation is encountered in the case of *free mem* parameter prediction. This parameter is very hard to predict because it has fast and vast value variations and tendency modifications and this is the reason why the errors are much more significant than those earlier discussed. Analyzing the experimental results, we observe three regions in the graphic, separated in Figure 12 using a vertical line. The first and the third zone are characterized by fast variations but no rapid tendency modifications and our new prediction approach based on cascade correlation architecture proved to offer very good results, improving the error with 15.4%. But in the second zone, characterized by very rapid tendency modifications, this architecture proved to be not proper to predict such a time series, in opposition with the decomposition prediction approach combined with a perceptron who offered the smallest error.

Multi-Step Ahead Prediction

A most relevant performance benchmark over all algorithms is given by the situation of multi-step ahead prediction. Also, one-step ahead prediction is often insufficient because, in order to optimize the resources utilization, a meta-scheduler needs an image over the future resources' state on a full period of time not only for a future moment of time.

Short-term prediction is preferred over a long-term one (Araujo & Barreto, 2004; Shoorehdeli et al., 2009) because on the fact that the scheduling mechanism must take decisions on process migration considering limited time and environment constraints. Besides, long-term prediction is not always as beneficial in distributed systems, as another task may start its execution, altering the node behavior unexpectedly.

Short-term prediction allows one to schedule the same task over different nodes if its behavior changes when necessary. Summarizing, it is more important to know what may happen in the next few seconds than in several hours. The multi-step ahead prediction experiments are made for the same system parameters, using the same performance criterion as in the previous case. The tested algorithms were put in the situation to predict the next interval of seven moments of time. The window for all classical algorithms is considered

Figure 12. Experimental results for free mem parameter

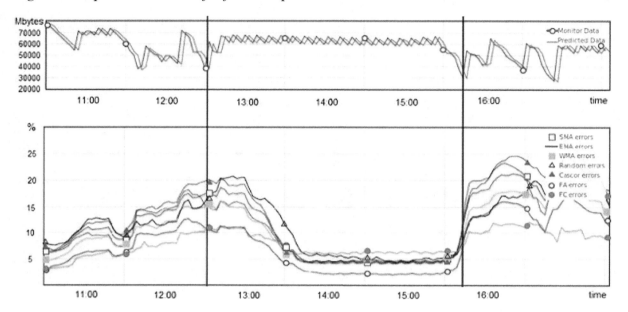

five and all approaches based on neural networks were trained using a training set with 30 elements.

As expected, for each algorithm, the errors are increasing more and more for each new prediction step in the case of the *idle* parameter, for instance. For all algorithms except FA (our new algorithm using a perceptron in the composition stage) the growth rate is similar for more than 5 future moments. Best results were obtained using our new prediction algorithm that uses in the composition stage a perceptron.

As experimental results emphasized, the multi-step ahead predictions are no very accurate and the errors are most significant than those obtained in the case of one-step ahead prediction because they are made using previous predictions, meaning that the error in the previous step is amplified in the further step. The accuracy is decreasing with each step of prediction and at some point it gets to make predictions just based on previous predictions made, meaning an error amplifier.

Best results were obtained by our approach using a perceptron in the composition stage. The improvement compared to the solution using in the composition stage consisting the Cascade

Correlation architecture is 32%. Compared to the classical predicted algorithms, we obtained a great improvement - 73%.

The prediction algorithms based on mean and standard deviation proved to be unable of accurate multi-step ahead prediction because of several factors. First of all, it should be mentioned their static prediction way (due to their fixed weights, inadequate to the current behavior and tendency of the system parameter's values). Also, the results of a (simple or weighted) mean cannot be greater than the maximum of the time series. If the time series we want to predict has an increasing tendency, such an algorithm will provide poor results because of this limitation. The decreasing situation is similar; the result of a mean algorithm cannot be smaller than its smallest input value.

Taking into account those observations, one can conclude that a complex architecture and learning algorithm are needed. Our prediction approach inspired from wave decomposition offered better results and a great error improvement.

As expected, bio-inspired algorithms offer accurate results been able to rapidly adapt to the dynamical character of large scale distributed systems and been able to capture fast and vast changes of system parameters.

CONCLUSION

This paper discussed and analyzed different classes of state prediction algorithms for distributed systems, algorithms ranged from classical approaches such as mean and standard deviation, to advanced techniques inspired from artificial intelligence, namely genetic algorithms and neural networks. Each technique can be applied for any system parameter type, but experiments proved that simple neural networks are able to accurately predict the state of parameters having fast but not vast variations. Complex neural networks, such as Cascade Correlation, are suited to predict the state of parameters having both fast and vast variations. One can conclude that the algorithm used to predict one parameter has to be chosen according to the parameter's general behavior. Current work can be improved with prediction algorithms aimed to identify patterns in parameters' behavior and for this purpose, neural networks are also very suited.

Monitoring and prediction information can contribute to improve the functionalities and the performance of resource management systems in large scale distributed systems in various ways. The immediate use of our work may be in a prediction based meta-scheduler in order to improve the scheduling decisions assuring the load balancing and optimizing the resources utilization.

ACKNOWLEDGMENT

The research presented in this paper is supported by CNCSIS-UEFISCSU national project "SORMSYS - Resource Management Optimization in Self-Organizing Large Scale Distributed Systems," Project "CNCSIS-PNII-RU-PD" ID: 201/2010 (5/28.07.2010).

REFERENCES

Araujo, A. F. R., & Barreto, G. A. (2004). Identification and control of dynamical systems using the self-organizing map. *IEEE TNN on Temporal Coding*, 1244-1259.

Cirstoiu, C. C., Grigoras, C. C., Betev, L. L., Costan, A. A., & Legrand, I. C. (2007, June 25). Monitoring, accounting and automated decision support for the Alice experiment based on the MonALISA framework. In *Proceedings of the Workshop on Grid Monitoring*, Monterey, CA (pp. 39-44). New York, NY: ACM Press.

Dinda, P. A., & O'Hallaron, D. R. (1999, August 3-6). An evaluation of linear models for host load prediction. In *Proceedings of the 8th IEEE International Symposium on High Performance Distributed Computing* (p. 10). Washington, DC: IEEE Computer Society.

Fahlman, S. E., & Lebiere, C. (1990). The cascade-correlation learning architecture. In Touretzky, D. S. (Ed.), *Advances in neural information processing systems 2* (pp. 524–532). San Francisco, CA: Morgan Kaufmann.

Girgin, S., & Preux, P. (2008, December 11-13). Basis function construction in reinforcement learning using cascade-correlation learning architecture. In *Proceedings of the Seventh International Conference on Machine Learning and Applications* (pp. 75-82). Washington, DC: IEEE Computer Society.

Jarvis, S. A., Spooner, D. P., Lim Choi Keung, H. M., Cao, J., Saini, S., & Nudd, G. R. (2006). Performance prediction and its use in parallel and distributed computing systems. *Future Generation Computer Systems*, 745–754. doi:10.1016/j.future.2006.02.008

Legrand, I., Voicu, R., Cirstoiu, C., Grigoras, C., Betev, L., & Costan, A. (2009). Monitoring and control of large systems with MonALISA. *Queue*, 7(6), 40–49.

Loc, N. T., Elnaffar, S., Katayama, T., & Bao, H.-T. (2006). Grid scheduling using 2-phase prediction (2PP) of CPU power. *Innovations in Information Technology*, 1-5.

Miikkulainen, R., & Stanley, K. O. (2009, July 8-12). Evolving neural networks. In *Proceedings of the 11th Annual Conference Companion on Genetic and Evolutionary Computation: Late Breaking Paper*, Montreal, QC, Canada (pp. 2977-3014). New York, NY: ACM Press.

Peck, C. C., & Dhawan, A. P. (1995). Genetic algorithms as global random search methods: An alternative perspective. *Evolutionary Computation*, *3*(1), 39–80. doi:10.1162/evco.1995.3.1.39

Pop, F., Costan, A., Dobre, C., & Cristea, V. (2009). Prediction based meta-scheduling for grid environments. In *Proceedings of the 17th International Conference on Control Systems and Computer Science*, Bucharset, Romania (pp.128-136).

Shoorehdeli, M. A., Teshnehlab, M., Sedigh, A. K., & Khanesar, M. A. (2009). Identification using ANFIS with intelligent hybrid stable learning algorithm approaches and stability analysis of training methods. *Applied Soft Computing*, *9*(2), 833–850. doi:10.1016/j.asoc.2008.11.001

Visan, A., Istin, M., Pop, F., & Cristea, V. (2010a, February 15-18). Automatic control of distributed systems based on state prediction methods. In *Proceedings of the International Conference on Complex, Intelligent and Software Intensive Systems* (pp. 502-507). Washington, DC: IEEE Computer Society.

Visan, A., Istin, M., Pop, F., & Cristea, V. (2010b). Decomposition based algorithm for state prediction in large scale distributed systems. In *Proceedings of the 9th International Symposium on Parallel and Distributed Computing*, Istanbul, Turkey.

Yang, L., Foster, I., & Schopf, J. M. (2003). Homeostatic and tendency-based CPU load predictions. In *Proceedings of the Parallel and Distributed Processing Symposium*, Nice, France (p. 9). Washington, DC: IEEE Computer Society.

Yang, L., Schopf, J. M., & Foster, I. (2003). *Conservative scheduling: Using predicted variance to improve scheduling decisions in dynamic environments. In* Proceedings of the ACM/IEEE Conference on Supercomputing and High Performance Networking and Computing *(p. 31). Washington, DC: IEEE Computer Society.*

This work was previously published in the International Journal of Distributed Systems and Technologies (IJDST), Volume 2, Issue 3, edited by Nik Bessis, pp. 1-18, copyright 2011 by IGI Publishing (an imprint of IGI Global).

Chapter 3
Reliability Based Scheduling Model (RSM) for Computational Grids

Zahid Raza
Jawaharlal Nehru University, India

Deo Prakash Vidyarthi
Jawaharlal Nehru University, India

ABSTRACT

Computational Grid attributed with distributed load sharing has evolved as a platform to large scale problem solving. Grid is a collection of heterogeneous resources, offering services of varying natures, in which jobs are submitted to any of the participating nodes. Scheduling these jobs in such a complex and dynamic environment has many challenges. Reliability analysis of the grid gains paramount importance because grid involves a large number of resources which may fail anytime, making it unreliable. These failures result in wastage of both computational power and money on the scarce grid resources. It is normally desired that the job should be scheduled in an environment that ensures maximum reliability to the job execution. This work presents a reliability based scheduling model for the jobs on the computational grid. The model considers the failure rate of both the software and hardware grid constituents like application demanding execution, nodes executing the job, and the network links supporting data exchange between the nodes. Job allocation using the proposed scheme becomes trusted as it schedules the job based on a priori reliability computation.

INTRODUCTION

The scientific community always thirsts for powerful computational tools and methods. This has resulted in enormous developments in the computing world with regard to processor speed, fast and large memory and efficient network devices for fast and reliable data transmission along with the advancement in software technology. The thirst for computational energy led to newer tools, which again fed back to improve the scientific research. The result of this self-feeding

DOI: 10.4018/978-1-4666-2647-8.ch003

cycle resulted in the aggregation of heterogeneous resources known as Grid, empowering towards collaborative engineering (Foster & Kesselman, 1998; Foster, 2002; Tarricone & Esposito, 2005; Taylor & Harrison, 2009).

A grid can be considered as consisting of a number of clusters with each cluster comprising of computing resources of nearly the same nature. Though, across the clusters the nature of the nodes may differ. Participants inside cluster agree to cooperate in problem solving thus making a virtual organization (VO). At any moment of time there could be many virtual organizations inside the grid with a dynamic constitution. Jobs may enter to the grid through any of the participating nodes. To harness the advantages of the grid these jobs should be scheduled over the grid so as to utilize the parallel and concurrent nature of the jobs. Scheduling is the problem of mapping the jobs over the grid resources and is said to be efficient if this mapping is done keeping in mind the job requirements e.g. the nature of the job, its inherent parallelism, proper load balancing etc. Since scheduling is an NP-hard problem many scheduling models have been proposed in the literature optimizing one or the other parameters.

Whenever a job enters the grid for execution the chances for its failure may spread from the application failure to the resource failure (node failure, etc.). Failure can be the result of many things viz. specification mistake (incorrect algorithms, architectures, etc.) hardware failures (hot crash, network partition etc.), software failure (numerical exception, failed application, etc.), implementation mistakes, component defects, external disturbance (radiation, electromagnetic waves, interference etc.), performance failures (application not completing within a specified time, etc.) or some other failures (machine rebooted by the owner, excessive CPU load, decreased priority by the local resource for the current task etc.) (Huda, Schmidt, & Peake, 2005). A fault tolerant system is one which continues to perform even in the presence of hardware and software failure. A fault is a physical defect, imperfection, or flaw that occurs within some hardware or software component, whereas an error is the manifestation of a fault and is a deviation from accuracy or incorrectness. Specifically, faults are the cause of error and errors causes the failures. Depending on the type of grid it may be susceptible to either or all types of faults.

Reliability is the ability of a system to perform and maintain its functions in routine circumstances, as well as hostile or unexpected circumstances. More the fault tolerance of the system more reliable it is. Reliability adds quality to the system and is an often desired parameter for schedulers owing to large size of the grid and the composition consisting of scarce resources. Failures can result in a huge loss both in terms of money and utilization of computational energy. Thus, it is always desired from a grid scheduler that it ensures the reliable environment to the job execution. Whenever a grid is designed, the hardware components are specified with a failure rate by the manufacturer and are supplied as a part of the hardware specifications. Software components also has failure rate specified during software design using software engineering paradigm. These failure rates reflect the reliability of the system, which is desired to be high. For the scheduling decision, reliability should be computed beforehand keeping in mind the contribution of both the hardware and the software so that the probability of successful job execution may increase. In this work, we propose a Reliability-based Scheduling Model (RSM) which allocates the modular job on the cluster of the grid that matches the job's requirements and offers the most reliable environment to the job execution.

The organization of the paper is as follows. First, we discuss the existing models in the literature with similar objective. Next we present the proposed RSM scheduler, data structures and notation used. This is followed by the cost estimation (fitness function) for the scheduler.

The algorithm, for the job allocation and the experimental results are presented next. The paper ends with the concluding remarks.

RELATED MODELS

Most of the work reported in the literature is based on the estimation of the reliability of the distributed computing system considering one or two parameters e.g. the reliability of the application, nodes or the distribution network. Also, these models do not consider the reliability before making scheduling decision. The existing models fail to present a realistic picture of the grid in reliability computation under the assumption that all the modules of the job are already allocated on the grid, which is an unrealistic situation, grid being a highly dynamic system. Unless the job comes for allocation, a reliability estimate done beforehand does not reflect the true reliability of the grid. In addition, the models do not consider the node attributes like processing speed of the node, previous workload assigned to them, nature of the job or communication requirements of the interactive jobs.

Fault tolerance and reliability have attracted attention of several researchers resulting in many relevant models. Importance of reliability for the grid computing systems has been highlighted in (Dabrowski, 2009). The work has described grid system based on various attributes distinguishing them from the distributed systems and has focused on various needs and parameters related to the reliability requirements of the grid. In (Shi, Jin, Qiang, & Zou, 2004) the reliability analysis is done for the grid but no architectural design, test bed deployment or allocation method is reported. An exclusive measurement of failure rates for distributed software has been done in (Chillarege, Biyani, & Rosenthal, 1995) but it does not take into account the failure of the computing and network resources. A reliability analysis confined only for the distribution network is also reported

developing a failure rate model based on failure statistics of the network (Pylvanainen, Jarvinen and Verho, 2004; Chen, 2004). The work provides guidance to consider the environmental and component based aspects in network management for controlling the planning process and can be used for optimizing the total life cycle costs of the network components.

Algorithms for task allocation to maximize reliability in Distributed Computing Systems have been proposed in (Shatz, Wang, & Goto, 1992). The work is based on the assumption that once the hardware is in place, the reliability mainly depends on the software design thereby neglecting the effect of reliability from the computational resource and network point of view. The effect of variation in parameters on reliability is studied in (Vidyarthi & Tripathi, 1998) but it does not propose any allocation strategy though it gives an insight in understanding the importance of reliability in scheduling. The work is further strengthened by exploring the use of simple GA for maximizing the reliability of task allocation in Distributed Computing Systems (Vidyarthi & Tripathi, 2001). The model considers only hardware failure thus being unsuitable for dynamic and unreliable grid environment. In another GA based task allocation scheme for distributed systems, the authors have proposed to maximize the system reliability by introducing redundancy which cannot be assumed to be the optimistic approach (Chiu, Hsu, & Yi, 2006). Also, the degree of redundancy is not specified.

A star topology based approach for executing a job on the grid is suggested in (Levitin, Dai, & Haim, 2006) in which a task is divided into subtasks and is sent to different specialized resources for execution with a centralized approach. The model does not specify how the job's requirements are considered while deciding the appropriate resources for it. Further, it is assumed that as soon as the subtask is allocated to a resource it starts executing which is unrealistic. In addition the allocation does not take into account the job's characteristics for scheduling. Reliability based task allocation by using clustering while introducing safety has been reported (Srinivasan & Jha, 1999). The model groups together highly communicated tasks in a single cluster. These clusters are then assigned to the same processor. But the model considers only a few parameters for the reliability analysis. Some soft computing techniques used for reliability analysis of the distributed computing system are also reported. Job replication for grid is proposed in one more fault tolerant scheduling approach with the assumption that if one executing site fails the other may take over (Abawajy, 2004). In this, the degree of replication is not clear. Further, the effect of job attributes, computing nodes and the network characteristics are not accounted. This approach is well suited under light workload but not for a system like grid. A reliability and trust based workflow job mapping on the grid has been proposed (Sedrakian, Badia, Kielmann, Merzky, Perez, & Sirvent, 2007). The scheduler allocates the job based on the trust ranking and identifying and acquiring the most available, least loaded and the fastest resources to run the application. A static grid scheduler has been reported in (Tao, Jin, &

Shi, 2007). It proposes a Markov Chain based model to predict node's availability in future by considering the data from the past. The scheduler does not consider the node characteristics, communication requirements of the job or the nature of the job while making the scheduling decision. A fault tolerant grid scheduling strategy, in which a history of the fault occurrences of the nodes is recorded while scheduling the jobs, has been reported in (Nazir & Khan, 2006). The work focuses only on node failures and does not considers other grid parameters for scheduling the job.

THE RSM SCHEDULER

The grid in consideration is comprised of a number of clusters as shown in Figure 1 with each cluster having its own specialization. The clusters, in turn, have number of nodes. A node may have a number of processors but the present work considers a node with a single processor only. Thus a reference to a node is the same as reference to the processor in the cluster. The proposed RSM scheduler assumes a multipoint entry for the job. Each cluster is as-

Figure 1. Computational grid

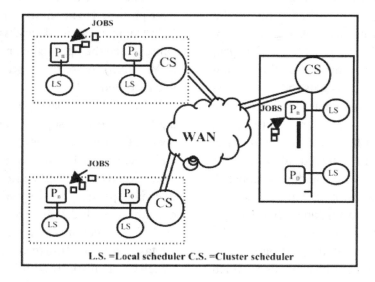

sociated with a Cluster Table (CT) which keeps track of the status of the cluster components and equipped with the following information:

- Number of clusters constituting the grid.
- Number of nodes in each cluster (Intra cluster distance).
- Processing speed of each node (processor) in a cluster.
- Failure rate of the node.
- Failure rate of the links connecting the nodes.

Each job (task) is assumed to be consisting of various subjobs or modules. In the case of the DCS or a grid, various subjobs (modules) need to be allocated possibly on different nodes based on some objectives in order to exploit the available resources efficiently and improve the execution characteristics of the given task (job) compared to its execution on a single processor system. In order to execute the job, these modules are executed in the order defined by the Job Precedence and Dependence Graph (JPDG). JPDG, a Directed Acyclic Graph (DAG), provides information about the order of execution of the job while the IMC accounts for the interactive jobs by specifying the degree of interaction required by the job modules in form of data exchange between them. Scheduling is the problem of mapping of the various modules of the job demanding execution on the

suitable grid resources (nodes) keeping in mind the precedence of the job's subjobs as specified in JPDG to the available processors which is illustrated in Figure 2 using an example (Vidyarthi & Tripathi, 1998; Vidyarthi, Sarker, Tripathi, & Yang, 2009).

The RSM scheduler proposes a scheduling strategy for the modular jobs. This is done by scheduling the modules of the job on the cluster nodes with the help of the CS in cooperation with CT. Since the grid is inherently dynamic in nature, the resources may enter and exit the grid any time. One of the reasons for this dynamic nature is the autonomy exercised on its resources by the owner of the VO constituting the grid. Another reason may be due to the failure of some nodes resulting in varying number of nodes available for computing. To accommodate these changes, CT is dynamically updated to reflect the correct grid composition. The scheduling policies of the individual nodes do not affect the scheduling decision. Once the modules of the jobs get allocated on the nodes, their execution is governed by the node's own Local Scheduler (LS) with local scheduling policy. It is under the autonomy of the node to schedule the modules allocated to it in a way convenient to it as per its own scheduling policy.

A job is assumed to be submitted along with the job attributes like number of modules in the job, module size, specialization (nature) of the

Figure 2. Mapping of job precedence and dependence graph to processor graph

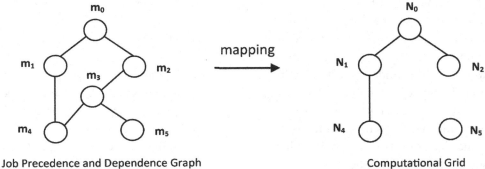

Job Precedence and Dependence Graph   Computational Grid

job, module's precedence in the form of the Job Precedence Graph (JPG) and the Inter Module Communication (IMC). It is assumed that during compilation (data flow analysis) the number of instructions and loop constructs in the modules are determined. Therefore, every submitted job contains the following information:

- Number of modules in the job.
- Nature of the job reflecting the job requirements in terms of resource specification.
- Inter Module Communication (IMC) requirement of the module. The IMC is considered as the number of bytes to be exchanged between two interactive modules.
- Failure rate of the modules.

The jobs submitted at various nodes are considered to be independent to each other. The RSM scheduler schedules the job of the cluster on the grid that matches the job requirements while being able to execute it with maximum reliability. This reliability offered to the job by the clusters is estimated considering both the hardware and software components as follows:

- Reliability of the application/job (Ri), which is submitted in form of modules. It can be calculated on the basis of the failure rates of its constituent modules. The reliability of the job's module is calculated for the time period during which it is to be executed on the computational resources. This time is evaluated on the basis of the processing time of the node with some correction factors added to account for the loop iterations and such other related constraints.
- Reliability of the nodes (Rki) on which the job is being considered for scheduling. This is important owing to the fact that if the job is allocated on a node which is failure prone, its chances to fail will be high. Further, for the resources being considered

for allocation, it is important that it should be both available and reliable for the time period the job needs it for its execution. The existing workload on the nodes should also be accounted for to reflect the node reliability as the previous workload will affect the time taken for the current job execution. Thus, the node reliability is a cumulative reliability obtained on the basis of the above mentioned factors.

- Reliability of the links (Rl) through which modules of interactive job residing on different nodes may communicate. The link reliability for the time period during which the communication takes place becomes important and needs proper attention for total reliability calculation.

Based on the above parameters, the job is scheduled on those resources matching the job specifications and offering the maximum reliability. The proposed model is realistic since it dynamically evaluates the reliability of the system before allocating the modules. The scheduler's performance is analyzed for the allocation strategy by carrying out the experiment to observe the effect of the previous workload on the nodes. This is done by scheduling the job initially with no existing load on the nodes and later evaluating it by considering the previous workload.

The various data structures and parameters used in the model are as follows.

- Cluster table (CT) indicates the status of the cluster with the following attributes.

$$C_n (P_k, S_n, f_k, T_{kn}, M_{ij}, \lambda_{kn}, \zeta_{kl}$$

- Job type J_j (j = 1 to J) represents the job specification or its specific type. For example, J_0 may stand for graphic specific job, J_1 for multimedia, J_2 for database specific job etc. The type J_p corresponds to the default job type i.e. which does not have any specialization or does not require a special treatment in terms of resource requirements.

- E_{ijkn}, processing time of a module mi of job J_j on node P_k of cluster C_n.

$$E_{ijkn} = I_i * (1/f_k) + n * \alpha \qquad (1)$$

where n is a multiplication factor to account for the loop constructs in the module and α is the average time taken in the loop. The processing time will be high for the nodes that have a lower clock frequency and vice versa.

- B_{ihj}, Bytes exchange between modules mi and m_h of job J_j.

Variants of the Matrixes of Weighing

The notation used in the paper is as follows:

J_j: Submitted job with specialization j.

m_i: i^{th} module of the submitted job.

I_i: Number of instructions in the module mi.

C_n: Cluster identifier.

S_n: Specialization of a cluster C_n.

P_k: kth node of a cluster C_n.

f_k: Clock frequency of node P_k.

λ_{kn}: Failure rate of node P_k in cluster C_n.

λ_{th}: Threshold failure rate for the cluster.

μ_{ij}: Failure rate of the module mi of job J_j.

ζ_{kl}: Failure rate of link connecting node P_k and P_l.

T_{kn}: Time to finish execution of the previously allocated modules on node P_k of cluster C_n.

M_{ij}: Module identifier. It helps in identifying association of a module with a job and is interpreted as module mi of job J_j.

N: Number of clusters comprising the grid.

K: Number of nodes in the cluster.

M: Number of modules in a job.

E_{ijkn}: Processing time of a module mi of job J_j on node P_k of cluster C_n.

B_{ihj}: Inter module communication (IMC) cost, in form of bytes exchange between modules mi and mh of job Jj.

D_{kln}: Hamming distance between nodes P_k and P_l of the cluster C_n. This corresponds to the number of links traversed between nodes P_k and P_l.

X_{ijk}: Vector indicating the assignment of module mi of job J_j on node P_k. It is 1 if the module is allocated to the node otherwise 0.

R_i: Reliability of the module mi under consideration.

R_{ki}: Reliability of the node P_k under consideration for module mi.

R_{kl}: Reliability of the link connecting the two nodes P_k and P_l the modules residing on which requires communication.

Execution Cost$_j$: Execution cost of the job J_j with the objective of minimizing the turnaround time of the job.

ModRel$_{ik}$: This is the reliability of the execution offered to a module m_i at node P_k in a cluster C_n of the grid. It represents the reliability of the module execution and is a function of the reliability of the module being considered for allocation, reliability of the node for possible allocation and the reliability of the links which may participate in data exchange of the current module with other modules residing on different nodes.

BR$_i$: This corresponds to the best reliability offered to a module mi and is equal to the maximum of ModRel$_{ik}$ for that module over all the nodes.

ClusRel$_{jn}$: Reliability of execution of a job J_j at cluster C_n.

GridRel$_j$: Reliability offered by the grid to the job.

Sendall: Keyword representing communicating the job to various clusters for evaluation.

Receiveall: Keyword representing communication of the evaluated reliability by the selected clusters to the calling node.

Cost Estimation

The cost of execution of any module mi on node P_k depends on the processing time of that module on that node (E_{ijkn}) and the inter module communication cost in terms of bytes (B_{ihj}) exchanged between various modules of the job allocated on the nodes separated by a distance D_{kln} between them. The execution of the previous modules of the same or other jobs assigned to the node also affect the current execution cost. The execution times of the previously allocated modules T_{kn} add up to the execution cost of the current module for which the allocation is being considered. Thus the time required to execute a given module on a node is equal to the sum of the processing time of the module on that node E_{ijkn}, communication cost of that modules with the preceding modules ($\sum B_{ihj} * D_{kln}$), and the time T_{kn}, required by the node to finish the modules already allocated on it.

An assignment vector x_{ijk} of matrix X can be defined indicating the assignment of a module on a node as

$$x_{ijk} =$$
$$\begin{Bmatrix} 1, & \text{if module } m_i \text{ of Job } J_j \text{ assigned to node } P_k \\ 0, & \text{otherwise} \end{Bmatrix}$$
(2)

Based on the above factors the execution cost of a job J_j consisting of M modules, to a cluster with K processing nodes can be written as

$$ExecutionCost_j =$$
$$\sum_{\substack{i=1 \\ \text{for all nodes} \\ \text{of} \\ \text{selected cluster } n}}^{M} \left(E_{ijkn}.x_{ijk} + \sum_{h=1}^{i-1} w\left(B_{ihj}.D_{k\ ln}\right)x_{ijk}.x_{hjl} + T_{kn} \right)$$
(3)

where w is the scaling factor to scale the term

$$\sum_{h=1}^{i-1} \left(B_{ihj}.D_{k\ ln}\right)x_{ijk}.x_{hjl}$$

into time unit and T_{kn} accounts for the execution time corresponding to the modules of the jobs already assigned on the cluster nodes. T_{kn} can be derived as

$$T_{kn} = \sum_{\substack{for\ all \\ g \neq j}} \left(E_{igkn}.x_{igk} + \sum_{h=1}^{i-1} w\left(B_{ihg}.D_{k\ ln}\right)x_{igk}.x_{hgl} \right)$$
(4)

Considering contributions from various factors, as discussed, the reliability of execution of any module mi on node P_k can be written as

$$\text{ModRel}_{ik} = (R_i * R_{ki} * R_{kl})$$
(5)

where

R_i = Reliability of a module mi of job J_j =
$$\exp\left\{-\mu_{ij}\left[E_{ijkn}.x_{ijk} + \sum_{h=1}^{i-1} w(B_{ihj}.D_{kl})x_{ijk}.x_{hjl}\right]\right\}$$
(6)

Equation 6 stresses on the fact that the system should be reliably available during the module processing time on a node and in addition during the time it is interacting with other modules.

R_{ki} =
Reliability of a node under consideration =
$$\exp\left\{-\lambda_{kn}\left[E_{ijkn}.x_{ijk} + T_{kn}\right]\right\}$$
(7)

Equation 7 concerns with the node reliability and thus deals with the processing time when the node is required to execute the module assigned to it.

R_{kl} = Reliability of a link connecting the two nodes P_k and P_l on which the communicating modules reside =
$$\exp\left\{-\xi_{kl}\left[\sum_{h=1}^{i-1} w(B_{ihj}.D_{k\ ln})x_{ijk}.x_{hjl}\right]\right\}$$
(8)

Equation 8 concerns itself with the link reliability and therefore the communication time during which the link is used by interactive modules.

From Equations 5, 6, 7, and 8 we get

$$Mod\,\mathrm{Re}\,l_{ik} =$$
$$\exp\left\{-\begin{bmatrix}(\mu_{ij}+\lambda_{kn})\left[E_{ijkn}.x_{ijk}\right]\\ +(\mu_{ij}+\xi_{kl})\left[\sum_{h=1}^{i-1}w(B_{ihj}.D_{k\,\ln})x_{ijk}.x_{hjl}\right]\\ +\lambda_{kn}\left[T_{kn}\right]\end{bmatrix}\right\} \tag{9}$$

The module is assigned to that node which results in the most reliable environment offered to the module and is referred as

$$BR_i = max\,(\mathrm{ModRel}_{ik}) \tag{10}$$

Therefore, the reliability of execution of job J_j consisting of M modules on cluster C_n can be written as

$$Clus\,\mathrm{Re}\,l_{jn} = \prod_{i=1}^{M}(BR_{ik})\,_{for\ all\ selected\ nodes\ of\ cluster\ C_n}$$
$$= \exp\left\{-\sum_{i=1}^{M}\begin{bmatrix}(\mu_{ij}+\lambda_{kn})\left[E_{ijkn}.x_{ijk}\right]\\ +(\mu_{ij}+\xi_{kl})\left[\sum_{h=1}^{i-1}w(B_{ihj}.D_{k\,\ln})x_{ijk}.x_{hjl}\right]\\ +\lambda_{kn}\left[T_{kn}\right]\end{bmatrix}\right\} \tag{11}$$

Finally, the job is assigned to the cluster offering the highest reliability to the job as

$$GridRel_j = max\,(ClusRel_{jn}) \tag{12}$$

THE ALGORITHM

The job is submitted in the form as discussed in the previous section. This job is sent to all the clusters of the grid for evaluation. For each cluster, the algorithm first searches the clusters with matching specialization of the job. The selected clusters are further evaluated for the best reliability it may offer to the job.

The allocation process starts by allocating each module of the job in the order suggested by its JPDG. For each module the reliability offered by each node $ModRel_{ik}$ is calculated as per Equation 9. The node which offers the highest $ModRel_{ik}$ is eventually selected for the module allocation with the reliability offered by it now becoming the BR_{ik}. The time taken by this node to execute the module equals the sum of the processing time of this node for the given module with the communication cost of the module with the preceding modules. The T_{kn} for the selected node is modified by adding the time taken to execute the new module. The process is repeated for the remaining modules.

For each cluster, selected for evaluation, the product of the BR_i for all the modules of the job gives the $ClusRel_{jn}$. The $ClusRel_{jn}$ values of the selected clusters are communicated to the calling node where these are compared to find the one offering the maximum reliability. The cluster offering this cost becomes the one chosen for the job execution. The cluster table of that cluster is updated to reflect the inclusion of the new job. The cost $ClusRel_{jn}$ offered by the selected cluster now becomes the cost offered by the grid $GridRe_{lj}$ to the job.

The RSM algorithm for the allocation is given in the Box 1. Although the algorithm considers the previous workload on the nodes, the same algorithm can be modified by eliminating T_{kn} from the equations where it is used.

THE SIMULATION RESULTS

A simulation program is written in MATLAB to carry out the experiment for the evaluation of the model. Input values conform to the values of similar other models. Experiments are conducted to study the two allocation schemes as stated below.

Case 1: Allocation of the job on the grid *without* the previous allocated modules as per Equation 11.

Case 2: Allocation of the job on the grid *with* the previous allocated modules as per Equation 12.

In one such experiment, a job J_1 is considered to be submitted in the desired format. All the data values are generated dynamically. The failure rates λ_{kn}, μ_{ij} and ζ_{kl} are randomly generated in the range 0.0001 to.0009. The range of B is set between 0 to 10 while the D is set to take a value between 0

Box 1. The RSM algorithm

RSM (Job)
begin
Submit the job J_j (with specialization) in the form of modules
// Submit the job J_j in the form of modules m_i (i = 1 to M)
Sendall // Send the jobs to all the clusters for evaluation of their suitability for the job execution
For all clusters C_n (n = 1 to N)
begin *// Evaluate all the clusters in parallel to find the suitable clusters matching the job's*
// requirements
Access the specialization of the cluster
// Access the specialization S_n of the clusters with the job to select the clusters with
// matching specialization
For the clusters with matching specialization of the Job J_j, compute processing time
matrix E_{ijkn} *// Compute E_{ijkn} as per eq. (i)*
end
For all selected clusters C_n *// For the suitable clusters, evaluate the reliability offered to the job to*
// find the cluster offering the maximum reliability
begin
For each module m_i (i = 1 to M) of job J_j
begin *// Allocate modules of the job J_j demanding allocation as per its JPDG*
For each node P_k (k=1 to K)
begin
Calculate $ModRel_{ik}$
// For each module calculate the reliability offered to it by each node P_k (k=1 to K)
// as per eq.(ix)
Find the best-fit node 'P_k' with
$BR_i = max (ModRel_{ik})$
// This is the node that results in maximum reliability of execution for the module
// considered for allocation
$T_{kn \text{ for the selected node k}} = T_{kn-1} + T_{kn \text{ for the current module}}$ *//*
// Update T_{kn-1} indicate time overhead of the previous load
end
end
Calculate $ClusRel_{jn} = \Pi (BR_i)$ (for i = 1 to M)
// The reliability offered to the job by the cluster is the product of BR_i
end
Receiveall
// Convey the reliability offered by all the selected clusters with matching specialization to the
// calling node
Find the best cluster offering the maximum cost as $GridRel_j = max (ClusRel_{jn})$
// The maximum value of $ClusRel_{jn}$ becomes the reliability offered to the job by the grid
Allocate and update
// Allocate the job J_j to the selected cluster C_n corresponding to its allocation pattern and
// update the CT of the cluster C_n
end

and 5. The other parameters are set dynamically and can take any value depending on the nature of the job and the grid composition. According to the algorithm, clusters with matching specialization are selected which in this case are Cluster C_1, C_5 and C_8 as shown below (Tables 1, 2, and 3). Although the following discussion presents the job allocation of a single job, the model takes into account the job modules already allocated on the nodes in terms of their execution time T_{kn}.

Table 1. Cluster table for C_1.

Node Number (P_k)	Clock Frequency (f_k in MHz)	Specialization (S_n)	Time to Finish (T_{kn} in μS)	Modules Allocated (M_{ij})	Node Failure Rate (λ_{kn})	Link Failure Rate (ζ_{kl})
P_0	10	1	19	11	0.004	0.003
P_1	8	1	15	31	0.007	0.007
P_2	5	1	15	71	0.004	0.003
P_3	9	1	17	12	0.004	0.005
P_4	9	1	19	32	0.003	0.005
P_5	7	1	15	33	0.006	0.006
P_6	10	1	19	51	0.004	0.002

Table 2. Cluster table for C_5.

Node Number (P_k)	Clock Frequency (f_k in MHz)	Specialization (S_n)	Time to Finish (T_{kn} in μS)	Modules Allocated (M_{ij})	Node Failure Rate (λ_{kn})	Link Failure Rate (ζ_{kl})
P_0	9	1	18	21	0.003	0.002
P_1	5	1	16	41	0.004	0.005
P_2	10	1	19	81	0.005	0.005
P_3	5	1	15	12	0.002	0.002
P_4	10	1	16	22	0.006	0.002
P_5	5	1	18	34	0.006	0.003
P_6	8	1	19	53	0.006	0.001

Table 3. Cluster table for C_8.

Node Number (P_k)	Clock Frequency (f_k in MHz)	Specialization (S_n)	Time to Finish (T_{kn} in μS)	Modules Allocated (M_{ij})	Node Failure Rate (λ_{kn})	Link Failure Rate (ζ_{kl})
P_0	6	1	16	51	0.005	0.004
P_1	5	1	16	71	0.005	0.007
P_2	9	1	18	12	0.005	0.003
P_3	9	1	18	42	0.008	0.003
P_4	7	1	15	52	0.003	0.003
P_5	6	1	18	62	0.002	0.003
P_6	8	1	16	72	0.002	0.004

Case 1

This is the case in which the previous workload is not considered. The allocation of modules to the various nodes of the selected clusters is shown below in Table 4.

The reliability *ClusRel*$_{jn}$ for clusters C_1, C_5 and C_8 is found to be 0.173, 0.237 and 0.173 respectively. Since cluster C_5 offers the maximum reliability, it is selected for the job execution. The reliability offered by it, therefore, becomes the *GridRel*$_j$.

Observations

Clusters were selected on the basis of their matching specialization with the specialization of the job.

It can be seen that the nodes with high clock frequency are the favored ones (node number 6 and 4), which are the ones with highest clock frequency (coincidently for all the clusters) as in these nodes the execution will take place in much

smaller time. Since the previous workload on the nodes is not considered, the allocation of the modules tends to be on the same faster node, till the execution cost on this node exceeds the same for other nodes or becomes comparable with them.

The allocation pattern is non uniform as only a few nodes are always the favored ones.

Case 2

In this case the RSM algorithm takes into account the previous workload T_{kn} on the nodes while estimating reliability offered to the job being considered for allocation. T_{kn} takes values between 10 and 20 but the algorithm works equally well for other range of values also. The allocation of modules to the various nodes of the selected clusters is shown below in Table 5.

The cluster execution cost for various clusters is found to be 0.0010, 0.0008 and 0.0022 for clusters C_1, C_5 and C_8 respectively. Since cluster C_8 offers the maximum reliability, it is selected

Table 4. Allocation of modules for the selected clusters in case 1

Module (M_{ij})	Selected Node on Cluster C_1	Selected Node on Cluster C_5	Selected Node on Cluster C_8
m_{01}	6	6	6
m_{11}	2	2	2
m_{21}	4	4	4
m_{31}	4	4	4
m_{41}	4	4	4
m_{51}	6	6	6
m_{61}	6	6	6
m_{71}	6	6	6
m_{81}	6	6	6
m_{91}	4	4	4
m_{101}	6	6	6
m_{111}	6	6	6
m_{121}	6	6	6
m_{131}	6	6	6
m_{141}	6	6	6

Table 5. Allocation of modules for the selected clusters in case 2

Module (M_{ij})	Selected Node on Cluster C_1	Selected Node on Cluster C_5	Selected Node on Cluster C_8
m_{01}	4	3	6
m_{11}	5	0	4
m_{21}	4	3	6
m_{31}	4	2	6
m_{41}	6	2	6
m_{51}	4	6	4
m_{61}	2	2	1
m_{71}	5	3	5
m_{81}	4	1	6
m_{91}	6	2	6
m_{101}	0	0	2
m_{111}	4	6	6
m_{121}	4	2	6
m_{131}	1	5	4
m_{141}	3	4	1

for the job execution. The cost offered by it becomes the GridRel$_j$.

Observations

The cluster offering the maximum reliability is selected for the job execution.

Since the previous workload on the nodes has been accounted, it leads to a uniform distribution of the modules over the nodes. This is because of the fact that now the allocation depends not only on the speed of the node and the degree of communication between the interactive modules but also on the previous workload on the nodes.

Reliability offered to the job comes out to be lesser in comparison to compared to the Case 1.

Many experiments have been performed all leading to same conclusion.

Effect of the Number of Modules and Number of Suitable Clusters on Reliability

Experiments have been conducted to observe the effect of number of modules and clusters on reliability. Keeping the number of clusters constant, the number of modules comprising the job is varied and the reliability offered by the system is obtained. The experiments are done by first considering the nodes already loaded with some work and then without considering any workload on the cluster nodes. Accordingly, a graph is plotted to study the effect of the change in the number of suitable clusters for a job and the number of modules in it on the reliability as shown in Figure 3 and Figure 4 respectively.

Observations

As the number of modules increases, the reliability of execution decreases in both the cases. This is because of the fact that with an increased number of modules, the allocation of modules result in an increased previous workload for the newer modules thereby increasing the processing time and eventually decreasing the reliability of the job execution.

As the number of clusters increases for a given number of modules, the reliability comes higher in both Case 1 and Case 2. This is a general observation owing to the fact that the chances of getting better reliability increases with availability of more clusters.

The reliability is lower, for the same number of modules, if we take into account the previous workload of the nodes.

While considering the previous workload on the nodes, the reliability drops much faster as the number of modules increases.

Figure 3. Reliability analysis with varying number of modules without considering the previous workload

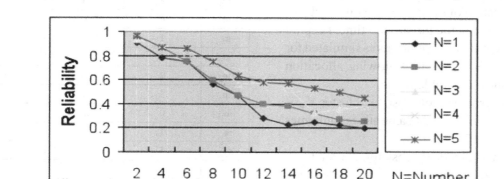

Figure 4. Reliability analysis with varying number of modules considering the previous workload

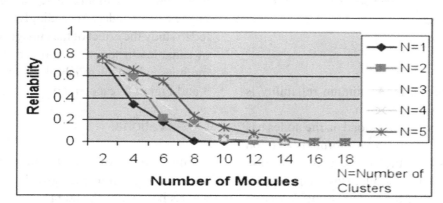

RSM vs. TSM Model

A comparison is made for the reliability and the corresponding turnaround time offered by the model with a turnaround-based scheduling model (TSM) is a scheduling model in which the allocation is based on the objective of minimizing the turnaround time for the job (Raza & Vidyarthi, 2008). The model works on the basis of the turnaround time for and accordingly allocating the modules to the node offering the minimum turnaround time. After allocation of all the modules of the job, the T_{kn} of the nodes on which allocation has been done gives the turnaround offered to the job. Reliability for the resulting allocation pattern is also obtained along with the turnaround time offered to the job with that model. Similarly, for the proposed RSM model, the turnaround time for the resulting allocation is calculated.

The allocation of the modules with the objective of minimizing the turnaround time, keeping the same environment conditions as simulated for RSM model results in the following allocation pattern as shown in Table 6.

The cluster execution cost for cluster C_1 is 95.71. The reliability for the same allocation comes out to be 0.00067.

The cluster execution cost for cluster C_5 is 101.40. The reliability for the same allocation comes out to be 0.00078.

The cluster execution cost for cluster C_8 is 111.57. The reliability for the same allocation comes out to be 0.00018.

The reliability for the job allocation based on the objective of minimizing the turnaround time of the job comes out to be 0.00078 with a turnaround time of 101.4 on cluster C_5. Thus it can be seen that the same model has resulted in

Table 6. Allocation of modules for the selected clusters in case 2

Module (m_j)	Selected Node on Cluster C_1	Selected Node on Cluster C_5	Selected Node on Cluster C_8
m_0	1	4	6
m_1	5	2	4
m_2	2	6	1
m_3	5	6	6
m_4	4	4	2
m_5	6	6	3
m_6	1	1	0
m_7	5	5	5
m_8	2	6	4
m_9	3	4	2
m_{10}	0	3	6
m_{11}	1	0	1
m_{12}	5	2	6
m_{13}	6	6	2
m_{14}	4	1	4

a lesser reliable environment for the job if the objective is other than maximizing the reliability. A graph is drawn to observe the variation in the reliability and the turnaround time of the job with the number of modules of the job as shown in Figure 5 and Figure 6.

Observations

The allocation pattern exhibits proper load balancing.

The reliability is calculated for both the schemes as mentioned above. Both the schemes resulted in different reliability offered to the job for the same number of modules. But the reliability for the scheme with the objective of maximizing

Figure 5. Reliability analysis with varying number of modules

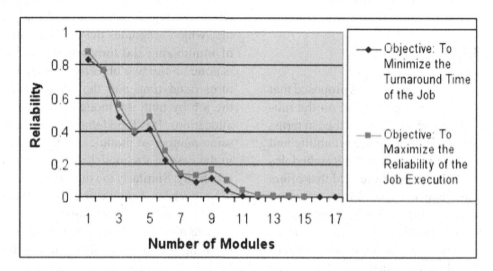

Figure 6. Turnaround time analysis with varying number of modules

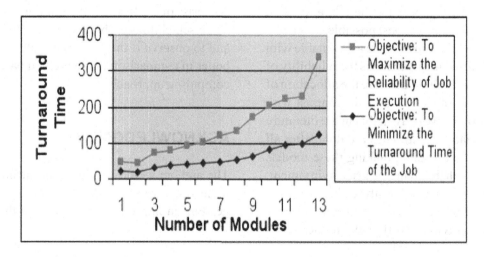

the reliability is found to be much higher than the scheduling with the objective of minimizing the turnaround time of the job execution.

Similarly, the turnaround time is calculated for both the scheme. It shows that the turnaround time offered by the scheme meant to minimize the job turnaround time resulted in a lesser turnaround time for the allocation obtained as compared to the scheme meant for maximizing the reliability.

The conclusion from this study is that the model optimizes the objective in consideration only and does not give attention to any other objectives.

CONCLUSION

In this paper, a scheduling model is proposed that schedules the job on the grid based on the reliability of the grid components described in terms of the application reliability, node reliability and the link (network) reliability. The model schedules the job on those resources of the grid that offers the most reliable execution environment to the job in the dynamic grid. The job submission is considered to be a multi-point entry system as it can be submitted at any node of the cluster of the grid. This makes the system scalable up to a fair extent. Also, since the scheduling criterion was based on the fact that it first checks for the suitability of the resource for the job, allocation results in the selection of best possible resources. The scheduling is more realistic and suitable with the dynamic grid environment as the reliability of the resources is evaluated before the allocation of each module of the job. This is in contrast with the majority of the work available in the literature where the reliability estimates are done after all the modules are allocated making these models non coherent with the changing grid environment.

In the model, the reliability estimation (and therefore scheduling) is done first without considering the previous workload on the nodes and in the other case by considering it. For the former case it led to a non uniform distribution of task as the allocation preferred the most reliable nodes whereas for the latter it led to uniform load balancing. This resulted in the distribution of the modules of the job over various suitable nodes thus harnessing the parallelism and concurrency in the job. Further, the model also takes into account the software reliability of the modules.

A comparative study is done to analyze the allocation pattern of a job with two different scheduling objectives. The performance of the RSM scheduler is compared with the TSM scheduler which schedules the job with the objective of minimizing the turnaround time. The study is done on the two objective parameters viz. the turnaround time and the reliability offered to the job by both the models for their respective allocations. It is found that the reliability, for the same number of modules, is found to be higher in the case of the model meant to maximize the reliability. Similarly the turnaround time is found to be much lesser for the model with the objective of minimizing the turnaround time.

The proposed RSM scheduler finds its use in ensuring the most reliable grid environment to the job. The model is a straight forward approach to scheduling problem of computational grid. As such the problem is NP-Hard. Future work may comprise of exploring soft computing methods to solve scheduling problem of computational grid and to observe if the proposed method performs better in comparison to the method based on soft computing approach.

ACKNOWLEDGMENT

The authors would like to thank the anonymous reviewers for their valuable comments and suggestions in improving the quality of this paper.

REFERENCES

Abawajy, J. H. (2004). Fault-tolerant scheduling policy for grid computing systems. In *Proceedings of the Eighteenth International Parallel and Distributed Processing Symposium* (p. 238).

Chen, Y. (2004). Bounds on the reliability of distributed systems with unreliable nodes and links. *IEEE Transactions on Reliability, 53*(2), 205–215. doi:10.1109/TR.2004.829152

Chillarege, R., Biyani, S., & Rosenthal, J. (1995). Measurement of failure rate in widely distributed software. In *Proceedings of the 25ᵗʰ International Symposium on Fault-Tolerant Computing* (p. 424).

Chiu, C., Hsu, C., Yeh, Y.-S., & Yi, S. (2006). A genetic algorithm for reliability oriented task assignment with k duplications in distributed systems. *IEEE Transactions on Reliability, 55*(1), 105–117. doi:10.1109/TR.2005.863797

Dabrowski, C. (2009). Reliability in grid computing systems. *Concurrency and Computation, 21*(8), 927–959. doi:10.1002/cpe.1410

Foster, I. (2002). What is the Grid? A three point checklist. *Grid Today, 1*(6), 22.

Foster, I., & Kesselman, C. (1998). *The Grid: Blueprint for a future computing infrastructure* (pp. 1–29). San Francisco, CA: Morgan Kauffman.

Huda Mohammad, T., Schmidt, W. H., & Peake, I. D. (2005). An agent oriented proactive fault-tolerant framework for grid computing. In *Proceedings of the First International Conference on e-Science and Grid Computing* (pp. 304-311).

Levitin, G., & Dai, H. (2006). Reliability and performance of star topology grid service with precedence constraints on subtask execution. *IEEE Transactions on Reliability, 55*(3), 507–515. doi:10.1109/TR.2006.879651

Nazir, B., & Khan, T. (2006). Fault tolerant job scheduling in computational grid. In *Proceedings of the Second International Conference on Emerging Technologies*, Pakistan (pp. 708-713).

Pylvanainen, J., Jarvinen, J., & Verho, P. (2004). Advanced reliability analysis for distribution network. *IEEE Transactions on Reliability, 2*, 457–462.

Raza, Z., & Vidyarthi, D. P. (2008). A fault tolerant grid scheduling model to minimize turnaround time. In *Proceedings of the International Conference on High Performance Computing, Networking, and Communication Systems*, Orlando, FL (pp. 167-175).

Sedrakian, A. A., Badia, R. M., Kielmann, T., Merzky, A., Perez, J. M., & Sirvent, R. (2007). *Reliability and trust based workflow's job mapping on the grid.* Retrieved from http://www.coregrid.net

Shahtz, S., Wang, J.-P., & Goto, M. (1992). Task allocation for maximizing reliability of distributed computer systems. *IEEE Transactions on Computers, 41*(9), 1156–1168. doi:10.1109/12.165396

Shi, X., Jin, H., Qiang, W., & Zou, D. (2004). Reliability analysis for grid computing. In H. Jin, Y. Pan, N. Xiao, & J. Sun (Eds.), *Proceedings of the Third International Conference on Grid and Cooperative Computing* (LNCS 3251, pp. 787-790).

Srinivasan, S., & Jha, N. K. (1999). Safety and reliability driven task allocation in distributed systems. *IEEE Transactions on Parallel and Distributed Systems, 10*(3), 238–251. doi:10.1109/71.755824

Tao, Y., Jin, H., & Shi, X. (2007). Grid workflow scheduling based on reliability cost. In *Proceedings of the Second International Conference on Scalable Information Systems*, Suzhou, China (p. 12).

Tarricone, L., & Esposito, A. (2005). *Grid computing for electromagnetics*. Boston, MA: Artech House.

Taylor, I. J., & Harrison, A. (2009) *From P2P and grids to services on the web- evolving distributed communities* (2nd ed.). London, UK: Springer-Verlag.

Vidyarthi, D. P., Sarker, B. K., Tripathi, A. K., & Yang, L. T. (2009). *Scheduling in distributed computing systems: Analysis, design, and models*. New York, NY: Springer. doi:10.1007/978-0-387-74483-4

Vidyarthi, D. P., & Tripathi, A. K. (1998). Studies on reliability with task allocation of redundant distributed systems. *Journal of the Institution of Electronics and Telecommunication Engineers*, 279–285.

Vidyarthi, D. P., & Tripathi, A. K. (2001). Maximizing reliability of distributed computing system with task allocation using simple genetic algorithm. *Journal of Systems Architecture*, 549–554. doi:10.1016/S1383-7621(01)00013-3

This work was previously published in the International Journal of Distributed Systems and Technologies (IJDST), Volume 2, Issue 2, edited by Nik Bessis, pp. 19-36, copyright 2011 by IGI Publishing (an imprint of IGI Global).

Chapter 4
Performance of Wireless Sensor Networks for Different Mobile Event Path Scenarios

Tao Yang
Fukuoka Institute of Technology, Japan

Makoto Ikeda
Seikei University, Japan

Gjergji Mino
Fukuoka Institute of Technology, Japan

Fatos Xhafa
Technical University of Catalonia, Spain

Leonard Barolli
Fukuoka Institute of Technology, Japan

Arjan Durresi
Indiana University-Purdue University Indianapolis, USA

ABSTRACT

In this paper, the authors investigate how the sensor network performs when the event moves with special movement path. Simulation results are compared with four scenarios: when the event is stationary, moving randomly, moving with simple 4 path, and boids path. The simulation results show that for the case when the event is moving randomly, the performance is the worst in the four scenarios. The characteristic of goodput decreases with the increase of number of sensor nodes. In the case of the boids model, the goodput is unstable when the T_r is lower than 10 pps. The consumed energy characteristic increases with the increase of T_r. Simulation results show that the consumed energy of random movement is the worst among the four scenarios. The consumed energy of boids model is the lowest in four cases. This shows that the event movement with boids model can decrease the consumed energy in large scale WSNs.

INTRODUCTION

In recent years, technological advances have lead to the emergence of distributed Wireless Sensor Networks (WSNs) which are capable of observing the physical world, processing the data, making decisions based on the observations and performing appropriate actions. These networks can be an integral part of systems such as battle-field surveillance and microclimate control in buildings, nuclear, biological and chemical attack detection, home automation and environmental monitoring (Akyildiz et al., 2004; Younis et al., 2004).

DOI: 10.4018/978-1-4666-2647-8.ch004

Wireless sensor network simulation is an important part of the current research. A large number of algorithms were first implemented and evaluated using several network simulators. Recently, there are many research works for sensor networks (Giordano et al., 2004; Al-Karaki et al., 2004). In our previous work (Yang et al., 2006), we implemented a simulation system for sensor networks considering different protocols (e.g: AODV, DSR, DSDV, OLSR.) and different propagation radio models. In Marco et al. (2006), we analysed the performance of WSNs considering different topologies and Shadowing radio model. Also, we analysed the performance of our proposed simulation system. But, we considered that the event node is stationary in the observation field. However, in many applications the event node may move. For example, in an ecology environment the animals may move randomly. Another example is when an event happens in a robot or in a car.

In this work, we want to investigate how the sensor network performs in the case when the event moves with special movement path. We carry out simulations for lattice topology and TwoRayGround radio model considering Adhoc On-demand Distance Vector (AODV) protocol. We evaluate the performance of WSN for 4 scenarios: when the event is stationary, moving randomly, moving with simple 4 path and boids path. The simulation results have shown that for the case when event is moving randomly the performance is the worst in the four scenarios. The characteristic of goodput decreases with the increase of number of sensor nodes. In the case of boids model, the goodput is unstable when the T_r is lower than 10 pps. The consumed energy characteristic increases with the increase of T_r. Simulation results show that the consumed energy of random movement is the worst among four scenarios.

PROPOSED NETWORK SIMULATION MODEL

In our WSN, every node detects the physical phenomenon and sends back to the sink node the data packets. We suppose that the sink node is more powerful than sensor nodes. In our previous work, the event node was stationary. In this work, we consider that the event moves with special movement path. We analyze the performance of the network in a fixed time interval. This is the available time for the detection of the phenomenon and its value is application dependent. A proposed network simulation model is shown in Figure 1.

A. Topology

For the physical layout of the WSN, two types of topologies have been studied so far: random and lattice topologies. In the former, nodes are supposed to be uniformly distributed, while in the latter one nodes are vertexes of particular geometric shape, e.g., a square grid. For lattice topology, in order to guarantee the connectedness of the network we should set the transmission range of every node to the step size, d, which is the minimum distance between two rows (or columns) of the grid (Allen et al., 2006; Cooper, 1993). In fact, by this way the number of links that every node can establish (the node degree D) is 4. Nodes at the borders have D = 2.

In the case of random networks, we suppose that the coordinates in the Euclidean plane of every sensor are random variables uniformly distributed in the interval [0,L]×[0,L]. Snapshots of lattice and random networks generated in simulations are shown in Figure 2 and Figure 3, respectively.

B. Radio Model

In order to simulate the detection of a natural event, we used the libraries from Naval Research Laboratory (NRL) (Network simulator). In this framework, a phenomenon is modeled as a wireless

Figure 1. Proposed network simulation model

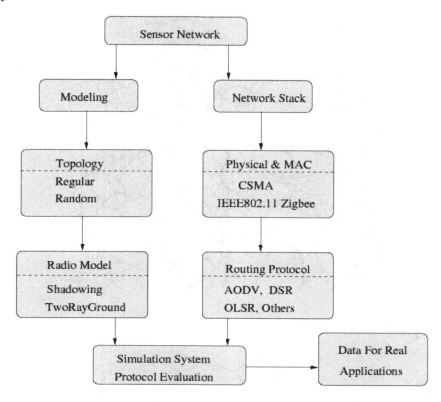

mobile node. The phenomenon node broadcasts packets with a tunable synchrony or pulse rate, which represents the period of occurrence of a generic event. These libraries provide the sensor node with an alarm variable. The alarm variable is a timer variable. It turns off the sensor if no event is sensed within an alarm interval. In addition to the sensing capabilities, every sensor can establish a multi-hop communication towards the sink by means of a particular routing protocol.

We assume that the MAC protocol is the IEEE 802.11 standard. This serves to us as a baseline of comparison for other contention resolution protocols. The receiver of every sensor node is supposed to receive correctly data bits if the received power exceeds the receiver threshold. This threshold depends on the hardware. As reference, we select parameters values according to the features of a commercial device (MICA2 OEM). In particular, for this device, we found that for a

carrier frequency of f = 916MHz and a data rate of 34KBaud, we have a threshold (or receiver sensitivity) λ |dB = −118dBm (Crossbow technology). In particular, the emitted power of the phenomenon is calculated according to a TwoRay-Ground propagation model (Rappaport, 2001). The received power Pr at a certain distance d is the same along all directions in the plane. For example, in the case of Line of Sight (LOS) propagation of the signal, the Friis formula predicts the received power as:

$$P_r(d) = P_t - \beta(dB),$$
$$\beta = 10\log(\frac{(4\pi d)^2 L}{G_t G_r \lambda^2}) \tag{1}$$

where G_r and G_t are the antenna gains of the receiver and the transmitter, respectively, λ is the wavelength of the signal, L the insertion loss

Figure 2. An example of lattice network

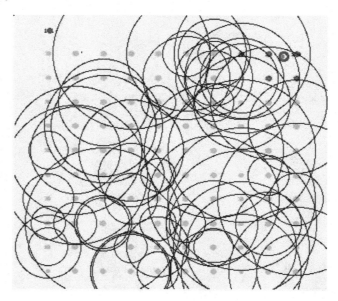

Figure 3. An example of random network

caused by feeding circuitry of the antenna, and β is the propagation pathloss. For omni-antennas, $G_R = G_t = 1$. The signal decay is then proportional to d^2. A more accurate model is TwoRay-Ground model, where in addition to the direct ray from the transmitter towards the receiver node, a ground reflected signal is supposed to be present. Accordingly, the received power depends also on the antenna heights and the pathloss is:

$$\beta = 10\log(\frac{(4\pi d)^4 L}{G_t G_r h_t h_r \lambda^2}) \tag{2}$$

where h_r and h_t are the receiver and transmitter antenna heights, respectively. The power decreases faster than Equation 1. The formula in Equation 2 is valid for distances d > dc (dc is the distance threshold of signal LOS propagation), that is far from the transmitting node (Zhou et al, 2006; Ye et al, 2004)).

C. Energy Model

The energy model concerns the dynamics of energy consumption of the sensor. A widely used model is as follows. When the sensor transmits k bits, the radio circuitry consumes an energy of kPT_xT_B, where PT_x is the power required to transmit a bit which lasts T_B seconds. By adding the radiated power $P_t(d)$ we have:

$$E_{T_x}(k, d) = kT_B(P_{Tx} + P_t(d)).$$

Since packet reception consumes energy, by following the same reasoning, we have:

$$E(k, d) = kP_{Tx}T_B + kT_BP_t(d) + kP_{Rx}T_B \qquad (3)$$

where PR_x is the power required to correctly receive (demodulate and decode) one bit.

D. Routing Protocols

We are aware of many routing protocols for ad-hoc networks (Perkins, 2001). We have implemented in our simulation system many routing protocols. But, in this work, we consider only AODV protocol. The AODV is an improvement of DSDV to on-demand scheme. It minimizes the broadcast packet by creating route only when needed. Every node in network maintains the route information table and participates in routing table exchange. When source node wants to send data to the destination node, it first initiates route discovery process. In this process, source node broadcasts Route Request (RREQ) packet to its neighbors. Neighbor nodes which receive RREQ forward the packet to its neighbor nodes. This process continues until RREQ reach to the destination or the node who know the path to destination. When the intermediate nodes receive RREQ, they record in their tables the address of neighbors, thereby establishing a reverse path. When the node which knows the path to destination or destination node itself receive RREQ, it send back Route Reply (RREP) packet to source node. This RREP packet is transmitted by using reverse path. When the source node receives RREP packet, it can know the path to destination node and it stores the discovered path information in its route table. This is the end of route discovery process. Then, AODV performs route maintenance process. In route maintenance process, each node periodically transmits a Hello message to detect link breakage.

E. Event Detection and Transport

For event detection and transport, we use the data-centric model similar to (Akan et al., 2005), where the end-to-end reliability is transformed into a bounded signal distortion concept. In this model, after sensing an event, every sensor node sends sensed data towards the Monitoring Node (MN). The transport used is a UDP-like transport, i.e. there is not any guarantee on the data delivery. While this approach reduces the complexity of the transport protocol and well fit the energy and computational constraints of sensor nodes, the event-reliability can be guaranteed to some extent because of the spatial redundancy.

The sensor node transmits data packets reporting the details of the detected event at a certain transmission rate. The setting of this parameter T_r depends on several factors, as the quantization step of sensors, the type of phenomenon, and the desired level of distortion perceived at the MN. For example, if we refer to event-reliability as the minimum number of packets required at sink in order to reliably detect the event, then whenever the sink receives a number of packets less than the event-reliability, it can instruct sensor nodes to use a higher T_r. This instruction is piggy-backed in dedicated packets from the MN.

This system can be considered as a control system, as shown in Figure 4, with the target event-reliability as input variable and the actual event-reliability as output parameter. The target event-reliability is transformed into an initial T_r^0. The control loop has the output event-reliability as input, and on the basis of a particular non-linear function f(·), T_r is accordingly changed. We do not implement the entire control system, but only a simplified version of it. For instance, we vary T_r and observe the behaviour of the system in terms of the mean number of received packets. In other words, we open the control loop and analyse the forward chain only.

EVENT MOBILITY IN MANY-TO-ONE MULTI-HOP WSN

The research works on the subject of event mobility in many-to-one multi-hop WSNs can generally be categorized based on the assumed type of event

trajectory. Types of mobile event trajectories most commonly studied in the literature include: fixed (stationary), random, 4 path and boids path model. We explain each of these four types of event trajectories in more details in following.

A. Stationary Event Model

In general, the event is stationary in the observed field. (For e.g., gas, fire). Sensor nodes which are around the event sense the event and send the information to the sink by multi-hop.

B. Movement with Random Path

As the name implies, the trajectory of a randomly moving event comprises a sequence of segments of arbitrary length and direction (Figure 5). The event's speed along each segment, and the pause time between movements along different segments, can also be arbitrary, although these two conditions do not to hold to satisfy the randomness requirement. In many applications the event node may move. For example, in an ecology environment the animals may move randomly. Another example is when an event happens in a robot or in a car.

Figure 4. Representation of the transport based on the event-reliability

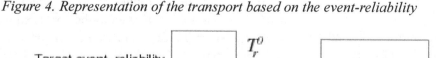
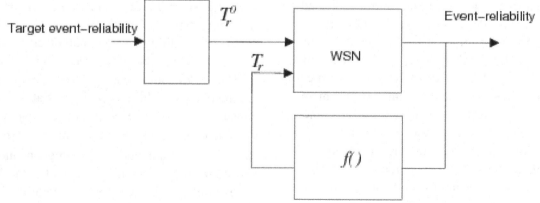

Figure 5. Multi-hop WSN with a random moving event

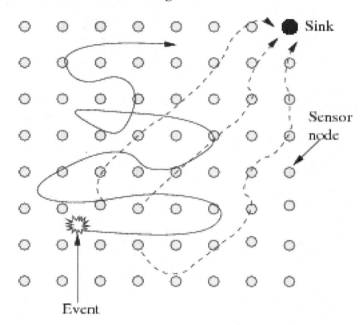

C. The Simple 4 Path Model

In contrast to the random trajectory, the fixed trajectory is fully deterministic - with this type of trajectory, the event is expected to continuously follow the same path through the network. The fixed trajectory is typically forced upon the mobile event by the nature of the physical terrain and/or presence of obstacles in the environment. An example of a research study that deals with this type of trajectory is (Tacconi et al., 2007). In this work, we set the mobile event with simple 4 path (Figure 6).

D. The Boids Path Model

As computer model of coordinated animal motion such as bird flocks and fish schools. It was based on three dimensional computational geometry of the sort normally used in computer animation or computer aided design. So called the generic simulated flocking creatures boids. The basic flocking model consists of three simple steering behaviours which describe how an individual boids moves based on the positions and velocities of its nearby flockmates (Figure 7).

Each boids has direct access to the whole scene's geometric description, but flocking requires that it reacts only to flockmates within a certain small neighborhood around itself. The neighborhood is characterized by a distance (measured from the center of the boids) and an angle, measured from the boids direction of flight. Flockmates outside this local neighborhood are ignored. The neighborhood could be considered a model of limited perception (as by fish in murky water) but it is probably more correct to think of it as defining the region in which flockmates influence a boids steering.

SIMULATION RESULTS

In this section, we present the simulation results of our proposed WSN. We simulated the network by means of NS-2 simulator, with the support of NRL libraries. In Tables 1 and 2, we summarise the values of parameters used in our WSN. Let

Figure 6. Multi-hop WSN with a simple 4 path-constrained movile event

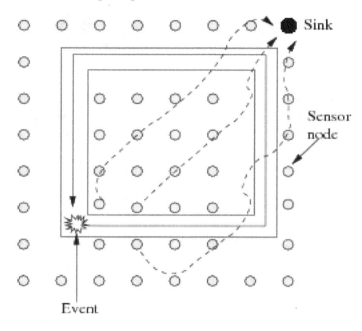

Figure 7. Boids model

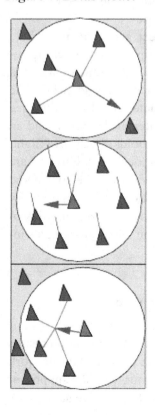

Separation:

Steer to avoid
crowding local
flockmates

Alignment:

Steer towards the
average heading
of local flockmates

Cohesion:

Steer to move toward
the average position
of local flockmates

us note that the power values concern the power required to transmit and receive one bit, respectively. They do not refer to the radiated power at all. This is also the energy model implemented in the widely used NS-2 simulator (Wei, 2005).

A. Performance Metrics

In this paper, we evaluated the performance of the proposed model with two performance metrics: goodput and depletion. The goodput is defined at the sink, and it is the received packet rate divided by the sent packets rate. Thus:

$$G(\tau) = \frac{N_r(\tau)}{N_s(\tau)} \tag{4}$$

where $N_r(\tau)$ is the number of received packet at the sink, and the $N_s(\tau)$ is the number of packets sent by sensor nodes which detected the phenomenon. Note that the event reliability is defined as

Table 1. Topology settings

Lattice	
Step	$d = \dfrac{L}{\sqrt{N}-1} m$
Service Area Size	L^2 =(800m×800m)
Transmission Range	$r_0 = d$
Number of Nodes	N=16,100,256

Table 2. Radio model and system parameters

Radio Model Parameters	
Path Loss Coefficient	α =2.7
Variance	σ^2_{dB} =16dB
Carrier Frequency	916MHz
Antenna	omni
Threshold (Sensitivity)	λ =-118dB
Other Parameters	
Reporting Frequency	T_r =[0.1,1000]pps(1)
Interface Queue Size	50 packets
UDP Packet Size	100 bytes
Detection Interval τ	30s
(1) packet per seconds	

$$G_R = \frac{N_\tau(\tau)}{R_\tau}$$

where R is the required number of packets or data in a time interval of τ seconds.

As long as the WSN is being used, a certain amount of energy will be consumed. The energy consumption rate directly affects the life-time of the network, i.e. the time after which the WSN is unusable. The energy depletion is a function of the reporting rate as well as the density of the

sensor network. Recall that the density of the network in the event-driven scenario correlates with the number of nodes that report their data. Accordingly, we define the consumed energy by the network in the detection interval τ as:

$$\overline{\Delta} = \frac{NE_I = \sum_{i=1}^{N} e_i(\tau)}{N_\tau} \qquad (5)$$

where $e_i(t)$ is the node energy at time τ and the means are computed over the number of nodes. The number of nodes N is set as power of integers in order to analyse the behavior of the scaled versions of the network.

B. Simulation Results and Discussion

For AODV routing protocol, the sample averages of Equation 4 and Equation 5 are computed over 20 simulation runs, and they are plotted from Figure 8 through Figure 13. In these figures, the vertical axis shows the goodput or consumed energy, while, the horizontal axis shows is the reporting frequency. We set the reporting frequency from 0.1 to 1000. At a particular value of T_r (~10pps), the goodput decreases abruptly, because the network has reached the maximum capacity. The goodput results are plotted from Figure 8 through Figure 10. As shown in Figure 8, for the case of 16 nodes, the goodput of stationary event model and boids model are unstable when the T_r is lower than 10 pps. When the T_r is larger than 10pps, the goodput of random path has the worst performance. When the number of sensor node increase to 100 nodes, as shown in the Figure 9, the goodput of stationary event is stable. The goodput of random path is lower compared with other cases. Also, the goodput for 100 nodes is lower than 16 nodes. The performance results have the same trend also for 256 nodes as shown in Figure 10.

Figure 8. Average goodput for 16 nodes

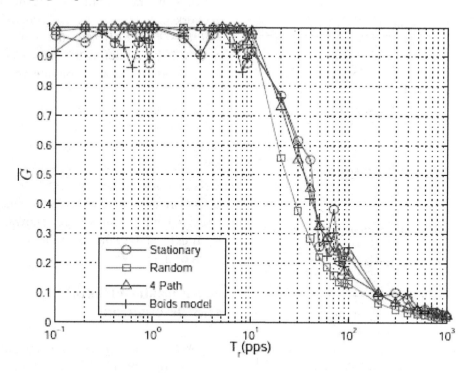

Figure 9. Average goodput for 100 nodes

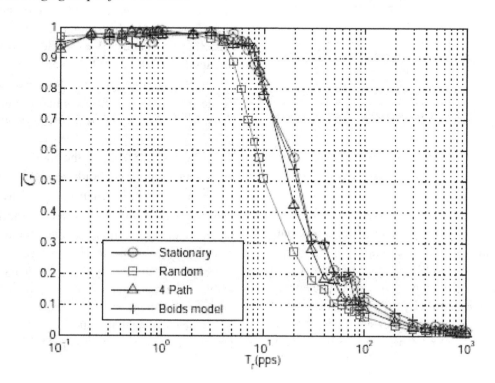

Figure 10. Average goodput for 256 nodes

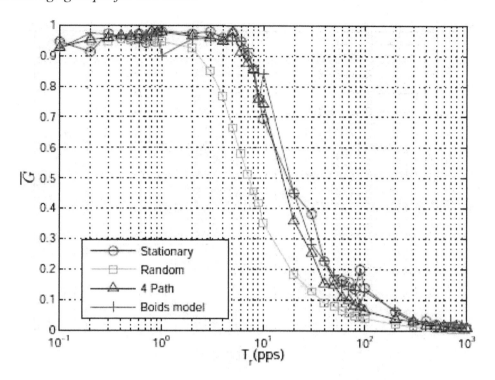

Figure 11. Average depletion for 16 nodes

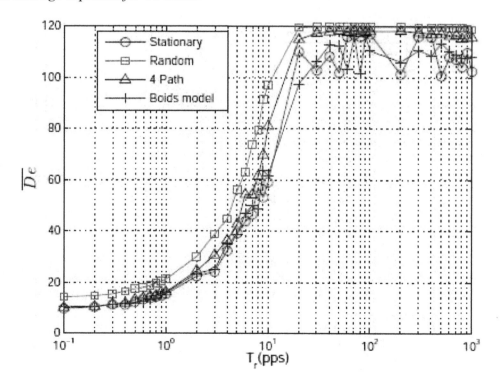

Figure 12. Average depletion for 100 nodes

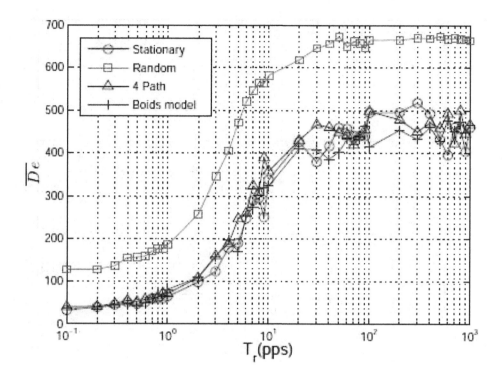

Figure 13. Average depletion for 256 nodes

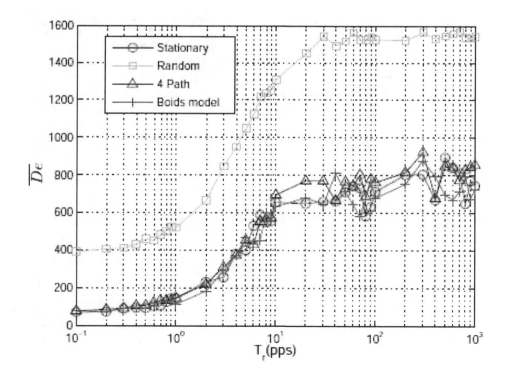

The results of consumed energy (depletion) are shown from Figure 11, Figure 12, and Figure 13. The consumed energy increases when the number of nodes is increased. In the case of 16 nodes, all the models perform the same, but the performance of random is not good. When the number of nodes increases from 100 to 256, the consumed energy of random path increases much more than the others models. The explanation of this effect is not simple, because it is intermingled with the dynamics of MAC and routing protocol. We also found that the consumed energy of boids model is the lowest in four cases. This shows that the event movement with boids model can decrease the consumed energy in the large scale WSNs.

CONCLUSION

In this paper, we presented our simulation results of WSN for four scenarios of event movement. We used the goodput and consumed energy metrics to measure the performance. From the simulation results, we conclude as follows.

- For the case of 16 nodes, the goodput of stationary event model and boids model are unstable when the T_r is lower than 10 pps.
- When the T_r is larger than 10 pps, the goodput of random path has the worst performance.
- When the number of sensor node increase to 100 nodes, the goodput of stationary event is stable.
- The goodput of random path is lower compared with other cases. Also, the goodput for 100 nodes is lower than 16 nodes. The performance results have the same trend also for 256 nodes
- The consumed energy increases when the number of nodes is increased.

- In the case of 16 nodes, all the models perform the same, but the performance of random is not good.
- When the number of nodes increases from 100 to 256, the consumed energy of random path increases much more than the others models.
- The consumed energy of boids model is the lowest in four cases. This shows that the event movement with boids model can decrease the consumed energy in the large scale WSNs.

In the future, we would like to increase the number of event nodes because the boids model can be applied for many event nodes. We also would like to consider the case of other routing and MAC protocols. We plan to evaluate the performance of WSNs for other metrics such as pathloss and routing efficiency.

ACKNOWLEDGMENT

The authors would like to thank KDDI Froundtion and Japanese Society for the Promotion of Science (JSPS) for supporting this work.

REFERENCES

Akan, Ö. B., & Akyildiz, I. F. (2005). Event-to-sink reliable transport in wireless sensor networks. *IEEE/ACM Transactions on Networking, 13*(5), 1003–1016. doi:10.1109/TNET.2005.857076

Akyildiz, I. F., & Kasimoglu, I. H. (2004). Wireless sensor and actor networks: Research challenges. *Ad Hoc Networks Journal, 2*(4), 351–367. doi:10.1016/j.adhoc.2004.04.003

Al-Karaki, J. N., & Kamal, A. E. (2004). Routing techniques in wireless sensor networks: A survey. *IEEE Wireless Communication, 11*(6), 6–28. doi:10.1109/MWC.2004.1368893

Allen, G. W., Lorincz, K., Marcillo, O., Johnson, J., Ruiz, M., & Lees, J. (2006). Deploying a wireless sensor network on an active volcano. *IEEE Internet Computing, 10*(2), 18–25. doi:10.1109/MIC.2006.26

Cooper, C. (1993). A note on the connectivity of 2-regular digraphs. *Random Structures and Algorithms, 4*(4), 469–472. doi:10.1002/rsa.3240040406

Crossbow Technology, Inc. (n. d.). *The smart sensors company.* Retrieved from http://www.xbow.com/

De Marco, G., Yang, T., & Barolli, L. (2006). Impact of radio irregularities on topology tradeoffs of WSNs. In *Proceedings of the NBiS/DEXA Conference*, Krakow, Poland (pp. 50-54).

Giordano, S., & Rosenberg, C. (2004). Topics in ad hoc and sensor networks. *IEEE Communications Magazine, 44*(4), 97. doi:10.1109/MCOM.2006.1632655

Information Sciences Institute. (n. d.). *The network simulator.* Retrieved from http://www.isi.edu/nsnam/ns/

Perkins, C. (Ed.). (2001). *Ad hoc networks.* Reading, MA: Addison-Wesley.

Rappaport, T. S. (2001). *Wireless communications.* Upper Saddle River, NJ: Prentice Hall.

Tacconi, D., Carreras, I., Miorandi, D., Casile, A., Chiti, F., & Fantacci, R. (2007, November). A system architecture supporting mobile applications in disconnected sensor networks. In *Proceedings of the IEEE Globecom Conference* (pp.484-497).

Wei, D. X. (2005). *Speeding up ns-2 scheduler.* Retrieved from http://netlab.caltech.edu/

Yang, T., De Marco, G., Ikeda, M., & Barolli, L. (2006). Impact of radio randomness on performances of lattice wireless sensor networks based on event-reliability concept. *International Journal of Mobile Information Systems, 2*(4), 211–227.

Ye, W., Heidemann, J., & Estrin, D. (2004). Medium access control with coordinated adaptive sleeping for wireless sensor networks. *IEEE/ACM Transactions on Networking, 12*(3), 493–506. doi:10.1109/TNET.2004.828953

Younis, O., & Fahmy, S. (2004). HEED: A hybrid, energy-efficient, distributed clustering approach for ad-hoc sensor networks. *IEEE Transactions on Mobile Computing, 3*(4), 366–379. doi:10.1109/TMC.2004.41

Zhou, G., He, T., Krishnamurthy, S., & Stankovic, J. A. (2006). Models and solutions for radio irregularity in wireless sensor networks. *ACM Transactions on Sensors Network, 2*(2), 221–262. doi:10.1145/1149283.1149287

This work was previously published in the International Journal of Distributed Systems and Technologies (IJDST), Volume 2, Issue 3, edited by Nik Bessis, pp. 49-63, copyright 2011 by IGI Publishing (an imprint of IGI Global).

Chapter 5
The Development of a Parallel Ray Launching Algorithm for Wireless Network Planning

Zhihua Lai
University of Bedfordshire, UK

Nik Bessis
University of Derby, UK &
University of Bedfordshire, UK

Guillaume De La Roche
University of Bedfordshire, UK

Pierre Kuonen
University of Applied Science of Western
Switzerland, Switzerland

Jie Zhang
University of Bedfordshire, UK

Gordon Clapworthy
University of Bedfordshire, UK

ABSTRACT

Propagation modeling has attracted much interest because it plays an important role in wireless network planning and optimization. Deterministic approaches such as ray tracing and ray launching have been investigated, however, due to the running time constraint, these approaches are still not widely used. In previous work, an intelligent ray launching algorithm, namely IRLA, has been proposed. The IRLA has proven to be a fast and accurate algorithm and adapts to wireless network planning well. This article focuses on the development of a parallel ray launching algorithm based on the IRLA. Simulations are implemented, and evaluated performance shows that the parallelization greatly shortens the running time. The COST231 Munich scenario is adopted to verify algorithm behavior in real world environments, and observed results show a 5 times increased speedup upon a 16-processor cluster. In addition, the parallelization algorithm can be easily extended to larger scenarios with sufficient physical resources.

DOI: 10.4018/978-1-4666-2647-8.ch005

INTRODUCTION

Propagation modeling serves as a fundamental input in the wireless network planning and optimization process. Especially, in order to determine the interferences for an indoor femtocell base station with the outdoor macrocell, accurate coverage predictions have to be obtained via propagation modeling (Zhang & De La Roche, 2010). Planning and optimization of a wireless network usually requires simulation of hundreds of User Equipments (UE) and the path loss between these UEs and base stations are obligatory to investigate the best servers and handovers etc.

Current propagation models can be divided into three categories: empirical models, semi-deterministic and deterministic models. Empirical models are the simplest models; which are usually based on simple factors such as the carrier frequency and distance. They are extremely fast because of statistical model environmental factors. The semi-deterministic models are enhanced by introducing relevant deterministic factors in the computation. Such models provide higher accuracy than empirical models, thus running time of semi-deterministic models is usually realistically acceptable upon conventional computing power, such as PCs.

The deterministic models consider environmental factors, e.g., buildings and walls, which are time-consuming compared to empirical and semi-deterministic models. However, the deterministic models provide the highest accuracy out of these categories.

Ray-based methods belong to deterministic models and they are based on geometry path finding algorithms (Haslett, 2008). Ray-based methods in general are divided into two subcategories: ray tracing and ray launching. Ray tracing adopts a backward path search technique, which guarantees that exact paths between transmitters and receivers can be computed (Glassner, 1989). Ray tracing offers high accuracy but it is extremely time consuming. The complexity grows exponentially

with the number of objects and the maximum ray iterations (Nagy, Dady, & Farkasvolgyi, 2009). Ray tracing is used for precise point-to-point predictions. Several acceleration techniques such as pre-processing (Wolfle, Gschwendtner, & Landstorfer, 1997) or the use of a General Purpose Graphic Processing Unit (GPGPU) (Rick & Mathar, 2007) have been proposed. The performance of ray tracing is usually limited by the inherent complex ray-object intersection tests and many techniques have been proposed over the past years to speed up computation (Degli-Esposti, Fuschini, Vitucci, & Falciasecca, 2009). Ray launching emits the rays from sources; which are separated by a small angle. This method is efficient in an area prediction because the rays are actively followed. However, this approach leads to two inherent problems. The first problem is angular dispersion of ray launching. The distant pixels are less likely to be visited by rays because rays disperse as they are propagated. For example, a distant small object may be missed by rays because a fixed angle is used to separate rays. Secondly, the ray double counting arises when a sample pixel is marked twice by the same rays, which should be avoided because it reduces the accuracy of ray launching. Ray launching is usually faster than ray tracing with less accuracy. The complexity of ray launching grows linearly with the number of objects and maximum ray iteration (Nagy et al., 2009).

In (Lai, Bessis, De La Roche, Song, Zhang, & Clapworthy, 2009), a new model based on discrete ray launching, namely the Intelligent Ray Launching Algorithm (IRLA), has been proposed to obtain fast propagation prediction (path loss and multipath components) within a realistic time scale. In (Lai et al., 2010), the authors extended this model to indoor prediction, which accurately predicts the multipath propagation in indoor environment. The IRLA model has been validated with measurement campaigns (Lai et al., 2010), which has led to the effective development for network applications. In (Lai et al., 2009), the authors proposed an efficient method to improve the accuracy of IRLA by solving angular dispersion problem of ray launching. This method has effectively improved the accuracy and avoids ray double counting. In (Lai et al., 2009), a parallel algorithm of IRLA is implemented based on a toolkit named Parallel Object-oriented Programming in C++ (POP-C++). Preliminary promising results have been presented, which show that parallel IRLA has improved the performance. This article is an extension of this work: issues related to performance and accuracy will be further addressed in this work. This article contributes to present a parallel propagation algorithm that accelerates the time-consuming prediction. The components of the IRLA model are analyzed so that the most time-consuming components are parallelized. Results show that with 16 processors, the performance can reach up to 5 for certain scenarios.

The rest of this article is organized as follows. At First, the IRLA model is briefly introduced. Secondly, the complexity of IRLA is studied, which serves as the fundamentals to develop the efficient parallel IRLA model. Then, the issues related to parallelization are detailed, which is followed by results that conclude this work.

THE RAY LAUNCHING MODEL: IRLA

IRLA is a discrete ray launching model that aims to provide highly improved prediction in terms of path loss and multipath components for wireless propagation prediction within a short time. In outdoor urban scenarios, a specific procedure has been developed to accelerate the computations of urban rooftop diffractions. IRLA can be easily extended to indoor, indoor-to-outdoor and outdoor-to-indoor scenarios due to the well designed mechanisms to avoid duplication of rays and angular dispersion (Lai et al., 2009). IRLA is based on discrete cubic data set, which can be extracted from vector building data. Typically,

building data for outdoor scenarios are simplified to 2.5-D which are described as polygon-shaped buildings with height information. For outdoor scenarios, the IRLA separates roof-top diffractions from horizontal diffractions and reflections. The algorithm quickly checks the number of roof-top diffractions required between the transmitter and receiver. The components of IRLA and their relationship are depicted in Figure 1. Given the input data (building, antenna, and network configuration), the discrete data set is built, based on which Line-of-Sight (LOS) component obtains secondary pixels for reflections and diffractions.

Horizontal Reflection Diffraction (HRD) and Vertical Diffraction (VD) are independent of each other and thus can be run in parallel. When these two components are completed, a post-processing procedure is carried out (such as antenna pattern adjustment and indoor coverage prediction) and final outputs include path loss and multipath components.

Computational Complexity

The discrete data set size is (N_x, N_y, N_z), which represents the number of cubes for *X, Y,* and *Z* dimensions respectively. The numbers of building cubes are known as N_{ground}, N_{wall} and N_{roof}, which represent the number of building ground, walls and roofs respectively. Therefore the total number of representing buildings can be denoted as

$$N_{\text{buildings}} = N_{\text{ground}} \cup N_{\text{wall}} \cup N_{\text{roof}}$$

For example, there are cubes; which are joint edges of walls and roofs. $N_{buildings}$ depends on the size of the scenario, the number of buildings and the resolution used for building the discrete data. $N_{buildings}$ usually impacts on the computation complexity. For example, greater $N_{buildings}$ causes larger computational complexity and vice versa.

The complexity of IRLA thus can be modeled by five parts: C_{pre}, C_{post}, C_{los}, C_{vd} and C_{hrd}, which represent the computation complexity for pre-

Figure 1. Structures of the ray launching model

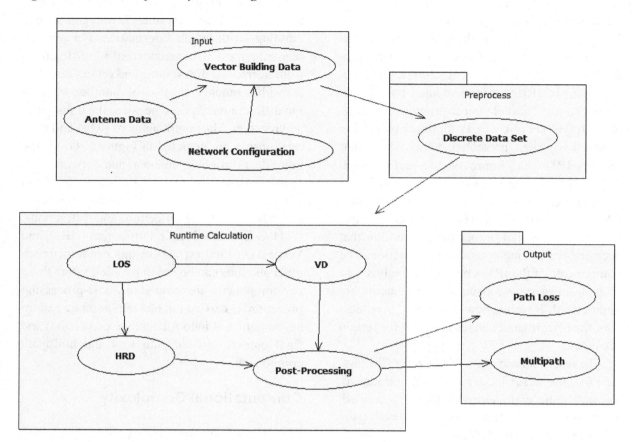

calculation, post-processing, component LOS, VD and HRD respectively. Let C be the total complexity of IRLA, then it is can be obtained as following:

$$C = C_{\text{los}} + C_{\text{vd}} + C_{\text{hrd}} + C_{\text{pre}} + C_{\text{post}}$$

C_{los} can be approximated based on the number of cubes on the fringe of scenario. The process of IRLA prediction starts with launching rays in all 3-D directions. Based on the discrete data set, the resolution and the number of cubes along each dimension (X, Y and Z) are known. Therefore the number of discrete rays required can be obtained by connecting the transmitter to all the cubes at the fringe of the scenarios (Lai et al., 2009), which is

$$N_{\text{fringe}} = 2N_x N_y + 2(N_z - 2)(N_x + N_y - 2)$$

where N is the number of discrete rays and N_x, N_y and N_z are the number of cubes in dimension X, Y and Z respectively.

This formula ensures no pixels are missing due to angular dispersion of ray launching (Lai et al., 2009) from component LOS. The use of such ray launching mechanism is useful in distribution of rays. N_{fringe} is the number of discrete rays launched by LOS. Suppose the transmitter is placed in cubic position (T_x, T_y, T_z), the distance function $D(x_1, y_1, z_1, x_2, y_2, z_2)$ acknowledges for the number of cubes that have to be checked on a particular discrete ray starting from (x_1, y_1, z_1) and the ending at position (x_2, y_2, z_2) (one of the fringe cubes). The maximum value of D is obtained if there is no obstacle found along the discrete ray being checked. In this case, D can be calculated as

$$D(x_1, y_1, z_1, x_2, y_2, z_2) = \max(|x_1 - x_2|, |y_1 - y_2|, |z_1 - z_2|)$$

The worst case for LOS occurs if it is an empty scenario (free space). Every single cube has to be checked. In this case, $N_{buildings} = 0$, C_{los} can be roughly approximated to

$$C_{\text{los}} = \sum_{i=1}^{N_{\text{fringe}}} D(T_x, T_y, T_z, x_i, y_i, z_i)$$

where x_i, y_i, z_i represents the cube coordinates of fringe at index i and N_{los} denotes the number of secondary cubes obtained via checking cubes on discrete rays if there are obstacles.

$$N_{\text{los}} = \sum_{i=1}^{N_{\text{fringe}}} H(T_x, T_y, T_z, x_i, y_i, z_i)$$

where x_i, y_i, and z_i represents the cube coordinates of fringe at index i.

$$H(T_x, T_y, T_z, x_i, x_y, z_i) = \begin{cases} 1 \text{ discrete ray } (T_x, \ T_y, \ T_z) \rightarrow \\ \quad (x_i, \ y_i, \ z_i) \text{ is blocked by obstacles} \\ 0 \text{ otherwise} \end{cases}$$

For indoor scenarios, $C_{vd} = 0$ because component VD (for rooftop diffractions) is not activated. For outdoor scenarios, N_{vd} represents the number of cubes that are checked by VD and can be approximated as

$$N_{\text{vd}} = \sum_{i=1}^{2(N_x + N_y - 2)} D(T_x, T_y, T_z, x_i, x_y, z_i) N_z$$

where D is assumed to reach its maximum value (no obstacles along the discrete ray).

For each cube in N_{vd}, a discrete scan-line is launched from the transmitter. The building blocks between these two cubes are checked. C_{vd} can thus be approximated by

$$C_{\text{vd}} = \sum_{i=1}^{N_{vd}} C_{vd - scan}(T_x, T_y, T_z, x_i, y_i, z_i)$$

where x_i, y_i, z_i represents the cube coordinates at index i being checked.

The procedure $C_{vd-scan}$ is to check the number of rooftop diffractions. In the worst case, each scan-line involves multiple visibility checks between two building blocks which are costly. In this case, the computation complexity can be approximated by counting the number of checks and their corresponding ray lengths.

$$C_{\text{vd-scan}} \simeq \sum_{i=1}^{N_{checks}} L_i$$

where N_{checks} represents the number of visibility checks and L_i represents length (the number of cubes) on discrete ray segment i.

However, due to caching techniques and the intelligence of using geometry to avoid possible checks, $C_{vd-scan}$ can be often be reduced to the complexity of constant $O(1)$.

IRLA incorporates the engine HRD to virtually launch and follow discrete rays. The number of rays is denoted as N_{los}, which is obtained from the LOS component. Depending on the complexity of scenario, current signal strength carried by discrete rays, the threshold and the number of ray iterations, the complexity varies from constant to exponentials i.e. the ray generates many secondary diffraction rays or a reflection ray. This can be greatly accelerated by the intelligent marking scheme; which avoids double marking and angular dispersion. C_{hrd} can be approximated to

$$C_{\text{hrd}} = \sum_{i=1}^{N_{\text{los}}} C_{\text{hrd-ray}}(i)$$

where $C_{hrd\text{-}ray}(i)$ returns the computational complexity of discrete ray i.

Pre-calculation C_{pre} and post-processing C_{post} usually involve operations on the entire discrete data set. In this case, C_{pre} and C_{post} can be approximated to $N_x N_y N_z$. The complexity of C is calculated based on one transmitter. Given n transmitters, the complexity can be sum to

$$\sum_{i=1}^{n} Ci$$

Parallelization

The components prototype of the IRLA model has been depicted in Figure 1. The HRD and VD components are dependent on the discrete data set but both can be executed in parallel. The outputs of these two components are merged and a post-processing procedure is carried. Since these two components are most time-consuming out of all other IRLA components, parallelization via splitting data or instructions has to be performed so that overall speed up can be observed. From the micro aspects of the view, parallelization can be possible even within components, e.g., HRD can easily be parallelized by distributing the rays among processors. These two possibilities offer speed up in the following two manners:

Single-Instruction-Multiple-Data (SIMD). From a micro aspect, computation-intense components can be parallelized via splitting the data. Each individual processor shares the same instructions but performs calculations on different portions of data (e.g. different rays). This can be efficiently and advantageously applied to components that are easily- parallelizable. For example, the inverse operation of an image can be parallelized by cutting images into pieces that are sent to parallel processors. The IRLA model

contains such similar components. For example, the calculation of HRD can be narrowed down to trace each discrete ray that can be treated in parallel. However, this approach requires different specific treatment for different components (i.e. parallelization implementation is different). A significant parallelization speedup is often gained when this approach is employed on data-intense components. In most of the cases, the data split causes the problem of simultaneously accessing the same piece of information by parallel objects/threads. Therefore, the success of this approach depends on the implementation of locks to critical sessions (i.e. a lock prevents other parallel objects/threads accessing important/critical information) (Silberschatz & Galvin, 2006).

Multiple Instruction Multiple Data (MIMD). From a macro aspect, different components can be scheduled on different processors, e.g., one or more processors handle HRD while at the same time the others handle VD. If two or more components are independent from each other, this approach introduces a light-weight (as compared to SIMD approach) parallelization technique. Independent models can be scheduled to different processors for computation simultaneously. However, if the running time from these models is largely different, some processors will be kept idle because usually a barrier is used. This can be avoided by continuous data/instructions fetch from a central node (for example, job manager or resource scheduler in distributed grid environment). However, this will increase the complexity and may increase the need of communication overhead (Bisseling, 2004).

Parallelization can be combined by both SIMD and MIMD approaches, which introduces a two-level parallelization scheme. For example, some faster processors target more data-intense components and the rest are handled by slower processors (MIMD), thus processors are virtually grouped into two. Inside each group, the second level of parallelization (SIMD) can be applied.

Finally, the results from both groups are merged. This is advantageous because it is more grid like and can be easily/slightly modified to suit a distributed grid environment.

Figures 2(a) and 2(b) display the overall parallel model of IRLA with and without a job manager respectively. A job manager is a scheduler that is responsible for deploying computation to available work nodes. If no job manager is used, worker nodes have to be manually given in the first place. This scheme is usually used within a cluster; which is locally limited and not flexible to extend. Without the central control of the job manager, the communication between user's node (N_0) and work nodes (from N_1 to N_n) are visible. In Figure 2(a), stage a represents the messages sent from user's node to work nodes. *b* corresponds to the stage where work nodes carry the parallel computation. *c* corresponds to the stage where all work nodes are stopped by a barrier. *d* corresponds to the stage where results are collected from work nodes and merged. Finally, at stage *e*, the results are sent to user's node. By contrast, if a job manager is used, N_0 is only visible to the job manager. In Figure 2(b), stage *b*, *c* and *d* are the similar to the stages in Figure 2(a) except that the results are sent to job manager instead of user's node. This scheme is often used in scalable and distributed grid environment (Foster & Kessel-man, 2003) where the number of work nodes can be easily extended.

Multithreading

In general, more threads increase the probability of resource competition. But this can be reduced by proper assignment of parallel sub-tasks. For example, the total number of tasks for VD and HRD can be determined before-hand. Each thread obtains a piece of the computation task. In order to reduce the conflict, threads handle pieces of rays that are far located, i.e., discrete rays are separated (greater than a resolution pixel) and unlikely to conflict with each other.

The computers have been equipped with multi-cores technology; which shares the memory via a high-speed system bus (Silberschatz & Galvin, 2006). This enables efficient message exchange between threads. The static data distribution scheme for threads can be described as follows.

Given the total number of jobs (e.g. discrete rays) $n(N_1$ to $N_n)$, and the number of threads to be used is represented by $T(T_1$ to $T_l)$. Assume each thread obtains approximately equal size of jobs, the size of jobs can be calculated by $J=N/P$. Assume adjacent jobs (N_i and N_{i+1}) represent adjacent rays. Define indices $j=(i-1)J+1$ and $k=j+1$. Hence, each thread T_i obtains an array

Figure 2. Parallel IRLA with and without job manager

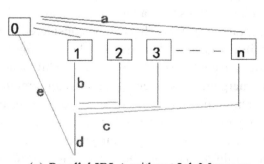

(a) Parallel IRLA without Job Manager

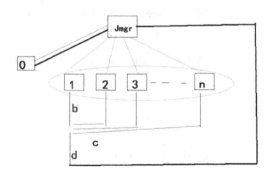

(b) Parallel IRLA with Job Manager

of jobs from N_j to N_k. This approach is easy to implement but has the disadvantage of keeping threads idle due to unequal computation time. For example, some threads may finish computations early and they have to be kept waiting until the rest of the threads have finished. In order to maximize CPU computation usage, more threads have to be created. However, this will lead to the increase of resource competition among threads and will possibly slow down computation. To solve this, a flexible and dynamic data distribution method is proposed, which eliminates the problem and is far more efficient.

Like static data distribution scheme, threads are assigned with a start index and the number of jobs to compute based on the total job number and the number of threads. However, the total number of jobs for each thread is not fixed in the dynamic distribution scheme. Threads continuously fetch next available job index until all computation jobs have been computed. The total job indices are treated as a virtual circular queue, as displayed in Figure 3. In order to reduce the possibility of resource competition from threads, continuous blocks of job indices are assigned to threads. Since the memory is effectively accessed by threads, synchronization techniques such as semaphores (Silberschatz & Galvin, 2006) are employed. Threads are computing simultaneously and when each job index is finished, a pointer indicating next job for each thread is incrementing. The current job index is checked if being locked by other threads and if it has been computed. In this case,

each thread will not be kept waiting unless there are no more jobs. It was verified by experiments that (Table 1, using 3 threads on T9300, 4GB RAM), on average, this parallelization scheme yields from 140% to 160% speedup over static data distribution scheme depending on the scenarios. The number of threads that is considered optimal in practice can be set to the number of physical cores because nearly all the time all the threads are active, which can be mapped to each core.

POP-C++

Parallel Object-oriented Programming in C++ (POP-C++) is a parallel-object oriented programming language in C++ (Nguyen, 2004). POPC++ is an extension of C++ which makes it easy to program parallel applications. It eliminates the need to explicitly invoke and handle message-passing between distributed nodes by introducing a parallel object model. All communication is handled via implicit object calls; which makes it efficient and flexible. Parallel objects represented in POP-C++ (Nguyen & Kuonen, 2007) are logical independent but can be geographically distributed. This provides parallelism via asynchronous methods invocation (asynchronous methods return immediately upon invocation).

Objects created by the POP-C++ runtime system carry the computation in parallel. There are two major schemes.

The first scheme is to create a central node (manager); which is responsible for splitting the data/instructions to available nodes and wait for the returned results. This can be considered as a flexible master-worker scheme where the master node is in control of job splitting, scheduling and data merging. This scheme leads to a large amount of communication because message-passing to send and receive results between master and worker nodes have to be considered. However, data splitting is dynamically accomplished at runtime, which is efficient because worker nodes

Figure 3. Dynamic data distribution of multithreading

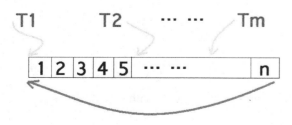

following send/receive principle can largely avoid the idle processors.

The second scheme eliminates the requirement for a central control. At the first stage, computation tasks are divided according to available nodes' capability (power, memory etc). Each node has been assigned for a piece of work. The nodes start computation. They send back results to the assigned node once the computation finishes. This scheme has a low communication overhead (there is no message-passing between work nodes). However, the parallel efficiency (resource utilization) largely depends on the static data distribution scheme. If faster nodes do not have a larger piece of a computation job, they idle and efficiency is compromised. Assume there are N nodes available during runtime and their performance indices P are known and calculated based on the CPU speed, memory, etc. P can thus be defined as

$$P_i = uM_i + vC_i$$

where i is the index for nodes, u, v are the weighting for the scores of memory M and CPU speed C, respectively. A percentage p to represent the portion of jobs for each node can be calculated as

$$p_i = \frac{P_i}{\sum_{i=1}^{N} P_i}$$

Based on p_i, Node N_i can thus compute the portion p_i of jobs and sends the results to an pre-assigned node which collects and merges the results. This scheme has no central control and thus can be easily extended if work nodes are increased. The idling time can be largely reduced by introducing the job splitting calculation.

In theory, IRLA can be parallelized via these two approaches. However, taking consideration of efficiency and flexibility, the parallelization of IRLA is accomplished via the second scheme described. The reasons are detailed as follows.

In a distributed grid environment (Coco, Laudani, & Pollicino, 2009), IRLA will benefit from an efficient grid resource scheduler that utilizes the resources.

A master-worker scheme is not flexible and cannot be easily adapted in a distributed grid environment where grid resources are usually dynamical. The use of a master node is inflexible and has the disadvantages of high-overload and overhead of communication. If the master node is faulty, the parallel simulation would crash or the performance would be degraded until an alternate master server is set up. The communication overhead would slow down the overall calculation time if data exchange is high.

Parallelization of the Components

The main computation components of IRLA are LOS, VD, and HRD. Low complex components such as post-processing are not parallelized because simply distributing the jobs of this module will not improve the overall performance rather it will incur extra communication overhead.

The objects are created in parallel. On creation, they are given an ID. Building data, antenna data and network configurations have to be loaded by all objects before actual simulation starts. This is ensured by setting up a barrier. As the time of loading data can usually be trivial, the cost of this barrier can usually be neglected. Because LOS engine has a lower computation complexity compared to other components, it will only be performed fully on the node where the result is stored (in this case, on the master node), while the rest of the nodes would simply just obtain LOS pixels for the use of a HRD engine. This will avoid unnecessary communication overhead spent on trivial tasks. The following details the parallelization of each component of IRLA.

Parallelization of LOS. LOS marks the visibility and collects direct paths from the transmitter. This component has low complexity and nowadays can be handled very fast on standard PCs. This component is expected to run with full functionality at the node; which is used to save results but a more light-weighted LOS component is accomplished at other worker nodes. The modified light-weighted LOS component does not calculate path loss at all and thus can be executed faster. However, at all nodes, LOS component marks the visibility area and collects secondary pixels for the HRD and VD. In this case, communication can be avoided and all processors can collect secondary cubes for the use of HRD.

Parallelization of VD. VD is an independent component mainly used for outdoor scenarios. The complexity of this component is $O(_n^3)$ (n denotes the number of border cubes at X-Y planes) i.e. $z = 0$ and ($x = 0$ or $x = N_x$ or $y = 0$ or $y = N_y$) where x, y, z represent the co-ordinates of cubes and N_x and N_y denotes the X and Y dimensions of scenario. By connecting the transmitter and these cubes, scan-lines are formed virtually. The principle thus can be easily parallelized because these scan-lines are independent from each other and they can be processed in parallel. The scan-line consists of building blocks comprising of a stack of pixels, which should be handled by only one scan-line. In a distributed environment, a processor shares global static information by message passing or accessing to a central node; which keeps the shared information. Message passing is costly and should be avoided wherever possible. The design of parallel IRLA is not centralized. The requirement to share global static variables is removed by a static data distribution scheme. In this case, there will be overlap of jobs assigned to each node because at this stage, nodes do not check if building blocks have been processed by other nodes. At the end of the calculations, results are sent to a node for collection and merged. Overlapping is also checked and only one piece of the result is considered for one building block. In order to avoid simultaneous access to the same building blocks, locks are used.

Parallelization of HRD. The number of discrete rays needed to be launched from the transmitter is known as N_{fringe}. As long as double counting is avoided, these rays can be considered independently, which offers the parallelism. The roughly-divide-and-solve approach as used in parallel VD can be also applied to HRD. Rays are roughly divided at the beginning of parallelization and they are calculated in independent memory space of the worker node. Double counting is avoided at each worker node. However, this approach does not guarantee the removal of all redundant pixels because rays may be repeatedly calculated at the worker nodes simply because close rays are launched at two nodes but there is no communication between them to avoid double counting. This can be solved at the last stage where results are collected at one node.

Efficiency. Assume D represents the number of conflicts caused by duplicated jobs (rays, building blocks etc) that have been produced due to distributed parallel simulation. Then smaller D leads to better efficiency and vice versa because duplicated jobs cost unnecessary computation time and cause an overhead of results sending and merging. It is preferable to mark continuous rays thus they can be efficiently computed locally on one node. Distributed HRD and VD employ similar strategy as allocating threads. Approximately, suppose job space is J_1 to J_n (n denotes the total number of jobs), and there are P distributed processors, then $D = P$.

Assume the overall performance of IRLA depends on N modules noted as M_1.. M_N. The approximate running time (percentage) for these modules is represented as p_1, p_2.. p_N. Thus,

$$\sum_{i=1}^{N} p_i = 1$$

The theoretical maximum speed up of M_i can be denoted as S_i and calculated by Amdahl's Formula (Bisseling, 2004). Hence max(S_i), $i \in$

[1, *N*] gives the most important component (with priority) that is optimised.

Optimization. Figures 4(a) and 4(b) depict two structures that can be applied to parallel IRLA: No-communications and master-worker schemes. The no-communication scheme (Figure 4(a)) does not require any communication between processors. All the results are stored on local machines as files and if necessary, the results are copied and merged after simulation. This eliminates the costly message-passing and processors are independent to each other. The master-worker scheme (Figure 4(b)) requires one-time collection from the master node at the end of simulation, which may cause delay if the message-passing takes time (if the data to send and receive is large). Usually, more processors to split the computation, less data is required to be sent from worker node at the end of simulation. This is due to the job splitting scheme, in which the total computations are virtualized as pieces of small work, which then are distributed among available processors.

Usually, if there are many parallel objects created on the same physical machine, they are considered as independent processors; which have independent memory space. This causes waste of memory because usually these objects are opening the same input data (building data, antenna, network parameters etc). Furthermore, files (resources) are treated as read-only and will not change during computation. Larger scenario (or higher resolution) will cause larger discrete data set, which needs to be loaded by each object. It will limit the performance and the number of objects that can be created on the same machine. To solve this, shared-memory between processes are adopted (Figure 5). Parallel objects (processes) will check if the resources are available before they load it. And they will make the resources visible to other objects if they are created on the same physical machine. In this manner, memory consumption is reduced and the number of objects that can be created on the same machines is increased.

Simulations

In order to test the parallelization efficiency of the parallel IRLA model via multithreading and distributed computing technologies, simulations are carried out on three platforms and results are analyzed. The specifications of machines (type A,

Figure 4. Parallel IRLA with and without communication

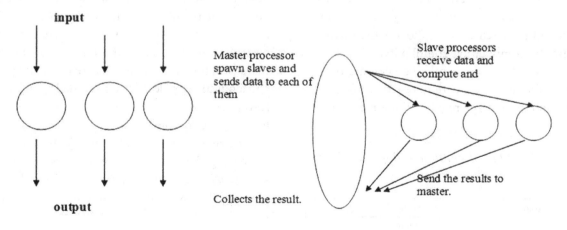

(a) No communications   (b) Master-worker scheme

Figure 5. Optimization via using shared-memory

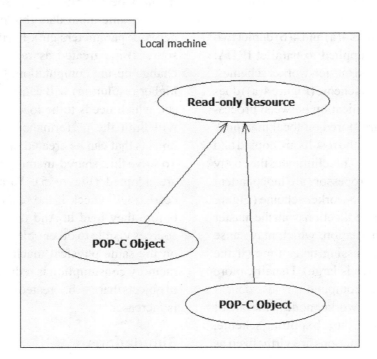

B, C) are listed in Table 1, in which "Estimated power" is an estimation score calculated via POPC++ runtime system.

The simulation scenario is based on COST231-Munich (Universitat Karlshrue, n. d.). In this scenario, the size (N_x, N_y, N_z) is equal to (483, 683, 23) when the resolution is set to 5 meter. In order to analyze the results more clearly, the ray-signal threshold is increased to 250 dB, which will increase the computation complexity.

In order to assure a relative accurate timing result, simulations are required to run several times and the average results are adopted (Figure

Table 1. Speedup of multithreading parallelization scheme

Speedup	Scenario
1.52	Munich
1.43	Paris

9). A simulation on the Kerrighed (1998) that is a distributed-shared-memory architecture is displayed in Figure 8.

The running time is displayed in Figure 6 and its corresponding speedup is displayed in Figure 7. It is observed that multi-threaded simulation generally dominates the single-threaded (the number of parallel objects is one) because the resources are more efficiently utilized by the system. However, when the number of threads increases, the performance has reached the peak and tends to degrade, which is limited by physical resources and possibly the resource competition tends to occur more often.

The running time can be greatly shortened by increasing the number of processors (the node specification can be found in Table 2) at the beginning. However, performance may degrade due to the unavoidable overhead for each object to load data and sends results at the end of calculations when more and more processors are used.

Figure 6. Running time via parallelization

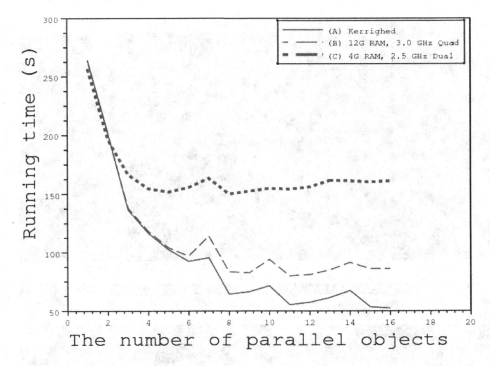

Figure 7. Speedup via parallelization

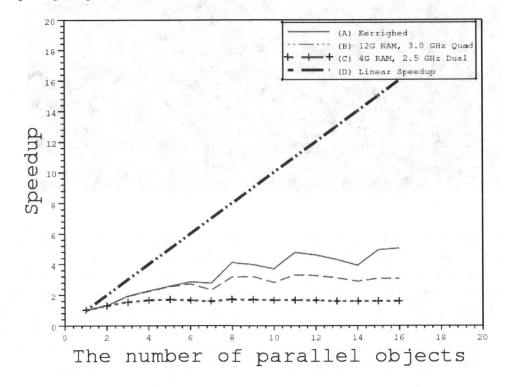

Figure 8. Run simulation on Kerrighed

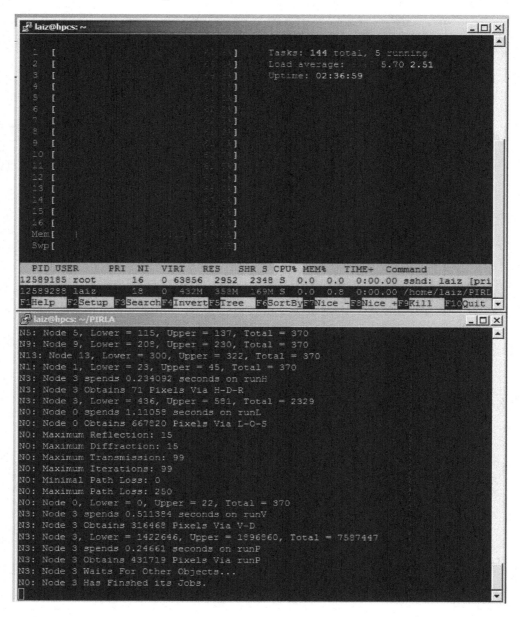

It has been observed that for some scenarios, the job distributed to each object is small and each object is capable of handling it even (because of cache hit in local memory). In this case, a super linear speedup may be observed.

It is also interesting to find that with two or three processors, multithreading may outperform distributed POPC++; which is mainly due to the overhead of communication or processor idling time from unfair distribution of jobs.

The running time of IRLA is greatly reduced by deploying parallel computation tasks to available nodes (Figure 8). It is also interesting to find that distributed memory is handled by Kerrighed behind scenes so that all objects created on the cluster virtually see a global large memory space

Figure 9. Test parallelization efficiency

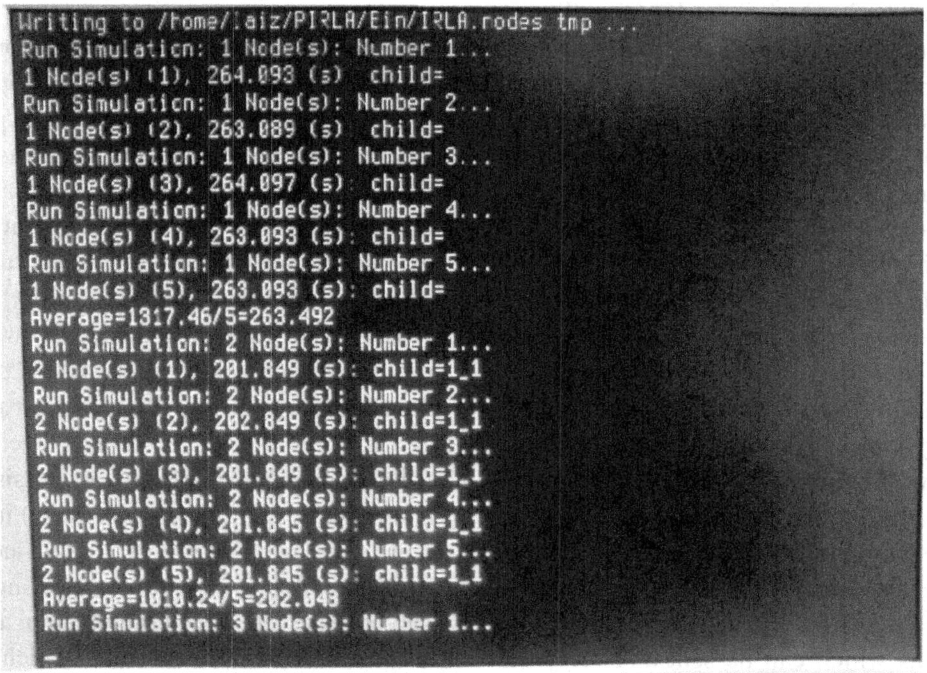

Table 2. Specification

Type	CPU (GHz)	Estimated Power	Cores	RAM (G)	OS
A (C)	3.0	5419	4	12	Fedora 10
B	2.5	4812	2	4	Ubuntu 9

and they can share the same data easily, which consume less memory (Figure 5).

The components of IRLA are of different complexity. Experiments show that different amount of time is spent on these components. For example, given Munich scenario, the running time for LOS, VD, HRD and post-processing is listed in Table 3. Apparently, the most time consuming parts are HRD and VD. It can be derived that the overall maximum speed for IRLA by parallelization is (based on the percentages of these components in Table 3).

$$\frac{1}{(1 - 0.211 - 0.628) + \dfrac{0.211 + 0.628}{N}}$$

N is the number of processors used; when N approaches infinity, the equation reaches 6.21. Each component can be further optimized by pinpointing the most time-consuming part. However, experiments show that usually the speedup hardly approaches 6.21, which is reasonable because of costly message-passing and the overhead of loading data etc. Figure 7 show that the maxi-

Table 3. Running time of components

Components	Running Time (s)	Percentage (%)
LOS	1.3	9.5
VD	2.9	21.1
HRD	8.6	62.8
Post-processing	0.9	6.6

mum speedup via Kerrighed cluster (16 objects) is approximately 5, which is far less than linear speedup. The explanations are twofold. The first is due to communication overhead that nodes have to send and collect results. The second is due to unpredictable amount of job tasks (rays distribution) and hence the timing to finish sub-computation tasks at each node is different, which incur barrier synchronization waiting time. This varies from scenario to scenario but at least this experiment indicates the same speedup pattern observed on the same scenario (Figure 7).

The communication overhead (measured in Mega Bytes) decreases as the number of parallel objects grows, Figure 10 indicates that to some extent, when the number of processors employed is high, the communication overhead can be minimized to a constant because the average data amount to be sent over the network is split into small portions which can be sent and received within a short time. Furthermore, the total speedup has a limit because of the aforementioned inherent parallelization strategy of IRLA.

CONCLUSION

Ray launching is extremely time consuming in large scenarios. Solving angular dispersion and avoiding double counting have been proposed in previous work. Intelligent algorithms have been developed to accelerate the computation. Parallelization has been focused in this article where the issues related to performance etc are described. The multithreading and POP-C++ version of IRLA was developed and speedup was obtained (up to five times faster with sixteen processors). Parallelization further reduces the running time of IRLA and this can be further extended to distributed grid environment (Lai, Bessis, Zhang, & Clapworthy, 2007; Lai et al., 2009) in the future work. By using POPC++ toolkit, computation tasks are deployed and performance speedup can be observed. The parallelization also helps to solve a more complex problem which may not be solved on a single computer, i.e., the memory may be a restricting factor for some large scenarios on a single computer.

Figure 10. Communication cost via parallelization

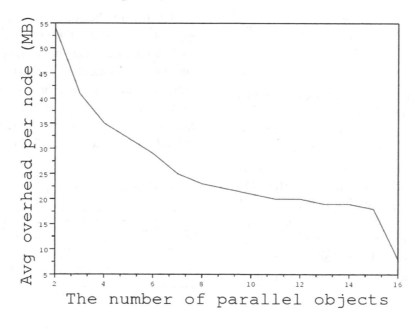

ACKNOWLEDGMENT

This work was supported by the EU-FP7 iPLAN and FP6 GAWIND under grant number MTKD-CT-2006-042783 ("Marie Curie Fellowship for Transfer of Knowledge").

REFERENCES

Bisseling, R. (2004). *Parallel scientific computation: A structured approach using BSP and MPI.* New York, NY: Oxford University Press.

Coco, S., Laudani, A., & Pollicino, G. (2009, March). Grid-based prediction of electromagnetic fields in urban environment. *IEEE Transactions on Magnetics, 45,* 1060–1063. doi:10.1109/TMAG.2009.2012577

Degli-Esposti, V., Fuschini, F., Vitucci, E., & Falciasecca, G. (2009). Speed-up techniques for ray tracing field prediction models. *IEEE Transactions on Antennas and Propagation, 57,* 1469–1480. doi:10.1109/TAP.2009.2016696

Foster, I., & Kesselman, C. (2003). *The grid2, blueprint for a new computing infrastructure.* Sanfrancisco, CA: Morgan Kaufmann.

Glassner, A. (1989). *An introduction to ray tracing.* San Francisco, CA: Morgan Kaufmann.

Haslett, C. (2008). *Essentials of radio wave propagation.* Cambridge, UK: Cambridge University Press.

Kerrighed. (1998). *What is Kerrighed?* Retrieved from http://www.Kerrighed.org

Lai, Z., Bessis, N., De La Roche, G., Kuonen, P., Zhang, J., & Clapworthy, G. (2009, November). A new approach to solve angular dispersion of discrete ray launching for urban scenarios. In *Proceedings of the Loughborough Antennas & Propagation Conference* Leicestershire, UK (pp. 133-136).

Lai, Z., Bessis, N., De La Roche, G., Kuonen, P., Zhang, J., & Clapworthy, G. (2010, April). On the use of an intelligent ray launching for indoor scenarios. In *Proceedings of the Fourth European Conference on Antennas and Propagation,* Barcelona, Spain.

Lai, Z., Bessis, N., De La Roche, G., Kuonen, P., Zhang, J., & Clapworthy, G. (2010, April). The characterisation of human-body influence on 3.5 GHz indoor path loss measurement. In *Proceedings of the Second International Workshop on Planning and Optimization of Wireless Communication Networks,* Barcelona, Spain (pp. 1-6).

Lai, Z., Bessis, N., De La Roche, G., Song, H., Zhang, J., & Clapworthy, G. (2009, March). An intelligent ray launching for urban propagation prediction. In *Proceedings of the Third European Conference on Antennas and Propagation,* Berlin, Germany (pp. 2867-2871).

Lai, Z., Bessis, N., Kuonen, P., De La Roche, G., Zhang, J., & Clapworthy, G. (2009, August). A performance evaluation of a grid-enabled object-oriented parallel outdoor ray launching for wireless network coverage prediction. In *Proceedings of the Fifth International Conference on Wireless and Mobile Communications,* Cannes, France (pp. 38-43).

Lai, Z., Bessis, N., Zhang, J., & Clapworthy, G. (2007, September). Some thoughts on adaptive grid-enabled optimisation algorithms for wireless network simulation and planning. In *Proceedings of the UK e-Science, All Hands Meeting,* Nottingham, UK (pp. 615-620).

Nagy, L., Dady, R., & Farkasvolgyi, A. (2009, March). Algorithmic complexity of FDTD and ray tracing method for indoor propagation modelling. In *Proceedings of the Third European Conference on Antennas and Propagation,* Berlin, Germany.

Nguyen, T. (2004). *An object-oriented model for adaptive high-performance computing on the computational grid.* Présentée à la faculté informatique et communications, Zurich, Switzerland.

Nguyen, T., & Kuonen, P. (2007, January). Programming the grid with POP-C++. *Future Generation Computer Systems, 23*(1), 23–30. doi:10.1016/j.future.2006.04.012

Rick, T., & Mathar, R. (2007, March). Fast edge-diffraction based radio wave propagation model for graphics hardware. In *Proceedings of the 2nd International ITG Conference* (pp. 15-19).

Silberschatz, A., & Galvin, P. (2006). *Operating system concepts with java* (7th ed.). New York, NY: John Wiley & Sons.

Universitat Karlshrue. (n. d.). *COST231 urban micro cell measurements and building data.* Retrieved from http://www2.ihe.uni-karlsruhe.de/forschung/cost231/cost231.en.html

Wolfle, G., Gschwendtner, B., & Landstorfer, F. (1997, May). Intelligent ray tracing - a new approach for the field strength prediction in microcells. In *Proceedings of the IEEE Vehicular Technology Conference,* Phoenix, AZ (pp. 790-794).

Zhang, J., & De La Roche, G. (2010). *Femtocells: Technologies and deployment.* New York, NY: John Wiley & Sons. doi:10.1002/9780470686812

This work was previously published in the International Journal of Distributed Systems and Technologies (IJDST), Volume 2, Issue 2, edited by Nik Bessis, pp. 1-18, copyright 2011 by IGI Publishing (an imprint of IGI Global).

Chapter 6
Soft–Checkpointing Based Hybrid Synchronous Checkpointing Protocol for Mobile Distributed Systems

Parveen Kumar
Meerut Institute of Engineering & Technology, India

Rachit Garg
Singhania University, India

ABSTRACT

Minimum-process coordinated checkpointing is a suitable approach to introduce fault tolerance in mobile distributed systems transparently. In order to balance the checkpointing overhead and the loss of computation on recovery, the authors propose a hybrid checkpointing algorithm, wherein an all-process coordinated checkpoint is taken after the execution of minimum-process coordinated checkpointing algorithm for a fixed number of times. In coordinated checkpointing, if a single process fails to take its checkpoint; all the checkpointing effort goes waste, because, each process has to abort its tentative checkpoint. In order to take the tentative checkpoint, an MH (Mobile Host) needs to transfer large checkpoint data to its local MSS over wireless channels. In this regard, the authors propose that in the first phase, all concerned MHs will take soft checkpoint only. Soft checkpoint is similar to mutable checkpoint. In this case, if some process fails to take checkpoint in the first phase, then MHs need to abort their soft checkpoints only. The effort of taking a soft checkpoint is negligibly small as compared to the tentative one. In the minimum-process coordinated checkpointing algorithm, an effort has been made to minimize the number of useless checkpoints and blocking of processes using probabilistic approach.

DOI: 10.4018/978-1-4666-2647-8.ch006

BACKGROUND

Mobile Hosts (MHs) are increasingly becoming common in distributed systems due to their availability, cost, and mobile connectivity. They are also considered suitable for effective and efficient disaster management. In case of disaster, the static connectivity may not work; therefore, we have to depend on mobile computing environments in such cases. An MH is a computer that may retain its connectivity with the rest of the distributed system through a wireless network while on move. An MH communicates with the other nodes of the distributed system via a special node called mobile support station (MSS). A "cell" is a geographical area around an MSS in which it can support an MH. An MSS has both wired and wireless links and it acts as an interface between the static network and a part of the mobile network. Static nodes are connected by a high speed wired network (Acharya & Badrinath, 1994).

A checkpoint is a local state of a process saved on the stable storage. In a distributed system, since the processes in the system do not share memory, a global state of the system is defined as a set of local states, one from each process. The state of channels corresponding to a global state is the set of messages sent but not yet received. A global state is said to be "consistent" if it contains no orphan message; i.e., a message whose receive event is recorded, but its send event is lost (Chandy & Lamport, 1985). To recover from a failure, the system restarts its execution from the previous consistent global state saved on the stable storage during fault-free execution. This saves all the computation done up to the last checkpointed state and only the computation done thereafter needs to be redone.

In coordinated or synchronous checkpointing, processes take checkpoints in such a manner that the resulting global state is consistent. Mostly it follows the two-phase commit structure (Chandy & Lamport, 1985). In the first phase, processes take tentative checkpoints, and in the second phase,

these are made permanent. The main advantage is that only one permanent checkpoint and at most one tentative checkpoint is required to be stored. In the case of a fault, processes rollback to the last checkpointed state (Elnozahy et al., 2002). The Chandy and Lamport (1985) algorithm is the earliest non-blocking all-process coordinated checkpointing algorithm. In this algorithm, markers are sent along all channels in the network which leads to a message complexity of $O(N2)$, and requires channels to be FIFO.

We have to deal with various issues while designing a checkpointing algorithm for mobile distributed systems (Acharya & Badrinath, 1994; Parkash & Singhal, 1996). These issues are mobility, disconnections, finite power source, vulnerable to physical damage, lack of stable storage etc. Prakash and Singhal (1996) proposed a nonblocking minimum-process coordinated checkpointing protocol for mobile distributed systems. They proposed that a good checkpointing protocol for mobile distributed systems should have low overheads on MHs and wireless channels; and it should avoid awakening of an MH in doze mode operation. The disconnection of an MH should not lead to infinite wait state. The algorithm should be non-intrusive and it should force minimum number of processes to take their local checkpoints. In minimum-process coordinated checkpointing algorithms, some blocking of the processes takes place (Koo & Toueg, 1987) or some useless checkpoints are taken (Cao & Singhal, 2001).

Cao and Singhal (2001) proposed minimum-process non-intrusive checkpointing algorithm by introducing the concept of mutable checkpoints. Kumar et al. (2003) avoided the formation of checkpointing tree and reduced the number of useless checkpoints. Singh and Cabillic (2003) proposed a minimum-process non-intrusive coordinated checkpointing protocol for deterministic mobile systems, where anti-messages of selective messages are logged during checkpointing. Higaki and Takizawa (1999) and Kumar et al. (2005) proposed hybrid checkpointing protocols where MHs checkpoint independently and MSSs checkpoint synchronously. Neves and Fuchs (1997) designed a time based loosely synchronized coordinated checkpointing protocol that removes the overhead of synchronization and piggybacks integer *csn* (checkpoint sequence number). Pradhan et al. (1996) had shown that asynchronous checkpointing with message logging is quite effective for checkpointing mobile systems.

Gao et al. (2008) developed an index-based algorithm which uses time-coordination for consistently checkpointing in mobile computing environments. In time-based checkpointing protocols, there is no need to send extra coordination messages. However, they have to deal with the synchronization of timers. This class of protocols suits to the applications where processes have high message sending rate.

Rao and Naidu (2008) proposed a new coordinated checkpointing protocol combined with selective sender-based message logging. The protocol is free from the problem of lost messages. The term 'selective' implies that messages are logged only within a specified interval known as active interval, thereby reducing message logging overhead. All processes take checkpoints at the end of their respective active intervals forming a consistent global checkpoint. Kumar and Khunteta (2010) proposed a minimum process coordinated checkpointing algorithm for mobile distributed

system, where no useless checkpoints are taken and an effort is made to minimize the blocking of processes. They have captured the transitive dependencies during the normal execution by piggybacking checkpoint sequence numbers onto normal computation messages. Garg and Kumar (2010) proposed a nonblocking coordinated checkpointing protocol for mobile distributed systems, where only minimum numbers of processes are required to commit the checkpoints. They have reduced the message complexity as compared to the algorithm proposed by Cao and Singhal (2001) algorithm, while keeping the number of useless checkpoints unchanged. Biswas and Neogy (2010) proposed a checkpointing and failure recovery algorithm where mobile hosts save checkpoints based on mobility and movement patterns. Mobile hosts save checkpoints when number of hand-offs exceed a predefined handoff threshold value.

INTRODUCTION

In the proposed checkpointing scheme, initiator process collects the dependency vectors of all processes and computes the tentative minimum set (Kumar et al., 2003; Cao & Singhal, 1998). Suppose, during the execution of the checkpointing algorithm, Pi takes its soft checkpoint and sends m1 to Pj as shown in Figure 1. Pj receives

Figure 1. Proposed checkpointing scheme

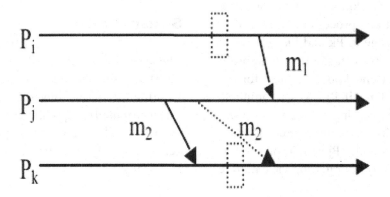

m such that it has not taken its checkpoint for the current initiation and it does not know whether it will get the checkpoint request or not. If Pj takes its checkpoint after processing m, m will become orphan. In order to avoid such orphan messages, we use the following technique (Awasthi & Kumar, 2007).

Pi sends m1 to Pj after taking its soft checkpoint. Pj receives m1 such that i) Pj has received the mset[] from the initiator process, ii) Pj does not belong to mset[] and iii) Pj has not taken its checkpoint for the current initiation. In this case we have two options: (i) Pj may take mutable checkpoint before processing m1, ii) m1 is buffered at Pj till Pj takes its soft checkpoint or Pj receives the tentative checkpoint request, whichever is earlier. We propose the probabilistic approach as follows. Suppose Pj has sent m2 to Pk and Pk belongs to mset[]. In this case, if Pk receives m2 before taking its soft checkpoint, then Pj will be included in the minimum set. Alternatively if Pk receives m2 after taking its soft checkpoint (shown by dotted message m2 in the Figure 1), then Pj wil not receive checkpoint request due to m2. Hence we can say that if Pj¬ has sent m2 to Pk such that Pk belongs to mset[] then most probably Pj will get the checkpoint request. In this case we propose that Pj should take its mutable checkpoint before processing m1. Here, if Pj gets the regular checkpoint request it will convert its mutable checkpoint into soft one. Alternatively, if Pj does not receive the checkpoint request, it will discard its mutable checkpoint on receiving tentative checkpoint request. Suppose there does not exist any process Pk such that Pj has sent some message to Pk and Pk belongs to mset[]. In this case, we can say that most probably Pj will not get checkpoint request for the current initiation. Here, if Pj takes its mutable checkpoint before processing m1, then most probably Pj will have to discard its mutable checkpoint. Therefore we propose that Pj should buffer m1. Pj will process m1 only after getting the tentative

checkpoint request or after taking the soft checkpoint whichever is earlier.

In minimum-process checkpointing, some processes may not be included in the minimum set for several checkpoint initiations due to typical dependency pattern; and they may starve for checkpointing. In the case of a recovery after a fault, the loss of computation at such processes may be unreasonably high (Kumar, 2007). In Mobile Systems, the checkpointing overhead is quite high in all-process checkpointing (Parkash & Singhal, 1996). Thus, to balance the checkpointing overhead and the loss of computation on recovery, we design a hybrid checkpointing algorithm for mobile distributed systems, where an all-process checkpoint is taken after executing of minimum-process algorithm for fifteen numbers of times.

In the first phase, the relevant MHs are required to take soft checkpoint only. Soft Checkpoint is stored on the disk of the MH and is similar to mutable checkpoint (Cao & Singhal, 2001). If any process fails to take its checkpoint in coordination with others, then all relevant processes need to abort their soft checkpoints only. In case of abort, the loss of checkpointing effort will be very low as compared to two phase algorithms. In mobile distributed systems, we may expect frequent aborts due to exhausted battery, abrupt disconnections etc.

THE PROPOSED CHECKPOINTING ALGORITHM

System Model

The system model is similar to Cao and Singhal (2001). A mobile computing system consists of a large number of MH's and relatively fewer MSS's. The distributed computation we consider consists of n spatially separated sequential processes denoted by P0, P1,..., Pn-1, running on fail-stop MH's or on MSS's. Each MH or MSS has one process running on it. The processes do no share common memory or common clock. Message passing is the only way for processes to communicate with each other. Each process progresses at its own speed and messages are exchanged through reliable channels, whose transmission delays are finite but arbitrary. We assume the processes to be non-deterministic.

Data Structures

Here, we describe the data structures used in the proposed checkpointing protocol. A process that initiates checkpointing is called initiator process and its local MSS is called initiator MSS. Data structures are initialized on completion of a checkpointing process if not mentioned explicitly. A process is in the cell of an MSS if it is running on the MSS or on an MH supported by it. It also includes the processes running on MH's, which

have been disconnected from the MSS but their checkpoint related information is still with this MSS (Tables 1, 2, and 3).

An Example

We explain the proposed minimum-process checkpointing algorithm with the help of an example. In Figure 2, at time t0, P4 initiates checkpointing process and sends request to all processes for their dependency vectors. At time t1, P4 receives the dependency vectors from all processes and computes the tentative minimum (mset[]) set, which in case of Figure 2 is {P3, P4, P5, P6} due to messages m1, m2 and m4 (Awasthi & Kumar, 2007). P4 sends this tentative minimum set to all processes and takes its own soft checkpoint. A process takes its soft checkpoint if it is a member of the mset[]. When P3, P5 and P6 get the mset[], they find themselves to be the members of mset[];

Table 1. Each process Pi maintains the following data structures, which are preferably stored on local MSS.

$d\_vect_i[]$:	a bit vector of size n; ; $d\_vect_i[j]$ =1 implies P_i is directly dependent upon P_j for the current CI; in Coordinated Checkpointing if P_i takes its checkpoint for an initiation and P_i is transitively dependent upon P_j, then P_j is also required to take its checkpoint in the current initiation to maintain consistency;
pr_block_i:	a flag which indicates that P_i is in blocking state;
$pr\_c\_state_i$:	a flag; set to '1' on the soft or mutable checkpoint or on the receipt of a message of higher csn during checkpointing;
$mutable_i$:	a flag; set to '1' on mutable checkpoint; reset on commit/abort or on tentative checkpoint;
$pr\_sendv_i[]$:	a bit vector of size n; $pr\_sendv_i[j]$=1 implies P_i has sent at least one message to P_j in the current CI;
pr_send_i:	a flag indicating that P_i has sent at least one message since last checkpoint;
pr_csn:	four bits checkpoint sequence no; initially, for a process pr_csn and pr_next_csn are [0000] and [0001] respectively; pr_csn is incremented as follows: pr_csn=pr_next_csn; pr_next_csn=modulo 16 (++pr_next_csn) ;

Table 2. Initiator MSS (any MSS can be initiator MSS) maintains the following data structures.

$mset[]$:	a bit vector of size n; mset[k]=1 implies P_k belongs to the minimum set; have given computation of minimum set on the bases of dependency vectors of all processes Cao and Singhal (1998).
$R1[]$:	a bit vector of length n; R[i] =1 implies P_i has taken its soft checkpoint in the first phase;
$R2[]$:	a bit vector of length n; R2[i] =1 implies P_i has taken its tentative checkpoint in the second phase;
$Timer1$:	a flag; initialized to '0' when the timer is set; set to '1' when maximum allowable time for collecting coordinated checkpoint expires;

Table 3. Each MSS (say MSSp) maintains the following data structures.

mss_local_p[]:	a bit vector of length n; mss_local$_p$ [i]=1 implies P$_i$ is running in the cell of MSS$_p$;
mss_loc_tent_p[]:	a bit vector of length n; **mss_loc_tent**$_p$[i]=1 implies P$_i$ has taken its tentative checkpoint at MSS$_p$;
mss_loc_soft_p[]:	a bit vector of length n; **mss_loc_soft**$_p$[i]=1 implies P$_i$ has taken its soft checkpoint in the first phase and P$_i$ is local to MSS$_p$;
mss_tent_req_p[]:	a bit vector of length n; **mss_tent_req**$_p$[i]=1 implies tentative checkpoint request has been sent to process P$_i$ and P$_i$ is local to MSS$_p$;
mss_soft_req_p[]:	a bit vector of length n; **mss_soft_req**$_p$[i]=1 implies soft checkpoint request has been sent to process P$_i$ in the first phase and P$_i$ is local to MSS$_p$;
mss_fail_bit:	a flag; set to '1' when some relevant process in its cell fails to take its checkpoint;
P$_{in}$:	initiator process identification;
g_chkpt:	a flag; set to '1' on the receipt of dependency request; it controls multiple checkpoint initiations;
rec_mset	a flag; set to 1 on the receipt of mset[] from the initiator MSS; set to '0' on commit/abort;
new_set[]	a bit vector of length n; it contains all new processes found for the minimum set at the MSS; on each checkpoint request: if (tnew_set≠φ) new_set=new_set∪tnew_set;
tnew_set[]	a bit vector of length n; it contains the new processes found for the minimum set while executing a particular checkpoint request. When a process, say P$_i$, takes its soft checkpoint, it may find some process P$_j$ such that P$_i$ is dependent upon P$_j$ and P$_j$ is not in the tentative minimum set known to the local MSS; in this case P$_j$ will be included in the minimum set and is updated in *tnew_set[]*;

therefore, they take their soft checkpoints. When P0, P1 and P2 get the mset[], they find that they do not belong to mset[], therefore, they do not take their soft checkpoints.

P5 sends m8 after taking its soft checkpoint and P1 receives m8 after getting the mset[]. When P5 sends m8 to P1, P5 also piggybacks pr_csn5 and pr_c_state5 along with m8. When P1 receives m8 it finds that csn[5]<m.pr_csn5 and m.pr_c_state5=1. P1 concludes that P5 has taken its checkpoint for some new initiation. P1 also finds rec_mset=1; it implies P1 has received the mset[] for the new initiation and P1 is not a member of mset[]. Further, P1 has not sent any message to any process of the mset[]. In this case, P1 concludes that most probably it will not be included in the minimum set for the current initiation; therefore P1 buffers m8 and processes it only after getting the tentative checkpointing request. After taking its soft checkpoint, P4 sends m11 to P2. At the time of receiving m11, P2 has received the mset[] and it P2 is not the member of the mset[]. P2 finds

that it has sent m3 to P3 and P3 is a member of mset[]. Therefore, P2 concludes that most probably, it will get the checkpoint request in the current initiation; therefore, it takes its mutable checkpoint before processing m11. When P3 takes its soft checkpoint, it finds that it is dependent upon P2, due to m3, and P2 is not in the mset[]; therefore, P3 sends soft checkpoint request to P2. On receiving the checkpoint request, P2 converts its mutable checkpoint into soft one. It should be noted that the soft checkpoint and mutable checkpoint are similar. Mutable checkpoint is a forced checkpoint and soft checkpoint is a regular checkpoint taken due to checkpoint request. In order to convert the mutable checkpoint into soft checkpoint, we only need to change the data structure (mss_local_soft[2]=1).

After taking its checkpoint, P3 sends m13 to P1. P1 finds that it has not sent any message to a process of tentative minimum set. It takes the bitwise logical AND of pr_sendv1[] and mset[] and finds the resultant vector to be all zeroes

Figure 2. An example of the proposed protocol

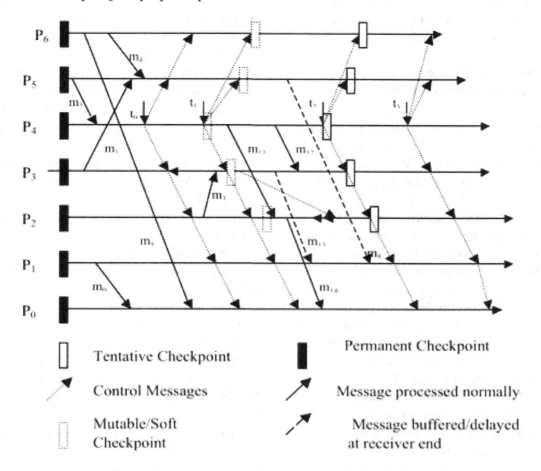

(pr_sendv1[]=[0000001]; mset[]=[1111000]). P1 concludes that most probably, it will not get the checkpoint request in the current initiation; therefore, P1 does not take mutable checkpoint but buffers m13. P1 processes m13 only after getting the tentative checkpoint request. P0 processes m14, because, it has not sent any message since last permanent checkpoint (pr_send0=0). After taking its checkpoint, P4 sends m12 to P3. P3 processes m12, because, it has already taken its checkpoint in the current initiation. At time t2, P4 receives positive responses to soft checkpoint requests from all relevant processes (not shown in the Figure 2) and issues tentative checkpoint request along with the exact minimum set [P2, P3, P4, P5, P6] to all processes. It should be noted that if any process fails to take its soft checkpoint, then all the relevant processes need to abort their soft checkpoints and not the tentative checkpoints. The effort of taking a tentative checkpoint is exceedingly high as compared to soft checkpoint in mobile distributed systems. In this way we try to reduce the loss of checkpointing effort if any process fails to take its checkpoint in coordination with others. On receiving tentative checkpoint request, all relevant processes convert their soft checkpoints into tentative ones and inform the initiator. A process, not in the minimum set, discards its mutable checkpoint, if any; or processes the buffered messages, if any. Finally, at time t3, initiator P4 issues commit. On receiving commit following actions are taken. A process, in the minimum set, converts its tentative checkpoint into permanent one and discards its earlier permanent checkpoint, if any.

The Minimum-Process Checkpointing Algorithm

Each process Pi can initiate the checkpointing procedure. If MHi wants to initiate checkpointing, it sends the request to its local MSS, called initiator MSS, that initiates and coordinates checkpointing procedure on behalf of MHi.

The initiator MSS sends a request to all MSSs to send the d_vect[] vectors of the processes in their cells. All d_vect[] vectors are at MSSs and thus no initial checkpointing messages or responses travel wireless channels. On receiving the d_vect[] request, an MSS records the identity of the initiator MSS (say mss_id= mss_idin) and sends back the d_vect[] of the processes in its cell, and sets timer1. If the initiator MSS receives a request for d_vect[] from some other MSS (say mss_id= mss_idin2) and mss_idin is lower than mss_idin2, the, current initiation (having mss_id= mss_idin) is discarded and the new one (having mss_id= mss_idin2) is continued. Similarly, if an MSS receives d_vect[] requests from two MSSs, then it discards the request of the initiator MSS with lower mss_id. Otherwise, on receiving d_vect[] vectors of all processes, the initiator MSS (MSSin) computes mset[], sends soft checkpoint request to all MSSs. On receiving positive responses from all relevant processes, MSSin issues tentative checkpoint request to all processes in the minimum set. If some process fails to take its soft checkpoint in the first phase, MSSin issues abort() request to all MSSs. When, MSSin comes to know that all concerned processes have taken their tentative checkpoint, it issues commit() request to all MSSs.

Concurrent executions of the minimum-process checkpointing algorithms may exhaust the limited battery life and congest the wireless channels. Therefore, the concurrent executions of the proposed protocol are not allowed. The pro-

posed protocol is distributed in nature; because, any process can initiate checkpointing. In case of concurrent initiations, only one is allowed to proceed. Hence, concurrent initiations of the proposed protocol do not cause its concurrent executions.

When an MSS (say MSSp) receives the soft checkpoint request along with the mset[] from MSSin in the first phase, it asks the relevant processes in its cell to take the soft checkpoint and stores them in mss_soft_reqp[]. The soft checkpoint of an MH is stored on the disk of the MH. When a process (say Pi) takes its soft checkpoint at MSSp; it is stored in mss_loc_softp[]. When it comes to know that all the relevant processes in its cell have taken their soft checkpoints (mss_soft_reqp[]=mss_loc_softp[]) or some process failed to take its soft checkpoint, MSSp sends the response to MSSin.

On receiving mset[] or tnew_set[] along with the checkpoint request, an MSS, say MSSj, updates tminset[] on the basis of mset[] or req.tnew_set[]. It sends the soft checkpoint request to any process Pi if (i) Pi belongs to the mset[] or req.tnew_set[], (ii) Pi is running in its cell (mss_localj[i]=1) and (iii) Pi has not been issued soft checkpoint request (mss_loc_softj[i]=0). If Pi has already taken its mutable checkpoint (mutablei=1), it simply converts its mutable checkpoint into soft checkpoint (mss_loc_softj[i]=1). On getting the soft checkpoint request, Pi takes its soft checkpoint. Pi processes the buffered messages, if any. For a disconnected MH, that is a member of the minimum set, the MSS that has its disconnected checkpoint, considers its disconnected checkpoint as the required checkpoint.

On receiving mset[], if MSSj finds a process Pk such that Pk is in blocking state and bitwise logical AND of mset[] and pr_sendvk[] is not all zeroes, Pk takes the mutable checkpoint, processes the buffered messages, if any.

On issuing checkpoint request to a process, says Pi, MSSj computes tnew_set[]. It contains the new processes for the minimum set. When a process Pi takes its soft checkpoint, it checks its dependency vector and the tentative minimum set computed so far known at the local MSS. If there is any process Pj such that Pi is dependent upon Pj and Pj is not in the tentative minimum set, then Pj is the new process found for the minimum set. A process Pj is in tnew_set[] only if Pj does not belong to the tminset[], and Pi is directly dependent upon Pj. If tnew_set[] is not empty, MSSj sends the checkpoint request to processes in tnew_set[]. MSSj also updates new_set[] and tminset[] on the basis of tnew_set[].

Suppose, Pi receives m from Pj, the different cases are described as follows:

Case 1: Pj has taken some permanent checkpoint after sending m.
   If (m.pr_csnj < csn[j]) then Pi processes m.
Case 2: If (Pi is in its blocking state (pr_blocki=1)) then (m is buffered for the blocking period of Pi).
Case 3: Pi has not entered the checkpoint state (pr_cstatei=0). Following sub-cases are possible:
   a. Pj has not taken any checkpoint before seding m.
       If (m.pr_own_csnj = csn[j]) then Pi processes m.
   b. Pj is in checkpointing state at the time of sending m but Pi has not sent any message since last committed checkpoint.
       If ((m.pr_c_statej) ∧ (pr_sendi==0)) then (Pi sets pr_c_statei, updates pr_csni and processes m).
   c. If ((m.pr_c_statej) ∧ (pr_sendi==1) ∧ (!rec_mset==1)) then (Pi sets pr_blocki and buffers m).
   d. If ((m.pr_c_statej) ∧ (pr_sendi==1) ∧ (rec_mset==1) ∧ (Bitwise logical AND of mset[] and sendvi[] is not all zeroes)) then (Pi takes mutable checkpoint before processing m, sets pr_c_state=1, and pr_own_csn=1).
   e. If ((m.pr_c_state) ∧ (pr_sendi==1) ∧ (rec_mset==1) ∧ (Bitwise logical AND of mset[] and pr_sendvi[] is all zeroes)) then (Pi sets pr_blocki flag and buffers m).
Case 4: Pi has entered the checkpoint state (pr_c_statei=1).
   a. *Pi processes m.* When an MSS learns that all of its relevant processes have taken their soft/tentative checkpoints successfully or at least one of its relevant process has failed to take its soft/tentative checkpoint, it sends the response message along with new_set to the initiator MSS. If, after sending the response message, an MSS receives the checkpoint request along with tnew_set, and learns that there is at least one process in the tnew_set running in its cell and it has not taken the soft checkpoint, the MSS requests such process to take checkpoint. It again sends the response message to the initiator MSS. Initiator MSS issues tentative checkpoint request only if every relevant process has taken its soft checkpoint.

When the initiator MSS receives a response from some MSS, it updates its mset[] on the basis of new_set received with the response. Finally, initiator MSS sends commit/abort to all processes. On receiving commit: if a process, say Pi, belongs to the minimum set, it converts its tentative checkpoint into permanent one and discards its earlier permanent checkpoint.

All Process Checkpointing Algorithm

Our all process checkpointing algorithm is an updating of Elnozahy et al. (1992). Initiator MSS sends soft checkpoint request to all MSSs. On receiving the soft checkpoint request, an MSS sends the request to all processes in its cell. A process takes its soft checkpoint if it has not taken the same during the current initiation. A process, after taking its tentative checkpoint or knowing its inability to take the checkpoint, informs its local MSS. When an MSS learns that all of its processes have taken their soft checkpoints, it informs the initiator MSS. When the initiator MSS receives positive response from all MSSs, it issues tentative checkpoint request to all MSSs. If any process fails to take soft checkpoint, initiator MSS issues abort request. Finally, initiator MSS issues commit request.

When a process sends a computation message, it appends its pr_csn with the message. When a process, say Pi, receives a computation message m from some other process, say Pj, Pi takes the soft checkpoint before processing the message if m.pr_csn > csn[j] ; otherwise, it simply processes the message.

All Process Checkpointing Algorithm

We use the following notations for performance analysis of the algorithms:

Nmss: Number of MSSs.

Nmh: Number of MHs.

Cpp: Cost of sending a message from one process to another.

Cst: Cost of sending a message between any two MSSs.

Cwl: Cost of sending a message from an MH to its local MSS (or vice versa).

Cbst: Cost of broadcasting a message over static network.

Csearch: Cost incurred to locate an MH and forward a message to its current local MSS, from a source MSS.

Tst: Average message delay in static network.

Twl: Average message delay in the wireless network.

Nmin: Number of minimum processes required to take checkpoints.

The Blocking Time

During the time, when an MSS sends the dependency vectors and receives the checkpoint request, all the processes in its cell remain in blocking period (Cao & Singhal, 1998). Koo and Toueg (1987) require processes to be blocked during checkpointing. Checkpointing includes the time to find the minimum interacting processes and to save the state of processes on stable storage, which may be too long. In the proposed scheme, a process Pi is blocked during checkpointing if i) Pi receives m from Pj such that Pj has taken its checkpoint for the current initiation before sending m and Pj has not; ii) Pi has not sent any message to a process of the tentative minimum set in the current CI. Pi comes out of blocking state immediately after taking its soft checkpoint or after getting the tentative checkpoint request, whichever is earlier.

Number of useless checkpoints. In the algorithm proposed by Cao and Singhal, (2001), every message of higher csn forces a mutable checkpoint on a process if it has not taken its checkpoint for the current initiation and sent atleast one message to some process in the current CI. In our scheme, a process takes its mutable checkpoint, if it is having a good probability of its inclusion in the minimum set. In this way, we try to reduce the number of useless checkpoints. We also reduce the checkpointing time by collecting dependency vectors and computing the minimum set in the beginning. In this way, we avoid the checkpointing tree which may be formed in other algorithms (Cao & Singhal, 2001; Koo & Toueg, 1987).

The Synchronization Message Overhead

The synchronization message overhead for the proposed scheme is computed as follows:

1. The initiator MSS broadcasts requests to all MSSs for dependency vectors, soft check-

points, tentative checkpoints and commit: 4Cbst.

2. The checkpoint request message from initiator process to its local MSS and its response: 2Cwl.

3. All MSSs send response to initiator MSS for dependency requests, soft checkpoint request and tentative checkpoint requests 3Nmss*Cst.

4. MSSs send soft and tentative checkpoint requests to relevant processes and receive response messages: 4Nmh*Cwl.

5. Total Message Overhead: 4Cbst + 2Cwl + 3Nmss * Cst + 4Nmh * Cwl.

The message overhead in the proposed scheme is greater than other minimum-process algorithms (Kumar et al., 2003; Kumar, 2007) by: Cbst+ Nmss*Cst+ 2Nmh* Cwl. The message overhead is increased, because, we add an extra phase for taking soft checkpoints. By doing so, we are able to reduce the loss of checkpointing effort, if any process fails to take its checkpoint in coordination with others. In this way, we are able to deal with the problem of frequent aborts in coordinated checkpointing scheme for mobile distributed systems.

Correctness Proof

Let $GC_i= \{C1,x, C2,y,..., Cn,z\}$ be some consistent global state created by our minimum process algorithm, where Ci,x is the xth checkpoint of Pi.

Theorem I: The global state created by the ith iteration of the checkpointing protocol is consistent.

Proof: Let us consider that the system is in consistent state when a process initiates checkpointing. The recorded global state will be inconsistent only if there exists a message m between two processes Pi and Pj such that Pi sends m after taking the checkpoint Ci,x, Pj receives m before taking the checkpoint Cj,y,

and both Ci,x and Cj,y are the members of the new global state. We prove the result by contradiction that no such message exists. We consider all four possibilities as follows:

Case I: Pi belongs to the minimum set and Pj does not:

As Pi is in the minimum set, Ci,x is the checkpoint taken by Pi during the current initiation and Cj,y is the checkpoint taken by Pj during some previous initiation i.e. $Cj,y \rightarrow Ci,x$. Therefore rec(m)$\rightarrow$ Cj,y and Ci,x$\rightarrow$ send(m) implies rec(m)$\rightarrow$ Cj,y$\rightarrow$ Ci,x$\rightarrow$ send(m) implies rec(m)$\rightarrow$ send(m) which is not possible. '$\rightarrow$' is the Lamport's happened before relation (Lamport, 1978).

Case II: Both Pi and Pj are in minimum set:

Both Ci,x and Cj,y are the checkpoints taken during current initiation. There are following possibilities:

a. Pi sends m after taking its soft checkpoint and Pj receives m before receiving request for dependency:

Any process can take the soft checkpoint only after initiator receives the dependencies from all processes. Therefore a message sent from a process after taking the soft checkpoint cannot be received by other process before getting the dependency request.

b. Pi sends m after taking the soft checkpoint and Pj receives m after sending the dependencies but before taking the checkpoint:

In this case Pj with take the mutable checkpoint before processing m or Pj will buffer m. In both the cases, Pj will process m after taking its checkpoint.

c. Pi sends m after commit and Pj receives m before taking its tentative checkpoint:

As Pj is in minimum set, initiator can issue a commit only after Pj takes tentative checkpoint and informs initiator. Therefore the event rec(m) at Pj cannot take place before Pj takes the checkpoint.

Case III: Pi is not in minimum set but Pj is in minimum set:

Checkpoint Cj,y belongs to the current initiation and Ci,x is from some previous initiation. The message m can be received by Pj:

a. Before receiving request for dependency.

b. After receiving request for dependency but before taking the checkpoint Cj,y. If m is received during (a), Pi will be included in the minimum set. If m is received during (b), Pj will find that mset[i]=0 and d_vectj[i]=1. In this case Pj will send the checkpoint request to Pi.

Case IV: Both Pi and Pj are not in minimum set: Neither Pi nor Pj will take a new checkpoint, therefore, no such m is possible unless and until it already exists.

CONCLUSION AND FUTURE RESEARCH DIRECTIONS

We propose a hybrid checkpointing algorithm, wherein, an all-process coordinated checkpoint is taken after the execution of minimum-process coordinated checkpointing algorithm for a fixed number of times. In minimum-process checkpointing, we try to reduce the number of useless checkpoints and blocking of processes using a probabilistic approach. Concurrent initiations of the proposed protocol do not cause its concurrent executions. In the first phase, all concerned processes take soft checkpoints only. In this way, we try to reduce the loss of checkpointing effort when any process fails to take its checkpoint in coordination with others. We have also reduced the size of the integer checkpoint sequence number to four bits. It is piggybacked onto normal computation messages. The present algorithm can be modified for its application in distributed systems and ad hoc networks. The actual number of useless checkpoints and number of messages blocked can be computed by simulation results.

REFERENCES

Acharya, A., & Badrinath, B. R. (1994). Checkpointing Distributed Applications on Mobile Computers. In *Proceedings of the 3rd International Conference on Parallel and Distributed Information Systems* (pp. 73-80).

Awasthi, L. K., & Kumar, P. (2007). A Synchronous Checkpointing Protocol for Mobile Distributed Systems: Probabilistic Approach. *International Journal of Information and Computer Security*, *1*(3), 298–314. doi:10.1504/IJICS.2007.013957

Biswas, S., & Neogy, S. (2010). A Mobility-Based Checkpointing Protocol for Mobile Computing System. *International Journal of Computer Science & Information Technology*, *2*(1), 135–151.

Cao, G., & Singhal, M. (1998). On the Impossibility of Min-process Non-blocking Checkpointing and an Efficient Checkpointing Algorithm for Mobile Computing Systems. In *Proceedings of the International Conference on Parallel Processing* (pp. 37-44).

Cao, G., & Singhal, M. (2001). Mutable Checkpoints: A New Checkpointing Approach for Mobile Computing systems. *IEEE Transactions on Parallel and Distributed Systems*, *12*(2), 157–172. doi:10.1109/71.910871

Chandy, K. M., & Lamport, L. (1985). Distributed Snapshots: Determining Global State of Distributed Systems. *ACM Transactions on Computer Systems*, *3*(1), 63–75. doi:10.1145/214451.214456

Elnozahy, E. N., Alvisi, L., Wang, Y. M., & Johnson, D. B. (2002). A Survey of Rollback-Recovery Protocols in Message-Passing Systems. *ACM Computing Surveys, 34*(3), 375–408. doi:10.1145/568522.568525

Elnozahy, E. N., Johnson, D. B., & Zwaenepoel, W. (1992). The Performance of Consistent Checkpointing. In *Proceedings of the 11th Symposium on Reliable Distributed Systems* (pp. 39-47).

Gao, Y., Deng, C., & Che, Y. (2008). An Adaptive Index-Based Algorithm Using Time-Coordination in Mobile Computing. In *Proceedings of the International Symposiums on Information Processing* (pp. 578-585).

Garg, R., & Kumar, P. (2010). A Nonblocking Coordinated Checkpointing Algorithm for Mobile Computing Systems. *International Journal of Computer Science issues, 7*(3).

Higaki, H., & Takizawa, M. (1999). Checkpoint-recovery Protocol for Reliable Mobile Systems. *Trans. of Information processing Japan, 40*(1), 236-244.

Kim, J. L., & Park, T. (1993). An efficient Protocol for checkpointing Recovery in Distributed Systems. *IEEE Transactions on Parallel and Distributed Systems*, 955–960. doi:10.1109/71.238629

Koo, R., & Toueg, S. (1987). Checkpointing and Roll-Back Recovery for Distributed Systems. *IEEE Transactions on Software Engineering, 13*(1), 23–31. doi:10.1109/TSE.1987.232562

Kumar, L., Kumar, P., & Chauhan, R. K. (2005). Logging based Coordinated Checkpointing in Mobile Distributed Computing Systems. *Journal of the Institution of Electronics and Telecommunication Engineers, 51*(6).

Kumar, L., Misra, M., & Joshi, R. C. (2003). Low overhead optimal checkpointing for mobile distributed systems. In *Proceedings 19th International Conference on IEEE Data Engineering* (pp. 686-688). Washington, DC: IEEE.

Kumar, P. (2007). A Low-Cost Hybrid Coordinated Checkpointing Protocol for Mobile Distributed Systems. *Mobile Information Systems, 4*(1), 13–32.

Kumar, P., & Khunteta, A. (2010). A Minimum-Process Coordinated Checkpointing Protocol For Mobile Distributed System. *International Journal of Computer Science issues, 7*(3).

Kumar, P., Kumar, L., & Chauhan, R. K. (2005). A low overhead Non-intrusive Hybrid Synchronous checkpointing protocol for mobile systems. *Journal of Multidisciplinary Engineering Technologies, 1*(1), 40–50.

Lamports, L. (1978). Time, clocks and ordering of events in distributed systems. *Communications of the ACM, 21*(7), 558–565. doi:10.1145/359545.359563

Neves, N., & Fuchs, W. K. (1997). Adaptive Recovery for Mobile Environments. *Communications of the ACM, 40*(1), 68–74. doi:10.1145/242857.242878

Pradhan, D. K., Krishana, P. P., & Vaidya, N. H. (1996). Recovery in Mobile Wireless Environment: Design and Trade-off Analysis. In *Proceedings of the 26th International Symposium on Fault-Tolerant Computing* (pp. 16-25).

Prakash, R., & Singhal, M. (1996). Low-Cost Checkpointing and Failure Recovery in Mobile Computing Systems. *IEEE Transactions on Parallel and Distributed Systems, 7*(10), 1035–1048. doi:10.1109/71.539735

Rao, S., & Naidu, M. M. (2008). A New, Efficient Coordinated Checkpointing Protocol Combined with Selective Sender-Based Message Logging. In *Proceedings of the International Conference on Computer Systems and Applications*. Washington, DC: IEEE.

Singh, P., & Cabillic, G. (2003). *A Checkpointing Algorithm for Mobile Computing Environment* (LNCS 2775, pp. 65-74).

Weigang, N., Vrbsky, S. V., & Sibabrata, R. (2004). Pitfalls in nonblocking checkpointing. *World Science's journal of Interconnected Networks, 1*(5), 47-78.

This work was previously published in the International Journal of Distributed Systems and Technologies (IJDST), Volume 2, Issue 1, edited by Nik Bessis, pp. 1-13, copyright 2011 by IGI Publishing (an imprint of IGI Global).

Section 2
State-of-the-Art Distributed Systems Applications

Chapter 7
Distributed Adaptive Windowed Stream Join Processing

Tri Minh Tran
University of Vermont, USA

Byung Suk Lee
University of Vermont, USA

ABSTRACT

This paper presents an adaptive framework for processing a window-based multi-way join query over distributed data streams. The framework integrates distributed plan modification and distributed plan migration within the same scope by using a building block called the node operator set (NOS). An NOS is housed in each node that participates in the join execution, and specifies the set of atomic operations to be performed locally at the host node to execute its share of the global execution plan. The plan modification and migration techniques presented are for the case of updating the NOSs centralized at a single node and the case of updating them distributed at each node. The plan modification is triggered by the change of stream statistics and adjusts the join execution order and placement greedily to satisfy a cost invariant. The plan migration uses the distributed track strategy to accelerate the migration of window extents to new nodes. The migration of all window extents is synchronized. Experiments confirm the effectiveness of the developed adaptive framework on reducing the join execution cost and indicate a small additional adaptation-overhead for distributing the NOS update.

INTRODUCTION

Distributed data stream processing (Amini, Jain, Sehgal, Silber, & Verscheure, 2006; Cormode, Muthukrishnan, & Zhuang, 2006; Das, Ganguly, Garofalakis, & Rastogi, 2004; Kumar, Cooper, & Schwan, 2005; Kumar, Cooper, Cai, Eisenhauer, & Schwan, 2005; Olston, Jiang, & Widom, 2003; Seshadri, Kumar, & Cooper, 2006; Sharfman, Schuster, & Keren, 2006) is a fast growing research area in the data stream field. The driving force behind this growth is the widely deployed and utilized diverse distributed computing environments such as the telecommunication networks,

DOI: 10.4018/978-1-4666-2647-8.ch007

web, sensor networks, and P2P networks as well as the evermore performance-demanding intelligence and monitoring applications in various sectors of the society.

In this paper, we focus on multi-way window-based stream join query which is an important class of queries in distributed stream applications. For example, in network packet monitoring, the network administrator may want to monitor the traffic of data packets passing though different routers with the objective of finding packets with the same destination IP address. For this task, a distributed stream join query is needed to join the streams of packets from those routers. As another example, in building-monitoring using sensor networks, one may want to keep track of the temperature, humidity, and light intensity measured by sensors in a room. The sensor readings of each measurement type are sent to their respective sinks as a stream. The monitoring task in each room can be specified as a distributed stream join query that joins on the same room id from three sensor reading streams. Similar distributed join queries are also needed in many other stream applications such as financial stock ticker analysis, telephone call monitoring, and news article filtering.

An important aspect of query processing today is the adaptivity, that is, adjusting the query execution plan adaptively to the changing data profile and system environment. In light of data stream query processing, the fluctuations of stream statistics (e.g., stream rates, join selectivity) or available system resources (e.g., memory, CPU time) are the changes to adapt to. This paper focuses on the former, i.e., stream statistics.

To the best of our knowledge, all existing research on adaptive stream join processing have been done in the centralized environment (Babu, Motwani, Munagala, Nishizawa, & Widom, 2004; Babu, Munagala, Widom, & Motwani, 2005; Zhu, Rundensteiner, & Heineman, 2004) and none in the distributed environment. In the distributed environment, a different query processing model

is needed because some or all join steps are performed at different nodes across the network and the communication overhead for these join steps should be taken into consideration in query execution planning, and thus the solutions developed in the centralized environment are not applicable.

Moreover, there is a division in the scope of the existing work. Adaptive query processing framework encompasses query plan *modification* and query plan *migration*. Query plan modification involves the process of updating current execution plan to a new, better plan, and query plan migration handles the switch from the current execution plan to the new plan. As far as we know, however, there does not exist any work done on adaptive stream query processing with both in one scope. All the existing work address either the query plan modification (Babu, Motwani, Munagala, Nishizawa, & Widom, 2004; Babu, Munagala, Widom, & Motwani, 2005) or the query plan migration (Zhu, Rundensteiner, & Heineman, 2004), not to mention they are not distributed. This disconnection naturally misses out the interaction between the two key aspects of adaptive query processing.

This paper aims to advance the state of the art by providing a solution to the distributed plan modification and migration problem for executing stream join queries adaptively within the same framework as the stream statistics change in a distributed environment.

The adaptation of query processing in this paper is triggered by an event defined as a significant change of stream statistics such as stream rate, join selectivity, and tuple size. One challenge in achieving this adaptivity in a distributed environment comes from the fact that the query execution plan specifies only the steps for executing a query but not specifically what each node needs to do. Thus, each node has to make its own local decision on what part of the distributed global plan it needs to execute, when to adjust its own part, and how to adjust it.

Our approach to meeting this challenge is to use an abstract data type called the node operator set (NOS). An instance of the NOS is stored in each node and used to specify what each node needs to do toward generating the global query result. Specifically, the elements of an NOS are the basic operators executed locally at the node as part of a distributed join execution plan. The operators include a one-way join operator, a window-update operator, and a tuple-shipping operator, and collectively represent the state of the node during the event-driven distributed join execution. Each node has a set of operators like these for executing its part of all execution plans.

Using the notion of NOS as a common building block, we develop an integrative solution that covers both distributed query plan modification and distributed query plan migration in an adaptive framework. The distributed plan modification is centered on updating the NOSs housed at individual nodes. The update of NOSs can be done either at a central node or distributed at individual nodes. In the centralized update, one node (usually the query site) maintains and updates the NOSs and sends updated NOSs to the nodes housing them (referred to as the *affected nodes*). In the distributed update, individual nodes communicate with their neighboring nodes and update their own NOSs locally if necessary. We address both update approaches in this paper. Both approaches are founded on the same greedy algorithm for plan generation, and thus always generate the same plan.

The distributed plan migration is executed at each node affected by the plan modification. The key requirement is to switch the current NOS to a new NOS locally without duplicating or missing any output tuple globally. The challenge comes from the fact that the switch-over is distributed, that is, when the plan changes, windows need to move to new nodes without disrupting the join execution. We call it the *distributed track strategy*. The approach used is to run the old NOSs and new NOSs together until the new NOSs start

generating the query output using full window contents and then have all affected nodes migrate to the new plan synchronously. In order to avoid the delay incurred until the new NOSs are ready, any window that needs to move to a different node during the switch-over is copied over as soon as possible so that the new NOSs do not have to start with empty windows. To enable the synchronized migration, we use a somewhat simple *two-phase migration* protocol.

A set of experiments has been done to evaluate how effective the proposed adaptive framework is compared with a non-adaptive one and to observe the extra adaptation-overhead of the distributed NOS-update approach (as opposed to the central) in return for the distributivity. The results show a significant reduction in the execution cost in the adaptive case despite substantial fluctuations of the stream rate and show an arguably small additional overhead of the distributed update approach.

Main contributions of this paper include, first, introducing the notion of a node operator set (NOS) which is a set of operators stored in each node to execute a join execution plan; second, proposing distributed plan modification and migration techniques with both centralized and distributed NOS update approaches; third, studying the performance of the adaptive framework through a set of experiments. To the best of our knowledge, this is the first work done to address the integrated problem of plan modification and plan migration for adaptively processing distributed windowed stream joins.

The rest of this paper is organized as follows. The second section presents the processing model and the cost model of distributed windowed stream join queries. The third section presents a basic plan generation algorithm for finding an efficient join execution plan. The fourth section introduces the concept of the node operator set and discusses the proposed distributed plan modification and migration techniques based on centralized and distributed NOS updates. The fifth section evaluates the performance of the proposed adaptive framework. The sixth section discusses related work. The final section concludes the paper and suggests future work.

PRELIMINARIES

This section provides two models associated with distributed stream join processing: query processing model and cost model.

Distributed Stream Join Processing Model

Queries are distributed window-based multi-way stream joins. A stream S_i is a sequence of tuples arriving in order. Each tuple in the stream has a timestamp, ts, and a join attribute, J, as part of the schema. In a distributed environment, a set of nodes (or sites) N1, N2,…,Nn are connected through a communication network. The model assumes only one stream per node, assuming all local processing (e.g., selection, projection) has been done at each node. It also assumes that the timestamp is synchronized across all nodes in the network.

All joins are window-based. For a given multi-way join, S_1 S_2 … S_m, there is a window W_i on each stream S_i ($i = 1, 2, …, m$). This join (Golab & Ozsu, 2003) is processed as follows. For each new tuple s_i arriving in S_i, probe the other $m-1$ windows in sequence and output the matching tuples, and then insert s_i into W_i and remove any expired tuples from W_i. Any type of join condition – equijoin or non-equijoin – is supported in our model. Note that in a distributed environment, the join processing model needs to consider other issues as well, such as the node synchronization over network latency and the batch processing of buffered tuples. These issues have already been addressed in our prior work on distributed stream join processing (Tran & Lee, 2010), and thus are not addressed in this paper.

A distributed multi-way join execution plan is characterized by join ordering, join placement, and join method (Ceri & Pelagatti, 1984). First, *join ordering* determines the sequence of joins in a multi-way join. We assume *linear* ordering (Viglas, Naughton, & Burger, 2003) which has proven to be effective in streaming scenarios (Gedik, Wu, Yu, & Liu, 2007; Zhou, Yan, Yu, & Zhou, 2006; Babu, Motwani, Munagala, Nishizawa, & Widom, 2004; Babu, Munagala, Widom, & Motwani, 2005; Srivastava, Munagala, & Widom, 2005). For a given *m*-way join query, linear ordering determines separate join sequences for each stream (which we call a *head stream*), thus *m* join sequences altogether. The join sequence associated with a head stream S_i is defined as an ordered set O_i of the other *m-1* streams that are joined in sequence for each new tuple s_i arriving in S_i. That is, $O_i = [Si_1, Si_2, …, Si_{m-1}]$ which is one of the *(m-1)!* possible orderings of $S_1, …, S_{i-1}, S_{i+1}, …$ and S_m.

Given such a join sequence (or ordering) O_i, a new tuple s_i arriving on the head stream S_i is used to probe the window Wi_1 on the first stream Si_1 in O_i to find matching tuples; if matching tuples are found, then each join output tuple is used to probe the window Wi_2 on the next stream Si_2 in O_i, and the same process repeats until the window Wi_{m-1} on the last stream Si_{m-1} in O_i or no matching tuple is found. In this paper we refer to the probing of a window Wi_k as a *one-way join* from the output stream of matching tuples from the previous probing (denoted as $S^i i_{k-1}$) to Si_k. (The head stream S_i is equivalent to Si_0 here.) Thus, given a linear join sequence O_i, there are *m-1* one-way joins executed to generate the output for each set of new arrival tuples.

Second, for each join in the sequence, *join placement* determines the node (or site) at which the join is processed. Specifically, a one-way join from S_s at N_s to S_d at N_d can be processed either at N_s by shipping the window W_d on the stream S_d to N_s (called the *source* placement) or at N_d by shipping the new tuples s_s arriving at S_s to

N_d (called the *destination* placement). Note that there may be delay or loss of tuple, and thus the join output might be not exact. However, in the scope of this paper, we assume no delay or tuple loss. Since there are *m-1* one-way joins in a join sequence O_i, there are *m-1* join placements, one for each one-way join. Thus, for each join ordering O_i, there is an associated sequence of join placement values. We call it the *join placement sequence* of O_i and denote it as $P_i = [pi_1, pi_2, ..., pi_{m-1}]$ where $pi_k = \{0,1\}$. Here, pi_k indicates whether the one-way join from S^i_{k-1} to Si_k is processed at the source node (i.e., $pi_k = 0$) or the destination node (i.e., $pi_k = 1$).

Third, for the join method, we consider only the nested loop join in this work, as considering other join methods only requires expanding the search space for finding an optimal plan and does not affect the plan modification and migration algorithms. Thus, only join ordering and join placement are the factors considered in the join execution plan.

To summarize, the execution plan of a multi-way stream join $S_1 ... S_m$ is defined as follows.

Definition 1: *Join Execution Plan (JEP)*. The plan of an *m*-way join query is a set of *m per-stream execution plans (SEPs)*, that is *{SEP_1, SEP_2, ..., SEP_m}*. Here each *SEP_i (i= 1,2,...,m)* is headed by stream S_i and is de-

fined as the pair (O_i, P_i) where $(O_i, P_i) = ([Si_1, Si_2, ..., Si_{m-1}], [pi_1, pi_2, ..., pi_{m-1}])$.

Example 1: Figure 1 illustrates one possible JEP of a three-way join query $S_1 S_2 S_3$. It consists of the following three SEPs, one for each head stream S_1, S_2, and S_3.

$$SEP_1 = (O_1, P_1) = ([S_2, S_3], [1,1])$$

$$SEP_2 = (O_2, P_2) = ([S_1, S_3], [0,1])$$

$$SEP_3 = (O_3, P_3) = ([S_1, S_2], [0,0])$$

Distributed Stream Join Cost Model

Table 1 summarizes the notations used to build the cost model.

Since data streams arrive continuously and unboundedly, we use the *unit-time cost* model proposed by Kang, Naughton, and Viglas (2003). That is, the cost is the time it takes to process the tuples arriving in unit time. Based on this, at any point in time, the execution cost of SEP_i is modeled as the sum of the total processing cost and the total transmission cost per unit time over all one-way join steps. That is, the cost of SEP_i, $CSEP_i$, is computed as the sum of the costs of *m-1* one-way joins:

$$CSEP_i = \sum_{k=1}^{m-1} C^i_{i_{k-l}, i_k}$$

Figure 1. An example join execution plan of a three-way join

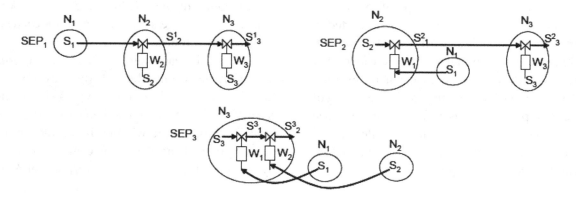

Table 1. Notations used in the cost model

Notation	Meaning ($i = 1,..,m$ and $k = 1,..,m-1$)
Join input streams and statistics	
r_i	The stream rate of S_i.
f_i	The join attribute selectivity factor of S_i, i.e., the average fraction of S_i tuples with the same join attribute value.
t_i	The size of a tuple in S_i.
w_i	The number of tuples in the window W_i of S_i.
Si_k	The kth stream in SEP_i
ri_k	The stream rate of Si_k
Join output streams and statistics	
$S^i i_k$	The output stream of the one-way join Si_k. ($S^i i_0 = S_i$)
$r^i i_k$	The stream rate of Si_k. ($r^i i_0 = r_i$)
$f^i i_k$	The join attribute selectivity factor of Si_k. ($f^i i_0 = f_i$)
$t^i i_k$	The size of a tuple in Si_k. ($t^i i_0 = t_i$)
$C^i i_{k-1}, i_k$	The cost of a one-way join from $S^i i_{k-1}$ to Si_k.
Join cost parameters	
c_p	Per-tuple window-probing cost.
c_u	Per-tuple window-update cost.
c_l	The latency of communication link in the network.
c_r	The transmission rate of communication link in the network.

The one-way join cost $C^i i_{k-1}, i_k$ is formulated as follows. On one hand, if the one-way join is executed at the source Ni_{k-1} (i.e., $pi_k = 0$), then the cost comprises the cost of shipping ri_k tuples from Ni_k to Ni_{k-1} per unit time, the cost of updating Wi_k at Ni_{k-1} per unit time, and the cost of probing Wi_k at Ni_{k-1} per unit time. That is,

$$C^i i_{k-1}, i_k \,|[pi_k = 0] = T(ri_k \times ti_k) \\ + ri_k \times c_u + r^i i_{k-1} \times c_p \times wi_k \qquad (1)$$

where $T(.)$ is a function $T(x) = c_l + x/c_r$ used as a model of the cost of transmitting x bytes of data between two nodes and the value of $r^i i_{k-1}$ is computed $r^i i_{k-1} = r^i i_{k-2} \times min(f^i i_{k-2}, f i_{k-1}) \times wi_{k-1}$ where $f^i i_{k-2}$ is estimated as the larger value between the two selectivity factors of the two streams that are joined, that is, as $max(f^i i_{k-3}, f i_{k-2})$. On the other hand, if the join is executed at the destination Ni_k (i.e., $pi_k = 1$), then the cost comprises the cost of shipping $r^i i_{k-1}$ tuples from Ni_{k-1} to Ni_k per unit time, the cost of updating Wi_k at Ni_k per unit time, and the cost of probing Wi_k at Ni_k per unit time. That is,

$$C^i i_{k-1}, i_k \,|[pi_k = 1] = T(r^i i_{k-1} \times t^i i_{k-1}) \\ + ri_k \times c_u + r^i i_{k-1} \times c_p \times wi_k \qquad (2)$$

where $t^i i_{k-1} = t^i i_{k-2} + ti_{k-1}$. Given these two cost formulas (Equations 1 and 2), the join placement value pi_k is determined depending on which one incurs the lower cost. In other words, if $C^i i_{k-1}, i_k |[pi_k = 0] \leq C^i i_{k-1}, i_k |[pi_k = 1]$, then $pi_k = 0$ and otherwise $pi_k = 1$. Thus, the one-way join cost $C^i i_{k-1}, i_k$ is computed as

$$C^i i_{k-1}, i_k = \\ min(C^i i_{k-1}, i_k |[pi_k = 0], C^i i_{k-1}, i_k |[pi_k = 1]) \qquad (3)$$

Basic Plan Generation Algorithm

Algorithm 1 is a plan generation (Figure 2) algorithm which finds SEP_i associated with each head stream S_i. The algorithm is used in two stages in the adaptive query processing framework. The first stage is to generate an initial plan which is disseminated to all participating nodes in the network. The second stage varies depending on the NOS update mechanism (either centralized

Figure 2. Algorithm 1: Basic plan generation algorithm

Input: Streams $\{S_1, S_2, ..., S_m\}$ and join graph
Output: Join execution plan $\{(O_1, P_1), (O_2, P_2), ..., (O_m, P_m)\}$

1 **begin**
2   **foreach** stream S_i *(i = 1, 2, ..., m)* **do**
3       $O_i = \emptyset$;
4       $P_i = \emptyset$;
5       $Temp = \{S_1, S_2, ..., S_m\} - S_i$;
6   **while** $Temp \neq \emptyset$ **do**
7   Find the stream S_{i_k} in $Temp$ with the smallest associated $C^i_{i_{k-1}, i_k}$ computed using Equation 3;
8   Insert S_{i_k} at the end of O_i;
9   Determine the join placement value p_{i_k} by comparing $C^i_{i_{k-1}, i_k}|[p_{i_k} = 0]$ (Equation 1) and $C^i_{i_{k-1}, i_k}|[p_{i_k} = 1]$ (Equation 2);
10   Insert p_{i_k} at the end of P_i;
11          $Temp = Temp - S_{i_k}$;
12   **end**
13   **end**
14 **end**

---

or distributed, to be discussed in the following section) – the entire algorithm is used as is if centralized whereas only the greedy property is used if distributed.

The algorithm takes the join graph and information about the participating streams as the input and returns the set of SEPs with each input stream as the head stream. For each head stream S_i, O_i and P_i are constructed together using a greedy approach to add the next stream and the next join placement value in each step. The next stream picked in each step is the one Si_k that has the lowest one-way join cost $C^i_{i_{k-1}, i_k}$ among streams $Si_k, ..., Si_{m-1}$.

$$C^i_{i_{k-1}, i_k} \leq C^i_{i_{k-1}, i_p}$$
for all p s.t. $1 \leq k < p \leq m-1$ (4)

Equation 4 is an invariant condition that should be satisfied throughout the continuous stream join processing despite the change of cost due to the fluctuation of stream statistics. The objective of the adaptive framework in this paper is to maintain the invariant condition online in a distributed environment. The next section presents the techniques developed to achieve it.

Note that the number of possible join execution plans is O(n!) (n is the number of joins in the query) which is exponential. In general, an optimal join plan generation is an intractable problem (Aho, Sagiv, & Ullman, 1979). For instance, the best known algorithm using dynamic programming approach (e.g., System R) takes $O(n2^{n-1})$. In contrast, the greedy approach used in this paper finds an efficient (but not necessarily optimal) plan in polynomial time $O(n^2)$ in the worst case. Note that this is the same whether the NOS update mechanism is centralized or distributed (to be discussed in the following sectios), as both are based on the same greedy property.

DISTRIBUTED ADAPTIVE STREAM JOIN PROCESSING

In this section, NOS is explained in previous sections with a focus on its formal definition and the construction algorithm. Section four describes the distributed plan modification with the centralized NOS-update strategy and the distributed NOS-update strategy, respectively. Section four discusses the distributed plan migration strategy.

Node Operator Set

Given a JEP, each node extracts the set of relevant operations needed to execute the JEP. There are three possible operators needed at each node, as summarized in Table 2. $Join(S_i, Sj)$ is the one-way join from S_i to Sj upon the arrival of a set of tuples of S_i. $Update(S_i)$ is the update of window W_i upon the arrival of a set of tuples of S_i. $Ship(S_i, N_k)$ is the shipment of a set of tuples of S_i to the node N_k. Thus, given the JEP of an m-way join, the NOS of a node N_k ($k = 1,2,...,m$) is composed of the sets of operations extracted from every SEP_i ($i = 1,2,...,m$) of the JEP. We denote the set extracted from SEP_i in N_k as NOS^i_k.

Definition 2: *Node operator set of N_k (NOS_k). $NOS_k = NOS^1_k \cup ... \cup NOS^m_k$ where NOS^i_k is the set of operators needed at the node N_k to execute SEP_i.*

Example 2: Continuing from Example 1, the NOS of each node is as follows:

$NOS_1 = NOS^1_1 \cup NOS^2_1 \cup NOS^3_1$
$= \{ship(S_1, N_2)\} \cup \{ship(S_1, N_2)\} \cup \{ship(S_1, N_3)\}$
$= \{ship(S_1, N_2), ship(S_1, N_3)\}$

$NOS_2 = NOS^2_2 \cup NOS^2_2 \cup NOS^3_2$
$= \{join(S_1, S_2), update(S_2), ship(S^1_2, N_3),$
$update(S_1), join(S_2, S_1), ship(S^2_1, N_3),$
$ship(S_2, N_3)\}$

$NOS_3 = NOS^1_3 \cup NOS^2_3 \cup NOS^3_3$
$= \{join(S^1_2, S_3), update(S_3), ship(S^1_3, N_0),$
$join(S^2_1, S_3), ship(S^2_3, N_0), join(S_3, S_1),$
$join(S^3_1, S_2), update(S_1), update(S_2),$
$ship(S^3_2, N_0)\}$

Table 2. Notations of operations

Notation	Meaning
$join(S_i, Sj)$	Perform one-way join from S_i to Sj.
$update(S_i)$	Update the window on S_i.
$ship(S_i, N_k)$	Ship tuples of S_i to node N_k.

NOS Construction Algorithm

In order to build the NOS for any give node, the algorithm constructs NOS^i_k from each SEP_i and then combines them to obtain NOS_k. Specifically, it locates the stream S_k in O_i and constructs NOS^i_k based on the join placement values of the one-way joins to S_k and its succeeding stream, respectively. The details of the algorithm for a given SEP_i are in Figure 3.

First, consider the one-way join to S_k in O_i. Let S_p and S_s be respectively the streams immediately preceding and immediately succeeding S_k in O_i. Let Np_- be the node at which S^i_p is generated. Note that Np_- can be any node, not necessarily Np, because the placement of the one-way join to S_p may not be at N_p. Depending on the join placement (p_k) of the one-way join to S_k, there are two alternative ways to construct the NOS operators. If $p_k = 0$ (Figure 3a), it means the one-way join to S_k is executed at N_{p-}. In this case, N_k needs to ship tuples to N_{p-} for the join execution there and, thus, an operator $ship(S_k, N_{p-})$ is added to NOS^i_k. If $p_k = 1$ (Figure 3b), it means the one-way join to S_k is executed at N_k. In this case, upon receiving tuples of S^i_p, N_k joins them with tuples in W_k on S_k and, thus, the operator $join(S^i_p, S_k)$ is added to NOS^i_k; additionally, W_k needs to be maintained at N_k and, thus, the operator $update(S_k)$ is added to NOS^i_k as well.

Next, consider the one-way join to S_s in O_i. Like the one-way join to S_k, there are two alternative ways to construct the operators. If $p_s = 0$ (Figure 3c), it means the one-way join to S_s is executed at N_k. In this case, N_s ships tuples to N_k and the join is executed at N_k and, thus, $join(S^i_k, S_s)$ and $update(S_s)$ are added to NOS^i_k. If $p_s = 1$ (Figure 3d), it means the one-way join to S_s is executed at node N_s. In this case, N_k ships the tuples of S^i_k to N_s and, thus, the operator $ship(S^i_k, N_s)$ is added to NOS^i_k; additionally, if S_k is the last stream (Si_{m-1}) in the join sequence, then the ship operator $ship(S^i_k, N_0)$ is added to NOS^i_k as well.

Figure 3. Construction of operators based on join placement

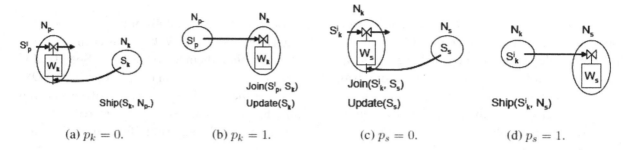

(a) $p_k = 0$.   (b) $p_k = 1$.   (c) $p_s = 0$.   (d) $p_s = 1$.

Note that if $p_s = 0$, that is, the one-way join to S_s is executed at N_k, then we need to consider the one-way join to the stream succeeding S_s, denoted as S_{s+1}, as well. The reason for this is that if $p_{s+1} = 0$ then this one-way join is executed at N_k as well and, thus, *join(S'_s, S_{s+1})* and *update(S_{s+1})* also need to be added to NOS'_k. This step proceeds with all succeeding streams ($S_{s+j}, j = 0,1,...,l \leq m-k-1$) until the first one-way join to a stream S_{s+l} with $p_{s+l} = 1$ is encountered or the last stream (Si_{m-1}) is encountered.

Given the NOSs constructed in that manner, the node N_k executes the operators in NOS_k upon the arrival of a set of tuples. The set of tuples comes from either the local node N_k or another node, and belongs to either the local stream S_k or the output stream S'_p. Each set of arrival tuples is associated with the stream identifier (streamID) of either S_k or S'_p, depending on where it is coming from. Upon the arrival of a set of tuples, the query executor executes all operators in NOS_k whose first argument matches the streamID.

Distributed Plan Modication

When the stream statistics at a node change significantly enough, any of the current SEPs (i.e., SEP_1, SEP_2,...,SEP_m) may become less efficient and in this case a new SEP needs to be generated to replace the current one for those affected SEP_i ($i = 1,2,...,m$). With the NOS in use for query processing, the plan modification involves updat-

ing the NOS at each affected node. In this section we discuss the centralized and the distributed approaches to making these updates.

As mentioned in previous sections, the invariant cost-condition (Equation 4) should always be satisfied by every SEP. Thus, the NOS update is essentially to adjust the NOS of the affected node so that all SEPs satisfy the cost condition again. The adjustment is triggered through a threshold mechanism, that is, when the change in the execution cost at a node exceeds the threshold. The threshold value is a system parameter and can be used to control the plan-modification frequency of the system.

Centralized Node-Operator-Set Update

The centralized NOS update is triggered whenever any of the participating nodes reports a change of stream statistics above the threshold. Once triggered, it generates a new JEP (comprising SEPs) based on the new stream statistics provided by the reporting nodes. For this, Algorithm 1 is used. It then extracts from the new SEPs the new NOS_k for each node N_k and if the new NOS_k is different from the old one then ships it to N_k to replace the old one. Algorithm 2 in Figure 4 summarizes these steps taken after the NOS update is triggered.

The computation cost of this algorithm in terms of the number of messages sent is $O(n)$ where n is the number of nodes. This is the worst case

Figure 4. Algorithm 2: Centralized NOS update

```
1  begin
2  |   A centralized node N_q runs Algorithm 1 to generate a new JEP (i.e., a set of SEPs);
3  |   foreach node N_i do
4  |   |   N_q generates a new NOS_i based on the new SEPs;
5  |   |   if the new NOS_i is different from the old NOS_i then
6  |   |   |   N_q ships the new NOS_i to N_i for an update;
7  |   |   end
8  |   end
9  end
```

cost, in which every node needs to be updated with a new NOS and thus N_q sends a new NOS to every node. Note that, in the algorithm, only those nodes whose old NOSs are different from the new NOSs receive the new NOSs from N_q. They are the only affected nodes. An affected node needs to switch from the old NOS to the new NOS after receiving a new NOS, and this switch-over should be handled online while not disrupting the generation of the correct output. This technique is presented in above.

In the centralized update approach, the information about the stream statistics as well as the NOSs of participating nodes is maintained all at the centralized node, and thus there is no cost of gathering the information from participating nodes; each participating node only needs to send a message to report the change of its stream statistics (so the NOS update is triggered) whenever the change exceeds the threshold. However, there always exists a possibility that the central node may be overloaded with too frequent update tasks in a volatile environment with frequent fluctuations of stream statistics. In a situation like this, the distributed NOS update strategy, in which each node communicates with only the neighboring nodes and updates its own NOS locally, is preferable.

Distributed Node-Operator-Set Update

The distributed NOS update is triggered locally at each node when its stream statistics change more than a threshold. Then, the plan modification is to reorder the streams in O_i and adjust the join placements in P_i so that the invariant cost-condition is satisfied again for every SEP. This is done at each node through communication with the neighboring nodes.

Let us consider a stream Si_k at node Ni_k. Remember that a SEP_i is constructed based on the greedy strategy that a stream Si_k is joined with S_p if and only if S_p has the lowest cost among all the streams that it can join to. A natural outcome of this strategy is that a stream with a lower join cost tends to be placed closer to the beginning of the join sequence and a stream with a higher cost tends to be placed farther from it. Thus, if the change of stream statistics makes $C^i_{i_{k-1}, i_k}$ increase, then the position of Si_k in O_i may need to shift toward the end, and if decrease then toward the beginning. Once the position of Si_k changes in O_i, other streams in O_i may need to be reordered as well to make sure the invariant cost-condition is satisfied by all streams. The reordering mechanism is similar to what happens during the insertion sorting.

Algorithm 3 in Figure 5 outlines the steps of modifying each SEP through distributed updates

Figure 5. Algorithm 3: Distributed NOS update

```
1   begin
2      for each SEP_i do
3         if C^i_{i_{k-1},i_k} has increased then
4            j = k;
5            begin // S_{i_j} moves toward the end of O_i
6               Determine S_{i_r} among {S_{i_{j+1}}, S_{i_{j+2}}, ..., S_{i_{m-1}}} to be swapped with S_{i_j} in O_i;
7               Update NOS_{i_r} and NOS_{i_j} to reflect the swap and send messages to the nodes of the
                 preceding and succeeding streams of S_{i_r} and S_{i_j}, respectively, to update their NOSs;
8               Update NOS_{i_r} to reflect a new join placement;
9            end
10           Repeat the steps 6 to 8 for j = k + 1 to m − 1;
11        end
12        else
13           begin // S_{i_k} moves toward the beginning of O_i
14              Determine S_{i_r} among {S_{i_1}, S_{i_2}, ..., S_{i_{k-1}}} to be swapped with S_{i_k} in O_i;
15              Update NOS_{i_r} and NOS_{i_k} to reflect the swap and send messages to the nodes of the
                 preceding and succeeding streams of S_{i_r} and S_{i_k}, respectively, to update their NOSs;
16              Update NOS_{i_k} to reflect a new join placement;
17           end
18           Repeat the steps 6 to 8 for j = r + 1 to m − 1; // Note:  not the steps 14 to 16
19        end
20     end
21  end
```

of NOSs. The algorithm is executed in two stages. The first stage is to move the stream that triggered the algorithm execution to the right position in O_i. The second stage is to continue to update the other streams affected by the move. The update of NOSs involves three steps. First, it determines the stream Si_r to be swapped with Si_k in the join sequence O_i. Second, it updates $NOS^i_{i_k}$ and $NOS^i_{i_r}$ and also the NOSs of the nodes of Si_{k-1} and Si_{k+1} in the join sequence. Third, it computes the join placements and, if necessary, updates NOS^i_k and $NOSi_r$ to reflect new join placements. Details of each step are presented now.

Stage 1: Update on the Triggering Stream

Step 1: Determine the Stream to be Swapped with Si_k in O_i

If $C^i i_{k-1}, i_k$ has increased, one of the succeeding streams $Si_{k+1}, ..., Si_{m-1}$ replaces Si_k in O_i. Let Si_r be the one that replaces Si_k. Then Si_r must be the one for which $C^i i_{k-1}, i_r \le C^i i_{k-1}, i_{k+}$ holds for all i_{k+} in $\{i_k, i_{k+1}, ..., i_{m-1}\}$. In order to find such an Si_r, streams in O_i are processed sequentially as follows. The initial lowest cost is the new cost of one-way join to Si_k, $C^i i_{k-1}, i_k$. Ni_k first sends a message to Ni_{k+1} with the instruction that Ni_{k+1} computes the cost $C^i i_{k-1}, i_{k+1}$ and compares it with $C^i i_{k-1}, i_k$. If $C^i i_{k-1}, i_{k+1} < C^i i_{k-1}, i_k$, then the cost of the join to Si_{k+1} is the lowest so far and thus, the lowest-cost stream is updated to Si_{k+1} (at the node Ni_{k+1}) and the lowest cost is updated to $C^i i_{k-1}, i_{k+1}$. Then, Ni_{k+1} sends a message to its succeeding stream in O_i with the same instruction. This relay propagates until the message reaches Ni_{m-1} while the lowest cost and the lowest-cost stream (and its node) are updated as necessary along the way. Then, Ni_{m-1} informs Ni_r that Sr should be swapped with S_k.

Figure 6a illustrates the process of determining the new position of S_2 when $C^1_{1,2}$ increases. N_2 first sends a message to N_3 to compute $C^1_{1,3}$ and compare it with $C^1_{1,2}$. If $C^1_{1,3} < C^1_{1,2}$, then N_3 is recorded as the node with the lowest cost. Then N_3 will communicate with N_2 to swap the position.

On the other hand, if $C^i i_{k-1}, i_k$ has decreased, one of the preceding streams $Si_1, ..., Si_{k-1}$ replaces Si_k. Let Si_r be the one that swaps with Si_k. Then, $C^i i_{r-1}, i_k < C^i i_{r-1}, i_r$ must hold. Finding Si_r needs more than considering the immediate preceding stream Si_{k-1}. The reason is that, even if $C^i i_{k-2}, i_k < C^i i_{k-2}, i_{k-1}$, it is possible that $C^i i_{(k)-1}, i_k < C^i i_{(k)-1}, i_k$ holds for some preceding stream Si_{k-} (i_{k-} in $\{i_1, i_2 ..., i_{k-1}\}$). Therefore, in order to find Si_r, we need to compare $C^i i_{j-1}, i_j$ with $C^i i_{j-1}, i_k$ for all Si_j starting from Si_1 until the first Si_j satisfying $C^i i_{j-1}, i_k < C^i i_{j-1}, i_j$ is found. This Sj is the wanted S_r. Figure 6b illustrates the process of determining the new position of S_3 when $C^1_{1,3}$ decreases.

In order to compute the execution costs using Equation 3 and compare them, each node Ni_k maintains metadata which includes the stream rate r^i_{k-1} and the tuple size t^i_{k-1} of S^i_{k-1} and the cost $C^i i_{k-1}, i_k$. In the case of increased $C^i i_{k-1}, i_k$, Ni_{k+} needs to know r^i_{k-1} and t^i_{k-1} to compute $C^i i_{k-1}, i_{k+}$, and thus the message sent from Ni_k includes the two values. In addition, the message includes the information about the lowest cost and the lowest-cost stream (and its node) so that Ni_{k+} can compare the computed $C^i i_{k-1}, i_{k+}$ with the lowest cost. In the case of decreased $C^i i_{k-1}, i_k$, Ni_{k-} needs to compare its cost $C^i i_{(k)-1}, i_{k-}$ with $C^i i_{k-1}, i_k$, and thus the message sent to Ni_{k-} includes ri_k, ti_k and Wi_k.

Step 2: Update NOSs to Reflect the Swap

Since each node maintains its NOS for join execution, in order to reflect the swap between Si_k and Si_r in O_i, the NOS^i_k at Ni_k and the $NOSi_r$ of Ni_r are updated. The update is done by swapping NOS^i_k of Ni_k and $NOSi_r$ of Ni_r and then replacing the streamID of the operators. Specifically, when Ni_r receives NOS^i_k from Ni_k, it replaces its $NOSi_r$ by NOS^i_k and changes the streamID of Si_k to the streamID of Si_r in each operator. Similarly, when Ni_k receives $NOSi_r$ from Ni_r, Ni_k replaces its NOS^i_k by $NOSi_r$ and changes the streamID of Si_r to the streamID of Si_k in each operator. When Ni_k and Ni_r finish updating their NOSs, they send messages to the nodes of the preceding stream and succeeding stream to instruct them to update their NOS by changing the streamID in the operators.

Note that the effect of swapping the positions of Si_k and Si_r is to swap the roles of these two streams in O_i and thus to swap NOS^i_k and $NOSi_r$.

Figure 6. Illustration of determining the stream to switch with S_3 in the join sequence O_1

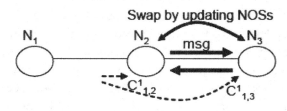

(a) When the one-way join cost to S_3 has increased.

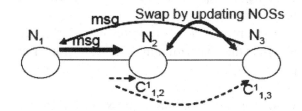

(b) When the one-way join cost to S_3 has decreased.

The replacement of the streamID of operators is necessary because $NOSi_r$ is at Ni_k after the swap of NOSs but there is Si_r at Ni_k and, thus, the streamID of Si_r should be changed to the streamID of Si_k. The streamID of Si_k should be replaced by the streamID of Si_r at Ni_r for the same reason. The nodes of the preceding stream and succeeding stream need to change the streamIDs because the succeeding stream and the preceding stream (i.e., either Si_k or Si_r) respectively are swapped with the other stream (i.e., either Si_r or Si_k).

Step 3: Update NOSs to Reflect a New Join Placement

As we see from Equation 3, the join placement of a one-way join is determined by the smaller execution cost between the placements at the source and at the destination. This join placement may change when the stream statistics change. Thus, the nodes need to compute the execution costs to determine the new join placement and then update the NOSs if it is different from the old one. Note that the join placement computed during the step 1 (while the stream to be swapped with is found) is not shipped all the way through the nodes in the sequence, as it can be simply recomputed at the swapped nodes.

The join placement may change from the source node to the destination node or the other way around. To accommodate these changes, the join operator and the update operator in the NOS of each affected node should be moved to the other node. Thus, the node from which the join operator is moved out adds a ship operator to its NOS for shipping the input stream of the join operator to the other node.

Example 3 below illustrates updating NOSs to reflect the update of join ordering (O_i) and join placement (P_i).

Example 3: Continuing from Examples 1 and 2, consider $SEP_1 = (O_1, P_1) = ([S_2, S_3], [1,1])$. In this SEP_1, $C^1_{1,2} < C^1_{1,3}$ holds. Now sup-

pose $C^1_{1,2}$ has increased and as a result the invariant cost-condition is violated. Further suppose that the ensuing plan modification tells that S_2 needs to be swapped with S_3 in O_1 and the new join from S_1 to S_3 needs to be executed in the source node. In other words, the new SEP_1 is $(O_1, P_1) = ([S_3, S_2], [0,1])$. In order to implement this change, the NOS in each node is updated as follows.

Before modification:

$NOS^1_1 = \{ship(S_1, N_2)\}$

$NOS^1_2 = \{join(S_1, S_2), update(S_2), ship(S^1_2, N_3)\}$

$NOS^1_3 = \{join(S^1_2, S_3), update(S_3), ship(S^1_3, N_0)\}$

After modification:

$NOS^1_1 = \{join(S_1, S_3), update(S_3), ship(S^1_3, N_2)\}$

$NOS^1_2 = \{join(S^1_3, S_2), update(S_2), ship(S^1_2, N_0)\}$

$NOS^1_3 = \{ship(S_3, N_1)\}$

Stage 2: Update on the Other Affected Streams

After the swap of Si_k and Si_r, depending on whether $C^i_{i_{k-1}, i_k}$ has increased or decreased, the positions of the other streams in O_i may need to change as well. Specifically, if $C^i_{i_{k-1}, i_k}$ has increased, it may happen that the subsequence $\{Si_1, ..., Si_{k-1}, Si_r\}$ satisfies the invariant cost-condition but the rest $\{Si_{k+1}, ..., Si_{r-1}, Si_k, Si_{r+1}, ..., Si_{m-1}\}$ does not. Thus, the update needs to continue from Si_{k+1}. In the same manner, if $C^i_{i_{k-1}, i_k}$ has decreased, it may happen that the subsequence $\{Si_1, ..., Si_{r-1}, Si_k\}$ satisfies the invariant cost-condition but the rest of the sequence $\{Si_{r+1}, ..., Si_{k-1}, Si_r, Si_{k+1}, ..., Si_{m-1}\}$ does not because the substitution of Si_k for Si_r affects the join cost to its succeeding streams. Thus, the update needs to continue from Si_{r+1}. Each update is performed following the stage 1 steps used in the case of increased cost (i.e., the steps 6 to 8 in Algorithm 3), as any necessary swaps are with another stream succeeding in the sequence.

The complexity of the algorithm in terms of the number of messages sent is $O(n^3)$ where n is the number of nodes, as there are n SEPs (one for each stream) and in the worst case there are n^2 NOS-swaps performed for each sequence.

Distributed Plan Migration

As mentioned in Introduction, the main challenge in the distributed plan migration is that windows are distributed over the nodes and thus, when the plan changes, the windows need to move to new nodes without disrupting the join execution. There should be no tuple missing or duplicated in the output. The proposed distributed track strategy is using the parallel track idea (Zhu, Rundensteiner, & Heineman, 2004) as the basis and exceeds its limit to address the distribution challenge.

In this strategy, window contents are moved to new nodes as soon as possible and each node runs the new NOS and the old NOS in parallel until the new NOS is ready, and at that point the old NOS is dropped and only the new NOS is used for join execution. In order to guarantee no missing tuple in the output, the new NOS is not ready until the old plan and the new plan generate the same output for every SEP. Note that the same output is generated only if for every window its content in the new node is the same as its content in the old node. In order to guarantee no duplicate tuples, join operators in a new plan are not executed until the window extent in the new node is filled up after the parallel runs of the new and old plans.

There are two technical issues to address in the distributed track strategy. One issue is the delay until the window content of the new plan is filled up, until when the plan migration cannot be completed. The delay is as long as the window size, which is inapplicable for large window sizes.

Our approach is to jump start the migration by copying the window extent from the old nodes to the new nodes as soon as the new nodes are identified during the plan modification. For this, for each stream the node that is maintaining its window should be kept track of, so that a new node can send a request to the old node and ask for the window content. The details are discussed below. The other issue is to make sure all the affected nodes start their own migration synchronously. This synchronized migration is important because otherwise one node may execute a new plan (after migration) while another node executes an old plan (before migration), thereby corrupting the distributed join result. This kind of synchronization has been well studied in the distributed computing area (e.g., two-phase commit), and we adopt a simple protocol approach described below.

Keeping Track of the Nodes Maintaining Windows

The distributed plan migration needs to keep track of which node currently maintains a window so that a request can be sent to the right node to ask for the window content. This issue is handled differently depending on the NOS update approach used in the distributed plan modification. In the centralized approach, all NOS updates are determined at the central node and thus the information on the window maintenance node is kept at a central node as well. In the distributed approach, the old node that currently has a window needs to communicate directly with the new node that will need the window. More specific steps are discussed next.

When the centralized NOS update approach is used, the central node Nq first compares the old NOS and the new NOS for each node to determine if a new window (e.g., W_i) is needed by the new NOS. A new window is needed by an NOS if it contains an update operator (e.g., $update(S_i)$). Then, the central node looks for the update operator in the old NOS. If found, it sends to the node of the old NOS a request to make the window (e.g., W_l) accessible to its new NOS. If not found, then it means the node of the new NOS needs to obtain the window content from another node. To identify the node that currently maintains the window, the central node checks the old NOSs of all nodes to find the NOS that contains the update operator (e.g., *update(S_l)*). Suppose NOS_p is the one. The central node then sends to the node of NOS_p (i.e., N_p) a request to move the window (e.g., W_l) to the node of the new NOS. Additionally, the central node makes the list of all affected nodes by comparing the new NOS and old NOS in each node. This list is needed in the synchronization step to be discussed below.

When the distributed NOS update approach is used, the information on the window maintenance node is recorded while NOSs are updated to reflect the NOS swap and the new join placement (see Step 2 and Step 3). More specifically, during the swapping of the new NOS in a node Ni_k and the old NOS in a node Ni_r, if the new NOS contains an update operator (e.g., *update(S_l)*) that is in the old NOS, then Ni_k sends a request to Ni_r to move the window (e.g., W_l) to Ni_k. Likewise, during the update of an NOS to reflect a new join placement, if an update operator (e.g., *update(S_l)*) is moved from one node (e.g., Ni_p) to another node (e.g., Ni_k), then Ni_k sends to Ni_p a request to move the window (e.g., W_l) to Ni_k. Additionally, each node (e.g., Ni_k) records the list of affected nodes which consists of the swapped node (i.e., Ni_r) and the nodes of the preceding stream and the succeeding stream of Ni_k (i.e., Ni_{k-1} and Ni_{k+1}). This list is used for the synchronization step, discussed next.

Synchronizing the Migration Among the Nodes

The NOS switch-over performed by all affected nodes should be synchronized. For this we use a two-phase migration protocol. Each node participating in the migration maintains two states, *local-ready* and *global-ready*, and follows the protocol outlined below.

1. When the window specified in the NOS at the node becomes full, the node enters the *local-ready* state. In this state, it sends a "local-ready" message to all the other affected nodes and waits to receive "local-ready" messages from them.

2. When the number of received "local-ready" messages becomes equal to the number of affected nodes, the first phase is complete, and the node enters the *global-ready* state. In this state, it sends a "global-ready" message to all the other affected nodes and waits to receive "global-ready" messages from them.

3. When the number of received "global-ready" messages becomes equal to the number of the other affected nodes, the second phase is complete, and the node starts performing the migration.

The first phase of this protocol guarantees that all affected nodes are ready to perform the migration and the second phase guarantees that all affected nodes start performing the migration altogether. There may be technical issues pertaining to distributed computing, such as dealing with lost messages or network partitioning, but these issues are beyond the scope of this paper.

This protocol assumes that every affected node knows which the other affected nodes in the plan modification are and the messages are exchanged point to point among the nodes. An alternative would be to elect a coordinator, in which case the total number of messages can be reduced in return for the overhead of electing a new coordinator every time a new plan migration is to be done.

PERFORMANCE EVALUATION

There are two objectives in the performance evaluation. One is to see how effective the proposed adaptive processing mechanism is compared with non-adaptive processing. The other is to examine the additional overhead paid by the distributed NOS update approach compared with the centralized approach. In this section we describe the design, setup, and results of these two sets of experiments.

Experiment Design

A prototype distributed data stream processing system has been built for the experiments. It runs on each node and comprises the three modules of optimizer, executor, and communicator. The optimizer generates the initial JEP, modifies the JEP, and extracts NOSs from a JEP. The executor performs the operations in the NOS, monitors the stream statistics, and notifies the optimizer if the change exceeds the threshold. The communicator delivers messages between the optimizers and the executors running on the distributed nodes. The prototype software program is written in Java 2 SDK 1.6.2 and uses TCP/IP as the communication protocol.

We have conducted the experiments in a network environment simulated using VMWare (VMWARE 1998). VMWare allows us to create multiple virtual machines that are connected through a virtual fully connected network in which the network bandwidth can be adjusted as needed. The network latency is not supported by VMWare, so we simulate it by injecting a fixed delay in every packet sent out to the virtual network. All virtual machines are created on a 2.0GHz Pentium Core 2 Duo computer with 2GB RAM; each virtual machine is configured to use the same CPU of the host computer and equally divided 192MB RAM of the host computer and runs Linux OS. We run multiple instances of the prototype on separate virtual machines which are the nodes participating in a multi-way join execution.

We have written a data generator to generate a stream data set as a sequence of tuples. Inputs to the data generator are the number of tuples to be in the data set, the stream rate, the tuple size (given as the number of 5-byte attributes in the stream schema), and the name, size, and join selectivity factor of each attribute in the schema. The values of the join attributes are assigned randomly with the uniform distribution. We use the string data type for all attributes. Each tuple has a timestamp, the value of which is determined based on the stream rate.

The performance metric is the total execution cost across all nodes, and is measured as follows. For a given query issued at a certain node (called the query node), the optimizer of the node generates a plan and disseminates it to all the nodes. Then, the executor of each node extracts its NOS and executes it. The execution cost, which includes the processing cost and the communication cost, is recorded at each node and sent to the query node for calculating the total execution cost.

Experiment Results

Experiment 1: Effectiveness of the Adaptive Processing

The approach in this set of experiments is to compare the total execution costs between the adaptive case and the non-adaptive case while changing the stream statistics. For the purpose of this experiment, it is adequate enough to switch between low and high for the rate of one stream. Thus, we have changed the stream rate at one arbitrary node between 50 tuples/sec and 200 tuples/sec. A four-way join query and an eight-way join query have been used, with a fully-connected join topology.[1] For this, we set up 4 nodes and 8 nodes for the four-way join query and the eight-way join query, respectively.

Figure 7 shows how the execution time of the non-adaptive and the adaptive processing changes as the stream rate changes at the interval of 2000 msec starting from the time 1500 msec. Both four- and eight-way join cases show the same performance curves, except for magnitude of the costs. (The eight-way join involves more nodes in the processing and, thus, the total execution cost is larger.) The costs fluctuate more in the eight-way join case.

In the figure we see that initially both non-adaptive and adaptive processing use the same execution plan, and thus they show the same execution cost. However, when the stream rate changes from low to high (at time 1500 msec), the non-adaptive processing cost increases by a much larger margin than the adaptive processing cost. Evidently, the reason is that the non-adaptive processing is still using the initial plan, while the adaptive processing has changed it to a more efficient plan. By the same token, when the stream rate changes from high to low (at time 3500 msec),

the adaptive processing switches back to the initial plan, which is the same plan the non-adaptive processing is using, and thus they have the same execution cost again.

We also see that there is hardly any difference between the two NOS update approaches (i.e., adaptive-CNU and adaptive-DNU) in the adaptive processing. It confirms that they always produce identical execution plans, since both NOS update approaches are based on the same greedy property.

The spike of the two costs when the stream rate changes from high to low in Figure 4(a) is interesting. This phenomenon can be explained as follows. During the plan migration in this case, a window content on the higher rate stream is copied from one node to another node and then the old NOS is switched to the new NOS for execution; at the beginning of the transition, however, the new NOS (generated for the lower-rate stream) is processing the higher-rate stream tuples still remaining in the window extent; this mismatch causes the cost to increase until the window content

Figure 7. Comparison between adaptive processing and non-adaptive processing

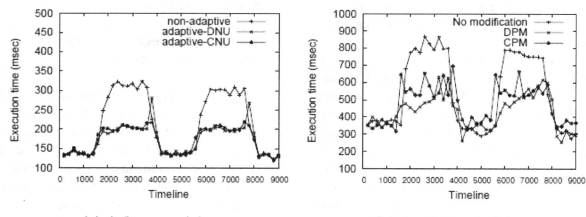

(a) A four-way join.

(b) An eight-way join.

Adapt-CNU refers to the adaptive processing using the *centralized* NOS update approach, and adapt-DNU refers to the adaptive processing using the *distributed* NOS update approach. The execution time is the average obtained from ten repeated runs. The default settings are as follows: tuples size = 150 bytes; stream rate = 100 tuples/sec; network bandwidth = 1024 Kbps; latency = 5 msec; selectivity factor = 0.01; window size = 500 msec; measurement interval = 200 msec.

Figure 8. Plan modification and migration overheads

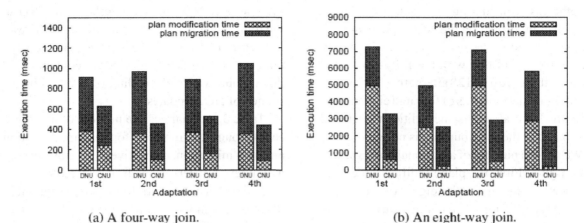

(a) A four-way join.   (b) An eight-way join.

The labels of the bars, DNU and CNU, refer to the adaptive processing using, respectively, the distributed and the centralized node update approaches. The default settings and the number of repeated runs are the same as those of Experiment 1 (Figure 4); the first and the third rounds correspond to the times at which the stream rate increases, and the second and the third rounds correspond to the times at which the stream rate decreases.

is replaced with the right (i.e., lower-rate stream) tuples. Another observation is that the spike in the adaptive-DNU is higher than in adaptive-CNU. The reason is that the former may need several rounds of NOS updates to reach a new efficient plan (see Stage 2) and, thus, may be using a less efficient plan than the latter during Stage 2. The spike is less visible in the eight-way join case (Figure 4(b)). This comes from the fact that we vary the rate of only one stream in our experiment setup and, therefore, the transient overhead is due to the migration of one window; as a result, the impact of the transient overhead caused by one out of eight windows (in the eight-way join case) is lower than that caused by one out of four windows (in the four-way join case).

Experiment 2: Overhead of the Adaptive Processing

Adaptivity requires plan modification and plan migration every time stream statistic changes at any node participating in the join. The objective of this set of experiments is to examine the overhead in terms of the costs of plan modification and

migration. The plan modification cost is measured as the total time all nodes spend to obtain new NOSs, and the plan migration cost is measured as the total time all nodes spend to switch over from old NOSs to new NOSs.

Figure 8 shows the experimental results. Each bar in the figure shows the sum of the plan modification cost and the plan migration cost, with the two distinguished using different patterns. The setup of the experiments is the same as the setup of Experiment 1, and thus the 1st and the 3rd pairs of bars in the figure look similar and so do the 2nd and the 4th. This is evident from the fact that those pairs are for the same changes of stream rates (see the changes at times 1500 msec and 5500 msec and at times 3500 msec and 7500 msec in Figure 4).

The figure shows that the total overhead (considering both plan modification and migration) of the adaptation using the distributed NOS update (DNU) approach is larger than the overhead in the centralized node update (CNU) approach by a factor of approximately 1.4 to 2.5 in the four-way join case and 2.1 to 2.7 in the eightway join case. There is no objective baseline to use to judge how acceptable these additional overheads are. Nonetheless, considering the facts that during query plan modification the NOS update at each node may occur multiple times in DNU but only once in CNU and that with the fully-connected topology there are 6 and 28 alternative join execution plans in the networks of four and eight nodes, respectively, we assert that the additional overhead to be paid for the distributivity is marginal.

We make a number of additional observations in the figure. First, the plan modification cost is significantly higher for the eight-way join than for the four-way join. This is obvious from the fact that there are more nodes involved in the modification process. Second, the plan modification cost is higher when the stream rate increases (the 1st and 3rd bars) than when it decreases (the 2nd and 4th bars). (It shows more clearly in the eight-way join case (Figure 5b).) This difference indicates that, given the parameter settings, there are more nodes whose NOSs are updated when the stream rate increases than when it decreases. Third, the plan modification cost is higher with DNU than CNU. This expected from the fact that the computation cost is $O(n^3)$ for DNU and $O(n)$ for CNU (where n is the number of nodes). Fourth, the plan migration cost is higher with DNU than CNU in the four-way join case (Figure 5a) but lower in the eight-way join case. This difference indicates that the migration overhead in DNU due

to multiple rounds of NOS updates is higher than the one-time NOS update overhead of CNU in the four-way join case but lower in the eight-way join case. (The migration cost depends on the number of shipments of window contents, and this number varies depending on the number of rounds of NOS updates.)

Table 3 summarizes the number of massages sent through the network for plan modification and plan migration, respectively. We now discuss a number of observations from this table.

In the plan modification part, first, the number of messages in CNU is the same as the number of nodes, n. This is because the messages consist of the message sent by a node to the central node to notify the change of its stream rate and $n-1$ messages sent by the central node to all the other nodes (which are all affected nodes with the experiment setting) to update their NOSs. Second, the messages in DNU consist of the messages sent through the nodes in a join sequence to determine the nodes to be swapped, the messages sent to update the NOSs of the other nodes to realize node swapping, and the messages sent to update the NOSs to realize join placement changes. The complexity of the DNU approach in term of the number of messages sent is $O(n^3)$.

In the plan migration part, the table shows the total number of migration messages and the number of synchronization messages. (Note the

Table 3. Number of messages for plan modification and migration

		When Stream Rate Increases			When Stream Rate Decreases		
		Number of modification messages	Number of migration messages	Number of synchronization messages	Number of modification messages	Number of migration messages	Number of synchronization messages
4-way join	CNU	4	34	24	4	27	24
	DNU	65	61	44	59	55	32
8-way join	CNU	8	131	112	8	115	112
	DNU	561	181	152	283	83	48

(The number of migration messages includes the number of synchronization messages. The number of messages reported in this table is measured each time the plan modification and plan migration algorithms are triggered. The measured numbers do not change through different repetitions, since the same steps in the algorithms are executed for each repetition.)

former includes the latter.) In CNU, the migration messages consist of the messages for requesting window movements and the messages for synchronization. With the two-phase synchronization in place, the number of synchronization messages is *2n(n-1)* since each node sends messages to all the other nodes in each of the two phases. In DNU, the migration messages consist of the messages for requesting the window movement each time NOSs swap or join placement changes and the messages for synchronization. The number of synchronization messages varies depending on the number of synchronized nodes and the number of synchronizations performed.

RELATED WORK

Major research on adaptive query processing has been for relational databases (Markl, Raman, Simmen, Lohman, & Pirahesh, 2004; Kabra & DeWitt, 1998; Cole & Graefe, 1994; Ioannidis, Ng, Shim, & Sellis, 1997; Antoshenkov & Ziauddin, 1996; Avnur & Hellerstein, 2000; Deshpande & Hellerstein, 2004; Babu, Bizarro, & DeWitt, 2005), and recently for data streams (Zhu, Rundensteiner, & Heineman, 2004; Tian & DeWitt, 2003; Babu, Motwani, Munagala, Nishizawa, & Widom, 2004; Babu, Munagala, Widom, & Motwani, 2005). In this section we give an overview of the related research in these two areas.

Adaptive Database Query Processing

We find two approaches based on *re-optimization*, which is the base of our proposed approach. Kabra and DeWitt (1998) introduce a *dynamic* re-optimization approach which detects the sub-optimality of a plan while executing the query and re-optimizes the plan in the midst of query execution if there is a significant difference between estimated and actual values. Similar to Kabra and DeWitt's (1998) approach, Markl, Raman, Simmen, Lohman, and Pirahesh (2004) propose a technique called *progressive* query optimization which adds one or more checkpoint operators to a plan to compare the optimizer's estimates with the actual values and triggers reoptimization if a pre-determined threshold on the estimation error is exceeded. There have been other approaches to adaptive query processing as well, such as the *competition* model (Antoshenkov & Ziauddin, 1996), *parametric* optimization (Cole & Graefe, 1994; Ioannidis, Ng, Shim, & Sellis, 1997), *tuple-routing* (Avnur & Hellerstein, 2000; Deshpande & Hellerstein, 2004), and *proactive* optimization (Babu, Bizarro, & DeWitt, 2005). In the *competition* model approach, multiple plans are executed together until one of the plans becomes better than the others and then the executions of the sub-optimal plans are stopped. The *parametric* optimization approach is to prepare separate plans optimal for different partitions of the parameter domain and choose a plan when the actual parameter values are known at run-time. The *tuple-routing* approach handles the query processing by routing tuples through a pool of operators. This mechanism is handled by an operator called *eddy* which continuously reorders operators in a query as it is running. In the *proactive* optimization approach, query plans are selected with possible re-optimization in mind, that is, to minimize it. The authors introduce bounding boxes to determine the uncertainty in the estimates of statistics and use these bounding boxes during optimization to generate robust and switchable plans that minimize the need for re-optimization as well as the cost of switching plans.

There has been some work done in distributed databases as well. Scheuermann and Chong (1997) present an adaptive algorithm for finding a query execution plan. This work, however, is not about adaptive query processing and does not address the problem of modifying a plan when the statistics or computing resources change. Zhou (2003) proposes an adaptive distributed query processing framework. It, however, only focuses on the scheme for learning the selectivity and workload of distributed servers. Besides, the adaptive mechanism is based on the eddy approach to reorder the operations at runtime.

All these adaptive approaches are for databases and are not geared for handling data stream query processing.

Adaptive Data Stream Query Processing

Adaptive query processing of data streams pose unique challenges due to the requirement of continuous and unbounded processing of arriving data. There have been some research done to address these challenges using the re-optimization approach (Babu, Motwani, Munagala, Nishizawa, & Widom, 2004; Babu, Munagala, Widom, & Motwani, 2005; Zhu, Rundensteiner, & Heineman, 2004; Yang, Kr¨amer, Papadias, & Seeger, 2007). Babu, Motwani, Munagala, Nishizawa, and Widom (2004) and Babu, Munagala, Widom, and Motwani (2005) study the problem of quickly detecting the change in stream statistics and efficiently switching to an equivalent yet more efficient plan. Specifically, the focus Babu, Motwani, Munagala, Nishizawa, and Widom (2004) is on adaptively ordering pipelined filters, where they introduce the *A-Greedy* algorithm which uses a greedy strategy to reorder the filters when the greedy property is violated. Then, the focus of Babu, Munagala, Widom, and Motwani (2005) is on handling the migration between join execution plans of a multi-way join query, where they introduce the *A-Caching* algorithm which stores the intermediate results of join subsequences to support the plan migration. These algorithms assume a centralized environment, and they do not work in a distributed environment because it requires a different model and techniques.

Zhu, Rundensteiner, and Heineman (2004) focus on the problem of plan migration and propose two solutions for the plan migration, a *moving state* strategy and a *parallel track* strategy. The mov-

ing state strategy temporarily suspends the query execution in order to produce an intermediate result for the new plan and then switches over to the new plan. The parallel track strategy runs both the new plan and the old plan in parallel and drops the old plan when it is not needed anymore. Yang, Kramer, Papadias, and Seeger (2007) proposes an improvement over Zhu, Rundensteiner, and Heineman (2004) approach by combining the two strategies. Besides the fact that these approaches are for centralized processing environment, the proposed techniques assume the tree ordering when moving an intermediate result during plan migration, which is inapplicable in our problem as we use the linear join ordering.

Another line of research on adaptive stream query processing is based on the tuple-routing mentioned above. This approach is different from the re-optimization approach. Tian and DeWitt (2003) consider the adaptive processing of stateful operators in a distributed environment. They use the *tuple-routing* approach (i.e,, eddies (Avnur & Hellerstein, 2000)) as the basis and extend it to work in a distributed environment with *multiple eddies*. Each eddy at a local node takes the input tuples and, based on pre-defined policies, determines the next operator (in another node) to forward the output tuples to. This technique requires metadata for each tuple to keep track of its processing progress, and it makes the system prohibitively expensive in terms of the communication overhead. Claypool and Claypool (2008) present an improvement over the eddies, called *trained eddies (TEddies)*. TEddies processes tuples in a batch instead of single tuples and has an adaptive scheduler module to adapt to the changes of the stream statistics and the number of tuples in a batch. TEddies is meant for a centralized environment.

Another work in distributed databases that has a similar distributed data model to our work is OGSA-DAI (OGSA-DAI 2002). In their model, multiple databases are placed in different nodes distributed over the network and can be queried through a server which makes the queried databases appear as one logical database. That is, given a query, the distributed query processor generates an initial query plan and then breaks it into operators that need to be executed at each node. Their work is fundamentally different from ours in two aspects. First, their query optimizer is rule-based, that is, the plan is optimized based on a set of predefined rules, whereas our query optimization algorithm is cost-based. Second, our work focuses on the adaptive query processing which modifies the execution plan when the stream statistics change, while their work does not.

CONCLUSION

In this paper, we have addressed the problem of adaptively processing multi-way windowed stream joins over distributed data streams. The key idea is to use a node operator set (NOS) to support the adaptivity locally while ensuring the correctness globally over the network. Based on the notion of NOS, we have presented two distributed plan modification techniques depending on whether the NOSs in all nodes are updated centrally or distributed. In the centralized update, one node maintains and updates the NOSs and sends updated NOSs to affected nodes. In the distributed update, individual nodes communicate with their neighboring nodes to update their own NOSs by themselves. Further, we have presented distributed plan migration techniques for centralized and distributed NOS updates. Both techniques guarantee a correct switch-over from an old plan to a new plan. Finally, we have conducted two sets of experiments to test the adaptivity of the developed techniques as a whole and to study the time overheads of the plan modification part and plan migration part in one view.

There are some directions we are considering for future work. First, the proposed adaptive framework assumes the entire window contents are migrated from one node to another as a result of plan modification. A more efficient mechanism that requires only a part of the window content would be more desirable. Second, the framework considers only the stream statistics as something to adapt to. The change of available system resources (e.g., memory, CPU time) is another factor commonly considered for adaptivity. If the system resources become short, then approximating the join results may be necessary. In this case, finding an adequate quality metric of the approximate result in a distributed environment and computing it efficiently will be an interesting problem. Third, the join processing model assumes the linear ordering in which intermediate join results are not buffered. Extending the model to maintain intermediate join results may improve the efficiency of join processing. The solution requires a technique to maintain and migrate intermediate results efficiently in our adaptive framework. Fourth, a variation of the distributed NOS update algorithm can be developed by limiting the number of streams to be searched in determining the stream to be swapped; in this way, the quality of the query plan (i.e., the execution time) might not be as good as that of our proposed algorithm, but the number of messages exchanged can be reduced.

REFERENCES

Aho, A. V., Sagiv, Y., & Ullman, J. D. (1979). Efficient optimization of a class of relational expressions. *ACM Transactions on Database Systems, 4*(4), 435–454. doi:10.1145/320107.32 0112doi:10.1145/320107.320112

Amini, L., & Jain, N. Sehgal, A. Silber, J., & Verscheure, O. (2006). Adaptive control of extreme-scale stream processing systems. In *Proceedings of the 26th IEEE International Conference on Distributed Computing Systems* (p. 71).

Antoshenkov, G., & Ziauddin, M. (1996). Query processing and optimization in Oracle RDB. *The Very Large Databases Journal*, *5*(4), 229–237. doi:10.1007/s007780050026doi:10.1007/s007780050026

Avnur, R., & Hellerstein, J. M. (2000). Eddies: Continuously adaptive query processing. In *Proceedings of the 19th International Conference on Management of Data* (pp. 261-272).

Babu, S., Bizarro, P., & DeWitt, D. J. (2005). Proactive re-optimization. In *Proceedings of the 24th International Conference on Management of Data* (pp. 107-118).

Babu, S., Motwani, R., Munagala, K., Nishizawa, I., & Widom, J. (2004). Adaptive ordering of pipelined stream filters. In *Proceedings of the 23rd International Conference on Management of Data* (pp. 407-418).

Babu, S., Munagala, K., Widom, J., & Motwani, R. (2005). Adaptive caching for continuous queries. In *Proceedings of the 21st International Conference on Data Engineering* (pp. 118-129).

Ceri, S., & Pelagatti, G. (1984). *Distributed databases: Principles and systems*. New York, NY: McGraw-Hill.

Claypool, K. T., & Claypool, M. (2008). Teddies: Trained eddies for reactive stream processing. In *Proceedings of the 11st International Conference on Database Systems for Advanced Applications* (pp. 220-234).

Cole, R. L., & Graefe, G. (1994). Optimization of dynamic query evaluation plans. In *Proceedings of the 13rd International Conference on Management of Data* (pp. 150-160).

Cormode, G., Muthukrishnan, S., & Zhuang, W. (2006). What's different: Distributed, continuous monitoring of duplicate-resilient aggregates on data streams. In *Proceedings of the 22nd International Conference on Data Engineering* (p. 57).

Das, A., Ganguly, S., Garofalakis, M. N., & Rastogi, R. (2004). Distributed set expression cardinality estimation. In *Proceedings of the 30th International Conference on Very Large Data Bases* (p. 312).

Deshpande, A., & Hellerstein, J. M. (2004). Lifting the burden of history from adaptive query processing. In *Proceedings of the 30th International Conference on Very Large Data Bases* (pp. 948-959).

Gedik, B., Wu, K.-L., Yu, P. S., & Liu, L. (2007). A load shedding framework and optimizations for m-way windowed stream joins. In *Proceedings of the 23rd International Conference on Data Engineering* (pp. 536-545).

Golab, L., & Ozsu, M. T. (2003). Processing sliding window multi-joins in continuous queries over data streams. In *Proceedings of the 29th International Conference on Very Large Data Bases* (pp. 500-511).

Ioannidis, Y. E., Ng, R. T., Shim, K., & Sellis, T. K. (1997). Parametric query optimization. *The Very Large Databases Journal*, *6*(2), 132–151. doi:10.1007/s007780050037doi:10.1007/s007780050037

Kabra, N., & DeWitt, D. J. (1998). Efficient mid-query re-optimization of sub-optimal query execution plans. In *Proceedings of the 17th International Conference on Management of Data* (pp. 106-117).

Kang, J., Naughton, J. F., & Viglas, S. D. (2003). Evaluating window joins over unbounded streams. In *Proceedings of the 19th International Conference on Data Engineering* (pp. 341-352).

Kumar, V., Cooper, B. F., Cai, Z., Eisenhauer, G., & Schwan, K. (2005). Resource-aware distributed stream management using dynamic overlays. In *Proceedings of the 25th IEEE International Conference on Distributed Computing Systems* (p. 783).

Kumar, V., Cooper, B. F., & Schwan, K. (2005). Distributed stream management using utility-driven self adaptive middleware. In *Proceedings of the 2nd International Conference on Autonomic Computing* (p. 3).

Markl, V., Raman, V., Simmen, D. E., Lohman, G. M., & Pirahesh, H. (2004). Robust query processing through progressive optimization. In *Proceedings of the 23rd International Conference on Management of Data* (pp. 659-670).

OGSA-DAI. (2002). *Welcome to OGSA-DAI.* Retrieved from http://www.ogsadai.org.uk/

Olston, C., Jiang, J., & Widom, J. (2003). Adaptive filters for continuous queries over distributed data streams. In *Proceedings of the 22nd International Conference on Management of Data* (pp. 563).

Scheuermann, P., & Chong, E. I. (1997). Adaptive algorithms for join processing in distributed database systems. *Distributed and Parallel Databases, 5*(3), 233–269. doi:10.1023/A:1008617911992doi:10.1023/A:1008617911992

Seshadri, S., Kumar, V., & Cooper, B. F. (2006). Optimizing multiple queries in distributed data stream systems. In *Proceedings of Workshop of the 22nd International Conference on Data Engineering* (p. 25).

Sharfman, I., Schuster, A., & Keren, D. (2006). A geometric approach to monitoring threshold functions over distributed data streams. In *Proceedings of the 25th International Conference on Management of Data* (p. 301).

Srivastava, U., Munagala, K., & Widom, J. (2005). Operator placement for in-network stream query processing. In *Proceedings of the 24th Symposium on Principles of Database Systems* (pp. 250-258).

Tian, F., & DeWitt, D. J. (2003). Tuple routing strategies for distributed eddies. In *Proceedings of the 29th International Conference on Very Large Data Bases* (pp. 333-344).

Tran, T. M., & Lee, B. S. (2010). Distributed stream join query processing with semijoins. *Distributed and Parallel Databases, 27*(3), 211–254. doi:10.1007/s10619-010-7062-7doi:10.1007/s10619-010-7062-7

Viglas, S., Naughton, J. F., & Burger, J. (2003). Maximizing the output rate of multi-way join queries over streaming information sources. In *Proceedings of the 29th International Conference on Very Large Data Bases* (pp. 285-296).

VMWARE. (1998). *VMWare Workstation 6.0.* Retrieved from http://www.vmware.com/

Yang, Y., Kramer, J., Papadias, D., & Seeger, B. (2007). Hybmig: A hybrid approach to dynamic plan migration for continuous queries. *IEEE Transactions on Knowledge and Data Engineering, 19*(3), 398–411. doi:10.1109/TKDE.2007.43doi:10.1109/TKDE.2007.43

Zhou, Y. (2003). Adaptive distributed query processing. In *Proceedings of PhD Workshop of the 29th International Conference on Very Large Databases*.

Zhou, Y., Yan, Y., Yu, F., & Zhou, A. (2006). Pmjoin: Optimizing distributed multi-way stream joins by stream partitioning. In *Proceedings of the 9th International Conference on Database Systems for Advanced Applications* (pp. 325-341).

Zhu, Y., Rundensteiner, E. A., & Heineman, G. T. (2004). Dynamic plan migration for continuous queries over data streams. In *Proceedings of the 23rd International Conference on Management of Data* (pp. 431-442).

ENDNOTES

[1]   This join topology is common in stream join queries. Examples are joins on IP addresses for network monitoring applications and joins on sensor IDs for sensor monitoring applications.

[2]   We may as well say that the overhead of the DNU approach over the CNU approach is a factor of 0.25 to 0.6 times per node in the four-way join case and 0.26 to 3.34 times per node in the eight-way join case.

This work was previously published in the International Journal of Distributed Systems and Technologies (IJDST), Volume 2, Issue 2, edited by Nik Bessis, pp. 58-80, copyright 2011 by IGI Publishing (an imprint of IGI Global).

Chapter 8
A Failure Detection System for Large Scale Distributed Systems

Andrei Lavinia
University Politehnica of Bucharest, Romania

Ciprian Dobre
University Politehnica of Bucharest, Romania

Florin Pop
University Politehnica of Bucharest, Romania

Valentin Cristea
University Politehnica of Bucharest, Romania

ABSTRACT

Failure detection is a fundamental building block for ensuring fault tolerance in large scale distributed systems. It is also a difficult problem. Resources under heavy loads can be mistaken as being failed. The failure of a network link can be detected by the lack of a response, but this also occurs when a computational resource fails. Although progress has been made, no existing approach provides a system that covers all essential aspects related to a distributed environment. This paper presents a failure detection system based on adaptive, decentralized failure detectors. The system is developed as an independent substrate, working asynchronously and independent of the application flow. It uses a hierarchical protocol, creating a clustering mechanism that ensures a dynamic configuration and traffic optimization. It also uses a gossip strategy for failure detection at local levels to minimize detection time and remove wrong suspicions. Results show that the system scales with the number of monitored resources, while still considering the QoS requirements of both applications and resources.

DOI: 10.4018/978-1-4666-2647-8.ch008

INTRODUCTION

Large scale distributed systems (LSDS) are hardly ever "perfect." Due to their complexity, it is extremely difficult to produce flawlessly designed distributed systems. While until recently the research in the distributed systems domain has mainly targeted the development of functional infrastructures, today new requirements have emerged among which fault tolerance is needed by more and more modern distributed applications, not only by the critical ones. The clients expect them to work despite possible faults occurring.

Although the importance of fault tolerance is today widely recognized and many research projects have been initiated in this domain, the existing systems often offer only partial solutions that follow a particular underlying distributed architecture. Traditional fault detection solutions, in particular, fail to work properly in the context of LSDS because of the large number of monitored processes involved, the high probability of message loss, the dynamic nature of the underlying topologies and the unpredictable delays in message delivery.

In this paper we present implementation details for a failure detector designed for highly dynamic LSDS. Based on the architecture previously proposed in (Dobre et al., 2009), it combines adaptive and accrual detection approaches with a hierarchical design, for scalability and performance, and uses gossip protocols for a more accurate detection. The detector is specifically designed to meet requirements of a reliable failure detector. Its architecture allows applications to specify different QoS detection levels, while offering scalability, generality and non-intrusive characteristics.

Failure detection consists in monitoring processes and failure detectors throughout the systems and detecting errors in the shortest time according to the fault tolerance requirements of the distributed applications. The interpretation of the monitoring information is based on the concept of suspicion level. The progressive detection feature brings a new approach in terms of predicting the time of arrival of the next heartbeat message, as well as interpreting and updating the suspicion level. The system is able to deal with both transitional and permanent errors.

The implementation of the system is based on two strategies. The first one uses a hierarchical approach based on dynamic clustering to solve the scalability issue. The second strategy leverages the gossiping technique in order to remove wrong suspicions and decrease the time needed to detect errors.

The solution proposed in this paper combines the advantages of existing approaches in order to minimize their limitations so as to effectively treat problems such as message explosion, scalability, flexibility, dynamism message delays and adjustment to variable network conditions and various fault tolerance requirements coming from applications.

The rest of this paper is structured as follows. First we present related failure detection strategies for distributed systems. The next section describes the proposed architecture, highlights key elements of the implementation of the failure detector, and details on the models and protocols being used. Experimental results demonstrating the validity and performance of the proposed solution are discussed next. Finally, we lay out the conclusions and future work.

RELATED WORK

Fault tolerance in LSDS is based on one form of a failure detection system. Such a failure detector is generally capable of running a detection algorithm and it can communicate with other services which it monitors. This model was first proposed, in the form of an "oracle" detection service, by Chandra and Toueg (1996).

The failure detection module is independent to the main application flow and is being responsible with the monitoring of a subset of the processes within the monitored system and maintaining a list of those it currently suspects to have crashed. A process can query its local failure detector module at any time to check its status. The list of suspected processes is permanently updated such that, at any time, new processes can be added and old ones removed. This failure detector is considered unreliable because it is allowed to make mistakes up to a certain degree. Therefore a module might erroneously suspect some correct process (wrong suspicion) or fail to detect processes that have already crashed. At any given time two failure detector modules may have different lists of processes.

The most common implementation of local failure detection is based on the heartbeat strategy. In this approach a failure detector module periodically sends a heartbeat message to other modules to inform them that it is still alive. When a module fails to receive a heartbeat from another module for a predetermined period of time (timeout) it concludes the remote process had crashed. There is a tradeoff, however, for the timeout values being considered. Short timeouts ensure quick detection, but with a high probability of wrong suspicions (some processes can take a longer time to respond due to temporary high load of the workstations on which they are running). Conversely, long timeouts decrease the probability of wrong suspicions, but cause penalties in the detection time. Also, this approach does not consider the heterogeneity of distributed systems. A fix timeout means the failure detection mechanism is unable to adapt to various changing conditions. Therefore a long timeout in some systems can turn out to be very short in others.

Except for the method of choosing the timeout threshold value, failure detectors adopt different strategies for choosing the set of monitored processes. In an LSDS, consisting of a large number of nodes, it is impractical to allow all failure detection modules to monitoring each other. A feasible solution is to arrange processes in a hierarchical structure (such as tree, forest, etc.) along which traffic is channeled. For example, one such solution relies on the use of a two-level hierarchy and was designed specifically for Globus toolkit (Stelling et al., 1998). However, because of the fixed and small number of hierarchy levels, the proposed solution fails to take full advantage of the hierarchical approach and, consequently, does not scale well for LSDS. An approach that focuses on the scalability of failure detection was proposed in (Bertier et al., 2002). However, the proposed system assumes simpler failure semantics such as crash failures.

An alternative technique for implementing failure detectors comes in the form of gossip-like protocols. In this approach each failure detector maintains a local list with monitoring data about the state of other processes in the system and periodically picks random partners with whom it exchanges information. Thus, the algorithm ensures with a high probability that all modules will obtain a piece of information eventually. An important advantage of this approach is the independence of the underlying topology resulting in a lower number of messages sent. Also, it tolerates lossy communication to the extent that an increased probability of message loss will result in a relatively small increase in detection time. However, detecting a specific type of fault may take a long time. One of the pioneering works in implementing gossip-style failure detectors is (Van Renesse et al., 1998). In their work the authors have identified a version of the protocol designed specifically for LSDS - multilevel gossiping. The idea is to define a multilevel hierarchy using the structure of Internet domains and sub-domains as defined by comparing IP addresses. But the protocol does not work well when a large number of components crash or become partitioned away.

Adaptive protocols come in response to the lack of adaptability of previous solutions (Defago et al., 2003). These protocols are designed to dynamically adjust to their environment and, in particular, adapt their behavior to changing network conditions. The approach is based on the heartbeat strategy with the difference that the timeout interval is not static but changes dynamically with the network conditions. It ensures a good compromise between detection time and number of wrong suspicions. However its limitation lies in flexibility, as the timeout can meet only the requirements of a single distributed application at a time. A protocol that adjusts the timeout by using the maximum arrival interval of heartbeat messages was proposed in (Fetzer et al., 2001). The protocol assumes a partially synchronous system model, being based on the assumption of an upper bound on message delays. (Chen et al., 2002) proposes a different approach based on a probabilistic analysis of network traffic. The protocol uses arrival times sampled in the recent past to compute an estimation of the arrival time of the next heartbeat. The timeout is recalculated on every heartbeat arrival according to the current estimation and a safety margin, based on application QoS requirements (e.g., upper bound on detection time) and network characteristics (e.g., network load).

A distinctive strategy of failure detection is represented by the accrual protocols. The family of accrual failure detectors consists in error detection modules that associate, to each of the monitored processes, a real number value that increases in time if the corresponding process has failed. One example of such an implementation is the φ-failure detector (Defago et al., 2003). The φ-failure detector samples the arrival time of heartbeats and maintains a sliding window of the most recent samples. The window is used to estimate the arrival time of the next heartbeat. A similar approach was proposed in (Bertier et al., 2002). However, the proposed failure detectors are poorly adapted to very conservative failure detection because of their vulnerability to message loss. In practice message losses tend to be strongly correlated (i.e., losses tend to occur in bursts). A proposed accrual detector designed to handle this problem is the k-failure detector (Hayashibara et

al., 2004). The k-failure detector takes into account both message loss and short-lived network partitions, each lost heartbeat contributing to raising the level of defined suspicion according to a predetermined schema.

Previous approaches fail to implement automatic detection of various failures in LSDS. Work still needs to be done to design appropriate failure detector solutions. The important problem with today's failure detectors is their incapacity to scale well, an important aspect when designing large distributed architectures. There are two important aspects to consider. First, the local failure detectors are limited by the resources they have at their disposal. This influences the number of nodes that they are able to monitor. Also, at a larger level, the problem of communicating fast the known faults to the entire system is still a problem. Adequate grouping solutions of the failure detectors and improved communication schema can lead to performances that would be acceptable for LSDS. We present a failure detection system which targets these problems. We present results proving its performance and capabilities.

ARCHITECTURAL AND IMPLEMENTATION DETAILS OF THE FAILURE DETECTOR

The architecture is based on the idea of making the fault detector available to applications as a service. This makes it suitable to be used with P2P, Grids and even Cloud systems. Such distributed systems can use the failure detection capabilities of the failure detector.

The system is composed of several failure detection agents running inside the distributed environment, each being responsible with the monitoring of a subset of processes and the update of the applications, through specialized modules, about the status of the monitored processes. Each detection agent implements several functions. The conceptual architecture of such a detection agent is represented in Figure 1. The agent represents the standalone process capable of executing locally the failure detection schema. Each agent is responsible with monitoring a number of applications. Such applications register with the agent and are periodically interrogated for their status.

The main objective of the *communication layer* is to create a scalable, fault tolerant and dynamic communication infrastructure between agents, to be used by the upper layer modules. For efficient communication the agents communicate according to a hierarchical clustering model. Within a LSDS a solution where each agent is in charge with monitoring every other agent is not feasible in terms of communication costs and scaling capabilities. The network and host resources are limited, while the geographical distribution of the system can be quite large. Therefore, we adopted a solution that groups agents into clusters, based on the geographical position of the workstations on which they are running, combined with metrics such as communication delays, load of the workstation, a load balancing cost, that together minimize the time needed to propagate updates among adjacent modules.

The system is therefore composed of several such clusters. Within each cluster an agent also has a coordination role. The main tasks of the *cluster coordinator* are *topology administration* (adding/removing nodes as agents enter or exit the system, dividing or unifying clusters), *intra-cluster and inter-cluster communication management*. The cluster coordinator is the agent that is aware of the topology of the cluster. All other agents need to know only the identity of the cluster coordinator. This approach aims to minimize the costs related to cluster information management. At the cluster level the coordinator acts as a gateway. Communication between clusters is routed through the coordinators. This topology leads to a hierarchical interconnecting network that ensures an optimal control schema and meets the requirements of LSDS.

Figure 1. The architecture of a detection agent

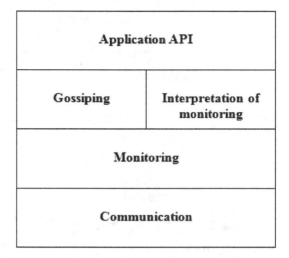

In order to ensure fault tolerance, within each cluster one agent acts as redundant *secondary replica* of the coordinator. This eliminates the possible single-point-of-failure aspect caused by the existence of a unique coordinator per cluster. The replica maintains a copy of the local topology and is asynchronously notified of any operation that could result in a topology change. This secondary replica becomes the new coordinator of the cluster when the current coordinator fails. The transition is quick and without loss of information - all unfinished operations (assuming for example that the last coordinator crashed unexpectedly) are evaluated and re-executed in order to bring the cluster to a consistent state.

Another aspect is the addressing solution being used to identify and locate agents. The solution consists in the use of a registry and lookup (LUS) service located at predefined IP addresses. Agents publish their public identity, the address of the workstation on which they are running and the listening port for incoming requests. The LUS is used to store information about all failure detection agents running inside the system (Figure 2).

When an agent starts it publishes its identity and joins a cluster (or it creates a new one if none is available). For that it estimates the best cluster

Figure 2. Information flow inside and outside the cluster

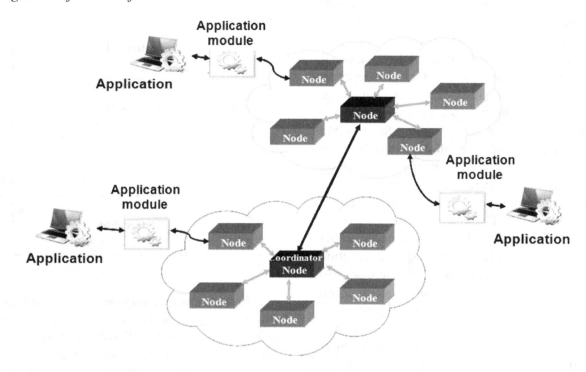

to connect to. The agent interrogates the LUS service to find all active coordinators. The received list is then ordered according to the proximity of each coordinator, and the number of agents in each cluster. The nearest cluster having the smallest dimension is then chosen and the agent connects to that cluster.

The number of coordinators and the size of their associated clusters are essential to maintaining efficiency of communication and fault detection schema. If the number of agents is too high compared to the number of coordinators, the cluster-level information becomes hard to manage, whilst if the number of agents is much smaller than the number of coordinators, the number of information and control messages exchanged between clusters increases greatly.

The solution consists in allowing the number of coordinators to dynamically adjust as the number of agents increases (new agents join the system) or decreases (agents exit the system). Thus, when the number of agents in a cluster is too large, a secondary coordinator is elected from the group of agents. The choice is based on the minimum principle applied to a unique internal identifier of each agent. Next the current cluster is divided in two balanced clusters, the agents are split in two groups and the agents belonging to the new cluster are notified of the coordinator change. Next the new coordinator registers itself as coordinator in the LUS service and establishes a new replica inside the newly formed cluster (Figure 3).

When the number of agents in a cluster becomes too small the cluster is eliminated by merging it with an adjacent cluster. For this the coordinator issues a merging request to the target cluster coordinator. This results in a merge of known topologies, followed by the notification of new members about the change of the coordinator and secondary replica. The old cluster coordinator also becomes the secondary replica of the newly merged cluster (Figure 4).

Figure 3. The creation of a new cluster

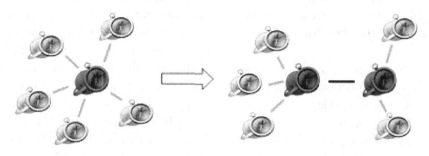

Figure 4. Merging of two clusters

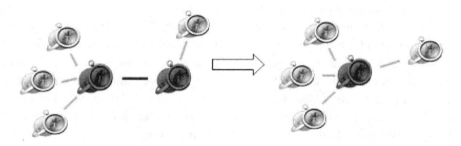

The *second level* (Figure 1) implements the monitoring and data logging functions. At this layer the agents monitor other agents based on a pull model. The agent periodically sends heartbeat messages to another agent and samples the timestamps of the received answers. Periodically, every number of seconds, a heartbeat message is sent to the associated agent. Based on the response, each agent keeps a list of suspicion values associated with each other monitored agent. This suspicion value represent the degree of confidence that the agent suspects the other agent failed (a value closer to 1) or not (a value closer to 0). Therefore, the suspicion value is a value between 0 and 1. The final interpretation of the suspicion value is left to the application.

An update of the suspicion value also triggers the logging of the current state. A registered application may require starting or stopping monitoring a certain process. When an agent receives a start monitor request, a discovery process is started to locate the agent to which the specified process is registered. First the agent searches agent to which to communicate inside the same cluster. There is a high probability that the monitored process runs inside the same cluster because schedulers generally schedule several tasks belonging to the same application for execution in the same cluster (or a relative small number of adjacent clusters) to minimize communication delays. If the process is not found in the local cluster, then the agent delegate the location function to the coordinator. The coordinator forwards the discovery request to all known coordinators. When receiving an inter-cluster discovery request each coordinator performs a local search. In case of a positive match, the coordinator further delegates a local agent to monitor the specified process and sends back a response to the primary source with the necessary monitoring information. Delegation is a particular case of monitoring as it is done remotely and the primary monitoring agent will only interrogate, on application request, the delegated agent about the status of the monitored process that is its associated suspicion level. Also, the delegated agent notifies the primary monitoring agent when the suspicion level exceeds the threshold given by the application.

Although the coordinator handles local communication, the monitoring function in particular is implemented using direct communication between agents. Therefore, to eliminate inconsistencies the coordinator notifies all members when a certain agent is removed from the cluster so that their monitoring is stopped and all involved applications notified of disconnection.

We also assume that processes can experience permanent or transient failures. In practice a process that cannot respond for a certain period of time is considered to be failed as no other process can use its services. A failure detection agent can decide that a process has failed due to several factors, such as the failure of the workstation on which the agent is running (e.g., hardware malfunction), the loss of a direct communication link with the monitored process, an increase in network traffic resulting in delayed responses from the interrogated agents, or a high load of the workstation on which the process is running

resulting in an increase in the response time which can be incorrectly detected as a failure (Figure 5).

It is difficult to determine the nature of an error that affects a certain process, even when using a sophisticated detection algorithm. In an unstable network, with frequent losses of messages or high process failure rate, any detection algorithm is almost irrelevant, because the agents cannot distinguish between permanent and transient failures. The *third level* of the architecture (see Figure 1) attempts to solve this drawback by using a gossiping algorithm whose role is to increase the confidence of an agent in the failure of a process. The gossiping schema aims to eliminate false negatives (wrong suspicions) and false positives (processes are considered to be running correctly even though they have failed). For this the agents monitor each other and periodically exchange local information containing the status of known agents. Also, at this layer the agent implements the solution for the interpretation of monitored data. The agent uses a special algorithm for the analysis and data processing to determine the current status of processes as quickly and thoroughly as possible.

Figure 5. Information flow within the failure detector

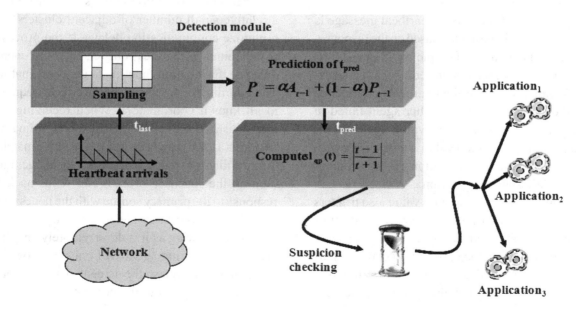

Heartbeat messages arrival times are sampled and used to estimate the time when the next heartbeat is expected to arrive. The estimation function relies on a modified version of the exponential moving average (EMA) method named KAMA (Kaufman's adaptive moving average). This method ensures a dynamic smooth factor based on the most recent timestamps. The predicted value is subsequently used to determine the suspicion level of the corresponding process. The contribution of a heartbeat H increases from 0, meaning that H is not yet expected, to 1, meaning that H is considered lost. Unlike other existing implementations of accrual detectors, the suspicious level in this case is not computed based only on local heartbeat contributions, but also considers the contributions received from other failure detectors located in the local cluster (received using the gossip approach).

The suspicion level represents the degree of confidence in the failure of a certain process. While in case of accrual detection the suspicion level increases on a continuous scale without an upper bound, in this case the suspicion level takes values in the [0, 1] interval. A value of 0 corresponds to a functional process, while as the value approaches to 1 the probability of failure increases as well. Each failure detector maintains a local suspicion level value $sl_{qp}(t)$ for every monitored process computed according to:

$$sl_{qp}(t) = \frac{t - 1}{t + 1}, \; where \; t = \frac{t_{now}}{t_{pred}} \qquad (1)$$

The contribution function limits the suspicion values to the [0, 1] interval, maintaining a relatively quick evolution in the [0, 0.8] interval and a very slow one in the [0.8, 1] interval. For a certain threshold the probability of failure is very high. When a process fails, its corresponding agent does not receives *alive requests*. This leads to an increase in the suspicion level associated to that particular process up to a value closer to 1. There-

fore, every heartbeat message that is not received leads to a higher suspicion level and so to a high probability of failure. On each *alive request* the monitoring agent updates the suspicion level of the queried process based on the current time and the last prediction. If no answer is received since the last update the predicted value is not changed. As the message is delayed the difference between current time and the last prediction increases and becomes and the suspicion value gets closer to 1.

The gossiping protocol is next responsible with the exchange of information between the nodes in the system. A traditional gossip protocol is based on a probabilistic model in which nodes randomly choose partners with whom they exchange information, leading to uneven distribution of monitoring data. Some agents might receive gossip messages more often than others and so the latter get to wrongly suspect or not at all the monitored processes. But, on the other hand, a traditional gossiping algorithm has several advantages: a simpler implementation, a fast dissemination of the monitoring data, no need to know the adjacent topology, the independence of the dimension of the clusters and topology changes, and it does not depend on a certain agent or on the delivery of a certain gossip message.

Because the traditional approach is unpractical, in the context of the current failure detection system a modified gossip protocol was used. First we reconsidered the drawbacks caused by the communication layer as it eliminated the initial advantage of independence of any topology change. In our approach no agent except for the coordinator and the secondary replica should know the topology. This technique is essential for minimizing the number of local messages, but in case of a traditional gossip algorithm this would require supplementary mechanisms to treat all inconsistencies generated by topology changes. This could further lead to a situation where agents in different clusters would communicate directly. In order to prevent such problems the coordinator might have to notify all agents in case of reconfiguration, providing the new topology as well, which would lead inherently to the transmission of large amounts of redundant information. On the other hand, because a probabilistic broadcast of information is not acceptable due to considerable penalties in terms of detection time and detection accuracy, we needed to create an optimized algorithm to disseminate gossiping information in a homogeneous manner. This is difficult to accomplish in an environment in which each agent knows only a subset of agents (the agents from which it received gossip messages) (Figure 6).

The designed solution consists in partitioning the cluster into groups of agents of a predetermined size (power of two). At each group level we apply a simple gossip algorithm, having the following properties:

- Each agent has a local view which changes dynamically, depending on the topology updates. Any agent from the same group has the same local view.
- Each agent also maintains a local list with gossiping information. A record of this list contains the identifier of the agent, the associated suspicion level and the timestamp of the last update.

- Each agent also maintains an internal counter to indicate the current round. The counter is reset when reaching the number of rounds necessary to disseminate the gossiping information to all members in the group.
- Periodically, every T_{gossip} seconds, each agent updates the local list by modifying the suspicion level for each entry, according to the Equation 1. Then it chooses a partner from the local view, based on a Round-Robin algorithm, to which it sends the local list.
- Periodically, every $T_{broadcast}$ seconds, each agent sends a broadcast request to the coordinator with local gossiping information. The coordinator then broadcasts the received data to all agents in other groups, but not outside the cluster.
- When receiving a gossip message from a group member, the agent merges the local list with the one received, choosing the minimum suspicion level for each entry on condition that the received value is more recent than the local value (meaning that it has been modified at a later time compared with the last local update).

Figure 6. Information flow in case of a gossip group consisted of 6 agents

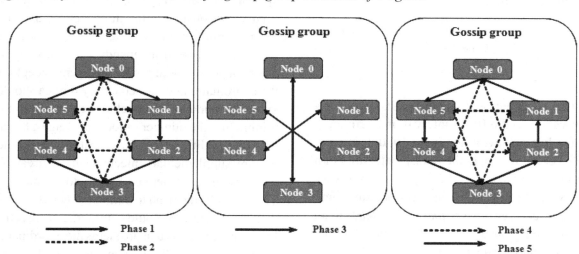

- When receiving a broadcasted gossip message, the agent checks the state of all monitored objects and updates the suspicion level if case as in the previous step. Furthermore an additional check is done to ensure that the new suspicion level value does not indicate failure. Therefore, if failure detected, that is the suspicion level exceeded the threshold of various applications, the concerned applications must be notified for specific actions to be executed.
- Every T_{gossip} seconds each agent also verifies the local list. If no gossip messages have been received from a group member more that $T_{cleanup}$ seconds and the associated suspicion level is large enough we can correctly assume the agent has failed and so requesting its exclusion from the cluster is perfectly justifiable.

In order to understand how gossiping actually works we can consider a simple case when upon request an agent monitors an agent from another group and from various reasons it loses touch with that agent and gets to suspect it. Then it receives a gossip message from a group member and/or a gossip broadcast revealing that the suspected object is still functional. The suspicion level is updated according to the received rumor and the monitored agent is no longer suspected. Until the transient failure disappears, the above process is likely to be repeated several times, but at some point the suspicion level will redress and indicate a functional object.

Finally, the *last layer* (Figure 1) is represented by the service capabilities being provided to various applications running on top of the LSDS. As in case of accrual failure detectors, we provide a complete decoupling between monitoring and interpretation. The failure detection architecture follows the SOA approach, the applications being able to invoke several functions of failure detectors using a standardized service approach. Also, this approach has the advantage of coping well with various existing service-based middleware platforms. Firstly an application must *register* to a failure detector in order to use its capabilities and *unregister* if failure detection is no longer needed. Upon registration the application will receive a *unique id* based on which all future requests will be issued. At this point only three actions are possible: *start monitoring* of a certain process with a given threshold so that if the suspicion level exceeds the specified threshold the application will be notified, *stop monitoring* when the monitored process is no longer of interest and *query* in order to obtain the status of a monitored process that is its associated suspicion level.

The architecture is designed to scale well and provide timely detection. For that, we combine the advantages of several proposed failure detection solutions. We believe that, in order to cope with the large scale nature of today's distributed systems, a failure detector must scale well and also the probability of false detections must not be influence by the number of monitored processes. For that, the gossip-based protocol provides several advantages: the probability that a member is falsely reported as having failed is minimized; the algorithm scales well and delivers minimum detection time and network loads. We combined these properties with those introduced by the accrual detectors. Such detectors provide a lower-level abstraction that avoids the interpretation of monitoring information (Figure 7).

A value that represents a suspicion level is associated with each process, which is then left to the application to be interpreted. In this way a real-time application could take quicker decision on processes being considered failed, while applications requiring a high-level of confidence in their decisions (such as a data warehouse synchronization service) might require higher level of confidence that a process has really failed. By setting an appropriate threshold, applications can then trigger suspicions and perform appropriate actions.

Figure 7. Structure of the accrual failure detectors. Monitoring and interpretation are decoupled. Applications interpret a common value based on their own interpretation

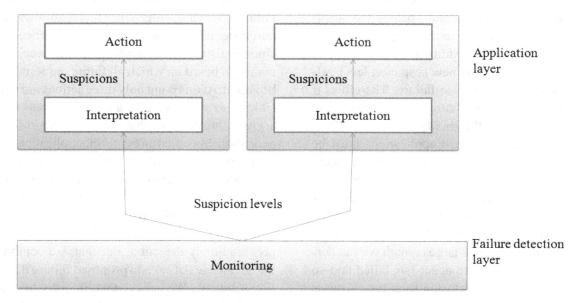

EXPERIMENTAL RESULTS

In order to evaluate the failure detection system we considered four scenarios. The purpose of the first scenario is to test the basic functionality, while the second highlights the overall performances. The following scenarios focus on the scalability of this solution. In the process of setting the scenarios we started from the idea that an agent must correctly detect failures in a reasonable time (scenario 1) and use a minimum amount of resources on the workstation where it runs, plus it should maintain a low number of messages sent for monitoring and control (scenario 2). The testbed involved four stations, two located in Switzerland, and two in Romania (Figure 8).

The first scenario consists of a set of simple experiments that evaluated the correct detection of failures. The idea was to simulate both permanent (forced crash of an agent) and transient faults (temporary interruptions in the network connections to simulate message loss). We also tested

Figure 8. The topology used in the experiments

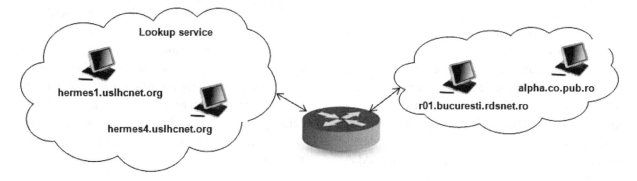

various values for configuration parameters such as the sliding *window size* and *gossip rate*.

On each node an agent has been started, while the LUS service has been running on *hermes1. uslhcnet.org*. For this experiment we considered a gossip group size of four.

The four agents form a cluster and also a gossip group. At one point, an agent is interrupted in order to see how the other agents react to its failure. The study shows how the window size influences the evolution of the suspicion level, given the fact that the smoothing factor used for prediction is closely related to the number of analyzed *actual values* (that is the size of the window). In addition, an important aspect of this scenario is the impact of a particular gossip rate over detection time.

The first experiment shows the evolution of the suspicion level of the failed agent within the three functional agents. For that we considered different values for the sliding window size (5, 10, 15) and various gossip rates (4, 6, 8, 16 seconds). The results show that the failure has been correctly detected in less than 20 minutes, which is a realistic result for a system where suspicions must follow a balanced growth in order to allow stations that experience transient faults to eventually recover from error. The results also show an increase in the detection time as the gossip rate increases regardless of the window size.

Therefore, the detection time can be adjusted accordingly by changing the gossip rate. In addition, the graph in Figure 9 shows that for a window size of 15 and a low gossip interval (4

Figure 9. The evolution of the suspicion level for a gossip interval of 4 seconds

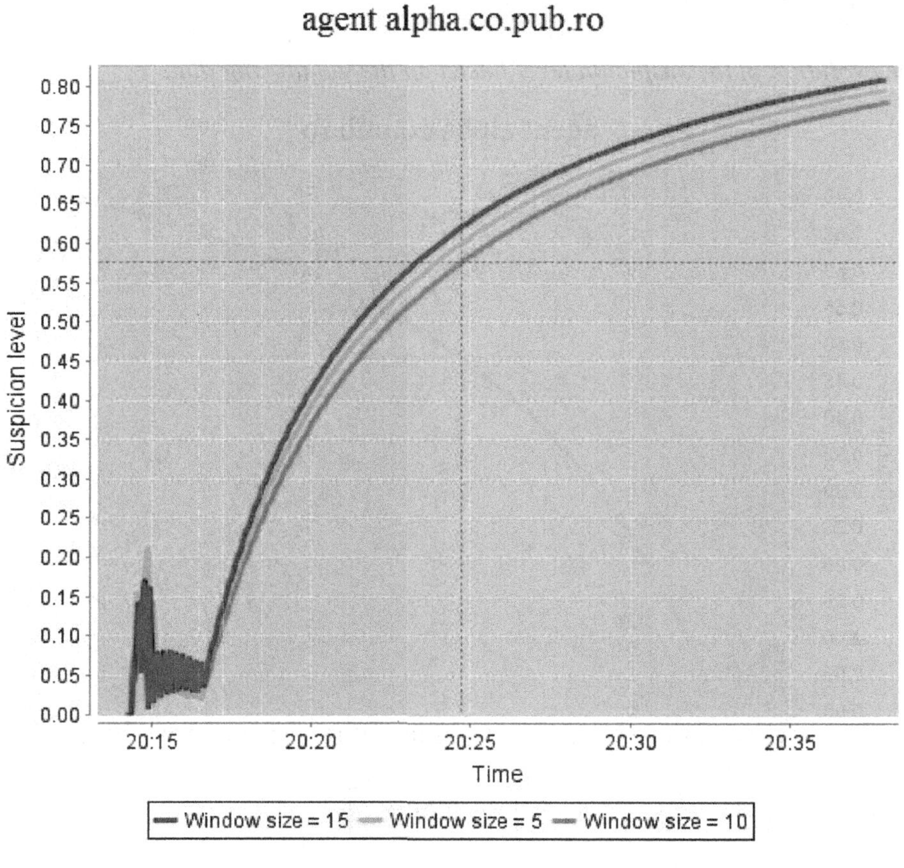

agent alpha.co.pub.ro

seconds, 6 seconds) we obtained the lowest detection time, while for larger gossip rates (8 seconds, 16 seconds) a smaller window size is better to be used, especially when fast detection is mandatory. Choosing a particular value for a configuration parameter largely depends on what we want to achieve through detection.

These results show that the suspicion level reaches the threshold of 0.7 in a reasonable time. An evolution beyond this threshold is slower in order to ensure the settlement of workstations that fail often. In conclusion, the algorithm used for updating the suspicion level successfully assures greater level of confidence in the failure of a station.

The second test evaluated the evolution of the suspicion level based on monitoring data. Here we have considered three applications using the detection service: one application only registers itself to its local failure detector, while the other two start monitoring it. At certain moments the applications query their detection modules about the status of the monitored process.

In this experiment both applications have used a suspicion threshold of 0.7. At one point the agent to which the monitored process is registered crashes. If before the failure the suspicion level remains close to 0, after the crash there is a continuous increase of it, so that when the threshold of 0.7 is crossed both applications received failure notifications. The graph obtained using monitoring data (Figure 10) is consistent with the one obtained based on gossiping information. Although given the fact that there is only one gossip group in this experiment, there was no need to update the local monitoring information through gossiping information, in large systems this is the only way to deal with transient errors, so it is important that the provided information is correct and as stringent as possible.

Figure 10. The evolution of the suspicion level based on the monitoring data

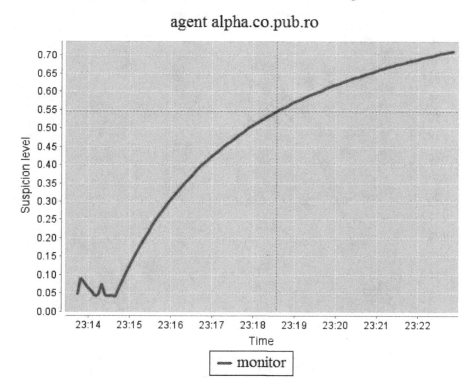

The second series of experiments assumed the use of LISA, a lightweight dynamic service that provides complete system and application monitoring (Dobre, et al., 2007). In this case the objective was to evaluate the network traffic and load of the workstations on which agents are running in order to demonstrate the non-intrusive characteristic of the failure-detection system.

These experiments were performed using gossip rates of four seconds and eight seconds, and demonstrate that the overhead caused by running agents is very low, both in terms of network traffic and CPU usage or system load.

The results in Figure 11 show that the peak traffic for this experiment did not exceed 1.20 Mbps for a gossiping rate of eight seconds. The increase in traffic corresponds to the entry of new agents in the cluster, which leaded to the reconfiguration of the groups and the transmission of data to all affected members. When the detec-

tion system stabilizes there is a decrease in the network traffic, even in the context of the gossip group enlargement. Also, the CPU remains idle at a rate of 97.05%.

In conclusion, the experimental results show that the detection system does not affect the performance of the system on which it runs (Figure 12). There are small increases in the load of the system observed in case of reconfigurations (when an agent enters or exits the cluster), but even in this case we demonstrated a small load on the workstations, even for frequent changes of topology. In addition, the network is not overloaded with control and monitoring messages.

The next experiments tested the scalability of the detection system. For these experiments we created a set of automatic tests to simulate various types of errors for a given amount of time and also at a specific rate.

Figure 11. The results for the evolution of the network traffic

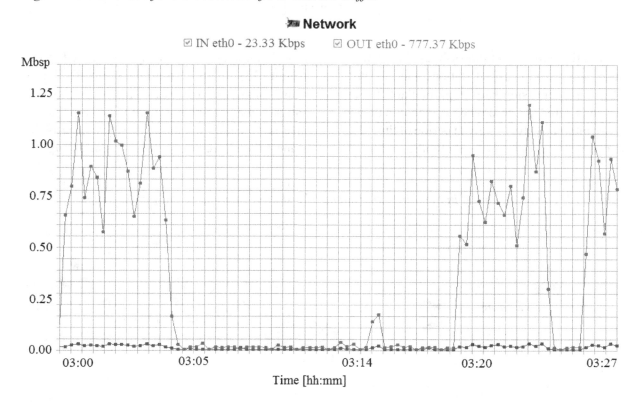

Figure 12. The results for the load

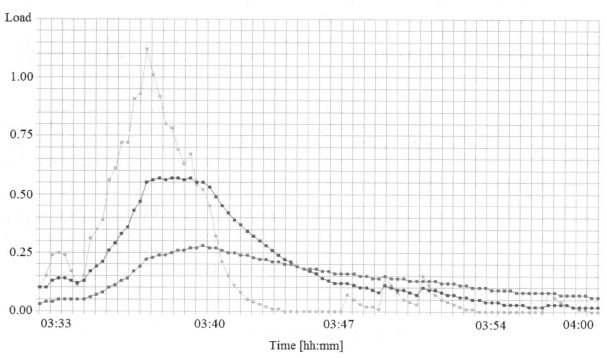

The first experiment shows the evolution of the suspicion level in case of stations that fail quite often. In order to simulate this particular behavior we considered the case when an agent is up and down alternatively for a given period of time. The experiments consisted of six rounds, each of 10 minutes, during which the agents marked in red (Figure 13) are up for 5 minutes and afterwards down for another 5 minutes. The cluster configuration considers one gossip group (gossip group size is 4): agent on *hermes1.uslhcnet.org* is the principal and agent on *hermes4.uslhcnet.org* the

Figure 13. The testbed used in the third experiment. The stations marked in red fail on a regular basis.

secondary replica. The configuration parameters values are window size of 10 and gossip rate of 8 seconds.

The results show an accurate detection flow within the functional agents. Figure 14 shows that both agents (on *hermes1.uslhcnet.org* and *alpha. co.pub*) are able to correctly detect the transient errors. When the faulty agents go *offline* their suspicion levels increase continuously. When agents go *online* the suspicion levels quickly drop close to 0. Also, agents on *alpha.co.pub* and *hermes1.uslhcnet.org* which don't experience any errors in the experiment have a very low suspicion level (very close to 0). Importantly, the suspicion level evolution adjusts to the faulty environment by suspecting less an agent that has suffered transient errors repeatedly. Therefore, considering the case of agent on *hermes4.uslhcnet.org* (Figure 14) for example, we can see that the maximum value reached by the suspicion level per round decreases every round. Also, the more time the agent is up and running, the higher the level of confidence is, which leads to a very low suspicion level that ensures a slower growth in case of an error. This proves that the agent adapts well to various error conditions and remains flexible while being independent on a particular type of error.

In conclusion this particular experiment underlines the capability of the agent to react correctly to an unstable environment regardless of geographic position and system load.

The next experiment targeted the reaction of agents when direct network link between two hosts is lost. In order to simulate this behavior we have considered the case when a firewall appears between two stations on a regular basis (Figure 15).

This experiment considered 6 rounds of the steps previously described. Each round lasts 10 minutes: 5 minutes correspond to firewall disabled while the other 5 minutes to firewall enabled. In order to simulate the firewall we used the *iptables* service from *xr01.bucuresti.rdsnet.ro* by adding rules to drop any packets sent to and received from *hermes1.uslhcnet.org* so that targeted stations will be unable to communicate. Thus any direct link will be lost and any communication attempt while firewall enabled will end with timeout.

```
iptables -t filter -I INPUT -s hermes1.uslhcnet.org -j DROP
iptables -t filter -I OUTPUT -d hermes1.uslhcnet.org -j DROP
```

The cluster configuration is slightly different from previous case: *hermes4.uslhcnet.org* is the principal, while *xr01.bucuresti.rdsnet.ro* is the

Figure 14. Suspicion level evolution in case of agent on hermes4.uslhcnet.org (left) and apha.co.pub.ro (right) as detected by agent on hermes1.uslhcnet.org

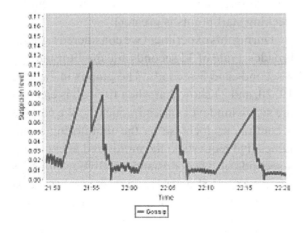
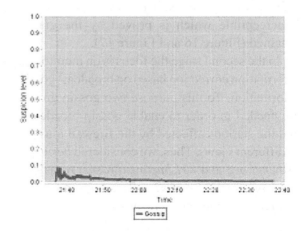

Figure 15. Testbed for the fourth experiment. A firewall is enabled between stations hermes1.uslhcnet. org and r01.bucuresti.rds.net on a regular basis.

secondary replica. In the first stage there is only one gossip group of size 4 as we are only interested in the correctness of the gossiping algorithm. As such *hermes1.uslhcnet.org* and *xr01.bucuresti.rdsnet. ro* must not suspect each other of failure due to received gossip messages from *hermes4.uslhcnet. org* and *alpha.co.pub.ro* that are not affected by firewall activation and so can communicate with any member of the cluster.

In this case *hermes1.uslhcnet.org* and *r01. bucuresti.rdsnet.ro* have no way to suspect each other as in one gossip cycle that ensures complete gossip data propagation (each member receives one gossip message from every other member) gossip messages received from *hermes4.uslhcnet. org* and *alpha.co.pub.ro* indicate that the unreachable peer is up and running. Given the size of the gossip group and low gossip rate (8 seconds) the effect is instantaneous that is the error is almost imperceptible which is proved by the graphs obtained (Figure 16 and Figure 17).

In the second stage the focus is on monitoring information correction based on broadcast gossip information. To this purpose two gossip groups are needed in order to enable gossip broadcasts and the stations affected by the firewall must be in different views. Thus, we considered *hermes4. uslhcnet.org* and *r01.bucuresti.rdsnet.ro* as one gossip group and *hermes1.uslhcnet.org* and *alpha. co.pub.ro* as the other. In order to activate the

monitoring service two applications are used of which one is registered to *r01.bucuresti.rdsnet. ro* while the other to *hermes1.uslhcnet.org* (Figure 18). Application 2 issues a monitoring request for Application 1 and so *hermes1.uslhcnet.org* (monitoring agent) begins to monitor *r01.bucuresti.rdsnet.ro* (monitored agent). Also, *application 2* will query the status of *application 1* repeatedly until threshold is exceeded or failure/disconnect notification is received. When the firewall is enabled the suspicion level of the monitored agent increases until corrected based on gossip broadcast received from *hermes4.uslhcnet.org*.

The suspicion level growth depends on the difference between the monitor rate and gossip broadcast rate. The greater the difference the more it is overdue the correction of the suspicion level and so the graph will have larger variations (that is the period of time between consecutive failure tracking start points is greater).

During this experiment we considered a gossip broadcast rate of 32 seconds and monitor rates of 4 seconds and 8 seconds. The graphs in Figures 19, 20, and 21 show that when firewall is enabled the suspicion level varies frequently. We can see a continuous increase as the monitoring agent issues live requests to the monitored agent every 4 seconds or 8 seconds and no alive response is received. Growth continues until gossip broadcast is received (~32 seconds) which shows that the

Figure 16. Suspicion level evolution in case of agent on r01.bucuresti.net.ro as detected by agent on hermes1.uslhcnet.org

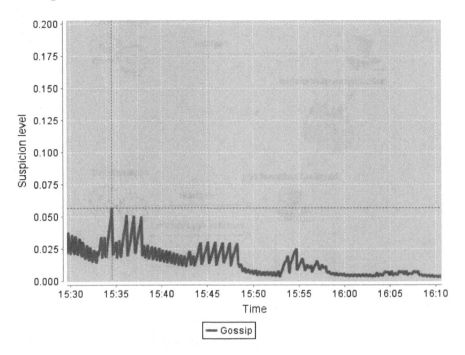

Figure 17. Suspicion level evolution in case of agent on hermes1.uslhcnet.org as detected by agent on r01.bucuresti.net.ro

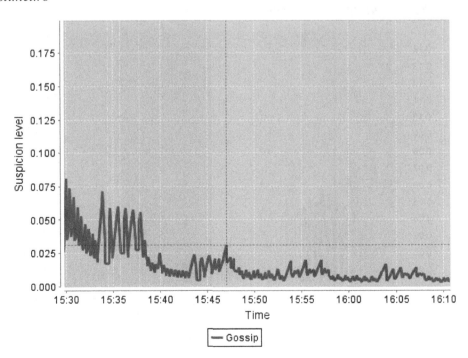

Figure 18. Monitoring configuration: Application 2 monitors Application 1 using our failure detection system

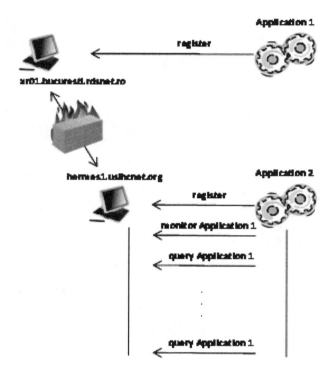

Figure 19. Suspicion level evolution in case of agent on r01.bucuresti.net.ro as monitored by agent on hermes1.uslhcnet.org (gossip rate of 4 seconds)

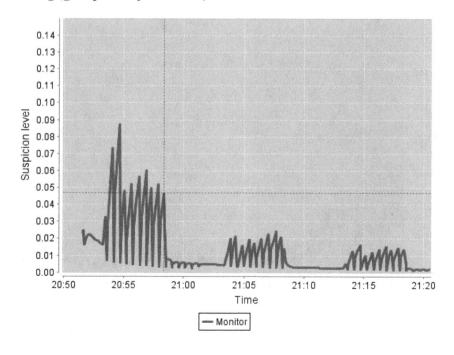

Figure 20. Suspicion level evolution in case of agent on r01.bucuresti.net.ro as monitored by agent on hermes1.uslhcnet.org (gossip rate of 8 seconds)

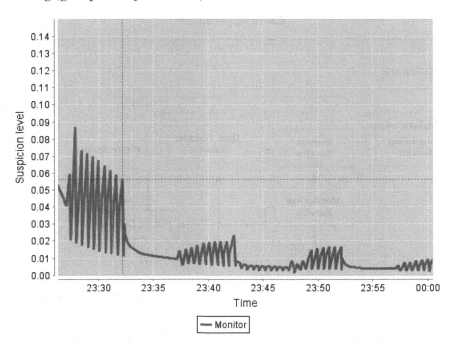

monitored agent is up and running and so local monitor data is updated based on gossip data. Consequently, the suspicion level drops significantly, but will resume growth until next gossip broadcast.

On the other hand, when firewall is disabled no variation is present as the suspicion level stabilizes near 0. Furthermore, as in previous case, the agent adapts to the faulty environment as shown by the decrease in the amplitude of the variations.

Relation with an Architecture for Dependable Large Scale Distributed Systems

The research presented in this paper for failure detection is part of a larger, unified solution for fault tolerance in LSDS. The software architecture for dependable LSDS follows a service-oriented design. The LSDS consists of a loosely-coupled set of services that use the functions of the op-

erating system and provide functions as required by higher-level applications. We approach fault tolerance at the operating system level, and also at the middleware level. The solutions for the middleware layer are presented in (Nastase et al., 2009). The operating system level solutions are presented in (Cristea et al., in press).

The middleware layer is composed of services providing functions such as communication, resource management, scheduling, data storage, etc. To these services we added several ones necessary for dependability. These services are capable to detect and recover from failures, using the solution proposed in this paper, or to enforce additional security mechanisms. The services are designed to cope with a wide-range of failures, both hardware and software. They can detect, react, and confine problems such that to tolerate failures. They can also learn and adapt the behavior of the system, and are able to predict possible failures. In addition, we make no assumption about the actual services composing the LSDS. The proposed services can

Figure 21. The architecture for dependable large scale distributed systems

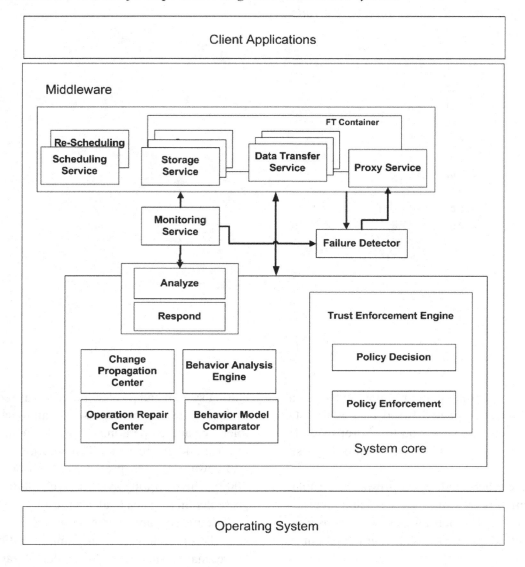

be used with various services for communication or monitoring for example. This promotes reuse and can simplify interoperability with existing large scale distributed infrastructures.

The software architecture of the dependable LSDS middleware is presented in Figure 21. The components that ensure the fault tolerance, job rescheduling, monitoring, fault detection, etc. are included. The system core, locating within the middleware, coordinates, integrates and provides a fault tolerant execution environment for these components. It also manages survivability and redundancy mechanisms. The architecture is designed to easily be integrated in existing distributed infrastructures, allows smooth extensions with other facilities and provides interoperability support to work with components developed using various technologies.

The architecture includes mechanisms to ensure resilience based on replicating components of the system that are responsible for communication, storage and computation. The replicas are further executed in fault-tolerant containers. These containers are supervised by a Proxy service that recovers the state of the system in the presence of failures. The Proxy service uses the information from Failure Detector and Monitoring services.

In addition, the architecture includes components that learn the conditions that led to failures such that to adapt and take proactive steps in recognizing faulty situations. The Analyze and Respond service (Figure 21) continuously analyzes data collected from an external monitoring system. The component responsible with the real-time analysis of monitored data is the Behavior Analysis Engine. The analyzer uses the services provided by the Behavior Model Comparator. This service contains behavior patterns that previously led to failures. A failure detector continuously monitors the state of the resources within the distributed system. When a failure is detected, the conditions that led to its manifestation are learned, and a behavior model is created. The Behavior Model Comparator is then further used to compute the probability of having the system pass through the chain of conditions which eventually lead to failure. When such a condition is detected the Operation Repair Center service initiates appropriate correction operations. This can be, for example, the instantiation of an alternative service that can replace the activity offered by the faulty service or could represent an instruction sent to a Scheduling Service to reschedule jobs. In (Cristea et al., in press) we also demonstrated the use of checkpointing coupled with virtualization techniques to be used to recover from failures. In this case the Operation Repair Center can be used to initiate a rollback action to a state previously saved. The correction mechanism can also use external services provided by the middleware (for example, for checkpointing Condor already provides a dedicated service). Once the repair action is determined it is propagated throughout the distributed system by the Change Propagation Center component.

The architecture includes several services. Some are internal, but we also use external services. For example, our proposed solutions involve communication with services providing functionalities in various parts of the distributed system. The data is collected by a monitoring service. The checkpointing capability involves dealing with a storage service. The state of the system is received from a central indexing service of the underlying middleware. A job failure can initiate a dialog between the services provided by the presented architecture and a scheduling service. The detection of failures, as well as propagation of recovery actions use a data transfer service. In this paper we presented a service constructed internally, within the service architecture, for fault tolerance. It provides the capability to adaptively detect faults.

With our approach, the process of dealing with faults is based on an accrual detector capable of dealing with both the QoS constraints coming from the applications, as well as the imperfect nature of the distributed environment. The error detection phase is complemented with the analysis of the data coming from a real-time monitoring of the distributed system by a monitoring module, using custom built modules within the MonALISA framework. The modules perform background audits that determine whether a service is functioning correctly or not. This approach was presented in Costan et al. (2010).

CONCLUSION

As society increasingly becomes dependent of distributed systems (Grid, P2P, network-based) it becomes more and more imperative to engineer solutions to achieve reasonable levels of dependability for such systems. Failure detection constitutes a fundamental abstraction for fault tolerant distributed systems.

In this paper we presented a failure detection system that combines the power of existing approaches: fast propagation of information as offered by gossip-based failure detection approaches together with the decoupling of monitoring and interpretation as offered by the accrual failure detection solutions. The solution is based on the use of prediction functions and a new alternative of computing the contribution function. The approach has several advantages, among which we mention a better estimation of the inter-arrival times of heartbeat messages and an increase level of confidence in the suspicions of processes being failed.

The approach considers both the various networking conditions of large scale distributed systems and the different QoS detection requirements coming from various applications. In our approach the interpretation of the suspicion level is left to the distributed application using it. In this way multiple applications, having different QoS requirements, use the same failure detectors in different ways. The application could take either conservative (slow and accurate) or aggressive (fast, but inaccurate) decisions.

In the future, we aim to fully deploy this solution in various existing system and compare the obtained performances against other existing solutions. We also plan to extend the architecture in order to include not only detection capabilities, but also means to allow application to automatically asses various recovery and masking (redundancy) mechanisms.

ACKNOWLEDGMENT

The research presented in this paper is supported by Romanian national project "TRANSYS – Models and Techniques for Traffic Optimizing in Urban Environments," Project "CNCSIS-PD" ID: 238.

REFERENCES

Bertier, M., Marin, O., & Sens, P. (2002). Implementation and performance evaluation of an adaptable failure detector. In *Proceedings of the International Conference on Dependable Systems and Networks*, Edinburgh, Scotland (pp. 354-363).

Chandra, T. D., & Toueg, S. (1996). Unreliable failure detectors for reliable distributed systems. *Journal of the ACM, 43*(2), 225–267. doi:10.1145/226643.226647

Chen, W., Toueg, S., & Aguilera, M. K. (2002). On the quality of service failure detectors. *IEEE Transactions on Computers, 51*(2), 13–32. doi:10.1109/12.980014

Costan, A., Dobre, C., Pop, F., Leordeanu, C., & Cristea, V. (2010). A fault tolerance approach for distributed systems using monitoring based replication. In *Proceedings of the 6th IEEE International Conference on Intelligent Computer Communication and Processing*, Cluj-Napoca, Romania (pp. 451-458).

Cristea, V., Dobre, C., Pop, F., Stratan, C., Costan, A., & Leordeanu, C. (in press). A dependability layer for large scale distributed systems. *International Journal of Grid and Utility Computing*.

Defago, X., Hayashibara, N., & Katayama, T. (2003). On the design of a failure detection service for large-scale distributed systems. In *Proceedings of the International Symposium on Towards Petabit Ultra Networks*, Ishikawa, Japan (pp. 88-95).

Dobre, C., Pop, F., Costan, A., Andreica, M. I., & Cristea, V. (2009). Robust failure detection architecture for large scale distributed systems. In *Proceedings of the 17th International Conference on Control Systems and Computer Science*, Bucharest, Romania.

Dobre, C., Voicu, R., Muraru, A., & Legrand, I. C. (2007). A distributed agent based system to control and coordinate large scale data transfers. *In Proceedings of the International Conference on Control Systems and Computer Science*, Bucharest, Romania.

Fetzer, C., Raynal, M., & Tronel, F. (2001). An adaptive failure detection protocol. In *Proceedings of the 8th IEEE Pacific Rim Symposium on Dependable Computing*, Seoul, Korea (pp. 146-153).

Hayashibara, N., Defago, X., & Katayama, T. (2004). *Flexible failure detection with K-FD*. (Tech. Rep. No. IS-RR-2004-006). Ishikawa, Japan: Japan Advanced Institute of Science and Technology.

Nastase, M., Dobre, C., Pop, F., & Cristea, V. (2009). Fault tolerance using a front-end service for large scale distributed systems. In *Proceedings of 11th International Symposium on Symbolic and Numeric Algorithms for Scientific Computing*, Timisoara, Romania (pp. 229-236).

Stelling, P., Foster, I., Kesselman, C., Lee, C., & von Laszewski, G. (1998). A fault detection service for wide area distributed computations. In *Proceedings of the 7th IEEE Symposium on High Performance Distributed Computing* (pp. 268-278).

Van Renesse, R., Minsky, Y., & Hayden, M. (1998). A gossip-style failure detection service. In *Proceedings of the Middleware Conference*, The Lake District, UK (pp. 55-70).

This work was previously published in the International Journal of Distributed Systems and Technologies (IJDST), Volume 2, Issue 3, edited by Nik Bessis, pp. 64-87, copyright 2011 by IGI Publishing (an imprint of IGI Global).

Chapter 9
Integrating Production Automation Expert Knowledge Across Engineering Domains

Thomas Moser
Vienna University of Technology, Austria

Stefan Biffl
Vienna University of Technology, Austria

Wikan Danar Sunindyo
Vienna University of Technology, Austria

Dietmar Winkler
Vienna University of Technology, Austria

ABSTRACT

The engineering of a complex production automation system involves experts from several backgrounds, such as mechanical, electrical, and software engineering. The production automation expert knowledge is embedded in their tools and data models, which are, unfortunately, insufficiently integrated across the expert disciplines, due to semantically heterogeneous data structures and terminologies. Traditional integration approaches to data integration using a common repository are limited as they require an agreement on a common data schema by all project stakeholders. This paper introduces the Engineering Knowledge Base (EKB), a semantic-web-based framework, which supports the efficient integration of information originating from different expert domains without a complete common data schema. The authors evaluate the proposed approach with data from real-world use cases from the production automation domain on data exchange between tools and model checking across tools. Major results are that the EKB framework supports stronger semantic mapping mechanisms than a common repository and is more efficient if data definitions evolve frequently.

DOI: 10.4018/978-1-4666-2647-8.ch009

INTRODUCTION

Industrial production automation systems depend on distributed software to control the system behavior. The behavior of automation systems must be testable and predictable to meet safety and quality standards. Modern automation systems have to be designed for better interoperability and flexibility to satisfy increasing customer needs for product variety, manufacturing agility, and low cost. In automation systems engineering (ASE) software engineering tasks depend on specification data and plans from a wide range of engineering expert domains in the overall engineering process, e.g., physical plant design, mechanical, and electrical engineering, and production process planning. This expert knowledge is embodied in domain-specific standards, terminologies, people, processes, methods, models, and software (Arndt Lüder, 2000).

However, a major challenge in current industrial development and research approaches is insufficient semantic model integration between the expert disciplines (Biffl, Moser, & Sunindyo, 2009; Schäfer & Wehrheim, 2007). Different and partly overlapping terminologies are used in these expert disciplines, which hampers understanding. Consequently, the weak tool support for semantic integration of the expert knowledge across domain boundaries hinders flexible engineering process automation and quality management, leading to development delays and risks for system operation.

The strategic goal of making the ASE process more flexible without delivering significantly more risky end products translates into the capability to efficiently re-configure the engineering process and tool instances of a project environment. While there are approaches based on a common repository that holds all relevant project data (Schäfer & Wehrheim, 2007), experience has shown that such a repository tends to get large, inflexible, and hard to maintain surprisingly fast, which makes the knowledge in the repository hard to reuse in new projects. Further, if several organizational units are involved in a project, even agreeing on a common data model is difficult. Thus a key goal is to allow all participants to continue using their own data models and provide a mechanism for translation between these data models. In the past several approaches for providing engineering knowledge in machine-understandable syntax have been investigated (Liao, 2005; Lovett, Ingram, & Bancroft, 2000; McGuire et al., 1993). However, these approaches focus primarily on storing existing homogeneous knowledge rather than providing support for managing and accessing heterogeneous knowledge, which is the focus of this work.

In this paper, we introduce an approach for semantic mapping in ASE with a focus on providing links between data structures of engineering tools and systems to support the exchange of information between these engineering tools and thus making ASE more efficient and flexible. The novel Engineering Knowledge Base (EKB) framework stores the engineering knowledge in ontologies and provides semantic mapping services to access design-time and run-time concepts and data. The EKB framework aims at making tasks, which depend on linking information across expert domain boundaries, more efficient. A fundamental example for such engineering tasks is checking the consistency and integrity of design-time and run-time models across tool boundaries (Wahyudin, Schatten, Winkler, Tjoa, & Biffl, 2008).

We evaluate the proposed approach with data from real-world use cases on assembly workshop engineering in the production automation domain. We compare the proposed EKB framework with the traditional approach using a repository with a common data schema for all involved tools. For the evaluation we compare the processes: a) setting up a translation mechanism using either the EKB framework or the common repository and b) using both evaluated approaches for the mentioned engineering task data model checking and analyses across tools for two use case scenarios.

For setting up the data exchange mechanism the major advantage of the EKB in comparison to the traditional approach is that the EKB framework needs no detailed common data schema. Additionally, the number of converters needed between n tool types with a common repository is $O(n^2)$ when using point to point integration, compared to $O(n)$ converters needed when using the EKB framework, since for the EKB for each engineering tool to be integrated only one mapping and transformation to the common domain concepts is needed, while for point to point integration transformations are needed for all possibly used combinations of engineering tools to be integrated. For model checking the EKB framework allows a more generic definition and execution of model checks on an application domain level, and additionally enables more advanced checks regarding the plausibility and semantic correctness of data structures by exploiting the querying capabilities of the EKB ontologies.

The remainder of this work is structured as follows: First we summarize related work on the domain of engineering production automation systems and on semantic integration of engineering knowledge across system boundaries. Then we motivate the research issues and introduce the EKB framework illustrated with real-world use case examples on assembly workshop engineering in the production automation system. We then evaluate the EKB framework and compare it with traditional approach such as a common repository and discuss the results of the comparison. Finally, we present the conclustion and suggest further work.

RELATED WORK

This section summarizes related work on engineering of Production Automation Systems and on Semantic Integration of Engineering Knowledge across systems.

Engineering of Production Automation Systems

Industrial production automation systems include manufacturing systems, such as assembly workshops that combine smaller parts into more complex products, e.g. cars or furniture. Several domains have to cooperate for manufacturing: (a) business order processing and work order scheduling, (b) technical processes for workshop and systems coordination, and (c) technical designs of a set of machines in a defined workshop layout (Lüder, Peschke, & Reinelt, 2006; Winkler, Biffl, & Östreicher, 2009).

Engineering models and Quality Assurance (QA) across disciplines. In engineering disciplines models (e.g., model-based design and testing (Baker, Zhen, Gabrowksi, & Oystein, 2008) help to construct new systems products and to verify and validate the solutions regarding the requirements, specification, and design models. Traditional systems engineering processes follow a water-fall like engineering process with late testing approaches (GAMP 5, 2008). Unfortunately, insufficient attention is paid in the field of automated systems engineering (ASE) to capabilities for QA of software-relevant artifacts and change management across engineering domains (Schäfer & Wehrheim, 2007), possibly due to technical and semantic gaps in the engineering team. Thus, there is considerably higher effort for testing and repair, if defects get identified late in the engineering process.

Engineering process data collection. A general challenge for process assessment is reliable and efficient data collection on the actual practices in a software development project as data collection mostly relies on human reporting and document analysis (Wahyudin et al., 2008). Despite positive findings in validation studies, there is still a gap between the published research results and the successful adoption of objective quality evaluation approaches in real-world projects due to the poor quality of available project data, heterogeneous data sources, and the effort required to extract and collect the necessary data (Fenton & Neil, 1999; Li, Herbsleb, & Shaw, 2005; Mockus, Weiss, & Zhang, 2003). Semantic integration approaches can help to improve data exchange and systematic tracing between models across these disciplines.

Figure 1 illustrates the interaction between some business and engineering roles to design and run a production automation system: workflows (e.g., work order scheduling, workshop coordination and machine assignment) and involved stakeholders (in our case: dispatcher, workshop integrator and operator, systems engineers, and machine vendors). During the engineering process efficient data exchange approaches are necessary to keep an overview on the process status and ensure that shared data elements are consistent at relevant milestones between individual stakeholders from different disciplines, i.e., engineers in the electrical, software, process, and mechatronic application domains. In production automation manufacturing systems a flexible systems design of the workshop layout is desirable to enable fast

Figure 1. Layout and workflow of a production automation system

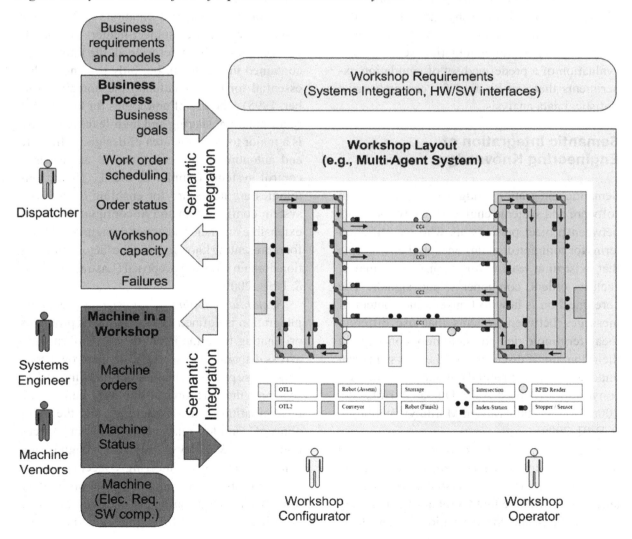

response to changed work orders and minimize systems downtime in case of changes or defects (Winkler et al., 2009).

Production automation research systems. As production automation system for research the Manufacturing Agent Simulation Tool (MAST) (Vrba, 2003) provides a unique combination of multi-agent-based manufacturing control features and a simulator of the manufacturing environment similar to the system illustrated in Figure 1. The system can represent the full range of roles involved in such a complex system: business orders, workshop scheduling strategies, robust workshop control, and control of individual machines in the workshop. The Simulator of Assembly Workshops (SAW) (Merdan, Moser, Wahyudin, & Biffl, 2008) is an extension of the original MAST simulator providing means for automatic execution and evaluation of a predefined set of simulation experiments that can be used for comprehensive statistical data analysis.

Semantic Integration of Engineering Knowledge

Semantic integration bridges semantic gaps in software and systems engineering environments between project participants who use different terms for common domain concepts, i.e., concepts that exist in at least two participating domains, such as orders, components, and signals. The core question is how to translate the content of messages between systems that use different local terminologies for common concepts in their domain of discourse, so these systems can understand each other and conduct a meaningful conversation (Aldred, Aalst, Dumas, & Hofstede, 2006; Hohpe, 2006; Moser, Mordinyi, Sunindyo, & Biffl, 2009).

Engineering knowledge representation with ontologies. A key concept of semantic integration is to provide a machine-understandable representation of knowledge that facilitates the mapping between facts and the derivation of new facts

from the modeled knowledge. In the production automation domain there exist several types of engineering knowledge: local engineering models of particular engineering tools (classes and instances), which use common concepts to enable data exchange, environment information, e.g., on stakeholder roles, processes, tools, and relationships between these entities, and meta-information on data elements, e.g., which stakeholder roles are interested in certain data entities. Ontologies provide effective mechanisms for storing all different types of engineering knowledge, while preserving the original syntax or terminologies and linking knowledge elements using mappings between them.

An ontology is a representation vocabulary for a specific domain or subject matter. The ontology does not seek to describe all the knowledge contained in a domain, but only the knowledge essential for conceptualizing the domain (Gruber, 1995). The use of ontologies for knowledge representation, sharing and high-level reasoning is a major topic in the area of designing flexible and autonomous systems, such as agent-based control systems (Obitko & Marik, 2002). Ontologies are necessary for enabling data-driven system configuration and re-configuration in an extensible manner. The use of domain ontologies for representing knowledge in the factory automation domain has been proposed (Lastra, Delamer, & Ubis, 2009).

Semantic mapping of knowledge. Semantic integration is defined as the solving of problems originating from the intent to share information across disparate and semantically heterogeneous data. These problems include the matching of data schemas, the detection of duplicate entries, the reconciliation of inconsistencies, and the modeling of complex relations in different sources (Noy, Doan, & Halevy, 2005). In an engineering context common engineering concepts can be used as basis for mappings between proprietary tool-specific engineering knowledge and more generic domain-specific engineering knowledge to support transformation between these engineering tools. Engineering knowledge descriptions in ontologies can be the basis to provide mappings between these ontologies to enable semantic integration. Noy (2004) identified three major dimensions of the application of ontologies for supporting semantic integration: the task of finding mappings (i.e., semantic correspondences) semi-automatically, the declarative formal representation of these mappings, and reasoning using these mappings. Semantic mappings can either consist of elements of the same granularity, such as 1:1 mappings of concepts or attributes, or in addition may be expressed using different levels of granularity, such as mapping the attribute of a concept to a target concept or mapping a concept to all inherited sub-concepts of a target concept.

RESEARCH ISSUES

The scope of our work is an ASE team consisting of experts from several engineering disciplines, who work on engineering process tasks with role-specific tools and systems that encapsulate engineering models and project data. As the engineers work together to deliver a product to the end user, they inevitably have to form common concepts on deliverables at interfaces between their work tasks. Such common concepts can be found in elements of requirements, design, and defect descriptions, which concern more than one role. Typical requirements for such engineering process tasks are low delay, i.e., in-time availability of information from other engineering tools and low effort for achieving the information exchange between the engineering tools.

Each engineering role has a tailored tool set that works on data relevant to the engineer's tasks. In order to support the data exchange between these engineering tools, an additional component is needed. Currently, in a typical process step in the engineering process an engineer exports data from

his tool to a transfer document (e.g., PDF of data table) and saves this document in a common repository accessible by a set of partner engineering tools. As alternative to the traditional approach we propose the novel Engineering Knowledge Base (EKB) framework. In comparison to a simple data storage such as a common repository, a knowledge base stores information (i.e., the original data plus meta-data describing links between data elements or annotations of data elements) which can be used to automate time-consuming tasks and support human experts in doing their work.

In this paper, we evaluate and discuss the benefits and limitations of the proposed EKB framework in comparison to a traditional solution using a common repository, in particular, more efficient support for data exchange between automation systems engineering tools. The key goal is to investigate to what extent the explicit and machine-understandable knowledge stored in the EKB helps support time-consuming ASE processes, such as data exchange between tools or model checking across tools. Relevant derived research issues for investigation are:

1. What are the advantages of using the EKB framework for these processes, compared to a common repository?
2. Investigate whether the EKB framework provides an overall more efficient and effective ASE process regarding typical requirements for engineering process tasks such as low delay, low effort for achieving the information exchange between the engineering tools, and flexibility of the approach regarding the involved engineering tools and data definitions.
3. Analyze how the extra effort for involving the EKB framework is likely to pay off in a typical engineering context.

For investigating the research issues we gathered requirements from a set of use cases from an industry case study. Based on these use cases we designed the architecture of the EKB framework and the empirical evaluation.

ENGINEERING KNOWLEDGE BASE FRAMEWORK AND USE CASE

This section introduces the Engineering Knowledge Base (EKB) framework and describes its architecture. Additionally, we identify a set of use cases from assembly workshop engineering, describe the use cases in the context of the SAW production automation research system, and show how these use cases are supported by the EKB framework.

The top part of Figure 2 illustrates the use case scenario with the EKB framework for engineering an assembly workshop for the SAW production automation system. In this example, there are two types of engineers (electrical engineer, software

engineer) who come from to different engineering domains respectively. These roles use specialized engineering tools for their tasks. These tools contain local data sources, which produce and/or consume data with heterogeneous data structures. The EKB is used to facilitate the efficient data exchange between these engineering tools and data sources by providing a so-called "virtual common data model". Based on this data exchange, more complex engineering process tasks like model checking across tools are supported. The bottom part of Figure 2 shows the internal architecture of the EKB.

The general mechanism of the EKB framework uses common engineering concepts identified beforehand as basis for mappings between proprietary tool-specific engineering knowledge and more generic domain-specific engineering knowledge to support transformation between these engineering tools. In the following, the internal architecture of the EKB is described in detail:

Figure 2. EKB use case scenario

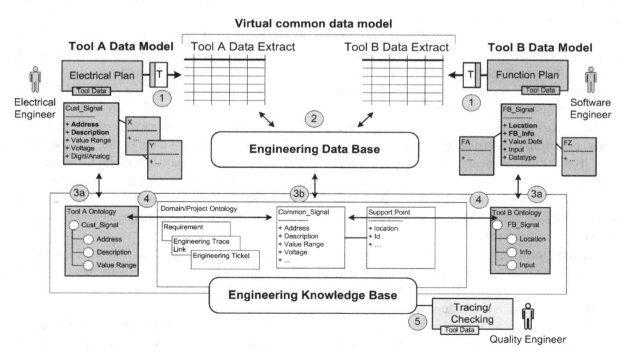

1. **Extraction of Tool Data:** As first step, the data elements contained in a particular tool need to be extracted in order to be available to the EKB framework. Since by now only a few engineering tools provide APIs for directly accessing the contained data, the export functionality of the tools is used. The exported data then is parsed and transformed into an internal format consisting of key-value pairs for each data attribute, which is easier to handle. This extraction mechanism is also a possible way of integrating legacy systems, which usually are hard to adapt or modify internally. However, the possibility of working with the extracted information of such legacy systems forms a powerful means of integrating such systems.

2. **Storage of Extracted Tool Data:** The extracted and transformed key-value pairs are stored using a Java Content Repository (JCR) (Java Community Process, 2009) implementation, the so-called Engineering Data Base (EDB). For data storage, a tree structure is used, and additional functionality like versioning or roll-back is provided. The EDB is indexed and can be queried using Apache Lucene (2010).

3a. **Description of Tool Knowledge:** The tool ontologies define the engineering-tool-specific, proprietary view on the information exchanged (e.g., a list of signals) in an integration scenario. This includes the view on the format of the information, but can also describe the meaning or the use of the specific view on the existing information, since there can exist multiple views for the same information. The most important part of this description is the definition of the exchanged information, i.e., the definition of the data structures either provided or consumed by a tool.

3b. **Description of Domain Knowledge:** The domain ontology contains the relevant shared knowledge between stakeholders in the particular application domain (in our case the Production Automation domain) and hence represents the collaborative view on the information exchanged in an integration scenario. In addition, the domain ontology is the place to model standardized domain-specific information (e.g., the description of concepts used throughout an application scenario such as the application domain independent description of business orders or machines in the context of the SAW production automation system). The proprietary information of the engineering tools, which is defined in the tool ontologies, is mapped to the more general information of the domain ontology in order to allow the interoperability with other engineering tools. In contrast to a common data schema, the knowledge stored in the domain ontology is defined on a more general domain level compared to the knowledge stored in the tool ontologies. This particular domain-specific knowledge described in the domain ontology can easily be updated or transferred to other EKB-based integration scenarios residing in the same domain. This approach allows a broad spectrum of new applications in a particular domain to benefit from the described domain knowledge. In order to support the creation of tool and domain ontologies, we assume that the models are available using well-established modeling standards, e.g., EER diagrams. The models can then easily be transformed into valid OWL ontologies, e.g., by using UML2OWL (http://diplom.ooyoo.de/). If required, the fine-tuning of the ontologies can be performed using an ontology editor, e.g., Protégé (http://protege.stanford.edu/).

4. **Mapping of Tool Knowledge to Domain Knowledge:** Each data structure segment described in the tool ontology is mapped to either exactly one particular corresponding domain concept or domain concept attribute

described in the domain ontology, or to e.g., all inherited sub-concepts of a target concept. In addition, the granularity of the mapped elements does not need to be the same, so that e.g., a concept can be mapped to the attribute of another concept, or vice versa. This defines the semantic context of the information contained in the segment and allows the detection of semantically similar information consumed and produced by other engineering tools. In addition, the format of the information is described, enabling an automated transformation from source to target format. The mapping process can be supported by applying Ontology Alignment methods to provide hints regarding possible mappings.

5. **Usage of the EKB:** The mapping of concepts described in the tool ontologies to common concepts described in the domain ontology allows the creation of transformation instructions. These transformation instructions are the foundation to transform data structures between two engineering tools, because the engineering tools may label or format their data structures in different ways.

Due to the mappings between tool ontologies and domain ontology data structures that are semantically equal can be identified, because they are either aligned to the same domain concept or belong to the same tree segment in the concept tree described in the domain ontology. The transformation instructions can be defined in XML syntax and consist of at least one input and output data structure segment. The segments contain a unique ID and instructions, how the input segment is transformed to an output segment. There is a set of basic transformations that can be combined to more complex transformations, like changing the name of a segment, converting the format using converters, merging or splitting a set of input segments or querying external services for transformation (Moser, Schimper,

Mordinyi, & Anjomshoaa, 2009). Based on these transformations, more complex applications can be implemented which use the integrated data of the virtual common data model to perform advanced tasks like tracing of artifacts, consistency checking across tool boundaries, change impact analyses or notification of stakeholders in case of changes.

Now that we have described the general mechanism and the internal architecture of the EKB framework, the next step is the setup and configuration of the EKB framework. As described in (Biffl, Schatten, & Zoitl, 2009), we suggest to use an enterprise service bus-based approach to integrate engineering tools by describing the data structures they produce and consume as services. The EKB framework acts as a component in the proposed technical integration solution, which performs its transformation service on the message transmitted using the enterprise service bus. After the EKB is set up and configured properly, we show how the EKB framework supports typical engineering tasks, illustrated in the context of the SAW production automation research system.

In this paper we focus on two fundamental use cases for model checking across tool boundaries in the production automation engineering context.

UC-1: *Model consistency checking across tool boundaries.* Model checking, i.e., the validation of model data elements regarding their integrity and consistency, typically is performed at project milestones before the model elements can be used in the next stage of engineering. For a safety-critical domain such as the production automation domain, model checking is required for obtaining relevant system certifications. Currently, model checking is limited to single engineering tools or domains. In addition to syntactical checks, plausibility checks of elements regarding their usage in other engineering domains are needed.

UC-2: *Impact analysis of model value changes.* In difference to single system models, where changes of model values have direct impacts on other model elements, model value changes in cross-domain modeling require additional transformation and checks before the actual impact of a value change can be estimated or measured. In the SAW research system model checks are necessary after concurrent engineering model changes to ensure that models do not violate design constraints. Design-time model checks include checking the workshop layout validity and the availability of all machine functions needed for valid production orders. Run-time model checks include checking sufficient machine capacity for producing orders planned for a shift and checking the impact of relevant machine/conveyor failures on the overall production output.

EVALUATION OF THE EKB SUPPORT FOR ENGINEERING TASKS

In this section, we evaluate the two use cases described both for a traditional approach using a common repository and for the novel EKB framework.

UC-1: Model Checking Across Tool Boundaries

Model checking refers in the evaluation study context to the inspection of model data elements regarding their consistency and integrity. As a first step towards comprehensive model checking, checks of local data structures belonging to a specific engineering tool can be performed. For these checks, no access to data structures of other engineering tools is needed. However, since the data structures of the single models are viewed independent of the data structures of other engineering tools, more advanced checks regarding a combination of data structure of multiple engineer-

ing models. For this use case, we focus on two types of models checks, namely a) consistency and integrity checks of model changes; and b) the derivation of runtime functionality for automated testing and monitoring.

An example for consistency and integrity checks of model changes is a hardware pump which supports a certain number of input/output signals (I/Os), and which is controlled by a pump control software using either analog or digital signal processors. Analog signal processors can handle 8 I/Os, digital 64 I/Os. If the signal processor type is changed in the pump control software model, it needs to be validated whether the new signal processor type can handle all available I/Os of the hardware pump. Respectively, if the I/Os are changed (e.g., new I/Os added) it has to be checked whether they all can be controlled using the chosen signal processor type of the pump control software.

Another example for the derivation of runtime functionality for automated testing and monitoring is again a hardware pump which can handle approximately 1000 liters per hour. A time-based analysis of the events originating from the reservoir located behind the hardware pump could show impossible conditions or sensor states, e.g., if the reservoir capacity of 10000 liters is reached within 5 hours starting from an empty condition.

Common Repository Approach. Using a common repository enables to perform advanced checks regarding the data structures of more than one engineering tool, such as checking the consistency of single data structure elements across tool boundaries or analyzing the possible impact of changes to data structures belonging to a specific engineering tool on the data structures of other engineering tools. The major drawback of this approach of performing model checks is the need for manual involvement of human experts. The experts need to explicitly define the checks and select the data they want to include in these checks. This definition needs to be updated after every change to the involved data elements. Additionally, the nature of the common repository allows only for syntactical checks (e.g., the availability of all obligatory data fields or the validity of data types regarding a certain data schema) of the data, but not for other checks such as regarding the semantic correctness or plausibility of data structures. Other checks, such as checks regarding logical connections of data elements, are not supported out of the box using a common repository, since the data elements in the repository are stored unaltered and without meta-information. However external analysis tools can use the data elements stored in the common repository for performing such model checks.

Engineering Knowledge Base (EKB) Approach. The EKB framework enables automated checks regarding both syntactical issues as well as plausibility checks regarding semantic correctness of data structures. The EKB framework exploits the querying capabilities of ontologies to allow even more advanced checks, such as checks regarding completeness of available information. Human experts define checks regarding specific domain or tool-specific concepts, which are then on-the-fly transformed into checks regarding tool-specific data structures accordingly. The results are then collected and again transformed into the domain concept level, allowing experts both to define checks as well as to view the results of the defined checks in their well-known syntax, terminologies and notations.

UC-2: Analyses Using Information from Multiple Stakeholder Domains

The problem described here corresponds to the sales manager's task of identifying the maximal amount of products that can be produced during a shift. To do this task, the sales manager needs to collect information from other stakeholders and make calculations based on the information collected before getting to the final result.

Common Repository Approach. All information of the process production is placed in the common repository. The sales manager retrieves the needed information out of the common repository, while the other stakeholders put the information in the common repository. The drawbacks of this approach are updates submitted by different stakeholders that are hard to handle concurrently, and different formats and syntax originating from different stakeholders. The sales manager has to deal with other data not necessarily needed for his tasks and manual and therefore error-prone steps are required to get the needed data from other stakeholders. See Box 1.

EKB Approach. By using the EKB framework, the automated analyses are supported using the following these steps (refer also to Figure 3 for a detailed description of these steps using simplified OWL syntax) (W3C, 2004): The sales manager queries the global view to find out the current shift time. The shift time is identified in the global view and the mapping of the shift time to the workshop manager's local view is exploited, and subsequently the shift time is queries in the workshop manager's local view and represented in the global view. As next step, information about the finishing time of the product type of product prod6 is queried in the global view, resulting again in an exploiting of the mapping to the business manager's local view, a query of this local view and a representation of the product type and finishing time of the product prod6 in the global view. Finally, in the global view the maximum amount of products that can be produced in the current shift is calculated using the previously queried information and the result is presented to the sales manager.

DISCUSSION

This section discusses the described EKB framework as well as the initial results of the evaluation with regard to the research issues regarding more efficient support for data exchange for automation systems engineering.

Box 1. EKB framework automated analyses

```
workshop:shift1 workshop:lasts workshop:14400
workshop:shift1 workshop:order workshop:prod6
business:prod6 business:finishingTime business:50
SELECT(?x) WHERE {sales:shift1 sales:lasts ?x}
SELECT(?x) WHERE {global:shift1 global:lasts ?x}
SELECT(?x) WHERE {manager:shift1 manager:lasts ?x}
Result: x = manager:14400
manager:14400 owl:equalTo global:14400
SELECT(?y) WHERE {global:prod6 global:finishingTime ?y}
SELECT(?y) WHERE {business:prod6 business:finishingTime ?y}
Result: y = business:50
business:50 owl:equalTo global:50
SELECT(?z) WHERE {?x owl:equalTo global:shiftTime
?y owl:equalTo global:finishingTime
global:prod6 global:has ?z: x/y)
Result: z = global:288
global:288 owl:equalTo sales:288
```

Figure 3. EKB framework example - identify the maximal amount of products which can be produced in a shift

```
workshop:shift1 workshop:lasts workshop:14400
workshop:shift1 workshop:order workshop:prod6
business:prod6 business:finishingTime business:50

SELECT(?x) WHERE {sales:shift1 sales:lasts ?x}
SELECT(?x) WHERE {global:shift1 global:lasts ?x}
SELECT(?x) WHERE {manager:shift1 manager:lasts ?x}
Result: x = manager:14400

manager:14400 owl:equalTo global:14400

SELECT(?y) WHERE {global:prod6 global:finishingTime ?y}

SELECT(?y) WHERE {business:prod6 business:finishingTime ?y}
Result: y = business:50

business:50 owl:equalTo global:50

SELECT(?z) WHERE {?x owl:equalTo global:shiftTime
?y owl:equalTo global:finishingTime
global:prod6 global:has ?z: x/y)
Result: z = global:288

global:288 owl:equalTo sales:288
```

1. *What are the advantages of using the EKB framework for these processes, compared to using a common repository?* The explicit and machine-understandable knowledge in the EKB framework helps to automate time-consuming automation systems engineering process steps like the exchange of data structures between heterogeneous engineering tools or consistency and completeness checks of data structures. Further, the EKB allows automating later integration processing steps, like automatically generating transformation instructions for data structure exchange between the integrated engineering tools. The major difference between the two evaluated approaches is the lack of the need for a common data schema when using the EKB framework, which can be seen as the main advantage of the EKB framework compared to a common repository. However, additional expert skills are necessary when using a fairly new technology in a quite traditional application context.

2. *Investigate whether the EKB framework provides an overall more efficient and effective ASE process regarding typical requirements for engineering process tasks such as low delay and low effort for achieving the information exchange between the engineering tools.* The advantage of centrally storing the domain knowledge together with the mappings of individual tool knowledge lies in the possibility of an automated QA and automation of further engineering process steps. As described in (Biffl, Mordinyi, Moser, & Wahyudin, 2008), using ontologies for storing the knowledge in the EKB framework, enables more efficient and effective QA for component-based systems such as production automation systems. The major differences between the two evaluated approaches are the amount of needed human involvement to define and perform model

checks, and the types of model checks which are supported by the approaches.

3. *Analyze how the extra effort for involving the EKB framework is likely to pay off in a typical engineering context.* The evaluation showed that the effort needed for certain automation systems engineering process steps with the EKB framework is slightly higher in case of performing it from the scratch, but comparatively a lot smaller when adaptations due to changing business needs have to be performed since new converters only need to be generated semi-automatically for each new or changed engineering tool in comparison to the need of creating or adapting a vast number of converters for each affected combination of the new or changed engineering tool manually.

The evaluation use cases supported the feasibility of the EKB approach and promising initial results. However, practical issues such as effort and defect rates for setting up an EKB with larger-scale data models and for semantic mapping with engineering experts need to be explored in settings with industrial experts.

CONCLUSION AND FUTURE WORK

Industrial production automation systems depend on distributed software to control the system behavior. In automation systems engineering (ASE) software engineering depends on specification data and plans from a wide range of business, process, and engineering expert domains in the overall engineering process, e.g., physical plant design, mechanical, and electrical engineering, and production process planning. In heterogeneous ASE environments capabilities for the effective and efficient integration of engineering systems and semantic integration of engineering knowledge are key enablers for flexible engineering process automation and advanced quality management.

However, a major challenge in current industrial research approaches is insufficient model integration between the expert disciplines.

In this paper, we introduced the novel Engineering Knowledge Base (EKB) framework for semantic mapping in ASE with a focus on providing links between data structures of engineering tools and systems to support the exchange of information between these tools and thus making ASE more efficient and flexible. Based on two real-world use cases of the SAW system, a research system for assembly workshop engineering in the production automation domain, we compared the proposed EKB framework with a traditional approach using a common repository.

The major difference between the two evaluated approaches is the lack of the need for a common data schema when using the EKB framework, which can be seen as the main advantage of the EKB framework compared to a common repository as the common data schema is a source of extra maintenance effort and tool evolution risk. Additionally, the number of needed converters is $O(n2)$ when using a common repository, compared to $O(n)$ converters needed when using the EKB framework, since for the EKB for each engineering tool to be integrated only one mapping and transformation to the common domain concepts is needed, while for point to point integration transformations are needed for all possibly used combinations of engineering tools to be integrated. Further, using the EKB framework allows a more generic definition and execution of model checks on an application domain level, and additionally enables more advanced checks regarding the plausibility and semantic correctness of data structures by exploiting the querying capabilities of ontologies.

Future Work. After evaluating the feasibility of the EKB approach next steps are studies that extend the scale of the data models involved and address the following research issues: efficient import of data models into EKB ontologies, robust semantic mapping, and performance of the EKB ontologies for larger data sets. Practical issues such as effort and defect rates for setting up an EKB with larger-scale data models and for semantic mapping with engineering experts need to be explored in setting with industrial experts. Once the EKB framework is set up properly, additional use cases can be supported in order to make ASE more efficient. Planned use cases to evaluate are the tracing of requirements between data structures across tools as well as the support for change management across tools.

ACKNOWLEDGMENT

The authors would like to acknowledge the works of the *Rockwell Automation Research Center*, Czech Republic, in the field of the Manufacturing Agent Simulation Tool (MAST), as well as *Liang Min* and *Uwe Szabo* for their work regarding design and implementation of the SAW prototype. This work has been supported by the Christian Doppler Forschungsgesellschaft and the BMWFJ, Austria, and partially funded by the Vienna University of Technology, in the *Complex Systems Design and Engineering Lab*.

REFERENCES

Aldred, L., Aalst, W. d., Dumas, M., & Hofstede, A. t. (2006). *Understanding the challenges in getting together: The semantics of decoupling in middleware.* Retrieved from http://bpmcenter.org/wp-content/uploads/reports/2006/BPM-06-19.pdf

Baker, P., Zhen, R. D., Gabrowksi, J., & Oystein, H. (2008). *Model-driven testing: Using the UML testing profile.* New York, NY: Springer.

Biffl, S., Mordinyi, R., Moser, T., & Wahyudin, D. (2008). Ontology-supported quality assurance for component-based systems configuration. In *Proceedings of the 6th International Workshop on Software Quality*, Leipzig, Germany (pp. 59-64).

Biffl, S., Moser, T., & Sunindyo, W. D. (2009). Bridging semantic gaps between stakeholders in the production automation domain with ontology areas. In *Proceedings of the 21st International Conference on Software Engineering and Knowledge Engineering*, Boston, MA (pp. 233-239).

Biffl, S., Schatten, A., & Zoitl, A. (2009). Integration of heterogeneous engineering environments for the automation systems lifecycle. In *Proceedings of the IEEE Industrial Informatics Conference* (pp. 576-581). Washington, DC: IEEE Computer Society.

Fenton, N., & Neil, M. (1999). A critique of software defect prediction models. *IEEE Transactions on Software Engineering, 25*, 15. doi:10.1109/32.815326

GAMP 5. (2008). *Good automated manufacturing practice.* Tampa, FL: International Society for Pharmaceutical Engineering (ISPE).

Gruber, T. (1995). Towards principles for the design of ontologies used for knowledge sharing. *International Journal of Human-Computer Studies, 43*(5-6). doi:10.1006/ijhc.1995.1081

Hohpe, G. (2006). *Conversation patterns.* Paper presented at the Dagstuhl Workshop.

Java Community Process. (2009). *JSR 283: Content repository for Java™ technology API version 2.0.* Retrieved from http://jcp.org/en/jsr/detail?id=283

Lastra, J. L. M., Delamer, I. M., & Ubis, F. (2009). *Domain ontologies for reasoning machines in factory automation.* Research Triangle Park, NC: ISA.

Li, P. L., Herbsleb, J., & Shaw, M. (2005). Forecasting field defect rates using a combined time-based and metrics-based approach: A case study of OpenBSD. In *Proceedings of the 16th IEEE International Symposium on Software Reliability Engineering* (pp. 193-202). Washington, DC: IEEE Computer Society.

Liao, S. (2005). Technology management methodologies and applications: A literature review from 1995 to 2003. *Technovation, 25*(4), 381–393. doi:10.1016/j.technovation.2003.08.002

Lovett, P. J., Ingram, A., & Bancroft, C. N. (2000). Knowledge-based engineering for SMEs - a methodology. *Journal of Materials Processing Technology, 107*(1-3), 384–389. doi:10.1016/S0924-0136(00)00728-7

Lucene. (2010). *Welcome to apache Lucene.* Retrieved from http://lucene.apache.org/

Lüder, A. (2000). *Formaler Steuerungsentwurf mit modularen diskreten Verhaltensmodellen* Unpublished doctoral dissertation, Martin-Luther-Universität, Halle-Wittenberg, Germany.

Lüder, A., Peschke, J., & Reinelt, D. (2006). *Possibilities and limitations of the application of agent systems in control.* Paper presented at the International Conference on Concurrent Enterprising.

McGuire, J. G., Kuokka, D. R., Weber, J. C., Tenenbaum, J. M., Gruber, T. R., & Olsen, G. R. (1993). SHADE: Technology for knowledge-based collaborative engineering. *Concurrent Engineering, 1993*(1), 137-146.

Merdan, M., Moser, T., Wahyudin, D., & Biffl, S. (2008). Performance evaluation of workflow scheduling strategies considering transportation times and conveyor failures. In *Proceedings of the IEEE International Conference on Industrial Engineering and Engineering Management* (pp. 389-394). Washington, DC: IEEE Computer Society.

Mockus, A., Weiss, D., & Zhang, P. (2003). Understanding and predicting effort in software projects. In *Proceedings of the International Conference on Software Engineering* (pp. 274-284). Washington, DC: IEEE Computer Society.

Moser, T., Mordinyi, R., Sunindyo, W., & Biffl, S. (2009). Semantic service matchmaking in the ATM domain considering network capability constraints. In *Proceedings of the 21st International Conference on Software Engineering and Knowledge Engineering* (pp. 222-227). Washington, DC: IEEE Computer Society.

Moser, T., Schimper, K., Mordinyi, R., & Anjomshoaa, A. (2009). SAMOA - a semi-automated ontology alignment method for systems integration in safety-critical environments. In *Proceedings of the 2nd IEEE International Workshop on Ontology Alignment and Visualization*, Fukuoka, Japan (pp. 724-729). Washington, DC: IEEE Computer Society.

Noy, N. F. (2004). Semantic integration: A survey of ontology-based approaches. *SIGMOD Record, 33*(4), 65–70. doi:10.1145/1041410.1041421

Noy, N. F., Doan, A. H., & Halevy, A. Y. (2005). Semantic integration. *AI Magazine, 26*(1), 7–10.

Obitko, M., & Marik, V. (2002). Ontologies for multi-agent systems in manufacturing domain. In *Proceedings of the 13th International Workshop on Database and Expert Systems Application*s (pp. 597-602). Washington, DC: IEEE Computer Society.

Schäfer, W., & Wehrheim, H. (2007). The challenges of building advanced mechatronic systems. *In Proceedings of the International Conference on the Future of Software Engineering* (pp. 72-84). Washington, DC: IEEE Computer Society.

Vrba, P. (2003). MAST: Manufacturing agent simulation tool. In *Proceedings of the Emerging Technologies and Factory Automation Conference* (pp. 282-287). Washington, DC: IEEE Computer Society.

W3C. (2004). *Semantics and abstract syntax.* Retrieved from http://www.w3.org/TR/owl-semantics/

Wahyudin, D., Schatten, A., Winkler, D., Tjoa, A., & Biffl, S. (2008). Defect prediction using combined product and project metrics: A case study from the open source "apache" *MyFaces Project Family.* In *Proceedings of the 34th Euromicro Conference on Software Engineering and Advanced Applications* (pp. 207-215). Washington, DC: IEEE Computer Society.

Winkler, D., Biffl, S., & Östreicher, T. (2009). Test-driven automation – adopting test-first development to improve automation systems engineering processes. In *Proceedings of the 16th EuroSPI Conference*, Madrid, Spain (pp. 1-13).

This work was previously published in the International Journal of Distributed Systems and Technologies (IJDST), Volume 2, Issue 3, edited by Nik Bessis, pp. 88-103, copyright 2011 by IGI Publishing (an imprint of IGI Global).

Chapter 10
Lightweight Editing of Distributed Ubiquitous Environments:
The CollaborationBus Aqua Editor

Maximilian Schirmer
Bauhaus-University Weimar, Germany

Tom Gross
University of Bamberg, Germany

ABSTRACT

Cooperative ubiquitous environments support user interaction and cooperative work by adapting to the prevalent situation of the present users. They are typically complex and have many environment components—interconnected devices and software modules—that realise new interaction techniques and facilitate collaboration. Despite this complexity, users need to be able to easily adapt their environments to the respective needs of the workgroups. In this paper, the authors present the CollaborationBus Aqua editor, a sophisticated, yet lightweight editor for configuring ubiquitous environments in groups. The CollaborationBus Aqua editor simplifies the configuration and offers advanced concepts for sharing and browsing configurations among users.

INTRODUCTION

Cooperative ubiquitous environments reach beyond single-user interaction and facilitate co-operation and collaboration among their users. They leverage interaction between users, artefacts, and devices, with the goal of softening or even eliminating the barrier between local and remote participants. For instance, a conference room can capture the positions of present persons and their actions, and then adapt the computer and projector configuration, the lighting, and the window shutters; and it could store these settings to support easy later resumption of a meeting.

The configuration of a cooperative ubiquitous environment describes the settings of the environ-

DOI: 10.4018/978-1-4666-2647-8.ch010

ment's components, as well as the degree and shape of the individual interaction between the components. Typically, the task of configuring an environment is realised by programmers or administrators, because it requires great insight into the underlying infrastructure and system architecture, and adequate programming skills. For instance, the rules for the adaptation behaviour of the above conference room are rather difficult to configure.

The configurations should cover the needs of the end-users and their workgroups. However, despite the progress in base technologies such as data acquisition, processing, and machine learning, creating and adapting configurations is still a complex process. In order to facilitate this process, users need empowerment for end-user configuration.

In this paper we present *CollaborationBus Aqua*—a sophisticated, yet light-weight editor for cooperative ubiquitous environments that supports elegant capturing and storing of data from the physical as well as electronic world, visual composition of configurations, and sharing and browsing of configurations among groups of configuration authors. In the next sections we discuss related work. We then present the concept and implementation of *CollaborationBus Aqua* and report on its user interaction. We exemplify the user interaction in a scenario. Finally, we conclude the paper.

END-USER EDITORS FOR UBIQUITOUS ENVIRONMENTS

There are several end-user editors for editing and managing configurations of ubiquitous environments. They provide inspiring concepts with respect to their enabling middleware (e.g., *eGadgets*), their scheme of the configurations (e.g., *iCAP*), and easy user interaction (e.g., *Jigsaw*). As a limiting factor they mostly focus

on individual end-users editing configurations of single-user settings.

In *eGadgets* (Mavrommati et al., 2004) a Gadgetware Architectural Style (GAS) framework for interconnecting reusable components in the form of devices, and a GAS editor for building custom compositions were developed. While an enabling middleware manages and controls all components within the framework, the editor hides complexity from users. The editor retains insight to the dataflow to avoid behaving like a black box for users. By means of connecting the components' inputs and outputs, users generate a range of scenarios consisting of home appliances that have been adapted to be accessible through the GAS platform. The GAS framework models individual components following a plug-synapse model, where each component offers a set of abilities and requests services from other components. Devices in the physical world are represented as plugs. When different plugs are instantiated and connected, they form synapses. This model abstracts and represents compatible data types and data flows, and thus effectively helps users understand which components can be interconnected. In contrast to the *eGadgets* editor, *CollaborationBus Aqua* focuses on a cooperative composing process for ubiquitous computing environments, and offers a sharing and browsing mechanism with synergy notifications.

Another related editor is the *iCAP* (Lim & Dey, 2009; Sohn & Dey, 2003) editor that allows users to prototype applications and scenarios for context-aware environments. Following a pen-based interaction technique, the system's components (input and output devices) may be interconnected to form a conditional rule-based construct in a user-friendly way. The *iCAP* editor allows users to draw their own sketches, which are used to represent the underlying devices within the editor environment. These sketches help to generate a deeper understanding of the constructed prototype and the interrelations between devices.

When components are connected, their rule-based interaction can be tested in the editor's run mode that allows the simulation of certain input states as well. Similar to the *eGadgets* editor, *iCAP* realises a single-user concept. In contrast, *Collaboration-Bus Aqua* aims at leveraging cooperative editing of ubiquitous computing compositions and offers synergy notifications.

The *Jigsaw* editor (Dey & Newberger 2009; Humble et al., 2003) is a graphical front-end to a user-oriented framework that supports users in configuring domestic ubiquitous environments. Users move dragging components (represented as jigsaw pieces) from the editor's list view onto a canvas to create compositions that interconnect hardware sensors and devices from a domestic environment. Differences among the jigsaw pieces (either output port, or input port, or both) reflect the connection properties of the underlying devices and help users to identify what devices are compatible and can be connected. The editor provides both visual and auditory feedback when interactions occur, and visualises the dataflow to help users keep track of sensor updates. In contrast to the Jigsaw editor, *CollaborationBus Aqua* relies on a sophisticated sensor-based ubiquitous computing event notification infrastructure with multifarious environment components and offers powerful mechanisms for filtering or further processing of gathered data.

The UBI-Designer toolkit (Vastenburg et al., 2009) is a web-based graphical editor for sensor networks and infrastructures for ubiquitous computing. The toolkit represents a high-level abstraction of the environment's underlying components and addresses designers of context-aware ubiquitous computing environments as end-users. The toolkit provides access to sensors, processors, and rules. *Sensors* are sources of information in the ubiquitous computing environment, gathered by either hardware sensors, or virtual sensors. Users can explore all available sensors and their current state, filter sensors according to projects, and simulate sensor values. *Processors*

represent software algorithms for the low-level interpretation of sensor data. Users can choose from a selection of pre-defined processors that implement algorithms such as pattern recognition. *Rules* trigger actuators in the environment, based on data gathered by sensors and processed by processors. Users create rules for their ubiquitous computing scenarios with a rule-editor that abstracts from the complexity of the underlying *JESS* rule engine. In the UBI-Designer toolkit, configurations of sensors, processors, and rules can be saved as *Projects*. Each project consists of links to the components and simplifies their clustering. In contrast to the UBI-Designer toolkit, *CollaborationBus Aqua* provides a rich graphical user interface with visual programming that allows users to interact directly with graphical representations of an environment's components.

The RePlay system (Newman et al., 2010) aims at designers of ubiquitous environments and enables them to recreate states of the environment. By simulating sensor data, replaying helps to test how a ubiquitous environment adapts to a prevalent context. Designers and developers can then adapt the configuration of the environment according to the simulation results. RePlay provides a graphical user interface that is very similar to multi-track audio or video editors and follows a scenario-based approach. Gathered sensor data is represented as *Clips* in a clip library. Users organise several clips from different sensors in *Episodes*. Furthermore, RePlay supports *Transforms* that can be applied on clips. Transforms are processing units that modify sensor data. Several pre-defined transforms are available, for example the Identity Transform for changing the associated user of sensor data, the Dwell Transform for creating delays in sensor data, and the GPS Noise Transform for manipulating GPS sensor data. In contrast to RePlay, the *CollaborationBus Aqua* editor allows users to configure the interconnections between components of a ubiquitous environment and provides a sharing mechanism for configurations.

The Topiary system (Li et al., 2004) is related to *CollaborationBus Aqua* because it presents an interesting approach for prototyping ubiquitous, location-enhanced applications. In Topiary, users model location contexts in a graphical user interface that consist of entities, which can be people, places, or things. People represent users in a location-enhanced ubiquitous application. Places are defined by boundaries that users draw on a map. Things are generic entities that can be associated with places. Topiary supports two distinct types of location contexts: presence contexts that describe the spatial relation of persons and things at places, and proximity contexts that model the adjacency of entities. Several location contexts form a scenario that represents a complex situation with a number of entities and location contexts. In contrast to the Topiary system, *CollaborationBus Aqua* goes beyond the prototyping of location-enhanced applications, and allows users to configure existing real-world components of ubiquitous environments.

Fokidou et al. (2008) have presented two interesting graphical user interface prototypes for configuring pervasive environments, which specifically address the requirements of elderly people (Bee Prototype) and young adolescents (Haring's World Prototype). The graphical user interface of the Bee Prototype follows the metaphor of a beehive that abstracts from the components of the ubiquitous computing environment. The actual configuration is created with the help of wizards and forms. The Haring's World Prototype provides a graphical user interface that leverages creativity. During the configuration process, users are able to communicate with others using the integrated instant messaging service. The prototype allows users to discover present artefacts of the ubiquitous environment, and to define associations between these artefacts. These associations are realised as a set of rules. In contrast to these prototypes, *CollaborationBus Aqua* is fully functionally and has been implemented and deployed as a graphical desktop application.

COLLABORATIONBUS AQUA CONCEPT

The requirements for *CollaborationBus Aqua* were from our own experience of developing cooperative ubiquitous environments for many years, and lessons learned from related work such as the examples described in the previous section. In this section we focus on the following three core concepts of *CollaborationBus Aqua:* advanced and easy capturing of data, composing configurations visually, and sharing and browsing configurations.

Advanced and Easy Capturing of Data

The *CollaborationBus Aqua* editor includes an ubiquitous sensor-based platform that distributes and processes gathered data in the form of sensor events. The powerful sensor-based platform *Sens-ation* (Gross et al., 2006) manages all the capturing, processing, and storing of the data for the users in the background. The combination of *CollaborationBus Aqua* and *Sens-ation* provides access to the environment components: sensors that gather data, inference engines that process gathered data, and actuators that trigger feedback in the user environment. Furthermore, *Sens-ation* offers a broad range of gateways as interfaces for the easy management of components and access to both raw and processed sensor data.

Sensors are either hardware sensors for light, movement, temperature, noise; or software sensors for applications such as email, Web browser, and office applications. The gathered data is used to abstract awareness information about the users in a cooperative ubiquitous environment.

Inference engines in the *Sens-ation* platform process incoming sensor data. This processing mechanism allows inferring higher-order information from the raw sensor data. Processing results vary from simple mathematical calculations (e.g., mean values) up to complex interdependent processing chains that involve multiple inference engines' results. Results from inference engines are transferred back to the platform as sensor events, so clients and actuators can access them through all available gateways.

Actuators realise actions within the environment according to the results of the inference process. Just like sensors, actuator components are either software applications or hardware devices. While hardware actuators change physical settings within the environment, software actuators typically serve as means of presenting notifications on a computer monitor.

Composing Configurations Visually

In *CollaborationBus Aqua* users visually compose configurations using the components of the platform. The editor follows the visual programming paradigm that supports configuration tasks by means of visually appealing graphical representations (Myers, 1986). These graphical representations abstract programmatic behaviour, yet still provide an indication of the underlying technology. The *CollaborationBus Aqua* editor uses distinct graphical elements for sensors, inference engines, and actuators.

Figure 1 shows our scheme of configurations consisting of one or more sensors, one or more inference engines, and one or more actuators. In this exemplary configuration, a user wants to be notified when the temperature measured by a temperature sensor has reached a defined threshold. The user has connected the sensor's output to an inference engine's input, and the inference engine's output to an actuator's input. The inference engine evaluates the incoming temperature and notifies the actuator.

Environment components are instantiated by drag-and-drop. Users create connections among them by drawing lines between two individual representations. The editor handles the necessary technical procedures in the background and provides an indication whether the established connections are correct on a technical as well as on a semantic level. The data type validation mechanism evaluates compatibilities and notifies users with a warning if they create connections that form incompatible relationships between components. This avoids that the composition results in unpredictable behaviour within the environment.

Typical examples for incompatibilities are: connecting two outputs of components (e.g., connecting the outputs of two sensors with each other, cf. Figure 2(a)), or connecting components with incompatible data types (e.g., connecting a temperature sensor with a Boolean inference engine Figure 2(b)). In the first case, there is no data flow because in the sensor model of *Sensation*, sensors only output data to the platform. In the second case, a movement sensor is connected with an inference engine that implements a logical AND operator. Clearly, the data types of both components are not compatible with each other. While the inference engine awaits Boolean values as input, the movement sensor only provides numerical float values as output.

Figure 1. Scheme of configurations including a sensor, inference engine, and actuator

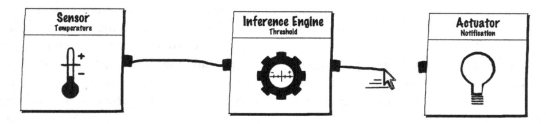

Figure 2. Incorrectly established sensor (a) and sensor-inference engine connections

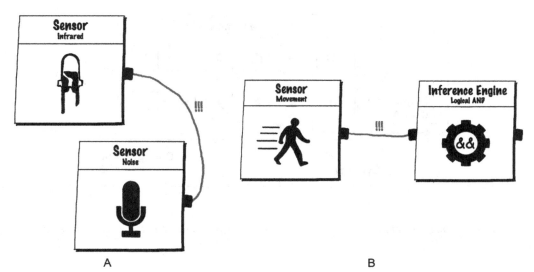

A   B

Sharing and Browsing Configurations

CollaborationBus Aqua encourages its users to share, explore, and reuse configurations. In *CollaborationBus Aqua* all configurations are accessible through a shared repository, which allows groups of authors to cooperate during the composing. This repository especially provides beginners, who do not have experience with configuring ubiquitous environments, with an entry point to the system (Mackay, 1990). With a growing number of configurations in the repository, beginners get a good sample of configurations and learn about their cooperative ubiquitous environment and configuration options therein.

Users can choose between sharing and privacy—that is, they can either place their configuration in a shared repository that every user in a group can access, or save their configuration in a private local file (see Greif & Sarin, 1986 for early findings on sharing and privacy).

The shared repository facilitates synergies among users. Components instantiated within the *CollaborationBus Aqua* editor refer to concrete physical artefacts or software instances. We define synergies as the similar use of the same components within the repository of available configurations. When users access components that are already part of other users' configurations, all users involved receive information about their mutual components. The notification encourages them to explore each other's configuration or contact each other to discuss synergies.

The underlying mechanism works as follows (cf. Figure 3): the shared repository of configurations is a set of components. Any configuration therein forms a subset of components. When the intersection of any number of configurations produces a set that is not the empty set, synergies occur.

CollaborationBus Aqua User Interaction

CollaborationBus Aqua consists of the Main Window (cf. Figure 4(a)) and the Inspector (cf. Figure 4(b)). The Main Window provides four parts: (aa) the Operation Mode toolbar on the top end of the window, (ab) the Component Browser below, (ac) the Composer in the centre of the window, and (ad) the Statusbar in the bottom of the window.

Figure 3. Synergies in shared cooperative ubiquitous environment configurations

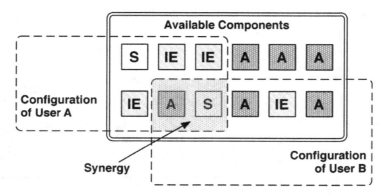

Figure 4. Graphical user interface of CollaborationBus Aqua, with (a) the main window, and (b) the inspector

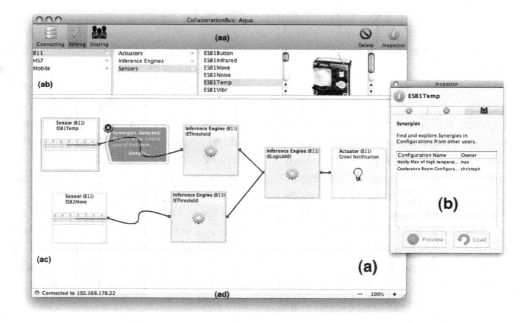

Connecting, Editing, and Sharing

The Operation Mode toolbar of the Main Window of *CollaborationBus Aqua* provides on the left side the access to three basic Operation Modes: Connecting, Editing, and Sharing. Switching to one of the modes changes the content of the Main Window. On the right side of the Operation Mode toolbar, two additional buttons allow users to

delete components and to open up the Inspector. In the Connecting Mode, users either enter the appropriate connection details of the *Sens-ation* instance they want to connect to or select one from the connection history list. Once users establish a connection, the Editing and Sharing Modes can be accessed. The Editing Mode is the core of the application and provides the Component Browser, the Composer, and the Inspector. From the Component Browser, components are instantiated by simply dragging them to the Composer, where they are transformed into graph nodes. The Inspector allows exploring and configuring selected components. In the Sharing Mode, users browse the repository of available configurations to learn about their environment or to find a template as a starting point for an editing process.

Exploring and Configuring Components

The Inspector provides detailed information and configuration options for components in the Editing Mode and dynamically changes its content in relation to selected components. For example, if users select a sensor component, the inspector only displays information about it and its recent events; if they select an inference engine or actuator component, the Inspector also provides means of configuring their parameters. The Inspector is a floating palette window always located on top of other windows of the editor. Figure 5 shows the Operation Modes of the Inspector. Changing

between Operation Modes follows the pattern of the Main Window: a toolbar with three different toggle buttons representing the associated modes.

The (a) General Information Mode displays common data about the selected component (e.g., its location, owner). This helps users to identify physical components in their environment. Furthermore, they provide a common ground for communication with other users of these components, because they allow explicit identification. The (b) Recent Events Mode provides an overview of the component's recent condition, which is mostly useful for sensor and inference engine components. It displays either a graphical or a tabular visualisation of the recent events, according to the component and its data type. For instance, a temperature sensor produces numerical event values, which can be visualised as a temperature graph, while an inference engine that evaluates a given input value against a threshold will output Boolean values, which require a tabular visualisation. The (c) Synergy Browser Mode allows user to quickly inspect a component's synergies within other configurations in the form of a tabu-

Figure 5. The operation modes of the inspector (from left): general information, recent events, and synergy browser

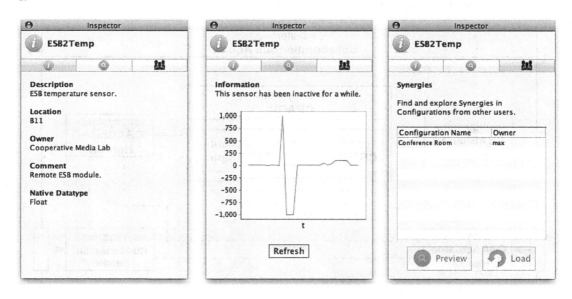

lar configuration listing. In the case of existing synergies, the Inspector provides two buttons for either previewing or loading a selected configuration with synergies.

CollaborationBus Aqua Implementation

The *CollaborationBus Aqua* editor is a stand-alone application implemented in Java 1.5.0_13, MySQL 5.0.41, and with Apache 2.0.59 on Mac OS X 10.4.9 and as such was straight-forward to implement and provides user interaction concepts that are well known to end-users. It acts as a client to the *Sens-ation* sensor platform.

CollaborationBus Aqua is comprised of five core subsystems that implement the main program logic (cf. Figure 6). The *CBAGUI* subsystem is responsible for managing both the *CBABrowser* component as well as the *CBAGraph* component that forms the editor's core. The *CBAGraph-Handler* subsystem manages the creation of the visual representations for the components and devices of the environment. The *CBASensation-Handler* subsystem communicates directly with the associated *Sens-ation* instance via XML-RPC

(Scripting News Inc., 2010) and distributes the gathered data and its available components to the *CBAGraphHandler*. The management and delegation of actuator components is realised by the *CBAActuatorHandler* subsystem. It manages all available and instantiated actuators and communicates directly to *Sens-ation* via XML-RPC. It provides actuator parameters for the graphical representations of actuator components to the *CBAGraphHandler*. The *CBASharing* subsystem directly relates to the *CBAGUI* subsystem. It handles access to the repository of shared configurations by delegating tasks to a database server. It also processes the related data for display within the graphical user interface and implements the synergy finding algorithm.

Subsequently, we explain how the concepts are implemented with the five subsystems. *CollaborationBus Aqua* has been completely implemented and deployed.

Deployment

We have deployed and tested *CollaborationBus Aqua* in a cooperative ubiquitous environment in our workgroup. In Figure 7, we introduce a

Figure 6. Component diagram of CollaborationBus Aqua

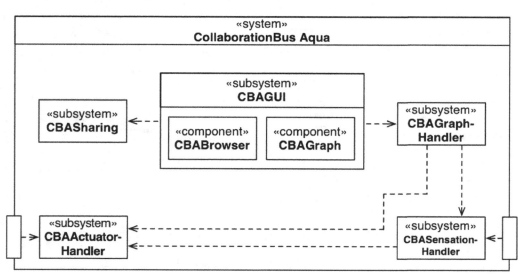

Figure 7. Deployment diagram of a typical CollaborationBus Aqua setup in our environment

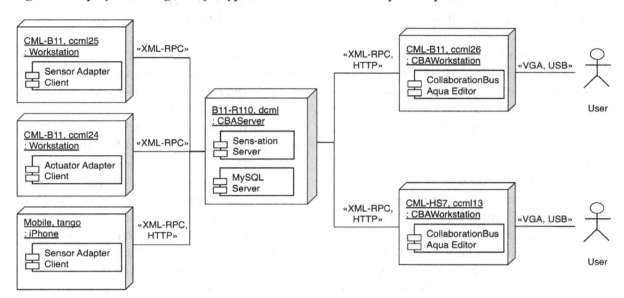

typical setup. This setup consists of two users on different workstation computers at two different buildings of our Cooperative Media Lab at the Bauhaus-University in Weimar. Each *CBAWorkstation* computer (*ccml13* and *ccml26* are 27-inch iMacs with 3.06 GHz Intel C2D, 4 GB of main memory, running Mac OS X 10.6.4) is equipped with the *CollaborationBus Aqua* editor. The workstation computers attach to the university's CAN (Campus Area Network) via a 100 MBit/s Ethernet connection. All instances of the *CollaborationBus Aqua* editor communicate with a central *CBAServer* using XML-RPC and HTTP.

The *CBAServer* is deployed on our *dcml* server, which is a PowerMac G5 with dual 1.8 GHz G5 processors, 1 GB of main memory, running Mac OS X 10.5.8. The *CBAServer* provides the *Sens-ation* platform (version 5.7) as well as a MySQL database server (version 5.0.41). The *Sens-ation* platform manages all environment components (i.e., sensors, inference engines, and actuators) of the cooperative ubiquitous environment. It also delegates the communication between the components, and the data exchange between clients. The database server persistently stores the

configuration repository of the *CollaborationBus Aqua* editor. This repository contains XML representations of the environment configurations.

In our setup, *Sensor Adapter Clients* and *Actuator Adapter Clients* are deployed on additional workstation computers (*ccml24* and *ccml25*, also iMac 27-inch C2D), and on an iPhone 3G (*tango*). *Sensor Adapter Clients* provide interfaces for environment sensors and send gathered sensor data to the *Sens-ation* platform of the *CBAServer*. The *Actuator Adapter Client* provides the necessary implementation for triggering environment reactions (e.g., displaying notifications on a computer display, controlling other computing devices, or manipulating real-world objects using servo motors).

Data Capturing

CollaborationBus Aqua requests and obtains data as a client for the *Sens-ation* platform. The editor implementation makes use of the XML-RPC gateways with synchronous communication. *CollaborationBus Aqua* relies on synchronous communication, because it is important to apprise all users of the current condition of the environment without noticeable delay. The *CBASensationHandler* subsystem of *CollaborationBus Aqua* implements communication management and initiation. It encapsulates connections to various *Sens-ation* platforms and keeps a history. The *CBASensationHandler* acts as a surrogate for the actual *Sens-ation* connection that is active. Instead of interacting directly with *Sens-ation*, all components of the *CollaborationBus Aqua* system direct their requests to the *CBASensationHandler*. The *Sens-ation* connection components make use of the Java XmlRpcClient implementation as well as the Java WebServer implementation (both from the corresponding Apache project framework Apache Software Foundation, 2010). While the XmlRpcClient is used to send requests to *Sens-ation* (e.g., for acquiring information about available sensors), the WebServer component listens for notifications that are sent from *Sens-ation* when a sensor event of an observed sensor occurs.

Visual Composing

Visual composing in the *CollaborationBus Aqua* editor is implemented in the *CBAGraphHandler* subsystem and based on a Model-View-Controller (MVC) pattern. The base of the visual composing graphical user interface is an interactive graph interface element, the *CBAGraph*. This graph implementation bases on the Java JGraph (JGraph Ltd, 2009) framework that provides a graph component for the Java Swing framework. The *CBAGraph* component in the *CBAGraphHandler* subsystem contains the *CBAGraphModel* with the necessary data for each node in the graph, as well as information about relationships between graph nodes. The *CBACellViewFactory*, *CBACellView*, and *CBAVertexRenderer* components realise the visual representations of these graph nodes, in conjunction with the *CBAGraphRouting* component that generates control points for the rendering of smooth spline-based edges between the nodes of the graph.

Sharing and Browsing Configurations

Sharing and browsing configurations are implemented in the *CBASharing* subsystem. Its *CBASharingDatabase* provides an abstraction layer to the underlying MySQL database and implements the functional behaviour to save and load configurations. An identifier string and the creator of the composition uniquely identify every composition. Each composition in the GUI is serialised to an internal XML representation, which facilitates their internal handling, and includes all necessary information to reload, edit, and share configurations. The identifier string, the creator, and the XML representation of the composition are stored persistently in the database.

The XML representation for all components of a configuration follows a simple structure (cf. Figure 8). Every component has a type identifier, a native data type (e.g., Float, String, Boolean), a location identifier, and a unique component identifier.

Figure 8. XML representation of a sensor component

```
<de.cmlab.collaborationbus.utility.VertexData
    serialization="custom">
  <map>
    <default>
      <loadFactor>0.75</loadFactor>
      <threshold>12</threshold>
    </default>
    <int>16</int>
    <int>4</int>
    <string>Type</string>
    <string>Sensor</string>
    <string>NativeDataType</string>
    <string>Float</string>
    <string>Location</string>
    <string>B11</string>
    <string>ID</string>
    <string>ESB1Temp</string>
  </map>
</de.cmlab.collaborationbus.utility.VertexData>
```

In order to detect synergies in shared configurations, a set of comparisons across all configurations in the repository is necessary. The components' identifiers and their locations are compared. When both the identifiers and the locations of two components match, a synergy is detected. For this purpose, an XML pull parser sequentially scans all configurations in the repository and evaluates the contained components. When a synergy is detected, a synergy flag is set for the corresponding component in the *CBAGraphModel*. During the graph rendering cycle, the *CBAGraphHandler* triggers the display of a graphical synergy notification for all graph nodes that are marked with the synergy flag. The synergy notification also contains the identifiers of configurations with synergies, as well as information about their authors. Users can directly explore and browse these configurations to find out more about them.

Scenario

In this section, we present a scenario to illustrate a typical editing situation in a cooperative ubiquitous environment. The scenario involves two users (Walter and Henry) who are using *CollaborationBus Aqua* for configuring devices and components in their research facility's cooperative ubiquitous environment.

Henry is a research and teaching assistant and Walter is the room administrator at the research facility that Tony is working at. It is Walter's responsibility to provide technical and administrative support for a number of conference rooms within the building.

Walter receives many calls from users of the conference rooms reporting a broken video projector. Most of the time he finds the project system perfectly intact, but the conference room users simply forgot to turn on the main power switch. This Switch is necessary to reduce the standby power output of the room's devices. It would simplify Walter's work a lot if there were

a system that automatically prepared the conference room for a meeting when a meeting situation is imminent.

With the help of the *CollaborationBus Aqua* editor, Walter creates a configuration of sensors, inference engines, and a simple actuator that controls a power switching relay. The configuration (cf. Figure 9) consists of a movement sensor (MovementRoom42) and a noise sensor (NoiseRoom42). Their gathered data is used by three inference engines in order to determine if there are people present in the conference room. Two of the inference engines are of the type IEThreshold, which means these inference engines evaluate incoming sensor data (in this case noise and movement levels) against user-specified thresholds. The third inference engine has the type IELogicAnd. It realises a logical AND operator for incoming sensor data. If both IEThreshold inference engines determine that their thresholds have been reached, the relay board actuator is triggered. The relay then powers the video projector on.

When Walter placed the actuator component in his configuration, he noticed a small dialogue window that appeared next to the component, stating that there are other configurations that make use of the power switching relay actuator in conference room 42 as well (cf. Figure 10).

Walter clicks the button "Details…", just like it is proposed in the dialogue to open the inspector window. Within the inspector, the synergy browser mode is activated and presents a list of other configurations (cf. Figure 11). These configurations contain components that are also present in Walter's configuration.

From the list of configurations in the synergy browser, Walter learns that a user named Henry has also created an environment configuration for conference room 42. Henry's configuration involves the power switch relay as well. Walter is curious to learn about Henry's configuration and uses the synergy browser to load it directly into his *CollaborationBus Aqua* editor application.

Figure 9. Walter's conference room configuration

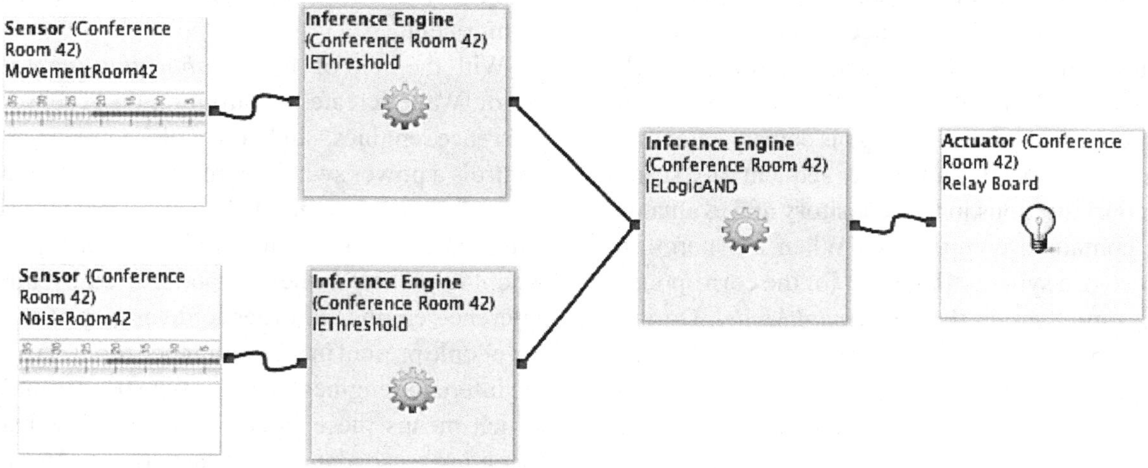

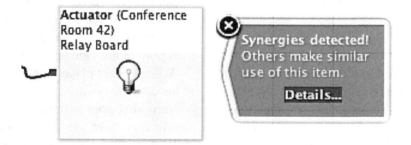

Figure 10. A synergy was detected in Walter's configuration

After exploring the configuration, he goes to see Henry. Henry is happy to introduce his configuration to Walter and explains what he did in great detail.

As it turns out, Henry is a regular user of the conference room and wanted to save the time required for turning on the main power switch over and over again every day. Henry organises all his appointments in a calendar application program on his computer. All the meetings in the conference room are included, as well. So he envisioned a system that would prepare the conference room just before a scheduled meeting begins.

Henry's configuration involved a calendar sensor that provides events right before an appointment is due, an inference engine that evaluates if the appointment is set to take place in the conference room 42, and the same relay board as actuator that Walter used in his configuration.

While they were discussing each other's configurations and the synergies they have created with them, Walter and Henry decide to work together on an even better configuration that works both for spontaneous, unscheduled meetings (like in Walter's configuration), and for scheduled meetings as well.

Figure 11. The synergy browser showing Walter's synergy with Henry

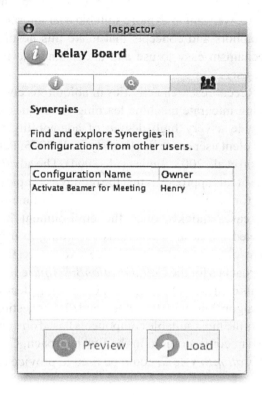

CONCLUSION AND FUTURE WORK

Cooperative ubiquitous environments combine aspects of ubiquitous computing with the general aim of supporting collaboration and cooperation in a shared information space, as envisioned in the core ideas of computer-supported cooperative work (Bannon & Schmidt, 1989). These environments require a lot of interconnected devices and software components in order to realise new interaction techniques and facilitate collaboration through them.

We introduced *CollaborationBus Aqua* that provides mechanisms and easy interfaces for accessing sensors and the event data they capture as well as for composing configurations. It is a continuation of our *CollaborationBus* editor

(Gross & Marquardt, 2007) with a special focus on end-users—combining easy handling with complex compositions. In particular, this editor is based on a sophisticated interaction concept that abstracts from the technical complexity of the cooperative ubiquitous environment and its components and allows users to focus on the semantics of their configurations. With the sharing and browsing mechanisms, users can exchange their configurations—this is particularly helpful for novice users who can browse existing configurations and do learning by example.

As our overview of related end-user editors for ubiquitous environments has shown, this particular field of research presents a lot of interesting challenges that cover several state-of-the-art topics in ubiquitous computing: sensor infrastructures and frameworks, natural and alternative user interaction, recording and replay of sensor data, use of location data, and new metaphors for graphical user interfaces. With *CollaborationBus Aqua*, we introduce means for cooperative editing of ubiquitous environments and therefore incorporate aspects from computer-supported cooperative work (CSCW). We think that this combination of ubiquitous computing and concepts of CSCW presents an important contribution to end-user editors for ubiquitous environments, and also for ubiquitous computing in general. Allowing users to easily share, discuss, and edit their configurations collaboratively, reduces the complexity of the configuration process.

Besides its regular deployment in our lab's ubiquitous environment, we have successfully deployed *CollaborationBus Aqua* in a media space setting (Gross et al., 2010). In this scenario, the editor allowed users of the media space to define what kind of information they disclose to others, and to specify a granularity level (ranging from undisclosed to full disclosure with two levels in-between). The graphical user interface of the editor, mostly the inspector window, was modified in this setting in order to provide the necessary mechanisms for controlling the disclosure level of media space sensors.

The *CollaborationBus Aqua* editor currently supports the management of sensors, inference engines, and actuators. For the future, users would benefit from including more capabilities for visualising and simulating sensor data. While users are presented with a simple configuration process, the editor in the current form has limitations concerning the scalability of the presentation of large configurations. This is particularly due to the fact that it can only display flat configurations, where up to ten components can be seen and manipulated at a time on a typical 17 inch screen. Introducing a nesting mechanism for components would allow users to divide and conquer their bigger configurations into multiple levels of abstraction.

Figure 12 presents a sketch of the proposed concept for a nesting mechanism in the *CollaborationBus Aqua* editor. In this case, the behaviour of an XOR inference engine is recreated with several inference engines that realise the logical equivalent to XOR, $(\overline{A} \wedge B) \vee (A \wedge \overline{B})$. In the future, we want to explore suitable user interface metaphors and concepts that make this nesting mechanism easy to use and understandable for end-users.

Recent research activities in ubiquitous computing integrate machine learning techniques to provide a very high degree of adaptability to prevalent user contexts (Fogarty et al., 2005; Patterson et al., 2003; Tapia et al., 2004). The advantage of this approach is that the required complexity for configuring ubiquitous environments decreases quickly once the environment has learned the desired reactions according to user input or user contexts. We see two interesting approaches for the *CollaborationBus Aqua* editor in this context: (1) configuring the machine learning algorithms with the editor, and (2) suggesting users the most suitable components based on their current configuration. In the first approach, *CollaborationBus Aqua* could be used to provide an

Figure 12. Nested inference engine components

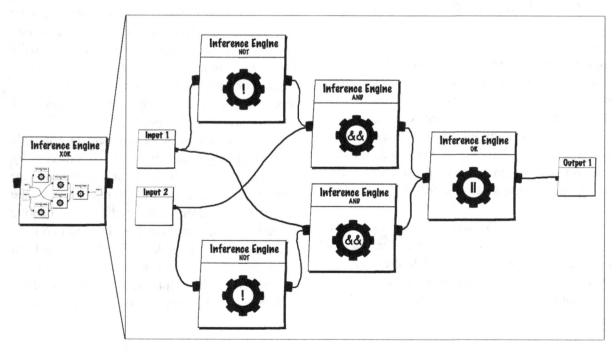

initial configuration of the ubiquitous environment, but also to create the configuration and composition of the machine learning algorithms. This would allow users to visually compose the processing chain from data acquisition to classification. In the second approach, the editor could be used to propose users the most suitable components, based on the components they are currently using in their configuration. This approach requires an analysis algorithm for detecting typical configurations with respect to commonly found combinations of components.

ACKNOWLEDGMENT

The authors would like to thank Christoph Beckmann, Mirko Fetter, Nicolai Marquardt and the other members of CML, as well as the anonymous reviewers for valuable feedback. Part of the work has been funded by the Federal Ministry of Transport, Building, and Urban Affairs and by the Project Management Juelich (TransKoop FKZ 03WWTH018).

REFERENCES

Apache Software Foundation. (2010). *About Apache XML-RPC*. Retrieved from http://ws.apache.org/xmlrpc/

Bannon, L. J., & Schmidt, K. (1989, September 13-15). CSCW: Four characters in search of a context. In *Proceedings of the First European Conference on Computer-Supported Cooperative Work*, Gatwick, UK (pp. 358-372).

Dey, A. K., & Newberger, A. (2009, April 4-9). Support for context-aware intelligibility and control. In *Proceedings of the Conference on Human Factors in Computing Systems*, Boston, MA (pp. 859-868). New York, NY: ACM Press.

Fogarty, J., Hudson, S. E., Akteson, C. G., Avrahami, D., Forlizzi, J., & Kiesler, S. (2005). Predicting human interruptibility with sensors. *ACM Transactions on Computer-Human Interaction*, *12*(1), 119–146. doi:10.1145/1057237.1057243

Fokidou, T., Romoudi, E., & Mavrommati, I. (2008, October 13-15). Designing GUI for the user configuration of pervasive awareness applications. In *Proceedings of the 5th IADIS International Conference Cognition and Exploratory Learning in Digital Age*, Freiburg, Germany (pp. 29-37).

Greif, I., & Sarin, S. (1986, December 3-5). Data sharing in group work. In *Proceedings of the ACM Conference on Computer-Supported Cooperative Work*, Austin, TX (pp. 175-183). New York, NY: ACM Press.

Gross, T., Beckmann, C., & Schirmer, M. (2010, February 17-19). The PPPSpace: Innovative concepts for permanent capturing, persistent storing, and parallel processing and distributing events. In *Proceedings of the Eighteenth Euromicro Conference on Parallel, Distributed, and Network-Based Processing*, Pisa, Italy (pp. 359-366). Washington, DC: IEEE Computer Society.

Gross, T., Egla, T., & Marquardt, N. (2006). Sensation: A service-oriented platform for developing sensor-based infrastructures. *International Journal of Internet Protocol Technology*, *1*(3), 159–167.

Gross, T., & Marquardt, N. (2007, February 7-9). CollaborationBus: An editor for the easy configuration of ubiquitous computing environments. In *Proceedings of the Fifteenth Euromicro Conference on Parallel, Distributed, and Network-Based Processing*, Naples, Italy (pp. 307-314). Washington, DC: IEEE Computer Society.

Humble, J., Crabtree, A., Hemmings, T., Akesson, K.-P., Koleva, B., Rodden, T., & Hansson, P. (2003, October 12-15). "Playing with the bits" user-configuration of ubiquitous domestic environments. In *Proceedings of the Fifth International Conference on Ubiquitous Computing*, Seattle, WA (pp. 256-263).

JGraph Ltd. (2009). *JGraph homepage*. Retrieved from http://www.jgraph.com

Li, Y., Hong, J. I., & Landay, J. A. (2004, October 24-27). Topiary: A tool for prototyping location-enhanced applications. In *Proceedings of the 17th Annual ACM Symposium on User Interface Software and Technology*, Santa Fe, NM (pp. 217-226). New York, NY: ACM Press.

Lim, B. Y., & Dey, A. K. (2009, September 30-October 3). Assessing demand for intelligibility in context-aware applications. In *Proceedings of the 11th International Conference on Ubiquitous Computing*, Orlando, FL (pp. 195-204). New York, NY: ACM Press.

Mackay, W. E. (1990, October 7-10). Patterns of sharing customisable software. In *Proceedings of the ACM Conference on Computer-Supported Cooperative Work*, Los Angeles, CA (pp. 209-221). New York, NY: ACM Press.

Myers, B. A. (1986, April 13-17). Visual programming, programming by example, and program visualisation: A taxonomy. In *Proceedings of the SIGCHI Conference on Human Factors in Computing Systems*, Boston, MA (pp. 59-66). New York, NY: ACM Press.

Newman, M. W., Ackerman, M. S., Kim, J., Prakash, A., Hong, Z., Mandel, J., & Dong, T. (2010, October 3-6). Bringing the field into the lab: Supporting capture and replay of contextual data for design. In *Proceedings of the 23nd Annual ACM Symposium on User Interface Software and Technology*, New York, NY (pp. 105-108). New York, NY: ACM Press.

Patterson, D. J., Liao, L., Fox, D., & Kautz, H. (2003, October 12-15). Inferring high-level behavior from low-level sensors. In *Proceedings of the Fifth International Conference on Ubiquitous Computing*, Seattle, WA (pp. 73-89).

Scripting News Inc. (2010). *XML-RPC homepage*. Retrieved from http://www.xmlrpc.com/

Sohn, T., & Dey, A. (2003, April 5-10). iCap: An informal tool for interactive prototyping of context-aware applications. In *Proceedings of Extended Abstracts of the Conference on Human Factors in Computing System*s, Fort Lauderdale, FL (pp. 974-975). New York, NY: ACM Press.

Tapia, E. M., Intille, S. S., & Larson, K. (2004, April 18-23). Activity recognition in the home using simple and ubiquitous sensors. In *Proceedings of the Second International Conference on Pervasive Computing*, Vienna, Austria (pp. 158-175).

Vastenburg, M. H., Fjalldal, H., & Mast, C. V. D. (2009, June 9-13). Ubi-Designer: A web-based toolkit for configuring and field-testing UbiComp prototypes. In *Proceedings of the 2nd International Conference on Pervasive Technologies Related to Assistive Environmen*ts, Corfu, Greece (pp. 1-6). New York, NY: ACM Press.

This work was previously published in the International Journal of Distributed Systems and Technologies (IJDST), Volume 2, Issue 4, edited by Nik Bessis, pp. 57-73, copyright 2011 by IGI Publishing (an imprint of IGI Global).

Chapter 11
Guaranteeing Correctness for Collaboration on Documents Using an Optimal Locking Protocol

Stijn Dekeyser
University of Southern Queensland, Australia

Jan Hidders
Delft University of Technology, The Netherlands

ABSTRACT

Collaboration on documents has been supported for several decades through a variety of systems and tools; recently a renewed interest is apparent through the appearance of new collaborative editors and applications. Some distributed groupware systems are plug-ins for standalone word processors while others have a purely web-based existence. Most exemplars of the new breed of systems are based on Operational Transformations, although some are using traditional version management tools and still others utilize document-level locking techniques. All existing techniques have their drawbacks, creating opportunities for new methods. The authors present a novel collaborative technique for documents which is based on transactions, schedulers, conflicts, and locks. It is not meant to replace existing techniques; rather, it can be used in specific situations where a strict form of concurrency control is required. While the approach of presentation in this article is highly formal with an emphasis on proving desirable properties such as guaranteed correctness, the work is part of a project which aims to fully implement the technique.

DOI: 10.4018/978-1-4666-2647-8.ch011

INTRODUCTION

Although some lesser known approaches exist (for example those described in Dekeyser et al., 2004; Oster et al., 2007), collaboration on documents is typically realized in one of two distinct ways. In the asynchronous setting collaborators typically check out a document from a central repository, make changes off-line over an extended time, and then check in their version of the document at which time they are typically asked to solve inconsistencies with the version currently stored in the repository. This type of collaboration has been possible since the introduction of the Source Code Control System (SCCS) in the early seventies of the previous century (Rochkind, 1975). Successors of SCCS have included RCS, CVS, and Subversion. The last of these remains in widespread use and for example provides the collaboration functionality of modern document collaboration systems such as ICE (Sefton et al., 2006).

The second approach to collaboration, found in most modern CSCW (Computer-Supported Cooperative Work) systems, involves synchronous collaboration where editors are aware of other users' changes while working on their own content. This approach requires on-line communication and uses a replicated architecture: shared documents are replicated at local sites such that each works on their own local copy and changes are propagated to other users. Such systems are called *real-time*: the response for local operations is quick and the latency for remote operations is relatively low. Examples of real-time editors include CoWord (Xia et al., 2004), Google Docs, and the short-lived Google Wave experiment (which was more than just a real-time editor, but that is beyond the scope of this article). The newest such systems call themselves *really* real-time: local operations are applied immediately, and remote operations are applied within seconds. EtherPad (Corneli, 2010), recently acquired by Google, is an example of a really real-time editor.

In this article we present an alternative approach that aims to preserve the strengths of the existing approaches while avoiding their weaknesses. A shorter preliminary version of this work was presented in Dekeyser and Hidders (2010).

The article is organized as follows: the next section will describe the two approaches mentioned above in greater detail and will compare them to our proposed technique. Subsequently we present the theory of piecemeal over a number of sections that progressively refine the model of documents that we work with; this concludes with a proof of the optimality of our protocol. Following this we discuss some practical implications for document servers and describe how off-line editing is supported. In the conclusion we summarize the article's contribution and list expected future work.

CURRENT TECHNIQUES

We briefly discuss existing collaboration techniques and highlight some of their strengths and drawbacks. We limit this discussion to the two dominant methods introduced above.

Version Control Systems

As discussed above, Subversion is currently the most widely used versioning control system and has its foundations in SCCS. The underlying collaboration technique is well understood and robust, although not grounded on a formal model or supported by a theory of correctness. While this technique sometimes fails to prevent conflicts, it seems to have an intuitive notion of conflict as well as a limited notion of transaction. The technique makes use of a so-called *diff* between two text documents, at the level of individual lines. At its most basic level, a diff is represented by individual lines of text that are marked as additions, lines that are marked as deletions and lines that are not marked and that are used as a context to help decide where a change was made in a document. This implicit notion of a context is one that we will formalize in our approach.

In contrast to techniques based on locking, the use of a diff cannot fully prevent conflicts between document versions. This is the main weakness of the version control approach for collaboration; users are asked to resolve conflicts if they occur. Other weaknesses include the *de facto* limitation to asynchronous communication and the lack of visual feedback on collaboration in the client. The main strength is in the technique's simplicity and that it does not require on-line connection allowing synchronization of documents that have been edited off-line over lengthy periods.

Compared to this approach, our proposed technique, dubbed *Piecemeal*, will maintain the simplicity (especially for clients), and seamlessly offer both real-time synchronous as well as off-line asynchronous operation. A comprehensive comparison is given in Table 1.

Operational Transformations

Most real-time and really real-time collaborative editors make use of the Operational Transformation technique (Ellis & Gibbs, 1989) as it is a highly optimistic method that fundamentally allows any operation to proceed at the local copy and then relies on appropriate transformation of the operation at remote sites. The transformation of an operation typically involves modifying the position in the local document where the operation needs to be applied. Hence, as in the previous approach, the technique is strongly tied to position in a sequential list of characters.

The consistency model used by OT relies on three properties: (1) *convergence* which means that ultimately copies of shared documents will become identical when all operations have been applied everywhere; (2) *causality preservation* which, simplified, means that dependent operations are executed in the same order on all sites;

Table 1. Comparison of main collaborative editing techniques to Piecemeal

Feature/Technique	CVS and SVN	OT	Piecemeal
Client software	Any text editor	Stand-alone or web applications with built-in support for OT protocol	Stand-alone or web applications with built-in support for Piecemeal protocol
Complexity of client	Very simple	Very complex (several erroneous implementations have been identified)	Simple
Complexity of server	Simple	No server necessary	Moderate
Support for off-line editing	Yes	No	Yes
Real-time propagation of changes to other connected clients	No	Yes	Yes
Overhead (time for local changes to be actioned on local copy)	Immediate	Immediate	After acquiring locks (some overhead)
Correctness guarantee	No	No	Yes
Manual conflict resolution needed in some cases	Yes	Yes	No
Granularity of updates	Per line	Individual characters	Can be set by user (from fine to coarse)
Support for UNDO	By checking out previous version	Problematic	Relatively simple

and (3) *intention preservation* which means that the intention of an operation is maintained at all sites (Wang et al., 2002).

The main advantages of OT are: that it is highly suitable for real-time collaboration because its optimistic approach results in high speed, that it does not require locks nor a central server, and that under most circumstances it works well (Sun & Ellis, 1998). However, the drawbacks of OT are also significant: there is no guarantee for correctness and the consistency model is problematic (Sun & Sun, 2009), implementation of a correct transformation for operations is difficult and has in fact been proven to be faulty in many systems (Imine et al., 2006), supporting undo operations is problematic (Ressel et al., 1996; Ressel & Gunzenhauser, 1999), and there is no inherent support for merging of document versions produced in an off-line manner.

In comparison to OT the proposed Piecemeal technique will seamlessly support both real-time as well as off-line operation, will formally guarantee correctness and show that its rules are as strict as they need to be but not stricter, and will enable simple, specification driven implementation. Piecemeal has the additional benefit that support for undo actions is comparatively straightforward. However, measured against OT our approach also has a number of perceived drawbacks which we briefly address:

- **Central Server:** While OT allows peers to communicate without a server, Piecemeal employs a scheduler that accepts or disallows operations. While this may be seen as a bottleneck, it is instructive to note that current OT-based really real-time editors are web-based: a central web server relays communication from client to client. Due to cloud-type implementation this setup does not lead to a bottleneck, and our approach would be comparable.
- **Stricter Strategy:** Our approach uses locks to allow a scheduler to determine

whether an operation can proceed or not. Such a strategy is by nature conservative and strict, even if applied by an optimistic scheduler, but leads to guaranteed correctness and is simpler to implement correctly.

- **Overhead:** Our server keeps track of locks, which is an overhead not incurred in OT. However, note that the number of locks in a collaborative editor is orders of magnitude less than in a database environment, as documents have relatively few concurrent editors and each editor typically holds only a few locks at a time due to the nature of text processing. Furthermore, our approach allows the user to decide on the size of context, making it possible to reduce the number of (read) locks held. Similarly, the size of constituent pieces in a document (the granularity of locking) is a parameter in our approach.

In Sun and Sosič (1999) the authors show that integrating locks in OT cannot solve any of the three problems of convergence, causality violation and intention violation. Crucially, what enables us to do so using locking (without the use of OT) is that we employ a fundamentally different document model (where position has been substituted by unique identifiers for 'blocks') and our operations are dependent on a context.

Table 1 compares Piecemeal to the two main techniques discussed above.

THE THEORY OF PIECEMEAL

The focus of this article lies in providing a solid theoretical foundation for Piecemeal such that both correctness and necessity of the proposed locking technique can be proven.

Our approach is inspired both by CVS and its successors, and traditional concurrency control theory for relational databases. The latter means that we will need to establish suitable notions of transactions (including read and update operations), conflicts, and isolation in the context of documents. We commence by defining a suitable model.

DOCUMENTS AND OPERATIONS

To simplify the final correctness proof we start from a relatively simple model and subsequently refine it. At first, documents will be modeled as general graphs where the nodes represent blocks that have a unique identifier and contain data (text, markup, or both) and the edges represent the fact that a block immediately precedes another block. The delimiters of a block (and hence its size) can be set by the system prior to the document being shared for collaborative editing. Since blocks have identifiers, clients will need to be able to create and manage globally unique identifiers. Operations on such graphs are modeled as graph-manipulation transformations that add and remove edges. For example, to create a new block (e.g. a paragraph of text), it will need to be positioned in the document by creating edges that connect it to existing blocks in the document. Later in the paper, when documents have been further restricted, this means that the new block will need a new incoming and outgoing edge and existing edges will need to be deleted.

Definition 1: *Instance and operation.* Given the set of blocks (or nodes) N, an *instance* is a set $I \subseteq N \times N$. The set of all instances is I. An *operation* is a tuple $o = (P, D, A)$ where P, $D, A \subseteq N \times N$ are respectively *pattern edges*, *deleted edges* and *added edges*, such that $D \cap A = \emptyset$.

Operations, through the A and D edges, encapsulate what needs to change in the document graph. The edges in D are removed and the edges in A are added. The P edges are the context in which these changes occur. They are in essence the formalization of the diff tools' non-marked lines and will correspond to read locks in our concurrency model. It is important to note that client editors may determine the size (and even the location) of the context for every individual operation, although the set of edges in the pattern will need to be at least a subset of the set of edges that are to be deleted (although we formally do not require this at this stage).

The semantics of an operation $o = (P, D, A)$ is defined as a partial function $o: I \rightarrow I$ such that $o(I) = (I - D) \cup A$ if $P \subseteq I$ and undefined otherwise. The concatenation of two such partial functions o_1 and o_2 is denoted as $o_1 \circ o_2$ and defined such that $(o_1 \circ o_2)(I) = o_1(o_2(I))$ if $o_1(o_2(I))$ is defined, and undefined otherwise.

Given the read and write operations as defined, we can now reuse standard notions of transaction management (Weikum & Vossen, 2001), including:

- **Schedules:** Lists of operations each of which is annotated with a transaction identifier.
- **Serial Schedules:** Schedules where operations belonging to different transactions are not interleaved.
- **Serializability:** A schedule is serializable if by reordering of operations we can obtain an equivalent serial schedule while preserving the relative order of operations within individual transactions.

A correct locking protocol must guarantee serializability. Locks are closely associated with conflicts; one kind of conflict is immediately apparent. There is a clear conflict between two operations if one removes the edges that the other one requires. Operation $o_1 = (P_1, D_1, A_1)$ is said to *disable* operation $o_2 = (P_2, D_2, A_2)$ if $P_2 \cap D_1 \neq \emptyset$.

Theorem 1: *Disabling operations.* Operation o_1 disables o_2 iff $o_2 \circ o_1$ is undefined for all instances.

Proof: Clearly if $P_2 \cap D_1 \neq \varnothing$ then $o_2 \circ o_1$ is undefined for all instances. Assume that $P_2 \cap D_1 = \varnothing$. Then let $I = P_1 \cup (P_2 - A_1)$. Clearly $o_1(I)$ is defined since $P_1 \subseteq P_1 \cup (P_2 - A_1)$, and so $o_1(I) = (I - D_1) \cup A_1$. We now show that $o_2(o_1(I))$ is defined by showing that $P_2 \subseteq o_1(I)$ because

$$o_1(I) = (I - D_1) \cup A_1$$
$$= ((P_1 \cup (P_2 - A_1)) - D_1) \cup A_1$$
$$= (P_1 - D_1) \cup (P_2 - A_1) \cup A_1 \text{ since } P_2 \cap D_1 = \varnothing$$
$$= (P_1 - D_1) \cup P_2 \cup A_1$$

Corollary: Two operations o_1 and o_2 are mutually disabling iff both $o_1 \circ o_2$ and $o_2 \circ o_1$ are undefined for all instances.

At this stage we have modeled documents as graphs where nodes represents blocks in a document and edges represent how the blocks are connected. To modify a document we use operations that alter edges. The creation of new blocks in a document (content) at this stage corresponds to linking new edges to a pre-existing node (in the infinite space of all nodes) that simply happens to contain the 'new' content. We will later refine this model but will use the current definitions to build a concurrency control technique for documents.

GRAPH LOCKING

Transaction-oriented concurrency control is usually based on the commutativity of operations that do not conflict, i.e., the fact that their order in a schedule can be changed without affecting the final outcome of the schedule. It is this notion that is used in traditional database concurrency control theory to show the correctness of a scheduler by demonstrating for example that under the absence of cycles in the conflict graph the schedule can be serialized, i.e., the operations can be moved around in the schedule without changing its se-

mantics to an order where the operations of the transactions are not interleaved. The challenge here is to come up with a notion of conflict that is optimal in the sense that the scheduler will disallow as little as possible schedules (and therefore stop certain operations from executing) that are in fact serializable, and thereby allows the maximum amount of parallelism.

We therefore now proceed with defining conflicts and showing operation commutativity in the relatively simple case where documents are graphs as defined in Definition 1. In subsequent sections we will refine this model.

Definition 2: *Conflicting operations.* Two operations $o_1 = (P_1, D_1, A_1)$ and $o_2 = (P_2, D_2, A_2)$ are said to conflict if at least one of the following holds:
C1: $P_1 \cap D_2 \neq \varnothing$
C2: $P_2 \cap D_1 \neq \varnothing$
C3: $P_1 \cap A_2 \neq \varnothing$
C4: $P_2 \cap A_1 \neq \varnothing$
C5: $D_1 \cap A_2 \neq \varnothing$
C6: $D_2 \cap A_1 \neq \varnothing$

Note that mutually disabling operations are also conflicting operations. The following theorem shows that if we only consider not-mutually disabling operations it holds that non-conflicting operations indeed do commute and that all commuting operation are non-conflicting or mutually disabling, i.e., for those combinations of operations the above definition of conflict is theoretically optimal.

Theorem 2: *Commutativity.* For all operations o_1 and o_2 that are not mutually disabling it holds that o_1 and o_2 do not conflict iff $o_1 \circ o_2 = o_2 \circ o_1$.

The proof is given in Dekeyser and Hidders (2009).

The conflict rules also have to deal with the case where both $o_1 \circ o_2$ and $o_2 \circ o_1$ are never defined, in which case the operations commute even though they conflict. We can show that this is indeed the only exception:

Proposition 1: For all operations o_1 and o_2 it holds that $o_1 \circ o_2 = o_2 \circ o_1$ iff o_1 and o_2 do not conflict or are mutually disabling.

A basic notion in transaction theory is that of schedules which represent a sequence of operations which would or would not be allowed by a scheduler. Since in practice a scheduler will only allow operations that have a defined result we proceed to syntactically characterize such schedules.

Definition 3: *Schedules.* A schedule is a non-empty sequence $S = \langle o_1, ..., o_n \rangle$ of operations. A schedule is said to be *sound* if there is an instance I such that $(o_n \circ ... \circ o_1)(I)$ is defined. A schedule $S = \langle o_1, ..., o_n \rangle$ is said to be *well-defined* if it holds that for any two operations $o_i = (P_i, D_i, A_i)$ and $o_j = (P_j, D_j, A_j)$ in S such that $i < j$ and edges $(v_1, v_2) \in D_i \cap P_j$ there is an operation $o_k = (P_k, D_k, A_k)$ such that $i < k < j$ and $(v_1, v_2) \in A_k$.

Theorem 3: *Well-definedness and soundness.* A schedule is sound if it is well-defined.

Proof: Clearly a schedule that is not well-defined will not have a defined result for any instance I and is therefore not sound.

For the other direction we start with assuming that $S = \langle o_1, ..., o_n \rangle$ with $o_i = (P_i, D_i, A_i)$ for all $1 \leq i \leq n$, is well-defined. Let $I = \cup_{1 \leq i \leq n} P_i$. We show with induction that for each $1 \leq i \leq n$ it holds that the result of $(o_i \circ ... \circ o_1)(I)$ is defined. Clearly for $o_1(I)$ this is the case. Assume it holds for i. For every edge (v_1, v_2) in P_{i+1} it holds that it is either not deleted or deleted in $o_i \circ ... \circ o_1$. In the first case it is in $(o_i \circ ... \circ o_1)(I)$. In the second case let $o_j = (P_j, D_j, A_j)$ be the last operation in $\langle o_1, ..., o_i \rangle$ that deletes (v_1, v_2). By the condition of well-definedness there is an operation o_k with $j < k < i+1$ that adds (v_1, v_2), so also then this edge is in

$(o_i \circ ... \circ o_1)(I)$. It therefore holds that $P_{i+1} \subseteq (o_i \circ ... \circ o_1)(I)$ and therefore $(o_{i+1} \circ o_i \circ ... \circ o_1)(I)$ is defined.

Piecemeal is a conservative concurrency control technique but not necessarily a pessimistic one. A document server may be implemented using either a commit scheduler or a conflict scheduler (Weikum & Vossen, 2001). The former one would be pessimistic in the sense that as soon as an operation arrives that causes a conflict, the scheduler would make the originating transaction wait until conflicting transactions have completed. However, a conflict scheduler, which is intrinsically more optimistic, would allow the conflicting operation to proceed and then ensure that subsequent operations do not generate a cycle in the so-called conflict graph. In addition to the normal conflict graph we also define a restricted conflict graph where the conflicts between mutually disabling operations are ignored, i.e., this graph indicates exactly when operations commute or not.

Definition 4: *Conflict graphs.* The conflict graph of a schedule $S = \langle o_1, ..., o_n \rangle$ is $G_S = (V, E)$ where $V = \{1, ..., n\}$ and E contains the edge (i,j) iff $i < j$ and o_i and o_j conflict. The *restricted* conflict graph of a schedule $S = \langle o_1, ..., o_n \rangle$ is $G^r_S = (V, E)$ where $V = \{1, ..., n\}$ and E contains the edge (i,j) iff $i < j$ and o_i and o_j conflict and are not mutually disabling. It can then be shown that the restricted graph is in terms of paths equivalent to the non-restricted graph.

Theorem 4: *Path equivalence.* For every sound schedule S and edge (i,j) in G_S there is a path from i to j in G^r_S.

Proof: We proceed with a proof of the theorem by induction upon $j - i$.

We first consider the base case where $j - i = 1$. Assume that $(i,j) \in G^r_S$. Since S is sound it holds that $P_{i+1} \cap D_i = \emptyset$ and so o_1 and o_2 are not mutually disabling. It follows that $(i,j) \in G_S$.

We now consider the case where $j - i > 1$. Assume that $(i,j) \in G^r_S$. Since S is sound it follows by

Theorem 3 that either (a) $P_j \cap D_i = \emptyset$ or (b) there is an operation $o_k = (P_k, D_k, A_k)$ in S such that $i < k < j$ and $A_k \cap D_i \neq \emptyset$ and $A_k \cap P_j \neq \emptyset$. In case (a) it holds that o_i and o_j are not mutually disabling, and therefore $(i,j) \in G_S$. For case (b) we observe that o_i and o_k conflict by rule **C5**, and also o_k and o_j by rule **C4**. It then follows by induction that there is in G'_S a path from i to k and from k to j, and therefore also a path from i to j.

It follows that an optimistic scheduler that bases its decisions on the presence of cycles, can use the simpler unrestricted conflict graph without disallowing serializable schedules and would therefore still be theoretically optimal.

From Graph Over Cyclic Instance to Document Locking

As an intermediate step towards restricting instances to true documents we first consider cyclic instances that consist of one or more disjoint simple cycles. To see why this step is useful, consider that we can model a document as a *single* cycle with one special edge that connects the end node with the begin node and cannot be removed. Hence cyclic instances approximate real-life documents very well. Figure 1 shows an example of this idea.

In the following, the set of nodes in a set of edges X is denoted as N_X. The set of incoming and outgoing edges of a node v in a set of edges X is denoted as $in_X(v)$ and $out_X(v)$, respectively. The indegree and outdegree of a node v in X are denoted as $|in_X(v)|$ and $|out_X(v)|$, respectively.

Definition 5: *Cyclic instance.* An instance I is said to be *cyclic* if it is finite and for every node v in N_I it holds that $|in_I(v)| = |out_I(v)| = 1$.

We now define what a cyclically sound operation is. Intuitively this is an operation where at least for one instance all additions are real additions, i.e., the edges were not yet in the instance, the deletions are real deletions, and the nodes not appearing in the pattern or the delete set are completely new. These restrictions are chosen such that they represent what might be expected of a correct operation that is specified by the user.

Definition 6: *Cyclically sound operation.* An operation $o = (P, D, A)$ is said to be *cyclically sound* if there is at least one cyclic instance I such that $I \cap A = \emptyset$, $D \subseteq I$, $N_I \cap (N_A - N_{P \cup D}) = \emptyset$ and $o(I)$ is defined and is a cyclic instance.

Examples: Figures 2 and 3 show examples of cyclically sound operations; in the first case $P = \{(1,2),(2,3),(3,4),(4,5)\}$, $D = \{(2,3),(3,4)\}$, and $A = \{(2,4)\}$. The operation removes node 3 if it is preceded by nodes 1 and 2, and followed by nodes 4 and 5. In the second example $P = \{(b,1), (1,2), (5,6), (6,e)\}$, $D = P$, and $A = \{(b,6), (1,e), (5,1), (6,2)\}$. The operation swaps node 1 and 6 if node 1 is the first (real) node of the document and node 6 is the final one.

The problem with Definition 6 is that it suggests that soundness of an operation must be tested by checking the instance. Since the instance can be very large, it would be better if we could determine soundness by looking only at the operation itself. The following definition is a syntactic approximation of a cyclically sound operation.

Figure 1. An example of a document modeled as a cyclic instance with one cycle

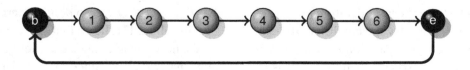

Figure 2. This cyclically sound operation removes node 3 given its context.

Figure 3. This operation swaps nodes 1 and 6 given their contexts.

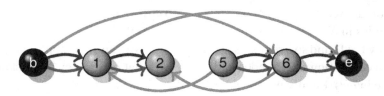

Definition 7: *Cyclically well-formed operation.* An operation $o = (P, D, A)$ is said to be cyclically well-formed if it holds that P, D and A are finite, for every node $v \in N_{P \cup D}$ it holds that $|in_{P \cup D}(v)| \le 1$ and $|out_{P \cup D}(v)| \le 1$, $P \cap A = \varnothing$ and for every node $v \in N_D \cup N_A$ one of the following holds:

Cwf1: $|in_A(v)| = 1, |out_A(v)| = 1, |in_{P \cup D}(v)| = 1, |out_{P \cup D}(v)| = 0$

Cwf2: $|in_A(v)| = 0, |out_A(v)| = 0, |in_D(v)| = 1, |out_D(v)| = 1$

Cwf3: $|in_A(v)| = 1, |out_A(v)| = 0, |in_D(v)| = 1, |out_D(v)| = 0$

Cwf4: $|in_A(v)| = 0, |out_A(v)| = 1, |in_D(v)| = 0, |out_D(v)| = 1$

Cwf5: $|in_A(v)| = 1, |out_A(v)| = 1, |in_D(v)| = 1, |out_D(v)| = 1$

Figure 4 illustrates the five rules for cyclically well-formedness given in Definition 7.

The following theorem states that the syntactical notion of cyclically soundness coincides with the syntactical notion of cyclically well-formedness.

Theorem 5: An operation is cyclically sound if it is cyclically well-formed.

The proof is given in Dekeyser and Hidders (2009).

The preceding theorem states that a cyclically well-formed expression might return a correct result. It can be shown that under the given restrictions for the input instance it in fact *must* return a cyclic instance.

Theorem 6: If an operation $o = (P, D, A)$ is cyclically well-formed and I a cyclic instance such that $D \subseteq I, A \cap I = \varnothing, N_I \cap (N_A - N_{P \cup D}) = \varnothing$ and $o(I)$ is defined, then $o(I)$ is a cyclic instance.

Figure 4. Graphical representation of cyclically well-formed rules as given in definition 7

Proof: All nodes in $o(I)$ are either in $D \cup A$ or not. In the latter case their indegree and outdegree is the same in I and $o(I)$. In the first case it holds that these nodes are in $N_D \cup N_A$. Let us first consider the case for nodes in $N_A - N_D$. These are not in N_D and therefore must satisfy **Cwf1** and therefore, because $N_I \cap (N_A - N_{P \cup D}) = \emptyset$, it is not in I and so they have indegree and outdegree 1 in $o(I)$. Next we consider the nodes in $N_D - N_A$. These nodes then must satisfy **Cwf2** and so o removes the only two edges containing these nodes and they will not be in $o(I)$. Finally we consider the nodes in both $N_A \cap N_D$. These nodes must satisfy **Cwf3**, **Cwf4** or **Cwf5**. Then, using $A \cap I = \emptyset$ and $D \subseteq I$, it is easily observed that in $o(I)$ their indegree and outdegree are 1 if they are 1 in I.

A reasonable restriction on operations is one where the delete set is a subset of the pattern; i.e., it is checked whether all edges that are to be deleted are indeed present in the instance. This restriction is useful in the remainder of the theory; hence, we give this property a name.

Definition 8: *Well-guarded operation.* An operation (P, D, A) is said to be well-guarded if $D \subseteq P$.

We will now show that if the result of a well-guarded cyclically well-formed operation is defined and the new nodes are indeed new nodes, then the result is a cyclic instance.

Lemma 1: For every cyclic instance I and cyclically well-formed operation $o = (P, D, A)$ it holds that if $D \subseteq I$, $N_I \cap (N_A - N_{P \cup D}) = \emptyset$ and $o(I)$ is defined then $A \cap I = \emptyset$.

Proof: Consider an edge $(v_1, v_2) \in A$. If v_1 or v_2 is not in $N_{P \cup D}$ then $(v_1, v_2) \notin I$ since $N_I \cap (N_A - N_{P \cup D}) = \emptyset$. Assume that v_1 and v_2 are in $N_{P \cup D}$. It follows that v_1 must satisfy **Cwf4** or **Cwf5**. It follows that $|out_D(v_1)| = 1$. Let

the outgoing edge of v_1 in D be (v_1, v_3) then, since $A \cap D = \emptyset$, $v_3 \neq v_2$. Since $D \subseteq I$ it follows that $(v_1, v_3) \in I$. Since I is cyclical it then holds that $(v_1, v_2) \notin I$.

Theorem 7: For every cyclic instance I and well-guarded cyclically well-formed operation $o = (P, D, A)$ such that $N_I \cap (N_A - N_{P \cup D}) = \emptyset$ and $o(I)$ is defined then $o(I)$ is a cyclic instance.

Proof: If $D \subseteq P$ and $o(I)$ is defined then $D \subseteq I$. It then follows by Lemma 1 that $A \cap I = \emptyset$. We can then apply Theorem 6 and derive that $o(I)$ is a cyclic instance.

We now have a simple way to check the syntax of an operation to determine whether it will yield a cyclic instance. We are now ready to revisit the notion of conflicts. We redefine it so that it coincides with the notion of conflict in a locking protocol where read-locks are requested for edges in P and write locks for edges in A and D.

Definition 9: *Lock-conflicting operations.* Two operations $o_1 = (P_1, D_1, A_1)$ and $o2 = (P_2, D_2, A_2)$ are said to conflict if at least one of the following holds:

LC1: $P_1 \cap D_2 \neq \emptyset$
LC2: $P_2 \cap D_1 \neq \emptyset$
LC3: $P_1 \cap A_2 \neq \emptyset$
LC4: $P_2 \cap A_1 \neq \emptyset$
LC5: $D_1 \cap A_2 \neq \emptyset$
LC6: $D_2 \cap A_1 \neq \emptyset$
LC7: $A_1 \cap A_2 \neq \emptyset$
LC8: $D_1 \cap D_2 \neq \emptyset$

Note that the conditions **LC1**, ..., **LC6** are the same as **C1**, ..., **C6** from Definition 2 regarding conflicting operations in the setting of graph instances. Only the conditions **LC7** and **LC8** are new, indicating that when we look at cyclic instances instead of graphs, operations can also cause a lock conflict when they both try to add or delete the same edges. This will then also imply an alternative notion of conflict graph.

Definition 10: *Lock-conflict graph.* The lock-conflict graph of a schedule $S = \langle o_1, \ldots, o_n \rangle$ is $G^l_S = (V, E)$ where $V = \{1, \ldots, n\}$ and E contains the edge (i,j) iff $i < j$ and o_i and o_j lock-conflict.

It can then be shown that this lock-conflict graph is in terms of paths equivalent to the preceding conflict graphs if we restrict ourselves to cyclically sound schedules. This result is required to show that our new lock-conflict rules remain optimal.

Theorem 8: For every cyclically sound schedule S and edge (i,j) in G^l_S there is a path from i to j in G_S.

Proof: If S is cyclically sound then by Theorem 5 it is cyclically well-formed. Assume that $(i,j) \in G^l_S$. If this is because one of **LC1** to **LC6** holds then because these conditions are those that define when two operations conflict and therefore whether there is an edge in G_S it follows that $(i,j) \in G_S$. If **LC7** holds because of an edge $(v_1, v_2) \in A_1 \cap A_2$ then there is a $i < k < j$ such that $(v_1, v_2) \in D_k$ and so there is in G_S an edge (i,k) because of **C6** and an edge (k,j) because of **C5**. If **LC8** holds because of an edge $(v_1, v_2) \in D_1 \cap D_2$ then by **Cwf3** there is a $i < k < j$ such that $(v_1, v_2) \in A_k$ and so there is in G_S an edge (i,k) because of **C5** and an edge (k,j) because of **C6**.

It therefore follows that although the notion of conflict is now more restrictive (with two additional rules), the scheduler that uses it will still be theoretically optimal for cyclically sound schedules. In other words, the locks are as strict as they need to be to guarantee correctness, but no stricter than they must be.

Documents

As already explained earlier, a document can be represented as a single cycle with a special irremovable edge that connects the last node with the first node. Unfortunately it is not possible to syntactically characterize the operations that preserve this property for true documents as it is possible for cyclic instances. This is because the same operation might, given a single cycle as input, sometimes return a single cycle and sometimes several cycles.

As an example, consider the operation $o = (P, D, A)$ with $P = D = \{(1,2), (3,4), (5,6)\}$ and $A = \{(1,6), (3,2), (5,4)\}$. Consider the instances $I_1 = (1-2-3-4-5-6)$ and $I_2 = (5-6-3-4-1-2)$. Then $o(I_1)$ results in the document $(1-6)$ plus the separate cycles $(2-3)$ and $(4-5)$, but $o(I_2) = (5-4-1-6-3-2)$. A second example is illustrated in Figures 5 and 6; the former shows the operation while the latter shows its effect on two different instances. Clearly the result in each case is a cyclic instance, but in the second case there are three cycles.

This of course does not mean that we cannot restrict the operations such that they always result in a document, but doing so would be excessively restrictive. Indeed, the above operation is generated by a fairly straightforward move that moves the blocks $(4-1)$ in instance I_2 from between the blocks 3 and 2 to between the blocks 5 and 6.

A consequence of this is that the document server will, in addition to the syntactical checks on just the operation, still have to check whether

Figure 5. A cyclically well-formed operation

Figure 6. The operation's effect on two documents

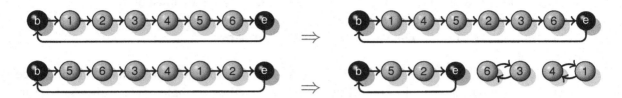

the result of the operation still correctly represents a document (i.e. a *single* cycle). However, there are indexing and optimization techniques that can be used to avoid computing the complete result and checking whether it constitutes a single cycle. Hence, even for large documents this server-side check does not need to be prohibitively expensive.

WORKING OFFLINE: OPERATION MERGING

The operations as defined in preceding sections are highly general in nature. We have seen that only some operations will be accepted and result in a document as defined above. Even so, they remain powerful and can encapsulate editing actions from diverse collaborative client editors on complex documents such as word processing files and serialized graphical content. Mapping client-side editing actions to Piecemeal operations can proceed on the basis of the needs of the editor and hence may depend on what sort of document is being edited.

However, the contents of individual operations need not only depend on editors' requirements. The generality of operations as allowed in our approach also makes it possible to vary the length or size of a single operation. Clients may decide to send minute changes to the server, resulting in a steady stream of tiny operations. Such operations may be seen by other clients (if they so wish) but only become 'permanent' upon committing a transaction. Alternatively, clients may decide to

go offline and concatenate all changes into one sole operation. Such a 'merged' operation has the advantage of acting as a diff between the version of the document as last seen from the server, and the one that the offline client currently manages. In addition, the merged operation is not simply the union of the individual P, A, and D sets; instead, it gives a condensed presentation of all changes since check-out occurred. A preliminary discussion of this issue is given in Dekeyser and Hidders (2009).

CONCLUSION

We have presented a novel conservative and strict technique for enabling collaborative editing of documents both on- and offline. Inspired by CVS's diff approach and its implicit context, we have given a formal foundation and proven that our technique guarantees correctness while limiting locking to the bare essential.

While requiring a central scheduler and incurring locking overhead, the approach offers an alternative to Operational Transformations in those situations where a correctness guarantee is critical, clients should be easy to implement (correctness being the responsibility of the document server), undo operations should be easy to deal with, and collaboration may occur in online and offline circumstances.

In future work we aim to formally define operation merging as well as describe how it would function in a practical system. We will also detail indexing and optimization techniques that a document server may employ to avoid having to check whether the result of a valid operation constitutes a single-cycle document.

ACKNOWLEDGMENT

This work was partially funded by IWT, the Flemish agency for innovation by science and technology, under grant nr. 070171. In addition the authors wish to thank Xenit B.V. for their support and participation in the execution and implementation of this research.

REFERENCES

Corneli, J. (2010, July 7-9). GravPad. In *Proceedings of the 6th International Symposium on Wikis and Open Collaboration*, Gdansk, Poland.

Dekeyser, S., & Hidders, J. (2009). *A notion of serializability for document editing and corresponding optimal locking protocols.* Retrieved from http://www.st.ewi.tudelft.nl/~hidders/docs/piecemeal-tr.pdf

Dekeyser, S., & Hidders, J. (2010). Piecemeal: A formal collaborative editing technique guaranteeing correctness. In *Proceedings of the IADIS International Conference on Collaborative Technologies*, Freiburg, Germany (pp. 125-131).

Dekeyser, S., Hidders, J., & Paredaens, J. (2004). A transaction model for XML databases. *World Wide Web Journal*, 7(1), 29–57. doi:10.1023/B:WWWJ.0000015864.75561.98

Ellis, C., & Gibbs, S. (1989). Concurrency control in groupware systems. In *Proceedings of the ACM SIGMOD Conference on Management of Data*, Seattle, WA (pp. 399-407).

Imine, A., Rusinowitch, M., Oster, G., & Molli, P. (2006). Formal design and verification of operational transformation algorithms for copies convergence. *Theoretical Computer Science*, 351(2), 167–183. doi:10.1016/j.tcs.2005.09.066

Oster, G., & Naja-Jazzar, H. (2007). Supporting collaborative writing of XML documents. In *Proceedings of the International Conference on Enterprise Information Systems*, Madeira, Portugal.

Oster, G., Urso, P., Molli, P., & Imine, A. (2006). Data consistency for P2P collaborative editing. In *Proceedings of the ACM Conference on Computer Supported Cooperative Work*, Banff, AB, Canada.

Ressel, M. (1996). An integrating, transformation-directed approach to concurrency control and undo in group editors. In *Proceedings of the ACM Conference on Computer Supported Cooperative Work*, New York, NY.

Ressel, M., & Gunzenhauser, R. (1999). Reducing the problems of group undo. In *Proceedings of the ACM Conference on Supporting Group Work*, Phoenix, AZ (pp. 131-139).

Rochkind, M. J. (1975). The source code control system. *IEEE Transactions on Software Engineering*, 1(4), 364–370.

Sefton, P. (2006, July 1-5). The integrated content environment. In *Proceedings of the 12th Australasian World Wide Web Conference: Making a Difference with Web Technologies*, Noosa, Australia.

Sun, C., & Ellis, C. (1998). Operational transformation in real-time group editors: Issues, algorithms, and achievements. In *Proceedings of the ACM Conference on Computer Supported Cooperative Work*, Seattle, WA (pp. 59-68).

Sun, C., & Sosič, R. (1999). Optimal locking integrated with operational transformation in distributed real-time group editors. In *Proceedings of the Eighteenth Annual ACM Symposium on Principles of Distributed Computing*, Atlanta, GA (pp. 43-52).

Sun, D., & Sun, C. (2009). Context-based operational transformation in distributed collaborative editing systems. *IEEE Transactions on Parallel and Distributed Systems*, *20*(10), 1454–1470. doi:10.1109/TPDS.2008.240

Wang, X., Bu, J., & Chen, C. (2002). A new consistency model in collaborative editing systems. In *Proceedings of the 4th International Workshop on Collaborative Editing*.

Weikum, G., & Vossen, G. (2001). *Transactional information systems: Theory, algorithms, and the practice of concurrency control and recovery*. San Francisco, CA: Morgan Kaufmann.

Xia, S., Sun, D., Sun, C., Chen, D., & Shen, H. (2004). Leveraging single-user applications for multi-user collaboration: The CoWord approach. In *Proceedings of the ACM Conference on Computer Supported Cooperative Work*, Chicago, IL (pp. 162-171).

This work was previously published in the International Journal of Distributed Systems and Technologies (IJDST), Volume 2, Issue 4, edited by Nik Bessis, pp. 17-29, copyright 2011 by IGI Publishing (an imprint of IGI Global).

Chapter 12
Collaboration Support for Activity Management in a Personal Cloud Environment

Liliana Ardissono
Università di Torino, Italy

Gianni Bosio
Università di Torino, Italy

Anna Goy
Università di Torino, Italy

Giovanna Petrone
Università di Torino, Italy

Marino Segnan
Università di Torino, Italy

Fabrizio Torretta
Università di Torino, Italy

ABSTRACT

This paper describes a framework supporting the development of open collaboration environments which integrate heterogeneous business services. The framework facilitates the user cooperation in the execution of shared activities by offering a workspace awareness support which abstracts from the business services employed to operate. The management of the workspaces of the user's collaborations is based on the functions offered by the Collaborative Task Manager (CTM), which offers a lightweight and flexible model for handling more or less complex collaborations. The CTM is integrated with business services in a loosely coupled way which supports the management of parallel workspaces for accessing the user's collaboration contexts, their objects and the related awareness information.

INTRODUCTION

User coordination support has been analyzed in the research on groupware environments for many years. However, until recently, the closed nature of such environments hampered their customization for answering the functional require- ments of specific user communities. In a sense, the "one size fits all" slogan has been applied at the functional level, forcing users to adopt fixed sets of business services for their activities, and often different sets of services, depending on the contexts in which such activities are carried out. For instance, Grimes and Brush (2008) discuss

DOI: 10.4018/978-1-4666-2647-8.ch012

that many working parents struggle to integrate different Web calendars, one used at home, and a different one at work, in order to achieve a unified view of their schedules.

As discussed in Pendyala and Shim (2009), private and corporate users are increasingly adopting online services to exploit the ubiquitous environment offered by the Internet for carrying out activities from any place, thus enabling distributed collaboration, as well as mobile work. However, we point out that, currently, this kind of support is offered by separate Web 2.0 services supporting specific types of activities, such as, e.g., distributed document writing, calendar sharing, and similar. In contrast, an open environment supporting the integration of services in a unified workspace does not exist. Therefore, when carrying out complex activities and projects, which require the execution of different types of operations, people have to switch among multiple applications, each one offering its own, separate, workspace for accessing the objects to be manipulated using it; see Ardissono et al. (2009c) for a discussion on this topic.

The provision of multiple, application-dependent workspaces (Erickson et al., 2009) is problematic because it exposes the user to separate views on such contexts, and separate access points to the involved entities (e.g., objects to be manipulated and actors participating to the shared activities). We claim that a user-centered perspective should be offered. Put in other words, the incredible potential of the Web 2.0 in supporting fast and flexible activity management is spoiled by the lack of integration of Web 2.0 services, which overload users with multiple representations of their coordination spaces (Introne & Alterman, 2006), and separate access points to their activity contexts.

As an attempt to address this issue, we propose an open framework which supports the integration of business services in order to offer a unified access point to the workspaces of the user's collaborations. The key component of this framework is a Collaborative Task Manager

(CTM) service which can be integrated with heterogeneous business services in order to enable the user to schedule and organize personal and shared activities using tools which provide different functionalities. The support offered by our framework, and in particular by the CTM, is characterized by the following features:

- **Direct Access to the Entities Involved in Collaboration:** The CTM offers a User Interface (UI) managing a separate workspace for each of the user's collaboration contexts. The workspace associated to a collaboration context is a single access point to the objects to be manipulated (e.g., documents), to the actors participating in the collaboration, and to the awareness information describing the events occurred in it, which can be reached by the user, and manipulated, by means of a click.
- **Flexible Coordination Support:** The CTM enables the user to define flexible processes, based on the specification of task networks, which can be easily managed and revised, in order to reflect frequent changes in the users' plans and schedules.
- **Awareness Support:** The framework supports the user in a quick assessment of the state of her/his collaborations by offering a customizable notification management service (aimed at answering individual notification preferences) as well as a structured, Web-based awareness space storing the history of awareness events directed to the user. In both cases, information is organized on the basis of the user's collaboration contexts and presented in a modality supporting its direct manipulation, e.g., in order to access the objects of the awareness events.

In the following, we describe the collaboration framework we propose, focusing on the Collaborative Task Manager service. This work builds on, and extends, the work described in Ardissono et al. (2010).

The remainder of this paper is organized as follows: Section *The problem* describes the issues we aim at addressing and provides some background on previous work. Section *A framework for the management of collaborative workspaces across applications* describes our collaboration support framework, focusing on the Collaborative Task Manager. Section *Discussion* compares our work with the related one and Section *Conclusion* concludes the paper.

THE PROBLEM

Most project management and groupware environments provide the user with a workspace supporting the execution of activities and shared tasks in closed environments, which offer a predefined set of business services to be exploited. For instance, BSCW (Horstmann & Bentley, 1997) and more recent services, such as DropBox (www.dropbox.com), support document sharing by offering distributed directories which users can access to manage and share documents, and an awareness space presenting the chronology of the operations carried out on such directories. Moreover, complex project management and groupware tools, such as Collanos (www.collanos.com/en/products) and ActiveCollab (www.activecollab.com), offer specific coordination services for the definition of projects and tasks, their assignment to users, and the monitoring of their execution. Such systems manage structured workspaces supporting the execution of operations and the user awareness, but they are based on vertical architectures and cannot be integrated with external business services.

We claim that, in order to offer an efficient support to the execution of personal and shared activities, such environments should be open, in order to enable the integration in the workspace of

business services supporting new types of activities, or simply largely adopted by the target users. Moreover, as suggested in some recent environments, such as TeamWox (www.teamwox.com), they should offer integrated workspaces enabling users to directly operate on the objects of their collaborations. Thus, for instance, the objects to be managed in a task should be made available when opening the task, together with the history of events concerning them, in a unified environment. Specifically, the following requirements can be identified:

- Offering an easy access to the entities of a cooperation in order to enable the user to interact with them in a seamless way, without changing application each time.
- Providing users with a flexible type of coordination support, which (1) enables them to easily manage more or less complex collaborations and to quickly revise their activity plans as needed, and (2) proactively supports the scheduling of activities, taking collaboration constraints into account, in order to improve the users' coordination.
- Supporting the users' awareness about their collaborations, in terms of who is involved, what has been done, when and where, in order to enable users to be timely informed about the occurred events.

As discussed in Mark and Su (2007), Czerwinsky et al. (2004), and Iqbal and Horvitz (2010), the users of online environments are involved in large numbers of collaborations and continuously switch between such different activity contexts, e.g., because of interruptions (phone calls, e-mails, etc.), but also spontaneously. In fact, such contexts represent streams of activity to be carried out in parallel and thus have to be continuously monitored. Until a few years ago, the involvement in many collaborations was typical of working environments, where users participate to several projects and have to interact with different groups of colleagues. For instance, usage data of BSCW show that some people use it handle up to 100-120 different collaborations. However, this phenomenon has recently started to interest users' personal activities as well; for instance, consider the success of social networks, such as Facebook (www.facebook.com) in helping users to manage their interaction and synchronization with different groups of friends.

Web 2.0 and cloud computing (Dikaiakos et al., 2009) bring a shift from the provision of closed environments offering families of integrated services to open *service clouds*, which make remote, heterogeneous services available, abstracting from their execution place and environment. The Software as a Service paradigm (SaaS) (Turner et al., 2003) proposes the provision of software as services that are accessible from the Internet, regardless of how the software runs, and of its execution platform. Based on SaaS, a Service Cloud is a set of integrated services and resources, typically associated to a Web desktop providing pointers for accessing its parts. In principle, a service cloud can include any services. Thus, besides the well-known service clouds available now, such as Amazon (www.aws.amazon.com) and Google (http://code.google.com/appengine/) ones, new service clouds can be created by technical users, or by federated service providers, in order to offer specific pools of services.

The service provision model proposed in cloud computing offers high flexibility in the development of customized collaboration environments. However, services are only integrated superficially. Therefore, each of them provides the user with its own workspace awareness, which must be externally managed in order to present a unified perspective on her/his activities. Given the high degree of specialization of business services, the management of a single collaboration context can become an ordeal if the activities to be carried out require the usage of many different applications. For instance, in a typical collaboration setting, users employ different tools in order to manage documents and tables, exchange e-mails and Instant Messages, handle their own calendars, schedule meetings, and so forth. Thus, they are forced to log in each application, and separately access its workspace in order to access the objects to be manipulated, and interact with their peers. The situation becomes even worse if users handle multiple collaboration contexts: in that case each context switch further demands for a resumption of the state of the related collaboration, in order to understand who has done what (Mark & Su, 2007).

In order to enable an efficient management of users' activities, an explicit support to user coordination, and to the management of the workspaces associated to each collaboration, is a major requirement. Our work attempts to answer this requirement by providing users with a unified Web desktop supporting a seamless management of their collaboration contexts, by abstracting from the perspectives proposed by the many business services used to handle them.

A FRAMEWORK FOR MANAGING COLLABORATIVE WORKSPACES ACROSS APPLICATIONS

We introduce the notion of *activity context*, as a representation of a collaboration context which the user establishes, or is involved in, in order to carry out a set of activities. The activity context is the core metaphor of our framework, which provides the functionality needed to support the scheduling and execution of activities, as well as the management of the associated awareness information. As described later on, the activity context is supported and managed by the Collaborative Task Manager.

Representation of the User's Activity Contexts

In order to model the user's collaboration contexts at different granularity levels, we model two types of activity contexts: the *activity frame* and the *task*. Central to both types of context is the information about who is involved in them, e.g., which users are allowed to create and view the entities belonging to such contexts, and to operate on them.

An *activity frame* represents a generic collaboration context involving a set of users who are interested in a certain topic, and/or participate in activities related to a topic. The activity frame supports lightweight collaboration management, which standard project management tools are just too complex to suit. Specifically:

- An activity frame models a loosely coupled collaboration defined in order to collect information and activities, represented as *tasks*, without necessarily organizing such activities in timelines with deadlines. At the same time, however, a fine-grained temporal organization of events is possible, by organizing tasks in partial order relations determining their correct scheduling.
- The hierarchical access right specification applied in standard task manager tools is replaced with a "frame sharing" model which specifies which users can jointly operate on an activity frame. Specifically, all the users sharing a frame with write privileges can access its objects, operate on them, create, delete, and modify tasks, and so forth; users sharing a frame with read-only privileges can view the frame content and its evolution.

In order to support the management of a workspace devoted to the presentation of an activity frame, as well as its management, the representation of an activity frame includes all its involved entities. Specifically, an activity frame is represented by a tuple (fn, c, Ur, Uw, O, T), where fn is the frame name, c is the container of the activity frame (either null, or a reference to a parent task - see below), Ur is the set of users sharing it with read access rights, Uw is the set of users sharing it with write access rights, O is the set of objects which have been associated to the frame by one of the users sharing it, T is the set of tasks included in the frame.

The meaning of the read and write access rights are standard: users sharing a frame with read privilege can view its content. Users having write privileges can view, modify and operate on the activity frame.

The *task* is aimed at supporting specific activities, interaction and synchronization in order to achieve a goal, possibly associated with a deadline. Similar to the activity frame, a task can have a set of associated objects, i.e., those to be accessed, or manipulated, in order to complete it. A task inherits the sharing specifications of the activity frame containing it, which can be modified in a very flexible way by restricting or expanding the users sharing it, as needed. Moreover, a task is explicitly assigned to a set of users (having write access right on it), in order to define responsibilities on its execution. Any user sharing a task in write mode can modify it, and operate on its objects.

The partial order relations among tasks are represented in a format supporting the specification of flexible processes, which users can easily modify, by updating the interested tasks. Specifically, following the traditional approach applied in Belief Desire Intention Agents (Rao & Georgeff, 1991), each task has a precondition describing whether the task is always enabled (true) or its enablement depends on the execution of some other tasks. The precondition is a Boolean condition on task completion and synchronization events, and supports the specification of AND/OR relations between tasks, thus enabling the definition of various types of workflow nets. In particular, we consider the following workflow patterns: parallel split, exclusive choice, synchronization and simple merge (van der Aalst & van Hee, 2002).

A task is thus represented by a tuple (*tn, c, Ur, Uw, A, O, g, P, s, d*) where *tn* is the name, *c* is the name of the container of the task (i. e., its activity frame), *Ur* and *Uw* are the sets of users sharing it in read/write mode, *A* is the set of assignees, *g* is the goal associated to it (if any), *P* is the precondition, *s* is its state (enabled, not enabled, done) and *d* is its deadline (if any).

In order to support the management of complex activities, requiring a hierarchical organization of sub-steps, a task *t* can be expanded by defining an activity frame devoted to its management and including smaller tasks, possibly organized in partial order dependencies. In that case, the container of the activity frame is set to *t*, as this is its "parent" task. Notice that a frame expanding a task *t* inherits the access right specification of *t*, but such properties can be modified in a very flexible way, in comparison to the strictly hierarchical organization of tasks in project management tools. For instance, the group of users sharing a frame can be smaller, but also larger than the one defined for its "parent" task.

CTM Support to the Management of Activity Contexts

The Collaborative Task Manager (CTM) service supports the management of the users' activity contexts by providing a User Interface which enables them to define collaboration contexts (internally represented as activity frames) and operate on them, e.g., by linking documents, creating and managing tasks, and so forth. Specifically, as far as activity frames are concerned, the CTM offers a user-friendly web graphical editor enabling the creation of tasks and connections using drag and drop. In particular, users are allowed to create:

- Task elements, characterized by a set of default properties (e.g., deadline), which can be modified, if needed. Users can as-

sign people to a task, set a deadline, include links to documents and other objects, and so forth.

- And/or elements exploited to set dependency conditions among tasks. These conditions are translated to the task preconditions by the CTM.
- Decision elements that allow creating alternative paths in a task network. Also the conditions specified in decision elements are translated by the CTM to the task preconditions.

For each activity frame/task, the CTM offers a unified access point to the related workspace, supporting its inspection and the execution of operations on it. Specifically, as far as tasks are concerned, the CTM presents an up-to-date view on their state, as well as of the ongoing activities. Moreover, the CTM offers an alert service which helps the user to be aware of deadlines, pending commitments, and similar.

The workspace of a collaboration context (activity frame) includes:

- The time-line of activities defined in such a context (if any), as specified in the partial order relations among tasks, including the state of such tasks, so that the user can immediately understand what has/can be done and where.
- The links to the associated objects, clickable in order to open/interact with them, and the references to the users involved in the same context, either as sharing users, or as assignees (reachable by e-mail or instant messages).
- The awareness information events related to the activity context, describing which operations have been carried out by the collaborators.

Figure 1 shows the workspace of a collaboration context (i.e., an activity frame) including

Figure 1. User interface supporting the management of activity frames (collaboration contexts)

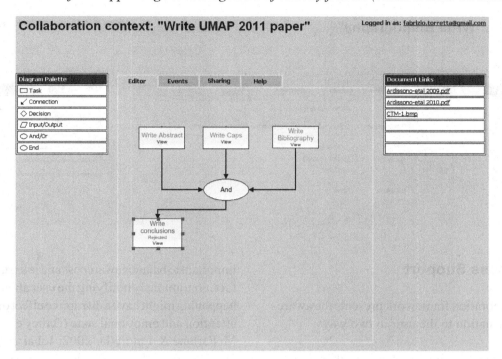

a simple task network defined to organize the preparation of a research paper. The workspace is presented in four tabs: the *Editor* one supports the management of tasks and objects within the activity frame. The *Events* one enables the user to view the related awareness information. The *Sharing* tab visualizes and links the users sharing the frame and the *Help* tab provides instructions and generic help. The *Editor* tab (in focus) is structured in three parts: at the left side, there is the palette supporting task creation and modification. The right portion of the tab shows the linked objects. The central part shows the tasks, represented by rectangles, and linked to each other according to the defined order dependencies. The state of tasks is depicted by coloring their titles in different ways (red for not enabled, green for enabled, grey for done).

Figure 2 shows the workspace associated to a task, enabling users to inspect its details and to operate on it. Besides showing the task name and the user currently logged in, the window is organized in three areas. On the left, the *Expand Task* button enables the user to expand the task by defining an activity frame for its management and including simpler tasks. On the right, the linked objects are listed. The central part of the window offers four tabs: the *Properties* one enables the user to view and modify task properties. As for activity frames, the *Events* tab enables the user to view the awareness information related to the task. The *Assignees* tab enables the visualization and the modification of the list of users in charge of the task, as well as the groups of users having read and write access on it, and the *Help* tab provides a generic help.

Figure 2. Task management window

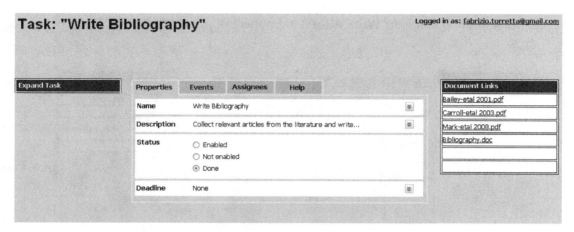

Awareness Support

Our collaboration framework presents the awareness information to the user in two ways:

- In an asynchronous, Web-based awareness space, structured according to the user's activity contexts. For each context, the space manages a tab presenting the history of the related awareness events, supporting multi-faceted browsing of information.
- As notification messages describing individual awareness events, submitted either as Instant Messages or as e-mails, depending on the user's preferences. In particular, IMs are submitted to the user as pop-ups in order to enable her/him to operate on them, different from the ephemeral balloons employed in other notification systems, which can only be visualized.

In both cases, awareness events are presented by including the involved entities (actor originating the event, object documents, etc.) as hypertextual links, which enable the user to operate on them by means of a click.

As largely discussed in the literature about attention and interruption management, the adoption of notification management policies is very important to balance awareness and interruption. In fact, continuously notifying the user about what is happening might have a disruptive effect on her/his attention and emotional state (Bailey et al., 2001; McFarlane & Latorella, 2002; Iqbal & Horvitz, 2007, Mark et al., 2008). Our framework enables the user to apply specific notification management policies to her/his activity contexts, in order to select the notifications (s)he wants to receive, or filter out. In particular, our framework offers two context-dependent policies which submit to the user the notifications concerning her/his current activity context, at different granularity levels, in the attempt to reduce the notification flow to the information related to the user's current activities: the *context filter* submits the notifications associated to the activity frame which the user is working at, when the awareness event is generated; the *task filter* submits the notifications belonging to the user's current task. See Ardissono et al. (2009a, 2009b) for details.

The context-dependent management of awareness events, and their presentation in a structured space, are based on a classification of events in the user's activity contexts. The CTM supports this contextualization of events thanks to (1) the explicit support offered to handle activity frames and tasks at the User Interface level, (2) the classification of objects in activity contexts (e.g., by tracking the activity frames/tasks which the user accesses objects from), and (3) an association of awareness events to activity contexts, depending on the objects which such events relate to. For instance, if the user creates a document x from the CTM window of a task t, then the object x is associated to t (by including it in the O element of t's tuple). As a consequence of this association, the CTM associates all the subsequent events generated while x is manipulated to the same task t. The meaning of such an association is an interpretation of the low-level events generated by services in terms of user intentions, aimed at supporting the tasks which users are carrying out; see Carroll et al. (2003).

As described in Section *Architecture*, the association of objects to activity frames and tasks, and the consequent contextualization of awareness events, are possible thanks to the integration of the CTM with the business services included in the collaboration environment.

Architecture

The CTM is included in the Personal Cloud Platform (Ardissono et al., 2009c), which supports the integration of services in a user-centered service cloud. The PCP supports the development of collaborative environments including heterogeneous business services; moreover, it provides the user with a Web desktop offering a unified access point to her/his collaborative workspaces. While the PCP alone synchronizes services with respect to the user's identities (single sign-on) and collaboration groups, the CTM enriches it with task management and workspace awareness support features.

The architecture of the PCP includes a set of core components supporting the management of the user's workspace across an extensible set of services. In order to develop a specific collaboration environment, its administrator has to integrate the required business services, wrapping them by means of adapters which enable them

to share information with the PCP. The adapter wrapping a service is exploited to retrieve, via APIs, the awareness events describing the operations performed by users on the application (e.g., document upload, deletion, and similar), and to invoke operations on the service (e.g., in order to synchronize business services with respect to the set of users sharing an activity frame).

The PCP bases the synchronization of software components on the publish and subscribe pattern, which supports a loosely-coupled interaction among heterogeneous software.

Figure 3 depicts the architecture of a collaboration environment integrating one external service. As shown, the core of the environment is represented by a coordination middleware (Pub-HUB/GIGA) which manages a shared context collecting the business information to be shared within the environment.

The coordination middleware receives the information items published by business services (via their adapters) and PCP core components (i.e., the Notification Manager, the CTM, and the User Agent in the figure), and propagates them to the rest of the environment on a subscription basis. The Web desktop functionality is provided by software components running within the user's browser.

For each user, the following components are devoted to the management of the workspace of activity contexts:

- A Collaborative Task Manager instance offers the User Interface for the management of activity frames and tasks. Moreover, it contextualizes the awareness events generated by the user's actions by associating them to the corresponding activity contexts.[1]
- A User Agent instance stores the user's notification preferences and tracks her/his current focus of attention over her/his activity frames and tasks, in order to support the application of the context-dependent

Figure 3. Portion of the architecture of a collaboration environment based on the PCP

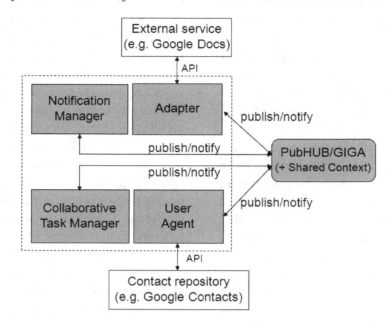

notification management policies offered by the collaboration framework.

- A Notification Manager instance collects the awareness information directed to the user and handles it, in the Web-based awareness space and as notifications.

The coordination middleware used in the PCP offers a fine-grained subscription mechanism, based on pattern matching on the event structure. Thus, each component subscribes exactly for the pieces of awareness information concerning its user. For instance, a user U's Notification Manager only receives the awareness information concerning U's collaborations. In other words, the specification of her/his activity frames is used as a control access list for the selection of the information pieces (s)he is allowed to receive. In this way, the propagation of user information in the collaboration environment is controlled, as each user can only receive the information directed to her/him.

The contextualization of awareness events is based on the following information flow:

- The CTM receives the awareness information generated by business services (via adapters) and classifies it in the user's activity contexts. Then, it publishes the contextualized awareness information in the shared context in order to make it available to the other PCP core components. It should be noticed that such information includes evidence about the user's focus of attention: each time the user opens a window of the CTM to work on a specific activity context, the CTM publishes a corresponding awareness event.
- The User Agent and the Notification Manager operate on the contextualized awareness information.

In particular, when the user creates/accesses an object o in the scope of an activity context ctx, the CTM associates o to ctx by adding the object identifier to the O element of ctx's tuple. This association enables the CTM to contextualize the subsequent actions performed on the same object.

Implementation Details

The prototype personal cloud implementing the Personal Cloud Platform (PCP) was developed by exploiting the Google Web Toolkit (GWT). The current dashboard is built as a iGoogle page, allowing the users to collect the Gadgets (http://code.google.com/intl/it/apis/gadgets) of their favorite apps, as well as those offered by the personal cloud. However, the goal of PCP is to allow the integration and synchronization of applications offering open APIs, therefore there is no architectural constraint to use Google APIs or Apps. The prototype is developed in Java and exploits Gigaspaces (Cohen, 2004), a publish and subscribe coordination middleware for managing the shared context and the synchronization of the services.

Figure 3 shows a portion of the architecture of the prototype collaboration environment we developed. The figure depicts the cloud in a shaded rectangle and, for simplicity, only shows the User Agent service, the Notification Manager one, and the Collaborative Task Manager, plus the adapter of an external service (Google Documents (Google, 2010)), hiding other services which are not central to the description of this paper. In the figure, the synchronized services are connected to the coordination middleware by arrows labeled as "publish/notify" that represent a bidirectional event flow between services and the publish-and-subscribe server. Those labeled as "API" indicate the exploitation of the service (open) API by core applications (e.g. the CTM) or by adapters wrapping external services.

In order to share activity frames and to enable collaborative work on tasks, activity frames have to be stored in a shared space. In our prototype, activity frames are stored as text files, using the JSON format (www.json.org), in Google Documents, exploiting the open Google Java API.

DISCUSSION

The integrated workspace offered by the Collaborative Task Manager (CTM), and its awareness support, provide users with a coordinating representation of shared activities which, as discussed in Introne and Alterman (2006), has a central role in preventing mistakes and supporting user coordination in any groupware environment. More generally, our work advances the state of the art in collaboration support in various ways.

With respect to standard project management tools and groupware environments, such as, e.g., Collanos (www.collanos.com/en/products), ActiveCollab (www.activecollab.com), TeamWox (www.teamwox.com), and eGroupware (www.egroupware.org), our CTM offers a lightweight management of activities, abandoning the traditional hierarchical task management model in favor for a flexible model, based on sharing activity contexts. Obviously, the management of a large, long-living project involving many people benefits from the adoption of one of such tools, but ordinary collaborations can benefit from a simpler coordination support, such as the one offered by our CTM. Notice also that the CTM operates in open environments, which can be extended with heterogeneous business services, while standard project management and groupware environments are closed.

With respect to task manager applications, such as, e.g., Doit (www.doit.im/) and Things (www.culturedcode.com/things/), our CTM is similar in the interpretation of activity management as "things to be done" and thus in the adoption of the Getting Things Done approach proposed in (Allen, 2003). However, it differs from the architectural and functional point of view: while such systems work in isolation with respect to the business services to be used for carrying out activities, the CTM is integrated with such services and thus supports a vivid presentation of the state of the user's collaboration contexts, supporting a direct interaction with them, by means of suitable workspaces.

With respect to workflow engines, the CTM supports simple processes (e.g., it does not deal with exception and transaction management), putting the user in charge of the decision making activities aimed at solving exceptional cases. While this simplification makes our approach unsuitable for the management of complex workflows, it makes the management of everyday collaboration much easier and lightweight, as it does not require the specification of complex workflows, which has been criticized in various works (e. g., van der Aalst, 1999).

With respect to other attempts to govern the complexity of application-oriented workspaces, e.g., the HP's Content Centered Collaboration Spaces (Erickson et al., 2009), our work has a different perspective: we do not want to model document-centered workspaces, but user-centered ones, taking into account the fact that user collaboration involves many different types of activity, and that document sharing is only a specific case.

CONCLUSION

This paper presented the collaboration and awareness support offered by an open collaboration framework integrating heterogeneous business services in a service cloud. Such support is based on (1) the management of a shared context supporting the synchronization of business services with respect to the user's activity contexts, and (2) the exploitation of a Collaborative Task Manager, which enables users to handle their activity contexts at different granularity levels (i.e., generic collaborations and tasks). On such a basis, our framework manages the workspaces of the users' collaborations, and presents the related awareness information, by abstracting from the specific services used to operate.

The Collaborative Task Manager supports the presentation of *intentional* information about the elementary awareness events which can be captured by interacting with business services. As discussed in various works, such as Carroll et al. (2003) and Gross and Prinz (2004), collaborative activities can articulate in non trivial processes. In such a situation, the information about the elementary operations performed by users (e.g., a document has been created, removed, etc.) is not enough to provide the user with an overview of the evolution of her/his activities. An effective presentation of the state of a collaboration, supporting a correct coordination of the user actions, has thus to be organized at a higher level, modeling the context of such actions.

An open issue of our work is the management of personal privacy preferences in the collaboration environment, which we intend to analyze in our future work. Our framework currently controls the propagation of user information at two levels: at the transport level, SSL is used to support the propagation of information between software components and shared context (the coordination middleware exploited for this purpose offers encrypted data transmission). At the application level, the composition of the collaboration groups involved in each activity context is used as an access control list to restrict the propagation of awareness information accordingly. Thus, each user only receives the awareness information concerning the collaborations (s)he is part of. Of course, this guarantees a correct diffusion of information only if all the business services integrated in the collaboration environment respect the users' privacy. Thus, a careful analysis of the data propagation patterns adopted by business services is needed in order to decide whether they can be integrated in the collaboration environment or not, or whether the kind of information they disclose has to be shaded in any way before publishing it in the shared context of the collaboration environment.

In addition to privacy preservation issues, our future work will be devoted to the design of a friendly User Interface for the management of the user's activity contexts and to the management of further experiments with users, in order to assess the usability of the overall framework and its applicability in real world settings.

REFERENCES

Allen, D. (2003). *Getting things done: The art of stress-free productivity*. Harlow, UK: Penguin.

Ardissono, L., Bosio, G., Goy, A., & Petrone, G. (2009a). Context-aware notification management in an integrated collaborative environment. In *Proceedings of the International Workshop on Adaptation and Personalization for Web 2.0* (pp. 21-30).

Ardissono, L., Bosio, G., Goy, A., Petrone, G., & Segnan, M. (2009b). Managing context-dependent workspace awareness in an e-collaboration environment. In *Proceedings of the International Workshop on Intelligent Web Interaction*, New York, NY (pp. 42-45). Washington, DC: IEEE Computer Society.

Ardissono, L., Bosio, G., Goy, A., Petrone, G., & Segnan, M. (2010). Open, collaborative task management in Web 2.0. In *Proceedings of the IADIS Multi Conference on Computer Science and Information Systems* (pp. 20-27).

Ardissono, L., Goy, A., Petrone, G., & Segnan, M. (2009c). From service clouds to user-centric personal clouds. In *Proceedings of the International Conference on Cloud Computing*, Bangalore, India (pp. 1-8). Washington, DC: IEEE Computer Society.

Bailey, B., Konstan, J., & Carlis, J. (2001). The effects of interruptions on task performance, annoyance, and anxiety in the user interface. In *Proceedings of the Conference on Human Computer Interaction*, Tokyo, Japan (pp. 593-601).

Carroll, J., Neale, D., Isenhour, P., Rosson, M., & Scott McCrickard, D. (2003). Notification and awareness: Synchronizing task-oriented collaborative activity. *International Journal of Human-Computer Studies*, *58*(5), 605–632. doi:10.1016/S1071-5819(03)00024-7

Cohen, U. (2004). *Inside GigaSpaces XAP - Technical overview and value proposition*. New York, NY: GigaSpace Technologies Ltd.

Czerwinski, M., Horvitz, E., & Wilhite, S. (2004). A diary study of task switching and interruptions. In *Proceedings of the Conference on Human Factors in Computing Systems*, Vienna, Austria (pp. 175-182).

Dikaiakos, M. D., Pallis, G., Katsaros, D., Mehra, P., & Vakali, A. (2009). Cloud computing: Distributed internet computing for IT and scientific research. *IEEE Internet Computing*, *13*(5), 10–13. doi:10.1109/MIC.2009.103

Erickson, J. S., Spence, S., Rhodes, M., Banks, D., Rutherford, J., & Simpson, E. (2009). Content-centered collaboration spaces in the Cloud. *IEEE Internet Computing*, 34–42. doi:10.1109/MIC.2009.93

Google. (2010). *Google documents*. Retrieved from http://www.google.com/google-d-s/tour1.html

Grimes, A., & Brush, A. J. (2008). Life scheduling to support multiple social roles. In *Proceedings of the Conference on Human Factors in Computing Systems*, Florence, Italy (pp. 821-824).

Gross, T., & Prinz, W. (2004). Modelling shared contexts in cooperative environments: Concept, implementation, and evaluation. *Computer Supported Cooperative Work*, *13*(3-4), 283–303. doi:10.1007/s10606-004-2804-6

Horstmann, T., & Bentley, R. (1997). Distributed authoring on the Web with the BSCW shared workspace system. *StandardView*, *5*(1), 9–16. doi:10.1145/253452.253464

Introne, J., & Alterman, R. (2006). Using shared representations to improve coordination and intent inference. *User Modeling and User-Adapted Interaction*, *3-4*(4), 249–280. doi:10.1007/s11257-006-9009-2

Iqbal, S., & Horvitz, E. (2007). Conversations admist computing: A study of interruptions and recovery of task activity. In *Proceedings of the 11th International Conference on User Modeling*, Corfu, Greece (pp. 350-354).

Iqbal, S., & Horvitz, E. (2010). Notifications and awareness: A field study of alert usage and preferences. In *Proceedings of the ACM Conference on Computer Supported Cooperative Work*, Savannah, GA (pp. 27-30).

Mark, G., Gudith, D., & Klocke, U. (2008). The cost of interrupted work: More speed and stress. In *Proceedings of the Conference on Human Factors in Computing Systems*, Florence, Italy (pp. 821-824).

Mark, G., & Su, N. (2007). Considering Web 2.0 technologies within an ecology of collaborations. In *Proceedings of the UMAP Workshop SociUM*, Corfu, Greece (pp. 50-59).

McFarlane, D., & Latorella, K. (2002). The scope and importance of human interruption in human-computer interaction design. *Human-Computer Interaction*, *17*(1), 1–61. doi:10.1207/S15327051HCI1701_1

O'Reilly, T. (2007). What is web 2.0: Design patterns and business models for the next generation of software. *Communications & Strategies*, *65*(1), 17–37.

Pendyala, V. S., & Shim, S. S. Y. (2009). The Web as the ubiquitous computer. *Computing Now*, *42*(9), 90–92. doi:10.1109/MC.2009.302

Rao, A., & Georgeff, M. P. (1991). Modeling rational agents within a BDI architecture. In *Proceedings of the International Conference on Principles of Knowledge Representation and Reasoning*, Cambridge, MA (pp. 473-484).

Turner, M., Budgen, D., & Brereton, P. (2003). Turning software into a service. *Communications & Strategies*, *36*(10), 38–44.

van der Aalst, W. (1999). Flexible workflow-management systems: An approach based on generic process models. In *Proceedings of the 10th International Conference on Database and Expert Systems Applications*, Firenze, Italy (pp. 186-195).

van der Aalst, W., & van Hee, K. (2002). *Workflow management - Models, methods, and systems*. Cambridge, MA: MIT Press.

ENDNOTES

[1] Sometimes, this contextualization fails, e.g., because the user actions are ambiguous and their reference activity context cannot be identified. In such cases, the awareness events are associated to an "unclassified" stream of awareness information, which is presented in a specific portion of the Web-based awareness space.

This work was previously published in the International Journal of Distributed Systems and Technologies (IJDST), Volume 2, Issue 4, edited by Nik Bessis, pp. 30-43, copyright 2011 by IGI Publishing (an imprint of IGI Global).

Chapter 13
Matrixes of Weighing and Catastrophes

José G. Hernández Ramírez
Universidad Metropolitana, Venezuela

María J. García García
Minimax Consultores C. A., Venezuela

Gilberto J. Hernández García
Minimax Consultores C. A., Venezuela

ABSTRACT

An easy to apply multi-criteria technique is the Matrixes Of Weighing (MOW), but many of the professionals that use it, in their respective fields, do it in intuitive fashion. In this regard, applications are rarely reported in specialized literature, which explains how few references exist about them. One of the application areas for MOW is the handling of catastrophes, in particular the pre-catastrophe and post-catastrophe phases where a series of problems are usually handled which solution leads to a choice, which could be done by using multi-criteria techniques. The objective of this investigation is to present the MOW with multiplicative factors, and showing their application in the pre-catastrophe phase, when choosing possible shelters and in the post-catastrophe phase, by aiding to hierarchies which infrastructures to be recovered after a catastrophe.

INTRODUCTION

The contribution of this work is mainly focused in establishing the essential concepts on Matrixes Of Weighing (MOW), to present its variants and how them can be used for group decision making, simultaneously presenting its applicability in decision support during a catastrophe, particularly in the pre and post catastrophe stages.

Of all the above the main objective of the investigation can be established, which is: To present the MOW with multiplicative factors, and to show their application the pre-catastrophe phase, when choosing possible shelters and in the

DOI: 10.4018/978-1-4666-2647-8.ch013

post-catastrophe phase, by aiding to hierarchies which infrastructures are to be recover after a catastrophe.

From this main objective, two specific objectives arise: Presenting the MOW, its variants and how they can be used in group decision making and presenting how this MOW can be used to aid the decision making when catastrophes occur.

To achieve this main objective and the specific objectives, it will be used as methodology the scientific method to solve problems, or applied to research operations (Hernández & García, in press; Hernández, García, & Hernández, 2009), in which, instead of proving hypothesis, a series of steps are followed:

- To define the problem, as indicated in the objectives is to present how the pre and post catastrophe phases can be aided by the MOW.
- Searching for data, particularly on aspects related to pre and post catastrophes and on MOW.
- Establishing alternatives, meaning the different models based in MOW, which can be used for supporting decision making in case of catastrophes.
- Evaluating alternatives, consisting in the feasibility of the proposed alternatives to achieve the desired objectives.
- Selecting the best alternative, based on previous evaluations and secondary objectives, whether tacit or explicit.
- Implementing the best alternative, in this case done by an hypothetical case of shelter selection and infrastructure to be recovered hierarchy, when affected by a catastrophe.
- Establishing controls that would be a mechanism to recognize if the proposed models remain current with time.

As results there will be two examples of how to use MOW on catastrophes, one for the selection of possible shelters, and other to hierarchies the order in which the affected infrastructure by the catastrophe should be recovered.

PRE- AND POST-CATASTROPHE

In this work, following Noji (1997) catastrophes will be defined as the result of an important ecological rupture of the relation between human beings and their environment, by sudden severe event (like an earthquake) or slow (like a drought) of such magnitude that the struck community will need extraordinary efforts to face it, often with external aid or international support.

The terms catastrophe and disaster, in this work, would be used as synonyms, and unless it is necessary, catastrophe will be used in general, without clarifying if they are caused by man or by nature.

Although there are other focuses (Cutter, 2003; Hsu, Wu, & Lin, 2005) a generally accepted scheme is to divide the catastrophes, whether they are of natural origin or caused by man, in three great phases: The pre-catastrophe, the catastrophe itself and the post-catastrophe.

Models, including mathematical models have been used to explain the catastrophes (Makowski, 2009; Yahaya, Ahmad, & Abdalla, 2010; Zhou et al., 2009) and to give support before, during or after them (Frysinger et al., 2007) and many of these models have been integrated to decision support systems (DSS) Hernández & García, (in press). Even though support systems to decision making could be of great use during a catastrophe (Borysiewicz, Potempski, & Galkowski, 2001; Gadomski et al., 2001; Mendonça, Beroggi, & Wallace, 2001; Sanders & Tabuchi, 2000) there is also a considerable value for them in the pre-catastrophe phase, when no event that caused an important rapture has occurred, but the population is preparing for such event, especially those that had been determined as possible shelter, as in the post-catastrophe phase, when the event has already occurred and the goal is to recover, at least, the life conditions that existed before the catastrophe.

In particular, in this work two aspects are paid special attention, the pre-catastrophe case, in the selection of possible shelters to which the affected population could be directed, and the post-catastrophe, in the order to be recovered the infrastructure damaged by the catastrophe.

MATRIXES OF WEIGHING

As indicated Matrixes Of Weighing (MOW) is one of the multi-criteria techniques simpler to implement and to use. As its name indicates, the MOW are no more than a numerical adjustment of rows and columns, as it is shown in Figure 1. But although extremely used, as it is indicated in Hernandez & García (in press), there are not many direct references of them and the majority is indirect and through similar matrixes (Environmental Management Systems, 1997; Monteiro & Rodrigues, 2006; Prasad, 1995; Shen & O'Hare, 2004).

Usually, as shown in Figure 1, the first column is used to identify the alternatives (Ak), the first two rows to identify criteria (Cj) and their range values PCji to PCjf, where sub index i means initial value and sub index f final value, and the rest of the matrix is filled with the value of alternative k for the criterion j (Pkj) and the last column is reserved to totalize the reached value for each one of the alternatives k (Total Ak). In occasions, when the criteria exceed the alternatives, it is recommended to invert the matrix.

For the value ranges of criteria it is normally used as initial value PCji zero or one, and for the final values PCjf a multiple of five or ten, although this is nor a rule, and any range of values can be used as long as the final value is higher than the initial value, in any case the higher the final value (PCjf) is because it is desired to give a greater relevance to this criterion and the bigger the difference (PCjf - PCji), is because greater differentiation through this criterion is desired.

How these ranks are defined and the possibility of using or not a fixed value of multiplication, allows differentiating the different variants from the MOW, as it is explained next.

Figure 1. General outline of a MOW

		Criteria (C_j) and its weights				
		Criterion 1	...	Criterion n-1	Criterion n	Total
	Weight $\longrightarrow$	PC_{1i} to PC_{1f}		PC_{n-1i} to PC_{n-1f}	PC_{ni} to PC_{nf}	---
Alternatives (A_k)	A_1	$P_{1,1}$	...	$P_{1,n-1}$	$P_{1,n}$	Total A_1
	A_2	$P_{2,1}$	...	$P_{2,n-1}$	$P_{2,n}$	Total A_2
	..	...	$P_{k,j}$	...	...	...
	A_{m-1}	$P_{m-1,1}$	...	$P_{m-1,n-1}$	$P_{m-1,n}$	Total A_{m-1}
	A_m	$P_{m,1}$	...	$P_{m,n-1}$	$P_{m,n}$	Total A_m

Variants of the Matrixes of Weighing

The first variant of the MOW is that where the ranges (PCj_f - PCj_i) coincide, meaning for all the criteria the initial values (PCj_i) coincide, as do the final values (PCj_f).

The second variant is given when the ranges (PCj_f - PCj_i) not coincide, meaning some of the criterion have one or both of the initial values (PCj_i) and final values (PCj_f) different.

The third and forth variants are equivalent to the first and second variants respectively, but for each criterion there will be a constant value of multiplication, as reflected in Equation 1, where the $P_{k,j}$, as was indicated are the values for the alternative k for each of the criteria j and the multiplication values (v_j) are usually whole numbers, generally no bigger than ten.

$$Total\ A_k = \sum_{j=1,n} v_j * P_{k,j} \qquad (1)$$

The fifth and sixth variants are equivalents to the third and fourth variants, but where the multiplication values are demanded to have an addition equal to one, as reflected on Equation 2.

$$1 = \sum_{j=1,n} v_j \qquad (2)$$

A resume of these six variants is presented on Table 1, where it is show that Equation 1 applies to all the variants, noting that for the first and second variant, the multiplication values (v_j) would be equal to one.

It is important to note that in spite of the applied variant, one of the greatest advantages present in MOW, is how easy they can be used in group decision making, therefore the next paragraph would be about this easiness.

MOW and Group Decision Making

As will be seen in the next section, the best form to apply the MOW is working in group, since it is recommended that when evaluating each criterion, the expert or group of experts in this criterion be the one who makes it. But aside from this direct form to work the MOW, there is another way to resort to the decisions in group using MOW.

That is to say, for group decision making with MOW, each one of the members of the group would make their evaluation separately and then all the evaluations would be consolidated to have the definitive valuation. In this case there are three different ways to do the valuation, the first and simpler is to add in direct form the results each alternative and to divide it equally, as always choosing the one that has the greater score in this average.

The second way is allowing different ponderations, that is to say, instead of a normal Arithmetic addition, a weighted average would be done, where each member of the equipment could have different ponderations, according to its experience or relevance in the organization, with respect to the decision being taken.

The third way to make use of group MOW, has to do with the natural way to work them, that is to say, in valuing each criteria by the respective expert, in this case, just as the second variant ponderations would be done, but within the criteria, where each one of the evaluators would have

Table 1. Variants of the MOW

Variant	Initial Value PCJ_i	Final Value PCJ_f	Multiplication Value (v_j)
First	All equals	All equals	All equals to 1
Second	Preferably equal	Different	All equals to 1
Third	All equals	All equals	Different, in general integers
Fourth	Preferably equal	Different	Different, in general integers
Fifth	All equals	All equals	Different and they add 1
Sixth	Preferably equal	Different	Different and they add 1

different weights in the different criteria, thus it would be the value of each criterion that would be weighed a priori, before having the final result for each alternative.

In any case the use of group MOW, is independent of the variant that is being used, just as it will be the steps to follow for its application, as they are explained next.

Steps to Construct and Apply Matrixes of Weighing

The steps to construct and to evaluate a MOW that are indicated next, in a certain manner conform a methodology, nevertheless is not a rigid methodology, since they are possible to be adapted to the own circumstances of the specific decision making for which the MOW is being used. These steps are:

1. To define clearly the decision objective. In general usually the MOW are used for two kinds of problems, those in which it is wanted to have a hierarchy of a group of alternatives or those in which it is needed to select the best of a set of alternatives.
2. To order to a group defining the evaluation criteria. In this step, like in all the rest that recommend the use of a group, of not being possible to have a group, it will be the person in charge of the decision making that must coordinate the operations.
3. To request to a new group, to search and to select all the alternatives to be evaluated. Nevertheless one of the great advantages of the MOW, is that he is not indispensable to have all the alternatives when constructing the model, since the alternatives are independent of the model itself.
4. To give responsibility to another group, to determine which of the six MOW variants is more advisable to use.
5. To make responsible a new group, in determining the ranks of ponderation of each

criterion and its values of multiplication if they were different from 1. In case of using multiplicative factors, which will be commented ahead, it would also be the moment for defining its ranks.

It is important to emphasize that some criteria can be qualitative or semi-qualitative, thus is necessary, with the ponderation ranks to establish the scales that will be used for each one of the criterion and multiplicative factors, in case of being used.

In case of descendent criteria, as it could be costs or losses, two options can be taken to value them in negative form, therefore worse, the most expensive one, has the most negative value, or in inverse form, that is to say, the one of greater cost has the smaller number of points. At any moment one is due to remember that the MOW is a maximization problem.

6. To establish the scales of acceptance and rejection of the different alternatives, in general is recommended that they are percentage of the maximum attainable value by the MOW being used.

    Another one of the great advantages of the MOW, is that with its application, it is knowing the acceptability or not of an alternative, independent if it had been evaluated against other alternatives, better or worse, a priori does not allow to establish a scale of acceptance and rejection of alternatives. There the MOW was constructed, from here begins the process of valuating alternatives.
7. To begin by the first criterion and to evaluate all the alternatives according to itself. It is preferable to establish expert or groups of experts for each criterion, and of being groups, all together must be in charge of evaluating all the alternatives, for the criterion of their experience. As was already commented each expert can have a different weight.
8. To evaluate the next criterion until there a no criteria left to evaluate. The recommen-

dations given in the previous steps must be followed.

9. To apply the valuation equation, when the evaluation of each alternative with each one of the criteria is concluded. Of being the values of multiplication (vj) different to one, it is recommended to make these multiplications, with the respective criterion that is being evaluated and to leave for the end, only the sum of the partial values and the multiplications by the multiplicative factors, in case last ones are being used these.

10. Hierarchize the alternatives from major to minor.

11. To apply to the scale of acceptance and rejection, thus to establish which alternatives are acceptable, which must be rejected and which need a greater revision to make a decision.

12. To present the list of acceptable alternatives or to indicate that no alternative reaches a sufficient value to be accepted. In case of a selection problem, if the list of acceptable alternatives is not empty, to propose as an alternative to be applied the first one on the list.

Although depending on the MOW variant that has been used, it is possible that the partial valuations by a predetermined value have been multiplied, this is not to be confused with the use of multiplicative factors, that have been mentioned already, will be explained next.

MOW and Multiplicative Factors

Multiplicative factors were taken from other multi-criteria model, the Multiattribute Models (MM) with multiplicative factors, as defined previously by Hernández and García (2007) and presented too in Hernández & García, (in press), mainly following Baucells and Sarin (2003), Ben-Mena (2000) and Ehrgott and Gandibleux (2002) and in interest of this investigation it is enough to pres-

ent the three equations that rule them, the (3) for MM without multiplicative factors and (4) and (5) with multiplicative factors.

$$Pts = \sum_i pc_i * (\sum_j pa_jc_i * va_jc_i) \tag{3}$$

where subindex i represents the criteria and subindex j the attribute, therefore pci will be the ponderation assigned to criterion i, pajci the ponderation for attribute j of criterion i, vajci corresponds to the assigned value to attribute j for criterion i, and Pts will be the total value achieved by the variable being studied. Equation 4 where these multiplicative factors appears.

$$Pts = \prod_k fg_k * (\sum_i f_i * pc_i * (\sum_j pa_jc_i * va_jc_i)) \tag{4}$$

maintains all of the variables in Equation 3 and introduces the multiplicative factors fgk and fi, where k takes account for the number of correction factors operating in the model, which would be called general factors, the fgk, and fi will represent the product of the correction factors operating in criterion i. The third Equation 5, shows the product of the criteria factors.

$$Pts = \prod_k fg_k * (\sum_i \prod_h f_{ih} * pc_i * (\sum_j pa_jc_i * va_jc_i)) \tag{5}$$

which maintains the nomenclature of Equations 3 and 4 and where h will be the accountant of the factors of each one of the criterion (fih), this way (5) turns to be the general expression, being able to use (4) if for every criteria there is only one multiplicative factors, and (3) in the case of not being multiplicative factors for the criteria or in general.

In the case of MOW, since there are no attributes for the criteria, there will be no sense in speaking of multiplicative factors of the criteria, but there will only be taken into account the general multiplicative factors, there Equation 6, becomes a combination from (1) and (4) maintaining the nomenclature of Equation 1, and where now the

Figure 2. General outline of a MOW with multiplicative factors

		Criteria (C_j) and its weights					
		Criterion 1	...	Criterion n-1	Criterion n	Factor fg_h	Total
	Weight →	PC_{1i} to PC_{1f}	...	PC_{n-1i} to PC_{n-1f}	PC_{ni} to PC_{nf}	Discreet or Continuous (0 to 1)	...
Alternatives (A_k)	A_1	$P_{1,1}$	...	$P_{1,n-1}$	$P_{1,n}$	f_1	Total A_1
	A_2	$P_{2,1}$	...	$P_{2,n-1}$	$P_{2,n}$	f_2	Total A_2
	..	...	$P_{k,j}$	...	...	f_k	...
	A_{m-1}	$P_{m-1,1}$	...	$P_{m-1,n-1}$	$P_{m-1,n}$	f_{m-1}	Total A_{m-1}
	A_m	$P_{m,1}$	...	$P_{m,n-1}$	$P_{m,n}$	f_m	Total A_m

fgh represents the general factors of the MOW, varying from h = 1 to H, with H being the number of total general factors, although in the MM, it is not recommended to be more than three (Hernández & García, in press), in the MOW there is usually a bigger amount of factors.

$$\text{Total } A_k = \prod_{h=1,H} fg_h * \sum_{j=1,n} v_j * P_{k,j} \qquad (6)$$

These general factors which are reflected in Figure 2, equivalent to Figure 1, through6out one column (Factor fgh), as was indicated it could be more than one, therefore the fk represents the value that for alternative k is assigned to the products of factors that affect it.

In the case of being used multiplicative factors, neither the group decision making, nor the steps to construct and to evaluate the MOW will be affected, the product by the multiplicative factors indicated in step 9 is the only one to do.

This last product by the multiplicative factors will be illustrated when presenting a pair of hypothetical applications of the MOW in catastrophes.

APPLICATIONS OF MOW IN CATASTROPHES

Following a pair of applications of the MOW will appear as support to decision making in the case of catastrophes and they be done through hypothetical cases, to display their generality, understanding that the models used here, could be adapted to the particular conditions of the problem to solve.

First an application will be done, in the selection of possible shelters and soon the order in which the infrastructures of a population must be recovered, after a catastrophe.

Matrixes of Weighing and Shelter Selection

One of the problems that must be handled in the pre-catastrophe phase is to identify all those possible places that could serve as shelter at the moment of a catastrophe. Antecedents in the solution to this problem see in Hernandez and García (in

Figure 3. Characteristic of the four hypothetical shelters to be evaluated

Criteria (Cj)	Alternatives (Ak)			
	A	B	C	D
Total space (Et) in m^2	2000	1500	1750	1500
Warehouse Area (% de Et)	30	27	25,5	25,5
Parking zone (% de Et)	10	8	9	8
Food service	Quite good	Slightly more than good	Good	Less than good
Medical assistance	Very good	Quite good	Slightly more than good	Good
Safety	Excellent	Very good	Very good	Good
Facilities for communications	Excellent	Good	Very good	Good
Access	Very good	Very good	A little more than good	Good
Energy and light	Excellent	Very good	Excellent	Excellent
Ventilation	Excellent	Very good	Excellent	Excellent
Sanitary facilities	Excellent	Excellent	Very good	Excellent
Potable water	No	Yes	Yes	Yes

press), where they make reference to Lopez and Perez (2006) and to Rodriguez and Zabala (2002).

In order to illustrate the use of the MOW in the selection of shelters, four hypothetical places will be chosen (A, B, C and D), whose characteristics are reflected in Figure 3 and for its selection with a MOW, following the previously indicated steps:

The objective, as it was already indicated is to hierarchize possible shelters to be used by the people affected by a catastrophe and the criteria to evaluate them are the ones expressed in the first column of Figure 3 and second column of Figure 4, in which, the four last columns reflect the reached values for each one of the alternatives.

The variant of MOW to use is the second, as it is possible to be seen in Figure 4, with criteria of different weights and without values from multiplication, but multiplicative factors will be used. In this Figure 4 also it is possible to observe,

in the third column, the values of each criteria and the total sum of these weights of the criteria.

In Table 2, making use of the criterion Warehouse area, it is illustrated how the scale can be established to value each criterion, the remaining scales are not detailed in the work, not to make it excessively extensive. The value of the criteria Warehouse area, is based on the area available for warehouse (AA) with respect to the percentage of the total space (Et).

For the scale of acceptance and rejection is established the shelter obtains a smaller score to 40% of the attainable maximum it is rejected, if the score is between 40% and 70% is necessary to analyze with greater care and if it is equal or superior to 70% it is accepted.

In Figure 4, the valuation of the first criteria stands in bold letter, since this must be the first valuation to make, for the remaining criteria and

Figure 4. General outline of a MOW for selection of shelters

		Weights	Alternatives (A_k)			
			A	B	C	D
Criteria (C_j) and its weights	Total space	(0 to 40)	**40**	**30**	**35**	**30**
	Warehouse Area	(0 to 20)	20	18	17	17
	Parking zone	(0 to 10)	10	8	9	8
	Food service	(0 to 60)	50	45	40	37
	Medical assistance	(0 to 50)	45	40	42	40
	Safety	(0 to 15)	15	12	12	11
	Facilities for communications	(0 to 10)	10	8	9	8
	Access	(0 to 15)	12	12	10	9
Multiplicative Factors	Energy and light	Continues (0 to 1)	1	0,95	1	1
	Ventilation	Continues (0 to 1)	1	0,95	1	1
	Sanitary facilities	Discreet (0, 0.75 or 1)	1	1	0,75	1
	Potable water	Discreet (0 or 1)	0	1	1	1
Results	Total	220#	0	157,9	130,5	**160 ***
	%	---	0,0	0,72	0,59	**0,73**
# = Maximum value that you can reach for an alternative						

Table 2. Valuation of the criterion warehouse area (WA)

If AA ≥ 30% of the Et, the value of the criterion WA will be between 60 and 80
If 25% ≤ AA < 30% of the Et, the value of the criterion WA will be between 80 and 100
If 20% ≤ AA < 25% of the Et, the value of the criterion WA will be between 60 and 80
If 15% ≤ AA < 20% of the Et, the value of the criterion WA will be between 40 and 60
If 10% ≤ AA < 15% of the Et, the value of the criterion WA will be between 20 and 40
If AA < 10% of the Et, the value of the criterion Warehouse Area will be between 0 and 20

the multiplicative factors are represented without emphasizing them.

In the last rows of Figure 4, are the definitive results, both in points as in percentage, emphasizing in bold letter and indicating with an asterisk, the best alternative.

It is important to notice, that without including the multiplicative factors the alternatives obtained the following scores: A, 202; B, 173; C, 174 and D, 160, nevertheless after applying the multiplicative factors the definitive order is:

1) D with 160, 2) B with 156.1, 3) C with 130.5 and 4) A with 0 points.

Of the previous values it is possible to be deduced that the alternative of shelter A should be rejected, whereas alternative C must be studied with more care, being accepted directly alternatives B and D, being the latter the first to be chosen.

Evidently with this hypothetical example, it is demonstrated, that with this model, or an adaptation of itself to the particular circumstances of the city being studied, the MOW can be used to make the selection of possible places to use as shelters in the case of a catastrophe.

MOW to Establish the Hierarchy to Recovered Infrastructures

When a catastrophe occurs the work of recovery of the areas affected by the tragedy is left, as the budgets usually are small, the first problem to solve is the order in which they are going to be restoring infrastructures. As a helpful element to establish this order of hierarchy, MOW can be used.

This illustration will also be made through a hypothetical case, to give greater generality to the explanation.

A population, as consequence of a catastrophe, in general needs to recover the following affected infrastructures: Houses, Clinics and hospitals, Schools and grammars school, Potable water networks, Served water networks, Telephony, Bridges, Highways, roads, avenues and freeways, Gas pipes, Electrical energy, Wharves, ports and airports, Food markets, Industries, Inns and Hotels, Stores and other commerce and Other infrastructures, that will include any non mentioned structure, except the tunnels, that will be contemplated within the highways or the water networks, according to the case.

In order to facilitate this type of analysis some infrastructures are usually subdivided. In order to illustrate these possible subdivisions, in the case of the highways, it is possible to speak of highways 1, highways 2, highways 3, according to the order in which they must be recovered.

Using these subdivisions, an infrastructure to recover can be handled in different stages. With all these infrastructures divided, as practical as possible, a precedence diagram is elaborated.

On the precedence diagram it is analyzed which sub-infrastructures do not require the recovery of a previous one, and those are analyzed in the first place. Updating this precedence diagram in time, according to recovered infrastructures, at any moment analyzing those infrastructures that are not preceded by another infrastructure that still is needed to recover.

For the illustration of the application of the MOW, as it will be shown in Figure 5, only nine possible infrastructures have been taken, in order to facilitate following the example and in addition understanding that some of non considered options could be recovered disposing from private capital and will be excluded from the study, and others are preceded by the recovery of some previous infrastructure.

In this sense the infrastructures to use in the illustration will be: Houses (A), Schools (B), Clinics (C), Bridges (D), Potable water networks (E), Served water networks (F), Electrical energy (G), Highways (H), Gas pipes (I).

As in the case of selecting possible shelters, to illustrate the use of MOW, the previously mentioned steps to construct and apply a MOW will be followed.

The objective will be to hierarchize the order in which infrastructures affected by the catastrophe must be recovered and criteria of evaluation, partially taken from Alessio and Vicuña (2003), who are referred by Hernandez & García (in press), will be: Impact in achieving normality for the affected population (01); Impact in the recovery of self-esteem in the affected population (02); Impact in the recovery of the sector to which the infrastructure belongs (03); Impact of the sector to which the infrastructure belongs to recover, with respect to the total to recover (04); Total

Figure 5. Characteristic of the infrastructures candidates to be recovered

Criteria (Cj)	Alternatives (A$_k$)								
	A	B	C	D	E	F	G	H	I
01	VH	Mo	Lo	Mo	VH	Hi	VH	Mo	Lo
02	VH	Hi	Hi	Mo	Hi	Mo	VH	VH	Hi
03	VH	Hi	Mo	VH	VH	VH	VH	Hi	VH
04	VH	Mo	Lo	Mo	Hi	Mo	VH	VH	Lo
05	Mo	Mo	Hi	Mo	Mo	Mo	VH	Hi	VH
06	Hi	Mo	Mo	Mo	Hi	Hi	VH	VH	VH
07	Mo	Hi	Hi	Lo	Lo	Lo	VH	VH	VH
08	Mo	Hi	Hi	VH	Mo	Lo	VH	Hi	Hi
09	VH	VH	VH	Hi	Mo	Hi	Mo	Hi	Mo
10	VH	VH	VH	VH	Hi	Hi	Hi	VH	Hi
11	Mo	Hi	Hi	Lo	Mo	Mo	VH	Hi	Mo
12	VH	VH	VH	Hi	VH	Hi	VH	VH	VH
13	VH	VH	VH	VL	VH	VH	VH	VH	VH
VH = Very High; Hi = High; Mo = Moderate; Lo = Low; VL = Very Low									

cost for the recovery (05); Necessary budget to initiate recovery (06); Amount of private capital that can be obtained for recovery (07); Necessary time to achieve recovery (08); Direct employment during recovery (09); Indirect employment during recovery (10); Employment to generate finished the recovery (11); Time to be able to begin the recovery works (12) and Technical feasibility of recovery (13). In any case, those criteria that can be handled as a percentage of a total, will be expressed in percentage.

In Figure 5, the infrastructures to study in this example appear, simultaneously given a valuation of them against the criteria to be considered.

The variant to use will be the fourth, with criteria of different weights and with values of multiplication and in addition multiplicative factors will be used. The ranks of the weights of

the criteria and the multiplicative factors can be seen in Figure 6.

In Table 3, using one of the less objective criteria, Impact in the recovery of self-esteem, a possible scale of valuation is illustrated and again the scales of all the criteria are not shown since escapes the objectives of this work and for reasons of space.

An acceptance scale will be used, similar to the one in the previous case: less of 30% of the attainable maximum implies that the infrastructure does not have to be recovered, at least at the moment, between 30% and 60% are due to study with more care before initiating their recovery, excepting the case of counting with sufficient resources and over 60% it is accepted directly, that is to say, efforts to obtain no available resources must be made, that allow initiating the

Figure 6. MOW for the hierarchy of the infrastructures to be recovered

				Alternatives (A_k)							
		Weights and Value	A	B	C	D	E	F	G	H	I
Criteria (C_j) and its weights	01	(0 to 100) 8	**90** **720**	**50** **400**	**40** **320**	**55** **440**	**85** **680**	**70** **560**	**95** **760**	**60** **480**	**30** **240**
	02	(0 to 100) 2	100 200	80 160	80 160	50 100	80 160	60 120	90 180	90 180	80 160
	03	(0 to 80) 4	80 320	65 260	45 180	75 300	80 320	80 320	80 320	60 240	80 320
	04	(0 to 100) 9	100 900	50 450	40 360	60 540	70 630	60 540	90 810	90 810	40 360
	05	(0 to 60) 3	35 105	25 75	40 120	25 75	35 105	25 75	50 150	40 120	60 180
	06	(0 to 60) 8	40 320	25 200	35 280	35 280	45 360	40 320	55 440	60 480	60 480
	07	(0 to 100) 1	60 60	70 70	65 65	40 40	30 30	30 30	90 90	100 100	100 100
	08	(0 to 100) 7	50 350	70 490	80 560	90 630	50 350	40 280	90 630	80 560	70 490
	09	(0 to 100) 8	100 800	100 800	100 800	80 640	60 480	70 560	60 480	80 640	60 480
	10	(0 to 80) 6	80 480	75 450	75 450	70 420	60 360	60 360	50 300	80 480	60 360
	11	(0 to 60) 5	25 125	45 225	40 200	20 100	30 150	35 175	50 250	45 225	30 150
	12	(0 to 100) 8	100 800	90 720	95 760	80 640	90 720	80 640	100 800	100 800	95 760
Multiplicative Factor	13	Discreet (0 or 1)	1	1	1	0	1	1	1	1	1
Results	**Total**	6060[#]	5180	4300	4255	0	4345	3980	*5210	5115	4080
	%	---	0,85	0,71	0,70	0,00	0,72	0,66	**0,86**	0,84	0,67
# = Maximum reachable value for an alternative											

Table 3. Scale of valuation of the criterion Impact in the recovery of the self-esteem

If the prospective impact is very high, the value of the criterion will be among 80 and 100
If the prospective impact is high, the value of the criterion will be among 60 and 80
If the prospective impact is moderate, the value of the criterion will be among 40 and 60
If the prospective impact is low, the value of the criterion will be among 20 and 40
If the prospective impact is very low, the value of the criterion will be among 0 and 20

recovery of the respective infrastructure immediately.

In Figure 6, appears the definitive valuation, where just as in the example of the possible shelters (Figure 4) the values of the first criterion stand out in bold letter and the final results are expressed in numerical form and percentage.

Before applying the only multiplicative factor used in this model, one sees that from a maximum of 6060 points the different infrastructures obtained: A, 5180; B, 4300; C, 4255; D, 4205; E, 4345; F, 3980; G, 5210, H, 5115 and I, 4080.

When applying the only multiplicative factor, Technical feasibility of recovery, that was discreet zero or one, only affected the infrastructure D, which of seventh position moves to the last one and leaves the definite order as: 1) G with 5210, 2) A with 5180, 3) H with 5115, 4) E with 4345, 5) B with 4300, 6) C with 4255, 7) I with 4080, 8) F with 3980 and 9) D with 0, that according to the scale allows to say that for all studied infrastructures the efforts to initiate recovery immediately must be done for all of them except D, for which it must be looked for another alternative of solution. Of these results, the first infrastructure that must be recovered is G, the electrical energy.

More than to analyze as infrastructure it is occupying the first position in the hierarchy, thus it must be taken care of the first, it is more important, to see the utility of the MOW to obtain this process of ordering, simultaneously allowing to visualize at least if it makes sense to recover some infrastructures at the moment.

Culminated this pair of examples of models of application of MOW in catastrophes, although still can to comment some other aspects, like facility that can to offer MOW to do analysis of sensitivity, or fact observed in evaluation of first criterion of this second example, where it is seen that no alternative reaches the maximum of the points, will go to present some conclusions.

CONCLUSION

The first conclusion is to reaffirm that the objectives have been fulfilled, that is to say, Matrixes Of Weighing (MOW) were presented, as a multicriteria model very simple to construct and to apply, simultaneously explaining this application on two associated cases to catastrophes, the selection of possible shelters, in the stage of pre-catastrophe and establishing the hierarchy of infrastructure to be recovered, in the post-catastrophe stage.

In addition to its simplicity, of the MOW is important to emphasize: its flexibility, since it is possible to use up to six variants of them; its great possibilities of being applied as techniques of group decision, where in addition the different members from the group can have different levels of influence in the decisions; its methodology of construction and application, that can be fit to anyone of the six variants and its facility to report in direct form strengths or weaknesses of an alternative.

Although greater emphasis in the work was not done, is important to emphasize the possibility of having experts who can evaluate the different alternatives for each one of the criteria, and also, the need of experts that are able to choose the MOW variant to use, the criteria to use and the weights that such must have in the model.

The multiplicative factors merits separate commentary that can completely change the valuation of an alternative, and even, to change the best alternative to one than must be rejected.

Once illustrated two possible applications of the MOW, to aide decision making in the handling of catastrophes with hypothetical examples, not only demonstrating the possibilities that MOW have, but also that they have a great capacity of adaptation, in this case to the different cities that are preparing for a catastrophe and are preselecting their possible shelters, or those that have undergone a catastrophe and want to recover their infrastructures.

Also it is important to specially emphasize, for the first hypothetical example, that when valuating an alternative, it can be known, which criteria have been less favoured and this even allows taking the pertinent measures to obtain its fortification, if this makes sense.

As far as the second example it was possible to known which aspects are necessary to cover, to make that an infrastructure has greater possibilities of being recovered in immediate form.

By all means, although here only two cases of application of the MOW in catastrophes were used, is evident that it is a field of very extensive work and that it will be easy to find other applications of the MOW.

FUTURE WORK

The MOW is before anything else a technical multi-criteria, reason why they will have application in all those fields where it is important to make decisions that depends on different parameters.

In particular in this work some possibilities of application of the MOW have been illustrated to give support in case of catastrophes, as much in the pre-catastrophe as in the post-catastrophe, from these it can be speculated that it could be used in other applications as in the pre-catastrophe, when deciding on types of vehicles to use for transport of the affected and in the post-catastrophe, when choosing the personnel that should be incorporated in the different recovery activities.

Equally applications can be had in the impact stage, when deciding on the members of rescue groups, or types and quantity of ambulatory services to install to assist the wounded and to make triage works.

But the applications of the MOW in the social field would not only be restricted to the case of catastrophes, but rather they could apply in many decisions that should be made by human groups and which involve several aspects to be evaluated as could be the selection of projects to choose for a certain social group to solve their daily problems.

REFERENCES

Alessio, M., & Vicuña, J. (2003). *Reestablecimiento de la normalidad a través de la gerencia de la logística de catástrofes de origen natural. Trabajo especial de grado*. Venezuela: Universidad Metropolitana.

Baucells, M., & Sarin, R. (2003). Group decisions with multiple criteria. *Management Science, 49*(8), 1105–1118. doi:10.1287/mnsc.49.8.1105.16400

Ben-Mena, S. (2000). Introduction aux méthodes multicritères d'aide à la decision. *Biotechnol. Agron. Soc. Environ., 4*(2), 83–93.

Borysiewicz, M., Potempski, S., & Galkowski, A. (2001). Computer network based decision support system for emergency response in case of chemical accidents. In *Proceedings of the international Conference on Emergency Managements (TIEMS 2001)*, Oslo, Norway.

Cutter, S. L. (2003). GI Science, Disasters, and Emergency Management. *Transactions in GIS, 7*(4), 439–445. doi:10.1111/1467-9671.00157

Ehrgott, M., & Gandibleux, X. (Eds.). (2002). *Multiple criteria Optimization: State of the art annotated bibliographic surveys*. Dordrecht, The Netherlands: Kluwer Academic Publishers.

Frysinger, S. P., Deaton, M. L., Gonzalo, A. G., VanHorn, A. M., & Kirk, M. A. (2007). The FALCON decision support system: Preparing communities for weapons of opportunity. *Environmental Modelling & Software*, *22*(4), 431–435. doi:10.1016/j.envsoft.2005.12.011

Gadomski, A. M., Bologna, S., Di Costanzo, G., Perini, A., & Schaerf, M. (2001). Towards intelligent decision support systems for emergency managers: the IDA approach. *Int. J. Risk Assessment and Management*, *2*(3 & 4), 224–242. doi:10.1504/IJRAM.2001.001507

Hernández, J. G., & García, M. J. (2007). Investigación de operaciones y turismo en Revista de Matemática. *Teoría y Aplicaciones*, *14*(2), 221–238.

Hernández, J. G., & García, M. J. (in press). Mathematical models generators of Decision Support Systems for help in case of catastrophes. An experience from Venezuela . In Asimakopoulou, E., & Bessis, N. (Eds.), *Advanced ICTs for Disaster Management and Threat Detection: Collaborative and Distributed Frameworks*. Hershey, PA: IGI Global.

Hernández, J. G., García, M. J., & Hernández, G. J. (2009). Influence of Location Management in supply chain Management. In *Proceedings of the Global Business and Technology Association (GBATA 2009)*, Prague, Czech Republic (pp. 500-507).

Hsu, P., Wu, S., & Lin, F. (2005). Disaster Management Using GIS Technology: A Case Study in Taiwan. In *Proceedings of the 26th Asia Conference on Remote Sensing*, Hanoi, Vietnam.

López, L., & Pérez, M. (2006). *Deslaves e inundaciones: Sistema de emergencia para el municipio Baruta. Trabajo especial de grado*. Venezuela: Universidad Metropolitana.

Makowski, M. (2009). Management of Attainable Tradeoffs between Conflicting Goals. *Journal Computer*, *4*(10), 1033–1042.

Mendonça, D., Beroggi, G. E. G., & Wallace, W. A. (2001). Decision support for improvisation during emergency response operations. *Int. J. Emergency Management*, *1*(1), 30–38. doi:10.1504/IJEM.2001.000507

Monteiro, R., & Rodrigues, G. (2006). A system of integrated indicators for socio-environmental assessment and eco-certification in agriculture-ambitec-agro. *Journal of Technology Management & Innovation*, *1*(3), 47–59.

Noji, E. K. (Ed.). (1997). *The public health consequences of disasters*. New York: Oxford University Press.

Prasad, B. (1995). JIT quality matrices for strategic planning and implementation. *International Journal of Operations & Production Management*, *15*(9), 116–142. doi:10.1108/01443579510099706

Rodríguez, D., & Zabala, J. (2002). *Trasporte para el traslado de heridos y afectados desde refugios a centros de asistencia y albergues. Trabajo especial de grado*. Venezuela: Universidad Metropolitana.

Sanders, R., & Tabuchi, S. (2000). Decision Support Systems for Flood Risk Analysis for the River Thames, United Kingdom. *Journal of the American Society for Photogrammetric Engineering & Remote Sensing*, *66*(10), 1185–1193.

Shen, S., & O'Hare, G. M. P. (2004). Agent-Based resource selection for grid computing. In *Proceedings of Workshop 4, the International Workshop on Agents and Autonomic Computing and Grid Enabled Virtual Organizations* (pp. 658-672).

Systems, E. M. (1997). (*EMS*) (pp. 1–44). Project Evaluation Matrix.

Yahaya, S., Ahmad, N., & Abdalla, R. F. (2010). Multicriteria Analysis for Flood Vulnerable Areas in Hadejia-Jama'are River Basin, Nigeria. *European Journal of Scientific Research*, *42*(1), 71–83.

Zhou, Y., Liu, G., Fu, E., & Zhang, K. (2009). An object-relational prototype of GIS-based disaster database. *Procedia Earth and Planetary Science*, *1*, 1060–1066. doi:10.1016/j.proeps.2009.09.163

Section 3
High-End Design Concepts for Future Distributed Systems

Chapter 14
Resource Management in Real Time Distributed System with Security Constraints:
A Review

Sarsij Tripathi
Motilal Nehru National Institute of Technology, India

Rama Shankar Yadav
Motilal Nehru National Institute of Technology, India

Ranvijay
Motilal Nehru National Institute of Technology, India

Rajib L. Jana
Motilal Nehru National Institute of Technology, India

ABSTRACT

The world has become a global village. Today applications are developed which require sharing of resources dispersed geographically to fulfill the need of the users. In most cases applications turn out to be time bound thus leading to Real Time Distributed System (RTDS). Online Banking, Online Multimedia Applications, Real Time Databases, and Missile tracking systems are some examples of these types of applications. These applications face many challenges in the present scenario particularly in resource management, load balancing, security, and deadlock. The heterogeneous nature of the system exacerbates the challenges. This paper provides a widespread survey of research work reported in RTDS. This review has covered the work done in the field of resource management, load balancing, deadlock, and security. The challenges involved in tackling these issues is presented and future directions are discussed.

DOI: 10.4018/978-1-4666-2647-8.ch014

INTRODUCTION

Today there are applications such as Online trading systems (Ahmed & Vrbsky, 1998), online multimedia applications, power grid distribution systems, etc., which require large amounts of computational resources dispersed geographically and cannot be executed on a single machine. Growing need of large computation intensive and data intensive applications demand sharing of resources particularly processing power geographical dispersed on different machines. Thus giving rise to distributed system where different computing nodes are interconnected with each other to fulfill the need of applications. These distributed systems can be homogeneous (Karatza & Hilzer, 2003) or heterogeneous (Radulescu & van Gemund, 2000) in nature. These applications which are distributed in nature sometimes require timely completion of task termed as real time distributed system. Online trading systems (Ahmed & Vrbsky, 1998), Online Banking, Online multimedia applications, Real time database system, Medical electronics (Gritzalis, 2004), Aircraft control systems (Abdelzaher et al., 2000), Scientific parallel computing (Connelly & Chien, 2002), Missile Tracking system (Mahafza et al., 1998), Power grid distribution system are examples of such type of applications which are growing very rapidly. These applications are distributed in nature and also require that they should adhere by the timing constraints imposed by application in form of deadline. For example, in an online multimedia applications which is used to view video online, let's say, of a live Football match, needs to transfer data (video and audio) within stipulated time otherwise the recipients will receive degradation in quality of received data(overlapping of video frames or voice overlapping). These applications are termed as soft real time applications where deadline miss of task degrades the application performance.

A Hard real time system e.g., missile tracking system, the deadline miss can cause catastrophic results which can be fatal sometimes e.g., lateness in tracking enemies' missiles. Another example could be flight control system (Liden, 1995) of fighter plane. In this system all the flight control tasks—including Guidance, Slow Navigation, Fast Navigation, Controller, and Missile Control—need to be executed in real-time to meet their deadlines. These five tasks are defined as follows: The "Guidance" task sets the reference trajectory of the aircraft in terms of altitude and heading; the "Controller" is responsible for executing the closed-loop control functions that deal with commands; the two "Navigation" tasks read sensor values distinguished by the required update frequency; and, finally, the "Missile Control" task is responsible for reading radar and firing missiles. These separate tasks are mandatory to control the aircraft during flight and they are all cyclic tasks with multiple versions. Deadline miss of any task can be fatal.

RTDS applications utilize the inherent features of distributed system such as resource sharing, openness, concurrency and scalability. To achieve RTDS applications requirements it is needed to organize, move, visualize and analyze massive amounts of data from different geographical locations, as well as employing large-scale computation. There are many challenges while fulfilling the requirements of RTDS. The most prior consideration is meeting deadline. The resources are dispersed and needed to be allocated fairly. The load in the system should be managed fairly and maximum system utilization should be achieved. However, due to openness of distributed system the applications are prone to attack thus application requires protection in terms of security and privacy of data. The different computing environment (heterogeneous) imposes another difficulty due to timing constraints because the mapping of execution time of task, security overhead, communication overhead etc. will differ from one node to another in heterogeneous environment. The solution of above discussed challenges required to be dynamic in nature such that minimum overhead should incur for different factors. These challenges can be broadly categorized as:

1. Resource Management, particularly Task Scheduling.
2. Load Balancing among the nodes.
3. Deadlock Management.
4. Protection, Security and Privacy.

Dealing with RTDS the challenges are exacerbated due to timeliness requirement of the real time task. Now to tackle different issues the first priority is to satisfy deadline constrained imposed by task. For example, for a RTDS where task execution is bounded by deadline its scheduling becomes more complex. Similarly heterogeneous nature of the distributed system e.g. nodes having different computing power will have affect over the different decision which has to be taken in regard of scheduling, load balancing, protection and communication. For example in case of different computing power of node the completion time of a task varies from one node to another thus the conventional scheduling algorithm available for distributed system cannot be applied in RTDS.

In this paper the next section briefs about preliminaries of distributed system, real time system, and scheduling. The third section surveys the resource management particularly task scheduling. The fourth section discusses the work done in the field of load balancing followed by a section, which covers deadlock management. Protection in terms of security and privacy is surveyed in the section next and finally concluding remarks are made in seventh section.

PRELIMINARIES

Distributed System

A lot of computational power is underutilized around the world in machines sitting idle. Combined processing power of multiple computers provides much more processing power than a centralized system with multiple CPUs. There are applications which in nature are distributed e.g. share trading system, power grid management, multimedia applications etc. also require large computation. Large commercial supercomputers are very expensive to be deployed for such type of applications. So distributed systems, in which computational nodes are interconnected by a high speed network, can be used to fulfill the demand of high computation required by the applications. The general definition can be given:

A distributed system is a collection of independent computers that appears to its users as a single coherent system (Tanenbaum & Maarten, 2007).

A distributed system can be characterized by the node computing power, communication channel bandwidth, resources available. A Distributed system can be broadly classified into two domains

1. Homogeneous Distributed System
2. Heterogeneous Distributed System

A homogeneous DS (Karatza & Hilzer, 2003) is a system in which all the nodes are having the similar configuration. Cluster computing is the example of homogeneous distributed system in which underlying hardware consists of a collection of almost similar workstations or PCs, loosely connected by means of a high speed local-area network. There is a cluster head and all the task assignment and resource management is done by cluster head. Whereas heterogeneous distributed systems (Radulescu & van Gemund, 2000) are those in which the resources differ from one node to another. Grid (Foster & Kesselman, 1999) computing is an example of heterogeneous distributed system which is often constructed as a federation of computer systems, where each system may fall under a different administrative domain, and may be very different when it comes to hardware, software and deployed network technology. Some applications which are distributed in nature are also constrained by there timing requirements such as multimedia applications, online trading system (Ahmed & Vrbsky, 1998), Power grid distribution system, Aircraft control system (Liden,1995). Thus to obtain parallel processing performance and to increase reliability, distributed architectures having processors interconnected by a communications network are increasingly being used for real-time systems giving rise to real time distributed systems (RTDS).

Real Time System

In a general purpose system the goal is to arrive at correct results, preferably as fast as possible but if the result is delayed it is generally of no great concern whereas a real-time system not only require correct results but also predictability as to when the results are available. A real-time system is a system in which computations must satisfy stringent timing constraints besides providing logi-

cally correct results i.e. a correct computation of the result must finish before its specified deadline.

Real Time System Classification

Depending on the activity a deadline can be either a hard deadline or a soft deadline (Figure 1). If a hard deadline is missed it is typically considered a catastrophe and can result in severe consequences for the environment the task was interacting with (for example aircraft control, missile tracking system). A soft deadline miss does not generally have dire consequences but may cause some slight grievances (for example multimedia application, online banking system, and online transaction system). Real-time systems does not necessarily equal fast computing, the goal is instead to achieve timely computing which means that all activities in the system have individual timing constraints.

A real time distributed system can be classified as hard real time distributed system and soft real time distributed system on the basis of applications. Tasks in these applications can be periodic, aperiodic or sporadic. If the tasks arriving frequency is fixed i.e. they arrive at fixed regular interval are known as periodic task. In other words we can say that these tasks are time-driven and recur at regular intervals such as Monitoring of temperature of a nuclear reactor. An aperiodic task arrival is not known in advance that means

Figure 1. (A) soft real time system (B) hard real time systems

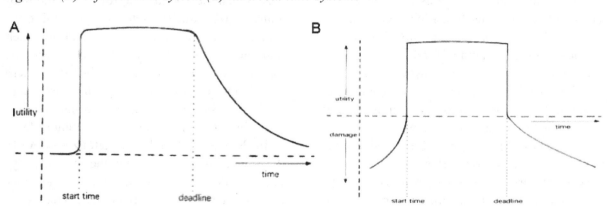

their occurrence is not fixed. These tasks are activated on the occurrence of certain events such as event of button is pushed. The sporadic tasks are those tasks whose arrival times are not known in advance, but any two consecutive instances of a sporadic task are separated by a minimum interval of time such as switching from autopilot to manual pilot (or vice-versa). A real time distributed system application can be periodic, aperiodic, sporadic or combination of these tasks.

Real Time Task Scheduling

Scheduling is defined as ordering of task in which they are going to execute. Real time task scheduling is very different from general scheduling. Ordinary scheduling algorithms attempt to ensure fairness among tasks, minimum progress for any individual task, and prevention of starvation and deadlock. To the scheduler of real-time tasks, these goals are secondary. The primary concern in scheduling real-time tasks is deadline compliance. When scheduling is done on the fixed parameters (period) assigned before the task is being executed is known as static scheduling (fixed priority) such as Rate Monotonic scheduling (Liu & Layland, 1973) whereas scheduling decisions based on dynamic parameters (deadline) that may change during system evolution is known as Dynamic scheduling (dynamic priority) such as Earliest deadline first (Stankovic et.al., 1998). Based on the time of when scheduling decision is taken scheduling algorithms are categorized as Offline and Online. In offline, scheduling is performed well before system starts functioning i.e. the schedule is generated for the entire task set before the tasks are activated however scheduling decision are taken at run time in case of online i.e. scheduling decisions are taken at run time every time a new task enters the system.

A scheduling policy can be pre-emptive (running task can be interrupted) or non pre-emptive (task, once started, is executed by processor until completion). The schedulability of a preemptive algorithm is always higher than its non preemptive version. However, the higher schedulability of a preemptive algorithm has to be obtained at the cost of higher scheduling overhead. A lot of scheduling algorithms are proposed to schedule real time tasks on uni-processor system. Rate monotonic (Liu & Layland, 1973) and Deadline monotonic (DM) are examples of fixed priority scheduling whereas Earliest deadline first (Stankovic et.al., 1998) and Least laxity first (LLF) are examples of dynamic priority scheduling. Scheduling task in distributed systems has been found to be NP-complete (Ullman, 1975). Thus, scheduling real time task on distributed system became open field of research in which variety of work has been reported.

RESOURCE MANAGEMENT IN RTDS

The main challenge in RTDS is resource management essentially by scheduling of task. Scheduling is an approach in which the tasks are ordered over the nodes available. The problem of scheduling in real time distributed system is to determine when and on which processor a given task is going to be executed. Meeting deadlines and achieving high resource utilization are the two main goals of task scheduling in real-time distributed systems. This can be done either statically (Gagne & Shepard, 1991) or dynamically (Dertouzos & Mok, 1989). In static algorithms task assignment on computing nodes is done before execution of task. Static algorithms are well suited for scheduling periodic tasks with hard deadlines. This scheduling approach guarantees the schedule if it exist. However, this approach is not applicable to applications where task characteristics are not known in prior e.g., aperiodic tasks. For scheduling tasks for such type of application, dynamic scheduling is done.

In dynamic scheduling (Dertouzos & Mok, 1989) when new tasks arrive, the scheduler dynamically determines the feasibility of scheduling these new tasks without affecting the guarantees that have been provided for the previously accepted tasks for execution. A feasible schedule is generated if the timing and resource constraints of all the tasks can be satisfied, i.e., if the schedulability analysis is successful. Dynamic scheduling algorithms can be either distributed or centralized. In a distributed dynamic scheduling scheme, tasks arrive independently at each processor. When a task arrives at a processor, the local scheduler at the processor determines whether or not it can satisfy the constraints of the incoming task. The task is accepted if they can be satisfied; otherwise, the local scheduler tries to find another processor which can accept the task. In a centralized scheme, all the tasks arrive at a central processor called the scheduler, from where they are distributed to other processors in the system for execution. The problem of scheduling task with resource constraints in real time distributed systems is NP- complete. These negative results motivated the need for heuristic approaches for solving the scheduling problem.

Conventional heuristic-based task scheduling algorithms such as OLB (opportunistic load balancing), UDA (user directed assignment), Min-Min, Fast Greedy, Max-Min (Armstrong, Hensgen & Kidd, 1998), are not appropriate for scheduling real time task on distributed systems. Because above approaches do not take deadline as a scheduling parameter. So, scheduling real time tasks on distributed systems is more intricate than scheduling non-real time tasks. Conventional real time task scheduling algorithms such as EDF (Stankovic, 1998), RM (Liu & Layland, 1973), and LLF have been proposed for uniprocessors. The above algorithms can be preemptive or non preemptive (Li, Kavi, & Akl, 2007) and are available in the literature. Apart from this heterogeneity of the distributed system also effects the scheduling of task. Thus heuristics developed for scheduling in homogeneous system can perform poorly in heterogeneous environment due to varying processor computation power and resource availability. This section reviews the research

work reported in scheduling of real time task in RTDS. Scheduling being a big research area and lot of parameters (such as dynamic, static, periodic, aperiodic, offline, online, pre-emptive, non pre-emptive, centralized and de-centralized) concerned it is difficult to categorize the reported work though we have classified it on the basis of types of RTDS i.e. Homogeneous and Heterogeneous based approaches.

Homogeneous Based Approaches

Ramamritham et al. (1990) have given a heuristic scheduling algorithm for real time multiprocessor (homogeneous) system with resource management. They have considered independent, aperiodic and non preemptive task and these tasks are scheduled by heuristic functions such as Minimum Deadline first, Minimum Processing Time first, Minimum Laxity first etc. and combination of these. Initially they take one task and create a partial schedule. The partial schedule is extended for remaining task according to the heuristic function 'H' applied for feasibility check. Their approach extends the partial schedule and if feasible schedule is not found than it backtracks. The resources are available in shared and exclusive mode. The tasks are scheduled according to the resource requirement. Their proposed approach is applicable to dynamic scheduling in real time system.

In (Hao, Liu, & Kim, 1992) authors have proposed a new scheme, called the All Sharing Task Scheduling (ASTS), for global task scheduling in a distributed system based on the synchronized bus network, in which the requesting nodes find serving nodes with incomplete global state information. The nodes in the system are organized in a logical ring. They have considered periodic and aperiodic task to be scheduled. The execution of periodic task is fixed on a particular node whereas if aperiodic task is not schedulable on the node where it arrived than it will be migrated to other node, which is having enough capacity to accommodate task, arranged in Ring order.

The proposed approach in (Spartiotis & Bestavros, 1993) has a decentralized heuristic for scheduling periodic tasks with sporadic tasks. The execution of periodic tasks is fixed and they are scheduled by local scheduler by EDF policy on local nodes but execution of sporadic tasks varies (in terms of node assignment for execution) according to the system condition and tasks characteristics. The node in distributed system consist of two processor in which one is meant for communication among nodes and other one is responsible for execution of scheduled task. The approach transfers sporadic task to other node if that node is idle for at least amount of time required for sporadic task to complete subject to deadline of that sporadic task is not violated. To perform this transfer, nodes require current load information of their neighboring nodes which is done by broadcasting and gossiping. Three different thresholds have been given for a node to decide when to broadcasts their load information.

Manimaran and Rammurthy (1998) have proposed a centralized dynamic scheduling algorithm for real time applications. The objective of their work is to propose a dynamic scheduling algorithm which exploits parallelism in tasks in order to meet their deadlines, thereby increasing the performance of the system. Their approach is based on task parallelizable model and heuristic is based on this. But its scope is limited to a task model where we can sub split the task. Executing sub task in parallel will incur overhead and synchronization problem will be there.

The work reported in (Abdelzaher, Atkins, & Shin, 1999) has presented an algorithm for offline task. This paper presents an algorithm for offline scheduling of communicating tasks with precedence and exclusion constraints in distributed hard real-time systems. Tasks are assumed to communicate via message passing based on a time-bounded communication paradigm, such as the real-time channel. The algorithm uses a branch-and-bound (B&B) technique to search for a task schedule by minimizing maximum task lateness (defined as the difference between task completion time and task deadline), and exploits the interplay between task and message scheduling to improve the quality of solution. This approach is applicable to applications where message delays and task completion time are known in advance. So the applicability of this is constrained by the above factors because when task are interdependent and share resources than calculating message delays is a bit complex. It can only be known when task is being scheduled in the system.

Ravindran and Devarasetty (2002) have used a feedback control mechanism to provide adaptive resource management in asynchronous real time distributed environment. The feedback control function gives information to create replicas of task. The number of replicas for a particular task is adaptively varies according to the feedback control. This approach distributes task onto different nodes in the form of replicas. The constrained are same as in the work reported in (Abdelzaher, Atkins, & Shin, 1999).

In Ravindran and Devarasetty (2002) authors have also proposed an adaptive resource management approach for periodic tasks in dynamic RTDS to create replicas of a task. Replicas are created based on task workload and processor utilization with the help of regression theory. The number of replicas is bounded by the load in the system and the processor utilization. After creating replicas the problem is to assign replicas to different processors and they have modeled this as a bin – packing problem and proposed two heuristics for this. Although the proposed approach is dividing the load in the form of replicas thus task completion time will be reduced but this does not focuses on what will be the effect of message communication between replicas of same task and of different task(for interdependent task).

Ammar and Alhamdan (2002) presented an algorithm to schedule real time task in homogeneous environment i.e., clusters. They have proposed a model in which nodes within a cluster are homogeneous and task assignment is done on the basis of processing power reservations. A processing power reservation table is been created for each node in the cluster for a fixed time interval (period) and it is updated regularly. The task assignment is done on the basis of minimum processing power required first. They have considered deadline violation thus this approach is not suitable for hard real time task. All the above approaches have taken homogeneous environment while scheduling tasks. A fault tolerance approach for scheduling in homogeneous environment is given in (Li, Ravindran, & Hegazy, 2003) where author have proposed two approaches RBA-FT and OBA FT which are heuristic algorithms that compute resource allocation decisions, the number of replicas that are needed for each subtask and the processors for executing them in polynomial-time. The approaches schedule periodic and aperiodic tasks in the presence of processor failure. The RBA-FT approach is based on minimum response time heuristic for scheduling resources and generating replicas of the task in a failure case, whereas OBA-FT is based on processor overload heuristic. They have not considered the replicas consistency while they are scheduled.

Lin et al. (2007) have proposed a divisible load scheduling approach for task, whose Computational loads can be arbitrarily divided into independent pieces, on homogeneous clusters. Their strategy is to assign number of nodes and task partitioning. The scheduling policy is EDF, FIFO and MWF (minimum workload derivative first). The task load assignment strategy has two variations either task load has been assigned to all the nodes or to required minimum number of nodes. Minimum number of nodes is calculated on the basis of task deadline and its execution time. The task partitioning is done by OPR (optimal partitioning rule) and EPR (equal partitioning rule). For dependent tasks which cannot be partitioned the applicability of approach is to be examined.

Bertogna, Cirinei, and Lipari (2009) reported a schedulability analysis for a set of periodic and sporadic task constrained by their deadline over homogeneous multiprocessors. Their approach considers a work conserving system in which task migration is allowed with task preemption. The main contribution of the paper is to give schedulability analysis of global scheduling algorithms for multiprocessor systems.

Heterogeneous Based Approaches

Gopalan and Kang (2007) have listed the challenges in resource management and in heterogeneous real time distributed environment. The challenges which they have considered are deadline partitioning among the subtask, runtime scheduling of multiple resources, statistical guarantee and feedback control mechanism across multiple resources. They have highlighted the challenges in determining the above factors. They have proposed an approach which has a global scheduler (GS) and local schedulers. GS have prior knowledge of tasks completion time, subtask deadline assignment, resource requirement and local schedulers. Local scheduler's schedules task on the basis of subtask deadlines and its utilization. The approach is not applicable for applications consisting of aperiodic tasks because prior information about the task parameters is not known in advance.

The work reported in Li et al. (2003) schedules periodic jobs with aperiodic jobs on heterogeneous clusters. Their approach is to schedule aperiodic jobs by using the spare time slots on cluster nodes where periodic jobs are already scheduled with EDF policy. Aperiodic jobs are parallel jobs modeled by Directed Acyclic Graphs (DAG). There is a Global scheduler which schedules aperiodic task according to the spare time left on cluster nodes. Cluster nodes are heterogeneous in nature and they are using EDF policy to schedule aperiodic task with previously scheduled periodic task thus it is more likely that aperiodic task will be pre-empted resulting in less number of aperiodic task will be completed.

The work reported in Kuo, Shih, and Kuo (2006) has developed a two-level resource allocation framework. The proposed framework allows the schedulers for subsystems or processors in distributed real-time systems to autonomously schedule local sub-tasks and the system performance is enhanced without heavy global optimization overhead. The approach has scheduled resources at two levels. At first level there is a global scheduler for entire system which is an offline scheduler, which schedules the resources conservatively. At the second level, there is a local scheduler at each processing node which is an online scheduler which schedules resources dynamically.

The paper (Rajasekaran, Ammar, & Hussein, 2007) schedules the dependent tasks on heterogeneous clusters. The approach is to minimize the communication delay between dependent tasks which is added as an overhead in execution time of tasks. This overhead significantly effects the scheduling decision. The approach is of two fold. The global scheduler searches for the optimal schedule that maximizes acceptance rate of the applications on the cluster by a multi-objective function that optimizes different performance criteria: namely processing power fragmentation, context switching, and communication cost. Each node in the cluster has its own local scheduler that is responsible for allocating and executing tasks on the processor.

The approach in Kalantari and Akbari (2008) focuses on online scheduling of real time applications in distributed environments. Performance dynamism of resources is modeled with the help of queuing techniques. A mathematical neural model is employed afterwards, to schedule subtasks of the application. Due to inherent overhead in neural model the approach is limited applicability.

Chen et al. (2008) proposes new anomaly prevention strategy when the system configuration is changed in embedded system. By system configuration they mean increase in the processor capacity and resource availability. Their work considers the non preemptible periodic real time task. Their idea is to schedule resources active

or passive by the use of inserting idle time slot thus higher priority task is not blocked. They have combined their approach with NCSP (non preemptible critical section protocol). The approach is for periodic task and for aperiodic task approach can't be applied.

The work reported in Lombardi, Milano, and Benini (2009) provides predictable and efficient non preemptive scheduling of multi-task applications with inter-task dependencies. Their approach schedules application which consist of set of dependent tasks that have to be periodically executed with in a deadline constraint, modeled as a task graph where task execution is characterized by known min-max intervals and inter-task dependencies are associated with a known amount of data communication. SenthilKumar et al. (2009) presents an approach for scheduling real time independent task in a Heterogeneous system. A heuristic known as MaxR-MinCT is applied where MaxR is a robustness of resource allocation i.e. scheduling and CT is the completion time of the task. The paper schedules task in the environment where the assumed scheduling parameters are deviated and still system is stable. The robustness metric is dependent on task completion time on a particular machine, modeled mathematically and is constrained by an upper bound of make span.

Zhu and Lu (2009) proposed multi-dimensional scheduling strategy, MDSS, considering timing constraints, QoS, throughput, load balancing and QoS fairness on heterogeneous clusters. Their approach schedules aperiodic task dynamically. Their approach is of three fold. They have adopted a centralized scheduler which initially accepts task with conventional RTS algorithm with minimum QoS. Later in second step a QoS level controller tries to increase QoS level of task which has been accepted for execution. Finally in third step there is an approach which tries to balance the load.

In Zhang, Gill, and Chen (2010), the paper proposes a set of configurable component middleware services supporting multiple admission control and load balancing strategies for handling aperiodic and periodic events. The configurable admission control (AC), load balancing (LB), idle resetter (IR) and task effector (TC) components are proposed which interact with each other. The work of each component is specific and working of each component adopts different strategies. Their work focuses on periodic and aperiodic tasks. The tasks are divided into subtask which is further divided into jobs and sub-jobs.

LOAD BALANCING

One of the issues in RTDS is the development of effective techniques/algorithms for the distribution of the processes/load of applications on multiple hosts to achieve goal(s) such as minimizing execution time, minimizing communication delays, maximizing resource utilization and maximizing throughput. Substantive research using queuing analysis and assuming job arrivals following a poisson pattern, have shown that in a multi-host system the probability of one of the hosts being idle while other host has multiple jobs queued up can be very high. Such imbalances in system load suggest that performance can be improved by either transferring jobs from the currently heavily loaded hosts to the lightly loaded ones or distributing load evenly/fairly among the hosts (Chhabra, Singh, Waraich, Sidhu, & Kumar, 2006).

The algorithms known as load balancing algorithms, helps to achieve the above said goal(s). These algorithms come into two basic categories - static and dynamic. static load balancing algorithms (SLB) take decisions regarding assignment of tasks to processors based on the average estimated values of process execution times and communication delays at compile time whereas dynamic load balancing algorithms (DLB) are adaptive to changing situations and take decisions at run time. The heterogeneous nature of real time distributed system causes difficulty while taking decision of migrating task from one node to another. It could be possible that a task

let say 'A' has been migrated from node N1 to node N2 where computing power of node N2 is less as compared to N1 thus completion of task A will require more time on N2 as compared to N1 which may lead to deadline miss. The challenges imposed by load balancing in RTDS are required to be tackled and very few works has been reported in the field RTDS load balancing. This section presents an overview of load balancing algorithm for distributed system and RTDS reported in past few years.

Dandamudi (1995) discussed the performance of two load balancing approaches sender initiated and receiver initiated in a distributed environment. It also compares the above approaches for non preemptive and preemptive task scheduling policies. It is hard to apply the comparison in real time systems.

Bestavros (1997) extends their previous work (Spartiotis & Bestavros, 1993). A load profiling approach is given for scheduling the tasks in the distributed system. Their approach considers real time periodic tasks whose execution time and deadline are known in advance. They also consider sporadic tasks. Each node have two processor out of which one processor is dedicated to execute the task and another one is for admission control and scheduling of task for minimizing the overhead. The EDF policy is been modified as EDL and EDS. Their approach is to schedule the sporadic task over the node which is best fit for scheduling it instead of equally dividing the load. Thus the approach uses concept of load profiling instead of load balancing. The limitation of the approach is the number of nodes in the system. For small number of nodes the approach is optimal but performance in large distributed system is to be examined.

The work in (Di Stefano, Lo Bello, & Tramontana, 1999) deals with the problem of allocating processes with the aim of achieving load balancing in a heterogeneous distributed system in order to improve response time. To measure the host's workload the concept of relaxation is introduced instead of process local queue at host. This states that the processor workload can be measured by observing the execution rate of the processes. A processor taking more time to execute a process will be termed as more relaxed. After calculating the relaxation parameter each node shares their relaxation value with each other after which the task assignment decision is taken.

The research work reported by Razzaque and Hong (2007) proposes a dynamic load balancing approach in homogeneous distributed environment by dividing the nodes into mutually overlapping subsets. The main problem in load balancing is to get the global system state which requires the communication overhead. By dividing the nodes into mutually overlapping subsets the node can get partial state of the system. In their approach the process scheduling decisions are driven by the desire to minimize turnaround time while maintaining fairness among competing applications and minimizing communication overhead. The work reported in the paper minimizes the communication overhead but maintaining mutually overlapping subsets will incur overhead.

Kermia and Sorel (2008) presented a heuristic for load balancing and efficient memory usage of homogeneous distributed real-time embedded systems. The approach is applied for periodic task in the real time embedded systems where the memory is limited thus efficient use of memory is required. The approach groups task into block and moving that block onto a node which has enough memory space. The approach considers the inter process communication overhead. Guangmin (2008) proposes a load balancing algorithm for heterogeneous nodes. The main purpose of the proposed approach is to improve the overall response time of the distributed system with minimum network traffic over heterogeneous workstations. This algorithm tries to keep the load difference between any two nodes within specified thresholds and shares CPU, memory and I/O resources with the best effort. Load balancing is done between all the nodes by cooperation of other subset of nodes during migration decision and thus reducing the traffic.

Finally we have reviewed the work by Dobber, Mei and Koole (2009) where comparative study between load balancing and job replication strategies for dynamic grid environment has been carried out. The approach is meant for bulk synchronous processes parallel programs where programs can be subdivided into jobs and each job can be executed in the same fashion. This involves iterations of jobs to be executed on processors. The work proposes a Load Balancing (LB)/Job Replication (JR) scheme. The selection of either LB or JR scheme is based on a statistical parameter derived from scheduling constraints.

DEADLOCK

Deadlock occurs when one or more tasks in a system are blocked by each other forever and their requirements can never be satisfied. A deadlock situation may arise if and only if the following four resource competition conditions hold in a system simultaneously:

1. Mutual exclusion
2. Hold and wait
3. No preemption
4. Circular wait

It is quite useful to consider each condition separately in analyzing and designing a deadlock free system. Principally, there are three strategies for dealing with the deadlock problem:

1. **Deadlock Prevention:** By ensuring that at least one of the deadlock conditions cannot hold.
2. **Deadlock Avoidance:** By providing a priori information so that the system can predict and avoid deadlock situations.
3. **Deadlock Detection:** By detecting and recovering from deadlock states.

The first two approaches guarantees that the system will never enter a deadlock state. Deadlock prevention is commonly achieved by guaranteeing that one of the four conditions will never occur e.g. hold and wait on resources conditions: by making all tasks to acquire resources a priori, allowing preemption: lower priority task will be preempted by higher priority task which requires a resource held by lower priority task. In deadlock avoidance system global safe state is checked and then task is been executed. The above two strategies are usually inefficient when applied in complex real time distributed systems. Deadlock prevention decreases system concurrency by restricting the execution of the tasks to avoid at least one of the deadlock conditions whereas in deadlock avoidance checking a safe state is computationally expensive. In a real time distributed system if tasks are required to acquire resources a priori (deadlock prevention), a group of tasks may get deadlocked in the resource-acquiring phase due to lack of a perfect global synchronization mechanism. Same problem will arise in deadlock avoidance case where due to imperfect global synchronization inconsistent local states will allocate resources assuming it safe. Another reason for not adopting the above two strategies are that they require prior knowledge of resource requirement which is not possible in many systems e.g. system with aperiodic tasks. Alternatively, by applying the third strategy, the system is allowed to enter a deadlock state and then it is detected and recovered from. The deadlock detection computation can be performed in parallel with the other normal system activities; therefore, it may not have a serious impact on the system performance.

There are two ways to detect the deadlock in Real time distributed system. One is how the system state information is stored i.e Centralized, Distributed or Hierarchal and another one is based on the technique used in searching the deadlock conditions e.g. path pushing, edge chasing etc. The problem with centralized detection strategy is that they are unreliable and have one point of

failure. Apart from this the control site or central site is prone to communication message overload.

In distributed deadlock detection algorithm each node manages only partial view of the system state. There is no one control or central site thus one point of failure is not there. The task experiencing the deadlock initiates deadlock detection algorithm. The communication messages are less and only nodes involved in deadlock are bothered. The one drawback associated with distributed deadlock detection is that deadlock resolution is difficult. The synchronization problem persists in both the approaches. Deadlock detection and resolution in real time distributed system is challenging issue due to timeliness requirement for task completion. The real time task required to be completed within its deadline thus it is important that the deadlock detection algorithm must detect deadlock and resolve it within slack time of that task. Thus due to intricacies involved in deadlock resolution in real time distributed system makes this an interesting and challenging open research area. Very little work has been reported in this field. This section gives a glimpse of research work reported in the field of distributed system and real time distributed system in past few years.

Sánchez et al. (2006) have proposed an approach for deadlock avoidance for distributed real time embedded systems. The paper gives protocols, based on annotations of call graphs, which are extra static information attached to the call graph nodes and inspected in the protocols. The main idea is to allocate threads on the basis of annotations associated with call graph which requires a thread. They have assumed that the call graph does not have cycle which is a very optimistic assumption.

The work reported in (Shiang & Stankovic, 1990) proposes deadlock detection algorithm. They have assumed a separate distributed run-time tasking supervisor and a deadlock agent on each node in the system. The functions of these components are to exchange messages among themselves and to detect deadlocks. A probe is being initiated whenever a task is being blocked by pending request and propagated in the backward direction of the edges of the Request Graph. The approach is for single source model. Their second approach is for AND model and it is also based on probe initiation and propagation.

The algorithm proposed Data and Ghosh (1990) is based on sending messages along the edges of the wait for graph, and is built on a prioritized signaling mechanism. The approach considers only one resource request to be granted by any task at a time. The scheme is based on prioritized signaling mechanism to coordinate among the tasks.

Yeung and Hung (1995) have given a deadlock detection algorithm for distributed real time database system. The detection process is comprised of two steps namely probe computation phase and cycle detection phase. The probe computation phase is initiated when a transaction is blocked. After this the deadlock manager will search for deadlock in the wait for graph over the remote sites and after receiving the probe the remote sites will initiate the cycle detection phase. The cycle detection phase will be terminated by finding a cycle and then the victim transaction based on the minimum slack value will be aborted.

Deng, Attie, and Sun (1996) have proposed an approach that generates the local wait for graph on the local node where deadlock is being detected. The approach is distributed in nature and less overhead is required. The approach detects deadlock if exist and no false deadlock is detected. The research work reported in Kshemkalyani and Singhal (1999) proposes a one-phase distributed algorithm for detecting generalized distributed deadlocks. The approach is meant for replicated databases where multiple copies of databases are available at different sites. The paper considers P out of Q model of resource requirement. The approach is based on reducing the wait for graph and if sufficient information is not present than lazy approach is used for graph reduction.

The paper (Xiao & Lee, 2008) proposes an approach which provides a fast and deterministic

deadlock detection mechanism for Multiprocessor System-on-Chips (MPSoCs) for multiunit resource system. The approach is based on the assumption that each type of resource has a fixed total number of units and each process request one resource at a time. The node stores RAG information in different matrices and information regarding search steps in different matrices. The MDDU algorithm is been realized using verilog HDL. The limitation of the approach is that it cannot be used in software deadlock detection due to running overhead.

Xiao and Lee (2010), have proposed a deadlock detection algorithm for single unit resource system on MPSoCs. The assumptions are same as it was in their previous work with a restriction over the number of unit of resources which is considered one here. They have minimized the computation time for finding sink node as compared to their previous work. The algorithm is meant for hardware supported deadlock detection rather than software support. Although the computation time is O(1) but due to hardware constrained it is not suitable for software deadlock detection approaches.

PROTECTION IN RTDS: SECURITY AND PRIVACY

To improve their utilization and share their resources to outside user's real time distributed systems are becoming open systems that are frequently exposed to public networks. One example of these type of real time distributed systems are Clusters which have become increasingly popular as the powerful and cost-effective platforms for executing computationally large or data-intensive applications (Zhu & Lu, 2008).

Now days many Real-time parallel applications on distributed systems are emerging in many domains, including online transaction processing systems, medical electronics, aircraft control, and scientific parallel computing. These applications require protection in terms of privacy and security of data due to vulnerability of environment which is open. The protection parameters can be data privacy (Connelly & Chien, 2002), data integrity check (Tuecke, Foster, Karonis, & Kesselman, 1998), software execution protection (Shi W., Lee H.H.S., Lu C., and Ghosh M., 2005) and authentication. To better understand the security threat to an application we will look into a example of stock quote update and trading application in which incoming requests coming from different business partner while outgoing response from an enterprise back-end machines are prone to security attack. These applications composed of a cluster that has to satisfy both timeliness of responses and security requirements. As cluster executes vast number of unverified application submitted by vast number of different types of user both applications and users can be source of security threats to cluster (Maheswaran, Ali, Siegel, Hensgen, & Freund, 1999). These applications are vulnerable to attacks such as: attack by malicious user, malicious application running on clusters itself. The malicious users intercept applications running and launch denial of service whereas blocking of resources is observed in the case of malicious applications. The security threats to these applications are primarily related to the authentication, integrity, and confidentiality of application.

An attacker may breach the above security service by spoofing, snooping and alteration kind of attack. These attacks are briefly defined below.

Spoofing attack is a situation in which one person or program successfully masquerades as another by falsifying data and thereby gaining an illegitimate advantage.

Snooping attack is not necessarily limited to gaining access to data during its transmission. Hacker may gain access to data while it is in transmission but can also gain access while the data is in not in transmission.

Alteration is a kind of attack in which a malicious user, which may be inside the cluster or outside the cluster, after gaining access to data performs unauthorized changes to it.

Thus, to provide protection to the applications security services are deployed on RTDS nodes so that the data processing in RTDS not being read or altered by malicious users, and only the person with access right is able to access the system. Deploying Security services, which are used to satisfy security needs of the applications, incurs computational overhead in terms of computation time due to running a particular security algorithm to combat the security threat.

Similarly computation overhead will occur for message passing. The computation overhead occurred due to above factors will significantly affect the scheduling of security critical real time tasks in RTDS. It is well-known that scheduling algorithms for Real time tasks play a key role to greatly improve the performance. Unfortunately, most traditional scheduling algorithms are merely devised to guarantee timing constraints while possibly posing unacceptable security risk. Thus, the conflicting requirements of good real-time performance and high quality of security protection imposed by security-critical real-time applications introduce a new challenge for resource allocation particularly scheduling schemes in form of how to make a judicious balance between the two conflicting requirements. Apart from this, heterogeneity of RTDS makes the scenario more difficult because same security requirement will incur distinct computations overhead for different nodes. This is due to the fact that computation overhead is node dependent. Being a new area of research very few work has been reported in the field of scheduling real time applications in distributed environment with security constraints. This section covers the work done in this field.

Tao and Xiao (2006) have proposed a security aware real time heuristic strategy known as SAREC for cluster environment. They have integrated the security and the real time scheduling algorithm namely EDF in cluster environment and proposed SAEDF. To map the security requirement quantitatively they have proposed a security overhead model. The security levels for confidentiality, authentication and integrity security requirements have been modeled. The model maps the security requirement of the task in a range of 0 to 1 according to the performance of different algorithms. This security overhead model is useful in calculating overhead for a security requirement needed by a task and can be extended for other services. The proposed SAEDF algorithm calculates the security overhead for the task and tries to enhance the security level of task at the time of feasibility by EDF policy. Their algorithm is greedy in nature because it tries to enhance security level of current task on the basis of present system conditions. Thus task arriving later will suffer the deadline miss because the current task will be given maximum security on the present slack available and thus later arriving task may not be accepted at their minimum security level.

Jiang, Wang, and Liu (2007) have presented security aware and fault tolerant algorithm based on adaptive job replications and shows the effect of security requirements on system performance. The paper uses adaptive replication scheme for jobs success according to the security level of the Grid environment. In the above approach they calculate different values such as SDi, TLj, TL, and 'replica'. SD is the security level of task, TLj is the trust level of node Mj (aggregation of historical security performance data of grid sites, such as prior successful job execution rate, cumulative site utilization, and intrinsic security attributes), TL is the grid security environment and 'replica' is the number of task replication required based on TL. TL of the grid is classified into five categories from very high to very low and number of 'replica' ranges from [0, 4]. Their algorithm schedules tasks on the nodes only when SD requirements of a task are fulfilled. It is also required that number of nodes available should be sufficient to schedule replicas required for a given task as a backup copy in case of fault.

The communication among primary and backup scheduler is done periodically and when task is completed the primary scheduler sends termination message to all which has been reserved for that task so that these sites can be used for other task in the scheduling event. The approach had not taken real time constraints in consideration thus cannot be deployed in RTDS.

In (Xiao & Tao, 2007) the authors deal with the scheduling of periodic tasks with security requirements in the embedded systems. The approach adds the security overhead experienced by the three security services (authentication, integrity, confidentiality) into the execution time of the task and then schedules the tasks for a Hyperperiod or planning cycle. The security level of a task will be fixed for all the instances or release of that task in the planning cycle. The security services of the tasks are increased on the basis of benefit –cost ratio function which is defined as measuring the increase of security level by unit security overhead. Thus task whose value for this function is more will be candidate for the increasing security. The approach is greedy in nature scheduling decision is based on benefit cost ratio which may result in some task to miss their deadline.

The paper (Tao & Xiao, 2007) gives a SATS algorithm for scheduling task on heterogeneous systems with security requirements. The main component of SATS is composed of five modules: (1) Execution time manager; (2) Security overhead manager; 3) Degree of security deficiency (DSD) calculator; (4) Security-adaptive window (SAW) controller; and (5) Task allocation decision maker. The approach tries to minimize an objective function SDSD (QoS) for a schedule X on nodes M, where SDSD is the sum of DSD (degree of security deficiency) of all tasks. DSD is the difference of the task security level and the node security level offered to that task where it is scheduled. This objective function is the qualitative measure of the security service achieved by the approach. The second measure is risk-free probability for QoS, which is the function of the probability of a task being executed & task risk rate. The algorithm SATS allocate tasks on different nodes by finding candidate nodes arranged in increasing order of task completion time on that node. After that the node offering the smallest DSD value is being selected from the candidate nodes. The approach is not meant for real time task and it is static in nature that means prior information of task attributes are required.

Tao and Xiao (2007) deal with scheduling data intensive Jobs with security requirements on Grids. The approach focuses on resources in grids that are computation, storage, software, and communications. There is a job acceptor which accepts job and dispatches to its corresponding site. E is a vector of execution times for the job on each site in M. The security overhead model considers four cases. a). Data & job are on same site. b).Data on remote site. c). Job on remote site. d).Both data & job are on remote site. To measure quality of security provided by the data grid they introduce concept of security discrepancy (SD). This is calculated as a job difference of Security requirement (code +data) with security provided by that site. Their scheduling algorithm known as SAHA which schedules job on FCFS basis with minimizing the value for Degree of SD for a schedule X for a given job set J. Later on they give a Risk free probability function which is dependent on execution time of jobs and security level provided to security services.

Songra et al. (2007) have proposed an approach for security critical real time tasks for cluster environment.. In the paper the authors have introduced the concept of task criticality and the security level of the task is increased according to its criticality thus introducing fairness in the approach. The criticality level of a task is being compared to a threshold which is dependent on the success ratio of the system and is adaptable in nature. The proposed approach exhibits better result in terms of success ratio.

In Tao and Xiao (2008) the authors have given approaches for homogeneous and heterogeneous environment. The security aware resource allocation scheme for homogeneous clusters proposes a Task Allocation for Parallel Applications with Deadline and Security Constraints Algorithm (TAPADS). This algorithm considers a parallel application modeled as J= (T, E, P).Here T is a set of non pre-emptable real time task, E is a set of weighted & directed edges use to indicate communication among task (Ti, Tj) belongs to E and P is the period that is a constant time interval between the two consecutive job instances of a parallel application J. The task is modeled as T= (ei, Li, Si) where ei is the execution time, Li is the amount of data and Si is the security level vector. The message overhead is modeled as eij/ Bka. Where eij is the amount of data to be transferred from task Ti to Tj and Bka is the bandwidth between node k and a. This approach is for scheduling periodic jobs on cluster. To meet deadline and precedence constraints, TAPADS assigns tasks to nodes in a way to maximize the security measured by PSC(X), which is the probability that all tasks are executed without any risk of being attacked and all messages are risk free during the course of transmissions. Furthermore, TAPADS can maintain a high schedulability measured by PSD(X), which is the probability that all tasks are timely completed. Their second approach is for Security Aware & Heterogeneity Aware Resource Allocation Parallel Jobs (SHARP) which models the security heterogeneity as job is going to be executed on Heterogeneous Cluster. Thus the execution time and security overhead will vary from one node to another. There are four security heterogeneity defined.

In paper (Lu & Zhu, 2009) approach schedules task onto heterogeneous clusters in two phase and algorithm is known as TPSS. First phase known as DSRF which comprises of three steps for feasibility check of arriving task. Second phase tries to balance the security level of different task on the nodes. In first step of DSRF approach tries to assign the maximal security level to a task Ti without violating the timing constraints of previously accepted task on a node Nj (Nj is the node where finish time of Ti is minimum.) and allocated according to EDF on that node. In 2nd step if task is not accepted with maximal security level than security level (SL) is degraded. In 3rd step a node is selected whose security level of the tasks in the local queue is maximum and degrades the security level up to minimum SL of tasks in LQ on Round Robin basis. In second phase there is a security level balancing algorithm known as FMSL (Fair & Maximal Security Level Algorithm). In this there is a security level controller on each node which tries to balance the security level of the entire task in the local queue of the nodes and to make the total security level higher than before. The strategy is to divide tasks in a LQ into two sets known as MaxSet and MinSet which consist of tasks with Maximal & Minimal SL respectively. First phase of TPSS i.e. DSRF is greedy in nature and incur overhead at runtime. As in DSRF the entire task are accepted at Maximal security level. So there is very little scope of enhancing the SL of tasks. Runtime overhead is a issue.

The research work reported in Tripathi, Yadav, and Ojha (2010) gives a scheduling algorithm for security sensitive real time applications in clusters. To achieve a balance and fairness between security values required and success ratio the concept of deferred approach has been used. By delaying the task feasibility, the approach gives more chance to tasks arriving later to schedule because it is more likely that tasks which are scheduled (present in local queue of nodes) according to their Worst Case Execution Time (WCET) will take less than their WCET. This will result in more slack time for waiting task in scheduler queue. Along with this load balancing is been used to mitigate the effect of over utilization and under utilization.

Srinivasan and Jha (1999) have proposed an approach for safe allocation of task with maximizing reliability. They also proposed a task based fault tolerance approach. The first phase of two-phase scheme allocates the tasks of the original task graph with reliability as the objective. The

allocation procedure uses the concept of clustering based on static levels. In the second phase, the fault tolerance tasks are allocated such that the decrease in reliability is minimized. The paper uses the concept of Exclusion Matrix and Preference Matrix. Their approach tries to allocate communicating tasks on the same processor to avoid Inter Process Communication overhead. If two inter communicating task are scheduled on different processors than communication is done on the most reliable link. Similarly the task having higher computation need have to be allocated on more reliable processor. The tasks are grouped into clusters that are exclusion compatible and preference compatible. The formation of clusters is done by giving static level to the tasks which is based on static level and communication cost.

CONCLUSION

There are several QoS parameters on which the performance of a scheduling algorithm is judged such as Makespan (the total running time of all jobs), Success rate (the percentage of job completed), Utilization (percentage of processing power allocated to user jobs out of total processing power available). Above all QoS parameters, success rate is the essential parameter for RTDS based applications where as others are desirable parameters. The main aim while scheduling real time task is to make maximum task to be completed before their stipulated deadline. Thus, several heuristics are developed to achieve the required QoS. Different systems can have different QoS requirements. For example an online trading stock exchange application needs security whereas a battery operated embedded application requires energy saving. Thus the Qos requirement of a RTDS varies from application to application.

RTDS applications are facing challenges which are discussed in this review and their existing solutions. The one of the main challenge is Resource management i.e. task scheduling. At the same time deadlock free resource allocation is also need of the applications so that maximum resource utilization can be achieved. Fairly distributing load among the sites is essential to achieve above QoS parameters. The security constraints also pose serious effect on scheduling. Quantitative model to measure the security is one of the main problems to be tackled. Heterogeneous nature of the distributed system complicates the problem domain.

This survey provides the current research issues in Real time distributed system and also provides the researchers an opportunity to update their reference list.

Presently these issues had been tackled individually. Now work is required for achieving a deep understanding on how to design a system that can optimally integrate all these issues.

REFERENCES

Abdelzaher, T. F., Atkins, E. M., & Shin, K. G. (2000). QoS negotiation in real-time systems & its application to automated flight control. *IEEE Transactions on Computers*, *49*(11), 1170–1183. doi:10.1109/12.895935

Abdelzaher, T. F., & Shin, K. G. (1999). Combined task & message scheduling in distributed real-time systems. *IEEE Transactions on Parallel and Distributed Systems*, *10*(11), 1179–1191. doi:10.1109/71.809575

Ahmed, Q., & Vrbsky, S. (1998). Maintaining security in firm real-time database systems. In *Proceedings of 14th Annual Computer Security Applications Conference*, Phoenix, AZ (pp. 83-90).

Ammar, R., & Alhamdan, A. (2002). Scheduling real time parallel structure on cluster computing. In *Proceedings of the 7th IEEE Symposium on Computers & Communications*, Taormina-Giardini Naxos, Italy, (pp. 69-74).

Armstrong, R., Hensgen, D., & Kidd, T. (1998). The relative performance of various mapping algorithms is independent of sizable variances in run-time predictions. In *Proceedings of the 7th IEEE Heterogeneous Computing Workshop*, Orlando, FL (pp. 79-87).

Bertogna, M., Cirinei, M., & Lipari, G. (2009). Schedulability analysis of global scheduling algorithms on multiprocessor platforms. *IEEE Transactions on Parallel and Distributed Systems*, *20*(4), 553–566. doi:10.1109/TPDS.2008.129

Bestavros, A. (1997). A methodology for scheduling real time tasks in a distributed system. In *Proceedings of the 17th International Conference on Distributed Computing Systems*, Baltimore, MD (p. 449).

Chen, Y. S., Chang, L. P., Kuo, T. W., & Mok, A. K. (2009). An anomaly prevention approach for real-time task scheduling. *Journal of Systems and Software*, *82*(1), 144–154. doi:10.1016/j.jss.2008.07.038

Chhabra, A., Singh, G., Waraich, S. S., Sidhu, B., & Kumar, G. (2006). Qualitative parametric comparison of load balancing algorithms in parallel & distributed computing environment. *World Academy of Science, Engineering & Technology*, 16.

Connelly, K., & Chien, A. A. (2002). Breaking the barriers: High performance security for high-performance computing. In *Proceedings of the 10th New Security Paradigms Workshop*, Virginia Beach, VA (pp. 36-42).

Dandamudi, S. (1995). Performance impact of scheduling discipline on adaptive load sharing in homogeneous distributed systems. In *Proceedings of the 15th International Conference on Distributed Computing Systems*, Vancouver, BC, Canada (pp. 484-492).

Data, A. K., & Ghosh, S. (1990). Deadlock detection in distributed systems. In *Proceedings of the 9th Annual International Phoenix Conference on Computers & Communications*, Scottsdale, AZ (pp. 131-136).

Deng, S. C. Y., Attie, P., & Sun, W. (1996). Optimal deadlock detection in distributed systems based on locally constructed wait-for graphs. In *Proceedings of the 16th International Conference on Distributed Computing Systems* (pp. 613-619).

Dertouzos, M. L., & Mok, A. K. (1989). Multiprocessor online scheduling of hard real-time tasks. *IEEE Transactions on Software Engineering, 15*(12), 1497–1506. doi:10.1109/32.58762

Di Stefano, A., Lo Bello, L., & Tramontana, E. (1999). Factors affecting the design of load balancing algorithms in distributed systems. *Journal of Systems and Software, 48*(2), 105–117. doi:10.1016/S0164-1212(99)00050-3

Dobber, M., Mei, R. V., & Koole, G. (2009). Dynamic load balancing & job replication in a global-scale grid environment: A comparison. *IEEE Transactions on Parallel and Distributed Systems, 20*(2), 207–218. doi:10.1109/TPDS.2008.61

Foster, I., & Kesselman, C. (1999). *The Grid: Blueprint for a new computing infrastructure*. San Fransisco, CA: Morgan Kaufmann.

Gagne, M., & Shepard, T. (1991). A pre-run-time scheduling algorithm for hard real time systems. *IEEE Transactions on Software Engineering, 17*(7), 669–677. doi:10.1109/32.83903

Gopalan, K., & Kang, K. D. (2007). Coordinated allocation & scheduling of multiple resources in real-time operating systems. In *Proceedings of the Workshop on Operating Systems Platforms for Embedded Real-Time Applications*, Pisa, Italy.

Gritzalis, S. (2004). Enhancing privacy & data protection in electronic medical environments. *Journal of Medical Systems, 28*(6), 535–547. doi:10.1023/B:JOMS.0000044956.55209.75

Guangmin, L. (2008). Adaptive load balancing algorithm over heterogeneous workstations. In *Proceedings of the 7th International Conference on Grid & Cooperative Computing* (pp. 169-174).

Hao, Y., Liu, J. C., & Kim, J. L. (1992). Task scheduling in hard real-time distributed systems on a bus local area network. In *Proceedings of the 11th Annual International Phoenix Conference on Computers & Communications*, Scottsdale, AZ (pp. 411-416).

He, L., Jarvis, S. A., Spooner, D. P., & Nudd, G. R. (2003). Dynamic scheduling of parallel real-time jobs by modeling spare capabilities in heterogeneous clusters. In *Proceedings of the IEEE International Conference on Cluster Computing* (pp. 2-10).

Jiang, C., Wang, C., & Liu, X. (2007). Adaptive replication based security aware & fault tolerant job scheduling for grids. *In Proceedings of the 8th ACIS International Conference on Software Engineering, Artificial Intelligence, Networking, & Parallel/Distributed Computing* (pp. 597-602).

Kachroo, P., Ravindran, B., & Hegazy, T. (2001). Adaptive resource management in asynchronous real-time distributed systems using feedback control functions. *In Proceedings of the 5th International Symposium on Autonomous Decentralized Systems* (pp. 39-46).

Kalantari, M., & Akbari, M. K. (2008). A parallel solution for scheduling of real time applications on grid environments. *Future Generation Computer Systems, 25*(7), 704–716. doi:10.1016/j.future.2008.01.003

Karatza, H. D., & Hilzer, R. C. (2003). Parallel job scheduling in homogeneous distributed systems. *Transactions of the Society for Modeling & Simulation, 79*(5), 287–298. doi:10.1177/003754903037148

Kermia, O., & Sorel, Y. (2008). Load balancing & efficient memory usage for homogeneous distributed real-time embedded systems. In *Proceedings of the International Conference on Parallel Processing - Workshops*, Portland, OR (pp. 39-46).

Kshemkalyani, A. D., & Singhal, M. (1999). A one-phase algorithm to detect distributed deadlocks in replicated databases. *IEEE Transactions on Knowledge and Data Engineering, 11*(6), 880–895. doi:10.1109/69.824601

Kuo, C. F., Shih, C. S., & Kuo, T. W. (2006). *Resource allocation framework for distributed real-time end-to-end tasks* (Tech. Rep. No. NTU/NEWS-6-0005). Taiwan: National Taiwan University.

Lee, J. J., & Xiao, X. (2010). A true O(1) parallel deadlock detection algorithm for single-unit resource systems & it's hardware implementation. *IEEE Transactions on Parallel and Distributed Systems, 21*(1), 4–19. doi:10.1109/TPDS.2009.38

Li, P., Ravindran, B., & Hegazy, T. (2003). Proactive resource allocation for asynchronous real-time distributed systems in the presence of processor failures. *Journal of Parallel and Distributed Computing, 63*(12), 1219–1242. doi:10.1016/S0743-7315(03)00111-4

Li, W., Kavi, K., & Akl, R. (2007). A non premptive scheduling algorithm for soft real time systems. *Computers & Electrical Engineering, 33*(1), 12–29. doi:10.1016/j.compeleceng.2006.04.002

Liden, S. (1995). The evolution of flight management systems. In *Proceedings of the 13th IEEE/AIAA Digital Avionics Systems Conference*, Phoenix, AZ (pp. 157-169).

Lin, X., Lu, Y., Deogun, J., & Goddard, S. (2007). Real-time divisible load scheduling for cluster computing. In *Proceedings of the 13th IEEE Real Time & Embedded Technology & Applications Symposium*, Bellevue, WA (pp. 303-314).

Liu, C. L., & Layland, J. W. (1973). Scheduling algorithms for multiprogramming in a hard real-time environment. *Communications of the ACM, 20*(1), 46–61.

Lombardi, M., Milano, M., & Benini, L. (2009). Robust non-preemptive hard real-time scheduling for clustered multicore platforms. In *Proceedings of the Design, Automation & Test in Europe Conference & Exhibition*, Nice, France (pp. 803-808).

Lu, P., & Zhu, X. (2009). A two-phase scheduling strategy for real-time applications with security requirements on heterogeneous clusters. *Journal of Computers & Electrical Engineering, 35*(6), 980–993. doi:10.1016/j.compeleceng.2008.11.022

Mahafza, B., Welstead, S., Champagne, D., Manadhar, R., Worthington, T., & Campbell, S. (1998). Real-time radar signal simulation for the ground based radar for national missile defense. In *Proceedings of the IEEE Radar Conference*, Dallas, TX (pp. 62-67).

Maheswaran, M., Ali, S., Siegel, H. J., Hensgen, D., & Freund, R. F. (1999). Dynamic matching & scheduling of a class of independent tasks onto heterogeneous computing systems. In *Proceedings of the 8th IEEE Heterogeneous Computing Workshop* (pp. 30-44).

Manimaran, G., & Rammurthy, C. S. (1998). An efficient dynamic scheduling algorithm for multiprocessor real-time systems. *IEEE Transactions on Parallel and Distributed Systems, 9*(3), 312–319. doi:10.1109/71.674322

Radulescu, A., & van Gemund, A. J. C. (2000). Fast & effective task scheduling in heterogeneous systems. In *Proceedings of the 9th Heterogeneous Computing Workshop*, Cancun, Mexico (229-238).

Rajasekaran, S., Ammar, R., & Hussein, A. (2007). Efficient scheduling of real-time tandem task graphs on heterogeneous clusters with network limitations. In *Proceedings of the 12ᵗʰ IEEE Symposium on Computers and Communications*, Aveiro, Portugal (pp. 227-232).

Ramamritham, K., Stankovic, J. A., & Shiah, P. (1990). Efficient scheduling algorithms for real time multiprocessor systems. *IEEE Transactions on Parallel and Distributed Systems, 1*(2), 184–194. doi:10.1109/71.80146

Ravindran, B., & Devarasetty, R. K. (2002). Adaptive resource management algorithms for periodic tasks in dynamic real-time distributed systems. *Journal of Parallel and Distributed Computing, 62*(10), 1527–1547.

Razzaque, M. A., & Hong, C. S. (2007). *Dynamic load balancing in distributed system: An efficient approach*. Retrieved from http://mnet.skku.ac.kr/data/2007data/JCCI2007/papers/pdf/P-II-10.pdf

Sánchez, C., Sipma, H. B., Manna, Z., Subramonian, V., & Gill, C. (2006). On efficient distributed deadlock avoidance for real-time & embedded systems. In *Proceedings of the 20ᵗʰ IEEE International Parallel & Distributed Processing Symposium*.

SenthilKumar, B., Chitra, P., & Prakash, G. (2009). Robust task scheduling on heterogeneous computing systems using segmented MaxR- MinCT. *International Journal of Recent Trends in Engineering, 1*(2), 63–65.

Shi, W., Lee, H. H. S., Lu, C., & Ghosh, M. (2005). Towards the issues in architectural support for protection of software execution. *ACM SIGARCH Computer Architecture News, 33*(1), 6–15. doi:10.1145/1055626.1055629

Shiang, C., & Stankovic, J. A. (1990). *Survey of deadlock detection in distributed concurrent programming environment & its applications to real time systems* (Tech. Rep. No. UM-CS-1990-069). Amherst, MA: University of Massachusetts.

Songra, A., Yadav, R. S., & Tripathi, S. (2007). Modified approach for secured Real time applications on clusters. *International Journal of Security, 1*(1).

Spartiotis, D., & Bestavros, A. (1993). Probabilistic job scheduling for distributed real - time applications. In *Proceedings of the IEEE Workshop on Real-Time Applications*, New York, NY (pp. 97-101).

Srinivasan, S., & Jha, N. K. (1999). Safety & reliability driven task allocation in distributed systems. *IEEE Transactions on Parallel and Distributed Systems, 10*(3), 238–251. doi:10.1109/71.755824

Stankovic, J. A., Spuri, M., Ramamritham, K., & Buttazzo, G. C. (1998). *Deadline scheduling for real-time systems: EDF & related algorithms*. Boston, MA: Kluwer Academic.

Tanenbaum, A. S., & Maarten, V. S. (2007). *Distributed systems: Principles & paradigms*. Upper Saddle River, NJ: Prentice Hall.

Tao, X., & Xiao, Q. (2006). Scheduling security-critical real-time applications on clusters. *IEEE Transactions on Computers, 55*(7), 864–879. doi:10.1109/TC.2006.110

Tao, X., & Xiao, Q. (2007). Performance evaluation of a new scheduling algorithm for distributed systems with security heterogeneity. *Journal of Parallel and Distributed Computing, 67*(10), 1067–1081. doi:10.1016/j.jpdc.2007.06.004

Tao, X., & Xiao, Q. (2008). Security-aware resource allocation for real-time parallel jobs on homogeneous & heterogeneous clusters. *IEEE Transactions on Parallel and Distributed Systems, 19*(5), 682–697. doi:10.1109/TPDS.2007.70776

Tripathi, S., Yadav, R. S., & Ojha, R. P. (2010). A utilization based approach for secured real time applications on clusters. In *Proceedings of the International Conference on Advances in Computing, Control, & Telecommunication Technologies*, Trivandrum, Kerala, India (pp. 433-438).

Tuecke, S., Foster, I., Karonis, N. T., & Kesselman, C. (1998). Managing security in high-performance distributed computations. *Cluster Computing*, *1*(1), 95–107.

Ullman, J. D. (1975). NP-complete scheduling problems. *Journal of Computer and System Sciences*, *10*(3), 384–393. doi:10.1016/S0022-0000(75)80008-0

Xiao, Q., & Tao, X. (2007a). Improving security for periodic tasks in embedded systems through scheduling. *ACM Transactions on Embedded Computing Systems*, *6*(3), 20. doi:10.1145/1275986.1275992

Xiao, Q., & Tao, X. (2007b). Security-driven scheduling for data-intensive applications on grids. *Cluster Computing*, *10*(2), 145–153. doi:10.1007/s10586-007-0015-x

Xiao, X., & Lee, J. J. (2008). A novel O(1) deadlock detection methodology for multiunit resource systems & its hardware implementation for system-on-chip. *IEEE Transactions on Parallel and Distributed Systems*, *19*(12), 1657–1670. doi:10.1109/TPDS.2008.56

Yeung, C., & Hung, S. (1995). A new deadlock detection algorithms for distributed real-time database systems. In *Proceedings of the 14th IEEE Symposium on Reliable Distributed Systems*, Bad Neuenahr, Germany (pp. 146-153).

Zhang, Y., Gill, C. D., & Chen, Y. (2010). Configurable middleware for distributed real-time systems with aperiodic & periodic tasks. *IEEE Transactions on Parallel and Distributed Systems*, *21*(3), 393–404. doi:10.1109/TPDS.2009.67

Zhu, X., & Lu, P. (2008). Study of scheduling for processing real-time communication signals on heterogeneous clusters. In *Proceedings of the 9th International Symposium on Parallel Architectures, Algorithms & Networks*. Sydney, Australia (pp. 121-126).

Zhu, X., & Lu, P. (2009). Multi-dimensional scheduling for real-time tasks on heterogeneous clusters. *Journal of Computer Science & Technology*, *24*(3), 434–446. doi:10.1007/s11390-009-9235-2

This work was previously published in the International Journal of Distributed Systems and Technologies (IJDST), Volume 2, Issue 2, edited by Nik Bessis, pp. 37-57, copyright 2011 by IGI Publishing (an imprint of IGI Global).

Chapter 15
A Meta–Design Model for Creative Distributed Collaborative Design

Li Zhu
Università degli Studi di Milano, Italy

Barbara Rita Barricelli
Università degli Studi di Milano, Italy

Claudia Iacob
Università degli Studi di Milano, Italy

ABSTRACT

As collaboration in creating software systems becomes more complex and frequent among multidisciplinary teams, finding new strategies to support this collaboration becomes crucial. The challenge is to bridge the communication gaps among stakeholders with diverse cultural and professional backgrounds. Moreover, future uses and issues cannot be completely anticipated at design time, and it is necessary to develop open-ended software environments that can be evolved and tailored in opportunistic ways to tackle co-evolution of users and systems. A conceptual meta-design model, the Hive-Mind Space (HMS) model, has been proposed to support multidisciplinary design teams' collaboration and foster their situated innovation. The model provides localized habitable environments for diverse stakeholders and tools for them to tailor the system, allowing the co-evolution of systems and practices. The authors explore the possibility of utilizing boundary objects within the HMS model to facilitate the communication amongst stakeholders as well as their participation in the creative distributed design process. Two concrete case studies, a factory automation and the Valchiavenna Portal, demonstrate the implementation of the HMS model and provide a possible solution to overcome the complex, evolving and emerging nature of the collaborative design.

DOI: 10.4018/978-1-4666-2647-8.ch015

INTRODUCTION

The most recent applications of Web technologies are geared to support user generated content activities as well as distributed collaborative design. There is a growing design culture shift in that stakeholders are not only passive software consumers but also can play the role of software designers and producers (Barbosa et al., 2001). The culture of participation (Fischer et al., 2004) allows all the stakeholders in the design process to be active producers and system co-designers, and supports them to express themselves creatively. This paper particularly addresses the distributed collaborative design which emerged as a response to the co-evolution of systems and stakeholders (Bourguin et al., 2001; Costabile et al., 2006). Co-evolution implies that, on one hand, the stakeholders' interaction strategies change by using systems because they become more and more experienced and their work practice changes over time. On the other hand, as an answer to that, systems need to change in order to adapt to the evolving stakeholders. Therefore, systems should present a set of characteristics shapeable by stakeholders according to their profile (in terms of culture, role and platform), in order to support situated practices and requirements. We address distributed collaborative design of software artifacts which involves groups of people who belong to different Communities of Practice (CoP), i.e. people who share a concern, a set of problems, or a passion about a topic and deepen their knowledge and expertise in this area by interacting on an ongoing basis (Wenger, 2002). In the design of complex systems, experts from different CoPs get together in order to collaborate in the design process; that is, they form a Community of Interest (CoI) (Fischer, 2001). In our approach, the notion of the CoP is refined, observing that stakeholders share not only the domain practice but also the technical languages and notations. Collaborative and distributed design activities therefore imply the use of different technical systems of signs, which

in turn lead to the existence of communication gaps among the CoPs involved in the process.

This paper is an extended work from Zhu et al. (2010), which presents the Hive-Mind Space (HMS) model, providing different work environments localized to the various CoPs involved in the collaborative design process. The aim of this model is to support the communication and common understanding of stakeholders belonging to different communities by providing them with opportunities to construct their own work environment and have control in the description of problems. Therefore, we have been developing tools and platforms to support these design communities, among whom there are non-professional software developers who are domain experts (e.g. physicians, archeologists, industrial designers, and so on). This will allow them to actively participate in the interaction design process, namely creating, modifying or extending software artifacts (Costabile et al., 2006). Our aim is to design a meeting space with new affordances (Torenvliet, 2003) to support stakeholders from different cultural and social domains, either as individuals or as members of specific CoPs and CoIs, empowering them to become active creative designers as well as creative knowledge *produsers* (Bruns, 2008). Moreover, we focus on the exchange of virtual boundary objects in a meeting space, the boundary zone, exploring its potential as a means for effectively tackling the collaboration difficulties. Software engineers, HCI experts, domain experts and users come together – each representing a CoP – and participate in the design of a software artifact. We provide annotation tools within the HMS model that can be used by stakeholders to express change requests. Therefore, professional software developers can evolve the system based on the stakeholder feedback.

The following section introduces an overview of works related to our research and that influence our approach. The HMS model is then presented. We describe its structure and present boundary zone and boundary object concepts. To make the

HMS model implementation concrete, two real-world cases are described. Further reflections and future works are discussed in the final section.

RELATED WORK

In literature, the design process has been defined as "human activity, involving communication and creative thought amongst groups of participants" (Gennari & Reddy, 2000). These groups of participants contribute to the collaborative activity bringing their skills, their expertise, and motor skills, all influenced by their background and culture. The diversity of the members that usually constitute a collaborative design team is well defined in the CoP concept (Wenger, 2002). Our research aims to bring together stakeholders of different CoPs, constituting a CoI. CoIs can be seen as "communities-of-communities" (Brown & Duguid, 2000) whose purpose is to develop their activities by learning, sharing and creating knowledge. However, none of the CoPs in a CoI has all the knowledge required to achieve these goals, which is tacitly distributed among the various CoPs (Kirsh, 1995).

Collaborative Design

The diversity of the stakeholders involved in a collaborative design process requires particular attention to knowledge sharing and communication. In fact, each stakeholder owns specific knowledge that is crucial to the design process but not sufficient to solve the whole puzzle.

Knowledge Sharing in Collaborative Design

This situation, defined as 'symmetry of ignorance' (Fischer, 2000; Rittel, 1984), requires each stakeholder to share her/his knowledge in order to integrate it with other stakeholders' knowledge. Stakeholders in the collaboration act as competent practitioners, in that "they exhibit a kind of knowing in practice, most of which is tacit" and they "reveal a capacity for reflection on their intuitive knowing in the midst of action and sometimes use this capacity to cope with the unique, uncertain, and conflicted situations of practice" (Schön, 1983). Competent practitioners use their (tacit) knowledge to interpret the documents they work with and to understand how to use their tools. For example, when using an interactive application, a significant portion of the information conveyed by the system is 'implicit information' (Costabile et al., 2006), i.e. embedded in the actual shape of the elements displayed and in the visual organization of the overall screen image. Such information can only be understood by users who possess (tacit) domain knowledge, as happens with sequences of images that illustrate sequences of actions to be performed. The sequence has to be organized according to the reading habits of the expected user, by taking into account the writing directions of her/his language (e.g. from left to right for Western readers and from right to left for some Eastern readers). Furthermore, certain icons, words, or images may be meaningful only to experts in a given discipline. Icons representing cells in a liver simulation, for instance, may have specific meaning only for physicians, while satellite images of mountains might be meaningful only to geologists (Carrara et al., 2000). Sharing and integrating knowledge among different CoPs often fails because similar concepts are expressed with different languages and notations within various CoPs, while similar expressions are associated with different meanings. In such situations, communication gaps arise between collaborating stakeholders who belong to different CoPs. Acknowledging the existence of the symmetry of ignorance is essential to bridging these gaps and appropriate solutions can lead to intelligent and creative results (Engelbart, 1995). Additionally, progressive semantization techniques (Tondl, 1981) need to be adopted and suitable tools should be created.

The boundary object concept is one that aims at helping in this context (Star & Griesemer, 1989). A boundary object is defined as an artifact used by different CoPs in their practices but viewed and used differently by each CoP. The use and view of the boundary object is affected by the CoP's members' culture, expertise and background. Boundary objects are used to express ideation and to sustain communication in real world collaboration, for example by using wooden models of buildings in architect-client discussions. Blueprints, sketches and drawings are used in design engineering, digital images in medicine and the natural sciences. Papers, electronic documents, and even glossaries play this role in transactions, while sketches are applied to interaction design (Henderson & Kyng, 1991; Verplank, 2009). Stakeholders in a design process interact and negotiate a concept by using the boundary object as a concrete representation of what they mean. Being aware of and discussing different interpretations of boundary objects leads to the emergence of social practices and to knowledge sharing (Jennings, 2005). Boundary objects serve as externalizations that capture distinct domains of human knowledge and hold the potential to increase social shared cognition and practice (Resnick et al., 1991). Stakeholders need a space in which to carry on these activities, and to this end Konkola (2001) introduces the concept of the boundary zone - that is, "an area which resembles a 'no-man's land,' free from prearranged routines or rigid patterns. It could also be considered a place where each activity system reflects its own structure, attitudes, beliefs, norms and roles." The HMS model adopts the definition of the boundary zone redefined by Andersen and Mørch (2009), which considers it as a common ground where CoPs can meet to exchange boundary objects that reflect the outcomes of their collaboration.

In order to make the exchange of boundary objects meaningful to different CoPs, internationalization and localization techniques (Esselink,

2000; Iacob & Zhu, 2010) are embedded in the HMS model. All the boundary objects exchanged within the boundary zone are described abstractly in term of the affordances they provide, and are enhanced with culture, role and platform related properties. For example, one possible affordance of a boundary object is the possibility of being annotated. This affordance is therefore materialized differently for each community, e.g. designers could annotate usability issues, while users can annotate change requests.

Communication Gaps in Collaborative Design

Human-computer interaction (HCI) literature pointed long ago the problem of communication gaps that arise between software designers and software users. The gaps arise since users, designers, and developers might not understand each others' jargon (Borchers, 2001; Lauesen, 2005; Majhew, 1992). An application's interaction style usually reflects its designer's culture, skill, and physical abilities rather than those of its users. Users are thus forced to adopt interaction styles alien to their culture, which consequently affect the performance of their activities (Carrara et al., 2000). Applications should, on the contrary, be designed to help end users in performing their daily work and activities without being aware of the complex hardware and software technology they are using. Therefore, the interaction style should be adapted to the users' cultures and capabilities, the context of use, and the task to be performed (Kuutti, 1996). Several solutions have been proposed to bridge communication gaps and to design usable interactive systems (Borchers, 2001; Costabile et al., 2007). These solutions explicitly recognize the existence of different cultures and of the communication gaps between users and system designers and suggest that the human-system interaction style must be adapted to end users' culture and capabilities. In order to overcome the communication gaps (Costabile et al., 2006) the symmetry of ignorance principle has to be taken into consideration.

In distributed collaborative design, collaboration of multidisciplinary CoPs is necessary. Hence, software engineers need to collaborate at the very least with domain experts, i.e. representatives of the software users. However, the collaboration needs to be mediated by HCI experts. (Borchers, 2001; Carrara et al., 2000; Costabile et al., 2007; Folmer et al, 2005).

In the HMS model, collaboration between these heterogeneous groups is facilitated by exchange of digital boundary objects. Each digital boundary object is a unique object, augmented by annotation as metadata. In practice, digital boundary objects are generally used online similarly to how they are used in face-to-face collaboration, for instance by using multi-touch whiteboards or virtual sticky notes (Branham et al., 2010; Maldonado et al., 2007).

End-User Development

According to Henderson and Kyng (1991), design is a process tightly coupled to use and it continues during the use of the system. The emerging paradigm of End-User Development (EUD) aims to explore the opportunities to enable development in use. EUD techniques propose various approaches that allow users of software systems, who are not professional software developers, to create, modify or extend software artifacts (Costabile et al., 2007). In this situation, end users can evolve from passive consumers of data and computer tools into active producers of information and software (Lieberman et al., 2006). EUD represents a shift in interpreting software as a continuous evolving artifact, which considerably contributes to the progress of software development. Consequently, more and more software architectures are geared to providing more opportunities for tailoring software artifacts in the use context.

Mørch (1997) introduced Component-Based Software Development (CBSD) into EUD and proposes three levels of EUD tailoring: customization, integration, and extension. Customization means to modify the parameters of existing components. Integration allows users to add new functionalities to an application by linking together predefined components without accessing the underlying implementation code. Extension refers to creating new components by writing program code. The FLEXIBEAN component model and the FREEVOLVE platform for CSCW (Stiemerling, 2000) have been developed under this line.

Taking the CBSD approach, the HMS model includes all these levels of tailoring in order to gradually bridge the tailoring gaps. The HMS model addresses EUD and adopts the meta-design approach and allows end users to design as well as to shape their own environments. The HMS model also emphasizes the need of developing different software environments for end users working in the collaborative design context from different domains and with different roles.

Nevertheless, EUD tends to solve the co-evolution (Bourguin et al., 2001) problem from a techno-centric perspective and mainly focuses on tailorability. It omits other technology-related communication, demonstration and negotiation activities (Pipek, 2005).

Meta-Design

In this context, meta-design tackles unanticipated or emerging problems by providing socio-technical environments to empower users to be active knowledge contributors (Fischer & Ostwald, 2002).

A meta-design model example is the SER (Seeding, Evolutionary growth, Reseeding) three-phase process model (Fischer et al., 1994). During the seeding phase, domain designers and environment developers work together to instantiate a domain-oriented design environment seeded with domain knowledge. The seed is defined as an "initial collection of domain knowledge that is designed to evolve at use time" (Fischer et al., 1994). Evolutionary growth is the phase of a decentralized evolution as the seed is used and extended to do work or explore a problem. During the evolutionary growth phase, domain designers add information to the seed as they use it to create design artifacts. Reseeding is constituted of deliberate and centralized efforts to organize, formalize and generalize information and artifacts created during the evolutionary growth phase. During the reseeding phase, environment developers help domain designers to reorganize and reformulate information so it can be reused to support future design tasks. SER describes a socio-technical environment for tailorable applications to be used over an extended period of time and in which the distinction is made between design time and use time. Moreover, it postulates that systems that evolve over a sustained time span must continually alternate between periods of unplanned evolutions and periods of deliberate (re)structuring and enhancement.

Another approach to meta-design has been proposed in Costabile et al. (2007): the Software Shaping Workshop (SSW). In SSW, the distinction among professional designers and users is blurred. The focus of SSW is on communicational aspects of HCI and on the communication process among all the stakeholders involved. Moreover the switch is moved from the distinction between design time and use time to the distinction between (meta) design activities and use time activities. In the SSW approach, the system is organized into various environments (called workshops), each one for a specific sub-community. The design and implementation of application workshops is incremental, in that communities design perpetual-beta artifacts and not final products (Bruns, 2008).

The HMS model inherits the SSW features and simplifies the communication means by introducing boundary objects and boundary zone concepts. Furthermore, internationalization and localization

techniques are utilized to improve the progressive semantization process among all the CoPs. In the HMS, localization considers three aspects of users' profile: culture, role in the context and digital platform in use (Barricelli et al., 2010).

Social Creativity

Creativity has been extensively studied from a multidisciplinary approach (Lawson, 2005). The heart of intelligent human performance is not the individual human mind but groups of minds with tools and artifacts (Norman, 1993). We explore a meta-design/socio-technical approach (Fischer et al., 2004), in the sense that we address the creativity of groups and communities rather than of any specific individual (Costabile et al., 2007).

Furthermore, the dynamic and complex nature of collaborative design problems certainly involves more comprehensive knowledge than an individual person or certain CoP can have (Rittel, 1984; Fischer, 2000); since neither of them have all the knowledge required, the knowledge associated with the design problem is tacitly distributed among the various CoPs (Fischer, 2001). Thus, involving all the stakeholders in problem solving collaboration is necessary and leads to social creativity.

However, communication among different CoPs often fails in that stakeholders are from different cultural backgrounds and employ different notations (Petre & Green, 1993) as well as languages to express their ideation. They interpret the same thing in very different ways. On the other hand, knowledge useful for solving the design problems is distributed tacitly among stakeholders. This means that there is no CoP which knows all the required knowledge, but rather that the knowledge of all involved parties is symmetrically important in the design problem solving process (Kirsh, 1995). Exploiting the power of the symmetry of ignorance can be achieved by providing users with opportunities to construct their own situations and have control in the description of problems. Additionally, bringing divergent viewpoints together and creating a shared common understanding will certainly help stakeholders to discover new insights and alternatives, and hence to solve problems more creatively (Fischer, 2000).

The HMS model enhances social creativity via encouraging diversity and user-driven innovation, in the sense of bringing design communities from different disciplines together as well as involving end users in the design process; allowing independence (Surowiecki, 2005), since the architecture of the HMS model is globally interconnected and locally controlled; framing a decentralized community of interest, hence design communities are able to specialize and draw on local knowledge (Anderson, 2006); providing localized environments reflecting design communities' culture, role, device in use; and allowing knowledge aggregation, therefore turning all individual contributions into collections and sharing them in the knowledge base.

THE HMS MODEL

HMS Structure

As mentioned in previous section, the HMS model evolves the Software Shaping Workshop (SSW) methodology (Costabile et al., 2007). According to the SSW methodology, the HMS model provides each CoP involved in the collaborative design with software environments that offer to the CoP's members all the essential tools they need to perform their activities and to participate in the design of the whole space, as well as its continuous evolution (Costabile et al., 2008). In the HMS model, the SSW network structure is inherited. The HMS model supports three different levels in the network (see Figure 1): 1) the meta-design level, which is inhabited by software engineers and domain experts who design and maintain the interactive systems to be

used at design level; 2) the design level, where domain experts design application environments for end users; 3) the use level, where end users tailor and use the applications.

Each level in the HMS model provides a CoP with habitable environments corresponding to the various environments of the SSW methodology. Each CoP is provided with a habitable environment that offers all and only the tools needed by its members to perform their activities. The HMS model has an open under-development infrastructure, i.e. further levels could be added to the network.

The novelty with respect to the SSW methodology is the introduction of a central communication channel serving as a boundary zone that allows the exchange and management of boundary objects. Since all the CoPs can access the boundary zone, they can send their requests as well as dispatches to other CoPs. This space supports CoPs communication by allowing the creation and transmission of the boundary objects and annotations.

The boundary objects can embed multimedia annotations, i.e. text annotation, voice input, emoticons, images and video, and can be different depending on the context of the implementation. As opposed to the communication mode of the SSW, the communication channel of the HMS provides the entire model with more flexible ways of communication and interaction.

In this HMS model, the communication gaps among different CoPs due to cultural differences are overcome by environments localized according to the user's culture, role and platform in use.

Boundary Zone and Boundary Objects in the HMS Model

In analogy with the real world, the HMS model provides a space to bring diverse CoPs together, within which social reasoning and creativity emerges from brainstorming sessions. The in-between boundary zone in the model allows CoPs to create and exchange boundary objects. Bound-

Figure 1. HMS model structure overview

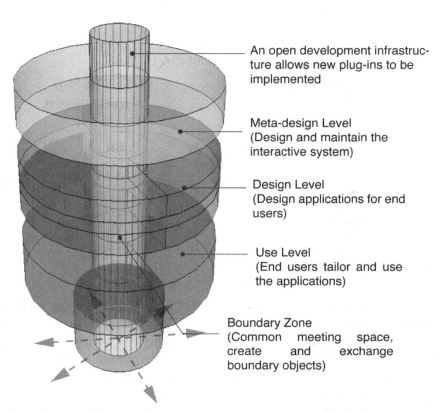

An open development infrastructure allows new plug-ins to be implemented

Meta-design Level
(Design and maintain the interactive system)

Design Level
(Design applications for end users)

Use Level
(End users tailor and use the applications)

Boundary Zone
(Common meeting space, create and exchange boundary objects)

ary objects serve as externalizations that capture distinct domains of human knowledge and have the potential to lead to an increase in socially shared cognition and practice (Resnick, 1991).

In the HMS model, CoPs are able to extend their activity and to create shared boundary objects within the boundary zone. Figure 2 illustrates CoPs as virtual organizations collaboratively designing software artifacts. Software engineers, HCI experts, domain experts and users come together – each representing a CoP – and participate in the design and exchange of software artifacts $(SA_1,\ldots, SA_4)$. The process is recursive and hence a continuous exchange of messages occurs among all the involved CoPs. The messages are, at each point, the software artifact under design in its current state. Based on the communication and understanding of the CoPs, the software artifact is

shaped at each step, converging towards a version usable for the CoP of users.

Boundary objects can be utilized to facilitate communication between heterogeneous CoPs. Each boundary object is a unique object and augmented by annotation as metadata of the boundary object, which is also a unique event within the message exchanging process.

In the HMS, the CoPs' members can communicate among each other using their habitable environments. They interact with their habitable environments through their notations and system of signs. In the HMS model, each CoP inhabits a certain interactive environment for reasoning and performing their activities inside it. Working in the habitable environments each participant develops and reasons on her/his model of the interaction process, works on prototypes and describes her/his

Figure 2. An example of collaborative design among software engineers, HCI experts, domain experts and users exchanging software artifacts

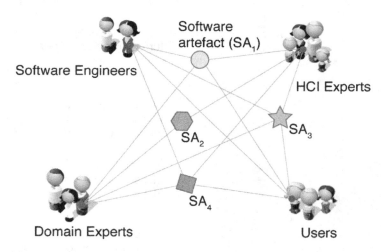

insights and proposed improvements. To guarantee efficient communication among these different participants, each environment is equipped with an annotation tool by means of which the participant can make observations about the exchanged information and proposals about possible changes of the system in order to improve it. In this way, each member of the team can directly experiment with the system, see and critique the recommendations and notes of other team members and can negotiate the system evolution. Hence, the different workshops allow the creation and management of a shared knowledge base.

Digital boundary objects are used to bridge the communication gaps among CoPs, aiming at supporting CoPs involved in a collaborative design process to effectively share and manage knowledge with each other.

HMS MODEL IMPLEMENTATION

The HMS model derives from observation of distributed collaborative design activities in the real world. The experience gained involving all the stakeholders in the collaborative design process has been applied to the implementation of the

HMS model. In this paper we introduce two real cases; the first is developed for a factory automation company, while the second is developed in the area of cultural heritage.

In both the cases, co-evolution of users and system is supported by the use of boundary objects and annotations. The design process is thus iterative and never ends. The diversity of the communities involved in the design process is considered. The domain-oriented environments, being localized to CoPs' systems of signs, support their creativity.

Factory Automation

The first HMS implementation case is for a factory automation company (Costabile et al., 2007). The company needs to develop software systems and user interfaces for the systems it sells to client companies. The systems created by the company should be usable, that is easy to learn and to use, and customized for users who are experts in factory automation but who are not familiar with programming.

The company also has to develop software tools for supporting its personnel in the development, testing, and maintenance of the factory automation systems. The company personnel is organized into different CoPs with different responsibilities and skills, and they need to perform various tasks with the software tools.

The requirements of the prototype ask for: 1) habitable environments which may be used by the clients of the company who are not software developers, but need to use factory automation tools, and 2) tools which allow the personnel of the company to develop, maintain, and test these systems.

Following on from the study of these requirements, a set of CoPs can be identified in the design of the prototype: the software engineers (SE), the domain experts (DE), the Company members (Company), the clients of the company (Client), the HCI experts, and the company's personnel (Personnel). Several other communities are present at the use level, e.g. mechanical testers and assembly-line operators.

Applying the HMS model to the design of the factory automation company prototype requires: 1) the grouping of these CoPs based on the design activities they perform, 2) the creation of a specific specialized habitable environment for each CoP and 3) the creation of a common space, the communication channel, through which these CoPs can exchange messages and communicate/collaborate with each other. Figure 3 shows a detailed section plan of the HMS model implementation in this case.

The meta-design level comprises the environments for the SE and DE in charge of developing the overall framework of habitable environments addressing each of the CoPs. They design, develop and maintain all the environments in the HMS system.

At the design level two sublevels are present. At each of the sublevels, the Company, HCI experts, the Personnel and the Client participate

Figure 3. The SF creates the assembly-line environment and the ALO annotates the assembly-line environment to communicate problems to the designers

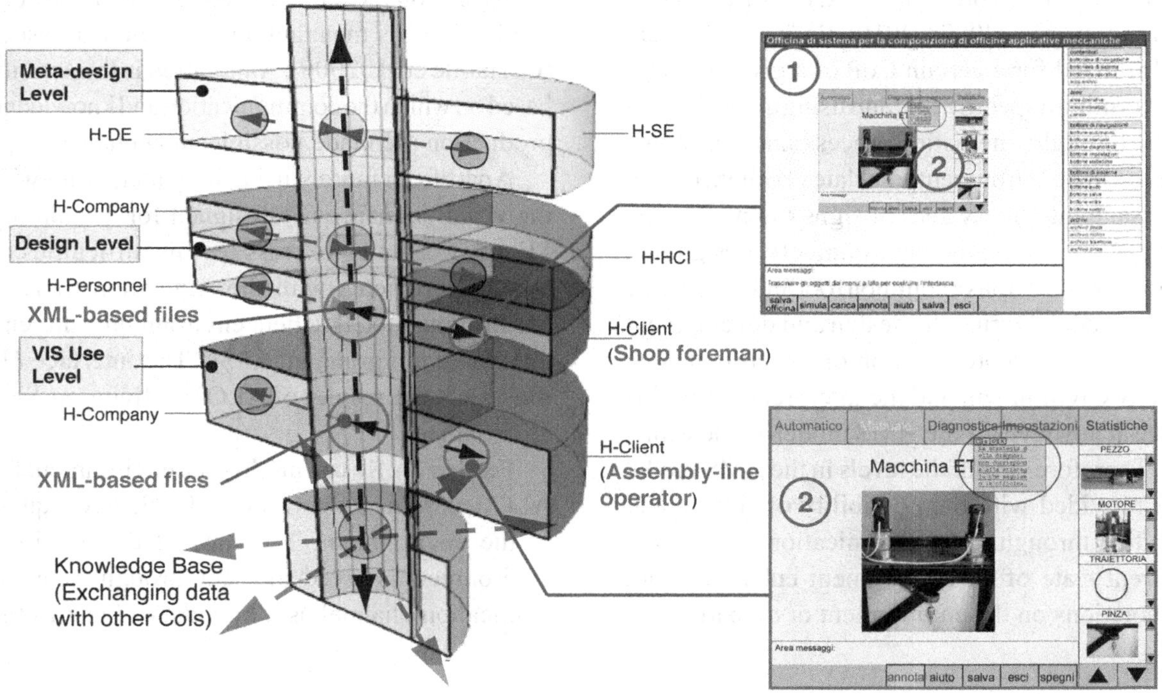

collaboratively in designing the localized habitable environments for the use level respecting the users' culture, roles and platform in use.

At the upper sublevel, a habitable environment is used by the Company which is in charge of creating all the tools to be managed at the lower plane; at the same level there is also a habitable environment for the community of HCI experts who are in charge of checking the tools created by the Company. At the bottom sublevel, the Personnel uses a habitable environment to generate the final habitable environments to be used by the use-level CoPs.

The use level in the case of the factory automation offers habitable environments for each CoP present at this level, e.g. mechanical testers and operators, who need to perform their specialized tasks.

The Communication Channel in the Factory Automation

All the habitable environments of the model are designed and implemented using a specific software framework – the BANCO framework (Barricelli et al., 2009a, 2010). Each environment is localized for a certain CoP of a given culture, performing a specific role and using a certain platform through a mediation process since an engine within the environment translates each incoming message into the system of signs oriented to the CoP. As a whole, the environments' design and implementation has a common root and follows the same model. During the design and development activities, the representation of the current state of any environment and the interpretation of this state at any level of the HMS model are possible.

Therefore, any of the levels in the HMS model are provided with the possibility of storing and sending through the communication channel the current state of an environment enhanced with annotations on the environment or on parts of it.

The state of the environments is represented in the form of a set of documents written in XML-based languages, acting as a boundary object, storing the current state of the environment, the attributes of its elements and the relationships between them.

On the other hand, all the other levels are embedded with means of recognizing and interpreting the documents describing the current state of an environment. The communication channel at this point acts as a transport channel. Any two ends of the communication channels are aware of the protocol used for communicating the annotated current states of the habitable environments.

Figure 3 shows the communication between an assembly-line operator (ALO) at the use level and a shop foreman (SF) at the design level, via exchanging the boundary object.

SF creates an environment for ALO by simply selecting essential components provided by her/his inhabited environment for the client (H-Client), identified by number (2) in Figure 3.

The annotation tool is used by SF and ALO to update the shared knowledge base, adding comments on the habitable environment in order to highlight its meaning and/or technical issues (Costabile et al., 2006). Annotation is the activity based on which the communication and knowledge production are made possible and enhanced.

Apart from merely using and interacting with the visual interface (2) designed for her/him by SF, ALO can also express her/his difficulties or new requirements with the annotation tools in her/his inhabited H-Client environment and send the whole environment to SF. The interface (1) illustrates the results of ALO's activity on SF's environment.

Further on, SF can modify the environment for ALO according to ALO's specific change request of the environment. The state of the modified environment is saved and sent through the communication channel as a boundary object to the

CoPs of the design and the meta-design levels, in charge of handling the user's request. The CoPs of the upper levels will receive the documents describing the environment's state, which will be materialized as in Figure 3, interface (1).

Communication and collaboration among the CoPs of the described case is grounded on the use of the boundary objects – in this case, the annotated state of the virtual environment.

In this way, the boundary object is the executable program exchanged between CoPs and becomes a dynamic artifact, since at each state of a habitable environment its representation may be enhanced by annotations. The annotations can be viewed as metadata of the boundary object. The purpose of the annotations is to explain the users' needs and thoughts on the environments. Figure 3 provides an example of an annotation in ALO's environment (circled in red).

Valchiavenna Portal

The Valchiavenna Portal (VCP) is a moderated map-based wiki, aiming to support tourists in their activities related to the Valchiavenna region (Barricelli et al., 2009b). VCP provides the tourists with tools to access, share, use, collaboratively reason on and update the knowledge base about the region. These tools are based on tagging and multimedia, multimodal annotation techniques. Figure 4 shows a detailed section plan of the HMS model implementation in the VCP case.

In this case, the set of CoPs that can be identified in the design of the prototype are: the software engineers (SE), the domain experts (DE) – such as historians and geologists – the Company members (Company), the HCI experts, stakeholders who manage the content publishing (Publisher), Senior Tourists – stakeholders with certain knowledge about the Valchiavenna region – and Tourists.

Figure 4. Localized habitable environments for Italian and Japanese tourists

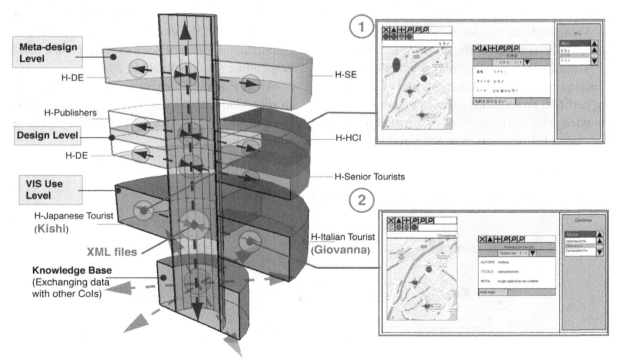

At the top meta-design level, communities of SE and DE, collaboratively design habitable software environments for other levels of the network.

The design level addresses several CoPs respectively, HCI experts, Publishers, DE, and Senior Tourists. All these CoPs collaboratively design habitable software environments to be used at the use level by Tourists.

The use level addresses the Tourists and consists of all the habitable environments facilitating them to browse the available information about the Valchiavenna region (stored in a knowledge base) or to create personal annotations, which can be shared through all levels in the network. The VCP knowledge base is the result of the social interaction among Tourists of different cultures, DE and the Publishers. They all jointly enrich the knowledge base with certified or personal annotations, which illustrate relevant topics referring to the maps or with impressions from their travels in the region represented by the map. The Publishers and the DE constitute a CoP of VCP actors using specialized languages and systems of signs to externalize their tacit knowledge.

At the meta-design level, SE design the habitable environments for the lower design level.

At the design level, the Publishers are in charge of accepting the user annotations and of publishing certified annotations on each element of the knowledge base. The creation of certified annotations is made by experts from several disciplines, which collaborate with the Publishers. Figure 4 shows the star operators, which are visual links to the certified annotations created and published by DE and the Publishers.

At the use level, Tourists can comment on certified annotations and the Publishers and the experts may decide to update them accordingly.

The Communication Channel in the Valchiavenna Portal

In the VCP case, the boundary objects are the digital map and annotation on it, which facilitate CoP communication and knowledge management.

Figure 4 shows two different habitable environments. Interface 1 is localized to Japanese culture, while Interface 2 is localized to Italian culture. Both Giovanna and Kishi can access the shared knowledge base and exchange their knowledge related to a certain region by creating annotations on the map. When Giovanna and Kishi access the map, which displays the same knowledge elements, they are able to perceive the map with two emoticons and two star operators appearing on it. However, the emoticons' shape, color and graphical representation are localized to the tourist's culture (Barricelli et al., 2010).

As an example, the emoticon associated with an appreciative annotation is represented with different colors and shapes for Italian and Japanese cultures (Figure 5).

Figure 5. Different appreciative annotations from Kishi and Giovanna

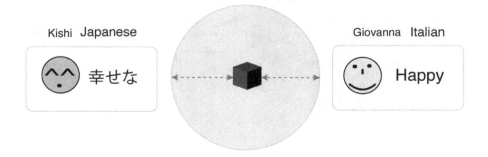

In this case, localization is not simply translation of the languages, but also considers the representation of graphical elements using different colors and shapes according to cultural conventions.

CONCLUSION AND FUTURE WORK

The HMS is a conceptual model based on meta-design and a culture of participation, which creates opportunities for creativity. The meta-design approach encourages collaboration across technological and cultural boundaries, offering the tools needed to socially negotiate communication gaps. However, assessing the meta-design framework and social creativity is challenging and needs long-term study.

For future work, we will focus on proposing a refinement of the HMS model to allow CoPs to design and exchange boundary objects according to their needs. This will support their communication through different levels during the collaborative design process. In addition, to enhance the common understanding among design teams, the next step aims to break down the concept of belonging to fixed roles, cultures and digital platform in use. Users will be able to switch to other CoPs' habitable environments to gain new perspectives. We are planning to provide other concrete implementations of the HMS for other domain-oriented design projects. The process of development will be continuously evaluated through informal meetings and experiments with all stakeholders involved in the creative collaboration in order to analyze the value of the model as well as redesign and improve its usability.

In general, this HMS model can be applied to any kind of localization-based distributed collaborative software design that needs to take language and cultural/domain differences into consideration. The HMS structure can be adapted

according to future development, the communication channel can serve as a boundary zone to support communication and message transmitting, and the multimedia annotations as boundary objects can overcome the communication gaps among the CoPs.

ACKNOWLEDGMENT

The authors would like to thank the late Piero Mussio for his insightful discussions. We acknowledge the contribution of Stefano Valtolina. The work of Li Zhu and Claudia Iacob was supported by the Initial Training Network "Marie Curie Actions," funded by the FP 7 – People Programme with reference PITN-GA-2008-215446 entitled "DESIRE: Creative Design for Innovation in Science and Technology."

REFERENCES

Andersen, R., & Mørch, A. I. (2009). Mutual development: A case study in customer-initiated software product development. In V. Pipek, M. B. Rosson, B. Ruyter, & V. Wulf (Eds.), *Proceedings of the Second International Symposium on End-User-Development* (LNCS 5435, pp. 31-49).

Anderson, C. (2006). *The long tail: Why the future of business is selling less of more.* New York, NY: Hyperion.

Barbosa, S. D. J., de Souza, C. S., & Prates, R. O. (2001). A semiotic engineering approach to HCI. In *Proceedings of Extended Abstracts on Human Factors in Computing, Seattle, WA* (pp. 55–56). New York, NY: ACM Press.

Barricelli, B. R., Iacob, C., & Zhu, L. (2009). Map-based wikis as contextual and cultural mediators. In *Proceedings of the Community Practices and Locative Media Workshop at MobileHCI.*

Barricelli, B. R., Iacob, C., & Zhu, L. (2010). BANCO web architecture to support global collaborative interaction design. In *Proceedings of the 9th International Workshop on Internationalization of Products and Systems* (pp. 159-162).

Barricelli, B. R., Marcante, A., Mussio, P., Parasiliti Provenza, L., Valtolina, S., & Fresta, G. (2009). BANCO: A web architecture supporting unwitting end-user development. *Interaction Design & Architecture(s). Design for the Future Experience*, 5-6, 23–30.

Borchers, J. (2001). *A pattern approach to interaction design*. Hoboken, NJ: John Wiley & Sons.

Bourguin, G., Derycke, A., & Tarby, J. C. (2001). Beyond the interface: Co-evolution inside interactive systems – A proposal founded on activity theory. In *Proceedings of the IHM-HCI Conference on People and Computers* (pp. 297-310).

Branham, S., Golovchinsky, G., Carter, S., & Biehl, H. T. (2010). Let's go from the whiteboard: Supporting transitions in work through whiteboard capture and reuse. In *Proceedings of the 28th International Conference on Human Factors in Computing* (pp. 75-84). New York, NY: ACM Press.

Brown, J. S., & Duguid, P. (2000). *The social life of information*. Boston, MA: Harvard Business School Press.

Bruns, A. (2008). *Blogs, Wikipedia, Second Life, and Beyond: From production to produsage*. New York, NY: Peter Lang.

Carrara, P., Fresta, G., & Rampini, A. (2000). Interfaces for geographic applications on the World Wide Web: An adaptive computational hypermedia. In *Proceedings of the 6th ERCIM Workshop on User Interfaces* (pp. 341-342).

Costabile, M. F., Fogli, D., Mussio, P., & Piccinno, A. (2006). End-user development: The software shaping workshop approach. In Lieberman, H., Paternò, F., & Wulf, V. (Eds.), *End user development* (pp. 183–205). Dordrecht, The Netherlands: Springer-Verlag. doi:10.1007/1-4020-5386-X_9

Costabile, M. F., Fogli, D., Mussio, P., & Piccinno, A. (2007). Visual interactive systems for end-user development: A model-based design methodology. *IEEE Transactions on Systems, Man, and Cybernetics. Part A, Systems and Humans, 37*(6), 1029–1046. doi:10.1109/TSMCA.2007.904776

Costabile, M. F., Mussio, P., Provenza, L. P., & Piccinno, A. (2008). Advanced visual systems supporting unwitting EUD. In *Proceedings of the Working Conference on Advanced Visual Interfaces* (pp. 313-316). New York, NY: ACM Press.

Engelbart, D. C. (1995). Toward augmenting the human intellect and boosting our collective IQ. *Communications of the ACM, 38*(8), 30–32. doi:10.1145/208344.208352

Esselink, B. (2000). *A practical guide to localization*. Philadelphia, PA: John Benjamins Publishing.

Fischer, G. (2000). Social creativity, symmetry of ignorance and meta-design. *Knowledge-Based Systems Journal, 13*(7-8), 527–537. doi:10.1016/S0950-7051(00)00065-4

Fischer, G. (2001). Communities of interest: Learning through the interaction of multiple knowledge systems. In *Proceedings of the 12th Annual Information Systems Research Seminar* (pp. 1-14).

Fischer, G., Giaccardi, E., Ye, Y., Sutcliffe, A. G., & Mehandjiev, N. (2004). Meta-design: A manifesto for end-user development. *Communications of the ACM, 47*(9), 33–37. doi:10.1145/1015864.1015884

Fischer, G., McCall, R., Ostwald, J., Reeves, B., & Shipman, F. (1994). Seeding, evolutionary growth and reseeding: Supporting the incremental development of design environments. In *Proceedings of the SIGCHI Conference on Human Factors in Computing Systems: Celebrating Interdependence* (pp. 292-298). New York, NY: ACM Press.

Fischer, G., & Ostwald, J. (2002). Seeding, evolutionary growth, and reseeding: Enriching participatory design with informed participation. In *Proceedings of the Participatory Design Conference* (pp. 135-143).

Folmer, E., van Welie, M., & Bosch, J. (2005). Bridging patterns: An approach to bridge gaps between SE and HCI. *Journal of Information and Software Technology, 48*(2), 69–89. doi:10.1016/j.infsof.2005.02.005

Gennari, J. H., & Reddy, M. (2000). Participatory design and an eligibility screening tool. In *Proceedings of the AMIA Annual Fall Symposium* (pp. 290-294).

Henderson, A., & Kyng, M. (1991). There's no place like home: Continuing design in use. In Greenbaum, J., & Kyng, M. (Eds.), *Design at work: Cooperative design of computer systems* (pp. 219–240). Mahwah, NJ: Lawrence Erlbaum.

Iacob, C., & Zhu, L. (2010). From the problem space to the web space: A model for designing localized web systems. In *Proceedings of the 9th International Conference on WWW/Internet* (pp. 112-119).

Jennings, P. (2005). Tangible social interfaces: Critical theory, boundary objects and interdisciplinary design methods. In *Proceedings of the 5th Conference on Creativity & Cognition* (pp. 176-186).

Kirsh, D. (1995). The intelligent use of space. *Artificial Intelligence, 73*(1-2), 31–68. doi:10.1016/0004-3702(94)00017-U

Konkola, R. (2001). Developmental process of internship at polytechnic and boundary-zone activity as a new model for activity. In Tuomi-Gröhn, T., Engeström, Y., & Young, M. (Eds.), *At the boundary zone between school and work – new possibilities of work-based learning* (pp. 148–186). Helsinki, Finland: University Press.

Kuutti, K. (1996). Activity theory as a potential framework for human-computer interaction research. In Nardi, B. (Ed.), *Context and consciousness: Activity theory and human-computer interaction* (pp. 17–44). Cambridge, MA: MIT Press.

Lauesen, S. (2005). *User interface design – A software engineering perspective*. Reading, MA: Addison-Wesley.

Lawson, B. (2005). *How designers think - The design process demystified*. New York, NY: Architectural Press.

Lieberman, H., Paternò, F., Klann, M., & Wulf, V. (2006). End-user development: An emerging paradigm. In Lieberman, H., Paternò, F., & Wulf, V. (Eds.), *End user development* (pp. 1–8). Dordrecht, The Netherlands: Springer-Verlag. doi:10.1007/1-4020-5386-X_1

Majhew, D. J. (1992). *Principles and guideline in software user interface design*. Upper Saddle River, NJ: Prentice Hall.

Maldonado, H., Lee, B., Klemmer, S. R., & Pea, R. D. (2007). Patterns of collaboration in design courses: Team dynamics affect technology appropriation, artifact creation, and course performance. In *Proceedings of the Computer-Supported Collaborative Learning Conference,* New Brunswick, NJ (pp. 486-495).

Mørch, A. (1997). Three levels of end-user tailoring: Customization, integration, and extension. In Kyng, M., & Mathiassen, L. (Eds.), *Computers and design in context* (pp. 51–76). Cambridge, MA: MIT Press.

Norman, D. A. (1993). *Things that make us smart.* Reading, MA: Addison-Wesley.

Petre, M., & Green, T. R. G. (1993). Learning to read graphics: Some evidence that 'seeing' an information display is an acquired skill. *International Journal of Visual Languages and Computing, 4*(1), 55–70. doi:10.1006/jvlc.1993.1004

Pipek, V. (2005). *From tailoring to appropriation support: Negotiating groupware usage.* Unpublished doctoral dissertation, University of Oulu, Oulu, Finland.

Resnick, L. B., Levine, J. M., & Teasley, S. D. (1991). *Perspectives on socially shared cognition.* Washington, DC: American Psychology Association. doi:10.1037/10096-000

Rittel, H. (1984). Second-generation design methods. In Cross, N. (Ed.), *Developments in design methodology* (pp. 317–327). Chichester, UK: John Wiley & Sons.

Schön, D. (1983). *The reflective practitioner: How professionals think in action.* London, UK: Maurice Temple Smith.

Star, S. L., & Griesemer, J. R. (1989). Translations' and boundary objects: Amateurs and professionals in Berkley's Museum of Vertebrate Zoology 1907-39. *Social Studies of Science, 19*(3), 387–420. doi:10.1177/030631289019003001

Stiemerling, O. (2000). *Component-based tailorability.* Unpublished doctoral dissertation, University of Bonn, Bonn, Germany.

Surowiecki, J. (2005). *The wisdom of crowds.* New York, NY: Anchor Books.

Tondl, L. (1981). *Problems of semantics.* Boston, MA: Reidel Publishing.

Torenvliet, G. (2003). We can't afford it! The devaluation of a usability term. *Interactions (New York, N.Y.), 10*(4), 12–17. doi:10.1145/838830.838857

Verplank, B. (2009, September). *Interaction design sketchbook.* Paper presented at the First International DESIRE Summer School Theories of Creative Design for Innovation in Science and Technology, Gargnano del Garda, Italy.

Wenger, R. E. (2002). *Cultivating communities of practice.* Boston, MA: Harvard Business School Press.

Zhu, L., Iacob, C., & Barricelli, B. R. (2010). New design strategies: Using the hive mind space model to enhance collaboration. In *Proceedings of the Multi Conference on Computer Science and Information Systems* (pp. 12-19).

This work was previously published in the International Journal of Distributed Systems and Technologies (IJDST), Volume 2, Issue 4, edited by Nik Bessis, pp. 1-16, copyright 2011 by IGI Publishing (an imprint of IGI Global).

Chapter 16
Adaptable Information Provisioning in Collaborative Networks:
An Object Modeling Framework and System Approach

Heiko Thimm
Pforzheim University, Germany

Karsten Boye Rasmussen
University of Southern Denmark, Denmark

ABSTRACT

Well-informed network participants are a necessity for successful collaboration in business networks. The widespread knowledge of the many aspects of the network is an effective vehicle to promote trust within the network, successfully resolve conflicts, and build a prospering collaboration climate. Despite their natural interest in being well informed about all the different aspects of the network, limited resources, e.g. time restrictions of the participants, often prevents reaching an appropriate level of shared information. It is possible to overcome this problem through the use of an active information provisioning service that allows users to adapt the provisioning of information to their specific needs. This paper presents an extensible information modeling framework and also additional complementary concepts that are designed to enable such an active provisioning service. Furthermore, a high-level architecture for a system that offers the targeted information provisioning service is described.

DOI: 10.4018/978-1-4666-2647-8.ch016

INTRODUCTION

In the recent years collaboration between companies in collaborative networks has been understood as a promising approach to cope with the challenges of the 21st century (Davidow & Malone, 1992; Snow et al., 1992). The ability to carefully form Virtual Enterprises (VEs) which refer to subsets of the entire network is considered as a factor of success for such networks (Camarinha-Matos & Afsarmanesh, 2005). VEs are formed to be assigned to business opportunities which they pursue by the completion of collaborative business processes. Successful collaboration in collaborative networks also depends on the informedness of the members concerning general aspects of the network, the network strategy, the forming of new VEs, and especially the current status of the network and the own company from a network point of view. The research presented in this article is grounded on the assumption that it is not only beneficial to individual members of a network if they are well informed about the network. We furthermore assume that a high level of informedness among the individual members entails benefits especially for the entire collaborative network, too. Evidence for this assumption can be found in the research literature on the relation between informedness and company profitability (Hitt & Brynjolfsson, 1996; Li, 2009). Our assumption has also been inspired by insights gained in earlier research on collaborative networks that included an empirical study of existing networks (Rasmussen & Thimm, 2009) and an investigation of support services for network moderation management (Thimm & Rasmussen, 2010).

The benefits that can result from well informed network members include trustworthy collaboration structures (Riemer & Klein, 2003), trust in the system, personal trust, and a reduced potential for conflicts within the network (Miles & Snow, 1995; Holland & Lockett, 1998). Especially conflicts that result from an overlap of competencies and/or overlap of target markets of members that lead to both a cooperation relation and competition relation between network members need to be addressed adequately (Bengtsson & Kock, 1999). Similar arguments motivating well informed networks can be found in the *Business Networking Architecture* proposed by Österle et al. (2001).

Even though the members of collaborative networks will naturally strive on staying well informed about the above mentioned aspects of networks often this interest conflicts with limited resources such as time restrictions. Typically such time restrictions do not allow network members to deal with the tedious tasks of searching for required information items in the various distributed information sources of a network and to combine them meaningfully for analytical purposes, for example. Our approach to solve this problem is to offer to network participants an IT based support service that is capable to provide for highly automated information provisioning in networks. A proposal for a first version of such a service can be found in (Thimm & Rasmussen, 2010b). We especially target an adaptable provisioning approach that delivers information not only on demand but permanently and actively. Through the targeted service the network participants are provided with information that is specifically prepared according to their individual requirements in terms of the concrete information objects, the level of detail, the visual form, and also the provisioning frequency. In order to meet these requirements as foundation for the targeted service an information modelling framework is needed that takes the specific requirements of information provisioning in networks into account. In this article we propose such an information modelling framework which is called the IPROVIN framework (Information Provisioning in Collaborative Networks) and also a corresponding system approach for active information provisioning. The IPROVIN framework consist of an extensible set of fine grain modelled information object types. These object types refer to the application specific information needs of network participants and they serve as basis for the definition of user defined report templates. In our approach it is reflected that the information needs can concern both a broad range of network specific and company specific indicators and also business processes executed in the network. Through the IPROVIN framework a corresponding provisioning service can support the concept of subscriptions for configurable report templates. Network participants will through this concept be provided with information in an automated way and under consideration of their individual subscription profiles.

This introduction is followed by a section which describes the IPROVIN object modelling framework and also complementary concepts for adaptable information provisioning in collaborative networks. A typical information report which is based on the IPROVIN framework is shown through an application example. Then we describe an approach for a system that offers the targeted active information provisioning service. Finally, major issues of our research and also related work are discussed, followed by our conclusions.

THE IPROVIN OBJECT MODELING FRAMEWORK

The information demand of network participants can be classified (Braha & Bar-Yam, 2004; Heck & Vervest, 2007). In the IPROVIN framework two information categories are considered. For each category an initial set of corresponding information object types is identified. The first information category concerns information about the global network status. The second category concerns information about business processes in the network (Saxena, 2009).

We expect that network members will typically be interested in receiving information objects that refer to the global network status according to relatively regular and similar information provisioning schemes. For example, we assume that network participants want to be provided with update information about the network's total revenue on a regular weekly or monthly basis.

Table 1 contains the skeletons of five sample object types that are part of the first information category of the IPROVIN framework. Each predefined object type is given an identifying and unique object type name such as *Inquiries Received SOT*. As discussed above the general nature of object types of the first category corresponds to network indicators that refer to network state

Table 1. Skeletons of sample object types to represent the global network status

Inquiries Received SOT	Quotations Given SOT	Orders Received SOT	VEs Formed SOT	Member Ranking SOT
Individual objects represent …				
external inquiries received	quotations given to customers	received orders	formed VEs	ranking of network members
Base content concerns number(s) and detailed statistical information about …				
inquiries received by network	quotations issued to customers	orders received	VEs formed	ranking of all network members
Complementary content concerns number(s) and detailed statistical information about …				
inquiries where own company is demanded as a supplier	quotations where own company is considered as a supplier	orders where own company is considered as a supplier	formed VEs with participation by own company	ranking of own company

information. Therefore, the postfix SOT which stands for *State Object Type* is part of each object type name of the first category. It is first explained in Table 1 what specific indicators the individual objects of the given types represent. Then, the *base content* and *complementary content* of each object type is described. These two concepts are similar to properties in object-oriented modeling (Rumbaugh et al., 1991). The base content specifies the information content provided by the object by default. From a semantic point of view the base content primarily refers to aggregated information about the entire network. For example, objects of type Inquiries Received SOT by default provide the number of external inquiries received by the network together with related statistical information. The complementary content corresponds to further complementary information from the analytical context of the object's base content. In contrast to the base content, the complementary content provides information that is specific to the own company. For example, while the base content of objects of type *Inquiries Received SOT* will provide the number of inquiries received by the entire network, the complementary content will

provide the number of received inquiries where the own company has been demanded as supplier.

The second information category of the IPROVIN framework concerns information about business processes executed in the network such as request handling, order fulfillment, and marketing campaign planning. It can be implied from the general role of a network participant that there is an intrinsic interest in information about such processes in order to feel well informed about the current status of the network. This process information can potentially concern the occurrence of new processes, process state transitions, and the conclusion of processes. However, we assume that the specific information demand of network members can vary to a large extent. We suppose that network members prefer a provisioning of information of this second category according to relatively irregular schemes and not at fixed points in time as for the first category of the IPROVIN framework.

Table 2 contains the skeletons of three sample object types that belong to the second information category. Each predefined object type is given an identifying and unique object type name such as

Table 2. Skeletons of sample object types to represent network business processes

Inquiry Handling POT	Order Fulfillment POT	Order Post Processing POT
Individual objects represent processes within the network that concern …		
Inquiry handling	Order fulfillment	Order fulfillment post administration
Processing states and corresponding base content (BC) and complementary content (CC)		
1. Inquiry Received Who issued inquiry? (BC) What product/service is demanded? (BC) Has the own company been requested as supplier? (CC) *2. Inquiry Decomposed* What are the elements of the inquiry? (BC) *3. VE Configured* Which partners are assigned to the inquiry? (BC) What are the VE configuration details of the own company? (CC) *4. Quotation Issued* …	*1. Order Received* To what offer is referred? (BC) *2. Suborders Issued* Which suborders have been issued? (BC) What are the details of the suborder issued to own company? (CC) *3. Suborders Completed* When were all suborders completed? (BC) What are the completion details of the suborder of the own company? (CC) *4. Order Completed* …	*1. Order Fulfilled* To what order is referred? (BC) *2. Post-Processing Data Prepared* What indicators are to be updated? (BC) What profit share is assigned to own company? (CC) How was the participation of the own company evaluated by the other VE members? (CC) *3. Order Post-Processing Completed* …

Inquiry Handling POT. As described above these object types correspond to business processes. Therefore, we consider as a naming convention for this category the postfix POT which stands for *Process Object Type.* The individual objects of these types can be regarded as proxy objects that represent real world business processes executed within the network. In our framework through these object types meaningful information about real world processes such as state information is made available. It is first explained in Table 2 what specific processes the individual objects represent. Then, each type is further specified in terms of the sequence of potential processing states which are of interest to network members. Note that in Table 2 the state sequences and state descriptions are not fully described. The description of each state consists of a state number and a unique state name such as *1. Inquiry Received.* Furthermore, a set of questions is given for each state. These questions describe the specific information items available in the given and also all following states. The information items that refer to the business process from the global view of the entire network are referred as the base content of the object which is specified by the acronym BC in the state descriptions of Table 2. The company specific process information items are referred as complementary content of the object (specified by CC).

In the context of our research information provisioning refers to the active dissemination of a set of information items that are selected from the above presented information objects and prepared according to user specific preferences. The instructions concerning the specific information items to be retrieved and further prepared are specified by the users in report templates. We show an example of a report template in the following. It is intended to illustrate through this example the typical content of reports and how this content is related to the information object types of the IPROVIN framework. In order to show these relations in our example it is referred to instances of the predefined information object types in the notation described in Figure 1. This notation is widely used in the literature on object-oriented modeling and programming techniques (Rumbaugh et al., 1991).

The sample partial report template shown in Table 3 is composed of process information items that refer to an inquiry handling process (rows 1 to 5) and, in case that this process leads to a customer order; a corresponding order fulfillment process (rows 6 to 8). Row 9 refers to the subsequent order post processing process in which network state indicators are updated. Finally, the report contains in rows 10 and 11 information items that concern the network state. Row 10 contains the aggregated profit of completed orders for the entire network whereas the number given in row 11 is a company specific profit value.

Report templates typically imply an active and reoccurring generation of concrete report instances. For example, the above described template implies that a first report is provided when a new

Figure 1. Notation for referencing information objects in report templates

The two general forms for referring to content of state information objects:
    an-Instance-of-<SOT object type name>.base-content
    an-Instance-of-<SOT object type name>.compl-content

The two general forms for referring to content of process information objects:
    an-Instance-of-<POT object type name>.<processing state name>.base-content
    an-Instance-of-<POT object type name>.<processing state name>.compl-content

Table 3. A sample partial report template composed of information items

	Caption	Content
1	New inquiry received:	an-Instance-of-Inquiry-Handling-POT.Inquiry-Received.base-content
2	Request elements resulting from inquiry decomposition:	an-Instance-of-Inquiry-Handling-POT.Inquiry-Decomposed.base-content
3	VE in charge of inquiry:	an-Instance-of-Inquiry-Handling-POT.VE-Configured.base-content
4	Quotation issued to customer:	an-Instance-of-Inquiry-Handling-POT.Quotation-Issued.base-content
5	Quotation result received from customer:	an-Instance-of-Inquiry-Handling-POT.Quotation-Result-Received.base-content
6	Order received:	an-Instance-of-Order-Fulfillment-POT.Order-Received.base-content
7	Suborders completed:	an-Instance-of-Order-Fulfillment-POT.Suborders-Completed.base-content
8	Order completed:	an-Instance-of-Order-Fulfillment-POT.Order-Completed.base-content
9	Order Post Processing completed:	an-Instance-of-Order-Post-Processing-POT.Order-Post-Processing-Completed.base-content
10	Order profit of all completed orders:	an-Instance-of-Orders-Completed-SOT.base-content
11	Company specific profit:	an-Instance-of-Orders-Completed-SOT.compl-content

inquiry handling process moves into the initial state referred as *Inquiry-Received*. The next report will then be provided when the same business process has progressed and thus reached the next state defined for the inquiry handling process referred as *Inquiry-Decomposed*. Further provisioning activities will follow. This includes reports that refer to state transitions as defined in the corresponding order fulfillment process. Through this assumed provisioning scheme a total number of nine specific reports will be delivered. In each of these reports the references are replaced by the corresponding information items that are available at the provisioning point of time.

APPLICATION SCENARIO TO ILLUSTRATE THE IPROVIN FRAMEWORK

In this section we illustrate how the IPROVIN framework can serve as a basis for active information provisioning in collaborative networks. The focus is on the use of the IPROVIN framework whereas the details of the provisioning service are left out. As an illustrating example we assume a fictitious company network named Seat-Tec-Net which is specialized on the joint development, production, and sales of passenger seats for planes, ships, trains, and busses. The further assumptions are as follows. Strategic and operative network related tasks are managed by a human network moderator (Sherer, 2003) that acts on behalf of the network. For example, the moderator is responsible for the dispatching and validation of inquiries from the external market and also the organization of the handling of inquiries by the network. We furthermore assume that an external request for quotation from a shipyard (referred by Volcano Ships) has been received by Seat-Tec-Net. In this request it is asked for a quotation for 400 passenger seats of the standard seat model Ocean Convenience which features an integrated infotainment system. This request will lead to an inquiry handling process in the network. In an early step of this process a proper VE is to be configured and then assigned to handle the request. We furthermore assume that the quotation issued by Seat-Tec-Net to the shipyard will lead to a corresponding order for the requested 400 passenger seats.

In the following we describe a report example that is provided to the network member Metal Gurus. Being a metal parts manufacturing company Metal Gurus is potentially in charge of the production of metal frames for seats that are manufactured according to a given customer order. We assume for the sample report that Metal Gurus is involved in both earlier mentioned processes. That is Metal Gurus is involved in the process that handles the inquiry from Volcano Ships and also the fulfillment of the resulting order within the network.

Note that through this sample report we intend to reveal the principle content of reports on the basis of the IPROVIN framework. The other issues of reports such as layout and presentation style are ignored in this article.

The sample report is generated based on a generic report template partially defined earlier. This template implies a series of nine reports with an increasing set of information about the referring inquiry management and order fulfillment process. Table 4 contains the last report that is

Table 4. A report composed of information about business processes and network indicators

Report-ID: 16112009-091624, Generation Date: 16.11.2009, Prepared for: Metal Gurus		
	Caption	**Content**
1	New inquiry received:	Inquiry ID: 210409-1654-59, Date inquiry received: 21-04-09 Inquiring company: Volcano Ships Inquiry Description: 400 seats model Ocean Convenience with final assembly at customer's site, Demanded delivery date: 30.12.2009
2	Request elements resulting from inquiry decomposition:	RE_1 *(provision of metal seat frame)*, RE_2 *(provision of seat upholsteries)*, RE_3 *(provision of circuit systems)*, RE_4 *(provision of monitors)*, RE_5 *(provision of harnesses)*, RE_6 *(final assembly of seat)*
3	VE in charge of inquiry:	$RE_1[M_3]$, $RE_2[M_6]$, $RE_3[M_9]$, $RE_4[M_9]$, $RE_5[M_{13}]$, $RE_6[M_7]$,
4	Quotation issued to customer:	Quote ID: 260409-1332-16, Date quote issued to customer: 26-04-09 Quote Description: Offer for 400 standard seats model Ocean Convenience with final assembly at customer's site. Offered Price: 880K€
5	Quotation result received from customer:	Quote ID: 260409-1332-16, Date quote result received: 02-05-2009 Quote result: positive Response of customer: Offer accepted without changes; will sign contract
6	Order received:	Order ID: 080509-0918-34, Date order received: 08-05-2009 Quote ID: 260409-1332-16
7	Suborders completed:	Order ID: 080509-0918-34 Date of completion of all suborders: 10-11-2009
8	Order completed:	Order ID: 080509-0918-34 Date of completion of order: 12-11-2009
9	Order Post Processing completed:	Order ID: 080509-0918-34 Date of completion of order post processing: 16-11-2009
10	Order profit of all completed orders:	Total profit value: 8.657K€
11	Company specific profit:	Profit value: 5.356K€

being provided to Metal Gurus. The details of this report are as follows. Information specific to the inquiry received is contained in row 1. Row 2 describes the request elements denoted by

$$RE_u(<a\,textual\,description>), u := 1, \ldots, k$$

needed from the network. It is the underlying assumption that orders are fulfilled collaboratively through the completion of a corresponding set of request elements. The identification of the needed set of request elements from the set of standardized product parts and production steps is defined in the Seat-Tec-Net network as a network moderator task. In our application example, six request elements are considered. Row 3 contains the VE in charge of the inquiry with details about the corresponding request elements and the assigned network members. Information about the quotation issued and the corresponding response received from the inquiring shipyard are contained in rows 4 and 5, respectively. Row 6 provides information about the resulting order received by the network. The primary purpose of the information contained in the rows 7 and 8 is to inform about the progress of the order fulfillment process. In row 9 it is referred to corresponding order post processing operations where network status indicators are updated. For example, in this post processing stage the obtained total profit of the completed order is divided into individual profit shares for the network participants according to a given profit sharing scheme. Information about order profit concerning all finished orders and profit information concerning finished orders where the own company participated in are given in rows 10 and 11, respectively.

SYSTEM APPROACH

We present in the following an approach for a system that offers the targeted active information provisioning service. The system is built upon the IPROVIN modeling framework described earlier. Recall that in the IPROVIN framework user specific requirements for information provisioning are defined in report templates. From these templates information provisioning operations demanded from the system are derived. The system operations are specified in the form of an information provisioning rule. A report template can result into a time-based or a condition-based provisioning rule. Time-based rules define points in time at which a report instance is to be delivered. Condition-based rules make the provisioning of reports dependent on specified conditions. A report template together with the derived provisioning rule and corresponding user data is in the following referred by the notion of *information provisioning scheme*.

Our system approach consists of a computing environment that performs active information provisioning according to a given set of information provisioning schemes. A conceptual overview of our approach is given in Figure 2. The Network Information Repository serves as central information repository in which general administrative data about the network are maintained such as the profiles and competency descriptions of the network partners. Furthermore, this repository also contains the two categories of information objects referred by status information objects and process information objects in the IPROVIN modeling framework. The set of individual objects of these types are a main part of the information pool maintained in order to enable active information provisioning.

It is obviously a requirement that the individual objects are continuously updated. Furthermore, new objects are to be created in order to accurately reflect corresponding real world events such as the creation of a new object of type *Inquiry Handling POT* to represent a corresponding new real world inquiry handling process. How these update tasks can be efficiently achieved

Figure 2. Conceptual system approach for active information provisioning

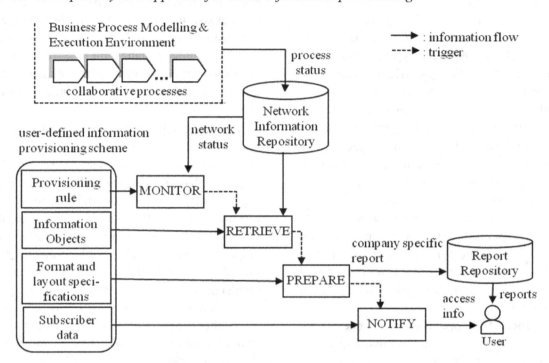

based on an integration with business process technology is currently studied by our group and will be the topic of another research article.

The system's overall processing for the targeted active information provisioning is structured into the operations MONITOR, RETRIEVE, PREPARE, and NOTIFY. The MONITOR operation continuously checks the provisioning rules of the provisioning schemes. For the determination of the rules' truth value the data items referred in the rules are first retrieved from the Network Information Repository and then evaluated. These data can be process status data of executing business processes and also network status data (i.e. values of network indicators).

To provide for the required active system capabilities we make use of the Event-Condition-Action (ECA) rule formalism which is the most used model for the specification of rules in active database systems (Paton & Diaz, 1999). The ECA model defines a rule to consist of three parts, event,

condition, and action. The semantic is that whenever the event happens, the condition is evaluated, and if satisfied then the action is taken. In our approach the provisioning rules contain both the event and condition part of the ECA formalism. The events as part of these rules belong to one of the following categories of events given in the events row (row one) in Table 5: (1) events that refer to value changes of network indicators, (2) events that refer to the registration of new business processes, (3) events that reflect state changes of business processes, (4) time controlled events. The condition part (row two) of the supported rules evaluates values of network indicators and values that refer to states of business processes. In particular, conditions are described that imply the usual comparison operations of numeric values. The conditions can be very short and only consist of a single comparison operation. But it is also possible to specify complex condition statements by combining several single comparison operations by logical binary operators. This approach for our conditions is described in Table 5 in the EBNF notation (International Organization for Standardization, 1996). The typical action specified in our information provisioning rules (row three) in general orchestrates an information report according to a user-defined report template.

When the given provisioning rule is evaluated to true the RETRIEVE operation is triggered. This operation will retrieve from the base content and complementary content of individual state objects and process objects a subset of information items. The specific subset of information items to be retrieved is specified in the report template of the provisioning scheme. When all specified information items have been retrieved from the network information repository the PREPARE operation is triggered.

The PREPARE operation will generate the report according to the format and layout specifications of the report template and store the result in the *Report Repository*. The PREPARE operation then triggers the NOTIFY operation. The NOTIFY operation in turn sends to the user a corresponding message that a new report has been prepared together with corresponding facilitating information to retrieve the report from the Report Repository.

The targeted information provisioning service implies complex data operations. These operations are to be performed on a large set of data objects for possibly many concurrent us-

ers. These requirements make the consideration of database technology the premier choice for our system approach. Note that most of today's standard database management systems through corresponding modeling primitives and system components allow for a proper implementation of ECA rules.

For an implementation of our system approach in the near future we consider a relational database system as foundation. We especially consider a single database scheme for both data repositories together, that is the Network Information Repository and the Report Repository. As a result a subset of the database objects maintained at runtime corresponds to individual SOT objects that represent the current status of the network. Information about currently executing and already completed business processes in the network is represented by another subset of database objects in the form of individual POT objects. The data are stored in flat tables for every defined SOT and POT type as separate tables. Another separate table is kept for each of the defined set of a process's states in order to administer process state information.

DISCUSSION AND RELATED WORK

We expect that through an active information provisioning service such as described in this article some of the difficulties can be resolved that

Table 5. Using the ECA rule model for Active Information Provisioning

Event	1. Update of SOT object	2. Creation of new POT object	3. Update of POT object	4. Update of a logical clock/ calendar
Condition	Given the database state at time t_i referred to by DB_{t_i} and given any pair of object items $OI_l, OI_k \in DB_{t_i}$ which are data values of SOT objects or POT objects, then a condition $cond$ is $cond = \left(cond_{single} \mid cond_{composite} \right)$ with $cond_{single} = OI_l (= \mid \neq \mid \leq \mid \geq) \left(OI_k \mid C \right) with C \in \mathbb{R}_0$ and $cond_{composite} = cond_{single} \{ \left(\wedge \mid \vee \right) cond_{single} \}_1$			
Action	Generation of individual report according to a user-defined report template and provision to user			

278

collaborative networks face today in achieving well informed network members. The re-occurring tedious manual tasks of searching, retrieving, augmenting, and preparing individualized information will be automatically completed by the service. We assume that the resulting gain in efficiency will encourage the network members to make intense use of the service and thus lead to an appropriate level of permanent informedness.

The use of such an information provisioning service in a network can also imply direct benefits for a human network moderator. Less time needs to be spent for manual information provisioning if such a service is available. As a result the moderator can use more time for other moderation management tasks (Sherer, 2003). Furthermore, through an automated information provisioning network members are less likely to accuse the moderator for unfair information sharing within the network.

Several researchers from the area of collaborative networks have stated that trust and a vital collaboration climate can be stimulated by setting a standard for the communication practice in the network (Österle et al., 2001). Our targeted provisioning service supports this kind of standardization of communication patterns.

The issue of trust and conflict prevention in the context of collaborative networks has been a subject of other researchers. The general role of business trust for the formation of collaborative networks has been investigated by Holland and Lockett (1998). While the focus of this study is on trust in the formation phase our focus is on maintaining and promoting trust during the operational phase of networks in order to promote collaborative business processes. More close similarities exist between our research focus and the classification of different approaches to promote and grow networkability of Österle (2001). The approaches proposed by these researchers include trust-creating measures, identification and control of goal conflicts, and information acquisition.

From a more technical point of view our approach to active information provisioning in networks shares some ideas that can also be found in the distributed information retrieval system developed by LogicaCMG and the University of Amsterdam (Mulder & Meijer, 2006) for the specific needs of collaborative networks. Like in our approach in this project it is attempted to relieve actors of networks from unnecessary complexity of specifying, searching, and obtaining relevant information. However, while this project has been primarily concerned with the network moderators' demand for information in order to get overviews about the network status and to make decisions our service also considers the need of network members for knowing about processing states of business processes.

CONCLUSION

The research results described in this article consist of an object modelling framework and system approach for adaptable information provisioning in collaborative networks. The proposed IPROVIN modelling framework supplies a predefined set of information object types that can be extended to specific needs of networks. While some of the predefined object types represent network indicators others represent network business processes. Every object type of our framework provides aggregated information for the entire network and company specific information prepared for a specific network member.

Our proposed service performs information provisioning operations. These operations are derived from user-defined report templates in which it is referred to individual IPROVIN objects. A database system is considered as foundation for our service. One of our next steps is targeted on a refinement and prototypical implementation of this approach. In this context we plan to investigate the use of XML based document management technologies and also information visualization techniques for the generation of the individual user reports.

We intend to evaluate our information modelling framework and the targeted provisioning service by conducting simulation studies and experiments through system prototypes. This will also involve the participation of existing collaborative networks where human moderators perform moderation management. We expect from these future research efforts a better understanding of the potential information content that the users want to receive through the generated reports. As a starting point for this investigation we intent to use the information exchange typology for virtual communities proposed by Burnett (2000). This typology includes information-oriented behaviours such as announcements, queries or specific requests for information, and directed group projects which can not only be observed in virtual communities but also in collaborative networks.

REFERENCES

Bengtsson, M., & Kock, S. (1999). Cooperation and competition in relationships between competitors in business networks. *Journal of Business and Industrial Marketing*, *14*(3), 178–193. doi:10.1108/08858629910272184

Braha, D., & Bar-Yam, Y. (2004). Information flow structure in large-scale product development organizational networks. *Journal of Information Technology*, *19*(4), 244–253. doi:10.1057/palgrave.jit.2000030

Burnett, G. (2000). Information exchange in virtual communities. *Information Research*, *5*(4), 82.

Camarinha-Matos, L. M., & Afsarmanesh, H. (2005). Collaborative networks: A new scientific discipline. *Journal of Intelligent Manufacturing*, *16*, 439–452. doi:10.1007/s10845-005-1656-3

Davidow, W. H., & Malone, M. S. (1992). *The virtual corporation: Structuring and revitalizing the corporation for the 21st century*. New York, NY: Harper Business.

Gomes-Casseres, B. (1994). Group versus group: How alliance networks compete. *Harvard Business Review*, 62–74.

Heck, E., & Vervest, P. (2007). Smart business networks: how the network wins. *Communications of the ACM*, *50*(6), 28–37. doi:10.1145/1247001.1247002

Hitt, L. M., & Brynjolfsson, E. (1996). Productivity, business profitability, and consumer surplus: Three different measures of information technology value. *Management Information Systems Quarterly*, *20*(2), 121–142. doi:10.2307/249475

Holland, C. P., & Lockett, A. G. (1998). Business trust and the formation of virtual organizations. In *Proceedings of the 31st Hawaii International Conference on System Sciences* (pp. 602-609).

International Organization for Standardization. (1996). *ISO/IEC 14977: ISO Standard for the EBNF*. Retrieved from http://www.iso.org/iso/iso_catalogue/catalogue_tc/catalogue_detail.htm?csnumber=26153

Jarillo, J. C. (1993). *Strategic networks: Creating the borderless organization*. Oxford, UK: Butterworth-Heinemann.

Kumar, K., & Diesel, H. G. (1996). Sustainable collaboration: Managing conflict and cooperation in interorganizational systems. *Management Information Systems Quarterly*, *20*(3), 279–300. doi:10.2307/249657

Li, T. (2009). Informedness and customer-centric revenue management (Doctoral dissertation, Erasmus University). *ERIM PhD Series in Research in Management*, 146.

Miles, R., & Snow, C. (1995). The network firm: A spherical structure built on human investment philosophy. *Organizational Dynamics, 23*(95), 5–18. doi:10.1016/0090-2616(95)90013-6

Mulder, W., & Meijer, G. T. (2006). Distributed information services supporting collaborative network management. In. *Proceedings of the IFIP Conference on Network-Centric Collaboration and Supporting Frameworks, 224*, 491–498. doi:10.1007/978-0-387-38269-2_51

Österle, H., Fleisch, E., & Alt, R. (2001). *Business networking - Shaping collaboration between enterprises*. Berlin, Germany: Springer-Verlag.

Paton, N., & Diaz, O. (1999). Active database systems. *ACM Computing Surveys, 31*(1). doi:10.1145/311531.311623

Rasmussen, K. B., & Thimm, H. (2009). Fact-based understanding of business survey non-response. *Electronic Journal of Business Research Methods, 7*(1), 83–92.

Riemer, K., & Klein, S. (2003). Challenges of ICT-enabled virtual organizations: A social capital perspective. In *Proceedings of the 14th Australasian Conference of Information Systems*, Perth, Australia (p. 8).

Rumbaugh, J., Blaha, M. R., Lorensen, W., Eddy, F., & Premerlani, W. (1991). *Object-oriented modeling and design*. Upper Saddle River, NJ: Prentice Hall.

Saxena, K. B. (2009). Business process management in a smart business network environment. In Vervest, P. H. M., van Liere, D. W., & Zheng, L. (Eds.), *The network experience*. Berlin, Germany: Springer-Verlag. doi:10.1007/978-3-540-85582-8_6

Sherer, S. A. (2003). Critical success factors for manufacturing networks as perceived by network coordinators. *Journal of Small Business Management, 41*(4), 325–345. doi:10.1111/1540-627X.00086

Snow, C. C., Miles, R. E., & Coleman, H. J. (1992). Managing 21st century network organization. *Organizational Dynamics, 20*(3), 5–20. doi:10.1016/0090-2616(92)90021-E

Thimm, H., & Rasmussen, K. B. (2010a). A decision and transparency support service for moderation management of virtual enterprises in collaborative networks. In *Proceedings of the 43rd Hawaii International Conference on System Sciences* (p. 44).

Thimm, H., & Rasmussen, K. B. (2010b) Information modeling for flexible information provisioning in collaborative networks. In *Proceedings of the IADIS International Conference on Collaborative Technologies*, Freiburg, Germany (p. 3-11).

This work was previously published in the International Journal of Distributed Systems and Technologies (IJDST), Volume 2, Issue 4, edited by Nik Bessis, pp. 44-56, copyright 2011 by IGI Publishing (an imprint of IGI Global).

Chapter 17
Design and Implementation of Hybrid Time (HT) Group Communication Protocol for Homogeneous Broadcast Groups

Isamu Tsuneizumi
Seikei University, Japan

Makoto Ikeda
Seikei University, Japan

Ailixier Aikebaier
Seikei University, Japan

Tomoya Enokido
Risho University, Japan

Makoto Takizawa
Seikei University, Japan

ABSTRACT

To realize the cooperation of a group of multiple peer processes (peers), messages sent by peers must be causally delivered to every peer. In a scalable group, it is necessary to reduce the communication overhead to causally deliver messages. In this paper, the authors take advantage of the linear time (LT) and physical time (PT) protocols, as the message length is O(n) for the number n of peers. However, some pairs are unnecessarily ordered, that is, even if a pair of messages is ordered in the protocols, the messages may not be causally ordered. The greater the number of messages that are unnecessarily ordered, the larger the overhead is implied since the messages must be kept in a receipt queue if a message is lost or delayed. This paper discusses a hybrid time group communication (HT) protocol that reduces the number of messages unnecessarily ordered. The HT protocol is evaluated in terms of the number of unnecessarily ordered messages compared with the PT and LT protocols. It is demonstrated that the number of unnecessarily ordered messages can be reduced in the HT protocol compared with the LT and PT protocols.

DOI: 10.4018/978-1-4666-2647-8.ch017

INTRODUCTION

In peer-to-peer (P2P) information systems (Schollmeier, 2001), a group of multiple peer processes (peers) are cooperating to achieve some objectives by exchanging messages with each other. A P2P system is in nature fully distributed with no centralized coordinator and is scalable. Here, messages are required to be causally delivered to peers (Nakamura & Takizawa, 1994). Each peer has to causally order messages received by using some types of clock. The vector time (VT) (Mattern, 1989) is widely used to causally deliver messages in group communication protocols (Birman & Van Renesse, 1994; Moser et al., 1991; Nakamura & Takizawa, 1994). Only and all the messages to be causally ordered can be ordered. However, it is difficult, maybe impossible to adopt the VT protocol due to the message overhead $O(n)$ for the number n of peers in a scalable P2P group. In addition, it is not easy to change the membership information in every peer in presence of the membership change so that a new peer joins or a member peer leaves a group.

Messages can be causally delivered to peers in the linear time (LT) protocol (Lamport, 1978) and the physical time (PT) protocol. Since the message length is $O(1)$ in the LT and PT protocols, the LT and PT protocols can be adopted for a scalable group. However, some messages are unnecessarily ordered. Suppose a peer receives a message m. The peer can deliver the message m only if the peer delivers every message which precedes the message m in the ordering rule of the protocol. If the peer does not receive some message m' preceding the message m, the peer has to wait for the message m' even if m' does not causally precede m.

Thus, the more number of messages are unnecessarily ordered, the longer it takes to deliver the messages. In order to realize an efficient scalable group protocol, we have to reduce the number of unnecessarily ordered messages.

A group is composed of multiple peers $p_1,...,p_n$ ($n>1$). Each peer p_i takes usage of its own physical clock c_i. Here, maximum gap of each physical time of c_i with accurate time is bounded to be some value λ_i. The accuracy λ_i of each physical clock of a peer p_i depends on the distance, i.e. number of routers and traffic between the peer p_i and the time server and on a type of operating system like Linux and Windows. Let d_{ij} be the minimum delay time between a pair of peers p_i and p_j. In this paper, we consider a homogeneous broadcast group where $\lambda_i=\lambda$ and $d_{ij}=d$ for every pair of peers p_i and p_j and each message is sent to every peer. Here, messages which are surely causally ordered in terms of the clock accuracy and minimum delay time are ordered in the physical time. Messages which cannot be ordered in the physical time are ordered in the LT protocol. In this paper, we discuss a hybrid time (HT) protocol which takes advantage of the PT and LT protocols. In the evaluation, we show the number of unnecessarily ordered messages can be reduced in the HT protocol compared with the LT and PT protocols for $d \geq 2\lambda$.

First, we present a system model. Next we discuss the linear (LT) and physical time (PT) protocols. We discuss how to order messages in a heterogeneous broadcast group with the hybrid time (HT) protocol. Finally, we evaluate the HT protocol in terms of the number of unnecessarily ordered messages compared with the PT and LT protocols.

GROUPS OF PEERS

A group G is composed of multiple peer processes (peers) $p_1, ..., p_n$ ($n>1$) and Global Positioning System (GPS) time servers (Hofmann-Wellenhof et al., 2001) which are interconnected in an underlying P2P overlay network. Each peer p_i is equipped with a physical clock c_i. A physical clock c_i of each peer p_i is synchronized with the GPS clock of the time server in the network time protocol (NTP) (Mills, 1985). We assume the maximum delay time between every pair of peers p_i and p_j is bounded to be some value D_{ij}. d_{ij} is the minimum delay time between a pair of peers p_i and p_j. It takes λ_{ij} time units to deliver a message from a peer p_i to another peer p_j where $d_{ij} \leq \lambda_{ij} \leq D_{ij}$.

While synchronized with the GPS clock in NTP, each physical clock does not show the same accurate UTC (Universal time coordinated) (Schmid, 1995) time. Let PT_i show physical time shown by the physical clock c_i of a peer p_i. $C(PT_i)$ indicates the accurate time when the physical clock c_i shows time PT_i. The gap $|C(PT_i) - PT_i|$ between the physical time PT_i and the accurate time $C(PT_i)$ gives the *accuracy* of the physical clock c_i of a peer p_i. The accuracy of the physical clock c_i is assumed to be bounded to be some constant value λ_i for every physical time PT_i as follows:

$$|C(PT_i) - PT_i| \leq \lambda_i \qquad (1)$$

In a Gigabit Ethernet (Pope & Riddoch, 2007) with a GPS time server in NTP as shown in Figure 1. Here, the clock accuracy λ_i is 1 to 10 [msec] according to our experiment (Nishimura et al., 2005). λ_i is about 100 to 500 [msec] in a system where computers are interconnected in a wide area network (WAN). The longer and more congested the network is, the less accurate the physical clock is. Since each peer p_i is synchronized with a time server in a high-speed local network, the clock accuracy λ_i is considered to be the order of millisecond in this paper. We consider a *homogeneous* group where $\lambda_i = \lambda$ for every peer p_i and $d_{ij} = d$ for every pair of peers p_i and p_j.

In this paper, we consider a fully distributed group G of multiple peers $p_1, ..., p_n$. Here, there is no centralized coordinator. Each peer directly communicates with other peers. A group is so scalable that a huge number of peers can be included. In this paper, we assume there is some

Figure 1. Group with time server

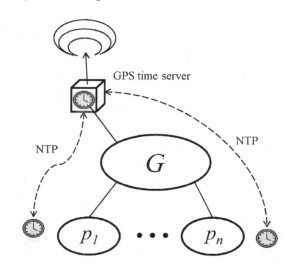

efficient mechanism to broadcast a message to every member peer in a group by using the P2P overlay network (Keshav, 2006). In addition, each peer is autonomous and makes a decision on the delivery order of messages and the membership by itself on the basis of information obtained by exchanging messages with the other peers.

In this paper, we consider a broadcast group where each message is sent to every peer and peer can receive every message sent. In a group G of multiple peers $p_1, ..., p_n$ $(n>1)$, messages sent by peers have to be causally delivered to destination peers (Birman & Renesse, 1994; Lamport, 1978). Let $s_i[m]$ and $r_i[m]$ denote sending and receipt events that a peer p_i sends and receives a message m, respectively. Lamport (1978) defines the famous *happen-before* relation $e_1 \rightarrow e_2$ between a pair of events e_1 and e_2 (e_1 *happens before* e_2) in a distributed system. For a pair of messages m_1 and m_2, the causally precedent relation $\rightarrow$ of messages are defined in terms of the happen-before relation $\rightarrow$ of events as follows:

- A message m_1 *causally precedes* another message m_2 ($m_1 \rightarrow m_2$) if and only if (iff) $s_i[m_1] \rightarrow s_j[m_2]$ (Lamport, 1978) (Figure 2).

Figure 2. Causal precedence ($m_1 \rightarrow m_2$)

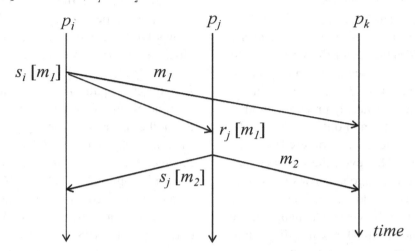

For example, a group G is composed of three peers p_1, p_2, and p_3 in a teleconference application. Suppose the peer p_1 sends a question message Q_1 to every peer and the peer p_2 sends an answer message A_1 of the question message Q_1. Here, since the answer message A_1 is meaningless without the question message Q_1, Q_1 causally precedes $A_1 (Q_1 \rightarrow A_1)$. Every peer p_k is required to deliver the question message Q_1 and then the answer message A_1.

TYPES OF CLOCKS

Logical Clocks

In order to causally deliver messages, synchronization mechanisms based on types of logical time; linear time (LT) (Lamport, 1978) and vector time (VT) (Birman & Van Renesse, 1994; Mattern, 1987, 1989) are used in traditional group communication protocols (Nakamura & Takizawa, 1994; Moser & Agrawala, 1991). In the LT protocol (Lamport, 1978), each peer p_i has a variable LT_i showing the linear time. Initially, $LT_i = 0$. A message m which a peer p_i sends carries the linear time $m.LT$ shown by the variable LT_i. Then, LT_i is incremented by one. On receipt of a message

m, the peer p_i changes the variable LT_i with the maximum value of LT_i and $m.LT$, i.e. $LT_i = max(LT_i, m.LT)$. A pair of the messages m_1 and m_2 received by a peer p_i are ordered as follows.

- **Rule for Ordering Messages in the LT Protocol:** A message m_1 precedes another message $m_2 (m_1 < m_2)$ in the LT protocol if $m_1.LT < m_2.LT$.

Here, it is noted $m_1.LT < m_2.LT$ if a message m_1 causally precedes another message $m_2 (m_1 \rightarrow m_2)$. However, $m_1 \rightarrow m_2$ may not hold even if $m_1.LT < m_2.LT$. A pair of messages m_1 and m_2 are *unnecessarily ordered* in the LT protocol iff $m_1 < m_2$ but $m_1 \rightarrow m_2$ does not hold. The more number of messages are unnecessarily ordered, the longer it takes to deliver messages. It is critical to reduce the number of messages to be unnecessarily ordered in order to improve the performance of the group communication protocol.

In the LT protocol, some messages are thus unnecessarily ordered while the message size is $O(1)$, independent of the number n of peers in the group G. In the vector time (VT) protocol (Mattern, 1987, 1989; Birman & Van Renesse, 1994), each peer p_i has a vector $\langle VT_1, \cdots, VT_n \rangle$ for a group of peers $p_1, \cdots, p_n (n > 1)$. Suppose a peer p_i would like to send a message m. First, the vector $VT = \langle VT_1, \cdots, VT_n \rangle$ is carried by the message m, $m.VT = \langle VT_1, \cdots, VT_n \rangle$. Then, the peer p_i sends the message m and the ith element VT_i of the vector VT is incremented by one ($i=1, \cdots, n$). On receipt of a message m, $VT_j = max(VT_j, m.VT_j)$ for $j= 1, \cdots, n$ ($j \neq i$) in the peer p_i. A message m_1 causally precedes another message $m_2 (m_1 \rightarrow m_2)$ if and only if (*iff*) $m_1.VT < m_2.VT$. There is no unnecessarily ordered message in the VT protocol. However, the message size is $O(n)$ since each message m carries the vector $m.VT$ of n elements. In addition, it is not easy for every peer to change the vector in change of the membership of the group. Hence it is difficult to adopt the VT protocol in scalable groups.

Physical Clocks

Each peer p_i has a variable PT_i showing the current physical time of the physical clock c_i. A peer p_i attaches a message m with the physical time $m.PT$, $m.PT = PT_i$. $m.PT$ shows the physical time when the peer p_i sends. Then, the peer p_i sends the message m in the group G. Here, the message length is the same $O(1)$ as the LT protocol. Let $C_i(PT_i)$ show the accurate time when the physical clock c_i of a peer p_i shows physical time PT_i. As assumed in the preceding section, $|PT_i - C_i(PT_i)| \leq$

λ_i for every physical time PT_i in every peer p_i. For every pair of peers p_i and p_j, $|C_i(PT) - C_j(PT)|$ shows the time gap between a pair of physical clocks c_i and c_j of peers p_i and p_j, respectively, when $PT_i = PT$ and $PT_j = PT$. $|C_i(PT) - C_j(PT)| \leq \lambda_i + \lambda_j$ for every pair of peers p_i and p_j.

It takes time for a peer to transmit a message to another peer. Suppose a peer p_i sends a message m at physical time PT_i and another peer p_j receives the message m at physical time PT_j as shown in Figure 3. $|C_i(PT_i) - C_j(PT_j)|$ shows the delay time λ_{ij} between a pair of peers p_i and p_j. In this paper, we assume the network is synchronous (Fischer et al., 1985), i.e. the maximum delay time between a pair of peers p_i and p_j is bounded to be a constant D_{ij}. For the minimum delay time d_{ij} and maximum delay time D_{ij}, $d_{ij} \leq \lambda_{ij} \leq D_{ij}$. Here, the following property holds for a pair of physical time PT_i and PT_j when a peer p_i sends a message m and another peer p_j receives the message m for a pair of clock accuracy λ_i and λ_j and minimal delay time d_{ij}:

$$-(\lambda_i + \lambda_j) + d_{ij} \leq PT_j - PT_i \leq (\lambda_i + \lambda_j) + d_{ij}: \quad (2)$$

Suppose another peer p_k receives a pair of messages m_i and m_j sent by peers p_i and p_j, respectively. The peer p_k has to decide which message

Figure 3. Delay time and clock accuracy

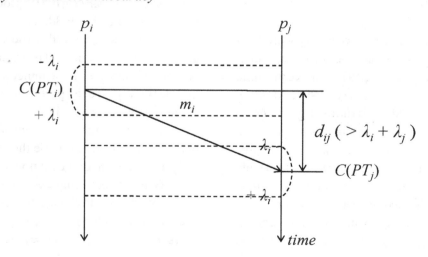

m_i or m_j precedes the other message by using a pair of physical time $m_i.PT$ and $m_j.PT$. In the physical time (PT) protocol, a pair of messages m_i and m_j are ordered as $m_i \Rightarrow m_j$ (m_j physically precedes m_i) as follows:

- **PT Protocol:** A message m_i physically precedes another message m_j ($m_i \Rightarrow m_j$) in the PT protocol if $m_j.PT - m_i.PT > \lambda_i + \lambda_j$.

The relation "$m_i \Rightarrow m_j$" means that a messages m_i is surly sent before m_j. A pair of messages m_i and m_j are physically concurrent ($m_i \parallel m_j$) if neither $m_i \Rightarrow m_j$ nor $m_j \Rightarrow m_i$.

For every pair of messages m_i and m_j, if m_i precedes m_j in the LT protocol ($m_i < m_j$), m_i physically precedes m_j in the PT protocol ($m_i \Rightarrow m_j$). If m_i causally precedes m_j ($m_i \rightarrow m_j$), $m_i \Rightarrow m_j$. However, $m_i \rightarrow m_j$ might not hold even if $m_i \Rightarrow m_j$ as discussed in the LT protocol. Thus, more number of messages are unnecessarily ordered in the PT protocol than the LT protocol.

HYBRID TIME (HT) PROTOCOL IN HOMOGENEOUS BROADCAST GROUPS

Ordering Rules

In this paper, we consider a homogeneous broadcast group $G = \{p_1, ..., p_n\}$ ($n \geq 1$) where $d_{ij} = d$, $D_{ij} = D$, and $\lambda_i = \lambda$ for every pair of peers p_i and p_j and every messages is sent to all the peers. Each message m carries two types of time, physical time $m.PT$ and linear time $m.LT$ of the source peer, when the source peer sends the message m, respectively.

A pair of messages m_i and m_j are ordered according to the following ordering rule in the hybrid time (HT) protocol.

- **Rules for Ordering Messages in the HT Protocol (HT Rules):** A message m_i precedes another message m_j ($m_i < m_j$) if one of the following conditions holds:
  1. $m_j.PT - m_i.PT \geq 2\lambda + d$.
  2. $|m_j.PT - m_i.PT| < 2\lambda + d$ and
     a. if $d > 2\lambda$: $m_j.PT - m_i.PT > d - 2\lambda$ and $m_i.LT < m_j.LT$.
     b. else /* $d \leq 2\lambda$: */ $m_i.LT < m_j.LT$.

In the rule 1, $m_i, ..., m_j$ means that a message m_i causally precedes a message m_j ($m_i \rightarrow m_j$). That is, m_i, m_j and $m_i \rightarrow m_j$ if $m_j.PT - m_i.PT \geq 2\lambda + d$. Here, there is no message unnecessarily ordered in the HT protocol. In the rule 2, if $d > 2\lambda$ and $|m_j.PT - m_i.PT| < d - 2\lambda$, a pair of messages m_i and m_j are not ordered. If $m_j.PT - m_i.PT > d - 2\lambda$, it is sure the message m_j is sent before the message m_i, $m_j \Rightarrow m_i$. Hence, we check if $m_i.LT < m_j.LT$. If $m_i.LT < m_j.LT$, m_i, m_j. Here, it is noted $m_i \rightarrow m_j$ might not hold even if m_i, m_j.

EVALUATION

Evaluation Model

We evaluate the hybrid time (HT) protocol in terms of number of messages unnecessarily ordered compared with the linear time (LT) and physical time (PT) protocols in the time based simulation. A homogeneous broadcast group G is composed of multiple peers $p_1, ..., p_n$ ($n > 1$). Here, the clock accuracy λ_i of each peer p_i is the same λ and the minimum delay time d_{ij} and maximum delay time D_{ij} are the same d and D, respectively. In addition, every message is sent to every peer in the group G

Each peer p_i sends a message with probability f at any accurate time t if the peer p_i had lastly sent a message at accurate time t' and $t > t' + \tau$. That is, τ is the minimum inter-transmission interval in each peer p_i. The average inter-transmission interval is $\tau + (1 - f)/f$ [time unit] in each peer p_i. In this evaluation, $f = 0.25$ and $\tau = 5$ [time unit]. The average inter-transmission interval is $5 + 3 = 8$ [time unit]. After a message m is sent by a peer p_i at accurate time t, the message m arrives at every peer p_j at time t_j. The arrival time t_j of the message m is randomly selected from $t+d$ to $t+D$. The physical time PT_i of a peer p_i at the accurate time t is randomly selected from $t - \tau$ to $t + \tau$.

Initially, a variable lt_i is $-\tau$ for each peer p_i. At each accurate time unit t, a sending event $s_i[m]$ is created for each peer p_i if $t \geq lt_i + \tau$ and mod($rand()$, $[1/f]) = 0$. $rand()$ is a function generating random number. Then, $lt_i = t$. If the sending event $s_i[m]$ is created at accurate time t, a receipt event $r_j[m]$ is created for every peer $p_j (j = 1, \ldots, n)$ at accurate time t_j. t_j is randomly selected from $t+d$ to $t+D$ for each peer p_j. In the evaluation, one configuration is thus created by one thousand times performing this step. One configuration is given as a collection of time based sequences of sending and receipt events randomly created for $t = 1, \ldots, 1000$. The events are stored in tables of a Mysql relational database.

For each message m created in one configuration, we first obtain the number $CN(m)$ of messages which causally precede the message m, $CN(m) = |\{m' | m' \to m\}|$. $LN(m)$, $PN(m)$, and $HN(m)$ show the numbers of messages which precede the message m in the LT, PT, and HT protocols, respectively, i.e. $LN(m) = |\{m' | m' < m\}|$, $PN(m) = |\{m' | m' \Rightarrow m\}|$, and $HN(m) = |\{m' | m' \; m\}|$. The numbers are obtained by using SQL on the tables for each configuration. Here, the numbers $LN(m) - CN(m)$, $PN(m) - CN(m)$, and $HN(m) - CN(m)$ give the numbers of messages unnecessarily ordered for a message m in the PT, LT, and HT protocols, respectively.

Evaluation Results

First, we consider a group of five peers, $n = 5$. For ratio λ/d, we obtain the average numbers PN, LN, and HN of unnecessarily ordered messages for each message in the PT, LT and HT protocols, respectively. The average numbers are obtained by taking the averages of 1000 configurations. Figure 4 shows the average numbers PN, LN, and HN of unnecessarily ordered messages in the PT, LT, and HT protocols, respectively. The horizontal axis shows the ratio λ/d where the minimum delay time d is 40 [time unit]. $\lambda/d = 0.025$ means that the clock accuracy λ is 1 [time unit]. For example, 4.01 messages are on the average unnecessarily ordered for each message in the HT protocol while 9.65 and 6.88 messages in the PT and LT protocols. As shown in Figure 4, the fewer number of messages are unnecessarily ordered in the HT protocol for $\lambda/d < 0.5$ than the LT and PT protocols. Especially, about 30% of the unnecessarily ordered messages are reduced for $\lambda/d < 0.1$ in the HT protocol compared with the LT protocol. The longer the minimum delay time d is, the fewer number of messages are unnecessarily ordered. For $\lambda/d \geq 0.5$, $LT = HN$ since every pair of messages ordered in the HT protocol are also ordered in the LT protocol.

Next, we measure the average numbers LN, PN, and HN of messages unnecessarily ordered for the number $n (= 10, \ldots, 100)$ of peers in a group. Figure 5 shows the average numbers LN, PN, and HN for n where $\lambda/d = 0.025$. The number of messages unnecessarily ordered is $O(n)$ as shown in Figure 5. For $n = 10$, the average numbers PN, LN, and HN are 17.2, 11.4, and 4.64, respectively. For $n = 100$, PN and LN are 169.5 and 116.5, respectively. On the other hand, HN is only 45.15. The increase rate of the messages unnecessarily ordered in the HT protocol for the number n of peers is 60% and 73% smaller than the LT protocol and PT protocol, respectively.

Figure 4. Average number of unnecessarily ordered messages for ratio λ/δ (n=5)

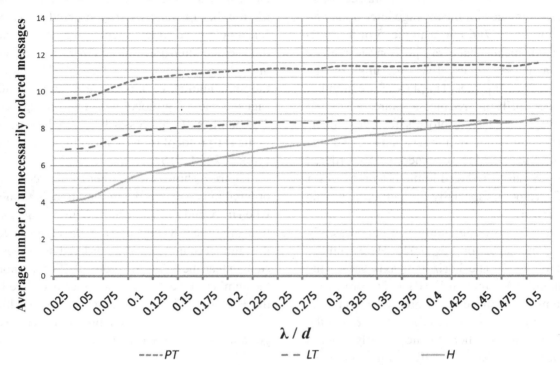

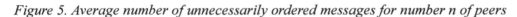

Figure 5. Average number of unnecessarily ordered messages for number n of peers

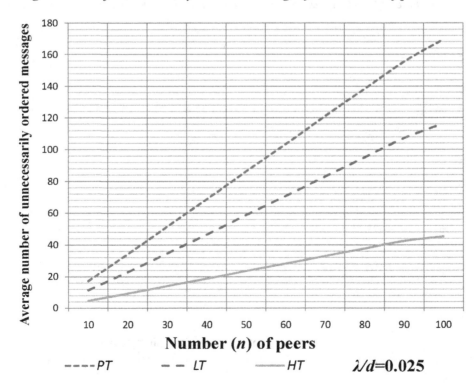

Figure 6 shows the number of unnecessarily ordered messages for the average inter-transmission time $\lambda + (1-f)/f$. For example, 5 of the horizontal axis means that every peer on the average sends a message every five time units on the average. The *HT* protocol implies a fewer number of unnecessarily ordered messages are transmitted than the PT and LT protocols for every inter-transmission time. In the evaluation, we can conclude the number of unnecessarily ordered messages can be reduced in the HT protocol for the LT protocol, especially for a group in a wide area network.

Figure 7 shows the number of unnecessarily ordered messages for $\lambda/\delta \leq 0.025$. Here, number of peers are 5. The horizontal axis shows the minimum delay time d. In the PT and LT protocols, the number of unnecessarily ordered messages is increased for the minimum delay time d. On the other hand, the number of unnecessarily ordered messages is almost independent of the minimum delay time d in the HT protocol. Figure 8 shows the number of unnecessarily ordered messages for the clock accuracy λ when $n=5$, $d=300$, and the average inter-transmission interval is 8 [time unit]. $\lambda=150$ means $\lambda/d=0.5$. Here, the HT implies the same number of unnecessarily ordered messages as the LT protocol as shown in Figure 4. The number of unnecessarily ordered messages in the HT protocol is one sixth of the LT protocol for $\lambda=5$, $\lambda/d=0.0167$.

Figure 8 shows the number of unnecessarily ordered messages for the minimum delay time d when $n=5$, and $\lambda=1$ [time unit]. The average inter transmit time is 8 [time unit]. In the HT protocol, the number of unnecessarily ordered messages is smaller than the PT and LT protocols. Furthermore, the number of messages unnecessarily ordered in the HT protocol almost invariable for d which increased in the LT and PT protocols. This is a good property of the HT protocol.

Figure 6. Average number of unnecessarily ordered messages for average inter transmission time

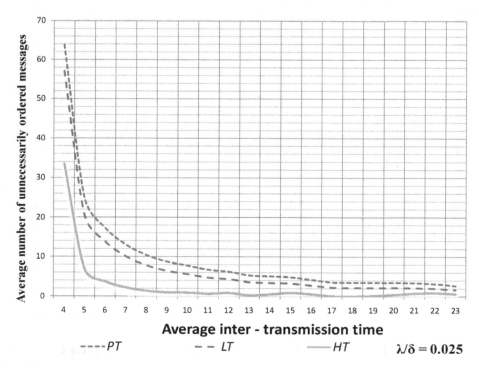

Figure 7. Average number of unnecessarily ordered messages for $\lambda/\delta \leq 0.025$, (n=5)

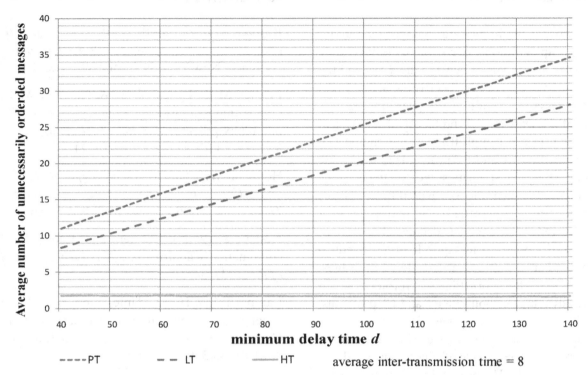

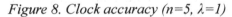

Figure 8. Clock accuracy (n=5, $\lambda=1$)

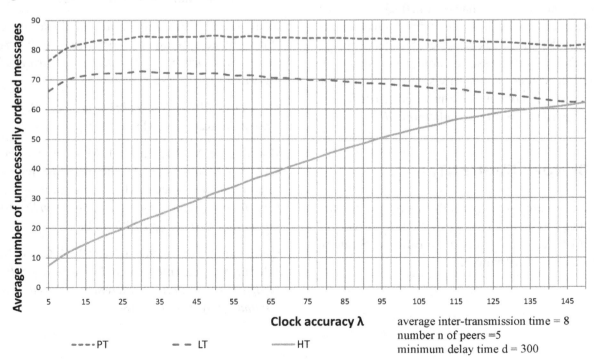

CONCLUSION

In this paper, we discussed a homogeneous broadcast group of multiple peers where the delay time between every pair of peers is the same and the clock accuracy of every peer is the same. Here, each message is sent to every peer in the group. Since the linear time (LT) protocol and the physical time (PT) protocol imply the message length $O(1)$, we can adopt LT and PT protocols to a scalable group. However, some messages are unnecessarily ordered in the protocols even if the messages are not causally preceded. The performance of the LT and PT protocols is decreased due to unnecessarily ordered messages. In order to reduce the number of unnecessarily ordered messages, we discussed the hybrid time (HT) protocol which take advantage of both the PT and LT protocols. In the evaluation, we showed the number of unnecessarily ordered messages can be reduced in the HT protocol. The number of unnecessarily ordered messages in the HT protocol is smaller than the LT protocol for $d > 2\lambda$. Especially, the number of unnecessarily ordered messages in the LT protocol can be reduced more than 60% in the HT protocol for $\lambda/\delta \leq 0.025$, i.e. if the delay time is forty times longer than the clock accuracy. Furthermore, the number of unnecessarily ordered messages in the HT protocol is not only smaller than the PT and LT protocol but also almost invariant for the change of the minimum delay time d.

ACKNOWLEDGMENT

This research was partially supported by the strategy research project of Seikei University and MEXT, Grant-in-Aid for Building Strategy Research Infrastructure.

REFERENCES

Birman, K. P., & Van Renesse, R. (1994). *Reliable distributed computing with the Isis toolkit (systems)*. New York, NY: John Wiley & Sons.

Fischer, M. J., Lynch, N. A., & Paterson, M. S. (1985). Impossibility of distributed consensus with one faulty process. *Journal of the ACM, 32*(2), 374–382. doi:10.1145/3149.214121

Hofmann-Wellenhof, B., Lichtenegger, H., & Collins, J. (2001). *Global positioning system (GPS): Theory and practice*. New York, NY: Springer.

Keshav, S. (2006). Efficient and decentralized computation of approximate global state. *Journal of the ACM, 36*, 69–74.

Lamport, L. (1978). Time, clocks, and the ordering of events in a distributed system. *Communications of the ACM, 21*, 558–565. doi:10.1145/359545.359563

Mattern, F. (1987). Algorithms for distributed termination detection. *Distributed Computing, 2*(3), 161–175. doi:10.1007/BF01782776

Mattern, F. (1989). Virtual time and global states of distributed systems. In *Proceedings of the International Workshop on Parallel and Distributed Algorithms* (pp. 215-226).

Mills, D. L. (1985). *Network time protocol (NTP)*. Marina del Rey, CA: RFC Editor.

Moser, L. E., Melliar-Smith, P. M., & Agrawala, V. (1991). Membership algorithms for asynchronous distributed systems. In *Proceedings of the 10th International Conference on Distributed Computing Systems* (pp. 480-488).

Nakamura, A., & Takizawa, M. (1994). Causally ordering broadcast protocol. In *Proceedings of the 14th IEEE International Conference on Distributed Computing Systems* (pp. 48-55).

Nishimura, T., Hayashibara, N., Takizawa, M., & Enokido, T. (2005). Causally ordered delivery with global clock in hierarchical group. In *Proceedings of the 11ᵗʰ IEEE International Conference on Parallel and Distributed Systems* (pp. 560-564).

Pope, S., & Riddoch, D. (2007). 10Gb/s ethernet performance and retrospective. *ACM SIGCOMM Computer Communication Review*, *37*(2), 89–92. doi:10.1145/1232919.1232930

Schmid, U. (1995). Synchronized universal time coordinated for distributed real-time systems. *Control Engineering Practice*, *3*(6), 101–107. doi:10.1016/0967-0661(95)00073-4

Schollmeier, R. (2001). A definition of peer-to-peer networking for the classification of peer-to-peer architectures and applications. In *Proceedings of the First International Conference on Peer-to-Peer Computing* (pp. 101-102).

This work was previously published in the International Journal of Distributed Systems and Technologies (IJDST), Volume 2, Issue 3, edited by Nik Bessis, pp. 37-48, copyright 2011 by IGI Publishing (an imprint of IGI Global).

Chapter 18
Information Communication Technology and a Systemic Disaster Management System Model

Jaime Santos-Reyes
SEPI-ESIME, Mexico

Alan N. Beard
Heriot-Watt University, UK

ABSTRACT

This paper presents some aspects of the 'communication' processes within a Systemic Disaster Management System (SDMS) model. Information and communication technology (ICT) plays a key part in managing natural disasters. However, it has been contended that ICT should not be used in 'isolation' but it should be seen as 'part' of the 'whole' system for managing disaster risk. Further research is needed in order to illustrate the full application of the ICT within the context of the developed model.

INTRODUCTION

Recent natural disasters have demonstrated the vulnerability of countries to such events. Also, past disasters have shown that their impact can be reduced significantly by taking adequate planning, preparedness and mitigation measures. A great deal of effort has been made, by academe, international organizations, and governments, practitioners, to investigate and develop approaches to address disaster risk (UN/ISDR, 2004; UNDP, 2004; McEntire, 2001; Lindell et al., 2007; Paton & Johnston, 2001; Moe & Pairote, 2006; Kurita et al., 2006; Aldunce & Leon, 2007; Kazusa, 2006; Jayawardane, 2006; Wilson, 2000; Iannella & Henricksen, 2007; Banipal, 2006).

DOI: 10.4018/978-1-4666-2647-8.ch018

On the other hand, information and communication technology (ICT) may be regarded as a key player in the process of disaster management. A number of studies and research has been conducted on ICT in relation planning, preparedness, mitigation, response and recovery (Murai, 2006; Kara-Zaitri, 1996; Mansor et al., 2004; De Silva, 2001; Quarentelli, 1997; Showalter, 2001; Billa et al., 2004; Brunn, 1995; Fedra & Reitisma, 1990; De Silva & Eglese, 2000; Johnson, 2000). For example, Showalter (2001) has examined articles published between 1972 and 1998 on remote sensing in hazard and disaster research. The review has found that the technique has been primarily used to detect, identify, map, survey and monitor existing hazards and/or their effects. Also, the author argues that remote sensing may help to provide damage assessments, improve planning, or provide data for mitigation, preparation, relief, response, and warning efforts (Brunn, 1995; Showalter, 2001). Moreover, remote sensing for a tsunami early warning system has been made possible by the use of existing technologies, such as radar, telemetry, telecommunication satellites, etc (Gonzalez et al., 1998). Other authors have conducted research on GIS and argue that it provides the primary advantage of displaying the critical information related to an incident on maps, satellite images, digital terrains (Billa et al., 2004; Fedra & Reitsma, 1990). Also, ICT technologies (e.g., Multimedia, CD-ROM, DVD, Internet, Web Sites and e-mail) are being applied to demonstrate how emergency planners may more effectively accomplish their mission to educate the larger community on a variety of issues such as the need to adopt proposed mitigation strategies, to respond to disaster warnings and evacuation suggestions (Fischer, 1998). Furthermore, ICT plays a critical role in facilitating the reconstruction process and in coordinating the return of those displaced by disasters to their original homes and communities. Disaster management activities, in the immediate aftermath of a disaster, can be made more effective by the use of appropriate ICT tools. These include tools for resource management and tracking, communication under emergency situations (e.g. use of Internet communications), collecting essential items for the victims, and national and international fundraising (Wattegama, 2007).

Following the 2004 Indian Ocean tsunami, the Asian Disaster Preparedness Centre (ADPC) and the International Telecommunication Union (ITU) have taken initiatives to study the current situation of emergency communications in the Asia-Pacific countries (Wattegama, 2007). Moreover, it is believed that assessments have been conducted in countries such as Bangladesh, Maldives and Sri Lanka on these emergency communication systems. The ADPC under the Indian Ocean Early-Warning System programme also introduced the Tsunami Alert Rapid Notification System Programme (TARNSP) with emphasis on robust ICT systems to disseminate information and warnings from the national to the community level (Wattegama, 2007).

Given the above, it may be argued that ICT cannot guarantee success in saving lives when used in 'isolation.' For example, it has been argued that had a tsunami early warning system (EWS) been operational in the Indian Ocean, the human toll might only have been a fraction of what it was (UNDP, 2005). It has been argued here and elsewhere (Santos-Reyes & Beard, 2010) that this may not be necessarily the case; an EWS should be seen as a component or part of a 'wider system'; i.e. a 'total disaster management system'. Moreover, an EWS may work very well when assessed individually but it is not clear whether it will contribute to accomplish the purpose of the total system; i.e. to prevent fatalities. For instance, a regional EWS may only work if it is well coordinated with the local warning and emergency response systems that ensure that the warning is received, communicated and acted upon by the potentially affected communities. It may be argued that without these local measures being in place, a regional EWS will have little impact in saving lives. Furthermore, communication should be effective so that the people receiving should acting upon it.

The paper presents examples of the application of ICT in the context of a Systemic Disaster management (SDMS) model. In particular, the paper addresses the 'communication' within the SDMS model.

ICT AND DISASTER MANAGEMENT

The previous section has demonstrated that ICTs play an important role in the process of disaster risk management. Overall, it may be argued that there are three distinct phases involved in this process; i.e. a) pre-disaster planning; b) activities during the disaster; and c) post-disaster (e.g. 'short' and 'long' term recovery). In what follows a brief description of each of these phases is presented.

Pre-Disaster

At this stage disaster risk should be assessed to take measures in order to eliminate disaster risk, prepare for emergencies. Effectively, ICT can play an important part for achieving this; e.g., ICTs can be used to transmit 'warnings' to the general public in order to take all the necessary actions to mitigate any potentially negative effects on themselves and property. Table 1 summarizes some examples of ICT that have been implemented or investigated for this stage of the disaster management process.

Disaster Response

In the aftermath of a disaster, often this stage has been regarded as one of the most difficult because it calls for prompt action within an exceptionally short period of time (Wattagama, 2007). That is, a significant number of individuals will be injured and/or displaced; some may require immediate

Table 1. Examples of ICTs in disaster management

Disaster Risk Stages	Examples of ICTs
Pre-Disaster (preparedness, early warning, mitigation) Activities including the assessment of disaster risk, mitigation, preparedness, response, and recovery needs.	GIS (Geographic Information System). (See or example Billa et al., 2004; Johnson, 2000; de Silva & Eglese, 2000; de Silva, 2000). TV (see Dunnette, 2006). Radio (see Coile, 1997; Acharya, 2005; Dunnette, 2006). Satellite radio (see Wattagama, 2007). Telephone (see Wattagama, 2007). Mobile phone (see Wattagama, 2007). 'Text Messages' also known as SMS (short message service) (see Clothier, 2005). Cell broadcasting (see Jagtman, 2010 and Wattagama, 2007). Internet/email (Fisher, 1998; Putnam, 2002) Amateur/community radio (see Coile, 1997; Acharya, 2005; Dunnette, 2006). Sirens
During Disaster (Response) All the activities following a disaster.	GIS (see Johnson, 2000). ICT based technology (internet, software, etc.) to address, for example the following issues: a. to trace missing persons; b. to coordinate donors; c. to record and coordinate temporary shelters; and d. Other. See for example, Fisher, 1998; Wattagama, 2007; Zincir-Heywood, 2002.
Post-Disaster ('short' & 'long' term recovery) All the activities necessary to bring all systems to normality	GIS in disaster recovery (see Johnson, 2000; Wattagama, 2007). Disaster Information Networks (e.g., UNDP's Tsunami resources and results tracking system). See Wattagama, 2007. FACTS (Food And Commodity Tracking System). See Wattagama, 2007. Internet. See for example, Zincir-Heywood, 2002.

medical attention, affected people may also be without food or other essential items; some might be waiting in temporary shelters, etc. Similarly, ICT may help authorities and organizations leading the response to assist those affected. Table 1 lists some examples of ICT for disaster response.

Post-Disaster

In general, disaster recovery involves two activities (Johnson, 2002): a) 'short-term' recovery involve those activities intended to return vital life-supply systems to minimum operating standards; e.g., temporary housing; and b) 'long-term' recovery activities are intended to continue for a number of years after the disaster. It may be argued that the purpose of this stage is to restore life to normality. A number of studies related to the application of ICT to disaster recovery are given in Table 1.

A SDMS MODEL

This section presents a brief overview of the fundamental characteristics of the Systemic Disaster Management System (SDMS) model.

The approach taken to formulate the SDMS builds on the Viable System Model (VSM) developed and proposed by Beer (1994), and the Failure Paradigm Method (FPM) proposed by Fortune and Peters (1995). Beer contends that in any viable system there are five necessary and sufficient subsystems interactively involved in any organism or organisation that is capable of maintaining its identity independently of other such organisms within a shared environment. The VSM facilitated an understanding to formulate the SDMS organisational structure. The FPM, inter alia, provided some best practices that helped to understand some human aspects. (It should be pointed out that the SDMS is a modified version of the Systemic Safety Management System (SSMS) model which has been applied to socio-technical systems; see for example Santos-Reyes and Beard (2001) for further details). The SDMS model aims to maintain disaster risk within an acceptable range in an organization's operations. The model is proposed as a sufficient structure for an effective disaster management system. It has a fundamentally preventive potentiality in that if all the sub-systems and connections are present and working effectively the probability of a failure should be less than otherwise. Table 2 lists some of the characteristics of the model.

Table 2. Some characteristics of the SDMS model

	Characteristic
1	A structural organization which consists of a 'basic unit' in which it is necessary to achieve five functions associated with systems 1 to 5. (See Figure 1). System 1: Disaster-policy implementation System 2: Disaster- total early warning coordination centre (TEWCC) System 2*: Disaster-local early warning coordination centre (LEWCC) System 3: Disaster-functional System 3*: Disaster-audit System 4: Disaster-development System 4*: Disaster-confidential reporting system System 5: Disaster-policy Note: whenever a line appears in Figure 1 representing the SDMS model, it represents a channel of communication.
2	'Communication Paradigm'
3	Other. See Santos-Reyes and Beard (2001, 2010) for details about these.

Structural Organization of the Model

A brief description of the structural organization of the model is given in what follows:

System 1: Disaster-policy implementation implements safety policies in the organization's operations. System 1 consists of one or more operations (e.g., disaster operations at the level of a country, or zone or region).

System 2: Disaster-TEWCC coordinates all the activities of the operations that form part of system 1 (see Figure 1) and in relation to the 'total environment.' Furthermore, it also coordinates other local early warning coordination centres (LEWCCs). System 2 along with system 1, implements the safety plans received from system 3.

System 2*: Disaster-LEWCC is part of system 2 and it is responsible for communicating advance warnings to other early warning coordination centres and to key decision makers in order to take appropriate actions prior to the occurrence of a major natural hazard event. (See next section for details about this).

System 3: Disaster-functional is directly responsible for maintaining disaster risk within an acceptable range in system 1 on a daily basis. It ensures that system 1 implements the organization's safety policy.

System 3*: Disaster-audit is part of system 3 and its function is to conduct audits sporadically into the operations of system 1. System 3* intervenes in the operations of system 1 according to the safety plans received from system 3.

System 4: Disaster-development is generally concerned with the 'total environment' and its function is to conduct research and development (R&D) for the continual adaptation of the organization. By considering strengths, weaknesses, threats and opportunities, sys-

tem 4 can suggest changes to the organization's safety policies.

System 4*: Disaster-confidential reporting system is part of system 4 and it is concerned with confidential reports or causes of concern from any person of the public about any aspects, some of which may require the direct intervention of system 5.

System 5: Disaster-policy is responsible for deliberating safety policies and for making strategic decisions. System 5 also monitors the activities of system 4 and system 3.

Hot-Line: Figure 1 shows a dash line directly from system 1 to system 5, representing a direct communication or 'hot-line' for use in exceptional circumstances; for example, during an emergency.

The full account of the main characteristics of the SDMS model is given in Santos-Reyes and Beard (2010).

Communication within a SDMS Model

Whenever a line appears, in Figure 1 representing the SDMS model, it represents a channel of information flow. For example, channels of communication between the system and its environment (i.e., 'total and disaster future environments', see Figure 1). Two way channels of communication connecting systems 1 to 5 as depicted in Figure 1. There is a particular concern in the SDMS about the nature of these channels and the information which flows in the communication channels. These channels of communication obey four organisational principles (see Annex-A). Finally, a special channel, represented as a dotted line in Figure 1, that connects system 1 with system 5 can be employed to communicate particular important safety information, which may require a direct intervention of system 5.

Figure 1. Channels of communication amongst systems 1-5 and the environment

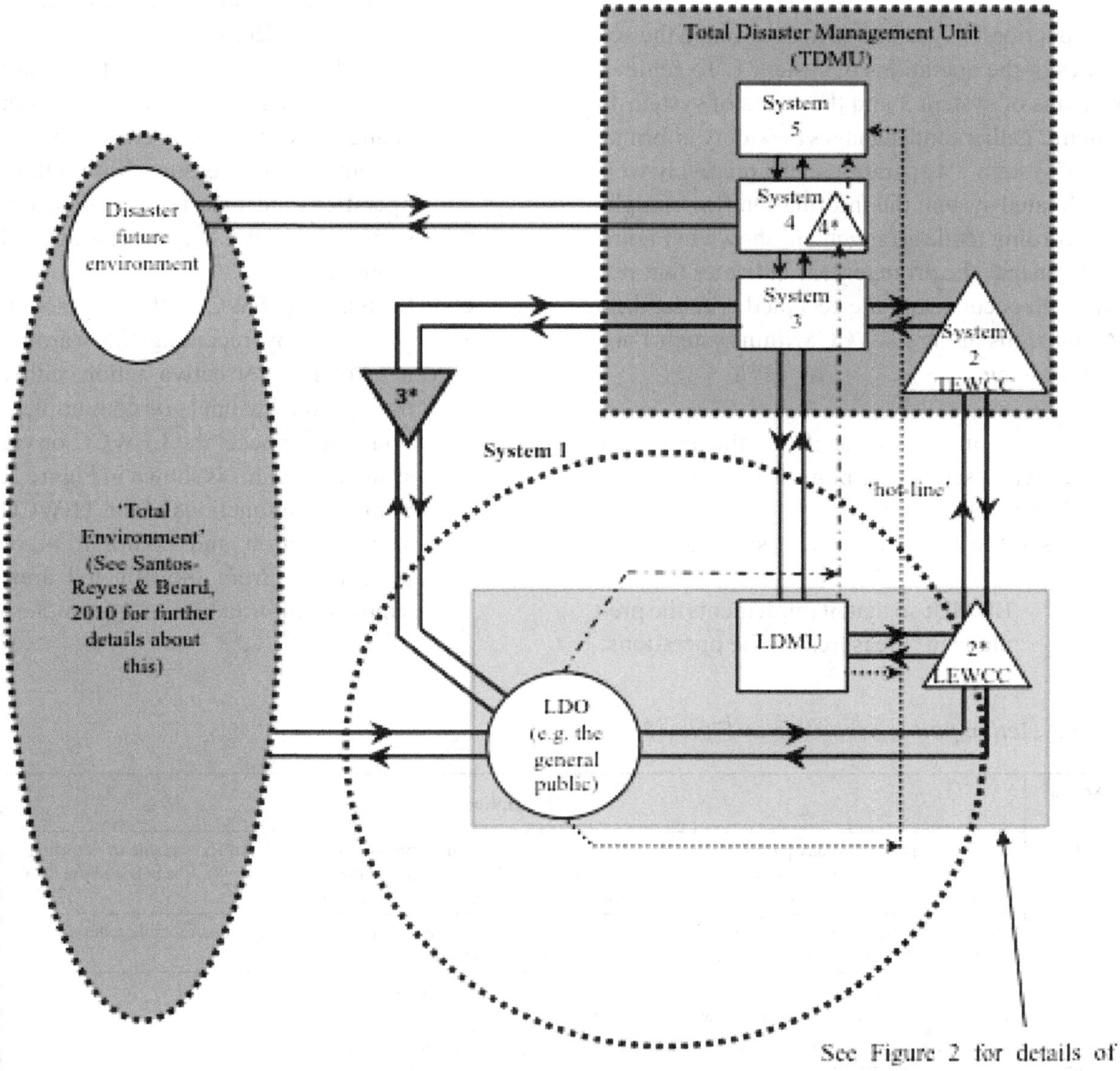

Acronyms:
TDMU = Total Disaster Management Unit
LDO = Local Disaster Operations
LDMU = Local Disaster Management Unit
TEWCC = Total Early Warning Coordination Centre
LEWCC = Local Early Warning Coordination Centre

Early Warning Coordination Centers

The function of system 2 is to coordinate the activities of the operations of system 1. To achieve the plans of system 3 and the needs of system 1, system 2 gathers and manages the safety information of system 1's operations. In a relatively well coordinated system the information flows might be according to the arrangement shown in Figure 2. In general, the arrangement indicates that if a deviation occurs from the accepted criteria, then the functions of the LEWCC within system 1 are the following:

1. Detect any deviation from the accepted criteria (see action point 2 in Table 3 and Figure 2).
2. Issue the disaster warning simultaneously to:
   a. LDMU; so that, it implements the preplanned 'measures' in the operations; see action points 3, 4, and 5 (e.g., evacuation, search and rescue, emergency medical services).
   b. Other LEWCCs through action point 2A. Similarly, these coordination centres have to assess consequences and implement measures within their operations and make reports quickly to system 2 (TEWCC); see Table 3 and Figure 2.
   c. System 2 (TEWCC) through action point 4A. By receiving the warning it takes fast corrective action, either through the channels of communication that connects the LEWCC or via system 3 and this is shown in Figure 2. Some of the functions of the TEWCC are: collection and compilation of information from the affected area, supply of information to System 3.

Table 3. Action points according to Figure 2

Action Point	Description
1	Flow of data related to any particular sensor system; for example "bottom pressure recorders" (BPRs) capable of detecting and measuring tsunamis with amplitudes as small as 1cm in 6000 m of water (Gonzalez et al., 1998). It is believed the data can be send to a 'companion surface buoy' with satellite transmitters for real-time communications.
2	Comparison/analysis of the data/information being received. If any deviation from the pre-planned acceptable criteria occurs then it issues the warning to action points '2A' & '3' as indicated in Figure 2.
2A	a. Communicates the warning to other LEWCCs (these are not shown in Figure 2). b. It also receives information from the TEWCC as shown in Figure 2.
3	The function of the LDMU is to respond to the warning and prevent fatalities due to the natural hazard.
4	Planning and taking measures in order to respond to the warning. For example, to develop appropriate emergency planning and be able to respond to warnings within minutes, and communicate them to local populations via sirens, mass media, specialized radio systems, and other notification technologies, etc. See Table 1. Regional workshops involving national agencies, institutes, broadcasting agencies and NGOs and warning experts and participants draw up plans to implement public awareness campaigns.
4A	Issues the warning to the TEWCC (See Figure 2) and by receiving all this information, the TEWCC enables to take a 'higher' order view of the total consequences. It will report to system 3, which is on the vertical command channel (see Figures 1 & 2).
5	a. The warning is issued. The public may be informed by a number of ICT; for example, via sirens, mass media, specialized radio systems, and other notification technologies. See Table 1. b. Implementation of pre-planned 'measures' to evacuate safely and prevent fatalities due to natural hazards; e.g., provision of medical services, search, rescue & evacuation. The primary concern should be the safety of the public; protection of property by the police and fire fighters.

Figure 2. Information flow amongst LDMU, LEWCC and the LDO (see Figure 1)

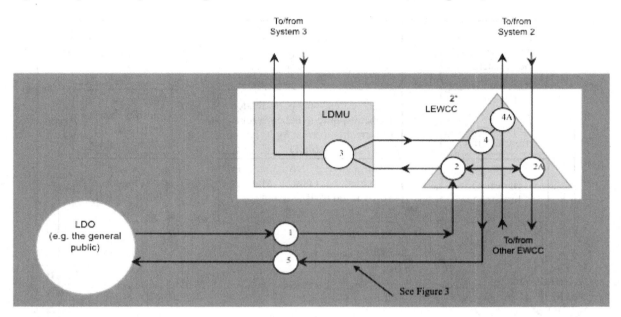

Acronyms:

LDMU = Local Disaster Management Unit; LDO = Local Disaster Operations
TEWCC = Total Early Warning Co-ordination Centre
LEWCC = Local Early Warning Co-ordination Centre

Disaster Risk Management in the Context of the SDMS Model

Figure 3 is intended to illustrate the process of disaster risk management in the context of the model. The Loop-1 is intended to illustrate the pre-disaster activities. Loop-2, on the other hand, addresses the activities involved in the 'response' phase during the disaster. Finally, Loop-3 illustrates the activities involved in dealing with post-disaster. It is clear that in all these activities ICTs play a key part. However, these technologies should be used on the right side of the 'equation'. The 'four organizational' principles may help to achieve this (see Annex-A). It should be pointed out that Figure 3 is intended to illustrate the general process of disaster risk management when using the model. However, a more detailed analysis of each phase of the disaster risk process should be conducted.

Communication Paradigm

Communication represents a central role in the SDSM model. Figure 2 shows an arrangement for an early warning and Figure 4 depicts an example of a channel of communication (action point 5); in particular it shows a dynamic two-way process of communication. According to the communication paradigm shown in Figure 4, an effective communication between the sender (i.e. action point 4 of Figure 2) and the receiver (i.e., the population within the LDO, see Figures 1 and 2) requires that: (a) the sender makes an appropriate selection from the agreed 'alphabet'; i.e., the 'alphabet' may be regarded as the set of signs from which the message may be constructed; (b) the 'message' can be transformed into a form of physical energy for transmission. With speech the message is first 'encoded' into nerve impulses that activate the mechanisms involved in the voice

Figure 3. Pre-disaster, response and recovery in the context of the SDMS model

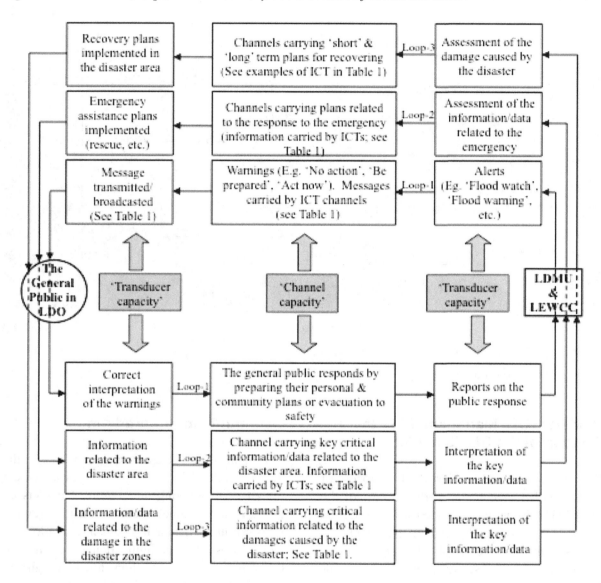

production, and then transformed into vibrations of the atmosphere; (c) the 'channel' (i.e., the radio) should be capable of transmitting the signal. This may depend on the channel capacity, (this may vary according to the information code used), the level of noise and the amount of distortion. It should be emphasised that the channel should be designed in such a way that in case of exceptional circumstances, such as an emergency, must be taken into account; (d) the received signal can be transformed back into a message using the same code; (e) the receiver has the same 'alphabet' as the sender and can therefore reconstruct and interpret the original message; and (f) the 'feedback verification' is intended to help the sender and the receiver to adapt to changes brought about by the level of noise. Also, the receiver's response to the sender's message can be used to modify subsequent messages.

Figure 4. Emergency "Evacuate" message between the sender and the population within the LDO ((see Figure 2) (The communication paradigm has been adapted from Fortune & Peters, (2005))

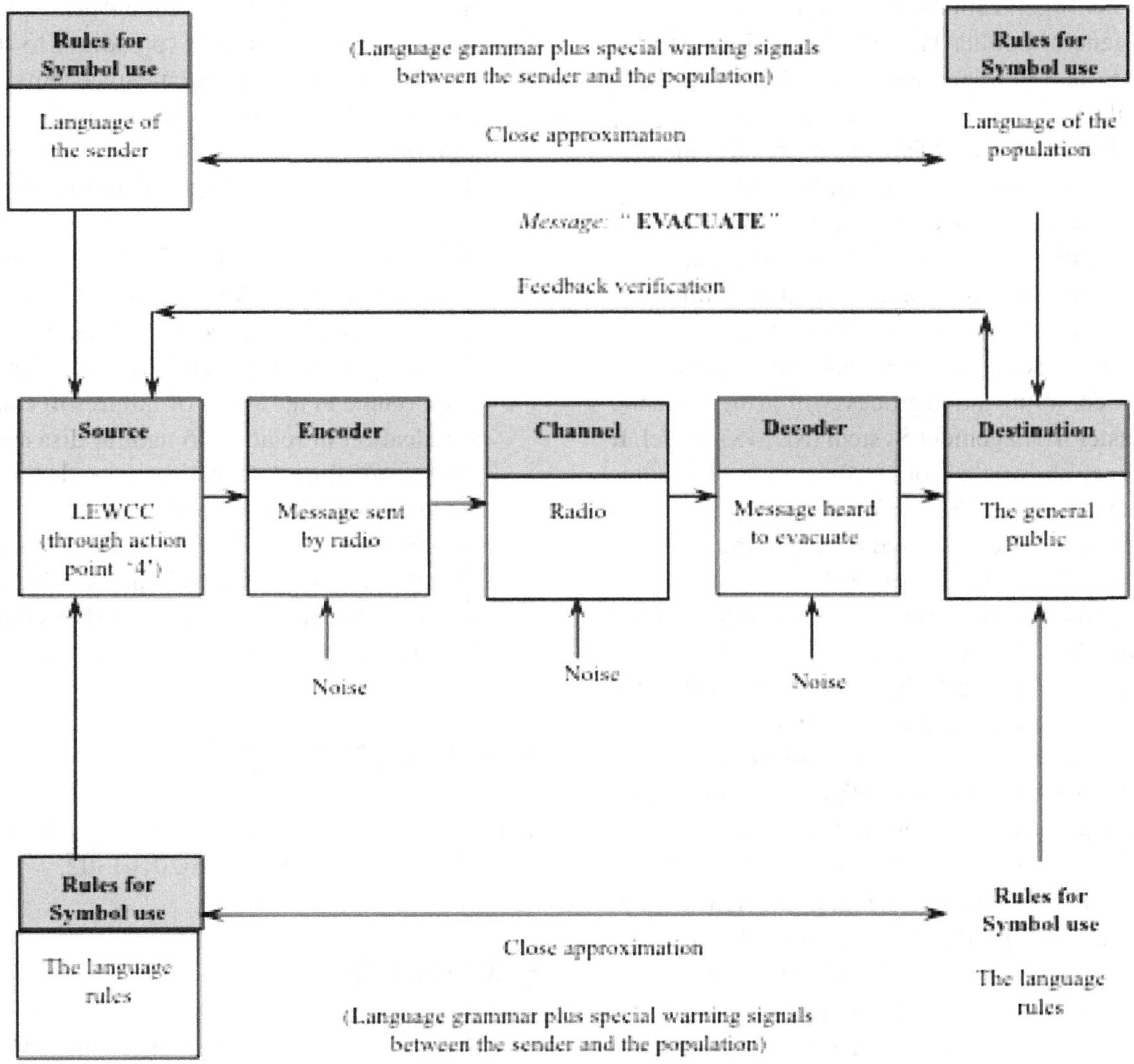

CONCLUSION

Natural disasters have demonstrated the vulnerability of countries to such events. Also, past disasters have shown that their impact can be mitigated by taking adequate early warning, preparedness and mitigation measures. Communication of information is central to the process of managing disaster risk. Information and communication technology (ICT) may be regarded as a key player in facilitating this process. However, ICTs also have the potential to harm and may lead to unacceptable decisions being made by those concerned (e.g., the general public, local and national governmental organizations, non-governmental organizations (NGOs), the media, the scientific community, etc.) in relation to disaster risk. For example, mass media organizations, such as TV networks and disaster organizations (e.g., civil protection) have different purposes and this may create conflicts; i.e., mass media organizations aim to attract viewers, listeners and readers while disaster organizations aim to assure the safety of the general public. This conflict of interest may lead to undesirable consequences. Moreover, ICTs should not be used in 'isolation' but should be considered as 'part' of a wider system for managing natural disasters. That is, ICT, for example, may successfully deliver the warning but if the general public does not know what actions need to be done, then the whole system will fail to accomplish the objective of saving lives.

The present paper has illustrated some aspect of the communication process within the Systemic Disaster Management System (SDMS) model. It has been shown that communication is a key component within the SDMS model; moreover, it has been emphasised the need to design the channels of communication amongst the key subsystems that constitute the structural organization of the model (i.e., Systems 1-5). In particular, these channels should be designed according to the four organizational principles (see Annex-A) in order to guarantee an effective communication. Also, an example of the application of the 'communication' paradigm has been presented. It may be argued that the example may be over simplistic but it highlights the need to address explicitly those aspects that may affect the communication process between organizations dealing with disasters and the general public when using ICTs.

However, more research is needed in order to illustrate the communication process throughout the whole SDMS model (see Figure 1). In particular, the following may be the way forward:

1. To model a flood disaster management system by applying the SDMS model. Then, apply the 'four organizational principles' to design the channels of communication (including ICTs) in every stage of the disaster risk management cycle; i.e., pre-disaster, during disaster and pos-disaster.

2. Similar to (1), except for the case of earthquakes.

3. To apply the 'four organizational principles' and the 'communication' paradigm to the existing 'disaster management systems' to assess the effectiveness of their communication processes.

4. The 'communication' paradigm used in the present paper is concerned only with the transmission and receipt of information and does not consider, for example, other factors such as human aspects (values, beliefs, or risk perception) that may be of great importance in the study of failures in communication in relation to natural disasters. This needs further investigation and should be incorporated into the SDMS model.

5. 'Communication' is a key component in the 'control' paradigm which is another feature of the SDMS model. Further work needs to be conducted in order to illustrate this.

ACKNOWLEDGMENT

This project was funded by SIP-IPN under the following grant: SIP-IPN: No-20101302.

REFERENCES

Acharya, M. (2005, January). Amateur Radio. A potential tool in emergency operations. *i4d Magazine, 3*(1). Retrieved May 20, 2010, from http://www.i4donline.net/jan05/amateur.asp

Aldunce, P., & Leon, A. (2007). Opportunities for improving disaster management in Chile: a case study. *Disaster Prevention and Management, 16*(1), 33–41. doi:10.1108/09653560710729794

Banipal, K. (2006). Strategic approach to disaster management: lessons learned from Hurricane Katrina. *Disaster Prevention and Management, 15*(3), 484–494. doi:10.1108/09653560610669945

Beer, S. (1994). *The heart of enterprise*. Chichester, UK: Wiley.

Billa, L., Mansor, S., & Mahmud, A. R. (2004). Spatial information technology in flood early warning systems: an overview of theory, application and latest developments in Malaysia. *Disaster Prevention and Management, 13*(5), 356–363. doi:10.1108/09653560410568471

Brunn, S. D. (1995). Geography's research performance based on Annals manuscripts, 1987-1993. *The Professional Geographer, 47*(2), 204–215. doi:10.1111/j.0033-0124.1995.00204.x

Clothier, J. (2005). *Dutch trial SMS disaster alert system. CNN*. Retrieved June 6, 2010, from http://edition.cnn.com/2005/TECH/11/09/dutch.disaster.warning/index.html

Coile, R. C. (1997). The role of amateur radio in providing emergency electronic communication for disaster management. *Disaster Prevention and Management, 6*(3), 176–185. doi:10.1108/09653569710172946

De Silva, F. N. (2001). Providing spatial decision support for evacuation planning: a challenge in integrating Technologies. *Disaster Prevention and Management, 10*(1), 11–20. doi:10.1108/09653560110381787

De Silva, F. N., & Eglese, R. W. (2000). Integrating simulation modelling and GIS: spatial decision support systems for evacuation planning. *The Journal of the Operational Research Society, 51*(4), 423–430.

Dunnette, R. (2006). Radio and TV Broadcasting for Disaster Relief and Public Warning. In *Proceedings of the Pacific Telecommunications Council '06*. Retrieved May 10, 2010, from http://www.ptc06.org/program/public/proceedings/Roxana%20Dunnette_paper_t151%-20(formatted).pdf

Fedra, K., & Reitsma, R. F. (1990). *Decision support and Geographical Information Systems. Geographical information systems for urban and regional planning* (Tech. Rep. No. RR-90-009). Laxenburg, Austria: ACA, International Institute for Applied Systems Analysis (IIASA).

Fisher, H. W. (1998). The role of the new information technologies in emergency mitigation, planning, response and recovery. *Disaster Prevention and management, 7*(1), 28-37.

Fortune, J., & Peters, G. (1995). *Learning from failure – the systems approach*. Chichester, UK: Wiley.

González, F. I., Milburn, H. B., Bernard, E. N., & Newman, J. (1998). *Deep-ocean Assessment and Reporting of Tsunamis (DART): Brief Overview and Status Report*. Retrieved April 15, 2010, from http://nctr.pmel.noaa.gov/dart_report1998.html

Iannella, R., & Henricksen, K. (2007). Managing Information in the Disaster Coordination Centre: Lessons and Opportunities. In B. Van de Walle, P. Burghardt, & C. Nieuwenhuis (Eds.), *Proceedings of the 4th International ISCRAM Conference*, Delft, The Netherlands (pp. 1-11).

International Strategy for Disaster Reduction (ISDR). (2004). *Living with risk: A global review of disaster reduction initiatives*. Geneva, Switzerland: United Nations.

Jagtman, H. M. (2010). Cell broadcast trials in The Netherlands: Using mobile phone technology for citizens' alarming. *Reliability Engineering & System Safety, 95*, 18–28. doi:10.1016/j.ress.2009.07.005

Jayawardane, A. (2006). Disaster mitigation initiatives in Sri Lanka. In *Proceedings of the International Symposium on Management System for Disaster Prevention*, Kochi, Japan.

Johnson, R. (2000). *GIS Technology for Disasters and Emergency Management*. Washington, DC: Environmental Systems Research Institute, Inc.

Kara-Zaitri, C. (1996). Disaster prevention and limitation: state of the art; tools and technologies. *Disaster Prevention and Management, 5*(1), 30–39. doi:10.1108/09653569610109541

Kasuza, S. (2006). Disaster management of Japan. In *Proceedings of the International Symposium on Management System for Disaster Prevention*, Kochi, Japan.

Kurita, T., Nakamura, A., Kodama, M., & Colombage, S. R. N. (2006). Tsunami public awareness and the disaster management system of Sri Lanka. *Disaster Prevention and Management, 15*(1), 92–110. doi:10.1108/09653560610654266

Lindell, M. K., Prater, C. S., & Peacock, W. G. (2007). Organizational Communication and Decision Making for Hurricane Emergencies. *Natural Hazards Review*, 50–60. doi:10.1061/(ASCE)1527-6988(2007)8:3(50)

Mansor, S., Shariah, M. A., Billa, L., Setiawan, I., & Jabar, F. (2004). Spatial technology for natural risk management. *Disaster Prevention and Management, 13*(5), 364–373. doi:10.1108/09653560410568480

McEntire, D. A. (2001). Triggering agents, vulnerabilities and disaster reduction: towards a holistic paradigm. *Disaster Prevention and Management, 10*(3), 189–196. doi:10.1108/09653560110395359

Moe, T. L., & Pairote Pathranarakul, P. (2006). An integrated approach to natural disaster management Public project management and its critical success factors. *Disaster Prevention and Management, 15*(3), 396–413. doi:10.1108/09653560610669882

Murai, S. (2006). Monitoring of disasters using remote sensing GIS and GPS. In *Proceedings of the International Symposium on Management System for Disaster Prevention*, Kochi, Japan.

Paton, D., & Johnston, D. (2001). Disasters and communities: vulnerability, resilience and preparedness. *Disaster Prevention and Management, 10*(4), 270–277. doi:10.1108/EUM0000000005930

Putnam, L. (2002, November). By Choice or by Chance: How the Internet Is Used to Prepare for, Manage, and Share Information about Emergencies. *First Monday, 7*(11). Retrieved May 10, 2010, from http://www.firstmonday.org/issues/issue7_11/putnam/index.html

Quarantelli, E. L. (1997). Problematical aspects of the information/communication revolution for disaster planning and research: ten non-technical issues and questions. *Disaster Prevention and Management, 6*(2), 94–106. doi:10.1108/09653569710164053

Santos-Reyes, J., & Beard, A. N. (2001). A Systemic Approach to Fire Safety Management. *Fire Safety Journal, 36*, 359–390. doi:10.1016/S0379-7112(00)00059-X

Santos-Reyes, J., & Beard, A. N. (2010). A systemic approach to managing natural disasters. In Asimakopoulou, E., & Bessis, N. (Eds.), *Advanced ICTs for Disaster Management and Threat Detection: Collaborative and Distributed Frameworks*. New York: Information Science Publishing.

Showalter, P. S. (2001). Remote sensing's use in disaster research: a review. *Disaster Prevention and Management*, *10*(1), 21–29. doi:10.1108/09653560110381796

United Nations Development Programme (UNDP). (2005). *Survivors of the tsunami: One year later*. Retrieved June 28, 2009, from http://www.iotws.org/ev_en.php?ID=1685_201&ID2=-DO_TOPIC

Wattagama, C. (2007). *ICT for disaster management. Asia-Pacific Development Information Programme-e-Primers for the Information Economy, Society and Policy*. Thailand: UNDP-APDIP and Asian and Pacific Training Centre for Information and Communication Technology for Development (APCICT).

Wilson, H. C. (2000). Emergency response preparedness: small group training- Part I- training and learning styles. *Disaster Prevention and Management*, *9*(2), 105–116. doi:10.1108/09653560010326987

Zincir-Heywood, N. A., & Malcolm, I. H. (2000). In the Wake of the Turkish Earthquake: Turkish Internet. In *Proceedings of the Internet Society's NET 2000 Conference*. Retrieved May 10, 2010, from http://www.isoc.org/inet2000/cdproceedings/8l/8l_2.htm

APPENDIX

The First Principle of Organization

"Managerial, operational and environmental varieties, diffusing through an institutional system, tend to equate; they should be designed to do so with minimum damage to people and to cost" (i.e., for a high viability system). An example could be an evacuation system designed to save lives in the case of a fire or explosion; then the evacuation capacity must be at least as great as the number of possible evacuees.

The Second Principle of Organization

"The four directional channels carrying information between the management unit, the operation, and the environment must each have higher capacity to transmit a given amount of information relevant to variety selection in a given time than the originating subsystem has to generate it in that time. Example, the channels carrying procedures of evacuation must have enough specificity so as to reduce ambiguities or eliminate unclear instructions."

The Third Principle of Organization

"Wherever the information carried on a channel capable of distinguishing a given variety crosses a boundary, it undergoes transduction; and the variety of the transducer must be at least equivalent to the variety of the channel. Example, in the case of means of escape for rail users, a transducer might be a fire safety instruction leaflet. This would 'transduce' between the person making up the evacuation rules and the people the rules are aimed at; then the notice must be comprehensive and clear."

The Fourth Principle of Organization

"The operation of the first three principles must be cyclically maintained through time, and without hiatus or lags." (That is, they must be adhered to continuously).

This work was previously published in the International Journal of Distributed Systems and Technologies (IJDST), Volume 2, Issue 1, edited by Nik Bessis, pp. 29-42, copyright 2011 by IGI Publishing (an imprint of IGI Global).

Chapter 19
A Next Generation Technology Victim Location and Low Level Assessment Framework for Occupational Disasters Caused by Natural Hazards

Nik Bessis
University of Derby, UK & University of Bedfordshire, UK

Eleana Asimakopoulou
University of Bedfordshire, UK

Peter Norrington
University of Bedfordshire, UK

Suresh Thomas
University of Bedfordshire, UK

Ravi Varaganti
University of Bedfordshire, UK

ABSTRACT

Much work is underway within the broad next generation technologies community on issues associated with the development of services to support interdisciplinary domains. Disaster reduction and emergency management are domains in which utilization of advanced information and communication technologies (ICT) are critical for sustainable development and livelihoods. In this article, the authors aim to use an exemplar occupational disaster scenario in which advanced ICT utilization could present emergency managers with some collective computational intelligence in order to prioritize their decision making. To achieve this, they adapt concepts and practices from various next generation technologies including ad-hoc mobile networks, Web 2.0, wireless sensors, crowd sourcing and situated computing. On the implementation side, the authors developed a data mashup map, which highlights the criticality of victims at a location of interest. With this in mind, the article describes the service architecture in the form of data and process flows, its implementation and some simulation results.

DOI: 10.4018/978-1-4666-2647-8.ch019

INTRODUCTION

Phenomena such as earthquakes, hurricanes, storms, landslides, forest fires, heavy snow and others take place daily and are considered as natural phenomena and as such, 'natural phenomena are normal and essential planetary actions' (Asimakopoulou et al., 2006). It has been said that an extreme natural phenomenon may be characterized as catastrophic and hazardous by the scope of people in relation to their lives, property, as well as their environment. In managing disasters and in particular during the response phase, it is apparent that a number of teams and individuals from multiple, geographically distributed organizations are required to communicate, cooperate and collaborate in order to take appropriate decisions and actions (Graves, 2004; Otten et al., 2004).

Various technological developments over the last years have facilitated users with numerous tools to support various levels of enquiry within the environment of their organisation or community. Specifically, the use of computer-based collaborative technologies has evolved over the years through developments in distributed computational science in a manner, which provides improved applicable intelligence to their problem-solving capabilities.

In fact, most of these technologies have emerged with the view of producing frameworks and standards to fully or partially – yet purposefully – support seamless integration processes within heterogeneous distributed environments. Emerging paradigms and their associated concepts highlighting their benefits include but are not limited to Web Services, Web 2.0, Ad-hoc mobile networks using wireless sensors, Pervasive, Grid and Cloud computing as well as Crowd sourcing and Situated computing. Their goal is to enable an approach relevant to collective resource utilization and thus, enhance multi-user participation in functioning as a coherent unit through the use of a Cyber Infrastructure (Bessis et al., 2010). That is, to purposefully work together, collaborate and

solve a well-defined problem of mutual interest from a multi-user point of view. As such, they typically enable the provision of shared and often real-time access to, centralized or distributed resources, such as applications, data, models, toolkits and sensors.

Within this in mind, the article aims firstly to present an occupational hazard case scenario as a means to describe stakeholders functional requirements; secondly to elaborate the case scenario by offering a brief overview of how emerging technologies could be utilized to enable some improved intelligence in decision making; thirdly to describe the service architecture in the form of data and process flow diagrams followed by its implementation. Finally, we conclude by providing a simulation experiment.

An Exemplary Occupational Disaster Management Scenario

We present here a previously published (Bessis et al., 2010) fictional yet typical occupational hazard scenario, which is used throughout the remainder of our article as a point of reference.

In an urban area a major earthquake of some significant magnitude on the Richter scale has occurred. The area is highly populated and characterized by multi-storey buildings, such as blocks of offices, malls and other public buildings. The occurrence of the earthquake caused a disastrous situation, as some of the buildings have collapsed and some people have been injured and trapped. Further to this, a number of secondary phenomena follow the occurrence of the main hazard, such as electricity failures, fires and a series of aftershocks.

The area's civil protection department has organised the emergency operation in order to respond to the disaster. According to the area plans and to the emergency calls that reach the emergency services, operational units (OU) have been sent on site to locate and rescue earthquake victims. The members of an OU have to work as a team and to report back to the operation centre about their status and progress. OU members have to find ways to locate (positioning) and then reach trapped victims within the collapsed buildings. This process is quite uncertain and surely dangerous, as the stability of the affected structural elements cannot be easily assessed. Further to this, the fact that aftershocks with different magnitudes and without lead-time occur in the area makes these attempts more difficult and dangerous. For example, imagine that while members of an OU-1 are inside of an affected multi-storey block of offices an aftershock occurs, which in turn results in some of the already affected structural elements of the building collapsing. Our assumption leads to a realistic scenario whereby some OU-1 members are injured and trapped inside the building alongside the originally trapped victims. Other OUs (e.g., OU-2 or OU-n) and the operation centre do not know the condition of OU-1 members: if they are alive, seriously injured, as well as their exact condition and location (positioning). The scenario yields even more uncertainties, increased workloads, pressures and problems, as other OUs have to locate and rescue their OU-1 colleagues, help assist in rescuing victims meant to be rescued by the OU-1 team as well as deliver their original rescue plan (issued to them prior to the aftershock) without compromising more lives. Rescuing OU-1 members is considered a top priority as these now-victim members are valuable personnel resource with significant immediate value and irreplaceable expertise in rescue operations.

The aforementioned scenario highlights a main concern that is to identify and locate the positioning of victims prior to the emergency managers' decision to send out their rescue teams. Our argument here is that it is of critical importance to move information requirements from speculative planning about the victims' population to actual management for and of the victims' population. In other words, disaster managers will need to know where people are: there is no benefit in sending OUs to a building, however certain its collapse may be, if there is no one actually there. Equally,

there is benefit in sending in an OU to a building not considered at great risk if someone injured is there. The view here is that it is easy to construct many plausible scenarios where knowledge of the number, whereabouts and health of people in an area struck by a disaster will significantly enhance the ability of disaster managers to respond to the reality of the situation.

Overview of Emerging Technologies to Improve Disaster Management Decision Making

The view here is for emergency management stakeholders including OU members to utilize next generation emerging technologies to provide, store, process and assess data about the location and health of victims of a disaster (i.e., an earthquake), which could enable them with some improved collective computational intelligence.

The task of identifying victims' exact positioning has been discussed in Asimakopoulou et al. (2010a; 2010b). Specifically, in previous works, we have suggested the use of current digital and wireless technology that is embedded in cell telephony and capable of reading, identifying and clustering groups of victims based on their exact positioning (cell area 1, cell area 2, etc). Data received could be analyzed in real-time and fed into a number of collaborative decision support systems encompassing a simulation tool, which could enable disaster managers with some improved intelligence. We therefore suggested combining simulation results with geographical maps as a means to illustrate the exact positioning of identified victims.

The main focus of this article is to extend our previous achievements by using next generation emerging technologies for grouping victims in relation to their health state. The motivation is also discussed in Bessis et al. (2010). In particular, it has been discussed that the goal of Grids and Clouds is to purposefully utilize resources (data, computational power, software, toolkits, expertise, etc) that are available from/to Virtual Organizations (VO) partners so they can more effectively solve mainly scientific (Grid) or commercial (Cloud) problems. Pervasive (also known as Ubiquitous) computing has been developed as a means to enable resource computation and utilization in a far more mobile or environmentally embedded manner. Pervasive computing embeds IT into our environments by integrating them seamlessly into our everyday lives. Situated Computing is an emerging paradigm dealing with computing devices that have the autonomous ability of adapting, detecting, interpreting and responding to the user's environment. Crowd sourcing (also known as Crowd Computing or Citizen Science) can utilize data captured from ordinary citizens' mobile phones and mobile sensors for various purposes. Finally, it is important to realize that Web 2.0 offers a platform where users as individuals or communities are able to share topics of interests using available social software. Readers are directed to a full emerging technologies review available in Bessis et al (2010). In this work, we have presented a visionary model architecture and an opportunity among various emerging technology paradigms including Grid, Cloud, Crowd, Pervasive and Situated Computing, to be integrated for a collective intelligence model to serve disaster management.

Herein, our recommendation involves that people working in OU members should have installed wearable sensors on their body when they are taking up a rescue task. Wearable sensors come in many forms: wrist watches, rings, smart clothes (shirts, shoes etc.), spectacles, plasters, or implanted devices (e.g., subcutaneous); and are known in different contexts or just with different usage under several generic names: wearable sensors, body sensors, disposable digital plasters or ambulatory monitoring, and extended into body sensor networks or body area networks (BANs). There are also various proofs-of-concept utilizing signals from a patient's chest, which monitor in real-time a range of vital signs such as ECG,

body temperature, respiration and physical activity (Smith, 2007). Such devices began clinical trials in November 2009 (ICL, 2009). The signals that smart body sensors measure include physiological vital signs such as heart rate, temperature, respiration or ECG rate, and other biological signs such as sweat production or glucose levels.

A further expectation is that buildings should have installed sensors and finally, we assume that victims have installed sensor APIs on their mobile devices. However, we do appreciate that the latter APIs would be limited in data transfer as well as in detecting and capturing a variety of signs. This is an additional reason to believe that the establishment of an ad-hoc network is of critical importance. In turn, data related to (identified and located) individual's state of health could enable disaster managers to cluster victims in groups of various priority levels (high – medium – low) and thus point to the location where maximum assistance is required. Similarly, it will help assist them in load-balancing resources.

SERVICE FUNCTIONALITY AND IMPLEMENTATION

This section briefly presents the broad functional requirements of the service illustrating various data and process flow diagrams. It also provides a brief description of the technologies used to develop the prototype service. With this in mind, the emergency management, as an end user, should be able to:

- View the occurrence of an earthquake in a dynamic way.
- Contextualise the occurrence in a specific geographical area on a map.
- Zoom to locate the exact area affected.
- Identify the exact positioning of people located in the affected area.
- Receive data (including health related) of people from various wireless sensors.

- Run a simulation incorporating data from all relevant sources.
- Group victims according to their health state and display them on the map.
- View alerts and define alert settings through triggering events.

The core functionality of the system is based on people who are connected with wearable sensors. Data collected from a sensor, which is above a defined threshold triggers a signal to be sent out to a consolidator (notification) agent. The notification service as described in Bessis et al. (2009) generates and illustrates an alert in the Google map. Similarly, data groupings that are related to the victims' health status enable the visualisation of clusters of victims in groups of various priority levels (high – medium – low) and thus point to the location where maximum assistance is required. This is shown in Figure 1 and a generic sequence diagram is shown in Figure 2.

The data mashup implementation involves various technologies including web services, Google™ map API and RSS feeds. Specifically,

web services are used to receive data from sensors attached to the victims. The wearable sensors capture the geographical coordinates and biological data (such as heart beat, body temperature, blood pressure) of the people who have the sensors installed on them. RSS feeds are used to receive real time data from seismological centres such as from the European Mediterranean Seismological Centre (EMSC). The Adobe Flash builder (FLEX) 4.0 is used as the integrated development environment for the Google map API. Specifically, Adobe Flash provides one of the efficient implementations of AJAX (Asynchronous JavaScript and XML). Adobe Flash provides a clear, rich and dynamic interface while AJAX support minimizes the traffic between server and client. The integration of Flex and XML feed generated from XML is done through PHP. A MySQL database has been used to aggregate the data. The dynamic RSS data does not persist in the database, but the data generated as the part of simulation does persist. Figure 3 shows a low-level data flow.

Figure 1. The low-level model architecture of the data mashup schematics

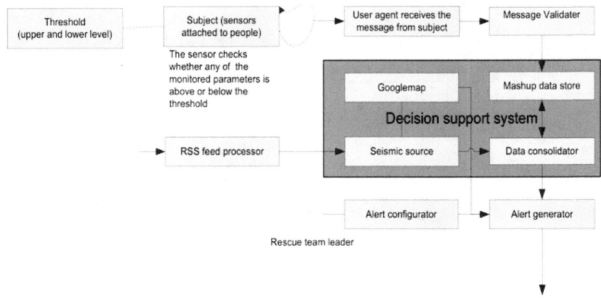

Figure 2. The data mashup sequence diagram

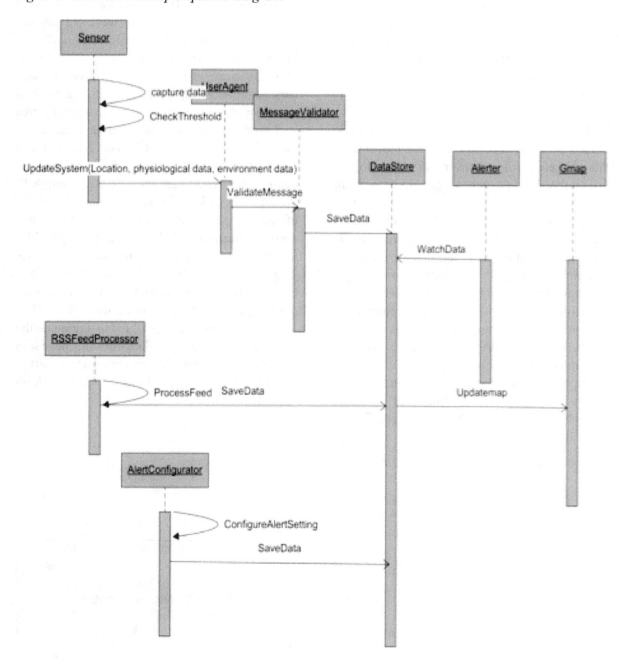

Figure 3. The data mashup service low-level data flow

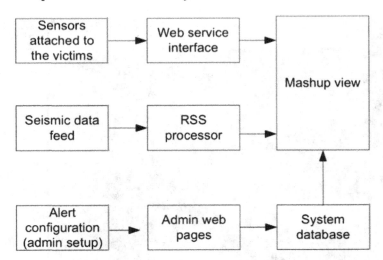

The implementation allows us to receive data and build a data mashup displaying the exact positioning and state of each of victim. Moreover, a configurator allows the emergency manager as an end user to define rules such as "if a person's heart beat is below 50 and blood pressure is 10% below the normal then show him on the map with red colour marker". The service is also able to monitor and alert changes to the state of the affected person. For example, the end user can set an alert if someone's body temperature drops drastically.

Simulation

The prototype service has been tested with various real life earthquakes. As part of the testing process the earthquakes is verified through EMSC seismic data provider's website. Figure 4 presents the end user web interface showing real data on October 2nd, 2010. The primary view has three frames built within Flash runtime. The left is the filter frame, which allows users to select the quake based on parameters. The right frame is derived from the dynamic RSS seismic feed. The right frame is dynamically refreshed with RSS updates. The earthquakes are categorised into different

magnitude ranges and are represented with different colours. Any earthquake more than 5 on the Richter scale is marked in red and is shown shaded red on the grid view. The size of the marker and rollover view are also an indication of the magnitude of the quake. The prototype also utilizes the Pan and Zoom functionalities from Google Maps. The earthquake view is equipped with a satellite map, which can be zoomed to visualize the area of human habitations, townships, offices, industrial areas etc.

We used a number of simulations to test the service functionality. The simulation experiment that it is presented here involves the:

- Creation of an arbitrary earthquake by selecting an epicentre and magnitude.
- Selection of an arbitrary depth of the earthquake epicenter.
- Set of a population pattern within the affected area.

In turn, the simulation will randomly make arbitrary state-changes of the victims. The simulation is performed by dragging and dropping a marker at a particular location. Figure 5 shows the simulation experiment illustrating magnitude scale, epicentre,

Figure 4. The data mashup service web interface

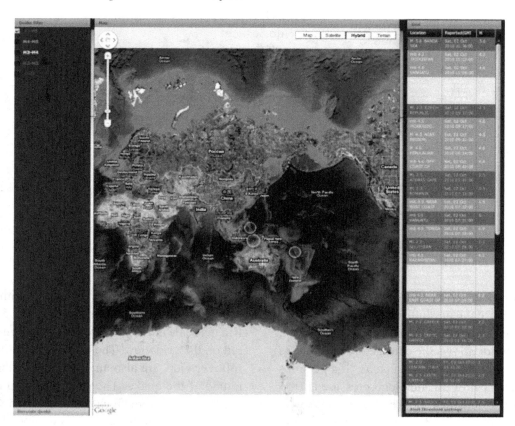

Figure 5. A random simulation experiment

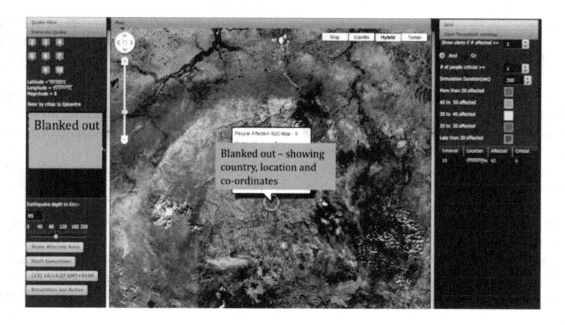

country, town and geographical co-ordinates. The zoom in function allows an end user to view the exact positioning and health state of victims. In this specific simulation experiment, sixty two affected people have been found, of which six have been found to be in a critical condition. That is to say, these six people require urgent attention and therefore an emergency manager can now utilize rescue team resource requirements from a previously speculative planning to an actual management for and of the victims' population. This is shown in Figure 6. The expectation here is that in an occupational hazard situation where all rescue teams who have wearable sensors installed on them and have been injured during a rescue operation can now identified, located and rescued appropriately.

CONCLUSION

In this experimental article, we have presented the implementation of data mashup service, which integrates data from various sources including wireless sensors with a view to identify and display the exact positioning and state of health of people affected by a disaster such as an earthquake. The data mashup provides the functionality to cluster victims in groups of various priority levels (high – medium – low), which in turn enables emergency managers to identify the location where maximum assistance is required.

Our future steps include the production of a technology-driven roadmap that clearly demonstrates the technical challenges and opportunities in making a realistic and feasible research agenda within the emergency management sector.

Figure 6. Displaying population density and clusters of victims in groups of priority levels (high–medium–low)

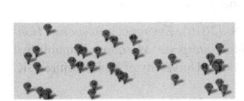

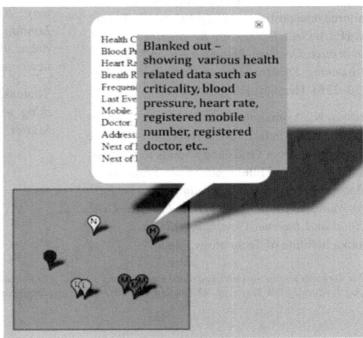

REFERENCES

Asimakopoulou, E., Anumba, C. J., Bouchlaghem, D., & Sagun, A. (2006, August). *Use of ICT during the response phase in emergency management in Greece and the United Kingdom*. Paper presented at the International Disaster Reduction Conference (IDRC), Davos, Switzerland.

Asimakopoulou, E., & Bessis, N. (Eds.). (2010a). *Advanced ICTs for Disaster Management and Threat Detection: Collaborative and Distributed Frameworks*. Hershey, PA: IGI Publishing.

Asimakopoulou, E., Bessis, N., Varakanti, R., & Norrington, P. (2010b). A Personalised Forest Fire Evacuation Data Grid Push Service – The FFED-GPS Approach. In Asimakopoulou, E., & Bessis, N. (Eds.), *Advanced ICTs for Disaster Management and Threat Detection: Collaborative and Distributed Frameworks* (pp. 279–295). Hershey, PA: IGI Global.

Bessis, N. (2009). Model architecture for a user tailored data push service in data grids. In Bessis, N. (Ed.), *Grid Technology for Maximizing Collaborative Decision Management and Support: Advancing Effective Virtual Organizations* (pp. 236–256). Hershey, PA: IGI Global.

Bessis, N., Asimakopoulou, E., French, T., Norrington, P., & Xhafa, F. (2010, November 4-6). The Big Picture, from Grids and Clouds to Crowds: A Computational Intelligence Case Proposal for Managing Disasters. *Proceedings of the Fifth International Conference on P2P, Parallel, Grid, Cloud and Internet Computing (3PGCIC)*, Fukuoka Institute of Technology, Japan.

European Mediterranean Seismological Centre. (2010). Retrieved from http://www.emsc-csem. org/#2

Graves, R. J. (2004, May). *Key technologies for emergency response*. Paper presented at the International Community on Information Systems for Crisis Response (ICSCRAM2004) conference, Brussels, Belgium.

ICL. (2009). *Digital 'plaster' for monitoring vital signs undergoes first clinical trials. News release. Imperial College London, Faculty of Medicine*. Retrieved from http://www1.imperial. ac.uk/medicine/news/20091102_di

Otten, J., Heijningen, B., & Lafortune, J. F. (2004, May). *The virtual crisis management centre. An ICT implementation to canalise information*. Paper presented at the International Community on Information Systems for Crisis Response Management (ISCRAM2004), Brussels, Belgium.

Smith, C. (2007). *A little plaster goes a long way. News and Events, Imperial College London*. Retrieved from http://www3.imperial.ac.uk/newsandeventspggrp/imperialcollege/newssummary/news_11-12-2007-9-27-28

Thomas, S. (2010). *Emergency Response Handling using Enterprise Mashups*. Unpublished Master's thesis, University of Bedfordshire, UK.

This work was previously published in the International Journal of Distributed Systems and Technologies (IJDST), Volume 2, Issue 1, edited by Nik Bessis, pp. 43-53, copyright 2011 by IGI Publishing (an imprint of IGI Global).

Compilation of References

Abawajy, J. H. (2004). Fault-tolerant scheduling policy for grid computing systems. In *Proceedings of the Eighteenth International Parallel and Distributed Processing Symposium* (p. 238).

Abdelzaher, T. F., Atkins, E. M., & Shin, K. G. (2000). QoS negotiation in real-time systems & its application to automated flight control. *IEEE Transactions on Computers, 49*(11), 1170–1183. doi:10.1109/12.895935

Abdelzaher, T. F., & Shin, K. G. (1999). Combined task & message scheduling in distributed real-time systems. *IEEE Transactions on Parallel and Distributed Systems, 10*(11), 1179–1191. doi:10.1109/71.809575

Acharya, A., & Badrinath, B. R. (1994). Checkpointing Distributed Applications on Mobile Computers. In *Proceedings of the 3rd International Conference on Parallel and Distributed Information Systems* (pp. 73-80).

Acharya, M. (2005, January). Amateur Radio. A potential tool in emergency operations. *i4d Magazine, 3*(1). Retrieved May 20, 2010, from http://www.i4donline.net/jan05/amateur.asp

Ahmed, Q., & Vrbsky, S. (1998). Maintaining security in firm real-time database systems. In *Proceedings of 14th Annual Computer Security Applications Conference*, Phoenix, AZ (pp. 83-90).

Aho, A. V., Sagiv, Y., & Ullman, J. D. (1979). Efficient optimization of a class of relational expressions. *ACM Transactions on Database Systems, 4*(4), 435–454. doi:10.1145/320107.320112doi:10.1145/320107.320112

Akan, Ö. B., & Akyildiz, I. F. (2005). Event-to-sink reliable transport in wireless sensor networks. *IEEE/ACM Transactions on Networking, 13*(5), 1003–1016. doi:10.1109/TNET.2005.857076

Akyildiz, I. F., & Kasimoglu, I. H. (2004). Wireless sensor and actor networks: Research challenges. *Ad Hoc Networks Journal, 2*(4), 351–367. doi:10.1016/j.adhoc.2004.04.003

Aldred, L., Aalst, W. d., Dumas, M., & Hofstede, A. t. (2006). *Understanding the challenges in getting together: The semantics of decoupling in middleware.* Retrieved from http://bpmcenter.org/wp-content/uploads/reports/2006/BPM-06-19.pdf

Aldunce, P., & Leon, A. (2007). Opportunities for improving disaster management in Chile: a case study. *Disaster Prevention and Management, 16*(1), 33–41. doi:10.1108/09653560710729794

Alessio, M., & Vicuña, J. (2003). *Reestablecimiento de la normalidad a través de la gerencia de la logística de catástrofes de origen natural. Trabajo especial de grado.* Venezuela: Universidad Metropolitana.

Al-Karaki, J. N., & Kamal, A. E. (2004). Routing techniques in wireless sensor networks: A survey. *IEEE Wireless Communication, 11*(6), 6–28. doi:10.1109/MWC.2004.1368893

Allen, D. (2003). *Getting things done: The art of stress-free productivity.* Harlow, UK: Penguin.

Allen, G. W., Lorincz, K., Marcillo, O., Johnson, J., Ruiz, M., & Lees, J. (2006). Deploying a wireless sensor network on an active volcano. *IEEE Internet Computing, 10*(2), 18–25. doi:10.1109/MIC.2006.26

Amini, L., & Jain, N. Sehgal, A. Silber, J., & Verscheure, O. (2006). Adaptive control of extreme-scale stream processing systems. In *Proceedings of the 26th IEEE International Conference on Distributed Computing Systems* (p. 71).

Ammar, R., & Alhamdan, A. (2002). Scheduling real time parallel structure on cluster computing. In *Proceedings of the 7ᵗʰ IEEE Symposium on Computers & Communications*, Taormina-Giardini Naxos, Italy, (pp. 69-74).

Andersen, R., & Mørch, A. I. (2009). Mutual development: A case study in customer-initiated software product development. In V. Pipek, M. B. Rosson, B. Ruyter, & V. Wulf (Eds.), *Proceedings of the Second International Symposium on End-User-Development* (LNCS 5435, pp. 31-49).

Anderson, C. (2006). *The long tail: Why the future of business is selling less of more*. New York, NY: Hyperion.

Antoshenkov, G., & Ziauddin, M. (1996). Query processing and optimization in Oracle RDB. *The Very Large Databases Journal*, 5(4), 229–237. doi:10.1007/s007780050026doi:10.1007/s007780050026

Apache Software Foundation. (2010). *About Apache XML-RPC*. Retrieved from http://ws.apache.org/xmlrpc/

Araujo, A. F. R., & Barreto, G. A. (2004). Identification and control of dynamical systems using the self-organizing map. *IEEE TNN on Temporal Coding*, 1244-1259.

Ardissono, L., Bosio, G., Goy, A., & Petrone, G. (2009). Context-aware notification management in an integrated collaborative environment. In *Proceedings of the International Workshop on Adaptation and Personalization for Web 2.0* (pp. 21-30).

Ardissono, L., Bosio, G., Goy, A., Petrone, G., & Segnan, M. (2009). Managing context-dependent workspace awareness in an e-collaboration environment. In *Proceedings of the International Workshop on Intelligent Web Interaction*, New York, NY (pp. 42-45). Washington, DC: IEEE Computer Society.

Ardissono, L., Bosio, G., Goy, A., Petrone, G., & Segnan, M. (2010). Open, collaborative task management in Web 2.0. In *Proceedings of the IADIS Multi Conference on Computer Science and Information Systems* (pp. 20-27).

Ardissono, L., Goy, A., Petrone, G., & Segnan, M. (2009). From service clouds to user-centric personal clouds. In *Proceedings of the International Conference on Cloud Computing*, Bangalore, India (pp. 1-8). Washington, DC: IEEE Computer Society.

Armstrong, R., Hensgen, D., & Kidd, T. (1998). The relative performance of various mapping algorithms is independent of sizable variances in run-time predictions. In *Proceedings of the 7ᵗʰ IEEE Heterogeneous Computing Workshop*, Orlando, FL (pp. 79-87).

Asimakopoulou, E., Anumba, C. J., Bouchlaghem, D., & Sagun, A. (2006, August). *Use of ICT during the response phase in emergency management in Greece and the United Kingdom*. Paper presented at the International Disaster Reduction Conference (IDRC), Davos, Switzerland.

Asimakopoulou, E., & Bessis, N. (Eds.). (2010). *Advanced ICTs for Disaster Management and Threat Detection: Collaborative and Distributed Frameworks*. Hershey, PA: IGI Publishing.

Asimakopoulou, E., Bessis, N., Varakanti, R., & Norrington, P. (2010). A Personalised Forest Fire Evacuation Data Grid Push Service – The FFED-GPS Approach. In Asimakopoulou, E., & Bessis, N. (Eds.), *Advanced ICTs for Disaster Management and Threat Detection: Collaborative and Distributed Frameworks* (pp. 279–295). Hershey, PA: IGI Global.

Avnur, R., & Hellerstein, J. M. (2000). Eddies: Continuously adaptive query processing. In *Proceedings of the 19th International Conference on Management of Data* (pp. 261-272).

Awasthi, L. K., & Kumar, P. (2007). A Synchronous Checkpointing Protocol for Mobile Distributed Systems: Probabilistic Approach. *International Journal of Information and Computer Security*, 1(3), 298–314. doi:10.1504/IJICS.2007.013957

Babu, S., Bizarro, P., & DeWitt, D. J. (2005). Proactive re-optimization. In *Proceedings of the 24th International Conference on Management of Data* (pp. 107-118).

Babu, S., Motwani, R., Munagala, K., Nishizawa, I., & Widom, J. (2004). Adaptive ordering of pipelined stream filters. In *Proceedings of the 23rd International Conference on Management of Data* (pp. 407-418).

Babu, S., Munagala, K., Widom, J., & Motwani, R. (2005). Adaptive caching for continuous queries. In *Proceedings of the 21st International Conference on Data Engineering* (pp. 118-129).

Bailey, B., Konstan, J., & Carlis, J. (2001). The effects of interruptions on task performance, annoyance, and anxiety in the user interface. In *Proceedings of the Conference on Human Computer Interaction*, Tokyo, Japan (pp. 593-601).

Baker, P., Zhen, R. D., Gabrowksi, J., & Oystein, H. (2008). *Model-driven testing: Using the UML testing profile*. New York, NY: Springer.

Banipal, K. (2006). Strategic approach to disaster management: lessons learned from Hurricane Katrina. *Disaster Prevention and Management, 15*(3), 484–494. doi:10.1108/09653560610669945

Bannon, L. J., & Schmidt, K. (1989, September 13-15). CSCW: Four characters in search of a context. In *Proceedings of the First European Conference on Computer-Supported Cooperative Work*, Gatwick, UK (pp. 358-372).

Barbosa, S. D. J., de Souza, C. S., & Prates, R. O. (2001). A semiotic engineering approach to HCI. In *Proceedings of Extended Abstracts on Human Factors in Computing, Seattle, WA* (pp. 55–56). New York, NY: ACM Press.

Barricelli, B. R., Iacob, C., & Zhu, L. (2009). Map-based wikis as contextual and cultural mediators. In *Proceedings of the Community Practices and Locative Media Workshop at MobileHCI*.

Barricelli, B. R., Iacob, C., & Zhu, L. (2010). BANCO web architecture to support global collaborative interaction design. In *Proceedings of the 9ᵗʰ International Workshop on Internationalization of Products and Systems* (pp. 159-162).

Barricelli, B. R., Marcante, A., Mussio, P., Parasiliti Provenza, L., Valtolina, S., & Fresta, G. (2009). BANCO: A web architecture supporting unwitting end-user development. *Interaction Design & Architecture(s). Design for the Future Experience, 5-6*, 23–30.

Baucells, M., & Sarin, R. (2003). Group decisions with multiple criteria. *Management Science, 49*(8), 1105–1118. doi:10.1287/mnsc.49.8.1105.16400

Beer, S. (1994). *The heart of enterprise*. Chichester, UK: Wiley.

Bengtsson, M., & Kock, S. (1999). Cooperation and competition in relationships between competitors in business networks. *Journal of Business and Industrial Marketing, 14*(3), 178–193. doi:10.1108/08858629910272184

Ben-Mena, S. (2000). Introduction aux méthodes multicritères d'aide à la decision. *Biotechnol. Agron. Soc. Environ., 4*(2), 83–93.

Bertier, M., Marin, O., & Sens, P. (2002). Implementation and performance evaluation of an adaptable failure detector. In *Proceedings of the International Conference on Dependable Systems and Networks*, Edinburgh, Scotland (pp. 354-363).

Bertogna, M., Cirinei, M., & Lipari, G. (2009). Schedulability analysis of global scheduling algorithms on multiprocessor platforms. *IEEE Transactions on Parallel and Distributed Systems, 20*(4), 553–566. doi:10.1109/TPDS.2008.129

Bessis, N., Asimakopoulou, E., French, T., Norrington, P., & Xhafa, F. (2010, November 4-6). The Big Picture, from Grids and Clouds to Crowds: A Data Collective Computational Intelligence Case Proposal for Managing Disasters. In *Proceedings of the Fifth International Conference on P2P, Parallel, Grid, Cloud and Internet Computing (3PGCIC)*, Fukuoka Institute of Technology, Fukuoka, Japan.

Bessis, N. (2009). *Grid technology for maximizing collaborative decision management and support: Advancing effective virtual organizations*. Hersey, PA: IGI Global. doi:10.4018/978-1-60566-364-7

Bessis, N. (2009). Model architecture for a user tailored data push service in data grids. In Bessis, N. (Ed.), *Grid Technology for Maximizing Collaborative Decision Management and Support: Advancing Effective Virtual Organizations* (pp. 236–256). Hershey, PA: IGI Global.

Bestavros, A. (1997). A methodology for scheduling real time tasks in a distributed system. In *Proceedings of the 17ᵗʰ International Conference on Distributed Computing Systems*, Baltimore, MD (p. 449).

Biffl, S., Mordinyi, R., Moser, T., & Wahyudin, D. (2008). Ontology-supported quality assurance for component-based systems configuration. In *Proceedings of the 6th International Workshop on Software Quality*, Leipzig, Germany (pp. 59-64).

Biffl, S., Moser, T., & Sunindyo, W. D. (2009). Bridging semantic gaps between stakeholders in the production automation domain with ontology areas. In *Proceedings of the 21st International Conference on Software Engineering and Knowledge Engineering*, Boston, MA (pp. 233-239).

Biffl, S., Schatten, A., & Zoitl, A. (2009). Integration of heterogeneous engineering environments for the automation systems lifecycle. In *Proceedings of the IEEE Industrial Informatics Conference* (pp. 576-581). Washington, DC: IEEE Computer Society.

Billa, L., Mansor, S., & Mahmud, A. R. (2004). Spatial information technology in flood early warning systems: an overview of theory, application and latest developments in Malaysia. *Disaster Prevention and Management, 13*(5), 356–363. doi:10.1108/09653560410568471

Birman, K. P., & Van Renesse, R. (1994). *Reliable distributed computing with the Isis toolkit (systems)*. New York, NY: John Wiley & Sons.

Bisseling, R. (2004). *Parallel scientific computation: A structured approach using BSP and MPI*. New York, NY: Oxford University Press.

Biswas, S., & Neogy, S. (2010). A Mobility-Based Checkpointing Protocol for Mobile Computing System. *International Journal of Computer Science & Information Technology, 2*(1), 135–151.

Borchers, J. (2001). *A pattern approach to interaction design*. Hoboken, NJ: John Wiley & Sons.

Borysiewicz, M., Potempski, S., & Galkowski, A. (2001). Computer network based decision support system for emergency response in case of chemical accidents. In *Proceedings of the international Conference on Emergency Managements (TIEMS 2001)*, Oslo, Norway.

Bourguin, G., Derycke, A., & Tarby, J. C. (2001). Beyond the interface: Co-evolution inside interactive systems – A proposal founded on activity theory. In *Proceedings of the IHM-HCI Conference on People and Computers* (pp. 297-310).

Braha, D., & Bar-Yam, Y. (2004). Information flow structure in large-scale product development organizational networks. *Journal of Information Technology, 19*(4), 244–253. doi:10.1057/palgrave.jit.2000030

Branham, S., Golovchinsky, G., Carter, S., & Biehl, H. T. (2010). Let's go from the whiteboard: Supporting transitions in work through whiteboard capture and reuse. In *Proceedings of the 28th International Conference on Human Factors in Computing* (pp. 75-84). New York, NY: ACM Press.

Brown, J. S., & Duguid, P. (2000). *The social life of information*. Boston, MA: Harvard Business School Press.

Brunn, S. D. (1995). Geography's research performance based on Annals manuscripts, 1987-1993. *The Professional Geographer, 47*(2), 204–215. doi:10.1111/j.0033-0124.1995.00204.x

Bruns, A. (2008). *Blogs, Wikipedia, Second Life, and Beyond: From production to produsage*. New York, NY: Peter Lang.

Burnett, G. (2000). Information exchange in virtual communities. *Information Research, 5*(4), 82.

Cai, M., Frank, M., Chen, J., & Szekely, P. (2003). MAAN: A multi-attribute addressable network for grid information services. In *Proceedings of the Fourth International Workshop on Grid Computing* (pp. 184-191). Washington, DC: IEEE Computer Society.

Camarinha-Matos, L. M., & Afsarmanesh, H. (2005). Collaborative networks: A new scientific discipline. *Journal of Intelligent Manufacturing, 16*, 439–452. doi:10.1007/s10845-005-1656-3

Cao, G., & Singhal, M. (1998). On the Impossibility of Min-process Non-blocking Checkpointing and an Efficient Checkpointing Algorithm for Mobile Computing Systems. In *Proceedings of the International Conference on Parallel Processing* (pp. 37-44).

Cao, G., & Singhal, M. (2001). Mutable Checkpoints: A New Checkpointing Approach for Mobile Computing systems. *IEEE Transactions on Parallel and Distributed Systems, 12*(2), 157–172. doi:10.1109/71.910871

Carrara, P., Fresta, G., & Rampini, A. (2000). Interfaces for geographic applications on the World Wide Web: An adaptive computational hypermedia. In *Proceedings of the 6th ERCIM Workshop on User Interfaces* (pp. 341-342).

Carroll, J., Neale, D., Isenhour, P., Rosson, M., & Scott McCrickard, D. (2003). Notification and awareness: Synchronizing task-oriented collaborative activity. *International Journal of Human-Computer Studies*, *58*(5), 605–632. doi:10.1016/S1071-5819(03)00024-7

Ceri, S., & Pelagatti, G. (1984). *Distributed databases: Principles and systems*. New York, NY: McGraw-Hill.

Chandra, T. D., & Toueg, S. (1996). Unreliable failure detectors for reliable distributed systems. *Journal of the ACM*, *43*(2), 225–267. doi:10.1145/226643.226647

Chandy, K. M., & Lamport, L. (1985). Distributed Snapshots: Determining Global State of Distributed Systems. *ACM Transactions on Computer Systems*, *3*(1), 63–75. doi:10.1145/214451.214456

Cheema, A. S., Muhammad, M., & Gupta, I. (2005). Peer-to-peer discovery of computational resources for grid applications. In *Proceedings of the 6th International Workshop on Grid Computing* (pp. 179-185). Washington, DC: IEEE Computer Society.

Chen, W., Toueg, S., & Aguilera, M. K. (2002). On the quality of service failure detectors. *IEEE Transactions on Computers*, *51*(2), 13–32. doi:10.1109/12.980014

Chen, Y. (2004). Bounds on the reliability of distributed systems with unreliable nodes and links. *IEEE Transactions on Reliability*, *53*(2), 205–215. doi:10.1109/TR.2004.829152

Chen, Y. S., Chang, L. P., Kuo, T. W., & Mok, A. K. (2009). An anomaly prevention approach for real-time task scheduling. *Journal of Systems and Software*, *82*(1), 144–154. doi:10.1016/j.jss.2008.07.038

Chhabra, A., Singh, G., Waraich, S. S., Sidhu, B., & Kumar, G. (2006). Qualitative parametric comparison of load balancing algorithms in parallel & distributed computing environment. *World Academy of Science, Engineering & Technology*, 16.

Chillarege, R., Biyani, S., & Rosenthal, J. (1995). Measurement of failure rate in widely distributed software. In *Proceedings of the 25th International Symposium on Fault-Tolerant Computing* (p. 424).

Chiu, C., Hsu, C., Yeh, Y.-S., & Yi, S. (2006). A genetic algorithm for reliability oriented task assignment with k duplications in distributed systems. *IEEE Transactions on Reliability*, *55*(1), 105–117. doi:10.1109/TR.2005.863797

Cirstoiu, C. C., Grigoras, C. C., Betev, L. L., Costan, A. A., & Legrand, I. C. (2007, June 25). Monitoring, accounting and automated decision support for the Alice experiment based on the MonALISA framework. In *Proceedings of the Workshop on Grid Monitoring*, Monterey, CA (pp. 39-44). New York, NY: ACM Press.

Claypool, K. T., & Claypool, M. (2008). Teddies: Trained eddies for reactive stream processing. In *Proceedings of the 11st International Conference on Database Systems for Advanced Applications* (pp. 220-234).

Clothier, J. (2005). *Dutch trial SMS disaster alert system. CNN*. Retrieved June 6, 2010, from http://edition.cnn.com/2005/TECH/11/09/dutch.disaster.warning/index.html

Coco, S., Laudani, A., & Pollicino, G. (2009, March). Grid-based prediction of electromagnetic fields in urban environment. *IEEE Transactions on Magnetics*, *45*, 1060–1063. doi:10.1109/TMAG.2009.2012577

Cohen, U. (2004). *Inside GigaSpaces XAP - Technical overview and value proposition*. New York, NY: GigaSpace Technologies Ltd.

Coile, R. C. (1997). The role of amateur radio in providing emergency electronic communication for disaster management. *Disaster Prevention and Management*, *6*(3), 176–185. doi:10.1108/09653569710172946

Cole, R. L., & Graefe, G. (1994). Optimization of dynamic query evaluation plans. In *Proceedings of the 13rd International Conference on Management of Data* (pp. 150-160).

Connelly, K., & Chien, A. A. (2002). Breaking the barriers: High performance security for high-performance computing. In *Proceedings of the 10th New Security Paradigms Workshop*, Virginia Beach, VA (pp. 36-42).

Cooper, C. (1993). A note on the connectivity of 2-regular digraphs. *Random Structures and Algorithms*, *4*(4), 469–472. doi:10.1002/rsa.3240040406

Cormode, G., Muthukrishnan, S., & Zhuang, W. (2006). What's different: Distributed, continuous monitoring of duplicate-resilient aggregates on data streams. In *Proceedings of the 22nd International Conference on Data Engineering* (p. 57).

Corneli, J. (2010, July 7-9). GravPad. In *Proceedings of the 6th International Symposium on Wikis and Open Collaboration*, Gdansk, Poland.

Costabile, M. F., Mussio, P., Provenza, L. P., & Piccinno, A. (2008). Advanced visual systems supporting unwitting EUD. In *Proceedings of the Working Conference on Advanced Visual Interfaces* (pp. 313-316). New York, NY: ACM Press.

Costabile, M. F., Fogli, D., Mussio, P., & Piccinno, A. (2006). End-user development: The software shaping workshop approach. In Lieberman, H., Paternò, F., & Wulf, V. (Eds.), *End user development* (pp. 183–205). Dordrecht, The Netherlands: Springer-Verlag. doi:10.1007/1-4020-5386-X_9

Costabile, M. F., Fogli, D., Mussio, P., & Piccinno, A. (2007). Visual interactive systems for end-user development: A model-based design methodology. *IEEE Transactions on Systems, Man, and Cybernetics. Part A, Systems and Humans*, *37*(6), 1029–1046. doi:10.1109/TSMCA.2007.904776

Costan, A., Dobre, C., Pop, F., Leordeanu, C., & Cristea, V. (2010). A fault tolerance approach for distributed systems using monitoring based replication. In *Proceedings of the 6th IEEE International Conference on Intelligent Computer Communication and Processing*, Cluj-Napoca, Romania (pp. 451-458).

Cristea, V., Dobre, C., Pop, F., Stratan, C., Costan, A., & Leordeanu, C. (in press). A dependability layer for large scale distributed systems. *International Journal of Grid and Utility Computing*.

Crossbow Technology, Inc. (n. d.). *The smart sensors company.* Retrieved from http://www.xbow.com/

Cutter, S. L. (2003). GI Science, Disasters, and Emergency Management. *Transactions in GIS*, *7*(4), 439–445. doi:10.1111/1467-9671.00157

Czajkowski, G. K., Fitzgerald, S., Foster, I., & Kesselman, C. (2001). Grid information services for distributed resource sharing. In *Proceedings of the 10th IEEE Symposium on High Performance Distributed Computing* (pp. 181-194). Washington, DC: IEEE Computer Society.

Czerwinski, M., Horvitz, E., & Wilhite, S. (2004). A diary study of task switching and interruptions. In *Proceedings of the Conference on Human Factors in Computing Systems*, Vienna, Austria (pp. 175-182).

Dabrowski, C. (2009). Reliability in grid computing systems. *Concurrency and Computation*, *21*(8), 927–959. doi:10.1002/cpe.1410

Dandamudi, S. (1995). Performance impact of scheduling discipline on adaptive load sharing in homogeneous distributed systems. In *Proceedings of the 15th International Conference on Distributed Computing Systems*, Vancouver, BC, Canada (pp. 484-492).

Das, A., Ganguly, S., Garofalakis, M. N., & Rastogi, R. (2004). Distributed set expression cardinality estimation. In *Proceedings of the 30th International Conference on Very Large Data Bases* (p. 312).

Data Grid. (2002). *EU DataGrid WP6: VOMS vs. EDG security requirements.* Retrieved from http://marianne.in2p3.fr/

Data, A. K., & Ghosh, S. (1990). Deadlock detection in distributed systems. In *Proceedings of the 9th Annual International Phoenix Conference on Computers & Communications*, Scottsdale, AZ (pp. 131-136).

Davidow, W. H., & Malone, M. S. (1992). *The virtual corporation: Structuring and revitalizing the corporation for the 21st century.* New York, NY: Harper Business.

De Marco, G., Yang, T., & Barolli, L. (2006). Impact of radio irregularities on topology tradeoffs of WSNs. In *Proceedings of the NBiS/DEXA Conference*, Krakow, Poland (pp. 50-54).

De Roure, D., Jennings, N. R., & Shadbolt, N. R. (2005). The semantic grid: Past, present and future. *Proceedings of the IEEE*, *93*(3), 669–681. doi:10.1109/JPROC.2004.842781

De Silva, F. N. (2001). Providing spatial decision support for evacuation planning: a challenge in integrating Technologies. *Disaster Prevention and Management, 10*(1), 11–20. doi:10.1108/09653560110381787

De Silva, F. N., & Eglese, R. W. (2000). Integrating simulation modelling and GIS: spatial decision support systems for evacuation planning. *The Journal of the Operational Research Society, 51*(4), 423–430.

Defago, X., Hayashibara, N., & Katayama, T. (2003). On the design of a failure detection service for large-scale distributed systems. In *Proceedings of the International Symposium on Towards Peta-bit Ultra Networks*, Ishikawa, Japan (pp. 88-95).

Degli-Esposti, V., Fuschini, F., Vitucci, E., & Falciasecca, G. (2009). Speed-up techniques for ray tracing field prediction models. *IEEE Transactions on Antennas and Propagation, 57*, 1469–1480. doi:10.1109/TAP.2009.2016696

Dekeyser, S., & Hidders, J. (2009). *A notion of serializability for document editing and corresponding optimal locking protocols.* Retrieved from http://www.st.ewi.tudelft.nl/~hidders/docs/piecemeal-tr.pdf

Dekeyser, S., & Hidders, J. (2010). Piecemeal: A formal collaborative editing technique guaranteeing correctness. In *Proceedings of the IADIS International Conference on Collaborative Technologies*, Freiburg, Germany (pp. 125-131).

Dekeyser, S., Hidders, J., & Paredaens, J. (2004). A transaction model for XML databases. *World Wide Web Journal, 7*(1), 29–57. doi:10.1023/B:WWWJ.0000015864.75561.98

Deng, S. C. Y., Attie, P., & Sun, W. (1996). Optimal deadlock detection in distributed systems based on locally constructed wait-for graphs. In *Proceedings of the 16th International Conference on Distributed Computing Systems* (pp. 613-619).

Dertouzos, M. L., & Mok, A. K. (1989). Multi-processor online scheduling of hard real-time tasks. *IEEE Transactions on Software Engineering, 15*(12), 1497–1506. doi:10.1109/32.58762

Deshpande, A., & Hellerstein, J. M. (2004). Lifting the burden of history from adaptive query processing. In *Proceedings of the 30th International Conference on Very Large Data Bases* (pp. 948-959).

Dey, A. K., & Newberger, A. (2009, April 4-9). Support for context-aware intelligibility and control. In *Proceedings of the Conference on Human Factors in Computing Systems*, Boston, MA (pp. 859-868). New York, NY: ACM Press.

Di Stefano, A., Lo Bello, L., & Tramontana, E. (1999). Factors affecting the design of load balancing algorithms in distributed systems. *Journal of Systems and Software, 48*(2), 105–117. doi:10.1016/S0164-1212(99)00050-3

Dikaiakos, M. D., Pallis, G., Katsaros, D., Mehra, P., & Vakali, A. (2009). Cloud computing: Distributed internet computing for IT and scientific research. *IEEE Internet Computing, 13*(5), 10–13. doi:10.1109/MIC.2009.103

Dinda, P. A., & O'Hallaron, D. R. (1999, August 3-6). An evaluation of linear models for host load prediction. In *Proceedings of the 8th IEEE International Symposium on High Performance Distributed Computing* (p. 10). Washington, DC: IEEE Computer Society.

Dobber, M., Mei, R. V., & Koole, G. (2009). Dynamic load balancing & job replication in a global-scale grid environment: A comparison. *IEEE Transactions on Parallel and Distributed Systems, 20*(2), 207–218. doi:10.1109/TPDS.2008.61

Dobre, C., Pop, F., Costan, A., Andreica, M. I., & Cristea, V. (2009). Robust failure detection architecture for large scale distributed systems. In *Proceedings of the 17th International Conference on Control Systems and Computer Science*, Bucharest, Romania.

Dobre, C., Voicu, R., Muraru, A., & Legrand, I. C. (2007). A distributed agent based system to control and coordinate large scale data transfers. *In Proceedings of the International Conference on Control Systems and Computer Science*, Bucharest, Romania.

Dunnette, R. (2006). Radio and TV Broadcasting for Disaster Relief and Public Warning. In *Proceedings of the Pacific Telecommunications Council '06.* Retrieved May 10, 2010, from http://www.ptc06.org/program/public/proceedings/Roxana%20Dunnette_paper_t151%-20(formatted).pdf

Ehrgott, M., & Gandibleux, X. (Eds.). (2002). *Multiple criteria Optimization: State of the art annotated bibliographic surveys*. Dordrecht, The Netherlands: Kluwer Academic Publishers.

El Samad, M., Hameurlain, A., & Morvan, F. (2008). Resource discovery and selection for large scale query optimization in grid environment. In Sobh, T. (Ed.), *Advances in computer and information sciences and engineering* (pp. 279–283). Berlin, Germany: Springer-Verlag. doi:10.1007/978-1-4020-8741-7_51

Ellis, C., & Gibbs, S. (1989). Concurrency control in groupware systems. In *Proceedings of the ACM SIGMOD Conference on Management of Data*, Seattle, WA (pp. 399-407).

Elnozahy, E. N., Johnson, D. B., & Zwaenepoel, W. (1992). The Performance of Consistent Checkpointing. In *Proceedings of the 11th Symposium on Reliable Distributed Systems* (pp. 39-47).

Elnozahy, E. N., Alvisi, L., Wang, Y. M., & Johnson, D. B. (2002). A Survey of Rollback-Recovery Protocols in Message-Passing Systems. *ACM Computing Surveys*, *34*(3), 375–408. doi:10.1145/568522.568525

Engelbart, D. C. (1995). Toward augmenting the human intellect and boosting our collective IQ. *Communications of the ACM*, *38*(8), 30–32. doi:10.1145/208344.208352

Erickson, J. S., Spence, S., Rhodes, M., Banks, D., Rutherford, J., & Simpson, E. (2009). Content-centered collaboration spaces in the Cloud. *IEEE Internet Computing*, 34–42. doi:10.1109/MIC.2009.93

Esselink, B. (2000). *A practical guide to localization*. Philadelphia, PA: John Benjamins Publishing.

European Mediterranean Seismological Centre. (2010). Retrieved from http://www.emsc-csem.org/#2

Fahlman, S. E., & Lebiere, C. (1990). The cascade-correlation learning architecture. In Touretzky, D. S. (Ed.), *Advances in neural information processing systems 2* (pp. 524–532). San Francisco, CA: Morgan Kaufmann.

Fedra, K., & Reitsma, R. F. (1990). *Decision support and Geographical Information Systems. Geographical information systems for urban and regional planning* (Tech. Rep. No. RR-90-009). Laxenburg, Austria: ACA, International Institute for Applied Systems Analysis (IIASA).

Fenton, N., & Neil, M. (1999). A critique of software defect prediction models. *IEEE Transactions on Software Engineering*, *25*, 15. doi:10.1109/32.815326

Fetzer, C., Raynal, M., & Tronel, F. (2001). An adaptive failure detection protocol. In *Proceedings of the 8th IEEE Pacific Rim Symposium on Dependable Computing*, Seoul, Korea (pp. 146-153).

Fischer, G. (2001). Communities of interest: Learning through the interaction of multiple knowledge systems. In *Proceedings of the 12th Annual Information Systems Research Seminar* (pp. 1-14).

Fischer, G., & Ostwald, J. (2002). Seeding, evolutionary growth, and reseeding: Enriching participatory design with informed participation. In *Proceedings of the Participatory Design Conference* (pp. 135-143).

Fischer, G., McCall, R., Ostwald, J., Reeves, B., & Shipman, F. (1994). Seeding, evolutionary growth and reseeding: Supporting the incremental development of design environments. In *Proceedings of the SIGCHI Conference on Human Factors in Computing Systems: Celebrating Interdependence* (pp. 292-298). New York, NY: ACM Press.

Fischer, G. (2000). Social creativity, symmetry of ignorance and meta-design. *Knowledge-Based Systems Journal*, *13*(7-8), 527–537. doi:10.1016/S0950-7051(00)00065-4

Fischer, G., Giaccardi, E., Ye, Y., Sutcliffe, A. G., & Mehandjiev, N. (2004). Meta-design: A manifesto for end-user development. *Communications of the ACM*, *47*(9), 33–37. doi:10.1145/1015864.1015884

Fischer, M. J., Lynch, N. A., & Paterson, M. S. (1985). Impossibility of distributed consensus with one faulty process. *Journal of the ACM*, *32*(2), 374–382. doi:10.1145/3149.214121

Fisher, H. W. (1998). The role of the new information technologies in emergency mitigation, planning, response and recovery. *Disaster Prevention and management*, *7*(1), 28-37.

Fogarty, J., Hudson, S. E., Akteson, C. G., Avrahami, D., Forlizzi, J., & Kiesler, S. (2005). Predicting human interruptibility with sensors. *ACM Transactions on Computer-Human Interaction, 12*(1), 119–146. doi:10.1145/1057237.1057243

Fokidou, T., Romoudi, E., & Mavrommati, I. (2008, October 13-15). Designing GUI for the user configuration of pervasive awareness applications. In *Proceedings of the 5th IADIS International Conference Cognition and Exploratory Learning in Digital Age*, Freiburg, Germany (pp. 29-37).

Folmer, E., van Welie, M., & Bosch, J. (2005). Bridging patterns: An approach to bridge gaps between SE and HCI. *Journal of Information and Software Technology, 48*(2), 69–89. doi:10.1016/j.infsof.2005.02.005

Fortune, J., & Peters, G. (1995). *Learning from failure – the systems approach*. Chichester, UK: Wiley.

Foster, I., Jennings, N. R., & Kesselman, C. (2004, July 19-23). Brain meets brawn: Why grid and agents need each other. In *Proceedings of the Third International Joint Conference on Autonomous Agents and Multiagent Systems*, New York, NY (pp. 8-15). Washington, DC: IEEE Computer Society.

Foster, I. (2002). What is the Grid? A three point checklist. *Grid Today, 1*(6), 22.

Foster, I., & Kesselman, C. (1998). *The Grid: Blueprint for a future computing infrastructure* (pp. 1–29). San Francisco, CA: Morgan Kauffman.

Foster, I., & Kesselman, C. (2003). *The grid2, blueprint for a new computing infrastructure*. Sanfrancisco, CA: Morgan Kaufmann.

Foster, I., Kesselman, C., & Tuecke, S. (2001). The anatomy of the grid: Enabling scalable virtual organizations. *International Journal of High Performance Computing Applications, 15*(3), 200. doi:10.1177/109434200101500302

Foundation for Intelligent Physical Agents (FIPA). (n. d.). *Welcome to FIPA*. Retrieved from http://www.fipa.org

Frysinger, S. P., Deaton, M. L., Gonzalo, A. G., VanHorn, A. M., & Kirk, M. A. (2007). The FALCON decision support system: Preparing communities for weapons of opportunity. *Environmental Modelling & Software, 22*(4), 431–435. doi:10.1016/j.envsoft.2005.12.011

Gadomski, A. M., Bologna, S., Di Costanzo, G., Perini, A., & Schaerf, M. (2001). Towards intelligent decision support systems for emergency managers: the IDA approach. *Int. J. Risk Assessment and Management, 2*(3 & 4), 224–242. doi:10.1504/IJRAM.2001.001507

Gagne, M., & Shepard, T. (1991). A pre-run-time scheduling algorithm for hard real time systems. *IEEE Transactions on Software Engineering, 17*(7), 669–677. doi:10.1109/32.83903

GAMP 5. (2008). *Good automated manufacturing practice*. Tampa, FL: International Society for Pharmaceutical Engineering (ISPE).

Gao, Y., Deng, C., & Che, Y. (2008). An Adaptive Index-Based Algorithm Using Time-Coordination in Mobile Computing. In *Proceedings of the International Symposiums on Information Processing* (pp. 578-585).

Garg, R., & Kumar, P. (2010). A Nonblocking Coordinated Checkpointing Algorithm for Mobile Computing Systems. *International Journal of Computer Science issues, 7*(3).

Gedik, B., Wu, K.-L., Yu, P. S., & Liu, L. (2007). A load shedding framework and optimizations for m-way windowed stream joins. In *Proceedings of the 23rd International Conference on Data Engineering* (pp. 536-545).

Gennari, J. H., & Reddy, M. (2000). Participatory design and an eligibility screening tool. In *Proceedings of the AMIA Annual Fall Symposium* (pp. 290-294).

Giordano, S., & Rosenberg, C. (2004). Topics in ad hoc and sensor networks. *IEEE Communications Magazine, 44*(4), 97. doi:10.1109/MCOM.2006.1632655

Girgin, S., & Preux, P. (2008, December 11-13). Basis function construction in reinforcement learning using cascade-correlation learning architecture. In *Proceedings of the Seventh International Conference on Machine Learning and Applications* (pp. 75-82). Washington, DC: IEEE Computer Society.

Glassner, A. (1989). *An introduction to ray tracing*. San Francisco, CA: Morgan Kaufmann.

Golab, L., & Ozsu, M. T. (2003). Processing sliding window multi-joins in continuous queries over data streams. In *Proceedings of the 29th International Conference on Very Large Data Bases* (pp. 500-511).

Gomes-Casseres, B. (1994). Group versus group: How alliance networks compete. *Harvard Business Review*, 62–74.

González, F. I., Milburn, H. B., Bernard, E. N., & Newman, J. (1998). *Deep-ocean Assessment and Reporting of Tsunamis (DART): Brief Overview and Status Report*. Retrieved April 15, 2010, from http://nctr.pmel.noaa.gov/dart_report1998.html

Google. (2010). *Google documents*. Retrieved from http://www.google.com/google-d-s/tour1.html

Gopalan, K., & Kang, K. D. (2007). Coordinated allocation & scheduling of multiple resources in real-time operating systems. In *Proceedings of the Workshop on Operating Systems Platforms for Embedded Real-Time Applications*, Pisa, Italy.

Graves, R. J. (2004, May). *Key technologies for emergency response*. Paper presented at the International Community on Information Systems for Crisis Response (ICSCRAM2004) conference, Brussels, Belgium.

Greif, I., & Sarin, S. (1986, December 3-5). Data sharing in group work. In *Proceedings of the ACM Conference on Computer-Supported Cooperative Work*, Austin, TX (pp. 175-183). New York, NY: ACM Press.

Grimes, A., & Brush, A. J. (2008). Life scheduling to support multiple social roles. In *Proceedings of the Conference on Human Factors in Computing Systems*, Florence, Italy (pp. 821-824).

Gritzalis, S. (2004). Enhancing privacy & data protection in electronic medical environments. *Journal of Medical Systems*, *28*(6), 535–547. doi:10.1023/B:JOMS.0000044956.55209.75

Gross, T., & Marquardt, N. (2007, February 7-9). CollaborationBus: An editor for the easy configuration of ubiquitous computing environments. In *Proceedings of the Fifteenth Euromicro Conference on Parallel, Distributed, and Network-Based Processing*, Naples, Italy (pp. 307-314). Washington, DC: IEEE Computer Society.

Gross, T., Beckmann, C., & Schirmer, M. (2010, February 17-19). The PPPSpace: Innovative concepts for permanent capturing, persistent storing, and parallel processing and distributing events. In *Proceedings of the Eighteenth Euromicro Conference on Parallel, Distributed, and Network-Based Processing*, Pisa, Italy (pp. 359-366). Washington, DC: IEEE Computer Society.

Gross, T., Egla, T., & Marquardt, N. (2006). Sensation: A service-oriented platform for developing sensor-based infrastructures. *International Journal of Internet Protocol Technology*, *1*(3), 159–167.

Gross, T., & Prinz, W. (2004). Modelling shared contexts in cooperative environments: Concept, implementation, and evaluation. *Computer Supported Cooperative Work*, *13*(3-4), 283–303. doi:10.1007/s10606-004-2804-6

Gruber, T. (1995). Towards principles for the design of ontologies used for knowledge sharing. *International Journal of Human-Computer Studies*, *43*(5-6). doi:10.1006/ijhc.1995.1081

Guangmin, L. (2008). Adaptive load balancing algorithm over heterogeneous workstations. In *Proceedings of the 7th International Conference on Grid & Cooperative Computing* (pp. 169-174).

Hao, Y., Liu, J. C., & Kim, J. L. (1992). Task scheduling in hard real-time distributed systems on a bus local area network. In *Proceedings of the 11th Annual International Phoenix Conference on Computers & Communications*, Scottsdale, AZ (pp. 411-416).

Harris, J., Hirst, L. J., & Mossinghoff, M. (2008). *Combinatorics and graph theory*. New York, NY: Springer.

Haslett, C. (2008). *Essentials of radio wave propagation*. Cambridge, UK: Cambridge University Press.

Hayashibara, N., Defago, X., & Katayama, T. (2004). *Flexible failure detection with K-FD*. (Tech. Rep. No. IS-RR-2004-006). Ishikawa, Japan: Japan Advanced Institute of Science and Technology.

He, L., Jarvis, S. A., Spooner, D. P., & Nudd, G. R. (2003). Dynamic scheduling of parallel real-time jobs by modeling spare capabilities in heterogeneous clusters. In *Proceedings of the IEEE International Conference on Cluster Computing* (pp. 2-10).

Heck, E., & Vervest, P. (2007). Smart business networks: how the network wins. *Communications of the ACM, 50*(6), 28–37. doi:10.1145/1247001.1247002

Henderson, A., & Kyng, M. (1991). There's no place like home: Continuing design in use. In Greenbaum, J., & Kyng, M. (Eds.), *Design at work: Cooperative design of computer systems* (pp. 219–240). Mahwah, NJ: Lawrence Erlbaum.

Hernández, J. G., García, M. J., & Hernández, G. J. (2009). Influence of Location Management in supply chain Management. In *Proceedings of the Global Business and Technology Association (GBATA 2009)*, Prague, Czech Republic (pp. 500-507).

Hernández, J. G., & García, M. J. (2007). Investigación de operaciones y turismo en Revista de Matemática. *Teoría y Aplicaciones, 14*(2), 221–238.

Hernández, J. G., & García, M. J. (in press). Mathematical models generators of Decision Support Systems for help in case of catastrophes. An experience from Venezuela. In Asimakopoulou, E., & Bessis, N. (Eds.), *Advanced ICTs for Disaster Management and Threat Detection: Collaborative and Distributed Frameworks*. Hershey, PA: IGI Global.

Higaki, H., & Takizawa, M. (1999). Checkpoint-recovery Protocol for Reliable Mobile Systems. *Trans. of Information processing Japan, 40*(1), 236-244.

Hitt, L. M., & Brynjolfsson, E. (1996). Productivity, business profitability, and consumer surplus: Three different measures of information technology value. *Management Information Systems Quarterly, 20*(2), 121–142. doi:10.2307/249475

Hofmann-Wellenhof, B., Lichtenegger, H., & Collins, J. (2001). *Global positioning system (GPS): Theory and practice*. New York, NY: Springer.

Hohpe, G. (2006). *Conversation patterns*. Paper presented at the Dagstuhl Workshop.

Holland, C. P., & Lockett, A. G. (1998). Business trust and the formation of virtual organizations. In *Proceedings of the 31st Hawaii International Conference on System Sciences* (pp. 602-609).

Horstmann, T., & Bentley, R. (1997). Distributed authoring on the Web with the BSCW shared workspace system. *StandardView, 5*(1), 9–16. doi:10.1145/253452.253464

Hsu, P., Wu, S., & Lin, F. (2005). Disaster Management Using GIS Technology: A Case Study in Taiwan. In *Proceedings of the 26th Asia Conference on Remote Sensing*, Hanoi, Vietnam.

Huang, Y., Bessis, N., Brocco, A., Sotiriadis, S., Courant, M., Kuonen, P., et al. (2009). Towards an integrated vision across inter-cooperative grid virtual organizations. In Y.-H. Lee, T.-H. Kim, W.-C. Fang, & D. Slezak (Eds.), *Proceedings of the 1st International Conference on Future Generation Information Technology and the 2nd International Conference on Grid and Distributed Computing*, Jeju Island, Korea (LNCS 5899, pp.120-128).

Huang, Y., Bessis, N., Kuonen, P., Brocco, A., Courant, M., & Hirsbrunner, B. (2009). Using metadata snapshots for extending ant-based resource discovery functionality in inter-cooperative grid communities. In *Proceedings of the International Conference on Evolving Internet*, Cannes, France.

Huang, Y., Brocco, A., Bessis, N., Kuonen, P., & Hirsbrunner, B. (2010). Community-aware scheduling protocol for grids. In *Proceedings of the 24th IEEE International Conference on Advanced Information Networking and Applications* (pp. 334-341). Washington, DC: IEEE Computer Society.

Huda Mohammad, T., Schmidt, W. H., & Peake, I. D. (2005). An agent oriented proactive fault-tolerant framework for grid computing. In *Proceedings of the First International Conference on e-Science and Grid Computing* (pp. 304-311).

Humble, J., Crabtree, A., Hemmings, T., Akesson, K.-P., Koleva, B., Rodden, T., & Hansson, P. (2003, October 12-15). "Playing with the bits" user-configuration of ubiquitous domestic environments. In *Proceedings of the Fifth International Conference on Ubiquitous Computing*, Seattle, WA (pp. 256-263).

Iacob, C., & Zhu, L. (2010). From the problem space to the web space: A model for designing localized web systems. In *Proceedings of the 9th International Conference on WWW/Internet* (pp. 112-119).

Iannella, R., & Henricksen, K. (2007). Managing Information in the Disaster Coordination Centre: Lessons and Opportunities. In B. Van de Walle, P. Burghardt, & C. Nieuwenhuis (Eds.), *Proceedings of the 4th International ISCRAM Conference*, Delft, The Netherlands (pp. 1-11).

ICL. (2009). *Digital 'plaster' for monitoring vital signs undergoes first clinical trials. News release. Imperial College London, Faculty of Medicine*. Retrieved from http://www1.imperial.ac.uk/medicine/news/20091102_di

Imine, A., Rusinowitch, M., Oster, G., & Molli, P. (2006). Formal design and verification of operational transformation algorithms for copies convergence. *Theoretical Computer Science, 351*(2), 167–183. doi:10.1016/j.tcs.2005.09.066

Information Sciences Institute. (n. d.). *The network simulator*. Retrieved from http://www.isi.edu/nsnam/ns/

International Organization for Standardization. (1996). *ISO/IEC 14977: ISO Standard for the EBNF*. Retrieved from http://www.iso.org/iso/iso_catalogue/catalogue_tc/catalogue_detail.htm?csnumber=26153

International Strategy for Disaster Reduction (ISDR). (2004). *Living with risk: A global review of disaster reduction initiatives*. Geneva, Switzerland: United Nations.

Introne, J., & Alterman, R. (2006). Using shared representations to improve coordination and intent inference. *User Modeling and User-Adapted Interaction, 3-4*(4), 249–280. doi:10.1007/s11257-006-9009-2

Ioannidis, Y. E., Ng, R. T., Shim, K., & Sellis, T. K. (1997). Parametric query optimization. *The Very Large Databases Journal, 6*(2), 132–151. doi:10.1007/s007780050037doi:10.1007/s007780050037

Iqbal, S., & Horvitz, E. (2007). Conversations admist computing: A study of interruptions and recovery of task activity. In *Proceedings of the 11th International Conference on User Modeling*, Corfu, Greece (pp. 350-354).

Iqbal, S., & Horvitz, E. (2010). Notifications and awareness: A field study of alert usage and preferences. In *Proceedings of the ACM Conference on Computer Supported Cooperative Work*, Savannah, GA (pp. 27-30).

Jagtman, H. M. (2010). Cell broadcast trials in The Netherlands: Using mobile phone technology for citizens' alarming. *Reliability Engineering & System Safety, 95*, 18–28. doi:10.1016/j.ress.2009.07.005

Jarillo, J. C. (1993). *Strategic networks: Creating the borderless organization*. Oxford, UK: Butterworth-Heinemann.

Jarvis, S. A., Spooner, D. P., Lim Choi Keung, H. M., Cao, J., Saini, S., & Nudd, G. R. (2006). Performance prediction and its use in parallel and distributed computing systems. *Future Generation Computer Systems*, 745–754. doi:10.1016/j.future.2006.02.008

Java Community Process. (2009). *JSR 283: Content repository for Java™ technology API version 2.0*. Retrieved from http://jcp.org/en/jsr/detail?id=283

Jayawardane, A. (2006). Disaster mitigation initiatives in Sri Lanka. In *Proceedings of the International Symposium on Management System for Disaster Prevention*, Kochi, Japan.

Jennings, P. (2005). Tangible social interfaces: Critical theory, boundary objects and interdisciplinary design methods. In *Proceedings of the 5th Conference on Creativity & Cognition* (pp. 176-186).

JGraph Ltd. (2009). *JGraph homepage*. Retrieved from http://www.jgraph.com

Jiang, C., Wang, C., & Liu, X. (2007). Adaptive replication based security aware & fault tolerant job scheduling for grids. *In Proceedings of the 8th ACIS International Conference on Software Engineering, Artificial Intelligence, Networking, & Parallel/Distributed Computing* (pp. 597-602).

Johnson, R. (2000). *GIS Technology for Disasters and Emergency Management*. Washington, DC: Environmental Systems Research Institute, Inc.

Kabra, N., & DeWitt, D. J. (1998). Efficient mid-query re-optimization of sub-optimal query execution plans. In *Proceedings of the 17th International Conference on Management of Data* (pp. 106-117).

Kachroo, P., Ravindran, B., & Hegazy, T. (2001). Adaptive resource management in asynchronous real-time distributed systems using feedback control functions. *In Proceedings of the 5th International Symposium on Autonomous Decentralized Systems* (pp. 39-46).

Kalantari, M., & Akbari, M. K. (2008). A parallel solution for scheduling of real time applications on grid environments. *Future Generation Computer Systems, 25*(7), 704–716. doi:10.1016/j.future.2008.01.003

Kang, J., Naughton, J. F., & Viglas, S. D. (2003). Evaluating window joins over unbounded streams. In *Proceedings of the 19th International Conference on Data Engineering* (pp. 341-352).

Karatza, H. D., & Hilzer, R. C. (2003). Parallel job scheduling in homogeneous distributed systems. *Transactions of the Society for Modeling & Simulation, 79*(5), 287–298. doi:10.1177/003754903037148

Kara-Zaitri, C. (1996). Disaster prevention and limitation: state of the art; tools and technologies. *Disaster Prevention and Management, 5*(1), 30–39. doi:10.1108/09653569610109541

Kasuza, S. (2006). Disaster management of Japan. In *Proceedings of the International Symposium on Management System for Disaster Prevention*, Kochi, Japan.

Kermia, O., & Sorel, Y. (2008). Load balancing & efficient memory usage for homogeneous distributed real-time embedded systems. In *Proceedings of the International Conference on Parallel Processing - Workshops*, Portland, OR (pp. 39-46).

Kerrighed. (1998). *What is Kerrighed?* Retrieved from http://www.Kerrighed.org

Keshav, S. (2006). Efficient and decentralized computation of approximate global state. *Journal of the ACM, 36*, 69–74.

Kim, J. L., & Park, T. (1993). An efficient Protocol for checkpointing Recovery in Distributed Systems. *IEEE Transactions on Parallel and Distributed Systems*, 955–960. doi:10.1109/71.238629

Kirsh, D. (1995). The intelligent use of space. *Artificial Intelligence, 73*(1-2), 31–68. doi:10.1016/0004-3702(94)00017-U

Konkola, R. (2001). Developmental process of internship at polytechnic and boundary-zone activity as a new model for activity. In Tuomi-Gröhn, T., Engeström, Y., & Young, M. (Eds.), *At the boundary zone between school and work – new possibilities of work-based learning* (pp. 148–186). Helsinki, Finland: University Press.

Koo, R., & Toueg, S. (1987). Checkpointing and Roll-Back Recovery for Distributed Systems. *IEEE Transactions on Software Engineering, 13*(1), 23–31. doi:10.1109/TSE.1987.232562

Kshemkalyani, A. D., & Singhal, M. (1999). A one-phase algorithm to detect distributed deadlocks in replicated databases. *IEEE Transactions on Knowledge and Data Engineering, 11*(6), 880–895. doi:10.1109/69.824601

Kumar, L., Misra, M., & Joshi, R. C. (2003). Low overhead optimal checkpointing for mobile distributed systems. In *Proceedings 19th International Conference on IEEE Data Engineering* (pp. 686-688). Washington, DC: IEEE.

Kumar, P., & Khunteta, A. (2010). A Minimum-Process Coordinated Checkpointing Protocol For Mobile Distributed System. *International Journal of Computer Science issues, 7*(3).

Kumar, V., Cooper, B. F., & Schwan, K. (2005). Distributed stream management using utility-driven self adaptive middleware. In *Proceedings of the 2nd International Conference on Autonomic Computing* (p. 3).

Kumar, V., Cooper, B. F., Cai, Z., Eisenhauer, G., & Schwan, K. (2005). Resource-aware distributed stream management using dynamic overlays. In *Proceedings of the 25th IEEE International Conference on Distributed Computing Systems* (p. 783).

Kumar, K., & Diesel, H. G. (1996). Sustainable collaboration: Managing conflict and cooperation in interorganizational systems. *Management Information Systems Quarterly, 20*(3), 279–300. doi:10.2307/249657

Kumar, L., Kumar, P., & Chauhan, R. K. (2005). Logging based Coordinated Checkpointing in Mobile Distributed Computing Systems. *Journal of the Institution of Electronics and Telecommunication Engineers, 51*(6).

Kumar, P. (2007). A Low-Cost Hybrid Coordinated Checkpointing Protocol for Mobile Distributed Systems. *Mobile Information Systems, 4*(1), 13–32.

Kumar, P., Kumar, L., & Chauhan, R. K. (2005). A low overhead Non-intrusive Hybrid Synchronous checkpointing protocol for mobile systems. *Journal of Multidisciplinary Engineering Technologies*, *1*(1), 40–50.

Kuo, C. F., Shih, C. S., & Kuo, T. W. (2006). *Resource allocation framework for distributed real-time end-to-end tasks* (Tech. Rep. No. NTU/NEWS-6-0005). Taiwan: National Taiwan University.

Kurita, T., Nakamura, A., Kodama, M., & Colombage, S. R. N. (2006). Tsunami public awareness and the disaster management system of Sri Lanka. *Disaster Prevention and Management*, *15*(1), 92–110. doi:10.1108/09653560610654266

Kuutti, K. (1996). Activity theory as a potential framework for human-computer interaction research. In Nardi, B. (Ed.), *Context and consciousness: Activity theory and human-computer interaction* (pp. 17–44). Cambridge, MA: MIT Press.

Lai, Z., Bessis, N., De La Roche, G., Kuonen, P., Zhang, J., & Clapworthy, G. (2009, November). A new approach to solve angular dispersion of discrete ray launching for urban scenarios. In *Proceedings of the Loughborough Antennas & Propagation Conference* Leicestershire, UK (pp. 133-136).

Lai, Z., Bessis, N., De La Roche, G., Kuonen, P., Zhang, J., & Clapworthy, G. (2010, April). On the use of an intelligent ray launching for indoor scenarios. In *Proceedings of the Fourth European Conference on Antennas and Propagation*, Barcelona, Spain.

Lai, Z., Bessis, N., De La Roche, G., Song, H., Zhang, J., & Clapworthy, G. (2009, March). An intelligent ray launching for urban propagation prediction. In *Proceedings of the Third European Conference on Antennas and Propagation*, Berlin, Germany (pp. 2867-2871).

Lai, Z., Bessis, N., Kuonen, P., De La Roche, G., Zhang, J., & Clapworthy, G. (2009, August). A performance evaluation of a grid-enabled object-oriented parallel outdoor ray launching for wireless network coverage prediction. In *Proceedings of the Fifth International Conference on Wireless and Mobile Communications*, Cannes, France (pp. 38-43).

Lai, Z., Bessis, N., Zhang, J., & Clapworthy, G. (2007, September). Some thoughts on adaptive grid-enabled optimisation algorithms for wireless network simulation and planning. In *Proceedings of the UK e-Science, All Hands Meeting*, Nottingham, UK (pp. 615-620).

Lamport, L. (1978). Time, clocks, and the ordering of events in a distributed system. *Communications of the ACM*, *21*, 558–565. doi:10.1145/359545.359563

Lastra, J. L. M., Delamer, I. M., & Ubis, F. (2009). *Domain ontologies for reasoning machines in factory automation*. Research Triangle Park, NC: ISA.

Lauesen, S. (2005). *User interface design – A software engineering perspective*. Reading, MA: Addison-Wesley.

Lawson, B. (2005). *How designers think - The design process demystified*. New York, NY: Architectural Press.

Lee, J. J., & Xiao, X. (2010). A true O(1) parallel deadlock detection algorithm for single-unit resource systems & it's hardware implementation. *IEEE Transactions on Parallel and Distributed Systems*, *21*(1), 4–19. doi:10.1109/TPDS.2009.38

Legrand, I., Voicu, R., Cirstoiu, C., Grigoras, C., Betev, L., & Costan, A. (2009). Monitoring and control of large systems with MonALISA. *Queue*, *7*(6), 40–49.

Levitin, G., & Dai, H. (2006). Reliability and performance of star topology grid service with precedence constraints on subtask execution. *IEEE Transactions on Reliability*, *55*(3), 507–515. doi:10.1109/TR.2006.879651

Li, P. L., Herbsleb, J., & Shaw, M. (2005). Forecasting field defect rates using a combined time-based and metrics-based approach: A case study of OpenBSD. In *Proceedings of the 16th IEEE International Symposium on Software Reliability Engineering* (pp. 193-202). Washington, DC: IEEE Computer Society.

Li, T. (2009). Informedness and customer-centric revenue management (Doctoral dissertation, Erasmus University). *ERIM PhD Series in Research in Management*, 146.

Li, Y., Hong, J. I., & Landay, J. A. (2004, October 24-27). Topiary: A tool for prototyping location-enhanced applications. In *Proceedings of the 17th Annual ACM Symposium on User Interface Software and Technology*, Santa Fe, NM (pp. 217-226). New York, NY: ACM Press.

Liao, S. (2005). Technology management methodologies and applications: A literature review from 1995 to 2003. *Technovation,* 25(4), 381–393. doi:10.1016/j.technovation.2003.08.002

Liden, S. (1995). The evolution of flight management systems. In *Proceedings of the 13th IEEE /AIAA Digital Avionics Systems Conference,* Phoenix, AZ (pp. 157-169).

Lieberman, H., Paternò, F., Klann, M., & Wulf, V. (2006). End-user development: An emerging paradigm. In Lieberman, H., Paternò, F., & Wulf, V. (Eds.), *End user development* (pp. 1–8). Dordrecht, The Netherlands: Springer-Verlag. doi:10.1007/1-4020-5386-X_1

Lim, B. Y., & Dey, A. K. (2009, September 30-October 3). Assessing demand for intelligibility in context-aware applications. In *Proceedings of the 11th International Conference on Ubiquitous Computing,* Orlando, FL (pp. 195-204). New York, NY: ACM Press.

Lin, X., Lu, Y., Deogun, J., & Goddard, S. (2007). Real-time divisible load scheduling for cluster computing. In *Proceedings of the 13th IEEE Real Time & Embedded Technology & Applications Symposium,* Bellevue, WA (pp. 303-314).

Lindell, M. K., Prater, C. S., & Peacock, W. G. (2007). Organizational Communication and Decision Making for Hurricane Emergencies. *Natural Hazards Review,* 50–60. doi:10.1061/(ASCE)1527-6988(2007)8:3(50)

Li, P., Ravindran, B., & Hegazy, T. (2003). Proactive resource allocation for asynchronous real-time distributed systems in the presence of processor failures. *Journal of Parallel and Distributed Computing,* 63(12), 1219–1242. doi:10.1016/S0743-7315(03)00111-4

Liu, S., Yu, J., Liu, Y., Wei, J., Gao, P., Li, W., et al. (2007). Make highly clustered grid a small world with shorter diameter. In *Proceedings of the Sixth International Conference on Grid and Cooperative Computing,* Xinjiang, China (pp. 109-116). Washington, DC: IEEE Computer Society.

Liu, C. L., & Layland, J. W. (1973). Scheduling algorithms for multiprogramming in a hard real-time environment. *Communications of the ACM,* 20(1), 46–61.

Li, W., Kavi, K., & Akl, R. (2007). A non premptive scheduling algorithm for soft real time systems. *Computers & Electrical Engineering,* 33(1), 12–29. doi:10.1016/j.compeleceng.2006.04.002

Loc, N. T., Elnaffar, S., Katayama, T., & Bao, H.-T. (2006). Grid scheduling using 2-phase prediction (2PP) of CPU power. *Innovations in Information Technology,* 1-5.

Lombardi, M., Milano, M., & Benini, L. (2009). Robust non-preemptive hard real-time scheduling for clustered multicore platforms. In *Proceedings of the Design, Automation & Test in Europe Conference & Exhibition,* Nice, France (pp. 803-808).

López, L., & Pérez, M. (2006). *Deslaves e inundaciones: Sistema de emergencia para el municipio Baruta. Trabajo especial de grado.* Venezuela: Universidad Metropolitana.

Lovett, P. J., Ingram, A., & Bancroft, C. N. (2000). Knowledge-based engineering for SMEs - a methodology. *Journal of Materials Processing Technology,* 107(1-3), 384–389. doi:10.1016/S0924-0136(00)00728-7

Lucene. (2010). *Welcome to apache Lucene.* Retrieved from http://lucene.apache.org/

Lüder, A. (2000). *Formaler Steuerungsentwurf mit modularen diskreten Verhaltensmodellen* Unpublished doctoral dissertation, Martin-Luther-Universität, Halle-Wittenberg, Germany.

Lüder, A., Peschke, J., & Reinelt, D. (2006). *Possibilities and limitations of the application of agent systems in control.* Paper presented at the International Conference on Concurrent Enterprising.

Lu, P., & Zhu, X. (2009). A two-phase scheduling strategy for real-time applications with security requirements on heterogeneous clusters. *Journal of Computers & Electrical Engineering,* 35(6), 980–993. doi:10.1016/j.compeleceng.2008.11.022

Ma, Y., Gong, B., & Zou, L. (2008). Resource discovery algorithm based on small- world cluster in hierarchical grid computing environment. In *Proceedings of the 7th International Conference on Grid and Cooperative Computing,* Lanzhou, China (pp. 110-116). Washington, DC: IEEE Computer Society.

Mackay, W. E. (1990, October 7-10). Patterns of sharing customisable software. In *Proceedings of the ACM Conference on Computer-Supported Cooperative Work*, Los Angeles, CA (pp. 209-221). New York, NY: ACM Press.

Mahafza, B., Welstead, S., Champagne, D., Manadhar, R., Worthington, T., & Campbell, S. (1998). Real-time radar signal simulation for the ground based radar for national missile defense. In *Proceedings of the IEEE Radar Conference,* Dallas, TX (pp. 62-67).

Maheswaran, M., Ali, S., Siegel, H. J., Hensgen, D., & Freund, R. F. (1999). Dynamic matching & scheduling of a class of independent tasks onto heterogeneous computing systems. In *Proceedings of the 8th IEEE Heterogeneous Computing Workshop* (pp. 30-44).

Majhew, D. J. (1992). *Principles and guideline in software user interface design.* Upper Saddle River, NJ: Prentice Hall.

Makowski, M. (2009). Management of Attainable Tradeoffs between Conflicting Goals. *Journal Computer, 4*(10), 1033–1042.

Maldonado, H., Lee, B., Klemmer, S. R., & Pea, R. D. (2007). Patterns of collaboration in design courses: Team dynamics affect technology appropriation, artifact creation, and course performance. In *Proceedings of the Computer-Supported Collaborative Learning Conference,* New Brunswick, NJ (pp. 486-495).

Manimaran, G., & Rammurthy, C. S. (1998). An efficient dynamic scheduling algorithm for multiprocessor real-time systems. *IEEE Transactions on Parallel and Distributed Systems, 9*(3), 312–319. doi:10.1109/71.674322

Mansor, S., Shariah, M. A., Billa, L., Setiawan, I., & Jabar, F. (2004). Spatial technology for natural risk management. *Disaster Prevention and Management, 13*(5), 364–373. doi:10.1108/09653560410568480

Marasovic, J., & Marasovic, T. (2006, September). CPM/PERT project planning methods as e-learning optional support. In *Proceedings of the International Conference on Software in Telecommunications and Computer Networks*, Dubrovnik, Croatia (pp. 352-356). Washington, DC: IEEE Computer Society.

Marcus, D. (2008). *Graph theory: A problem oriented approach.* Washington, DC: Mathematical Association of America.

Mark, G., & Su, N. (2007). Considering Web 2.0 technologies within an ecology of collaborations. In *Proceedings of the UMAP Workshop SociUM,* Corfu, Greece (pp. 50-59).

Mark, G., Gudith, D., & Klocke, U. (2008). The cost of interrupted work: More speed and stress. In *Proceedings of the Conference on Human Factors in Computing Systems*, Florence, Italy (pp. 821-824).

Markl, V., Raman, V., Simmen, D. E., Lohman, G. M., & Pirahesh, H. (2004). Robust query processing through progressive optimization. In *Proceedings of the 23rd International Conference on Management of Data* (pp. 659-670).

Mattern, F. (1989). Virtual time and global states of distributed systems. In *Proceedings of the International Workshop on Parallel and Distributed Algorithms* (pp. 215-226).

Mattern, F. (1987). Algorithms for distributed termination detection. *Distributed Computing, 2*(3), 161–175. doi:10.1007/BF01782776

McEntire, D. A. (2001). Triggering agents, vulnerabilities and disaster reduction: towards a holistic paradigm. *Disaster Prevention and Management, 10*(3), 189–196. doi:10.1108/09653560110395359

McFarlane, D., & Latorella, K. (2002). The scope and importance of human interruption in human-computer interaction design. *Human-Computer Interaction, 17*(1), 1–61. doi:10.1207/S15327051HCI1701_1

McGuire, J. G., Kuokka, D. R., Weber, J. C., Tenenbaum, J. M., Gruber, T. R., & Olsen, G. R. (1993). SHADE: Technology for knowledge-based collaborative engineering. *Concurrent Engineering, 1993*(1), 137-146.

Mendonça, D., Beroggi, G. E. G., & Wallace, W. A. (2001). Decision support for improvisation during emergency response operations. *Int. J. Emergency Management, 1*(1), 30–38. doi:10.1504/IJEM.2001.000507

Merdan, M., Moser, T., Wahyudin, D., & Biffl, S. (2008). Performance evaluation of workflow scheduling strategies considering transportation times and conveyor failures. In *Proceedings of the IEEE International Conference on Industrial Engineering and Engineering Management* (pp. 389-394). Washington, DC: IEEE Computer Society.

Miikkulainen, R., & Stanley, K. O. (2009, July 8-12). Evolving neural networks. In *Proceedings of the 11th Annual Conference Companion on Genetic and Evolutionary Computation: Late Breaking Paper*, Montreal, QC, Canada (pp. 2977-3014). New York, NY: ACM Press.

Miles, R., & Snow, C. (1995). The network firm: A spherical structure built on human investment philosophy. *Organizational Dynamics*, 23(95), 5–18. doi:10.1016/0090-2616(95)90013-6

Mills, D. L. (1985). *Network time protocol (NTP)*. Marina del Rey, CA: RFC Editor.

Mockus, A., Weiss, D., & Zhang, P. (2003). Understanding and predicting effort in software projects. In *Proceedings of the International Conference on Software Engineering* (pp. 274-284). Washington, DC: IEEE Computer Society.

Moe, T. L., & Pairote Pathranarakul, P. (2006). An integrated approach to natural disaster management Public project management and its critical success factors. *Disaster Prevention and Management*, 15(3), 396–413. doi:10.1108/09653560610669882

Monteiro, R., & Rodrigues, G. (2006). A system of integrated indicators for socio-environmental assessment and eco-certification in agriculture-ambitec-agro. *Journal of Technology Management & Innovation*, 1(3), 47–59.

Mørch, A. (1997). Three levels of end-user tailoring: Customization, integration, and extension. In Kyng, M., & Mathiassen, L. (Eds.), *Computers and design in context* (pp. 51–76). Cambridge, MA: MIT Press.

Moser, L. E., Melliar-Smith, P. M., & Agrawala, V. (1991). Membership algorithms for asynchronous distributed systems. In *Proceedings of the 10th International Conference on Distributed Computing Systems* (pp. 480-488).

Moser, T., Mordinyi, R., Sunindyo, W., & Biffl, S. (2009). Semantic service matchmaking in the ATM domain considering network capability constraints. In *Proceedings of the 21st International Conference on Software Engineering and Knowledge Engineering* (pp. 222-227). Washington, DC: IEEE Computer Society.

Moser, T., Schimper, K., Mordinyi, R., & Anjomshoaa, A. (2009). SAMOA - a semi-automated ontology alignment method for systems integration in safety-critical environments. In *Proceedings of the 2nd IEEE International Workshop on Ontology Alignment and Visualization*, Fukuoka, Japan (pp. 724-729). Washington, DC: IEEE Computer Society.

Mulder, W., & Meijer, G. T. (2006). Distributed information services supporting collaborative network management. In. *Proceedings of the IFIP Conference on Network-Centric Collaboration and Supporting Frameworks*, 224, 491–498. doi:10.1007/978-0-387-38269-2_51

Murai, S. (2006). Monitoring of disasters using remote sensing GIS and GPS. In *Proceedings of the International Symposium on Management System for Disaster Prevention*, Kochi, Japan.

Myers, B. A. (1986, April 13-17). Visual programming, programming by example, and program visualisation: A taxonomy. In *Proceedings of the SIGCHI Conference on Human Factors in Computing Systems*, Boston, MA (pp. 59-66). New York, NY: ACM Press.

Nagy, L., Dady, R., & Farkasvolgyi, A. (2009, March). Algorithmic complexity of FDTD and ray tracing method for indoor propagation modelling. In *Proceedings of the Third European Conference on Antennas and Propagation*, Berlin, Germany.

Nakamura, A., & Takizawa, M. (1994). Causally ordering broadcast protocol. In *Proceedings of the 14th IEEE International Conference on Distributed Computing Systems* (pp. 48-55).

Nastase, M., Dobre, C., Pop, F., & Cristea, V. (2009). Fault tolerance using a front-end service for large scale distributed systems. In *Proceedings of 11th International Symposium on Symbolic and Numeric Algorithms for Scientific Computing*, Timisoara, Romania (pp. 229-236).

Nazir, B., & Khan, T. (2006). Fault tolerant job scheduling in computational grid. In *Proceedings of the Second International Conference on Emerging Technologies*, Pakistan (pp. 708-713).

Neves, N., & Fuchs, W. K. (1997). Adaptive Recovery for Mobile Environments. *Communications of the ACM, 40*(1), 68–74. doi:10.1145/242857.242878

Newman, M. W., Ackerman, M. S., Kim, J., Prakash, A., Hong, Z., Mandel, J., & Dong, T. (2010, October 3-6). Bringing the field into the lab: Supporting capture and replay of contextual data for design. In *Proceedings of the 23nd Annual ACM Symposium on User Interface Software and Technology*, New York, NY (pp. 105-108). New York, NY: ACM Press.

Nguyen, T. (2004). *An object-oriented model for adaptive high-performance computing on the computational grid.* Présentée à la faculté informatique et communications, Zurich, Switzerland.

Nguyen, T., & Kuonen, P. (2007, January). Programming the grid with POP-C++. *Future Generation Computer Systems, 23*(1), 23–30. doi:10.1016/j.future.2006.04.012

Nishimura, T., Hayashibara, N., Takizawa, M., & Enokido, T. (2005). Causally ordered delivery with global clock in hierarchical group. In *Proceedings of the 11th IEEE International Conference on Parallel and Distributed Systems* (pp. 560-564).

Noji, E. K. (Ed.). (1997). *The public health consequences of disasters*. New York: Oxford University Press.

Norman, D. A. (1993). *Things that make us smart*. Reading, MA: Addison-Wesley.

Noy, N. F. (2004). Semantic integration: A survey of ontology-based approaches. *SIGMOD Record, 33*(4), 65–70. doi:10.1145/1041410.1041421

Noy, N. F., Doan, A. H., & Halevy, A. Y. (2005). Semantic integration. *AI Magazine, 26*(1), 7–10.

O'Reilly, T. (2007). What is web 2.0: Design patterns and business models for the next generation of software. *Communications & Strategies, 65*(1), 17–37.

Obitko, M., & Marik, V. (2002). Ontologies for multi-agent systems in manufacturing domain. In *Proceedings of the 13th International Workshop on Database and Expert Systems Applications* (pp. 597-602). Washington, DC: IEEE Computer Society.

OGSA-DAI. (2002). *Welcome to OGSA-DAI.* Retrieved from http://www.ogsadai.org.uk/

Olston, C., Jiang, J., & Widom, J. (2003). Adaptive filters for continuous queries over distributed data streams. In *Proceedings of the 22nd International Conference on Management of Data* (pp. 563).

Oster, G., & Naja-Jazzar, H. (2007). Supporting collaborative writing of XML documents. In *Proceedings of the International Conference on Enterprise Information Systems*, Madeira, Portugal.

Oster, G., Urso, P., Molli, P., & Imine, A. (2006). Data consistency for P2P collaborative editing. In *Proceedings of the ACM Conference on Computer Supported Cooperative Work*, Banff, AB, Canada.

Österle, H., Fleisch, E., & Alt, R. (2001). *Business networking - Shaping collaboration between enterprises*. Berlin, Germany: Springer-Verlag.

Otten, J., Heijningen, B., & Lafortune, J. F. (2004, May). *The virtual crisis management centre. An ICT implementation to canalise information*. Paper presented at the International Community on Information Systems for Crisis Response Management (ISCRAM2004), Brussels, Belgium.

Padmanabham, A., Wang, S., Ghosh, S., & Briggs, R. (2005). A self-organised grouping (SOG) method for efficient grid resource discovery. In *Proceedings of the International Workshop on Grid Computing* (p. 6). Washington, DC: IEEE Computer Society.

Paton, D., & Johnston, D. (2001). Disasters and communities: vulnerability, resilience and preparedness. *Disaster Prevention and Management, 10*(4), 270–277. doi:10.1108/EUM0000000005930

Paton, N., & Diaz, O. (1999). Active database systems. *ACM Computing Surveys, 31*(1). doi:10.1145/311531.311623

Patterson, D. J., Liao, L., Fox, D., & Kautz, H. (2003, October 12-15). Inferring high-level behavior from low-level sensors. In *Proceedings of the Fifth International Conference on Ubiquitous Computing*, Seattle, WA (pp. 73-89).

Peck, C. C., & Dhawan, A. P. (1995). Genetic algorithms as global random search methods: An alternative perspective. *Evolutionary Computation, 3*(1), 39–80. doi:10.1162/evco.1995.3.1.39

Pendyala, V. S., & Shim, S. S. Y. (2009). The Web as the ubiquitous computer. *Computing Now, 42*(9), 90–92. doi:10.1109/MC.2009.302

Perkins, C. (Ed.). (2001). *Ad hoc networks*. Reading, MA: Addison-Wesley.

Petre, M., & Green, T. R. G. (1993). Learning to read graphics: Some evidence that 'seeing' an information display is an acquired skill. *International Journal of Visual Languages and Computing, 4*(1), 55–70. doi:10.1006/jvlc.1993.1004

Pipek, V. (2005). *From tailoring to appropriation support: Negotiating groupware usage*. Unpublished doctoral dissertation, University of Oulu, Oulu, Finland.

Pop, F., Costan, A., Dobre, C., & Cristea, V. (2009). Prediction based meta-scheduling for grid environments. In *Proceedings of the 17th International Conference on Control Systems and Computer Science*, Bucharset, Romania (pp.128-136).

Pope, S., & Riddoch, D. (2007). 10Gb/s ethernet performance and retrospective. *ACM SIGCOMM Computer Communication Review, 37*(2), 89–92. doi:10.1145/1232919.1232930

Pradhan, D. K., Krishana, P. P., & Vaidya, N. H. (1996). Recovery in Mobile Wireless Environment: Design and Trade-off Analysis. In *Proceedings of the 26th International Symposium on Fault-Tolerant Computing* (pp. 16-25).

Prakash, R., & Singhal, M. (1996). Low-Cost Checkpointing and Failure Recovery in Mobile Computing Systems. *IEEE Transactions on Parallel and Distributed Systems, 7*(10), 1035–1048. doi:10.1109/71.539735

Prasad, B. (1995). JIT quality matrices for strategic planning and implementation. *International Journal of Operations & Production Management, 15*(9), 116–142. doi:10.1108/01443579510099706

Putnam, L. (2002, November). By Choice or by Chance: How the Internet Is Used to Prepare for, Manage, and Share Information about Emergencies. *First Monday, 7*(11). Retrieved May 10, 2010, from http://www.firstmonday.org/issues/issue7_11/putnam/index.html

Pylvanainen, J., Jarvinen, J., & Verho, P. (2004). Advanced reliability analysis for distribution network. *IEEE Transactions on Reliability, 2*, 457–462.

Quarantelli, E. L. (1997). Problematical aspects of the information/communication revolution for disaster planning and research: ten non-technical issues and questions. *Disaster Prevention and Management, 6*(2), 94–106. doi:10.1108/09653569710164053

Radulescu, A., & van Gemund, A. J. C. (2000). Fast & effective task scheduling in heterogeneous systems. In *Proceedings of the 9th Heterogeneous Computing Workshop,* Cancun, Mexico (229-238).

Rajasekaran, S., Ammar, R., & Hussein, A. (2007). Efficient scheduling of real-time tandem task graphs on heterogeneous clusters with network limitations. In *Proceedings of the 12th IEEE Symposium on Computers and Communications*, Aveiro, Portugal (pp. 227-232).

Ramamritham, K., Stankovic, J. A., & Shiah, P. (1990). Efficient scheduling algorithms for real time multiprocessor systems. *IEEE Transactions on Parallel and Distributed Systems, 1*(2), 184–194. doi:10.1109/71.80146

Ramos, T. G., & de Melo, A. C. M. A. (2006). An extensible resource discovery mechanism for efficient grid resource discovery. In *Proceedings of the Sixth IEEE International Symposium on Cluster Computing and the Grid* (pp 115-122). Washington, DC: IEEE Computer Society.

Rao, A., & Georgeff, M. P. (1991). Modeling rational agents within a BDI architecture. In *Proceedings of the International Conference on Principles of Knowledge Representation and Reasoning*, Cambridge, MA (pp. 473-484).

Rao, S., & Naidu, M. M. (2008). A New, Efficient Coordinated Checkpointing Protocol Combined with Selective Sender-Based Message Logging. In *Proceedings of the International Conference on Computer Systems and Applications.* Washington, DC: IEEE.

Rappaport, T. S. (2001). *Wireless communications.* Upper Saddle River, NJ: Prentice Hall.

Rasmussen, K. B., & Thimm, H. (2009). Fact-based understanding of business survey non-response. *Electronic Journal of Business Research Methods, 7*(1), 83–92.

Ravindran, B., & Devarasetty, R. K. (2002). Adaptive resource management algorithms for periodic tasks in dynamic real-time distributed systems. *Journal of Parallel and Distributed Computing, 62*(10), 1527–1547.

Raza, Z., & Vidyarthi, D. P. (2008). A fault tolerant grid scheduling model to minimize turnaround time. In *Proceedings of the International Conference on High Performance Computing, Networking, and Communication Systems*, Orlando, FL (pp. 167-175).

Razzaque, M. A., & Hong, C. S. (2007). *Dynamic load balancing in distributed system: An efficient approach.* Retrieved from http://mnet.skku.ac.kr/data/2007data/JCCI2007/papers/pdf/P-II-10.pdf

Resnick, L. B., Levine, J. M., & Teasley, S. D. (1991). *Perspectives on socially shared cognition.* Washington, DC: American Psychology Association. doi:10.1037/10096-000

Ressel, M. (1996). An integrating, transformation-directed approach to concurrency control and undo in group editors. In *Proceedings of the ACM Conference on Computer Supported Cooperative Work*, New York, NY.

Ressel, M., & Gunzenhauser, R. (1999). Reducing the problems of group undo. In *Proceedings of the ACM Conference on Supporting Group Work*, Phoenix, AZ (pp. 131-139).

Rick, T., & Mathar, R. (2007, March). Fast edge-diffraction based radio wave propagation model for graphics hardware. In *Proceedings of the 2nd International ITG Conference* (pp. 15-19).

Riemer, K., & Klein, S. (2003). Challenges of ICT-enabled virtual organizations: A social capital perspective. In *Proceedings of the 14th Australasian Conference of Information Systems*, Perth, Australia (p. 8).

Rittel, H. (1984). Second-generation design methods. In Cross, N. (Ed.), *Developments in design methodology* (pp. 317–327). Chichester, UK: John Wiley & Sons.

Rochkind, M. J. (1975). The source code control system. *IEEE Transactions on Software Engineering, 1*(4), 364–370.

Rodríguez, D., & Zabala, J. (2002). *Trasporte para el traslado de heridos y afectados desde refugios a centros de asistencia y albergues. Trabajo especial de grado.* Venezuela: Universidad Metropolitana.

Rumbaugh, J., Blaha, M. R., Lorensen, W., Eddy, F., & Premerlani, W. (1991). *Object-oriented modeling and design.* Upper Saddle River, NJ: Prentice Hall.

Russel, S., & Norvig, P. (2003). *Artificial intelligence: A modern approach.* Upper Saddle River, NJ: Pearson Education.

Sánchez, C., Sipma, H. B., Manna, Z., Subramonian, V., & Gill, C. (2006). On efficient distributed deadlock avoidance for real-time & embedded systems. In *Proceedings of the 20ᵗʰ IEEE International Parallel & Distributed Processing Symposium.*

Sanders, R., & Tabuchi, S. (2000). Decision Support Systems for Flood Risk Analysis for the River Thames, United Kingdom. *Journal of the American Society for Photogrammetric Engineering & Remote Sensing, 66*(10), 1185–1193.

Santos-Reyes, J., & Beard, A. N. (2001). A Systemic Approach to Fire Safety Management. *Fire Safety Journal, 36*, 359–390. doi:10.1016/S0379-7112(00)00059-X

Santos-Reyes, J., & Beard, A. N. (2010). A systemic approach to managing natural disasters. In Asimakopoulou, E., & Bessis, N. (Eds.), *Advanced ICTs for Disaster Management and Threat Detection: Collaborative and Distributed Frameworks.* New York: Information Science Publishing.

Saxena, K. B. (2009). Business process management in a smart business network environment. In Vervest, P. H. M., van Liere, D. W., & Zheng, L. (Eds.), *The network experience*. Berlin, Germany: Springer-Verlag. doi:10.1007/978-3-540-85582-8_6

Schäfer, W., & Wehrheim, H. (2007). The challenges of building advanced mechatronic systems. *In Proceedings of the International Conference on the Future of Software Engineering* (pp. 72-84). Washington, DC: IEEE Computer Society.

Scheuermann, P., & Chong, E. I. (1997). Adaptive algorithms for join processing in distributed database systems. *Distributed and Parallel Databases*, *5*(3), 233–269. doi:10.1023/A:1008617911992doi:10.1023/A:1008617911992

Schmid, U. (1995). Synchronized universal time coordinated for distributed real-time systems. *Control Engineering Practice*, *3*(6), 101–107. doi:10.1016/0967-0661(95)00073-4

Schollmeier, R. (2001). A definition of peer-to-peer networking for the classification of peer-to-peer architectures and applications. In *Proceedings of the First International Conference on Peer-to-Peer Computing* (pp. 101-102).

Schön, D. (1983). *The reflective practitioner: How professionals think in action*. London, UK: Maurice Temple Smith.

Scripting News Inc. (2010). *XML-RPC homepage*. Retrieved from http://www.xmlrpc.com/

Sedrakian, A. A., Badia, R. M., Kielmann, T., Merzky, A., Perez, J. M., & Sirvent, R. (2007). *Reliability and trust based workflow's job mapping on the grid*. Retrieved from http://www.coregrid.net

Sefton, P. (2006, July 1-5). The integrated content environment. In *Proceedings of the 12th Australasian World Wide Web Conference: Making a Difference with Web Technologies*, Noosa, Australia.

SenthilKumar, B., Chitra, P., & Prakash, G. (2009). Robust task scheduling on heterogeneous computing systems using segmented MaxR- MinCT. *International Journal of Recent Trends in Engineering*, *1*(2), 63–65.

Seshadri, S., Kumar, V., & Cooper, B. F. (2006). Optimizing multiple queries in distributed data stream systems. In *Proceedings of Workshop of the 22nd International Conference on Data Engineering* (p. 25).

Shahtz, S., Wang, J.-P., & Goto, M. (1992). Task allocation for maximizing reliability of distributed computer systems. *IEEE Transactions on Computers*, *41*(9), 1156–1168. doi:10.1109/12.165396

Sharfman, I., Schuster, A., & Keren, D. (2006). A geometric approach to monitoring threshold functions over distributed data streams. In *Proceedings of the 25th International Conference on Management of Data* (p. 301).

Shen, S., & O'Hare, G. M. P. (2004). Agent-Based resource selection for grid computing. In *Proceedings of Workshop 4, the International Workshop on Agents and Autonomic Computing and Grid Enabled Virtual Organizations* (pp. 658-672).

Sherer, S. A. (2003). Critical success factors for manufacturing networks as perceived by network coordinators. *Journal of Small Business Management*, *41*(4), 325–345. doi:10.1111/1540-627X.00086

Shi, X., Jin, H., Qiang, W., & Zou, D. (2004). Reliability analysis for grid computing. In H. Jin, Y. Pan, N. Xiao, & J. Sun (Eds.), *Proceedings of the Third International Conference on Grid and Cooperative Computing* (LNCS 3251, pp. 787-790).

Shiang, C., & Stankovic, J. A. (1990). *Survey of deadlock detection in distributed concurrent programming environment & its applications to real time systems* (Tech. Rep. No. UM-CS-1990-069). Amherst, MA: University of Massachusetts.

Shi, W., Lee, H. H. S., Lu, C., & Ghosh, M. (2005). Towards the issues in architectural support for protection of software execution. *ACM SIGARCH Computer Architecture News*, *33*(1), 6–15. doi:10.1145/1055626.1055629

Shoorehdeli, M. A., Teshnehlab, M., Sedigh, A. K., & Khanesar, M. A. (2009). Identification using ANFIS with intelligent hybrid stable learning algorithm approaches and stability analysis of training methods. *Applied Soft Computing*, *9*(2), 833–850. doi:10.1016/j.asoc.2008.11.001

Showalter, P. S. (2001). Remote sensing's use in disaster research: a review. *Disaster Prevention and Management, 10*(1), 21–29. doi:10.1108/09653560110381796

Silberschatz, A., & Galvin, P. (2006). *Operating system concepts with java* (7th ed.). New York, NY: John Wiley & Sons.

Silberschatz, A., Galvin, P., & Gagne, G. (2000). *Applied operating system concepts.* New York, NY: John Wiley & Sons.

Singh, P., & Cabillic, G. (2003). *A Checkpointing Algorithm for Mobile Computing Environment* (LNCS 2775, pp. 65-74).

Smith, C. (2007). *A little plaster goes a long way. News and Events, Imperial College London.* Retrieved from http://www3.imperial.ac.uk/newsandeventspggrp/imperialcollege/newssummary/news_11-12-2007-9-27-28

Snow, C. C., Miles, R. E., & Coleman, H. J. (1992). Managing 21st century network organization. *Organizational Dynamics, 20*(3), 5–20. doi:10.1016/0090-2616(92)90021-E

Sohn, T., & Dey, A. (2003, April 5-10). iCap: An informal tool for interactive prototyping of context-aware applications. In *Proceedings of Extended Abstracts of the Conference on Human Factors in Computing Systems*, Fort Lauderdale, FL (pp. 974-975). New York, NY: ACM Press.

Songra, A., Yadav, R. S., & Tripathi, S. (2007). Modified approach for secured Real time applications on clusters. *International Journal of Security, 1*(1).

Sotiriadis, S., Bessis, N., Huang, Y., Sant, P., & Maple, C. (2010). Towards decentralized grid agent models for continuous resource discovery of interoperable grid virtual organizations. In *Proceedings of the 3rd International Conference on the Applications of Digital Information and Web Technologies: Distributed Information and Applied Collaborative Technologies,* Istanbul, Turkey (pp. 530-535). Washington, DC: IEEE Computer Society.

Sotiriadis, S., Bessis, N., Huang, Y., Sant, P., & Maple, C. (2010, February). Defining minimum requirements of inter-collaborated nodes by measuring the heaviness of node interactions. In *Proceedings of the International Conference on Complex, Intelligent and Software Intensive Systems*, Krakow, Poland.

Sotiriadis, S., Bessis, N., Sant, P., & Maple, C. (2010). A mobile agent migration strategy for grid interoperable virtual organisations. In *Proceedings of the 1st International Conference on Collaborative Technologies*, Freiburg, Germany.

Sotiriadis, S., Bessis, N., Sant, P., & Maple, C. (2010). Encoding minimum requirements of ad-hoc inter-connected grids to a genetic algorithm infrastructure. In *Proceedings of the 1st International Conference on Collaborative Technologies*, Freiburg, Germany.

Spartiotis, D., & Bestavros, A. (1993). Probabilistic job scheduling for distributed real - time applications. In *Proceedings of the IEEE Workshop on Real-Time Applications*, New York, NY (pp. 97-101).

Srinivasan, S., & Jha, N. K. (1999). Safety and reliability driven task allocation in distributed systems. *IEEE Transactions on Parallel and Distributed Systems, 10*(3), 238–251. doi:10.1109/71.755824

Srivastava, U., Munagala, K., & Widom, J. (2005). Operator placement for in-network stream query processing. In *Proceedings of the 24th Symposium on Principles of Database Systems* (pp. 250-258).

Stankovic, J. A., Spuri, M., Ramamritham, K., & Buttazzo, G. C. (1998). *Deadline scheduling for real-time systems: EDF & related algorithms.* Boston, MA: Kluwer Academic.

Star, S. L., & Griesemer, J. R. (1989). Translations' and boundary objects: Amateurs and professionals in Berkley's Museum of Vertebrate Zoology 1907-39. *Social Studies of Science, 19*(3), 387–420. doi:10.1177/030631289019003001

Stelling, P., Foster, I., Kesselman, C., Lee, C., & von Laszewski, G. (1998). A fault detection service for wide area distributed computations. In *Proceedings of the 7th IEEE Symposium on High Performance Distributed Computing* (pp. 268-278).

Stiemerling, O. (2000). *Component-based tailorability.* Unpublished doctoral dissertation, University of Bonn, Bonn, Germany.

Sun, C., & Ellis, C. (1998). Operational transformation in real-time group editors: Issues, algorithms, and achievements. In *Proceedings of the ACM Conference on Computer Supported Cooperative Work*, Seattle, WA (pp. 59-68).

Sun, C., & Sosič, R. (1999). Optimal locking integrated with operational transformation in distributed real-time group editors. In *Proceedings of the Eighteenth Annual ACM Symposium on Principles of Distributed Computing*, Atlanta, GA (pp. 43-52).

Sun, D., & Sun, C. (2009). Context-based operational transformation in distributed collaborative editing systems. *IEEE Transactions on Parallel and Distributed Systems, 20*(10), 1454–1470. doi:10.1109/TPDS.2008.240

Surowiecki, J. (2005). *The wisdom of crowds.* New York, NY: Anchor Books.

Systems, E. M. (1997). (*EMS*) (pp. 1–44). Project Evaluation Matrix.

Tacconi, D., Carreras, I., Miorandi, D., Casile, A., Chiti, F., & Fantacci, R. (2007, November). A system architecture supporting mobile applications in disconnected sensor networks. In *Proceedings of the IEEE Globecom Conference* (pp.484-497).

Tanenbaum, A. S., & Maarten, V. S. (2007). *Distributed systems: Principles & paradigms.* Upper Saddle River, NJ: Prentice Hall.

Tao, Y., Jin, H., & Shi, X. (2007). Grid workflow scheduling based on reliability cost. In *Proceedings of the Second International Conference on Scalable Information Systems*, Suzhou, China (p. 12).

Tao, X., & Xiao, Q. (2006). Scheduling security-critical real-time applications on clusters. *IEEE Transactions on Computers, 55*(7), 864–879. doi:10.1109/TC.2006.110

Tao, X., & Xiao, Q. (2007). Performance evaluation of a new scheduling algorithm for distributed systems with security heterogeneity. *Journal of Parallel and Distributed Computing, 67*(10), 1067–1081. doi:10.1016/j.jpdc.2007.06.004

Tao, X., & Xiao, Q. (2008). Security-aware resource allocation for real-time parallel jobs on homogeneous & heterogeneous clusters. *IEEE Transactions on Parallel and Distributed Systems, 19*(5), 682–697. doi:10.1109/TPDS.2007.70776

Tapia, E. M., Intille, S. S., & Larson, K. (2004, April 18-23). Activity recognition in the home using simple and ubiquitous sensors. In *Proceedings of the Second International Conference on Pervasive Computing*, Vienna, Austria (pp. 158-175).

Tarricone, L., & Esposito, A. (2005). *Grid computing for electromagnetics.* Boston, MA: Artech House.

Taylor, I. J., & Harrison, A. (2009) *From P2P and grids to services on the web- evolving distributed communities* (2nd ed.). London, UK: Springer-Verlag.

Thimm, H., & Rasmussen, K. B. (2010). A decision and transparency support service for moderation management of virtual enterprises in collaborative networks. In *Proceedings of the 43rd Hawaii International Conference on System Sciences* (p. 44).

Thimm, H., & Rasmussen, K. B. (2010) Information modeling for flexible information provisioning in collaborative networks. In *Proceedings of the IADIS International Conference on Collaborative Technologies*, Freiburg, Germany (p. 3-11).

Thomas, S. (2010). *Emergency Response Handling using Enterprise Mashups.* Unpublished Master's thesis, University of Bedfordshire, UK.

Tian, F., & DeWitt, D. J. (2003). Tuple routing strategies for distributed eddies. In *Proceedings of the 29th International Conference on Very Large Data Bases* (pp. 333-344).

Tondl, L. (1981). *Problems of semantics.* Boston, MA: Reidel Publishing.

Torenvliet, G. (2003). We can't afford it! The devaluation of a usability term. *Interactions (New York, N.Y.), 10*(4), 12–17. doi:10.1145/838830.838857

Tran, T. M., & Lee, B. S. (2010). Distributed stream join query processing with semijoins. *Distributed and Parallel Databases, 27*(3), 211–254. doi:10.1007/s10619-010-7062-7doi:10.1007/s10619-010-7062-7

Tripathi, S., Yadav, R. S., & Ojha, R. P. (2010). A utilization based approach for secured real time applications on clusters. In *Proceedings of the International Conference on Advances in Computing, Control, & Telecommunication Technologies*, Trivandrum, Kerala, India (pp. 433-438).

Tuecke, S., Foster, I., Karonis, N. T., & Kesselman, C. (1998). Managing security in high-performance distributed computations. *Cluster Computing*, *1*(1), 95–107.

Turner, M., Budgen, D., & Brereton, P. (2003). Turning software into a service. *Communications & Strategies*, *36*(10), 38–44.

Ullman, J. D. (1975). NP-complete scheduling problems. *Journal of Computer and System Sciences*, *10*(3), 384–393. doi:10.1016/S0022-0000(75)80008-0

United Nations Development Programme (UNDP). (2005). *Survivors of the tsunami: One year later*. Retrieved June 28, 2009, from http://www.iotws.org/ev_en.php?ID=1685_201&ID2=DO_TOPIC

Universitat Karlshrue. (n. d.). *COST231 urban micro cell measurements and building data*. Retrieved from http://www2.ihe.uni-karlsruhe.de/forschung/cost231/cost231.en.html

van der Aalst, W. (1999). Flexible workflow-management systems: An approach based on generic process models. In *Proceedings of the 10ᵗʰ International Conference on Database and Expert Systems Applications*, Firenze, Italy (pp. 186-195).

van der Aalst, W., & van Hee, K. (2002). *Workflow management - Models, methods, and systems*. Cambridge, MA: MIT Press.

Van Renesse, R., Minsky, Y., & Hayden, M. (1998). A gossip-style failure detection service. In *Proceedings of the Middleware Conference*, The Lake District, UK (pp. 55-70).

Vastenburg, M. H., Fjalldal, H., & Mast, C. V. D. (2009, June 9-13). Ubi-Designer: A web-based toolkit for configuring and field-testing UbiComp prototypes. In *Proceedings of the 2nd International Conference on Pervasive Technologies Related to Assistive Environments*, Corfu, Greece (pp. 1-6). New York, NY: ACM Press.

Verplank, B. (2009, September). *Interaction design sketchbook*. Paper presented at the First International DESIRE Summer School Theories of Creative Design for Innovation in Science and Technology, Gargnano del Garda, Italy.

Vidyarthi, D. P., Sarker, B. K., Tripathi, A. K., & Yang, L. T. (2009). *Scheduling in distributed computing systems: Analysis, design, and models*. New York, NY: Springer. doi:10.1007/978-0-387-74483-4

Vidyarthi, D. P., & Tripathi, A. K. (1998). Studies on reliability with task allocation of redundant distributed systems. *Journal of the Institution of Electronics and Telecommunication Engineers*, 279–285.

Vidyarthi, D. P., & Tripathi, A. K. (2001). Maximizing reliability of distributed computing system with task allocation using simple genetic algorithm. *Journal of Systems Architecture*, 549–554. doi:10.1016/S1383-7621(01)00013-3

Viglas, S., Naughton, J. F., & Burger, J. (2003). Maximizing the output rate of multi-way join queries over streaming information sources. In *Proceedings of the 29th International Conference on Very Large Data Bases* (pp. 285-296).

Visan, A., Istin, M., Pop, F., & Cristea, V. (2010a, February 15-18). Automatic control of distributed systems based on state prediction methods. In *Proceedings of the International Conference on Complex, Intelligent and Software Intensive Systems* (pp. 502-507). Washington, DC: IEEE Computer Society.

Visan, A., Istin, M., Pop, F., & Cristea, V. (2010). Decomposition based algorithm for state prediction in large scale distributed systems. In *Proceedings of the 9ᵗʰ International Symposium on Parallel and Distributed Computing*, Istanbul, Turkey.

VMWARE. (1998). *VMWare Workstation 6.0*. Retrieved from http://www.vmware.com/

Vrba, P. (2003). MAST: Manufacturing agent simulation tool. In *Proceedings of the Emerging Technologies and Factory Automation Conference* (pp. 282-287). Washington, DC: IEEE Computer Society.

W3C. (2004). *Semantics and abstract syntax*. Retrieved from http://www.w3.org/TR/owl-semantics/

Wahyudin, D., Schatten, A., Winkler, D., Tjoa, A., & Biffl, S. (2008). Defect prediction using combined product and project metrics: A case study from the open source "apache" *MyFaces Project Family*. In *Proceedings of the 34th Euromicro Conference on Software Engineering and Advanced Applications* (pp. 207-215). Washington, DC: IEEE Computer Society.

Wang, X., Bu, J., & Chen, C. (2002). A new consistency model in collaborative editing systems. In *Proceedings of the 4th International Workshop on Collaborative Editing*.

Wattagama, C. (2007). *ICT for disaster management. Asia-Pacific Development Information Programme-e-Primers for the Information Economy, Society and Policy*. Thailand: UNDP-APDIP and Asian and Pacific Training Centre for Information and Communication Technology for Development (APCICT).

Wei, D. X. (2005). *Speeding up ns-2 scheduler*. Retrieved from http://netlab.caltech.edu/

Weigang, N., Vrbsky, S. V., & Sibabrata, R. (2004). Pitfalls in nonblocking checkpointing. *World Science's journal of Interconnected Networks, 1*(5), 47-78.

Weikum, G., & Vossen, G. (2001). *Transactional information systems: Theory, algorithms, and the practice of concurrency control and recovery*. San Francisco, CA: Morgan Kaufmann.

Wenger, R. E. (2002). *Cultivating communities of practice*. Boston, MA: Harvard Business School Press.

Wilson, H. C. (2000). Emergency response preparedness: small group training- Part I- training and learning styles. *Disaster Prevention and Management, 9*(2), 105–116. doi:10.1108/09653560010326987

Winkler, D., Biffl, S., & Östreicher, T. (2009). Test-driven automation – adopting test-first development to improve automation systems engineering processes. In *Proceedings of the 16th EuroSPI Conference*, Madrid, Spain (pp. 1-13).

Winton, L. J. (2005). A simple virtual organisation model and practical implementation. In *Proceedings of the Australasian Workshop on Grid Computing and e-Research* (Vol. 44, pp. 57-65).

Wolfle, G., Gschwendtner, B., & Landstorfer, F. (1997, May). Intelligent ray tracing - a new approach for the field strength prediction in microcells. In *Proceedings of the IEEE Vehicular Technology Conference*, Phoenix, AZ (pp. 790-794).

Xia, S., Sun, D., Sun, C., Chen, D., & Shen, H. (2004). Leveraging single-user applications for multi-user collaboration: The CoWord approach. In *Proceedings of the ACM Conference on Computer Supported Cooperative Work*, Chicago, IL (pp. 162-171).

Xiao, Q., & Tao, X. (2007). Improving security for periodic tasks in embedded systems through scheduling. *ACM Transactions on Embedded Computing Systems, 6*(3), 20. doi:10.1145/1275986.1275992

Xiao, Q., & Tao, X. (2007). Security-driven scheduling for data-intensive applications on grids. *Cluster Computing, 10*(2), 145–153. doi:10.1007/s10586-007-0015-x

Xiao, X., & Lee, J. J. (2008). A novel O(1) deadlock detection methodology for multiunit resource systems & its hardware implementation for system-on-chip. *IEEE Transactions on Parallel and Distributed Systems, 19*(12), 1657–1670. doi:10.1109/TPDS.2008.56

Yahaya, S., Ahmad, N., & Abdalla, R. F. (2010). Multi-criteria Analysis for Flood Vulnerable Areas in Hadejia-Jama'are River Basin, Nigeria. *European Journal of Scientific Research, 42*(1), 71–83.

Yang, L., Foster, I., & Schopf, J. M. (2003). Homeostatic and tendency-based CPU load predictions. In *Proceedings of the Parallel and Distributed Processing Symposium*, Nice, France (p. 9). Washington, DC: IEEE Computer Society.

Yang, L., Schopf, J. M., & Foster, I. (2003). *Conservative scheduling: Using predicted variance to improve scheduling decisions in dynamic environments*. In Proceedings of the ACM/IEEE Conference on Supercomputing and High Performance Networking and Computing *(p. 31). Washington, DC: IEEE Computer Society.*

Yang, Y., Kramer, J., Papadias, D., & Seeger, B. (2007). Hybmig: A hybrid approach to dynamic plan migration for continuous queries. *IEEE Transactions on Knowledge and Data Engineering, 19*(3), 398–411. doi:10.1109/TKDE.2007.43doi:10.1109/TKDE.2007.43

Yang, T., De Marco, G., Ikeda, M., & Barolli, L. (2006). Impact of radio randomness on performances of lattice wireless sensor networks based on event-reliability concept. *International Journal of Mobile Information Systems, 2*(4), 211–227.

Yeung, C., & Hung, S. (1995). A new deadlock detection algorithms for distributed real-time database systems. In *Proceedings of the 14ᵗʰ IEEE Symposium on Reliable Distributed Systems*, Bad Neuenahr, Germany (pp. 146-153).

Ye, W., Heidemann, J., & Estrin, D. (2004). Medium access control with coordinated adaptive sleeping for wireless sensor networks. *IEEE/ACM Transactions on Networking, 12*(3), 493–506. doi:10.1109/TNET.2004.828953

Younis, O., & Fahmy, S. (2004). HEED: A hybrid, energy-efficient, distributed clustering approach for ad-hoc sensor networks. *IEEE Transactions on Mobile Computing, 3*(4), 366–379. doi:10.1109/TMC.2004.41

Zhang, J., & De La Roche, G. (2010). *Femtocells: Technologies and deployment*. New York, NY: John Wiley & Sons. doi:10.1002/9780470686812

Zhang, Y., Gill, C. D., & Chen, Y. (2010). Configurable middleware for distributed real-time systems with aperiodic & periodic tasks. *IEEE Transactions on Parallel and Distributed Systems, 21*(3), 393–404. doi:10.1109/TPDS.2009.67

Zhou, Y. (2003). Adaptive distributed query processing. In *Proceedings of PhD Workshop of the 29th International Conference on Very Large Databases*.

Zhou, Y., Yan, Y., Yu, F., & Zhou, A. (2006). Pmjoin: Optimizing distributed multi-way stream joins by stream partitioning. In *Proceedings of the 9th International Conference on Database Systems for Advanced Applications* (pp. 325-341).

Zhou, G., He, T., Krishnamurthy, S., & Stankovic, J. A. (2006). Models and solutions for radio irregularity in wireless sensor networks. *ACM Transactions on Sensors Network, 2*(2), 221–262. doi:10.1145/1149283.1149287

Zhou, Y., Liu, G., Fu, E., & Zhang, K. (2009). An object-relational prototype of GIS-based disaster database. *Procedia Earth and Planetary Science, 1*, 1060–1066. doi:10.1016/j.proeps.2009.09.163

Zhu, L., Iacob, C., & Barricelli, B. R. (2010). New design strategies: Using the hive mind space model to enhance collaboration. In *Proceedings of the Multi Conference on Computer Science and Information Systems* (pp. 12-19).

Zhu, X., & Lu, P. (2008). Study of scheduling for processing real-time communication signals on heterogeneous clusters. In *Proceedings of the 9ᵗʰ International Symposium on Parallel Architectures, Algorithms & Networks*. Sydney, Australia (pp. 121-126).

Zhu, Y., Rundensteiner, E. A., & Heineman, G. T. (2004). Dynamic plan migration for continuous queries over data streams. In *Proceedings of the 23rd International Conference on Management of Data* (pp. 431-442).

Zhu, X., & Lu, P. (2009). Multi-dimensional scheduling for real-time tasks on heterogeneous clusters. *Journal of Computer Science & Technology, 24*(3), 434–446. doi:10.1007/s11390-009-9235-2

Zincir-Heywood, N. A., & Malcolm, I. H. (2000). In the Wake of the Turkish Earthquake: Turkish Internet. In *Proceedings of the Internet Society's NET 2000 Conference*. Retrieved May 10, 2010, from http://www.isoc.org/inet2000/cdproceedings/8l/8l_2.htm

About the Contributors

Nik Bessis is currently Head of Distributed and Intelligent Systems (DISYS) research group, a full Professor and a Chair of Computer Science in the School of Computing and Mathematics at University of Derby, UK. He is also an academic member in the Department of Computer Science and Technology at University of Bedfordshire (UK). He obtained a BA (1991) from the TEI of Athens, Greece and completed his MA (1995) and PhD (2002) at De Montfort University (Leicester, UK). His research interest is the analysis, research, and delivery of user-led developments with regard to trust, data integration, annotation, and data push methods and services in distributed environments. These have a particular focus on the study and use of next generation technologies methods for the benefit of various virtual organizational settings. He is involved in and leading a number of funded research and commercial projects in these areas. Prof. Bessis has published over 150 papers, won 2 best paper awards and is the editor of several books and the Editor-in-Chief of the *International Journal of Distributed Systems and Technologies* (IJDST). In addition, Prof. Bessis is a regular reviewer and has served several times as a keynote speaker, conferences/workshops/track chair, associate editor, session chair, and scientific program committee member.

* * *

Ailixier Aikebaier received his BE and ME degrees in Computers and Systems Engineering from XinJiang University, China and Tokyo Denki University, Japan, in 2004 and 2008, respectively. He is currently a PhD candidate student at Department of Computer and Information Science, Seikei University. His research interests include distributed systems, P2P networks, consensus problems, and fault tolerant systems. He is a member of IEEE.

Liliana Ardissono is an Associate Professor at the Computer Science Department of the Università di Torino, where she obtained her University Degree and her Ph.D in Computer Science. Her research interests include User Modeling, Adaptive Hypermedia and Service Oriented Computing. She is Secretary of the Board of Directors of User Modeling Inc. and she is a member of the Editorial Board of User Modeling and User-Adapted Interaction - The Journal of Personalization Research.

Eleana Asimakopoulou has a first degree (University of Luton, UK) and an MA (University of Westminster, UK) in Architecture and a PhD (Loughborough University, UK) in managing natural disasters using Grid technology. Dr Asimakopoulou is currently a visiting lecturer at the Department of Computer Science and Technology at the University of Bedfordshire. Eleana is the editor of a book workshops chair and a regular reviewer in several international conferences and journals. Her research interests include emergency management, response and planning for disasters, business continuity, construction and risk management, and also advanced ICT methods (such as grid and other forms of applicable collaborative technologies) for disaster management.

Leonard Barolli is a Full Professor in Department of Information and Communication Engineering, Fukuoka Institute of Technology (FIT), Japan. He has published more than 350 papers in Journals, Books and International Conferences. He has served as a Guest Editor for many Journals and has been PC Co-Chair and General Co-Chair of many International Conferences. He is Steering Committee Chair of International Conference on Complex, Intelligent and Software Intensive Systems (CISIS). His research interests include wireless networks, ad-hoc networks, sensor networks, fuzzy logic and genetic algorithms. He is member of IEEE, IEEE Computer Society, IPSJ and SOFT.

Barbara Rita Barricelli is currently a PhD Candidate at the Department of Computer Science and Communication of Università degli Studi di Milano, Italy. In the same university, she obtained a B.Sc. in Digital Communication and a M.Sc. in Information and Communication Technologies. Her research topics are related to End-User Development (EUD), computer semiotics, internationalization and localization of virtual interactive systems.

Alan N. Beard studied physics at Leicester University and in 1972 was awarded a Ph.D. in theoretical physics from Durham University. After carrying out research in medical physics at Exeter University and the University of Wales, in 1977 he started fire research at Edinburgh University, leaving in 1995 to go to Heriot-Watt University, Edinburgh, where he has been Reader in Fire Safety Engineering since 2003. His research is in the very broad area of modelling in relation to safety and fire safety in particular; including deterministic and probabilistic modelling as well as qualitative research, in particular applying the concepts of systems to safety management. His research has covered buildings, offshore installations and railways amongst other things. Since 1993, a major research interest has been in the field of tunnel fires and he co-edited 'The Handbook of Tunnel Fire Safety'. In 2008 he published a report commissioned by the European Parliament on tunnel safety decision-making; available on the European Parliament web-site. He has conducted research for both government departments and industrial companies. Further, his papers have been used as key references by the International Standards Organization and some of his research has been translated into Japanese. More generally, he is concerned to help to develop a framework for the acceptable use of fire models in safety decision-making and to pursue a systemic approach to safety management.

Stefan Biffl is an associate professor of software engineering at the Institute of Software Technology and Interactive Systems, Vienna University of Technology. He received his MSc and PhD in Computer Science from the Vienna University of Technology in 1989 and 1991, respectively, as well as a MS degree in social and economic sciences from the University of Vienna. In 2001 he received an Erwin-Schrödinger research scholarship and spent one year as researcher at the Fraunhofer Institute of Experimental Software Engineering (headed by Dieter Rombach), focusing on quality management and empirical software engineering. Also, in 2001 he received the Habilitation degree Venia Docendi for work on empirical software engineering in project management and quality management. In 2006 he worked as guest researcher at Czech Technical University, Department of Cybernetics (headed by Vladimir Marik). He is actively involved in research in the fields of Software Engineering, Empirical Software Engineering, Software Process and Product Improvement.

Gianni Bosio received the Bachelor degree in Communication Science in 2004 and a Master degree in Communication for the Information Society in 2007. He is currently a PhD student in Computer Science at the Computer Science Department of the Università di Torino. His research activity comprises: human computer interaction, usability studies, collaborative technologies, user centric technologies, cloud architectures for computer supported collaborative work, notification systems and user interfaces.

Gordon J. Clapworthy received a BSc (Hons., Class 1) in Mathematics and a PhD in Aeronautical Engineering from the University of London, and an MSc, with Distinction, in Computer Science from The City University, London. He is a Professor of Computer Graphics in the Department of Computer Science & Technology and Head of the Centre for Computer Graphics & Visualization (CCGV) at the University of Bedfordshire, UK. His interests include medical visualisation, computer animation, biomechanics, virtual reality, surface modelling, and fundamental computer graphics algorithms. Clapworthy has published over 150 refereed articles and has been involved in 25 international projects in recent years, mostly funded by the European Commission; he coordinated 8 of these. He is a member of the ACM, ACM SIGGRAPH and Eurographics.

Valentin Cristea is a Professor at Computer Science department in University Politehnica of Bucharest. His main fields of expertise are Grid Computing, e-Learning, e-Business, e-Government, Distributed Systems and Web-based Application Development. He is the Director of the National Center for Information Technology. Prof. Valentin Cristea has a long experience in the development, management and/or coordination of research national and international projects on distributed computing, Grid computing, High Performance Computing, and e-Learning.

Stijn Dekeyser obtained his PhD in 2003 from the University of Antwerp in Belgium having completed research in the area of database theory and concurrency control for XML. Stijn is also interested in educational technology and computer science education. He is currently the Head of Department of Mathematics and Computing at the University of Southern Queensland in Australia.

Guillaume De La Roche has been working as a research fellow at the Centre for Wireless Network Design (CWiND), United Kingdom, since 2007. From 2001 to 2002 he was a research engineer at Infineon, Munich, Germany. From 2003 to 2004 he worked in a small French company where he deployed WiFi networks. From 2004 to 2007 he was with the CITI Laboratory at the National Institute of Applied Sciences (INSA), France. He holds a Dipl-Ing from CPE Lyon, France, and M.Sc. (2003) and Ph.D. (2007) degrees in wireless communications from INSA Lyon. He is a co-author of the book Femtocells: Technologies and Deployment (Wiley, 2010).

Ciprian Dobre, PhD, is lecturer with the Computer Science and Engineering Department of the University Politehnica of Bucharest. The main fields of expertise are Grid Computing, Monitoring and Control of Distributed Systems, Modeling and Simulation, Advanced Networking Architectures, Parallel and Distributed Algorithms. Ciprian Dobre is a member of the RoGRID (Romanian GRID) consortium and is involved in a number of national projects (CNCSIS, GridMOSI, MedioGRID, PEGAF) and international projects (MonALISA, MONARC, VINCI, VNSim, EGEE, SEE-GRID, EU-NCIT). His research activities were awarded with the Innovations in Networking Award for Experimental Applications in 2008 by the Corporation for Education Network Initiatives (CENIC).

Arjan Durresi is an Associate Professor of Computer Science at Indiana University Purdue University Indianapolis (IUPUI), USA. His current research interests include network architectures, heterogeneous wireless networks, security, QoS routing protocols, traffic management, optical and satellite networks, performance testing, multimedia systems, and bioinformatics. He has authored more than 70 papers in journals and more than 130 in conference proceedings. He is on the editorial boards of *Ad Hoc Networks Journal* (Elsevier) and *Journal of Ubiquitous Computing and Intelligence*.

Tomoya Enokido received B.E. and M.E. degrees in Computers and Systems Engineering from Tokyo Denki University, Japan in 1997 and 1999, respectively. After he worked for NTT Data Corporation, he joined Tokyo Denki University as a research associate in 2002. He received his D.E. degree in Computer Science from Tokyo Denki University in 2003. He is currently an associate professor in the Faculty of Business Administration, Rissho University. He is a member of IEEE and IPSJ.

María J. García García has a Bachelor's in Chemistry and mastery in Operations Research. She, José G. Hernández Ramírez, and Gilberto J. Hernández García have combined their managerial and educational experience to increase their investigations, already above one hundred and seventy, mainly in the areas of Evaluation and Management of Projects, Managerial and Social Decision making, Logistics, Risk Management and Operations research. They have been presented or published in different countries, having publications and offering their reports, chats or conferences in: Germany, Italy, Czech Republic, Iceland, Lithuania, Spain, France, Portugal, United States, Panama, Paraguay, Uruguay, Brazil, Cuba, Mexico, Argentina and Chile besides attending as guest speaker, in reiterated occasions, in lectures to relevant events in Colombia, Peru, Costa Rica, Brazil and their own country, Venezuela. From the year 1999, come working the topic of the catastrophes, either of natural origin as caused by men, including there the industrial accidents. They have presented a big number of works in national and international congresses, where they demonstrate the applicability of some models of the field of the operations research, in the help to confront situations of catastrophes, this principally across decision support systems.

Rachit Garg obtained his MCA from Periyar University, Salem (India) in 2001 and MPhil (Computer Science) from Periyar University, Salem (India). He has contributed several technical papers in various national journals and international journals. His areas of research interest include Distributed Systems, Mobile Computing, and Routing in Ad-hoc Networks. He joined Department of Computer Science & IT, Lyallpur Khalsa College in 2001 as Lecturer. He worked as Asst Prof in Department of Computer Science & IT (with additional charge of Placement Officer) from June, 2001 to till date. He has been dedicatedly working towards the growth of technology related issues since the last more than one decade. He also takes interest in various sports.

Anna Goy is a Researcher at the Computer Science Department of the Università di Torino, where she works in the area of web-based systems. She obtained her Ph.D in Cognitive Science at the same university, with studies in the area of lexical semantics. She carries on her research and development activity about intelligent web-based systems providing personalized services, distributed web-based applications, "open" architectures in the Web 2.0, and context-aware systems at the Computer Science Department.

Tom Gross is professor and chair of Computer-Supported Cooperative Work at the Bauhaus-University Weimar, Germany. His research interests are particularly in the fields of Computer-Supported Cooperative Work, Human-Computer Interaction, and Ubiquitous Computing. In these areas he has published numerous articles in journals, conference proceedings, books and book chapters. And he has been teaching at various universities across Europe. He has participated in and coordinated activities in various national and international research projects. He is an expert member of the IFIP Technical Committee on 'Human Computer Interaction' (TC.13). He has been conference co-chair and organiser of many international conferences (e.g., most recently program co-chair of the ACM GROUP 2010 and INTERACT 2009 conference). Further information can be found at: http://www.tomgross.net.

Gilberto J. Hernández García has a Bachelor's in Chemistry and a master in Technology of Foods. He, José G. Hernández Ramírez, and María J. García García have combined their managerial and educational experience to increase their investigations, already above one hundred and seventy, mainly in the areas of Evaluation and Management of Projects, Managerial and Social Decision making, Logistics, Risk Management and Operations research. They have been presented or published in different countries, having publications and offering their reports, chats or conferences in: Germany, Italy, Czech Republic, Iceland, Lithuania, Spain, France, Portugal, United States, Panama, Paraguay, Uruguay, Brazil, Cuba, Mexico, Argentina and Chile besides attending as guest speaker, in reiterated occasions, in lectures to relevant events in Colombia, Peru, Costa Rica, Brazil and their own country, Venezuela. From the year 1999, come working the topic of the catastrophes, either of natural origin as caused by men, including there the industrial accidents. They have presented a big number of works in national and international congresses, where they demonstrate the applicability of some models of the field of the operations research, in the help to confront situations of catastrophes, this principally across decision support systems.

José G. Hernández Ramírez is a Chemical Engineer and has mastery in Operations Research. He, María J. García García, and Gilberto J. Hernández García have combined their managerial and educational experience to increase their investigations, already above one hundred and seventy, mainly in the areas of Evaluation and Management of Projects, Managerial and Social Decision making, Logistics, Risk Management and Operations research. They have been presented or published in different countries, having publications and offering their reports, chats or conferences in: Germany, Italy, Czech Republic, Iceland, Lithuania, Spain, France, Portugal, United States, Panama, Paraguay, Uruguay, Brazil, Cuba, Mexico, Argentina and Chile besides attending as guest speaker, in reiterated occasions, in lectures to relevant events in Colombia, Peru, Costa Rica, Brazil and their own country, Venezuela. From the year 1999, come working the topic of the catastrophes, either of natural origin as caused by men, including there the industrial accidents. They have presented a big number of works in national and international congresses, where they demonstrate the applicability of some models of the field of the operations research, in the help to confront situations of catastrophes, this principally across decision support systems.

Jan Hidders received his PhD in 2001 from Eindhoven University of Technology in the Netherlands and subsequently completed a stint as a post-doctoral researcher at the University of Antwerp in Belgium. Jan's research interests are broad and focused on web information systems. He is currently an assistant professor at the University of Delft in the Netherlands.

Claudia Iacob is currently a PhD student at Università degli Studi di Milano, Department of Computer Science. She obtained her B.Sc. and her M.Sc. in Computer Science from the Department of Computer Science of Babes-Bolyai University, Cluj-Napoca. She is a Marie Curie early stage researcher and her research topics relate to interactive design patterns and tools for supporting creative design process through visual languages.

Mihai Istin received his BSc in Computer Science in 2008 within the Computer Science department at the University Politehnica of Bucharest. His research interests include scheduling in large scale distributed systems, evolutionary computing, time series prediction and peer to peer networks. He is involved in the DEPSYS Romanian national research project, working on these subjects. He is currently master student in Parallel and Distributed Computer Systems at Vrije University, Amsterdam.

Makoto Ikeda is an Assistant Research Fellow, at the Center for Asian and Pacific Studies, Seikei University, Japan. He received BE, MS, and PhD degrees from Fukuoka Institute of Technology (FIT), Japan, in 2005, 2007 and 2010, respectively. He was a Japan Society for the Promotion of Science (JSPS) Research Fellow, from April 2008 to March 2010. He is a member of IEEE, ACM, IPSJ and IEICE. His research interests include wireless networks, mobile computing, high-speed networks, P2P systems, mobile ad-hoc networks, wireless sensor networks and vehicle ad-hoc networks.

Rajib L. Jana received his B.Tech degree in Computer Science & Engineering from West Bengal University of Technology, Kolkata, India in 2006. He is currently working towards the M.Tech degree in Information Security with Computer Science & Engineering department, MNNIT, Allahabad, India. His current research interests include distributed system, real-time system and information security. He is a member of CRSI.

Parveen Kumar obtained his Ph.D. degree in Computer Science from Kurukshetra University, Kurukshetra (India) in 2006. His title of PhD thesis is "Checkpointing-Based Fault Tolerance in Mobile Distributed Systems". He Did his MS [Software Systems] from BITS Pilani in 2001. He did his MCA from Dept. of Computer Sc & Applications, Kurukshetra University, Kurukshetra in 1989. He has contributed more than thirty five technical papers in various journals, which includes twenty papers in international journals. He is working with MIET Group of Institutions as Professor (CSE) with the additional charge of Director MCA since Sept. 2009.

Pierre Kuonen received a Master in Electrical Engineering from the Swiss Federal Institute of Technology (EPFL) in 1982. After six years of experience in the industry, he joined the Computer Science Theory Laboratory at EPFL in 1988 and began working in the field of parallel and distributed computing. He received his Ph.D. in computer science from the EPFL in 1993. Since 1994 he has worked regularly in the field of parallel and distributed computing. First at EPFL where he founded and directed the GRIP (Group for Research in Parallel Computing) and then at the University of Applied Sciences of Valais. Since 2003 he is full professor at the University of Applied Sciences of Fribourg in the Information and Communication technologies department (ICT), where he is leading the Grid & Ubiquitous Computing Group. Since 1993, besides his teaching activity, he was constantly involved in national or international research projects particularly for applications in the field of telecommunications or wave propagation.

Zhihua Lai received a bachelor in Computer Science in University of Luton, UK. After that he started a PhD studentship in University of Bedfordshire, UK. His current research is wireless propagation algorithms. At the third year of study, he has been offered a chance to study in University of Applied Science in Western Switzerland, Fribourg, Switzerland where he designs and implements parallel propagation algorithms. Zhihua enjoys programming during the leisure time and he believes a good program can make a difference in research.

Andrei Lavivia received her BSc in Computer Science in 2008 within the Computer Science department at the University Politehnica of Bucharest. Her research interests include Distributed Systems, Fault Tolerance. She is involved in the DEPSYS Romanian national research project, working on these subjects.

Byung Suk Lee is an Associate Professor at the Department of Computer Science in The University of Vermont, U.S.A. He received a BS degree from Seoul National University, South Korea, an MS degree from KAIST, South Korea, and a Ph.D. degree from Stanford University, U.S.A. His research interests include database systems, data stream processing, and event processing.

Carsten Maple is currently Pro-Vice Chancellor (Research and Enterprise) at the University of Bedfordshire. He was a Head of the Computer Science and Technology Department at the same University and was appointed Professor of Applicable Computing in 2004. He has an international research reputation and extensive experience of institutional strategy development and interacting with external agencies as well as substantial experience of chairing and participating in committees and boards at all levels of an HE institution. Professor Maple obtained his PhD at the University of Leicester where his thesis was "A Special Method for Solving Hamilton Eigen problems Arising from Ordinary Differential Equations." His research interests are in the area of applicable computing, information security, trust and authentication distributed systems, graph theory and optimisation techniques. He is involved in and leading a number of funded research and commercial projects in these areas. Professor Maple has published numerous papers and articles in international conferences and journals, and he is the co-editor of the International Journal of Applied Informatics. In addition, Professor Maple is a regular reviewer of several journals and conferences and has served as a guest speaker, an associate editor, a conference chair, a scientific program committee member, and a session chair in numerous international conferences.

Gjergji Mino was graduated in Electronics at Tirana Polytechnic University, Albania in 1995. After the graduation, he was working for different telecommunication companies in Albania. From 1997, he worked for different companies such as Digital Corporation, Compaq, Computer Technology Solutions and Peripheral Computer Support in USA. Presently, he is a PhD candidate at Graduate School of Engineering, Fukuoka Institute of Technology (FIT), Japan. His research interests include wireless networks, CAC, handover and fuzzy logic.

Thomas Moser received his master and PhD degrees in business informatics at the Vienna University of Technology and works as a post-doc researcher in the research area "Semantic Integration" in the Christian Doppler Laboratory Software Engineering Integration for Flexible Automation Systems since 2010. His main research areas are data modeling and semantic web technologies for model engineering knowledge and the connection of design-time and runtime engineering processes.

Peter Norrington received his PhD from the University of Bedfordshire in 2009 with a thesis in cognitive authentication techniques, focusing on human factors and their security implications. He currently works there as Graduate Outcomes Project Officer on system development projects for educational design to improve graduate employability. He has worked in the education, hospitality and journalism sectors. His research interests center around cooperative and collaborative systems, particularly their usability and security.

Florin Pop, PhD, is assistant professor of the Computer Science and Engineering Department of the University Politehnica of Bucharest. His research interests are oriented to: scheduling in Grid environments (his PhD research), distributed system, parallel computation, communication protocols and numerical methods. He received his PhD in Computer Science in 2008 with "Magna cum Laudae" distinction. He is member of RoGrid consortium and participates in several research projects in these domains, in collaboration with other universities and research centers from Romania and from abroad developer. He has received an IBM PhD Assistantship in 2006 (top ranked 1st in CEMA out from 17 awarded students) and a PhD Excellency grant from Oracle in 2006-2008.

Giovanna Petrone is a researcher of Computer Science at the Università di Torino. Her research interests concern two main areas: Multi-agent systems (with specific interest for distributed systems and Web Services) and Intelligent User Interfaces (with specific attention to personalization in Web-based services). Previously, she has worked for several years as a software engineer and architect in large US and Italian computer companies and she was also Visiting Scholar at the Stanford University.

Ranvijay is presently pursuing Ph.D from Motilal Nehru National Institute of Technology Allahabad. He has received B. Tech. degree from Purvanchal University and M.Tech in computer science and Engineeirng form Motilal Nehru National Institute of Technology Allahabad, India. He has worked as lecturer at a Institute of Northern India Engineering College Lucknow. He has authored more than 12 research papers in international conference and reputed journal/book chapters. Mr. Ranvijay's areas of interest are Real-Time System, Computer Architecture, Energy Aware Scheduling and Mobile Computing.

Zahid Raza is currently an Assistant Professor in the School of Computer and Systems Sciences, Jawaharlal Nehru University, India. He has a Master degree in Electronics, Masters degree in Computer Science and Ph.D. in Computer Science. Prior to joining Jawaharlal Nehru University, he served as a Lecturer in Banasthali Vidyapith University, Rajasthan, India. His research interest is in the area of Grid Computing and has proposed a few models for job scheduling in a Computational Grid. He is a member of IEEE.

Paul Sant is currently a senior lecturer (assistant professor) in the Department of Computer Science and Technology at University of Bedfordshire (UK). He obtained a BSc (Hons) first class in Computer and Information Systems from the University of Liverpool and completed his PhD in Computer Science (Algorithmic Graph Theory) at Kings College London (UK). His research interests lie in the area of algorithm design, and more recently, in the area of trust modelling. Dr. Sant has published papers and articles in international conferences and journals and serves as a conference and workshop organizer as well as being a reviewer for The Computer Journal and the Journal of Discrete Algorithms.

Jaime Santos-Reyes is a lecturer at SEPI-ESIME, Zacatenco, Instituto Politecnico Nacional (IPN), Mexico, whose main research interests are safety management systems, accident and risk analysis, reliability engineering and natural disasters. He obtained a PhD from Heriot-Watt University, UK, in 2001 for his thesis 'The Development of a Fire Safety Management System (FSMS)' model. Since then he has used the systemic safety management system model that he developed to look at safety management on offshore installations, on the UK railway network, in tunnels and on natural disasters. He is currently using the model to analyse a number of accidents that have occurred in other industries as well as past natural disasters. Jaime has a degree in Mechanical Engineering from the IPN, Mexico and an MSc in Thermal Power and Fluid Engineering from UMIST, UK. He has spent 3 years working as a research associate at Heriot-Watt University, Edinburgh, Scotland, UK. He also spent some years working in the oil and gas industry.

Maximilian Schirmer is a Ph.D. student and research and teaching assistant at the Computer-Supported Cooperative Work group of the Bauhaus-University Weimar, Germany. He received a Master of Science degree in Media Systems at the Bauhaus-University. His research interests focus on Ubiquitous Computing, Computer-Supported Cooperative Work, and Recommender Systems. For further information (including a list of publications), please visit http://www.maximilianschirmer.net.

Marino Segnan is a Researcher at the Computer Science Department, Università di Torino, working with the Advanced Service Architectures group. His recent research activities deal with interaction models for Web Services, choreographies, monitoring. His previous activity focused on the development of a Qualitative Simulation Tool for Model-Based Diagnosis. Previously, he worked with several companies, mainly on projects involving Integrated Development Environments, User Interfaces, compilers, Transaction Management.

Stelios Sotiriadis is currently a PhD student in the Department of Computer Science and Technology at University of Bedfordshire (UK). He obtained a BSc first class in Computer Science, and an MSc in Computer and Internet Application from the University of Bedfordshire. His research interests are in the area of distributed computing (Grid and Cloud Computing), and Artificial Intelligent Agents.

Wikan Danar Sunindyo received his master degree in computational logic at the Dresden University of Technology, Germany, and works as a PhD researcher at the Vienna University of Technology in the research area "Complex Systems" since 2008. His main research areas are data warehousing and semantic web technologies to better integrate heterogeneous engineering environments.

Makoto Takizawa is currently a Professor of Seikei University, Japan. He received his BE and ME in Applied Physics and DE in Computer Science from Tohoku University, Japan. He was on the Board of Governors (2003 - 2008) and is a Golden Core member of the IEEE Computer Society. He is a fellow of IPSJ. He chairs many international conferences. He founded IEEE AINA. He is a member of the IEEE, ACM and IPSJ.

Suresh Thomas, Senior Technical Analyst, has been working with Thomson airways (part of TUI AG) for the last 4 years. He has been consulting the Airline division of the company on the applications of computing on Airlines operations and maintenance. His expertise includes multi tier airline IT systems and software tools for optimising airline operations and engineering maintenance and have been working with geographically dispersed team to deliver large IT solutions. He has also recently completed his master is Computer science from University of Bedfordshire. Prior to joining Thomson, he has been working on various IT consulting roles from programmer to technical architect for a number of American and European clients for more than 10 years. His expertise include implementation of Sun Grid Engine cloud computing into Airline crew rostering, multi tier web technologies and other middle tier distributed computing frame works such as COM+ and CORBA. His recent interest includes enterprise mashups and other new developments in WEB2 and their applications in social computing and web reusability.

Sarsij Tripathi is presently pursuing a Ph.D. from Motilal Nehru National Institute of Technology Allahabad. He has received B. Tech. in Computer Science and Engineering degree from M.J.P Rohailkhand University, Bareilly, India and M.Tech in Computer Science and Engineering form Motilal Nehru National Institute of Technology Allahabad, India. He has worked as lecturer at Institute of Foreign Trade and Management, Moradabad. Mr. Tripathi areas of interest are Real-Time System, Distributed System, Security, Scheduling and Computer Networks.

Fabrizio Torretta is a collaborator at the Computer Science Department of the Università di Torino where he obtained his Master degree in Computer Science. He actively participated to a National Project with Thales Alenia Space, concerning collaborative workflow management. His research interests include Web 2.0 technologies and Cloud Computing.

Tri Minh Tran is a Ph.D. candidate in Computer Science at the University of Vermont, U.S.A. He received the B.Eng. degree in Information Technology from Hanoi University of Technology, Vietnam in 2001 and the MS degree in Mathematics from Ohio University, U.S.A. in 2003. He is currently working as a Software Engineer in the Query Optimizer group at Teradata Corporation. His main research interests include query optimization, data stream processing and database systems.

Isamu Tsuneizumi received his BE in 2010 and is now a graduate student in Computer and Information Science, Seikei University. His research interests include distributed systems, P2P networks, group communication protocol.

Deo Prakash Vidyarthi received a Master Degree in Computer Application in 1991 and PhD in Computer Science in 2002. Dr. Vidyarthi has published many research papers in various peer reviewed International Journals and Transactions, peer-reviewed International conferences, Edited books etc. He has authored a book entitled "Scheduling in Distributed Computing Systems: Design, Analysis and Models" published by Springer, USA. Dr. Vidyarthi is member of IEEE, International Society of Research in Science and Technology (ISRST), USA and senior member of the International Association of Computer Science and Information Technology (IACSIT), Singapore. Research interest includes Parallel and Distributed System, Grid Computing, Mobile Computing.

Andreea Visan is currently a master student at Parallel and Distributed Computer Systems at Vrije University Amsterdam. She received her BSc in Computer Science in 2009 within the Computer Science department at the University Politehnica of Bucharest. Her research interests include parallel and distributed systems, fault tolerance and data structures. She is involved in the DEPSYS Romanian national research project, working on these subjects.

Dietmar Winkler is researcher and lecturer at the Vienna University of Technology and member of the research group for Quality Software Engineering at the Institute of Software Technology and Interactive Systems. Additionally he is working as a consultant for quality assurance and process management in software engineering and as quality management consultant in the automotive business area. Since 2010 he is working as project assistant in the Christian Doppler Laboratory "Software Engineering Integration for Flexible Automation Systems."

Fatos Xhafa joined the Department of Languages and Informatics Systems of the Technical University of Catalonia as an Assistant Professor in 1996 and is currently an Associate Professor and member of the ALB-COM Research Group of this department. His current research interests include parallel algorithms, combinatorial optimization, approximation and meta-heuristics, distributed programming, Grid and P2P computing. He has published in leading international journals and conferences and has served in the organizing committees of many conferences and workshops. He is also a member of editorial board of several international journals.

Rama Shankar Yadav is currently Professor at Motilal Nehru National Institute of Technology, Allahabad. He received Ph.D. degree from IIT, Roorkee, M.S. degree from B.I.T.S. Pilani and B.Tech degree from I.E.T, Lucknow. Dr. Yadav has extensive research and academic experience. He has woked in leading institutions such as GBPEC, Pauri Garhwal, BITS, Pilani. He has authored more than 50 research papers in National/International conference and referred Journals/Book chapters. Dr. Yadav's areas of interest are Real-Time System, Embedded System, Fault Tolerant System, Energy Aware Scheduling, Computer Architecture, Distributed Computing and Cryptography.

Tao Yang received a B.E. from Hunan University, China in 2001 and MS from Fukuoka Institute of Technology (FIT), Japan in March 2007, respectively. He received the PhD degree from Intelligent Information and System Engineering, Fukuoka Institute of Technology, Japan in 2010. He is a Japan Society for the Promotion of Science (JSPS) Research Fellow (PD) at FIT. He also is a Part-time Lecturer at Department of Information and Communication Engineering, FIT. His research interests include routing protocols, wireless networks, mobile networks, ad-hoc networks and wireless sensor networks. He is a member of IPSJ.

Jie Zhang is Professor of Wireless Communications and Networks at the Department of Computer Science and Technology, University of Bedfordshire (UoB), UK. He received his MEng and PhD degrees from the Department of Automatic Control and Electronic Engineering, East China University of Science and Technology, Shanghai, China. From 1997 to 2002, he was a Research Fellow with University College London, Imperial College London, and Oxford University. He is the founding Director of the Centre for Wireless Network Design, which is one of the best-funded and leading research groups in wireless network design and femtocell research in Europe. Since 2003, he has been awarded more than 19 projects worth over £4.0 million (his share).He has published over 120 journal and conference papers, and is a lead author of the first technical book on femtocells - "Femtocells: Technologies and Deployment," which was published by Wiley in Jan. 2010.

Li Zhu received her Bachelor degree in Architecture. She obtained an M.Arch Studies degree in Advanced Architecture Studies from the University of Sheffield and a M.Sc degree in Design and Digital Media from the University of Edinburgh, earning distinctions in both. She is currently a PhD student at Università degli Studi di Milano and a Marie Curie researcher. Her research is investigating end-user development and meta-design approaches for supporting creative collaborative software design.

Index

A

B

C

D